# MOIRA

*Fate, Good, and Evil in Greek Thought*

LONDON : HUMPHREY MILFORD
OXFORD UNIVERSITY PRESS

# MOIRA

## *Fate, Good, and Evil in Greek Thought*

WILLIAM CHASE GREENE

*Professor of Greek and Latin and*

*Tutor in Classics*

*in Harvard University*

HARVARD UNIVERSITY PRESS

CAMBRIDGE MASSACHUSETTS

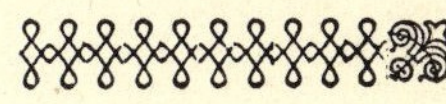

1944

PRINTED AT THE HARVARD UNIVERSITY PRINTING OFFICE

CAMBRIDGE, MASSACHUSETTS, U. S. A.

*To the Memory*
*of*
A. M. G.

# PREFACE

Fate, good, and evil; the relation of power to goodness, and the origin and nature of evil: here is a group of fundamental ideas and problems that challenges inquiry, even if it defies any complete answer. The Greek word *Moira*, with its fringe of associations, comes perhaps nearer than any other single word to suggesting this group of ideas, and may serve as a title for such an inquiry.

The present study began a number of years ago when I attempted to interpret, so far as I was able, various works in Greek literature, both in poetry and in prose, which express these ideas. Naturally I found that one problem leads to another, so that eventually I must consider most of the literature of the classical period; indeed, since it proved impossible to set any arbitrary limit in antiquity, I felt free to follow single threads of Greek thought as far as Milton. In the course of my investigations I have profited by reading a multitude of works by modern scholars, as will appear from a glance at the footnotes; in the Select Bibliography I have indicated a few of the works that have seemed to me most valuable or that bear most directly on phases of the general problem. But since I could find no single work that undertakes to deal with the group of questions that confronted me, what I have set down for my own enlightenment may prove helpful also to others.

If centuries of Greek thought did not solve all the questions that it raised, if indeed some of them are likely to remain forever unsolved, nevertheless they are necessary questions both for ancient Greeks and for modern men to ask. I trust that I have been able at least to throw into relief the character of the Greeks' inquiries, the extent of their success, and the extent to which they had recourse to poetry or myth as the appropriate approach toward certain baffling fields of experience.

The reader who is curious to discover at once the argument of the book will find in the brief introductory chapter an attempt in rather abstract terms, without detail and without discussion of any individual thinker, to indicate the nature of the problem and the direction of the most important Greek thought about it; this is not only an introduction but something like an outline and an index of much that follows. The remaining chapters deal first with poetry and its next of kin, and then chiefly with prose; this is in general the chronological order of Greek literature, if allowance be made for a certain amount of overlapping, especially in the fifth century B.C.

One chapter in this book (II) appeared in preliminary form in *Harvard Studies in Classical Philology*, in 1935, but has received considerable revision. A few pages at the beginning of Chapter VIII represent some of the content of another article published in the same periodical in 1936. For criticism and advice I am grateful to the kindness of my colleagues Professors A. D. Nock and J. B. Munn, who read the whole of my manuscript, and to Professor Werner Jaeger, who read portions of it. For assistance in preparing my manuscript for publication I am indebted to a grant from the Joseph H. Clark Bequest in Harvard University. In compiling the Indices I have had the coöperation of Mr. and Mrs. Cedric H. Whitman and of Mr. Norbert T. Byrnes.

W. C. G.

CAMBRIDGE, MASSACHUSETTS,
May, 1942.

# CONTENTS

# MOIRA

*Fate, Good, and Evil in Greek Thought*

# CHAPTER I

## FATE, GOOD, AND EVIL

THAT this is on the whole a good world, and that man is on the whole happy, we are generally agreed; at least man struggles to prolong his life as if it were worth living. Yet he is confronted also by pain and sorrow and vice, and their origins are often obscure. Even good is sometimes turned to evil; even evil seems sometimes mysteriously to contain elements of good. We assume that everything must have its cause, and we ordinarily push the ultimate cause of all things back to God. Yet this very assumption results in making God responsible for evil as well as for good, and at least raises the question whether man is responsible for his actions, good or evil. Shall we suppose that God is imperfectly good, or that He is good but not omnipotent? Shall we set Fate above God? Shall we suppose that God is still developing, or is manifesting Himself only gradually? Shall we break the world apart, and recognize a Devil as well as a God? Shall we, in order to preserve the freedom of the human will and its goodness, dispense with divinity, and recognize only a material universe in which moral values are of purely human origin and relevance?

These are not new questions. They troubled the Greeks, and have lifted their heads in almost every succeeding age, to the confusion of philosophy, theology, and practical affairs. But the problem is perhaps simpler in the world of the Greeks, and often more concrete. Why is it, we may ask, that the Greeks, on the whole a healthy, cheerful, successful people, were nevertheless constantly visited by melancholy? On the other hand, why does their tragic drama, dealing largely with suffering and evil, give pleasure? How do their thinkers contrive to explain the persistence of evil in an orderly, rational universe? Or do they, indeed, explain it?

The problem, thus simplified, is at least intelligible. Yet it is not wholly simple, for the various phases of the problem arise at different times and in different ways. The instinct of the Greeks, as of all men, would be to dwell on the goodness and activity of Nature and of whatever powers there be in the world, rather than to stress the evil, thwarting powers and the oppressiveness of Law; we think more easily in positive than in negative terms. It would be only after the general goodness and rationality of the prevailing power had been already accepted and was perceived to be vitiated by the existence of evil that a problem of evil could arise; and it would be only persistent suffering that would arouse a suspicion that there may be some evil power at work. Injustice would not be imputed to the gods if justice had not generally been taken for granted. Moreover there could be no question of the freedom of the will if there were not already an idea of law or causality, a determinism against which freedom could be measured or contrasted. Whether this standard was identified with the will of the gods, as usually by the poets, or with law or power of a less personal sort, as by the philosophers, or with Fate, as by men generally, it provided a background against which the strength of men's wills and their sense of their own deserts might be set forth, as the conception of human personality and the value of human objectives were being defined in the process of living. Thus the moral struggles of life, and their counterpart on the tragic stage and in the pages of the philosophers and historians, were made possible. Presently, as faith in the existence of an external moral order was abated, except as the central tradition of the philosophers stemming from Socrates maintained it, man assumed for a time the helm of his destiny. At a later period, Chance, a creature with little moral character, came to hold a greater sway in his imaginings. Finally, in the decay of the ancient world, recourse was had once more to the simpler forms of religious faith, or to a philosophic interpretation of Fate that tended to identify it with Providence, and that recognized the freedom of man's will. The Greek philosophic tradition was largely absorbed by the Christian tradition, and also flowered again in the thought of the Renaissance.

To trace the emergence of successive problems and of the various attempts by myth and rational discussion to meet these problems will be our task in the following chapters. All Greek poetry, we shall immediately observe, is shot through with figures and ideas that were ingrained in the minds of the Greek people. Most of them had acquired connotations and associations which we can only with difficulty recapture, so that the understanding of identical words found in different contexts requires resourcefulness and a historic sense on the part of the interpreter. Similarly in philosophy it seems at times as if the terms and arguments of philosophers engaged in polemic are like the soldiers in a stage army marching forever before us; yet they are really marshalled each time in a new setting and for a new purpose. Even though the problems of fate, good, and evil may admit of no simple and perhaps of no metaphysical solution, it will not suffice to take refuge in the brilliant satire of Lucian, who presents Zeus as discomfited when he is cross-examined with regard to the relations between Destiny, the Moirai, the gods, human responsibility, and Providence;[1] nor will it do merely to echo the perplexity of Milton's fallen angels, lost in the mazes of metaphysical argument about "Providence, foreknowledge, will and fate." [2] For the synoptic eye can discern a pattern in the movements of Greek thought.

Therefore before we survey in turn the successive stages of Greek thought, with its recurrent images and ideas that form and change and regroup themselves with kaleidoscopic variety, but also with a forward movement like that of the waves of an incoming tide, it will be helpful to attempt to take in at a single rapid glance the general trend of this tide. So let us for the moment neglect the names of authors and the special historical settings of the developments to be studied later, and let us merely note the various types of answer to our problem that sprang up at different periods. I will not insist that my order is even roughly chronological, except in the sense that the most significant ideas were most recurrent, lasted longest, and are still valid, while others suffered eclipse and oblivion.

The spectacle, and still more the experience, of life's vicissitudes*[3] has always been the parent of perplexity. Disappointed hopes, the prosperity of the wicked, the suffering of the innocent, even the little ironies of circumstance, invite men to question whether the ultimate power in the universe is good or evil. One type of answer, common among the ancient Greeks, takes a dark view of human life. It ranges from brooding melancholy* to stark pessimism* and the cry that "it were best never to have been born" (μὴ φῦναι*); from kindly consolation* of others, and counsels of moderation* (*sophrosyne**) and the avoidance of risks ("the half is better than the whole"; "excess in nothing," μηδὲν ἄγαν*, "live in obscurity," λάθε βιώσας*, "endure and renounce," ἀνέχου καὶ ἀπέχου*) to manly endurance* of hardship (*tlemosyne**), or even to the discovery that wisdom may come through suffering* (πάθει μάθος*), which is a school of character. So far we have followed the path of caution, of the quiet life, of resignation and passive endurance.

Another type of answer springs from a tendency to think in terms of time; our present life cannot be all. Time itself (χρόνος*) or the special moment (καιρός*) has a vital power, for better or for worse. The inclination to look back wistfully to a supposed Golden Age* in the past opens to the imagination a world of innocence and happiness; to the believer in such a primitivism*, human history, or even cosmic history, has been a tale of degeneration*, marked by the moral decline* or fall of man.* Yet another and even stronger inclination is to look to the future.

[1] Lucian, "Zeus Catechized," Loeb ed., vol. II, pp. 60–87.

[2] Milton, *P. L.*, II, 557–569, quoted below, p. 397.

[3] Words and phrases in pp. 5–9 marked with asterisks represent key-ideas, further illustrations or discussions of which may be found by reference to the Indices.

If the body (σῶμα*) is mortal, not so is it with the soul* (ψυχή*), which passes through a cycle* of rebirths (κύκλος γενέσεως*) till it wins a final release and a blessed immortality*; such is the faith of the "mystery* religions,"* based not only on asceticism* and purification* but on a conviction that divine justice* must compensate hereafter for injustice* in this life. Hence the glowing colors of the myths* in which the mystics clothe their eschatology.*

But these hopes are not for every man, nor for the Greek who seeks to find his good here and now. He will strive rather to order his life by custom and established law* (*nomos**) within the orbit of his state (*polis**), achieving such happiness (*eudaimonia**) as he can by personal excellence (*arete**) and courage, by skill (*techne**) and intelligence. This is the code of humanism.* Yet he will recognize his own limitations, encompassed as he is by his fellows and by the external world, or Nature* (*physis**), which is blind to his aspirations and his moral code. Gradually it dawns on him that Nature has her own customs no less regular (perhaps even more regular), than those of the *polis*; she is a *cosmos**, with a way or justice* (*dike**) of her own, a harmony*, a law of nature.* For her, some things are impossible (ἀδύνατα*). He will not often suppose her to feel with him (by what has been called the "pathetic fallacy"); only at a late period will he occasionally feel the unity of Man-and-Nature* so strongly as to speak of a "sympathy" * of the *cosmos* in which human events are linked with cosmic events, and to resort to astrology.* To be sure he may sometimes find in Nature a sanction for rebelling against man-made law or the conventions of the *polis*. But he may also find in the cosmic system a pattern for human life and the social order. At any rate he will be disposed to recognize a justice* or a moral law* that binds human nature. So he will trace the inevitable sequence of man's error (*hamartia**); if prosperity (*olbos**) or a sense of surfeit (*koros**) leads a man to a deed of excess (*hybris**), he will suffer retribution* (*nemesis**), or ruin (*ate**). That is in fact justice (*dike*). Indeed he may for a time suppose that mere prosperity, apart from any misdeed, may involve a man in such *ate*, because it has aroused the jealousy* (*phthonos**) of the gods (φθόνος θεῶν*).

The "gods" of every-day Greek thought, whether conceived as vague *daimones** or as fully anthropomorphic *theoi**, are at first primarily powers, and only secondarily the authors of good and evil, or of good alone. They are causality realizing itself in a world whose processes demand some sort of propitiation in cult, of explanation in myth* or speculation. According as the course of human lives appears to be frustrated, rescued from threatened ruin, or permitted to move onward happily toward an intelligible goal, the gods show different aspects. They seem to interfere because of caprice or jealousy* (*phthonos**); to sanction a human oath* (*horkos**) or curse*; to intervene as saviors vouchsafing a divine dispensation or grace (θεία μοῖρα*, or θεία τύχη*); to impart something of the divine foreknowledge* of the future by means of oracles* or prophecies*, sometimes in the form of conditional oracles*; or, finally, to exercise continuously a divine will* or purpose* or law*, which is the highest form of reason* (νοῦς*). This they manifest alike in the ordering of the *cosmos**, by bringing "persuasion" * to bear on refractory "necessity" * (*ananke**) or on matter*, (ὕλη*), and in the vindication of a moral law* among men by punishment* of the guilty (even, it was supposed at times, by punishment of the innocent children of the guilty*), and by allowing the righteous to order their lives, by freedom of the will*, in a favorable environment, so as to win happiness (*eudaimonia**) either in this life or in a future state. If this is not precisely a divine love of individual man, it is the divine justice* or providence* (πρόνοια*), and affords some grounds for belief that all things are planned for a good end (*teleology**). "The best world for a moral agent is one that needs him to make it better." [4]

It would be blind optimism, however, to assert that life as we see it exhibits so perfect an adjustment of rewards to merits. Even if the framework within which we order our lives is roughly calculated to give us a fair prospect of happiness, even if the divine justice be ultimately meted out, clearly this is a world in which the innocent often suffer, and the wicked often prosper. Justice and law are abstract, and have no respect for individual persons, who moreover are partly at the mercy of force and of chance; and we are all of us individual persons. Here is a conflict of principles*, the physical and the moral, which is of the essence of tragedy*, and which demands some kind of reconciliation.* Here is the realm of fear and pity*, of pathetic contrast* between rewards and merits, of irony* in the inevitable outcome of misguided or blind endeavor (*peripeteia**). If Greek tragedy has not often exhibited in its action that nice adjustment of rewards to merits which has been termed "poetic justice," * it has done something better by directing our attention from the external action to the moral forces involved and to the inner life of the characters, from appearance (δόξα*) to reality (ἀλήθεια*); the *arete* of the hero, his

[4] J. Royce, *The World and the Individual*: Vol. II, *Nature, Man, and the Moral Order* (New York, 1901), p. 340. This little sentence really says everything; but for fuller discussion of the views implied in it, cf. the whole of the work that contains it, and the same author's *Studies of Good and Evil* (New York, 1899), supplemented by A. E. Taylor, *The Faith of a Moralist*: Vol. I, *The Theological Implications of Morality* (London, 1930).

For pointed and far-reaching criticism of Royce's philosophy, and for the contention that good is only an "island of relative permanence" built by man amid the vast and cruel flux of cosmic events, see G. Santayana, "A Brief History of My Opinions," in *Contemporary American Philosophy: A Symposium* (New York, 1930).

*tlemosyne** and his final vindication.* Here, indeed, justice of a higher order is done.

But it is not only Greek tragedy that is penetrated by the conception of divine power surrounding struggling mortals. Greek philosophy as a whole seeks to mediate between more or less abstract forces and individual human aspirations toward some good. It always utilizes, like popular speech and like the language of the poets, the various terms that suggest the ineluctable data of experience with some suggestion of a fate exterior to man: the due portion or share assigned (*moira**, *aisa**, *heimarmene**), the apportioners (the Moirai*), the *fait accompli* (πεπρωμένη*), that which must be, or ought to be (τὸ χρεών*). Here moral interpretations and value judgments begin to supplant mere implications of fact. Similarly the conception of necessity* (*ananke**) comes to acquire overtones of moral blame or moral approval. Meanwhile the living, divine stuff or process (*physis**) which the earlier thinkers conceive of as the underlying unity and cause of all phenomena is replaced by two rival conceptions: on the one hand, by matter, now increasingly regarded as inert, and sometimes as actually evil in itself; on the other hand by such conceptions as form* or idea* (εἶδος*), as living soul* or spirit* (ψυχή*), and as reason (*nous**).

The question of causality* (*aitia**) now becomes acute, and moves from the field of physics to the field of ethics and metaphysics, and finally of religion. Indeed it is from the early law-courts, where the question of accountability (*aitia*) for actions arose, that the idea of causality was transferred to the consideration of *physis* and the *cosmos*. But when what we should call material agencies no longer sufficed to explain value judgments and the moral responsibility* of man, the debate turned on the extent to which rational man is master of his actions. It could be argued by some that man is wholly in the power of an external destiny* or fate, or of the gods; that is the contention of determinism*, or of fatalism*, and of its offshoot, astrology.* Others could reply that to the extent to which man's reason partakes of the universal reason or spirit, to that extent there are things "in our power" (ἐφ' ἡμῖν*), so that we acquire wills and personalities and may deliberately choose actions in conformity with nature and reason. That is the case, in its briefest form, for freedom of the will.* On the fringe of the debate is that external group of indeterminate factors which all men recognize and which we call "chance" * (*tyche**; fortune*; accident*; coincidence*; contingency*; *Lachesis**). They are forces which affect nature and therefore life most powerfully, but which cannot be foreseen, and which in themselves have little or no moral quality unless viewed either as a happy divine dispensation (θεία τύχη*) or as a challenge to man's endurance (*tlemosyne**). Only a late period in Greek thought, losing faith both in the elder gods and in man's power and reason, made of Tyche a major deity.

The whole trend of Greek thought, therefore, in its higher levels if not in the consciousness of average men, is from an external toward an internal conception of life. It turns its gaze from prosperity (ὄλβος*) to happiness* (*eudaimonia**) or even blessedness* (*beatitudo**); from passive endurance (*tlemosyne*) of external evil to the positive creations of the will and character. "A man's character is his destiny" (ἦθος ἀνθρώπῳ δαίμων*); "the responsibility lies with him who chooses; God is blameless" (αἰτία ἑλομένου, θεὸς ἀναίτιος*). It finds in events and the body, existing in space and time, only the imperfect instruments through which a soul or will or reason may find expression; and it finds ultimate good and evil (the absence or incompleteness of good) only in the conscious purposes which they may elect. Thus crude fatalism is abandoned as an edifice built on semblances, in favor of a rational or idealistic humanism. Yet man did not create himself and his world, nor is the good that is in process of emerging from nature and man yet complete. Therefore the final step taken by some Greek thinkers is to subordinate humanism to the conception of divine providence* (πρόνοια*), within which man may seek by his own free choice the good that is gradually unfolded to his reason.

# CHAPTER II

## EARLY GREEK POETRY

GREEK literature begins, for us, with Homer. Yet we cannot fail to recognize in his poems, and still more in the survivals of ritual in the historic period, the traces of earlier, possibly pre-Hellenic, ways of recognizing men's dependence on the powers of Nature, the universal Mother. She is a creative life-force, a *daimon* dispensing food and warmth and shelter, hardship and suffering, a force wonderful in her variety, a force neither wholly good nor wholly evil. She continues through the cycle of days and months and years, and her way is the way of *Dike*.[1] As Mother Earth, *Gaea*, she receives the vegetation rites that are supposed to bring food, and that become the symbols of the cycle of birth, death, and rebirth.[2] So proclaims the (late) Homeric Hymn (XXX) to Earth the Mother of All: "I will sing of well-founded Earth, Mother of All, oldest of all beings; she feeds all creatures. . . . Through thee, O queen, men are blessed in their children and blessed in their harvests; and to thee it belongs to give means of life to mortal men and to take it away. Happy is the man whom thou delightest to honor; he hath all things in abundance. . . ."

But Earth was not the only *daimon*; for offshoots of divinity were felt in the baleful *Keres*, winged creatures that brought the infection of disease and age and death, and that later could be identified with Fate; or again, in the *Erinys*, the "wrathful" and avenging ghost of a murdered man, that could later become the stern guardian of law and justice. In time the older *daimones*, invested with something like human qualities, had to resist the invasion of Zeus and his glorious Olympians, as both myth and cult testify. But even after Themis,[3] the new divine counterpart of human conscience and human ideals of conduct, had been wedded to Zeus and eclipsed *Dike*, the Way of Things, the new dynasty found themselves compelled to continue, along with their new rôle as anthropomorphic beings presiding over a social order, something of the rôle of nature gods. Even when the victory of Zeus was complete, and he had dethroned old Cronos and defeated the Titans and wedded reluctant

[1] Cf. R. Hirzel, *Themis, Dike und Verwandtes*, pp. 56–64; 210–227; J. E. Harrison, *Themis*, pp. 516–518; and see below, p. 224.

[2] See below, pp. 49–50; 64 f.

[3] See Appendix 1: *Themis*.

Hera[4] and many another divinity or local spirit, he had to take over the attributes and functions of his defeated rivals. The older *daimones*, even if vanquished, could well afford to bide their time; for in a later day, when the Greeks found their human gods all too human, and powerless to help them in time of trouble, it was the older *daimones* who became their deliverers in the religious revival of the mystery cults.[5] For behind the gods of Olympus there was still the divine Life-force, the spirit of growth, something felt rather than apprehended by the intellect, and therefore something that lent itself to poetry and life. And the Greeks, whose Zeus was never regarded as the creator of the visible *cosmos*, found in the old worship of divine powers abundant materials for a cosmogony, a philosophy of history, and a theology that becomes both a science of nature and a guide to human life. These matters will concern us later; at present we must observe that it was precisely the dual rôle of the Olympians, as nature gods and as gods of a social order, that first made acute the problem of evil.

Recognizing, as we must, that the *Iliad* and *Odyssey* represent a long tradition of oral verse-making, in which many strata of ideas are fused, we shall not expect to find systematic theology; moreover, the poet's aim is to delight with his story, rather than to instruct. So we shall not easily distinguish traditional elements from the poet's own thought. Yet his ethics, if I may so put the point, is nobler than his theology. His gods, as Xenophanes and Plato will complain, are guilty of sins which neither they nor mortals condone among ordinary men. Even Zeus, though he can smile as well as frown, is sometimes no more than a clumsy, hot-tempered *pater familias*, whereas the swineherd Eumaeus has all the virtues.

We may waive the moral inadequacy of the gods as individuals, their lack of true affection for men,[6] their failure to maintain justice constantly in this world or in another world,[7] the polytheistic system or lack of system; these blemishes the Greeks could in time recognize, and in the course of centuries they did to some extent purify their theology. But the dual rôle of Zeus, who besides pretending to hold the sceptre of law and justice over his own régime, which is a "succession monarchy" founded on the débris of a great war, has perforce to assume the liabilities of his predecessors, makes him both arbiter of justice and weather god. And

[4] Cf. the Homeric Hymn (III) to Pythian Apollo, 305–355, emphasizing Hera's connection with the earth and her hostility to Zeus. See also below, p. 64.

[5] See below, pp. 49–63.

[6] "This is the lot the gods have spun for miserable men, that they should live in pain; yet themselves are sorrowless" (*Il.* 24, 525 f; cf. *Od.* 1, 325–352; *Hom. Hymn* III (Apollo) 189–193); cf. also *Il.* 6, 311; 13, 631–639; *Od.* 9, 551–555; 20, 201–203.

[7] See Appendix 2: Afterlife in Homer.

this ascription to Zeus of responsibility for the processes of nature, apparently so obvious and so religious a point of view (does not Job's Jehovah speak "out of the whirlwind"? [8]), is really charged with a dangerous explosive power. To the extent to which the Olympic gods take over the nature religion and express it in anthropomorphic form, to that extent they are unmoral, if not positively vicious. The rain falls alike upon the just and upon the unjust; the thunder and the lightning strike the good and the evil alike. Let this remain a matter of blind Nature's power, which knows nothing of human distinctions, and no harm is done to our moral sense; Nature knows no better.[9] But give this same power to gods in our own form, recognizing our standards of good and evil, and we are confronted by gods who are arbitrary and capricious when they are not passionate and cruel. Translate into human terms the various fertility-cults that are supposed to prosper the crops, and we shall have polygamous gods, fickle gods, gods of whose powers we shall often have reason to be sceptical. For like political parties that claim the credit for a period of prosperity, the human gods of Homer must also assume the blame for catastrophes and periods of depression. Monarchs who reign but do not rule, delegating their authority to ministers, evade having imputed to them the responsibility for all imperfections, as does the divine creator in Plato's *Timaeus*.[10] Homer's less calculated solution is perhaps polytheism and divided responsibility, and an occasional recourse to *Moira*. Some imputation of evil, moreover, Zeus escapes by not being the creator of the *cosmos*; he uses the materials provided by his predecessors.

Even after the gods have been differentiated, the idea of power lingering in the vaguer *daimon* [11] or *daimonion* often provides an easier explanation of the divine cause of things than could some more departmentalized god in human form,[12] and thus comes near to standing for the idea of Fate; in particular it emphasizes what is external to a man's will, what he does in passion or infatuation; indeed the adjective *daimonios* is regularly used of what is incomprehensible or blameworthy.[13] And since it is in times of misfortune, rather than of normal prosperity, that men are most apt to suppose that higher powers have actually interfered,[14] the tendency

[8] *Job*, 38, 1.

[9] Even the conservative Aristophanes allows himself, in the character of Socrates, to point out, *Clouds* 397–402, that Zeus does not strike with lightning the perjurers, but his own temple and the oak trees.

[10] See below, pp. 307–309.

[11] The more plausible etymology of the word, from stem *da-* (cf. δαίω, δατέομαι, "to share"; cf. Hesychius, *s.v.* δαίμων) suggests that the *daimon*, or "sharer," apportions things among men.

[12] See Appendix 3: *Daimon*.

[13] Homer does not know the word *eudaimon* ("attended by a kindly *daimon*," the common classical word for "happy"), but does use its opposite, *dusdaimon*.

[14] *Od*. 3, 166; 7, 248; 12, 295.

in Greek literature from Homer down is to attribute to "the *daimon*," or to some unnamed god, or to the gods collectively, whatever arises to thwart the wills or hopes of men, as well as whatever sudden inspiration occurs to them. It is more often a *theos* who dispenses favors, and (the) *daimon* who, if not neutral, exerts a baleful influence.[15] Already the *daimon* seems to have gone far on the path from the rôle of divinity to the rôle of devil (the later *demon*).[16] In Homer, however, the problem of evil is not solved by a simple recourse to a dualistic separation between powers of light and powers of darkness, as in various oriental religions. In only one passage does Homer seem to adopt so drastic a solution: "a hateful *daimon* attacked him . . . but the gods delivered him from evil."[17] Even here, however, the *daimon* does only what an angry god might elsewhere do. Homer's *daimon*, like his *Moira*, is inscrutable, and at times hostile; his gods have human failings. But Homer has no absolutely evil god, no devil, unless it be *Ate*; and her rôle is, after all, a minor one.[18]

Yet, though Homer is not a thorough-going dualist, he recognizes, as all must recognize, the stubborn fact that there are evils in the world, disorders and maladies, pains and disappointments, ruin and deaths that shock our moral sense. Mere optimism will not do; men and even gods must struggle, must suffer. What is more, a poem that is to have movement and action must allow some freedom of human wills within the divine framework, or even in opposition to divine wills. The setting forth of the unimpeded will of a perfect Zeus might be good theology, but would not result in a great poem. Polytheism, however, not only has its artistic advantages but provides in the conflicting wills of the gods a loophole for a certain amount of human freedom and a plausible explanation of many an evil.

Beyond the carrying out of momentary purposes, have Homer's gods any more far-reaching purpose, moral or providential? There is, of course, the "Plan" of Zeus (*Dios Boule*, *Il.* 1, 5; cf. *Od.* 11, 297), and the persistent care of Athene, aided by Zeus, for Odysseus. Moreover it has been observed that when the gods act collectively they show "a certain gravity, a sense of duty, and consciousness of moral responsibility for the use of their power over men."[19] For there stands behind the gods a shadowy reality,

[15] 14 times in the *Iliad*; 20 in the *Odyssey*. Good examples are: *Il.* 9, 600; *Od.* 3, 166; 7, 248; 12, 295.

[16] See below, pp. 310; 369.

[17] *Od.* 5, 396 f. Cf. further J. A. Hild, *Étude sur les Démons*, pp. 36–75.

[18] See below, pp. 20–22.

[19] W. E. Gladstone, *Landmarks of Homeric Study* (London, 1890), p. 65; cf. E. Ehnmark, *Idea of God in Homer*, pp. 87; 95–101, connecting this attitude of the gods with *dike* (which thus rises superior to *themis*), and with the moral order decreed by fate which has no power of its own unless it becomes operative through their agency (p. 80). Less trustworthy, but of

a fixed order rather than a power,[20] a divine conscience, at times gathering moral grandeur, at times dreadful and oppressive to man, the reality known as *Moira*. If *Dike*, in the pre-Homeric world, stands for a rhythm in the time-flow of things, *Moira* suggests their orderly division in space, — men's lands and just portions, the rôles and prerogatives of men and gods.[21] It is almost equivalent to *Physis*; as Hermes shows Odysseus the *physis* of the plant *moly*,[22] so Penelope remarks to him that men cannot keep awake indefinitely, "since the immortals have made for mortals a *moira* for each thing," [23] which is as much as to say that "you can't fight against Nature." The exact color of the word *moira* depends, of course, on its context in each case; sometimes neutral, sometimes suggesting what must be and therefore should be, it often tends, particularly when it refers to the one lot that all must accept, the *μοῖρα θανάτου*, to acquire, like *daimon*, an unfavorable meaning, and is given uncomplimentary epithets.[24] Thus in a polytheistic world *Moira* keeps order and assigns limits; she is just, or at least not capricious; not yet has the word *tyche* come into use.

So far the idea of Fate has ethical possibilities. But how is *Moira* related to the gods? Are the two ideas identical? Or are they opposed? Is *Moira* superior to the gods? The fundamental task of assembling the passages that bear on the question was done by Nägelsbach;[25] and although he forced on Homer a greater degree of logical consistency than is to be expected of the poet, whose attitude is one of religious faith rather than of philosophic conviction, it is fair to say that on the whole Homer recognizes no essential conflict, as did certain later poets and philosophers, between the power of Fate and the will of Zeus (and other gods), between the remote power and the immediate agency.[26] Both express the cause of events which man is powerless to alter, and it is only the demand of the story that determines whether the more abstract or the more vividly personified agent shall be invoked on a given occasion. Sometimes a tradi-

---

some interest, is P. E. Eberhard, *Das Schicksal als Poetische Idee bei Homer* (Paderborn, 1923).

[20] Ehnmark, p. 75.

[21] See Appendix 4: Etymologies of *Moira*, etc.

[22] *Od.* 10, 303.

[23] *Od.* 19, 591–597. Cf. K. Lehrs, "Zeus und die Moira," in *Populäre Aufsätze*, pp. 216–218.

[24] E.g., *Il.* 21, 83. Cf. A. Mayer, *Moira in Griechischen Inschriften* (Giessen, 1927); Moira in inscriptions of all periods tends to mean misfortune, death, or even a goddess of death.

[25] *Hom. Theol.*[3], pp. 116–141.

[26] M. P. Nilsson, *Arch. f. Rel. Wiss.* 33 (1936), pp. 89 f., warns against the fallacious idea that Homer contains philosophic fatalism, and that the attempt to define in theological terms the relation between Destiny and Zeus existed in his age.

tional formula, expressing the rôle of fate or of a god respectively, and ready to hand, may determine in a given line which turn of expression is the more convenient for the exigency of an oral versifier.

Frequently Fate and gods seem to be interchangeable in their functions.[27] If Fate spins men's lots, so also do the gods.[28] When man's lot seems sad and inscrutable it is natural to think of the gods as ill-disposed; for all things "lie on the knees of the gods" (*Od.* 1, 267). Oedipus had to suffer "through the destructive plan of the gods" (*Od.* 11, 276); the death of Patroclus, the sufferings of Odysseus, and the painful struggles of the Greeks and the Trojans all came to pass "by the will of the gods." [29] Zeus plans the happy outcome of the wanderings of Odysseus, and attributes it to *moira* (*Od.* 5, 41 f.; 114 f.), while Odysseus attributes his troubles to Zeus (*Od.* 9, 38; 67; 12, 405) or to the "evil *aisa* of Zeus" (*Od.* 9, 52), or again to a *daimon* (*Od.* 12, 295) or to "the gods of heaven" (*Od.* 7, 242). But Eustathius, twelfth century commentator on Homer, oversimplifies the matter when he states that the will of Zeus and destiny are synonymous.[30] Not only is Poseidon subject to *moira* (*Od.* 9, 528–535), but even Zeus is powerless to avert the death of his own son Sarpedon, though he apparently can postpone the day of his doom.[31] The death of Patroclus is variously ascribed to Zeus (*Il.* 16, 252; 647; 800), to the purpose of Zeus (688), to the gods (693), to Apollo (791; 804; 816), to Zeus and Apollo (844), to *Moira* and Apollo and Euphorbus and Hector (849 f.). Sometimes divine responsibility is limited to foreknowledge of what must be, as in the case of Sarpedon's death.[32] Sometimes Zeus shows a certain vacillation of purpose (*Il.* 16, 644–655). But at the critical moments of the poems the will of Zeus tends to be connected with *Moira*; and once his mind is made up, the consequences follow inexorably. He may even warn mortals by thunder and lightning (*Il.* 8, 75; 133) or by a star (*Il.* 4, 75–84) that the dread moment has come.

It seems likely that the figure of the Jars, in the great speech of Achilles,[33] in which evils outnumber blessings two to one, is a traditional one, and is the germ of the single Jar of Pandora, containing only evils, by which Hesiod was to account in part for the evil in the world.[34] Tradi-

[27] Cf. *Il.* 21, 83 f.: "destructive *Moira* has given me into your hands; I must be hated by father Zeus, who gave me to you"; similarly *Il.* 16, 687–694; 18, 115 f.; and for verbal connections *Il.* 9, 608: *Διὸς αἴσῃ*; *Od.* 22, 413: *μοῖρα θεῶν*.

[28] See below, p. 16, and n. 37.

[29] *θεῶν ἰότητι*, *Il.* 19, 9; *Od.* 7, 214; 12, 190 = 17, 119.

[30] Eustathius, p. 1686; *ἔστι δὲ ταὐτὸν Διὸς βουλὴν εἰπεῖν καὶ θεοῦ μοῖραν.*

[31] *Il.* 16, 433–461. For Cicero's interpretation of this passage, cf. *De Div.* II, 25 (see below, p. 362 and note 186).

[32] Cf. also *Od.* 20, 75 f.; 4, 399; 468.

[33] *Il.* 24, 525–533; see below, pp. 26 f.

[34] See below, pp. 30 f.

tional, too, in all probability, is the other principal figure by which Zeus is represented as the chief dispenser of good and evil, the "golden scales." [35] The poet is not suggesting that Zeus is in doubt as to the issue and is leaving the decision to something external; for the fate of Hector, at any rate, was already settled,[36] and the scales serve but to dramatize the turn in the tide of battle. Nor are the scales symbolic, like the "Scales of Justice," of any specially moral purpose; emphasizing tragic events which are essential to the story, they suggest, like the Jars and the spinning of Fate (and of the gods),[37] the necessary evil that the gods send or at least permit.

It was only in the poets who folllowed Homer that Fate was at times definitely separated from the gods and sometimes even set above them. Moreover it was chiefly in the post-Homeric period that *Moira*, a single order, gave place to the *Moirai*, the Fates. Only once in Homer (*Il.* 24, 49) do we find the plural; but in Hesiod (*Theog.* 217 ff.) we find not only the three *Moirai* and their pedigree but their familiar names (Clotho, "the Spinner," Lachesis, "the Dispenser of Lots," and Atropos, "She who cannot be turned"). In Homer it is sometimes the gods who "spin men's destiny," sometimes *Moira* or "*Aisa* and the stern spinning women." [38] Often such destinies are spun for men at the moment of their birth (*Od.* 4, 208; cf. *Il.* 10, 70 f.), which is a more vivid way of asserting the determining influence of heredity, though it links each individual directly with Fate, rather than with his forebears. And because mortal spinners often sing over their work, it is natural for these superhuman spinners to sing, foretelling in words what they are creating with their hands; hence the "Song of the Fates" of later ages.[39] Here, of course, we have something very close to fatalism of the oriental type.

Other divine agencies, hardly personified and by no means yet individualized, are such vague powers as *Eris* (Strife), *Phobos* (Fear), *Kydoimos* (Uproar) and *Ossa* (Rumor); but the age of vigorous personification begins only with Hesiod. From the earlier age, however, linger the *Keres*, the spirits that cut short the thread of man's life, and when least

[35] *Il.* 8, 69–72; 22, 209–213; cf. 16, 658; 19, 223 f.; *Hom. Hymn* IV (Hermes), 324; Theognis, 155–158.

[36] *Il.* 22, 179; 22, 185. Cf. E. Ehnmark, *Idea of God in Homer*, p. 78: "Zeus weighs the fates, just as other objects are weighed: to ascertain their weight. When the lot containing death sinks, Zeus knows whose fate it is to die. This by no means implies that he is subject to a power, but rather that there exists an order to which he conforms. The weight of a commodity is not determined by a power, but is conceived as a quality inherent in the very structure of matter."

[37] *Il.* 20, 127 f.; 24, 209 f.; 24, 525; *Od.* 1, 17; 3, 208; 7, 197; 8, 579; 11, 139; 16, 64.

[38] See the previous note.

[39] Cf. Plato, *Rep.* 617 bd (see below, pp. 315 f.); the Roman *Parcae Veridicae* (*Fatidicae*); Catullus 64; Virgil, *Buc.* 4; and the Norse "Weird Sisters."

personified are equivalent to the moment of death.[40] Only once, in a powerful scene (*Il.* 18, 535–540), is "destructive *Ker*" fully personified, along with *Eris* and *Kydoimos*, as a grim angel of death. Elsewhere the *Keres* are akin to such powers as *Gorgons*, *Sirens*, *Sphinxes*, and *Erinyes*.

The *Erinys*, originally the angry soul of a murdered man,[41] appears in Homer not as the soul but as the avenger of the soul, and of offenses against kindred, particularly against parents or against the eldest born (*Od.* 11, 280). They know no pity, nor any excuse or justification for crime; they are interested only in the deed, and avenge especially the sins for which primitive human law provides no redress. Nowhere in Greek mythology do the *Erinyes* pursue Clytaemnestra for the murder of her husband, for he was no blood relation of hers. Yet not only the family but strangers and even beggars can invoke their protection (*Od.* 17, 475); not merely murder but perjury and other crimes are their concern, and they can be called upon for the fulfilment of curses.[42] Even the gods are subject to the stern power of the *Erinyes* (*Il.* 21, 410–414; cf. 15, 204); in other words, they have become the avengers of all offenses against the moral law, or, in more positive terms, the champions of the moral order in every sphere. Finally, as in the moral sphere they have punished what may be called "unnatural" conduct, they assume a guardianship over even natural law. Here their rôle is very close to that of *Moira*, the order of things. So when Xanthus, Achilles' horse, spoke, prophesying the death-day that "a mighty god and powerful *Moira*" were soon to bring him, and "when he had thus spoken the *Erinyes* stayed his voice," it was not merely to reprove the unnatural prodigy of a speaking horse (for "Hera gave him speech"). The horse is the spokesman of *Moira*; and when the *Erinyes*, acting as coadjutors of *Moira*, stay his voice, it is because he has spoken to the full.[43] So the *Erinyes*, beginning as *daimones*, spirits of instinctive vengeance crudely expressing *Physis*, have been purified by *Themis* (or *Nomos*), and have then strangely returned again to *Physis*, as upholders of *Moira*.

The gods and their agents, then, sustaining and expressing the power of *Moira*, uphold both the natural order and the moral order. What is the attitude of Homer's mortals toward this system (if we may call it a system)? They recognize in it a limit to the boons that they can expect of

[40] Cf. κείρω, "to cut, shear." See also above, p. 10. κὴρ θανατοῖο is a frequent formula.

[41] See above, p. 10.

[42] *Il.* 19, 258–260; *Od.* 2, 135; 9, 449–457; 9, 566–572. An oath (*Horkos*) involves a "fence" by which one has bound oneself; like the curse, its sanction is the power of subterranean divinities. See also below, p. 20.

[43] *Il.* 19, 404–418; J. E. Harrison, *Prolegomena*, p. 16; but see also H. J. Rose, *Handbook of Greek Mythology* (London, 1928), p. 84. For Heraclitus on the *Erinyes* as guardians of natural law, see below, p. 225.

the gods, and to the acts that they can themselves commit with impunity. So far as they themselves are concerned, it is *Aidos*, a sense of shame or conscience or personal honor, that acts negatively and forbids them to do certain things. If we ask what things, seeking a content for this vague, constraining emotion, we find that it is most often concerned with the treatment of the aged, the weak, the socially unfortunate, whose rights are guarded by the gods. Thus aged Priam and the swineherd Eumaeus can both invoke *Aidos*.[44] And if *Aidos* is the sense of honor on its negative side, its positive character is expressed by *Thumos*, the proud, courageous, high-spirited self, eager to assert itself and win glory (*Kudos*). (For *θυμός*, *Od.* 8, 178; for *κῦδος*, *Il.* 22, 390.) But this spirit, "very manly" (*ἀγήνωρ*), and self-seeking, may also pass over into *Hybris*, arrogance, wanton violence, insolence; this is the fault of Ajax, son of Oïleus, who boasted that he had escaped death despite the gods, and thus incurred death through the vengeful wrath of Poseidon.[45] In varying degrees, *hybris* is the sin of the suitors of Penelope, and even of Achilles when he maltreats the body of Hector, casting away pity and *Aidos* (*Il.* 24, 39–45).

If such deeds as *Aidos* forbids are nevertheless committed, other men feel a just indignation, *Nemesis*. One may, to be sure, feel *Aidos* in good season, and thus avoid such social obloquy. Thus Hector, dissuaded from battle by the appeal of Andromache, cannot give in to her entreaty: "for I have sore shame (*aidos*) of the Trojans and Trojan women with trailing robes, if like a coward I shrink from battle; moreover my own spirit (*thumos*) forbiddeth me."[46] Here we find as a powerful motive not merely self-respect but the face of public opinion, the idea of what will arouse blame, the voice of Mrs. Grundy. Penelope "respects (has *aidos* for) her lord's couch and the talk (*φάτις*) of the people." (*Od.* 16, 75; cf. 21, 323–329.) Telemachus appeals to the suitors to resent (feel *nemesis* for) his own intolerable plight and to have regard (*aidos*) for their neighbors, and to fear the wrath of the gods, beseeching them in the name of Zeus and of *Themis* (*Od.* 2, 64–68). For himself he fears, if he should obey the suitors, not only the punishment of the gods and of the *Erinyes* but the blame (*nemesis*) of men (*Od.* 2, 134–137). But the suitors "had no fear of the gods nor of the indignation (*nemesis*) of men hereafter" (*Od.* 22, 39 f.).

In *Aidos* and *Nemesis*, then, the Homeric world felt two forms of

[44] *Il.* 24, 503–506; *Od.* 14, 56–58; 83 f.; 388 f. On *aidos* and related matters, from Homer to Democritus, see further C. E. frhr. von Erffa, "ΑΙΔΩΣ."

[45] *Od.* 4, 499–511. For the similar *hybris* of Ajax, son of Telamon, see below, p. 148. The word *ὕβρις* is perhaps cognate to *ὑπέρ*, suggesting therefore excess, lack of moderation.

[46] *Il.* 6, 441–444; cf. 22, 105–107; *Il.* 15, 661 f.

*Themis*, one self-regarding, the other social, and both constraining men to observe certain limits. *Nemesis*, in particular, involves a sentiment of disapproval, in varying degrees, of all violations of duty or of any excess or disproportion, of all temerity or presumption; it is quick to emerge at the sight of undeserved misfortune, or at the triumph of the wicked. It is a moral sentiment, in that resentment is felt against the offender even if one is not personally offended by him. And if men feel *nemesis* at overweening acts, so also do the gods. Many are the myths that tell of human temerity and divine punishment (e.g. Thamyris, Niobe, the Ajaxes, Tantalus, Phaethon, etc.). In the *Iliad* each satisfaction of passion or pride is paid for by sorrow or death; the *Odyssey* triumphantly vindicates the divine order, and virtue and vice receive their rewards. In the epic, far more than in tragedy, what has been called "poetic justice" [47] is illustrated; yet the epic is also not without tragic elements, especially in the *Iliad*. Indeed Aristotle distinguishes the *Iliad*, as "pathetic," from the *Odyssey*, which he calls "ethical." [48] The most obvious instance of *hybris* followed by *nemesis* is the punishment of the suitors of Penelope; in fact she feels that it cannot be Odysseus, it must be some god who has slain them (*Od.* 23, 62–64).

Just anger is thus reflected in the *Nemesis* of the gods; they jealously maintain the moral order, and punish any overstepping of its boundaries. Yet there are times when they seem to send calamities to men without just cause and to be jealous of their own superiority and prerogatives, or even to be animated by ill-will at the sight of the prosperity of others.[49] Perhaps this is indeed the earlier form of anger known to the gods; they love their friends and hate all who threaten their own security, and there is nothing theological about the matter. If the gods are chiefly responsible for human affairs, they must at times seem niggardly when things go wrong. Menelaus, a special favorite of Zeus, would gladly have welcomed Odysseus to his own land, and shared it with him: "however the god himself, methinks, must have been jealous, who from that hapless man alone cut off his returning" (*Od.* 4, 181 f.). And Penelope, excusing her caution in welcoming her husband, pleads: "Be not angry with me, Odysseus. . . . It is the gods that gave us sorrow, the gods who begrudged us that we should abide together and have joy of our youth and come to the threshold of old age." [50] The word used of the grudging attitude of

[47] See below, pp. 93–97.

[48] See Appendix 5: *Odyssey* ethical.

[49] J. Adam, *Religious Teachers*, pp. 36–39; also, for Homer and later authors, S. Ranulf, *The Jealousy of the Gods and Criminal Law at Athens: A Contribution to the Sociology of Moral Indignation* (Copenhagen and London, 1933–1934), esp. I, pp. 20–114; 146–158; II, 28–74; and cf. below, p. 20, n. 52.

[50] *Od.* 23, 209–212; cf. 5, 118–120.

the gods in each of these passages (ἄγαμαι, "be amazed at," "be vexed," "begrudge") introduces an idea, though not the precise word, that was destined in later times to play an important rôle in Greek thought: the "Envy" or "Jealousy" of the gods (φθόνος θεῶν, in post-Homeric writers). The germ of the idea is here, as well as the attitude that pious or cautious mortals should adopt with regard to possibly jealous gods; it is an attitude of moderation, of scrupulous care not to offend by presumption. Menelaus, for example, will not let his palace, lordly though it is, be compared with that of Zeus (*Od.* 4, 78–81). "Think, son of Tydeus," cries Apollo, "and shrink, and desire not to match thy spirit with gods; since there is nothing common to the race of the immortal gods and to the men who walk upon the earth" (*Il.* 5, 440–442). "Never boast, in folly," counsels the neatherd, "but leave speech to the gods, since they are far stronger than we" (*Od.* 22, 287–289). And how far this spirit of distrust can go we learn from the words of the pious Telemachus, when he beholds his father, still unknown to him, transfigured by the power of Athene; and he "marvelled at him, and looked away for fear lest it should be a god," and prayed to him: ". . . surely thou art a god, one of those who keep the wide heaven. Nay then, be gracious, . . . and spare us" (*Od.* 16, 178–185).

This instinctive feeling of a barrier between man and god, this fear that any presumption on the part of man may cause the gods to take offense, lies behind not only the ethical ideas of the Homeric age but the prudential morality of the historic period.[51] Fear of overstepping barriers is the element common to the Homeric *Aidos* and the sanctity of oaths (*horkoi* = "barriers") and to the classical ideal of *Sophrosyne* (the word is post-Homeric). "Excess in nothing"; "think only human thoughts"; avoid *hybris* and you will not have to fear *nemesis*; be warned betimes; tempt not the gods, or fate; the quiet, obscure life is the safest and happiest; the form of expression will vary throughout Greek literature, but the thought will be much the same. It is the reply of *Themis* to *Moira*, of *Nomos* to *Physis*; it is the attempt, by shrewdness and self-discipline, to circumvent the innate dangers of life. The later history of the idea of *Nemesis* and of the Jealousy (*Phthonos*) of the gods, and of the repudiation of the latter idea by certain Greeks, must concern us again;[52] divine jealousy is not prominent in Homer, nor is *Nemesis* personified.

Nevertheless men are guilty of *hybris* and there must be a reason. In fact Homer recognizes two reasons: the abuse of the human freedom of

[51] For Pindar, see below, pp. 74–78.

[52] See below, *Indices*; s.vv. Phthonos (φθόνος); Jealousy. Cf. also E. Tournier, *Némésis et la Jalousie des Dieux*; H. V. Canter, "Ill Will of the Gods in Greek and Latin Poetry," *C.P.* 32 (1937), pp. 131–143; F. Wehrli, ΛΑΘΕ ΒΙΩΣΑΣ; J. A. K. Thomson, *Irony*, pp. 93–115, finding in Homer not the Jealousy of the gods, but (chiefly because of Achilles' foreknowledge of his destiny, and other similar considerations) Tragic Irony.

the will, resulting in a hardened character, which is *atasthalie*; and something so terrible, so blinding, that men would fain disown it and impute it to the gods, the heaven-sent power of evil, which is *Ate*,[53] the "eldest daughter of Zeus" (*Il.* 19, 90). Here, at last, is something satanic, a very Devil, who beguiles at times even the gods (*Il.* 19, 95–124); and Zeus in turn would fain disown her (*Il.* 19, 125–133), though he employs her for ends beyond men's understanding. However much the rôle of *Ate* in men's moral downfall was to be justified and regularized by later poets in a sequence,[54] there is no moral justification for Homer's *Ate*. It is not the result of man's own freedom to sin (that is *atasthalie*); it is always external, and is almost equivalent to a verdict of "temporary insanity." Agamemnon lamely pleads that not he himself was to blame for his share in the quarrel with Achilles, "but Zeus and *Moira* and *Erinys*, who cast angry *Ate* in his mind" (*Il.* 19, 86–88; 134–137); and if it be urged that Agamemnon is merely seeking to excuse himself, let it be remembered that elsewhere Zeus is represented by the poet as wilfully deceptive.[55] If Homer had been content to leave *Ate* a child of *Physis* (which she is), instead of making her a daughter of Zeus, much moral confusion might have been avoided.

When Phoinix seeks to overcome the stubbornness of Achilles, arguing that even the gods are prevailed upon to forgive transgressions when men approach them with sacrifice and prayer, he continues: "For Prayers (*Litai*) are daughters of mighty Zeus, halting and wrinkled, and of eyes askance, whose care it is to go following after *Ate*. For *Ate* is strong and swift of foot, wherefore she far outrunneth all Prayers, and goeth before them over all the earth, and doeth men hurt; but they follow behind, to heal the harm. Now whoever revereth (feels *aidos* for) the daughters of Zeus when they draw near, him they greatly bless, and hear his entreaties; but whoever refuseth them, and harshly denieth, from him do they depart and beseech Zeus, son of Cronos, that *Ate* may come upon him, that he may be hurt and suffer atonement" (*Il.* 9, 502–512). Why do the Prayers lag behind *Ate*? Surely because men are slower to repent than to sin. And why is that? We might answer to-day, in order to save our pride, in terms of inhibitions and complexes; Homer's bit of allegory projects the conflict into the divine scene. Nevertheless Homer recognizes also, besides the momentary blindness of *Ate* (which is merely the result of yielding to the solicitations of external temptation) something more deliberate, a

[53] Ἄτη, and ἀάω, "hurt," "wound"; from which come suggestions of moral blinding, delusion, and ruin; *Od.* 21, 288–300; *Il.* 10, 391; 24, 28; *Hom. Hymn* II (Demeter) 256–258.

[54] See below, pp. 36; 37 f.; 40 f.; 43 f.

[55] *Il.* 2, 1–40; 4, 70–72; cf. Aesch. frag. 156 Sidgwick, quoted below, p. 107, n. 20; for Sophocles and Euripides, p. 139 and n. 6; p. 146 and n. 54.

deeper moral blindness: this is the wickedness of a hardened character that perversely and perhaps deliberately sins against the light, against an external moral law. It is *Atasthalie*.

During the classical period of Greek thought, as is often remarked, Greek equivalents for the English word "sin," and even the idea of sin, are all but absent. We find instead various expressions that imply "going too far," "overshooting the mark," "disturbing the right proportion" or "mean."[56] Even the striking and characteristic idea of *Hybris* is probably founded on the notion of excess.[57] Sometimes it is said, with some measure of truth, that Greek ethics is largely intellectual or aesthetic. However true that may be of the classical period, the *Hybris* and still more the *Atasthalie* of Homer represent the idea of sin, with the emphasis not on intellectual error, or even on a yielding to external seduction, but on innate and growing proneness to mischief, on a deliberate choice of evil.[58] They are the result of an aggravated wilfulness,[59] of a failure to observe *Aidos*; and they lead to *Nemesis* and the punishment of the gods. So the suitors, as one of them admits, have met a shameful death through their own deeds of *atasthalie* (*Od.* 22, 317).

For deeds of *atasthalie* men are themselves responsible; yet there remains *Moira*. But to ask whether Homer believes in fate or in freedom of the will is to ask an idle question; like most men, he believes in both — in the power of external forces (*Moira*, given expression by Zeus), and in man's own choices. The double answer appears clearly in the words of Odysseus, over the dead bodies of the suitors: "These men hath the *Moira* of the gods overcome *and* their own cruel deeds. . . . Wherefore they have met with an unseemly doom through their deeds of *atasthalie*" (*Od.* 22, 413–416). Against any one-sided answer,[60] and particularly against imputing every evil to the gods, Zeus himself protests in what may be called the *locus classicus* for this problem in Homer, in the council of the gods at the beginning of the *Odyssey*.[61] "Lo, how vainly do mortals blame the gods! For from us do they say that evils come, whereas they themselves through

[56] E.g. *ἁμαρτία*, on which see below, pp. 93 f.; 96; 98 f.

[57] See above, p. 18, n. 45; cf. *ὑπερβασίη*, *Il.* 16, 17 f.; *Od.* 22, 64; and *Od.* 1, 368: *μνηστῆρες ὑπέρβιον ὕβριν ἔχοντες*.

[58] Gladstone, *Juventus Mundi*, pp. 90 f, well compares the relation of *ἀτασθαλίη* to *ἄτη* with that of Aristotle's *κακία* to *ἀκρασία* (see below, p. 328), though, as he points out, Homer's moral law is more objective (or religious) than Aristotle's.

[59] Cf. *thumos*, above, p. 18.

[60] An example of one-sided criticism, denying choice and free will to Homeric man, appears to be C. Voigt's *Ueberlegung und Entscheidung* (Berlin, 1934). This work I have not seen; it is reviewed by H. L. Lorimer, *C. R.* 19 (1935), pp. 174 f.; cf. also L. A. Post, *T.A.P.A.* 70 (1939), p. 166, n. 9.

[61] *Od.* 1, 32–43: possibly a late portion of the Homeric poems. For Solon's development of the idea, see below, pp. 36 f.; and for the connection of Solon with Homer, cf. W. Jaeger, in *Sitzber. preuss. Akad. Wiss.* (Berlin, 1926), pp. 71 ff., and his *Paideia*, pp. 137–144.

their deeds of *atasthalie* bring sorrows beyond what is ordained," [62] — that is, beyond the ills that are common to the condition of mortals, provoking the vengeance of the gods for attempting to disturb the moral equilibrium, and in the case of Aegisthus, to which Zeus refers, despite the express warning of the gods. There is no predestination here; rather an opportunity offered and refused. ("It is hard to kick against the pricks.") Athene, assenting, proceeds to contrast with the deserved ruin of Aegisthus the undeserved sufferings of her favorite Odysseus. Not wholly undeserved, gently retorts Zeus; Odysseus has offended Poseidon in the blinding of Polyphemus; yet the gods may well help Odysseus homeward, and Poseidon had better forget his resentment. And so the story goes forward, with a clear picture of a world in which both Fate, represented by the wills of the gods, and the choices of human beings have their parts to play.

Not to be overlooked in the speech of Zeus is the explicit warning that he says the gods sent by Hermes to Aegisthus (*Od.* 1, 37–39). If it was predestined that Aegisthus should woo Clytaemnestra and slay Agamemnon in any case, what was the use of sending the warning? Clearly Zeus, who desires to disclaim sole responsibility for the ruin of Aegisthus, intends by citing the warning to emphasize the free choice that lay before Aegisthus. The warning is a command followed by a reason (the penalty that will follow the violation of the command). That is very different from foretelling as an ineluctable certainty the ruin of Aegisthus; it is analogous to the "twain fates" which are bearing Achilles to the issue of death, and between which he is permitted to choose: either to win imperishable fame, by remaining at the siege of Troy, and dying there, or to forego fame by returning home, and thus to live long.[63] This is not predestination, for of course Achilles, like Aegisthus, must die some day; the question is merely when and how. The prophecy of Teiresias with regard to the return of Odysseus (*Od.* 11, 100–137) is at first based on a condition [64] which is later dropped: If Odysseus and his men refrain from hurting the cattle of Helios, he will return, though in evil plight; if he does not refrain, he will return in an evil plight *and late*; and the rest of the prophecy assumes the latter alternative. If we encounter in Greek

[62] *ὑπὲρ μόρον*, *Od.* 1, 34; the expression is common. So also *ὑπὲρ αἶσαν*, as *Il.* 6, 487: no man shall send Hector to Hades "before his appointed time," though (488 f.) no man can escape *Moira* altogether.

For a general sketch of the development of the problem of moral responsibility that was set for the Greeks by the Homeric passage, cf. R. Mondolfo, *Problemi del Pensiero Antico*, pp. 3–20.

[63] *Il.* 9, 410–416; cf. 1, 415–418; 18, 95 f.; 19, 408–410; similar is the case of Echenor, *Il.* 13, 663–672.

[64] *Od.* 11, 105; 110; 112; 113; cf. *Od.* 12, 137–141 (Circe's prophecy).

tragedy prophecies and oracles that seem to bind the characters inexorably, we shall do well to consider whether they, too, may not be conditional.[65]

Although the Homeric poems are above all else poems of heroic action, they contain incidentally a surprising amount of reflection on human life and destiny, sometimes in the form of brief gnomic utterances, traditional in character, and not especially appropriate to the speakers, sometimes developed into the *rhesis.* Such utterances, like that of Zeus, just mentioned, the accepted maxims and ideas of the epoch, were destined to be developed further by the elegiac poets; and they provide a running commentary on the action almost comparable to the lyric choruses of full-grown tragedy.

Since the ideas of the Homeric world were far from systematic or even consistent with regard to the relation of Fate and the gods to Good and Evil, there were *gnomai* to several different effects which Homer's characters could cite as occasion arose. It would be hard to find in Homer an ascription to Zeus or to the gods of human happiness unmingled with suffering. What appears at first to be such an ascription proves to be a consolation for hardship — the remark of Nausicaa to shipwrecked Odysseus.[66] That the gods bestow on men a diversity of gifts is the theme of Odysseus himself, taunted by Euryalus for his unathletic appearance; and he develops the theme by antithesis, passing back and forth from one side of the matter to the other, in a style that was to be characteristic of the elegy.[67] That the gods are all-powerful is another commonplace, from which is deduced moreover a reflection on the grudging nature of gods who do so much less for man than they might.[68] Still more pointed is the reproach addressed to Zeus himself by Menelaus, exasperated by the Trojans, who, not content with having wantonly carried off his wife, are now insatiate of battle, apparently with the connivance of Zeus. "O father Zeus, they say that thou dost excel in wisdom all others, both men and gods; and all these things are from thee. How wondrously art thou favoring men of violence (*hybris*), even the Trojans!" etc.[69] It is with a more general sense of universal pity that the neatherd, welcoming the hapless stranger who is none other than Odysseus, and surmising that Odysseus may well be in similar plight, reproaches the god who should have treated the stranger better: "Father Zeus, none other god is more baneful than thou; for thou hast no pity on men when thou hast begotten

[65] See Appendix 6: Conditional Prophecy.

[66] *Od.* 6, 188–190; quoted below, p. 27.

[67] *Od.* 8, 166–185; cf. 1, 347–349; 15, 486–490; J. T. Stickney, *Les Sentences dans la Poésie grecque*, pp. 28–34; 94–96.

[68] *Od.* 10, 306; cf. *Il.* 13, 632; 16, 687–691; 19, 90; *Hom. Hymn* II (Demeter) 147 f.

[69] *Il.* 13, 631–639. Here not only are "all things" ascribed to the gods but "all these things," things that revolt the moral sense.

them, but dost give them fellowship with evil and with bitter pains" (*Od.* 20, 201–203). Here is the germ of the reproach, now bitter, now brooding, that later poets were to take up.[70]

Other Homeric *gnomai* crowd upon the memory. "By the event is even a fool made wise" is a saying with which both Menelaus and Achilles conclude speeches.[71] Familiar commonplaces are the feebleness of man,[72] man who is "even as the generation of leaves," [73] and the inevitability of death,[74] a thought which does not deter Hector from battle [75] and which actually heightens the resolution of Sarpedon. "Ah, my friend, if once escaping this battle you and I were to be ever ageless and immortal, neither would I myself fight in the van nor would I send thee into battle, that gives glory. But now, since ten thousand forms of death (κῆρες θανάτοιο) beset us none the less, which no mortal may shun nor escape, let us go forward, and bestow glory on another, or let him bestow it on us" (*Il.* 12, 322–328). Rare is the deeper note of pessimism and the incipient philosophy of history that meets us in the words of Athene, who, in the guise of Mentor, stirs up Telemachus with the idea of the progressive degeneracy of mankind: if he be indeed his father's son, he will act; if not, there is no hope. "For few children, to be sure, are like their father; the most are worse, yet a few are better than their sire." [76] And there is a difference between the melancholy of Homer at the spectacle of high hopes and powers untimely cut short and the cynical, middle-aged sort of pessimism that a later age was to experience. Indeed, Homer's age feels the death in battle of a young warrior like Achilles to be glorious as well as pathetic.[77] Still less does any Homeric character suggest, as will some later Greeks, that life is not good in itself, and that it were better never to have been born, or, having been born, to die as soon as possible.[78] On the contrary, for Homer, as for Mimnermus and for Horace and for Omar

[70] E.g., Theog. 373–392; 731–752. See below, pp. 40–42.

[71] *Il.* 18, 32; 20, 198; cf. Hes. *W.D.* 218.

[72] *Od.* 18, 130 f.; cf. *Il.* 17, 446 f., in a quite different sense.

[73] *Il.* 6, 145–149; cf. 21, 464–466, and echoes in Mimnermus, etc.

[74] *Od.* 16, 447.

[75] *Il.* 6, 486–493. Later (*Il.* 12, 243), in reply to a warning that an evil omen has been observed, Hector replies: "One omen (εἷς οἰωνός) is best, to fight for our country." Thus humanism, or rationalism, answers primitive superstition.

[76] *Od.* 2, 276 f. Note the antithetical gnomic form of expression; it was not really to the point to mention an improvement of son over sire. The decline of successive generations will meet us again in Hesiod's Myth of the Ages of Men (see below, pp. 31–33).

[77] S. H. Butcher, "The Melancholy of the Greeks," in *Some Aspects of the Greek Genius*, pp. 136–141; C. M. Bowra, *Tradition and Design in the Iliad* (Oxford, 1930), pp. 234–237; 248 f.; also, on the more general aspects of the whole subject, J. Adam, "Ancient Greek Views of Suffering and Evil," in *Vitality of Platonism*, pp. 190–212; H. Diels, "Der Antike Pessimismus"; W. Nestle, "Der Pessimismus und seine Überwindung bei den Griechen."

[78] For the commonplace, μὴ φῦναι, see below, p. 42, n. 189.

Khayyam, this life is good, in spite of its ills, though Homer's heroes prize it for other things than the roses, and the shades whom Odysseus calls up in the land of the Cimmerians are pale and meagre ghosts, envious of the living, and not at all themselves to be envied.

What, beyond occasional melancholy, is the attitude of Homer's characters, or of the poet himself, in the face of the evils of life? First, a manly endurance; this we shall learn to call *tlemosyne* (although that word will not appear before Archilochus).[79] Apollo contrasts with Achilles many another man who has suffered a grievous loss but who "has nevertheless brought his wailing and lamentation to an end; for an enduring soul (*τλητὸν . . . θυμόν*) have the *Moirai* given to men." [80] Or again Nausicaa, consoling the shipwrecked Odysseus, urges that "Zeus himself dispenseth happiness to men, to the good and to the evil, to each one as he listeth; and it is doubtless he that hath given thee this lot, and thou must endure (*τετλάμεν*) it in any case." [81] Then, in the second place, the Homeric characters may rely on their frank recognition of the power of the gods, which leads to a wholesome fear or even distrust of them, and to that cautious attitude of moderation which we have already noted.[82] If one could be certain that such precautions would avail, how happy life would be! Yet there remains the dark inscrutability of Fate and the gods; some evils come from our own folly, others from the jealousy of the gods or from *Ate*, and we can seldom draw the line clearly between the two sources of evil. However much we learn, however great our power, however long we live, in the shadow lies the unknown, frustration and ruin, the grave, often confronting us when we least expect them. Here is matter for tragedy, or, if the mood be less of sympathy than of intellectual apprehension, for irony. Both have their roots in Homer.

In two striking speeches put into the mouths of the two principal heroes of the respective poems, and throwing light on their characters, the philosophy of Fate, Good, and Evil is developed systematically and with an application to the special situation. In the last book of the *Iliad*, the "Ransoming of Hector," Priam and Achilles are brought together. Contrasted as strongly as possible, — Trojan with Greek, aged king with youthful warrior, weakness with fiery pride, — they are at last made equal

[79] See below, p. 35.

[80] *Il.* 24, 46–49; but cf. *Il.* 24, 549–551 (Achilles to Priam) quoted below, p. 27.

[81] *Od.* 6, 188–190; cf. *Od.* 18, 134–137 (Odysseus to Amphinomus), quoted below, p. 27; n.b. *τετληότι θυμῷ* (line 135); *Il.* 2, 299: *τλῆτε, φίλοι, κτλ.* (Odysseus); *Od.* 20, 17: *τέτλαθι δή, κραδίη· καὶ κύντερον ἄλλο ποτ' ἔτλης* (with which cf. Archilochus 7 and 67a; and see below, p. 35; *Od.* 12, 208 and 293; Virgil, *Aen.* 1, 198 f.; 202 f.; 207; Horace, *Odes* I, 7, 30–32); *Hom. Hymn* II (Demeter) 147: *θεῶν μὲν δῶρα καὶ ἀχνύμενοί περ ἀνάγκῃ | τέτλαμεν ἄνθρωποι· δὴ γὰρ πολὺ φέρτεροι εἰσιν*; and the (late) "Epigram" attributed to Homer (quoted below, p. 65, n. 86).

[82] See above, pp. 18–20.

by sorrow. To the moving appeal of Priam, Achilles in pity speaks his winged words:

Ah hapless man, many evils hast thou endured in thy heart. . . . But come now, sit upon a seat, and we will let our sorrows lie in our hearts, grieved though we be, for nothing availeth chill lament. For thus did the gods spin the lot for wretched mortals, that they should live in pain; but they themselves are sorrowless. For upon the floor of Zeus stands two Jars (πίθοι) of the evil gifts that he giveth, and another of blessings. To whomsoever Zeus, whose joy is in the lightning, giveth a mingled lot, he chanceth now on evil, now on good; but to whomsoever he giveth only of the evil, him he bringeth to outrage, and evil hunger driveth him over the goodly earth, and he is a wanderer honored neither of gods nor of men.[83]

And Achilles continues with a personal application of this thesis, first to the case of his own father, and then to the lot of Priam. "Endure (ἄνσχεο)," he concludes, "and lament not overmuch in thy heart; for nought wilt thou avail by grieving for thy son, nor wilt thou bring him to life ere thou suffer some new evil." [84] What is the kernel of this hard-earned philosophy of Achilles? Acceptance of the good, resignation before the evil, that the gods bestow, and at last a pity born of fellow-suffering.

In the course of his response to the kindly words of the half-decent suitor Amphinomus, Odysseus remarks:

Nothing feebler than man doth the earth nurture, of all the creatures that breathe and move upon the face of the earth. Lo, he thinketh that never shall he suffer evil in time to come, while the gods give him prosperity, and his limbs move easily. But when the blessed gods bring to pass evil things, these too he bears, though reluctantly, with steadfast heart (τετληότι θυμῷ). For the spirit of mortals is of the selfsame sort as the fortune (ἦμαρ) unto which the father of men and gods leadeth them. I, too, was once like to have been prosperous among men, but many a deed of *atasthalie* did I do, in hardihood and boldness of spirit, trusting in my father and my brethren. Wherefore let no man ever be lawless any more, but let him keep quietly the gifts of the gods, whatsoever they may give.[85]

And the unknown Odysseus continues with an application of this general principle to the presumption of the suitors, who will surely be punished when Odysseus returns, and prays, too late as it proves,[86] that some *daimon* may withdraw Amphinomus from this encounter. Good and evil, it

[83] *Il.* 24, 518–533; this is our earliest example of the "Consolation"; see below, p. 232; cf. A. D. Nock, *Harv. Theol. Rev.* 33 (1940), p. 309.

[84] *Il.* 24, 549–551. ἀνέχεσθαι will be the favorite Stoic expression for *tlemosyne*; see below, Appendix 58.

[85] *Od.* 18, 130–142.

[86] *Od.* 18, 155.

appears in this speech, are alike the gift of the gods; but man's own folly aggravates the evil or nullifies the good. Most striking is the mention of the "spirit of man" that is commensurate with the fortunes that the gods bestow. This quality, whether it be a "grace" divinely vouchsafed or a moral good of human origin, is destined to play a great part in later Greek thought; good and evil, Odysseus suggests, are not merely objective "things" but are also attitudes of the mind. But neither Homer nor any other Greek will go so far as to say that "there is nothing either good or bad, but thinking makes it so"; evil is evil, but may be minimized by a manly endurance (*tlemosyne*) that rises to the occasion, and this is a good. And in the counsel to "keep quietly the gifts of the gods" Odysseus characteristically supplies the other half of his philosophy, the prudent acceptance of good in such a way as not to tempt Providence. The philosophy of the quiet life begins thus early, and comes well from one who has experienced the strenuous life.[87]

Homer's world is complete. If it preserves stubborn inconsistencies, of Nature and Law, of Fate and Free Will, of the things that are and the things that should be, of pessimism and courage, they are inconsistencies naïvely or frankly accepted, as eternal mysteries. If Homer looks back on ancient wars in heaven and the emergence of a new order, the wars are long past and the results accepted; certainly he entertains no hopes of a better order to come, and little fear of a worse.

With Hesiod it is different. The sense of movement is all-important. The *Theogony* seeks to explain how the existing order of divinities came to be; the *Works and Days*, finding toil and injustice in the world, seeks to account for their genesis, and then to show how to make the best of a weary world.

We may well accept the *Theogony* not as by Hesiod but as Hesiodic, in the sense that it continues the Boeotian didactic tradition and is to be dated not long after Hesiod;[88] much of the matter is earlier, borrowing from ancient religious poetry, hymns and myths, Homeric or even pre-Homeric. In its attempt to classify the divine powers[89] and define their relationships, it proceeds on two main principles. One is the idea of generation, or *Physis*, the struggle of the powers of Nature and the birth of successive *daimones*. Here there is little suggestion of good or evil; the poet is content to narrate.[90] The other idea is that of progress, from

[87] Cf. Plato, *Rep.* 620 c-d; Odysseus in the Myth of Er chooses an obscure lot.

[88] For a brief defense of Hesiodic authorship of the *Theogony* cf. P. Mazon, *Hésiode* (Paris, 1928), pp. 3 f.; W. Jaeger, *Paideia*, pp. 57–73, also accepts both *Theogony* and *Works and Days* as by Hesiod.

[89] Homer is sparing in his use of personification; Hesiod is the great personifier. Cf. O. Kern, *Religion der Griechen*, I, pp. 255–258; G. H. Macurdy, *The Quality of Mercy*, pp. 59–64; and my article on "Personifications" in the forthcoming *Oxford Classical Dictionary*.

[90] See further below, pp. 53–55.

anarchy and violence to order, with a climax in the triumph of Zeus over the Titans and the establishment of his reign (881–885). And here, it is to be noted, it is definitely good that has triumphed over evil. Not that the poet is wholly consistent either with Homeric tradition or with himself. We note in particular the double pedigree of *Moira*: first the *Moirai* are described as daughters of Night, along with *Moros*, the *Keres*, and *Nemesis* and other powers (211–225); they are birth-goddesses, "Klotho, Lachesis, and Atropos, who give men at their birth both evil and good to have," though they also punish the transgressions of men and of gods (217–222). Later, in the new régime, the *Moirai* appear, along with the *Horai* (*Eunomia* and *Dike* and *Eirene*), as the honored daughters of Zeus and Themis, dispensing evil and good.[91] But they have nothing to do with the philosophy of history of the *Theogony*, such as it is.[92] The truth of the matter is that the poet is but slightly concerned with justice and human good and evil, though he provides stern sanctions against perjury. Even the myth of Prometheus, as he tells it, is partly aetiological,[93] and partly told to enforce the moral that "it is not possible to deceive Zeus" (613). The poet is a priest.

Hesiod, on the other hand, the author of the *Works and Days*, is a prophet.[94] He, too, knows his Homer, and the Boeotian traditional didactic poetry, and the oracles that are coming from Delphi on the further side of Parnassus,[95] as well as the proverbial sayings and fables that one might hear in winter at the crowded *lesche* of the smithy (493). But he is smarting under the sense of social and personal injustices, and his whole poem is, among other things, a protest against *hybris* and a plea for *dike*. He wishes to believe that the just flourish (225–237), and that the gods punish injustice (249–264); indeed he contrasts Nature, "red of tooth and claw," with man, whose distinguishing mark is justice (276–280). But it is hard to believe; so often, in his Iron Age, do the facts belie his faith. "The earth is full of evils and the sea is full" (101). Disease stalks silently abroad (102–104); Zeus himself, for all his power and justice,[96] oft punishes a whole city for the sin of one evil man.[97] And the alternative to

[91] 904 f.; see below, p. 55. Cf. W. Jaeger, *Paideia*, pp. 67 f.

[92] The idea of Fate behind the successive dynasties is slight; but note 464; 475; 894.

[93] *Theog.* 556 f.; cf. M. P. Nilsson, *Hist. of Greek Religion*, pp. 62 f.; 95.

[94] Cf. T. A. Sinclair, *Hesiod, Works and Days* (London, 1932), Intro., Chap. III, "The Prophet of Justice."

[95] Hes. *W.D.* 285; cf. Herod. 6, 86.

[96] 5–8; cf. *Od.* 16, 211 ff.; *Il.* 20, 242.

[97] Hes. *W.D.* 240–247; cf. 260–262. These are the first gnomic expressions in Greek literature of the theory of vicarious atonement by one person or by a people for the wickedness of another, and are given as proof of the justice and power of Zeus, which are not questioned by Hesiod. Narratives illustrating such vicarious atonement are, of course, abundant; cf. *Il.* 1, 9–12; Hes. *W.D.* 47–49. Probably the notion, as found in Homer and Hesiod, is rooted in the primitive feeling that the prosperity of a people depends on the

injustice is, for most men, back-breaking toil. How can Hesiod reconcile all this?

To be honest, he cannot reconcile it wholly. He can repeat traditional sentiments, but despite his attempts at a systematic "didactic and admonitory epistle"[98] his gift is not consistency, skill in architectonic structure; rather he writes what may well be called "paragraph poetry,"[99] with awkward transitions and superfluous antitheses like those characteristic of the later elegy. But he does stubbornly attempt to explain the genesis of evil and toil, in two famous myths; and he attempts also to suggest to Perses what can be done to make a virtue of necessity by finding a good in toil.

We are not likely to understand Hesiod's use of the story of Prometheus[100] unless we constantly remember that it is introduced wholly in order to account for the origin of toil, and that toil is, in the myth, regarded as wholly evil. Toil was not always necessary;[101] it is part of the penalty inflicted by Zeus in his anger at the original deception of Prometheus in the matter of the sacrifice.[102] After Zeus had hidden men's means of livelihood[103] and fire (50), and Prometheus had retaliated by stealing fire back again,[104] Zeus in reprisal (57) sent Pandora, from whose *pithos* issued all the evils of men.[105] The unnamed woman in the myth of the *Theogony* is represented by the misogynist author, somewhat in the vein of Semonides of Amorgus, as herself evil and as the source of evil;[106] Pandora in the *Works and Days* is the innocent but baleful creature whose *pithos* (abruptly mentioned) holds and sends forth all evils, — all save *Elpis*. Why does Hope remain in the *pithos*? Because it is a good, or

---

magical powers of their king or (later) on his righteousness; cf. *Od.* 19, 109–114, and Nilsson, *Homer and Mycenae* (London, 1933), p. 220. For the punishment of the innocent children of the guilty, cf. Solon (below, p. 36); contrast Theognis (below, pp. 41 f.).

[98] Sinclair, *op. cit.*, p. x.

[99] Cf. Stickney, *Sentences*, pp. 58; 65.

[100] Clearly a traditional story; from it Hesiod appropriates in an allusive style only what he needs for his purpose, as does the author of the *Theogony*. Hesiod, for example, but not the *Theogony*, omits the story of the final punishment of Prometheus. Originally the myth doubtless grew out of the hostility of the Titan Prometheus to the Olympians, and his attempt to upset the equilibrium (*moira*) of Zeus. With this is combined the conflict between the native Prometheus, a culture-hero, and his rival the oriental, but naturalized, Hephaestus. Cf. L. Malten, *P. W.*, s. v. *Hephaistos*.

[101] Hes. *W.D.* 90–92; cf. 43–46; 111 f.

[102] The story of the sacrifice, not recounted here, as irrelevant, appears in *Theog.* 535–564; cf. above, p. 29, n. 93.

[103] *W.D.* 47; sc. *βίον* from 42.

[104] *αὖτις*, 50; there should be no question that Hesiod, unlike Aeschylus, thought of fire as originally available to man.

[105] *κήδεα λυγρά*, 95, apparently referring to the evils just described in 91–92, rather than to the more remote gifts mentioned in 82.

[106] *Theog.* 570–612; cf. Sem. Amorg. 7, esp. ll. 1, 21 f., 68, 71 f., 94–118. All citations from the elegiac and iambic poets are from E. Diehl, *Anthologia Lyrica* (Leipzig, 1922–25).

because it is an evil? Because it is available to man, or because it is denied to man? I agree with T. A. Sinclair[107] that it is not to the purpose to collect passages from Greek literature proving that Hope is sometimes a good, sometimes an evil; but I do not accept his contention that Hope is imprisoned because she is denied to man, whose condition is "hopeless." Better is the suggestion of S. M. Adams[108] that Hesiod "is drawing a distinction between those evils for which man is at least partially responsible and those others which assail him for no ascertainable cause."

The vindictiveness of Zeus, and the plight of mankind, at all points worse off than before, are the two essential elements in this myth of degeneration, which ends, as does the myth of the *Theogony*, with the moral that there is no way to escape from the will of Zeus.[109] Here is indeed matter for tragedy, if not for irony, in the spectacle of the good intentions of Prometheus frustrated.[110] Or is it rather satire on the supposed blessings of civilization, the attempt of *techne* to supplant *physis*?[111] Or are we, with W. Headlam,[112] to see in Prometheus, not the benefactor of man, the culture-hero, but the serpent who caused man to leave the Garden of Eden? The suggestion is tempting; but it is only from the point of view of Zeus that Prometheus is evil; and the Zeus of Hesiod's myth is himself anything but kindly. We must read neither Aeschylus nor Shelley into Hesiod.[113] Nor should we identify the toil of the myth, which is an evil, with the noble kind of strife mentioned early in the *Works and Days*.[114] The two are cleverly fused, to be sure, by Virgil,[115] and developed in the gospel of toil, which is Hesiodic, despite the myth of Prometheus. Virgilian *labor*, however, is not Hesiodic πόνος.[116]

Degeneration and the inevitability of toil are the themes also of the Myth of the Ages, which immediately follows. Instead of the dynastic sequence of the *Theogony*, moving from chaos to order, it presents a dissolving view of steady physical and moral decline. The Golden Age, the "dream of a tired peasant," as M. Croiset well called it,[117] the age of

[107] Sinclair, *Hesiod*, p. 13.

[108] "Hesiod's Pandora," *C. R.* 46 (1932), pp. 193–196. Convincing also is the suggestion that in the πίθος Hesiod is combining the idea of Homer's πίθοι with the idea of the Pithoigia. Cf. J. E. Harrison, "Pandora's Box," *J. H. S.* 20 (1900), pp. 99–114.

[109] Hes. *W.D.* 105; cf. *Theog.* 613.

[110] For Aeschylus, *P.V.* 250–252, see below, p. 120; for the use of Prometheus by Protagoras (or Plato), pp. 245 f.

[111] Cf. F. Wehrli, ΛΑΘΕ ΒΙΩΣΑΣ, p. 63; E. Tournier, *Némésis*, pp. 9–14.

[112] "Prometheus and the Garden of Eden," *C. Q.* 28 (1934), pp. 63–71.

[113] Nor even Horace, despite the similarities detected by E. K. Rand, in "Horatian Urbanity in Hesiod's 'Works and Days,'" *A. J. P.* 32 (1911), pp. 131–165.

[114] Hes. *W.D.* 17–24.

[115] *Georg.* 1, 121 f.: *pater ipse colendi* | *haud facilem esse viam voluit*, etc.

[116] See below, p. 32.

[117] See Appendix 7: Golden Age.

primitive innocence, of the "good old days," is painted with a nostalgic longing. Cronos, not the brutal Titan of the *Theogony*, but the kindly earth-*daimon* of the lingering ritual of the Cronia, gives place to Zeus, one infers, at the end of the Golden Age; kindly *physis* and the sweet disorder of the ἀρχαῖος βίος [118] to the *nomos* and tolerated *hybris* of later ages; union with the gods (108; 112; 120) to enmity and the appearance of intermediate *daimones*; ease and abundance to toil; good to evil.

In his masterly analysis of the sequence of the ages, E. Meyer [119] calls attention to the inevitable moral decline that accompanies the natural degeneration from gold to silver (a pair of fantasy pictures), and from bronze to iron (pictures based on some understanding of history).[120] The idleness of the Golden Age leads to the enervation and the presumption of the Silver Age; the physical violence of the bronze men leads to the impiety and intellectual craftiness of the iron men. A tribute to Homer may be read in the Age of Heroes that interrupts the scheme; their violence is tempered by their justice (158). And this momentary halt in the hitherto steady degeneration of the ages may suggest that Hesiod sees a ray of hope for better days to follow him.[121] But in the Iron Age, Hesiod's and our own, *Dike* and *Aidos* are no longer present, for *Aidos* and *Nemesis* have long since gathered their white garments about them and fled to Olympus (192–201).

The Myth of the Ages is more than a philosophy of history; it has its moral for Perses. Even a Utopia of idleness cannot last, but leads to degeneration; nor can the resort to intellect, a stronger tool than brute force, survive if it leads to mere craftiness and injustice. The moral is, then, that Perses had better not trust to Utopian dreams of wealth easily to be won, or to injustice; he had better be upright, and work.[122] The point is helped by the apparent freedom of will granted to the successive generations. To be sure, the stage is set and the story manipulated more mechanically than in Plato's account of the progressive decline of society in the *Republic*;[123] and each race lives up to the quality bestowed by its creator, and is "in character." Yet the illusion exists that each race could act otherwise if it willed so to do; certainly to each race except the men of

[118] Cf. *Od.* 9, 106–115.

[119] "Hesiods Erga und das Gedicht von den fünf Menschengeschlechten," in *Kleine Schriften*, II (Halle, 1924), pp. 17–66.

[120] Cf. T. R. Glover, "Metallurgy and Democracy," in *Greek Byways* (Cambridge, 1932), pp. 58–77.

[121] So, too, in line 175 (if it is authentic): ἢ πρόσθε θανεῖν ἢ ἔπειτα γενέσθαι. (H. G. Evelyn-White, *C. R.* 30 (1916), p. 72, finds in lines 169c–201 evidence of double recension, both versions being Hesiodic.) But not too much is to be made of this passing antithetical remark.

[122] Meyer, "Hesiods Erga," pp. 56 f.

[123] Books VIII and IX.

gold and the heroes blame is attached for its conduct, and the men of silver and of iron definitely incur the anger of their creator (138; 180), whereas the men of gold and the heroes earn a kind of blessed immortality.[124] Perses had better be warned betimes.

As in the Myth of Prometheus, so in the Myth of the Ages the anger of Zeus has brought on man the necessity of toil. But a virtue may be made of this necessity; a peasant may attain to a philosophy of hardship and manly endurance as noble in its way as that of Achilles or Odysseus. If "the gods have placed between us and goodness the sweat of our brows,"[125] and a long, steep way, the way becomes easier through resolution (291–293). This is the noble kind of *Eris*, appointed by Zeus, which is good for men (17–24). Note that Hesiod does not say that Zeus appointed it for man's good; it is man's discovery, despite the niggardliness of the gods, that toil brings courage, intelligence, and satisfaction, as well as wealth to offset what Zeus concealed from man (293–319). What is more, men who deal justly with their fellows find that something like the Golden Age returns among men, and "with merry-making they tend the fields which are all their care."[126] And as Hesiod goes on to tell of the *Days*, as well as the *Works*, of the peasant's life, one feels that the regularity of the seasons and the heavenly bodies (in other words, of *Physis*) serves not merely as a calendar but as a moral pattern for an orderly human society.[127]

The leaven of Homer and of Hesiod was at work in the seventh and sixth centuries, in which elegiac and iambic verse made familiar to men the proverbial wisdom of the Greek race. Whatever view be taken of the origin and use of the elegy during the earlier part of its career, it is clear at least that it is accretional, full of phrases and commonplaces echoed from epic and from earlier elegy, sometimes twisted into new uses; that it is full of antitheses, and lacking in consistency and systematic structure; and that it tends ordinarily to preserve a gnomic character, addressing itself to a definite listener or reader, or, in a special social setting, to a group.[128]

[124] *W.D.* 116–126; 166–169b. I venture to differ with Meyer's remark (p. 44) about the identity of the *δαίμονες ἁγνοὶ ἐπιχθόνιοι* (l. 122). I agree that they are not the 3000 *ἀθάνατοι φύλακες* of l. 253 (as Hild supposes, *Démons*, p. 88; apparently so also E. Rohde, *Psyche*, Eng. Trans., New York, 1925, pp. 70–72), despite the similarity of their functions. But they are not, as Meyer strangely states, Cronos and the Titans; surely they are simply the men of the Golden Age (109–120) just mentioned as *τοῦτο γένος* (121).

[125] *W.D.* 289 f.; cf. Simonides, 37.

[126] 231; cf. 225–237; and on *Dike* as the champion of justice among man, 219–224; 256–262.

[127] Cf. W. Jaeger, *Paideia*, pp. 70 f.; and see below, p. 225.

[128] Stickney, *Sentences*, pp. 79–102; R. Reitzenstein, *Epigramm und Skolion* (Giessen, 1893), pp. 49–86.

Homeric diction[129] and Homeric ideas naturally color the elegies of Callinus and Tyrtaeus, and even of Mimnermus. That death, the *μοῖρα θανάτου*, is inevitable, but that if it be met in a manly fashion it is glorious, is a recurrent theme in the more martial poets.[130] In Mimnermus, of course, it is the negative aspect that prevails: man's life like the leaves, the woes that Zeus bestows, the hatefulness of old age.[131] In his passionate conviction that after youth has passed life is not worth living, Mimnermus almost anticipates the even more overwhelmingly pessimistic commonplace, first phrased by Theognis, that it were best never to have been born;[132] yet Mimnermus clutches at the fleeting joys of youth, less wise than Epicurus and Horace, or even than Archilochus.

The pessimism of Semonides of Amorgus extends beyond his misogyny to a vast distrust of Zeus and all his works. In a poem preserved by Stobaeus in the long section entitled "That life is short, of little account, and full of cares," Semonides ascribes to Zeus omnipotence, to man a stupid gullibility, and proceeds to show how all man's hopes are cheated by age or by death: "So true is it that nothing is without ills; nay ten thousand are the dooms of men and their woes and sorrows past reckoning."[133]

That remarkable soldier of fortune, Archilochus, whom the ancients admired so greatly as to puzzle many modern critics, was an innovator in many ways; and this, together with his abounding verve, is perhaps what the ancients chiefly admired in him. Even in dealing with our present theme he is a pioneer, though less in thought than in expression, and though not attaining to consistency. What controls man's destiny? In two, or possibly three, gnomic fragments Archilochus answers the question. *πάντα τύχη καὶ μοῖρα, Περίκλεες, ἀνδρὶ δίδωσιν.*[134] The attribution of all things to *moira* is Homeric enough; but the introduction of *tyche* is a new note in Greek poetry.[135] Yet again it may be Archilochus who writes: *πάντα πόνος τεύχει θνητοῖς μελέτη τε βροτείη,*[136] which has a Hesiodic ring. Elsewhere he counsels: *τοῖς θεοῖς τιθεῖο πάντα*, and gives us the first example of the commonplace, developed by Solon and others, that the

[129] For the diction, cf. T. Hudson-Williams, *Early Greek Elegy* (Cardiff, 1926).

[130] Callinus, 1, 8; 1, 12–15; Tyrtaeus, 5, 5; 6; 7; 8, 5 f.; 9, 35.

[131] Mimnermus, 2; cf. *Il.* 6, 146–149; 9, 410–416; Semon. Amorg. 29; Mimn. 4, 2; 1, 10; 6, 2.

[132] Mimn. 2, 10: *τεθνάμεναι βέλτιον ἢ βίοτος.* Cf. 4; Theognis, 425, and other poets, cited below, p. 42 and n. 189.

[133] Stobaeus, *Anth.* (ed. Wachsmuth and Hense, Vol. V, p. 289); Semon. Amorg. 1. For Solon's use of this poem and of 29, in his "Prayer to the Muses," see below, pp. 36 f.

[134] Archil. 8. For *Τύχη* personified, cf. the "Archilochus Monument," as restored by J. M. Edmonds, *Elegy and Iambus* (Loeb ed.), II, p. 164, lines 56–58.

[135] I am not overlooking Hes. *Theog.* 360, a hint as yet undeveloped. *Hom. Hymn* XI, 5 is later. On *τύχη* in Archilochus, see further W. Jaeger, *Paideia*, p. 122.

[136] Archil. 14. The attribution to Archilochus is doubtful.

gods raise upright the fallen and overthrow the prosperous.[137] That there is nothing in the world that man need not expect or that he should swear impossible or marvellous, in view of the eclipse that Zeus has caused, is the moral that the poet puts into the mouth of "the father." Both the turn of phrase of the first lines,

> χρημάτων ἄελπτον οὐδέν ἐστιν οὐδ' ἀπώμοτον
> οὐδὲ θαυμάσιον, κτλ.,

and the development of the series of impossibilities now to be expected (beasts and dolphins exchanging their haunts, etc.), institute new and fruitful motives in Greek (and Latin) poetry.[138]

Homeric, once more, is the counsel that Archilochus addresses to a certain Pericles: manly endurance (τλημοσύνη) is the remedy which the gods have ordained for woes that are incurable, such as afflict one man to-day and another to-morrow, and are not to be alleviated by womanish grief.[139] The thought is that of Achilles and Odysseus, but the turn of phrase is new,[140] and is to be echoed frequently by Theognis and later poets.[141] Novel, too, and destined to be imitated, is the self-address of another fragment, in which the poet bids his soul, confounded by hopeless troubles, to rise up and defend itself, not too exultant at victory, not too much vexed by evils, and conscious of the "rhythm" that controls mankind.[142] But Archilochus, be it noted, does not stress, as do Solon and even Theognis, the worth of virtue and piety in attaining to peace of mind. For all his protestation that the gods control the world (58), it is τύχη and μοῖρα that apparently are in his thought the sovereign dispensers of men's goods and evils (8), and πόνος and μελέτη βροτείη (14), and τλημοσύνη (7), that win for men in an inscrutable and largely unfriendly world such happiness as they can hope for. And perhaps he is speaking for himself in the resolute and independent words which, according to Aristotle, he puts in the mouth of Charon the carpenter, the despiser of the wealth of Gyges.[143]

[137] Archil. 58, the "Magnificat" (with a difference) of Archilochus. Cf. Solon, 1, 65–70 (see below, pp. 36 f.); Sem. Amorg. 1, more pessimistically (see above, p. 34).

[138] Archil. 74; Arist. *Rhet.* 1418b 28; cf. Theognis, 659: οὐδ' ὀμόσαι χρὴ τοῦθ', ὅτι μή ποτε πρῆγμα τόδ' ἔσται. For the later history of the idea, cf. H. V. Canter and E. Dutoit (see below, p. 220, n. 3).

[139] Archil. 7; cf. 11: κρύπτωμεν ⟨δ'⟩ ἀνιηρὰ Ποσειδάωνος ἄνακτος | δῶρα, the "dreadful gifts of Poseidon" apparently referring to a shipwreck.

[140] See above, pp. 26–28; cf. Hudson-Williams, *Early Greek Elegy*, p. 87.

[141] Theog. 591–592; 355–360; 441–446; 991–992; see below, p. 44; cf. Wehrli, ΛΑΘΕ ΒΙΩΣΑΣ, pp. 14–20.

[142] Archil. 67a: θυμέ, θύμ' ἀμηχάνοισι κήδεσιν κυκώμενε, ἀνάδυ, κτλ.; cf. *Od.* 20, 17 (above, n. 81); Theog. 1029–1036: τόλμα, θυμέ, κακοῖσιν ὅμως ἄτλητα πεπονθώς, κτλ.; also 393–398; 593–594; 657–658; and see below, p. 45.

[143] Archil. 22; Arist. *Rhet.* 1418b 42.

Not for any new thought bearing on our problem is Solon important, but for his determined setting forth of accepted Greek views about justice and moderation and order, and for his attempt to apply them in practise to a world that was inclined to forget them.[144] Furthermore he gave definite form for the first time to a creed, hitherto vaguely held, about the moral decline of man. Though it is impossible to arrange with certainty all the fragments, we shall not do violence to the probable development of his thought if we suppose that the longest poem (1), the "Prayer to the Muses," comes fairly early in his life, before his political activity, and expresses the inherited and tested creed of an Athenian gentleman who has engaged in trade.[145] Throughout the first part of the poem (ll. 1–32), the emphasis is on justice, the security of wealth justly won with the approval of the gods, and the retribution that attends injustice[146] — if not immediately, at any rate in the end, perhaps striking the innocent children of those guilty persons who have themselves escaped the θεῶν μοῖρα. (Solon accepts this doctrine without criticism, and without any suggestion of Orphic beliefs of punishment in another world.) So far Solon's attitude is one of conservative piety; the gods are just, *ate* follows *hybris*, and meets with retribution (τίσις); Zeus oversees all, and his vengeance is as sure, though perhaps not as swift, as the clearing away of the clouds in spring by the wind. That is, moral law is as certain as natural law, or as what will presently be called *Physis*.[147] Both a deep-seated moral conviction of the power of justice and observation of the world of affairs impel Solon to dread ill-gotten gains and to proclaim that justice is the best policy.

Observation, however, has taught Solon also something about the vicissitudes of life. The second part of the poem (ll. 33–76) therefore emphasizes the uncertainty of man's lot and his various undertakings and the deceptiveness of his hopes; both good and evil come from *Moira* (63), and the gifts of the gods may not be refused (64); so inscrutable is their will that they often afflict with great and sore *ate* him who strives to act nobly,[148] and to another who is acting ill God gives good fortune and a release from his folly.[149] Here the justice of the goods seems at first sight almost to be doubted, or at least not emphasized. The point has already been made in similar terms by Semonides of Amorgus,[150] but with a

[144] Cf. I. M. Linforth, *Solon the Athenian*, esp. pp. 104–123.

[145] Cf. M. Croiset, *C.-R. de l'Acad. des Inscr. et Belles-Lettres* (Paris, 1903), pp. 581–596; Linforth, *Solon*, p. 104.

[146] Hesiod provides a close parallel, *W.D.* 320–326; the thought recurs in Theognis, 197–208 (see below, p. 40); cf. Aesch. *Eum.* 553–565.

[147] For this idea, and the converse, in later thought, see below, p. 225; and cf. Confucius: "As surely as water always runs downward, so surely is there some good in all men."

[148] Solon, 1, 67; cf. Archil. 58.

[149] Solon, 1, 70; i.e., a pardon of his folly (ἀφροσύνη), and a cancellation of its consequences.

[150] Sem. Amorg. 1; cf. 29. See above, p. 34.

counsel of utter despair. Yet if we are right in supposing that Solon, for all his conventional reference to *Moira*, believed that men have a full measure of responsibility for their careers, and if moreover we may agree with F. Wehrli[151] in taking ἐξ αὐτῶν (l. 75) as referring to the men themselves, as the source of *ate*, rather than to the κέρδεα (l. 74) bestowed by the gods, we shall conclude with Solon that though wealth is the root of all evil, it is not wealth alone but the greed that it so often engenders that works ruin. And Solon ends the poem, as he all but begins it, on the note of retribution.[152] Unexplained, and perhaps unexplainable, is the affliction with *ate* of even him who is striving to do nobly;[153] here is the stubborn residuum of evil that every philosophy finds it difficult to justify on purely moral grounds. Solon accepts it in the spirit of faith, and returns to his convictions.

Not absolute consistency, then, but a faith maintained in spite of misgivings,[154] is the achievement of this poem. Nor is it perfectly constructed as a work of art, despite the attempts of H. Weil and others to discover in it a strophic structure;[155] it is still "paragraph poetry," loosely composed of elegiac couplets, and breaking into two main parts. Nevertheless it traces with something like a system for the first time in Greek poetry the moral decline of man; and it is to be noted that, allowing for one or two ellipses, the sequence is identical in the two parts of the poem: πλοῦτος (9; 71); κόρος (not mentioned in the first part; 73); ὕβρις (11, 16; not mentioned in the last part, but perhaps implied in ἐξ αὐτῶν, 75); ἄτη (13; 75); τίσις (25, 29; 76).

This generalized creed Solon proceeds in another poem (3) to apply to the grievous plight of Athens, afflicted not by "the *aisa* of Zeus or the will of the blessed immortal gods," but by the folly and greed of her own people, whose *hybris* leads to injustice; they give no heed to justice, who, though now silent, will in time demand retribution. The moral which Solon proclaims is the need of *eunomia*, the practical expression of justice,

[151] Wehrli, ΛΑΘΕ ΒΙΩΣΑΣ, p. 12, n. 1. K. Reinhardt, *R. M.* 71 (1916), p. 132, though not quite explicit, seems to take the words in the same sense. Linforth, *Solon*, pp. 241 f., rejects a similar suggestion by Kynaston, and consequently has to hold (p. 110) that "this time [i.e., at the end of the poem] there is no distinction between honest and dishonest riches." Wilamowitz, *Sappho und Simonides* (Berlin, 1913), pp. 263; 267, also retains the older interpretation. Cf. *Od.* 1, 32 (see above, pp. 22 f.); W. Jaeger, *Sitzber. preuss. Akad. Wiss.* (Berlin, 1926), p. 74; and, for Solon, W. Jaeger, *Paideia*, pp. 142–144.

[152] *N. b.* τεισομένην (76); if Zeus sends *ate*, it is not arbitrarily but in just recompense.

[153] Solon, 1, 67. This is of the essence of tragedy, though it provides no theory of the nature of the tragic ἁμαρτία.

[154] Linforth, *Solon*, p. 111, calls it "the normal attitude of pious perplexity." The more positive description of Solon's position applies also to Solon, 4, 9–10 (cf. Theog. 315–318); the more negative description to Solon, 17: πάντῃ δ' ἀθανάτων ἀφανὴς νόος ἀνθρώποισιν.

[155] Cf. Linforth, *Solon*, pp. 242 f.

to check *koros* and make *hybris* dim and wither budding *ate*.[156] Here is an explanation of human good and evil in purely human terms, albeit under the rule of friendly and powerful gods. The pedigree of *hybris* is vaguely suggested once more.

Possibly it is only a little later, and still before his political reforms, that Solon, an aristocrat whose career and personal fortune have made of him a member of the middle class, as Aristotle remarks, "urges the rich not to be greedy."[157] "Calm the eager tumult of your hearts. Ye have forced your way to a surfeit (κόρος) of good things; confine your swelling thoughts within moderate bounds," etc.[158] Almost certainly it is after the archonship that he phrases, in an appeal to the *demos* to find a mean between excessive freedom and excessive restraint, the classic statement of the pedigree of *hybris*, though without tracing its consequences: "For *koros* giveth birth to *hybris*, when great prosperity (ὄλβος) followeth after men whose minds are not sound."[159] Once more the emphasis is on human responsibility and sanity of mind, not on fatalism or jealous gods. And still later, after the tyranny of the Peisistratids is established, Solon writes (8): "If ye have suffered the dire consequences of your own fault, blame not the gods for this evil fortune; ye have yourselves exalted these men," etc.

Even so robust a figure as Solon provides at least one passage for the melancholy section of Stobaeus devoted to the proposition "that life is short, of little account, and full of cares": "Nor is any mortal happy, but wretched are all they upon whom the sun looks down."[160] Such pessimism, one may suppose, came late in Solon's life, as the fruit of disappointment. He stops short, however, of declaring that it were better never to have been born.[161] And it is tempting to suppose further that it was largely from this couplet, and any others like it that he may have written, that Herodotus or his informant manufactured the famous story of the interview between Solon and Croesus, and Solon's reluctance to count a man happy before his death has ended a perfect life.[162] But

[156] For *eunomia* in Hesiod, see above, p. 29; in later thought, pp. 55; 66; 75, n. 156; 83; 235. Cf. further Jaeger, *Sitzber. preuss. Akad. Wiss.* (Berlin, 1926), pp. 69–85; V. Ehrenberg, "Eunomia," in *Charisteria* (Festschrift Rzach, Reichenberg, 1930), pp. 16–29.

[157] Arist. Ἀθ. Πολ. 5.

[158] Solon, 4, 5–8; cf. 23, 16–24; 24; 25, written after the reforms.

[159] Solon, 5, 9–10; cf. Theog. 153 f., noting his change; see below, p. 45. The idea is doubtless proverbial before Solon, but hardly the definite expression, despite the citation of the hexameter by the schol. on Pindar, *Ol.* 13, 12, as Homer's.

[160] Stob. *Anth.* (ed. Wachsmuth and Hense, Vol. V, p. 833); Solon, 15. Cf. Theog. 167–168, and see below, p. 42.

[161] See below, p. 42, n. 189.

[162] Hdt. 1, 32; cf. 1, 31, the tale of Cleobis and Biton with the moral ὡς ἄμεινον εἴη ἀνθρώπῳ τεθνάναι μᾶλλον ἢ ζώειν; 86, Croesus on the pyre remembers the "inspired saying of Solon," τὸ μηδένα εἶναι τῶν ζωόντων ὄλβιον. Cf. further Theognis, 161–164 (see below,

Solon's retort to Mimnermus, setting fourscore years as the goal of a good life, argues no bitterness of spirit.[163]

The work that has come down to us under the name of Theognis represents the ideas that prevailed in the late sixth century. Accepting as authentic much of the first book, which is all that happens to concern our problem, and even the passages borrowed from Tyrtaeus, Mimnermus, and Solon as deliberately borrowed and exploited for a purpose,[164] we have as in the *Works and Days* a body of verse, mainly didactic, and addressed mainly to an individual, though it lends itself also to sympotic[165] and to educational uses. It likewise attempts a systematic discussion of good and evil in human life, and is fraught with inconsistencies, achieving at best a balance of conflicting half-truths. It is for the most part still "paragraph poetry," still antithetical in style, a composite of traditional nuggets, loosely connected, and suggesting a collection, a sort of Greek *satura*; it invites comparison with the Hebrew *Book of Proverbs*, with *Poor Richard's Almanack*, and with Martin Farquhar Tupper's *Proverbial Philosophy: A Book of Thoughts and Arguments Originally Treated*. The poet expressly tells Cyrnus (27 f.): "I shall give thee the counsels that I learned from good men when I was a lad"; yet he, like Solon, reckons with the political stress of his age, ever fearing the fruits of *hybris* and *stasis*.[166] Both poets stress human responsibility for human evils; the difference is in the narrower political sympathies of the later poet and his deeper pessimism.

The order of the parts is not of great significance, especially after the first 254 lines; no injustice will be done to the thought of Theognis if we make a cento of the passages that bear upon our problem. So abundant is the material that we must be content for the most part to select one or two passages to illustrate each theme, giving mere references to other passages of similar import.

Of especial prominence is the old thought that "man proposes, but God disposes."

No man is himself the cause of loss (ἄτη) and gain (κέρδος), Cyrnus; the gods are the givers of them both; nor doth any that laboreth know in his heart whether he moveth to a good end or to a bad. For often when he thinketh he

n. 167); Soph. *O. T.* 1528–1530; Eur. *Androm.* 100–102, and schol. *ad. loc.*; *Troad.* 509 f.; Aristotle on Solon's dictum, *Eth. N.* 1100a 10–1101a 21.

[163] Solon, 22.

[164] Cf. E. Harrison, *Studies in Theognis* (Cambridge, 1902), pp. 100–120; *pace* T. Hudson-Williams, *The Elegies of Theognis* (London, 1910), pp. 43–50; 74–78. W. Jaeger, *Paideia*, pp. 186–192, holds that to the original "Sayings to Cyrnus" of Theognis was added an anthology containing poems by Theognis and by other poets.

[165] Cf. R. Reitzenstein, *Epigramm und Skolion* (Giessen, 1893).

[166] Theog. 39–42; cf. 43–52; Solon, 3 and 8.

shall do evil he doeth good, and doeth evil when he thinketh he shall do good. Nor doth any man get what he wisheth; for the barriers of sore perplexity hold him back. We men consider vain things, knowing naught, while the gods accomplish all according to their own mind.[167]

The gods are not only omnipotent but inscrutable. " 'Tis very hard to understand how God will accomplish the end of a matter yet undone; for there is darkness outstretched, and the barriers of perplexity are not for mortals to comprehend, before what is to be."[168] Elsewhere, in an echo of Solon's comparison between the secure possessions won justly from Zeus and the fruits of injustice for which the gods require retribution, Theognis, like Solon, accepts without question the doctrine that the malefactor's innocent children may suffer for his sins; but he stresses not so much the certainty of the retribution as the uncertainty of the moment when it may strike: "in the end [unjust gain] becometh evil, and the mind of the gods overcometh [the offender]; but these things deceive men's understanding, for the Blessed Ones demand not retribution for wrongdoing at the moment," etc.[169]

Such inscrutability amounts almost to ill-will or niggardliness on the part of the gods; and a belief in that, too, and in the unsatisfactory character of the gifts of the gods finds a place in the creed of Theognis.[170] In fact the prosperity of the wicked troubles Theognis, like many another good man. "Possessions doth Heaven (δαίμων) give even to the wicked, Cyrnus, but the boon (μοῖρα) of virtue cometh to but few."[171] For all that, Theognis does not envy the prosperity of the useless and the wicked; it is valor and virtue that endure.[172] Nevertheless he gives voice in a famous passage to a protest, upbraiding omnipotent Zeus for bestowing the same *moira* on *hybris* and on *sophrosyne*; the wicked enjoy *olbos*, the just receive *penia*, mother of perplexity (ἀμηχανίη), which corrupts their wits

[167] Theog. 133–142. Cf. Solon 1, 33–76 (above, pp. 36–37), which Theognis here (and possibly in 585–590; see below, pp. 44 f.) imitates in his own way, but without here reckoning with the first half of Solon's poem, 1, 1–32 (above, p. 36), which he imitates in 133–142 (below, pp. 44 f.); on the unsatisfactory character of this pair of poems which deal piece-meal with a problem which Solon has seen as a whole, cf. W. Jaeger, *Paideia*, pp. 201 f. With Theognis 133–142 contrast moreover 833–836 (see below, p. 44). Cf. 155–158, noting the figure of the scale of Zeus, 157; (cf. 169–170; 171–172); 161–164, noting the rôles of the *daimon*, both good and evil (cf. 165 f.; 349 f.), and the uncertainty of the τέλος, as well as the antithetical structure of the quatrain; 1187–1190, the inevitability of death and misfortunes (controlled by μοῖρα) and of care (sent by θεός).

[168] Theog. 1075–1078; cf. 381 f.; also 903–930 (if authentic).

[169] Theog. 197–208; cf. Solon, 1, 1–32. But cf. also Theog. 731–752 (below, p. 41).

[170] Theognis uses the word νέμεσις only once (280), however, and even here of just retribution, not of jealousy. For the gifts of the gods, cf. 25 f.; 801–804; 271–278.

[171] Theog. 149 f.; παγκάκῳ, 149, is here surely ethical, as the context shows, though elsewhere political. Cf. 336, on the difficulty of attaining virtue by one's own efforts.

[172] Theog. 865–868; 683–686; cf. 315–318 (= Solon, 4, 9–12).

by strong necessity (ἀνάγκη) into evil-doing (ἀμπλακίη).[173] This is indeed a courageous protest, tracing incidentally the moral decline of man in a new terminology,[174] and throwing the blame on Zeus in a tone of apparently respectful though bewildered resentment. A. Croiset well remarks: "Here is the great enigma of moral theology boldly posed; this is a memorable date in the history of Greek thought."[175] Shall we call this the protest of a troubled but orthodox thinker, or the disillusionment of a renegade? Shall we find in the passage that immediately follows,[176] on the uses of adversity, and in another passage[177] bidding mortals not to sit in judgment on immortals, signs of a recovery of orthodoxy? Or shall we find in the parallel protest tokens of a settled attitude of pessimism and cynicism?

Father Zeus [he cries], I would it were the gods' pleasure that *hybris* should delight the wicked if they so choose, but that whosoever did abominable acts intentionally, with no regard for the gods, should pay the penalty himself, and the deeds of *atasthalie* of the father should not become a misfortune to his children after him. . . . But as it is, the doer escapeth, and another beareth the misfortune afterwards. Yet how can it be just, O king of the immortals, that a man who hath no part in unjust deeds, committing no transgression nor perjury, but being just, should not fare justly?

And the poet goes on to ask how, in view of this situation, men could stand in awe of gods who permit such moral confusion.[178] Like all his contemporaries, he believes that the gods punish the innocent children of the wicked;[179] but apparently he is the first who believes this to be bad, a blot on a dispensation that pretends to be just. As a matter of fact, we know that the innocent often suffer through the fault of the guilty or the careless; that is perhaps a matter of *physis*, rather than of *dike* or of special interference by the gods. For the primitive Greek, who thought of guilt as something tangible, all but physical, it was logical enough for guilt to be inherited, like diseases or debts.[180] For Herodotus, the punishment of the guilty is merely just (δίκαιον), and that of their sons something divine (θειότατον . . . θεῖον πρῆγμα), that is, a sign of the active *nemesis* of the

[173] Theog. 373–392. Harrison, p. 192, regards 373, Ζεῦ φίλε, θαυμάζω σε, as "perhaps unique in serious poetry; but it is quite in keeping with the flippant earnestness of this poem."

[174] πενίη, ἀνάγκη, ἀμηχανίη, κακὰ πάντα.

[175] See Appendix 8: Theognis on Zeus.

[176] Theog. 393–398.

[177] Theog. 687–688.

[178] Theog. 731–752. Cf. Soph. *O. T.* 883–896; Eur. *I. T.* 386–391, and Fr. 294, 6: *εἰ θεοί τι δρῶσιν αἰσχρόν, οὐκ εἰσὶν θεοί.* See also above, p. 24.

[179] Cf. Theog. 197–208, cited above, p. 40.

[180] Bion of Borysthenes (third cent. B.C.) points out that for the gods to punish the sons of the guilty is more ridiculous than for physicians to dose the descendants of the sick; Mullach, *Frag. Phil. Graec.* II (Paris, 1881), p. 427, no. 42.

gods.[181] It is the more remarkable that Theognis, beginning to realize that morality must be defined in terms of the will, should have made his protest in terms even faintly suggestive of a Hebrew prophet.[182]

For the rest, it is not surprising that Theognis, looking at the externals of life, should have voiced at times a thoroughgoing pessimism. With Mimnermus[183] and Alcaeus[184] and Horace[185] and Omar, he shares the darker side of the "Epicurean" creed. "I play rejoicing in youth; for long is the time that I shall lie underground without life, like a speechless stone, and leave the lovely light of the sun; and good though I be, I shall see nothing more."[186] Or again, "one man hath this ill, another that, and not one of all that the sun beholdeth is happy in very truth."[187] A darker vein of brooding runs through one of four passages that begin with the Delphic counsel of moderation: "Be not over-eager in any matter; best is due measure in all human affairs; oft is a man eager in pursuit of gain, only to be misled into great loss (*ἀμπλακίῃ*) by an eager spirit (*δαίμων πρόφρων*) which easily maketh what is evil seem to him good, and what is good seem evil."[188] Here is once more the stuff of tragedy. But seldom does Greek tragedy plumb the very abyss of pessimism that meets us, and for the first time, in Theognis, and that was to become the familiar commonplace *μὴ φῦναι*. "Best of all for mortals were it never to have been born, nor to have seen the rays of the burning sun; but if once born, to pass as soon as may be the gates of Hades, and to lie under a goodly heap of earth."[189]

This is the "De Profundis" of Theognis, and he rarely sinks to such despairing utterance. Granted that this world is largely evil, and that the

[181] Hdt. 7, 137. See below, p. 87.

[182] Cf. *Ezekiel*, 18 (early sixth cent.); the thought is strikingly similar.

[183] Mimn. 2.

[184] Alcaeus, 73.

[185] Horace, esp. the spring poems.

[186] Theog. 567–570; cf. 877 f.

[187] Theog. 167 f.; cf. Solon, 15; Theog. 1013–1016.

[188] Theog. 401–406. Cf. E. G. Wilkins, *The Delphic Maxims in Literature* (Chicago, 1929), pp. 19–48; P. E. More, "Delphi and Greek Literature," in *Shelburne Essays*, Second Series (New York, 1905), pp. 188–218.

[189] Theog. 425–428. For the later tradition of this *τόπος*, cf. Bacchyl. V, 160 and Jebb *ad loc.*; Bacchyl. Frag. 28 (Jebb); Aesch. Frag. 401 (Sidgwick); Soph. *O. C.* 1225–1229; *O. T.* 1186–1196; Soph. Frags. 488 and 556 (Pearson); Eur. Frags. 285 and 449 (Nauck, *Trag. Graec. Frag.*[2]); Alexis, Frag. 141 (Kock), 15 f.; Menander, Frag. 125 (Kock); *Certamen Homeri et Hesiodi*, 73–74 (at least as late as Hadrian, though derived from Alcidamas the Sophist (fourth cent.); the lines are here put in the mouth of Homer; cf. *Il.* 23, 71; Mimn. 2, 10); Plut. *Consol. ad Apollon.* 109 D; 115 C (= Arist. Frag. 44, Rose); J. W. Mackail, *Select Epigrams from the Greek Anthology* (London, 1890), pp. 82 f.; Cic. *Tusc.* 1, 114 f. (See also below, *Index*, s.v. *μὴ φῦναι.*) The form of the passage in Theognis may well suggest sympotic origin or use, in its ranking of goods; cf. Theog. 255 f.; Attic Scolia, 7; Solon, 13.

gods give little help, he knows, like Homer and Hesiod, like Archilochus and Solon, how to face hardship with wisdom and resolution, and even piety. "Choose rather to dwell with little wealth in piety than to be rich with possessions unjustly gained; justice is the whole sum of virtue, and every man is good, Cyrnus, if he be just."[190] E. Harrison[191] and J. T. Stickney[192] find irony in the position of another quatrain,[193] a commendation of justice, immediately following the protest against the suffering of the righteous and the escape of the wicked; but Theognis nowhere draws from the prosperity of the wicked the conclusion that injustice is to be preferred. Rather is he orthodox in setting forth the pedigree of *hybris* and its fruits. "To an evil man whose place he is about to remove, Cyrnus, God first giveth *hybris*."[194] Note that it is not a malicious god who acts, and that it is an evil man who is afflicted with *hybris*.[195] This point explains well enough the turn that Theognis gives to Solon's couplet on the pedigree of *hybris*[196] by substituting *κακῷ* for *πολύς*; the thought is substantially the same in both poets, but in borrowing from Solon the later poet gives every possible emphasis to the character of the mortal, "to lay stress on the fact that it is not the quantity of the good fortune [*πολὺς ὄλβος*, Solon] but the quality of the recipient's mind [*κακῷ . . . ἀνθρώπῳ*, Theognis] which determines his fate."[197] Finally, in adapting to his purpose the last six lines of Solon's "Prayer to the Muses," the lines dealing with the insatiate greed bred of wealth, and its dire results, Theognis makes, together with insignificant changes, a major substitution:[198] whereas Solon writes, "the immortals give mortals possessions, yet ruin (*ἄτη*) stands revealed coming from them" (i.e. from mortals), Theognis substitutes "the possessions of mortals turn to folly (*ἀφροσύνη*) and ruin (*ἄτη*) stands revealed coming from it." Hudson-Williams,[199] writing on

[190] Theog. 145–148.

[191] Harrison, p. 201.

[192] Stickney, *Sentences*, p. 107.

[193] Theog. 753–756.

[194] Theog. 151 f.

[195] J. Adam seems to overstate the case, *The Religious Teachers of Greece*, p. 88, when he writes: "*Hybris*, Theognis says, is the first and greatest evil; and God is its author," and cites 151, comparing 133 ff. Theognis is trying to vindicate the ways of God and assert a measure of human responsibility. But of course he does not achieve complete consistency, as Adam also remarks on the same page.

[196] Theog. 153 f.; Solon, 5, 9 f.; see above, p. 38.

[197] Harrison, p. 113. Hudson-Williams, pp. 48 f., is scornful of such a theory of appropriation by Theognis; yet he writes (255) that "a change in the sense was introduced in order to emphasize the effects of *κόρος* upon the *bad* man," and cites Clement of Alexandria (*Str.* VI, 8), who "knew that the popular version was ascribed to Theognis, and he may have read it himself in a MS. of the Megarian poet." That is indeed the very least to be made of Clement's explicit statement: *Σόλωνος δὲ ποιήσαντος 'τίκτει γὰρ κόρος ὕβριν, ὅταν πολὺς ὄλβος ἕπηται,' ἄντικρυς ὁ Θέογνις γράφει 'τίκτει τοι κόρος ὕβριν, ὅταν κακῷ ὄλβος ἕπηται.'*

[198] Theog. 227–232; Solon, 1, 71–76; see above, pp. 36 f.

[199] Hudson-Williams, p. 191.

the substitution in this passage (which he does not attribute to Theognis himself), remarks that Solon's line "was replaced by 230 to avoid holding the gods responsible." According to the interpretation of Solon's lines accepted above (p. 37), Solon also avoids holding the gods responsible; but the substituted lines are still more explicit in holding man and his folly accountable.[200]

What is the practical result of the philosophy of Theognis? First, a faith in prudential maxims of conduct, especially with regard to moderation, as in drinking, a mean between two extremes.[201] "Be not too eager in any matter; the mean is the best in all things; and thus, Cyrnus, thou shalt have virtue, which is a thing hard to get."[202] He believes, moreover, in the power of the human mind. "Judgment (γνώμη), Cyrnus, is the best thing the gods give mortals; judgment holdeth the end of all things. O happy he that hath it in his mind! He is far stronger than baleful *hybris* and dolorous *koros*, and these are of those evils than which there is none worse for mortals; for every evil, Cyrnus, cometh from them" (1171–1176). It follows that man is largely responsible for his condition. "All things here are among the crows and perdition, nor is any of the blessed immortal gods, Cyrnus, to blame; rather the violence of men and their base gains and their *hybris* have cast us from much good into evil" (833–836). This is doubtless spoken with pious intent, to divert blame for evil from gods to men;[203] but it is palpably at variance with the idea that man proposes and God disposes.[204] Elsewhere, also in the interest of piety, Theognis adapts the passage of Solon's "Prayer to the Muses" on the uncertainty of the results of human activities, good or bad, with a real change of meaning.[205] Whereas Solon says that one who is seeking to "do well" (εὖ ἔρδειν) falls unexpectedly into *ate*, and one who is "doing ill" (κακῶς ἔρδοντι) is delivered by God into good fortune, Theognis makes the contrast between one who is merely seeking a fair reputation (εὐδοκιμεῖν) and fails, and one who is really acting well (καλῶς ποιεῦντι) and is prospered by God, even his blunders coming to a good end.[206] This violent

[200] ἀφροσύνη I suppose to have been suggested by Solon, 1, 70, on the "folly" from which God may deliver man. "χρήματα, ἀφροσύνη, ἄτη form a sort of genealogy like κόρος, ὕβρις, ἄτη," remarks Hudson-Williams (p. 191), comparing 153 f.; I have already called attention (above, p. 41) to the still different genealogy in 373–392, in which Zeus is held accountable. In Theognis, 232, τειρομένοις, "wretched," looks like a mere scribal corruption of τισομένην (Solon, 1, 76), which is certainly better in both contexts. Cf. Harrison, p. 106, n. 2.

[201] Theog. 837–840.

[202] Theog. 335 f.; cf. 401–406; 593 f.; 463 f.; Hes. *W.D.* 289–292.

[203] Cf. 687 f.; it is not *themis* to sit in judgment on the gods; and 897–900: man fares better at the hands of the gods than he deserves.

[204] Cf. 133–142; see above, pp. 39 f.

[205] Theog. 585–590; Solon, 1, 65–70; see above, pp. 36 f.

[206] Harrison, p. 106.

perversion of Solon's thought is certainly made "to 'justify the ways of God to man.' "[207]

Between the divine dispensation and the activity of man, then, Theognis holds that much good may emerge. "Never swear that a thing cannot be, for the gods resent it, and the end is theirs. Yet do *something*; good may come of bad, and bad of good," etc.[208] Here is at least a sporting chance in an uncertain world. And at the very worst, Theognis, like Archilochus, counsels endurance and manliness. "We ought to endure (τολμᾶν) what the gods give mortal men and bear patiently either lot" (591 f.; cf. 555 f.). "Neither make thy heart too sick with evils nor too quickly glad of good, ere thou see the final end" (593 f.; cf. 393–398; 657 f.). "Bear up (τόλμα), Cyrnus, in ill fortune, because once thou didst rejoice in good, when *Moira* enjoined that thou shouldst share in that," [and pray, rather than display thy misery] (355–360). And Theognis takes his own medicine: "It is not possible, Cyrnus, to avoid what it is our lot (*moira*) to suffer; and what it is my lot to suffer, I fear not to suffer" (817 f.). Homeric in some of its diction, and indebted to Archilochus for the form of self-address,[209] but full of a noble resignation and a noble resolution that come from Theognis himself, is an address to his own soul.

Endure (τόλμα), my soul, in misfortune, though thou hast suffered the intolerable; 'tis sure the heart of the baser sort is quicker to wrath. Be not thou in great distress or anger over deeds that cannot be done, nor grieve thy friends and gladden thy foes. Not easily shall mortal man escape the destined gifts of the gods, neither if he sink to the bottom of the purple sea, nor when he be held in murky Tartaros (1029–1036).[210]

Perhaps the conclusion of the whole matter, for Theognis, is expressed in his emphasis on human character as something that can rise superior to circumstances. "Nobody is all-happy in all things; but the good man, if he have evil, yet endureth, though men know it not, whereas the bad man knoweth not how to abide and restrain his heart either in weal or in evil. Of all sorts are the gifts that come of the immortals to mortals; yet endure we must to keep the gifts they send, of whatsoever sort they be" (441–446). Surely this attitude, which the tragic poets were soon to rediscover among the uses of adversity, is a positive and a precious moral gain; all may be lost, save honor and τλημοσύνη. And it is a step toward the philosophy of happiness of Plato and Aristotle.

[207] Hudson-Williams, p. 46 (not accepting the lines as belonging to Theognis). Cf. also Theog. 865–868; 315–318 (Solon, 4, 9–12).

[208] Theog. 659–666; cf. Archil. 74; and see above, p. 35.

[209] Cf. Archil. 67a; see above, p. 35.

[210] Cf. Herodotus 5, 56, the riddling oracle spoken to Hipparchus in a dream, just before his death in 514 B.C.: τλῆθι λέων ἄτλητα παθὼν τετληότι θυμῷ.

The centuries that preceded the rise of Greek tragedy and of Greek philosophy were thus incessantly preoccupied with the problem of Fate, Good, and Evil. However much the problem was to grow later out of the form of tragedy itself and the great myths of tragedy, however stubbornly the philosophers were to attempt an intellectual solution, however much the Orphic cult was to transform Greek ideas of the soul and moral values, the Greeks had already built a solid structure of thought about the problem. Though not wholly consistent, it is a single tradition from Homer to Theognis and beyond, drawing from heroic action, peasant and civic life, and personal vicissitudes its touch of reality, and pouring its thought into gnomic form, often in antithetical half-truths. Its trend is from *Physis* to *Nomos*; it comes to distrust Nature and the gifts of the gods, and to find whatever of good the world affords more in social justice and the wise and brave acceptance and use of what Fate brings.

Each of the major poets, as we have seen, makes his contribution to the development of this tradition. For Homer, seeking to reconcile natural phenomena with anthropomorphic divinities, *Moira* and the *daimones* are equivocal ethical forces, bringing now good, now evil, and *nemesis* is barely ethical. Despite his distinction between *Ate* and *atasthalie*, Homer permits Menelaus to reproach Zeus for conniving with the wicked Trojans. Yet Zeus himself disclaims responsibility for what men suffer ὑπὲρ μόρον, and Achilles and Odysseus lay the foundations of a philosophy of endurance. In the myths of Hesiod, the source of evil is involved in a theory of cosmic degeneration, and human good is founded on the acceptance of the inevitable and on prudence and industry. The gnomic poets seek, though with misgivings, to maintain their orthodoxy. Archilochus, bewildered by the vicissitudes of life, introduces the idea of τύχη; but he develops the philosophy of τλημοσύνη, initiating moreover the literary device of self-address in the expression of it. Solon's emphasis is on the moral responsibility of man; and he is the first to trace systematically the sequence of moral decline. He is troubled by the spectacle of the suffering of good men, along with the wicked, for both good and evil come from *Moira*, and the gifts of the gods may not be refused; he is not troubled by the punishment of the innocent children of the wicked. Theognis, however, protests against such a miscarriage of justice, as he protests against the prosperity of the wicked; and he launches the pessimistic commonplace μὴ φῦναι. Nevertheless he qualifies his pessimism with counsels of piety and moderation and prudence. And if he is inconsistent, like his predecessors, in attributing evil now to the gift of the gods, now to the *hybris* of men, like them he also proclaims the need of activity and endurance.

# CHAPTER III

## ORTHODOXY AND MYSTICISM

THE attitude of the Greeks toward their gods and the unseen powers that molded their lives was expressed principally in two ways: in ritual and in the writings of their poets and thinkers. During the long period that falls between the eighth and the fifth centuries both cult and thought were dominated, for the most part, by the conceptions that had been set forth in the poems of Homer and Hesiod, only slightly modified by the ideas of the gnomic and lyric poets. Herodotus, in fact, expressed (II, 53) the prevalent view of his age when he declared that Homer and Hesiod "composed for the Greeks the generations of the gods, and gave the gods their titles and distinguished their several provinces and special powers that marked their forms." Even though ritual preserved, more than the Greeks of this period realized, the religion of the pre-Homeric period, nevertheless the orthodox ritual of the city-states had been largely reformed and expanded in accordance with the fully developed and anthropomorphic conceptions of Homer and Hesiod. Furthermore the orthodox theology of this period is to be sought in the poetry and the art that flowed from Homeric sources; there is as yet no other "Bible." Even the lyric and dramatic poets of the sixth and fifth centuries continue, to a large extent, this tradition, being, as it were, the "Fathers of the Church." But there was no compulsion, save that of social convenience, on any Greek to accept any theological view. He took part, as a matter of course, in the ritual observances of his city-state: but he was free to criticize myths and ideas, or to take part, in addition to participating in the cults of the state, in other forms of religious expression. That heterodoxy and individualism did emerge, and for good reason, we shall presently observe, and we shall trace their effects both in social movements and in the writings of poets and philosophers. But we must first notice the character of the orthodox religion of the average citizen of the city-state.

For the average Greek during this period, the goodness of the gods, though theoretically implied in the idea of divinity, is far from absolute. Some gods are more kindly than others; but none is consistently gracious or merciful. Nevertheless, though the gods are not the creators of the world, they sustain both the physical and the moral order, and govern not only the fortunes of men but their moral natures, admitting men to some extent, through their freedom of will, into partnership with the divine responsibility. From the sixth century on, Zeus increasingly asserts his sovereignty over the other gods, and the power of Fate is all but merged in him. The whole effect of the anthropomorphic religion reflected in the Homeric poems, in Hesiod, in the gnomic poets, and even in later literature, is to suggest that the gods are powerful, remote, and not wholly kindly; they give both good and evil, and somewhat capriciously; and there is little to hope for beyond the grave. The wisdom of the "Seven Sages," like the Delphic Sayings inculcating self-knowledge and the avoidance of excess, also counsel submission to powers beyond the control of the individual, and may end in quietism. The result, if it is not pessimism, is at least an attitude of resignation before the inevitable; and the fear of the gods (*deisidaimonia*) may easily become mere superstition, even panic.

The civic religion is an attempt to direct such dangerous tendencies into regular, legalized channels. If the gods will at least listen to prayers, and will at times accept sacrifices, the state will do all that organized effort can accomplish to maintain friendly relations with the gods by such means. So temples and cult images, processions and sacrifices, hymns and dances, are the answer of the state to this demand. (Something of the sort the Roman state, in turn, was to attempt in its highly organized and legalized systems.) To the beauty and majesty of the ritual our best witness is the Parthenon, with the marbles that still show us the figures of the gods of Olympus and their human worshipers. Such a cult may well serve a useful civic purpose at times in diverting to a social activity the minds of suffering individuals who are tormented by doubts or a sense of injustice. The cults of local gods and heroes, closely linked with the fortunes of a given city-state, focus the patriotic instincts, if they do not meet the deeper religious needs, of a people. Yet to persistent doubters, the answer of orthodoxy is only to reiterate the old conviction that *hybris* is punished by *nemesis*, insolence by retribution, or that the gods are actually jealous of prosperity (the φθόνος θεῶν).

The answer of orthodoxy could not forever satisfy all Greeks. Something could be done to mitigate the apparent harshness of the older conceptions. "Zeus who hearkens to supplication," "Zeus the compassionate" (Ζεὺς Ἱκετήσιος, Αἰδοῖος) found worshipers; there were even cults of Reverence (*Aidos*) and of Pity (*Eleos*) in Athens.[1] To Greeks as early as Pittacus and Thales, when asked, "Are the gods cognizant of every sin that a man commits?" was credited the reply, "Yes, and of every evil

[1] Cf. L. R. Farnell, *The Higher Aspects of Greek Religion*, p. 111.

intention."[2] And the Delphic oracle rebuked the Spartan Glaucus for contemplating the theft of some money that had been entrusted to him.[3] The inwardness of good and evil, as rooted in character, not in circumstances, was suggested also by the gnomic poets in their more daring moods.[4] Drama was to deal even more stubbornly with the problem of divine justice. But the more drastic solution of the problem was the abandonment, save for artistic and imaginative purposes, of the anthropomorphic conception of the gods. Philosophers replaced it by more abstract conceptions of the divine power that governs all things;[5] ordinary men tended more and more to resort to mystical religious experience.[6] Both tendencies are to some extent fused in the thought of Socrates and Plato.

The mystical revival of the sixth century has its roots in the oldest religious experience in the Greek world of which we have any knowledge, — the pre-Homeric religion, not of personal, anthropomorphic divinities but of natural powers and vague *daimones*, of vegetation rituals and taboos; a religion in which man and divinity are parts of Nature not utterly separate one from the other. But although the mysticism of the sixth century was in a sense a revival of this old and perennial attitude, it was revived under special forms that had entered Greece chiefly after the Homeric age: the cults of Eleusis, of Dionysus, and of the Orphic and the Pythagorean sects.[7] The evidence for all these matters is obscure, particularly as to dates, so that it is often necessary to rely on later testimony with regard to very early movements.[8] But it is clear that what is common to all these movements is a belief about the nature of the human soul and its destiny and the happiness in another life that awaits those who have received a certain kind of initiation in this life. Ecstasy, the going forth of the soul from the body, which is felt to take place under certain conditions of emotional excitement, is held to be evidence of the possibility of union with a god and of immortality. With these beliefs there is apt to be connected a myth, and in some cases a cosmogony.

The Eleusinian mysteries, the ancient fertility rites of the Attic village

[2] Diog. Laert. I, 76; 35.

[3] Herodotus, VI, 86.

[4] See above, pp. 38; 43; 45.

[5] See below, pp. 220; 224–226.

[6] On mysticism in general a valuable commentary may be found in parts of W. James, *The Varieties of Religious Experience* (New York, 1902); n.b. especially pp. 34–52, on the glad acceptance of the universe as the religious attitude; 78–123, on "healthy-mindedness," which recognizes no evil; 127–165, on "the sick soul," all too conscious of it; 379–429, on mysticism as a hopeful personal method and hypothesis; 488–519, contrasting the repudiation of personality by science with the interest of religion in personality.

[7] It is especially to the attitude of mind of these groups that I refer when I use the convenient though not wholly satisfactory term "mystery religions"; see further below, pp. 62 f.

[8] See below, pp. 52 f.

of Eleusis, held at the time of the autumn sowing, and symbolizing or seeking to assist the rebirth of the dead plant-world each year, were transformed into a ritual that symbolized the hope of human immortality. The beautiful Homeric *Hymn to Demeter* (II) is an aetiological myth, in which the institution of the cult is connected with the story of the loss, by the grain-goddess Demeter,[9] of her daughter Persephone, and of her recovery: only by the faithful performance of the ritual could the prosperity of the crops be insured.[10] But the emphasis was transferred from the conception of reviving crops to that of human immortality. As the cycle of the seasons beholds all losses restored by the rebirth of the buried seed in a new plant, so, the mystic argues, man's destiny comes full circle when life and death are followed by resurrection and a new life.[11]

Because the Eleusinian initiates were pledged to secrecy,[12] we are in the dark as to the precise character of the ritual; but it seems likely that apart from the preliminary ritual of ceremonial purification the central part consisted in the witnessing of a sacred drama that reënacted the experience of Persephone. All the initiates are promised (and all Greeks are eligible for initiation) such bliss as Homer reserves for Menelaus, the favored of Zeus, who is spared from death to enjoy forever the Elysian fields,[13] or such as Hesiod ascribes to the fabulous race of the Golden Age.[14] No moral qualifications were required of the Eleusinian initiate; and the ethical potentialities of the cult were lower than were those of Orphism. Nor did the initiate receive any secret dogma; his craving for immortality received no intellectual confirmation, but rather imaginative support; at the most, he felt a comforting sense of having entered into the

[9] That Demeter is not "Mother Earth" but the "Grain Mother" is argued by M. P. Nilsson, in *Archiv für Religionswissenschaft* 32 (1935), especially at pp. 102 ff., and in his *Greek Popular Religion* (New York, 1940), pp. 50–55. The usual interpretation of Δημήτηρ (= Γῆ μητήρ) is supported by H. Diels, "Ein orphischer Demeterhymnus," *Festschrift für T. Gomperz* (Wien, 1902), pp. 1–15; H. Diels, *Vorsokratiker*[5] 1 B 21, l. 1; O. Kern, *Orph. Frag.*, 47. Nilsson also argues that the months when Kore (Persephone) is absent are not the winter season, when as a matter of fact the fields in Mediterranean lands are green, but the parched summer months after the spring harvest, when the seed is stored underground until the autumn planting. His argument seems valid, despite the reference in the *Hymn* (lines 401 and 455) to "spring" flowers that attend the return of the daughter. (Possibly the reference is to the "second spring" that follows the autumn rains in Mediterranean lands.)

[10] Cf. further H. Diels, "Ein orphischer Demeterhymnus," pp. 1–15.

[11] The Epicurean, by conviction or by temperament, will deny the validity of the analogy, perhaps contrasting the cycle of night and day or of the moon's phases with man's everlasting eclipse (see below, p. 337 and n. 32). Similarly Aristotle, *De Gen. et Corrupt.* 338 a4–b19, answering Plato's argument for immortality in the *Phaedo*, based on the alternation of opposites in nature. The pseudo-Platonic *Axiochus* (early third century B.C.) is a reply to the Epicurean argument; cf. A. E. Taylor, *Epicurus*, pp. 98–105.

[12] *μύω*, "to keep the eyes shut"; *μυέω*, "to initiate into a *μυστήριον*, *mystery*."

[13] *Od.* 4, 561–569; see Appendix 2: Afterlife in Homer.

[14] See above, pp. 31 f.

experience of a goddess, who might therefore feel sympathy with him. And certain it is that he felt a deep assurance that he was a privileged person both in this life and in the life to come. Let the Homeric *Hymn* speak: "Blessed among men upon the earth is he who has seen these things; but he that is uninitiate in the rites and has no part in them has never an equal lot in the cold place of darkness."[15] Or again let us hear Sophocles:[16] "Thrice happy are those mortals who see these rites before they depart for Hades; for to them alone is it granted to have true life on the other side. To all the rest there is evil." Of these lines Diogenes of Sinope asked: "What do you mean? Is Pataikion the thief going to have a 'better lot' after death than Epaminondas, just because he was initiated?"[17]

It was from Thrace that Dionysus, the spirit of growing things, worshiped under various names, made his way into Greece, and focussed the natural cravings of man for a release from the restraints of the bodily, material world, through the use of wine and the orgiastic dance. The myth of the death and rebirth of Dionysus, besides expressing the annual death and revival of vegetation and the corresponding hope of human immortality, is also a projection of the ritual dismemberment (the *Sparagmos*) and eating of bulls (the *Omophagia*) practised by his worshipers at nocturnal festivals, and is so far aetiological. It was later given a new interpretation by the followers of Orpheus in such a fashion as to provide an account of the origin of man and of his dual moral nature, partly good and partly evil.[18]

The greater excesses of the new cult of Dionysus were curbed as it was admitted to the Greek city-states: the *Bacchae* of Euripides, with all its sympathetic expression of the Dionysiac frenzy, nevertheless reflects also the suspicion with which the *polis* regarded it. At Delphi the cult was kept within bounds, under the influence of Apollo: and the two gods of inspiration henceforth shared men's devotion,[19] and contributed together to the birth and growth of tragedy.

[15] Homeric *Hymn to Demeter* (II), 480–482; cf. lines 488 f., promising wealth to the initiates.

[16] *Soph. Frag.* 837 (Pearson). For Pindar, see below, pp. 78–81. Cf. also Aristophanes, *Frogs*, 454–459; the whole passage (ll. 312–459), which follows the twelve-mile procession of the initiates (*Mystai*) from Athens along the Sacred Way to Eleusis, is a mingling of burlesque and truly religious feeling, as was doubtless the actual procession. The same poet's *Clouds* represents the initiation of Strepsiades into the new learning under forms that parody Eleusinian (and Orphic) initiation.

[17] Plutarch, *De Aud. Poet.* 21 F.

[18] See below, pp. 59 f.

[19] Cf. A. D. Nock, *Conversion* (Oxford, 1933), pp. 25 f. But prophecy was in the province of Apollo, not of Dionysus; cf. K. Latte, "The Coming of the Pythia," *Harv. Theol. Rev.* 33 (1940), pp. 9–18.

But it was another Thracian, the seer or "shaman" Orpheus, who was supposed to have done most to give a wide currency to mystical ideas. Orpheus "invented the mysteries of Dionysus," says Apollodorus, quite bluntly;[20] and even if it be held that "Orpheus" never existed, nevertheless it remains true that the sect which claimed him as its founder did take over, as we shall see, the myth of Dionysus.[21] To Orpheus were attributed also hymns and theogonies, of which later versions still exist, and above all the foundation of secret rites of initiation.[22] By the latter part of the sixth century the local Orphic groups were firmly established both in Greece and in southern Italy, in Athens largely through the efforts of the "minister of cults" of the Peisistratids, Onomacritus, who was even given credit for the authorship of Orphic poems as well as for instituting ritual representations of the suffering of Dionysus at the hands of the Titans. Certainly Athens became the chief literary center for the diffusion of Orphism, a religion distinguished by its sacred books and by its way of life.[23]

There are few traces in Homer of interest in what became the leading subjects for speculation among the men of the later age, — the origin of the world, the origin and nature of the human soul, and the destiny of the soul after death. Homer's vision is fixed for the most part on a world that is stationary; his one great glimpse of the dead gives men no grounds for hopes of a better life;[24] as for theogony, Oceanus is the father (*genesis*) and Tethys ("suckler") the mother of all the gods.[25] Yet behind the gods stands a power in awe of whom even Zeus, the mightiest of the reigning gods, checks his impulses, — "Night, that subdues both gods and men."[26] Here we seem to find something older than Homer, older than Zeus.[27]

In the cosmogonies and theogonies of the centuries that followed the Homeric age we observe the imaginative efforts of men without scientific instruments to find some principle of order, and perhaps of goodness, in the world. "Hesiod," Pherecydes, Epimenides, Aristophanes, and the late "Orphic" writers all preserve in their several ways some record of this attempt. The relative ages of the various Orphic theogonies and cosmogonies cannot be precisely determined; accounts of them are preserved for us chiefly in the writings of the Platonic and Neoplatonic philosophers, notably by Damascius, head of the Neoplatonic school in Athens in the early sixth century A.D. Undoubtedly the germs of the cosmogonies are

[20] *Bibliotheca*, I, 3, 2.
[21] See below, pp. 59 f.
[22] Cf. [Euripides], *Rhesus*, 943: Aristophanes, *Frogs*, 1032.
[23] See Appendix 9: Orphism.
[24] *Odyssey*, 11; see Appendix 2: Afterlife in Homer.
[25] *Il.* 14, 201; 246; 302.
[26] Il. 14, 258–261.
[27] Cf. Damascius, *De Princ.* 124 (= Diels, *Vorsokratiker*[5], 1 B 12).

earlier than the Homeric poems, but are influenced by "Hesiod," by oriental beliefs, and by later philosophical interpretations. The "Rhapsodies"[28] have been dated as early as the sixth century B.C. and as late as the period just before the Neoplatonic age, though in the latter case they would admittedly preserve traces of much earlier poetry. In any case it appears that the materials of the Orphic theogonies and cosmogonies rolled up like a snowball, and we must note the content without expecting to trace the precise development of the ideas.[29]

The purpose of "Hesiod," the author of the *Theogony*, is to explain systematically how the existing order of things came into being; and this he undertakes to do both by tracing a sequence of powers or divinities growing naturally one from another by the process of generation (*Physis* expressing herself, as it were, without any moral trend), and also by suggesting at times a deliberate policy of action, culminating in the triumph of order over disorder (*themis* or *nomos* over *physis*).[30] In one of the Preludes the poet expresses what may be the traditional idea of the source of the gods, "those that were born of Earth and starry Heaven, and gloomy Night, and those that the salt sea reared" (106 f.). But in the poem proper, the poet's own idea is set forth; he boldly looks back further than Homer, and places at the very beginning not Oceanus, or even Night, but Chaos, the primeval "gap" or "void," — an abstraction. "Verily at the first Chaos came to be, but next wide-bosomed Earth, the ever-sure foundation of all, . . . and dim Tartarus in the depth of the wide-pathed Earth . . . and Eros, who moves the limbs and overcomes the mind and wise counsels of all gods and all men within them" (116–122). There is little more than a sequence here, hardly an idea of generation, certainly not one of scientific causality or evolution. Neither Chaos nor, as it proves in the sequel, Eros is really used effectively to suggest the function, in the one case of matter, in the other of a vital, procreative force. Yet the description of Eros as a psychological rather than a cosmic force is remarkable; the epithet λυσιμέλης is the very one that Sappho uses of him,[31] though Sappho takes liberties with the genealogy of Eros, making him the "dearest offspring of Earth and Heaven." Quite possibly "Hesiod" is borrowing from an earlier source;[32] but though Chaos and Eros and

[28] See below, pp. 57 f.

[29] Cf. E. Zeller, *History of Greek Philosophy*, I, 98; T. Gomperz, *Greek Thinkers* (Eng. Trans., London, 1906), I, 90; O. Kern, *Orph. Frag.*, pp. 140 f.; O. Kern, *Orpheus* (Berlin, 1920), pp. 41 f.; M. Nilsson, *Harv. Theol. Rev.* 28 (1935), p. 182; I. F. Burns, "Cosmogony and Cosmology (Greek)," in Hastings, *Enc. Rel. Eth.* IV, 145–151; Guthrie, *Orpheus*, pp. 74–91; 115–130; A. Rivaud, *Devenir*, pp. 5–81.

[30] Cf. above, p. 28.

[31] Sappho, 137 Diehl.

[32] But cf. W. Jaeger, *Paideia*, p. 63: "Hesiod's Eros is a philosophical conception of his own: a new idea which was to have profoundly stimulating effects on later speculation."

Night are Orphic powers, as we know, the cosmic egg that the Orphics are apt to associate with Eros is not here.[33] Yet the poet deserves credit for introducing ideas that are to be used more successfully by the Orphic and philosophic writers. The gods, it must be noted, have not yet appeared, or any idea of purpose.

The account goes on: "from Chaos came forth Erebus and black Night; but of Night were born Aether and Day, whom she conceived and bore from union with Erebus. And Earth first bore starry Heaven, equal to herself, to cover her on every side, and to be an ever-sure abiding-place for the blessed gods" (123–128). In this last phrase there is a suggestion of a purpose in nature. In what follows (the birth to Earth of the Mountains and the Sea, and to Earth and Heaven of Oceanus and the other Titans and finally of Cronos, and of the Cyclopes and the Hundred-armed), no explicit use is made of the power of Eros, even if the process is that of procreation (129–153). A real myth or folk-tale is used to explain the origin of the Erinyes, the Giants, the Meliae (Nymphs) and Aphrodite; these spring from the plot of Earth and Cronos against Heaven, and their mutilation of him (154–210). Allegory seems to intrude itself into this interpretation of the powers of *physis*, where Eros and even Himeros (Longing) are allotted to the retinue of Aphrodite, the goddess whose *moira* is human love in all its manifestations (201–206).

The children of Night are also largely abstractions, — Doom (*Moros*) and black Fate (*Ker*) and Death, Sleep and the Tribe of Dreams; the *Moirai*, *Nemesis*, and various moral abstractions, chiefly baleful, and among them *Ate* (211–232). Hesiod's Night, unlike the Night of the Orphics, is not the "mother of the gods"; she has an elementary power, to be sure, but nothing else in common with the Orphic Night save the name.[34]

We may pass over the "Hesiodic" account of the matings of the Titans and their progeny (aspects of nature, and monsters) and the tale of the outwitting of Cronos by Rhea, which results in the Triumph of Zeus, and the Tale of Prometheus;[35] but we must note that there is nothing ethical in these myths, which are clearly aetiological and are told in order to account for the superseding of the older cults by the Olympians (233–616). The wars of Zeus and the Olympians against the Titans, and the imprisonment of the defeated Titans in Tartarus, like the account of Typhoeus, suggest the rebellious forces of nature, chiefly subterranean, which Zeus brings under control and order (617–885). But there is no

[33] Cf. Gomperz, I, 89; Burnet, *Early Greek Philosophy*[4], p. 7; Harrison, *Proleg.*, p. 626; see also below, p. 57, n. 46.

[34] O. Kern, *De Orphei Epimenidis Pherecydis Theogoniis* (Berlin, 1888), p. 18.

[35] See above, p. 52 f.

suggestion yet of Tartarus as a place of punishment for men, nor of the birth of man from the ashes of the Titans;[36] these are Orphic ideas.

The remainder of the poem, dealing with the successive marriages of Zeus, and tapering off into the marriages and progeny of other divinities, clearly represents an accretion of miscellaneous material (preserved partly in double recension).[37] Somewhat sophisticated is the introduction of many more or less abstract ideas: Styx, goddess and river (of "loathing"), by whom even the gods may not swear falsely without doing penance (775–806); Metis, the first of the wives of Zeus, whom he swallowed, and thus brought forth her child Athene himself, thus ensuring that he should be the fount of all wisdom (889–900; 924–929 t); and the children of his second wife, Themis, — the *Horai* (*Eunomia*, *Dike*, *Eirene*), and the *Moirai*.

The *Theogony* of "Hesiod," then, is not a very original treatment of its theme, nor does it carry out consistently a single hypothesis. But many of its ingredients and its general method of tracing a sequence of stages in a natural process were to be taken over both by the Orphic composers of theogonies and by more scientific or philosophic thinkers.

In the sixth century the making of cosmogonies was a common undertaking of men who sought to supplement the Hesiodic account by Orphic and other ideas. Pherecydes of Syros, one of earliest Greek writers of prose, and possibly one of the earliest Greeks to promulgate the immortality of the soul, lived at Athens at the court of the Peisistratidae, along with the Orphic Onomacritus.[38] Whereas "Hesiod" had put first in his *Theogony* the spatial abstraction *Chaos*, Pherecydes in his treatise on the genesis of the gods sets at the head three first-principles (ἀρχαί): *Zas* (Zeus, spelled in such a way as to suggest that he is the principle of "life"), Chronos (the abstraction, Time) and *Chthonie* (the principle of Earth whom Zas wedded, and to whom is given *Ge*, the material Earth (D 7 B 1 and 2); it was *Chronos* who made from his seed Fire and Air (πνεῦμα) and Water, from which came the gods in five families or provinces (μυχοί) (D 7 A 8). Possibly it is going too far to see in these primal beings (or substances, or gods) an anticipation of the elements of Empedocles; he is still a myth-maker, rather than a philosopher. Later eyes were inclined to read allegory into his scheme (D 7 B 2; 4; 5; 6). A great imaginative idea appears in the statement that when Zeus was about to accomplish the creation he transformed himself into Eros.[39] Furthermore Zeus

[36] See below, p. 59.

[37] Cf. the double pedigree of the *Moirai*, 217; 904; and see above, p. 29.

[38] Diels, *Vorsokratiker*[5], 7 A 1–5.

[39] Proclus on Plato's *Tim.* 32C (= D 7 B 3). Proclus continues with a philosophical interpretation (the motive of Zeus is the desire to produce a harmony of opposites); and one

made a great robe, and embroidered on it the Earth and Ogenos (Oceanus), and spread it on a wing-borne oak tree (D 7 B 2); later, there was a great battle between Chronos[40] and a serpent-god of the earth, Ophioneus, and his hosts, in which Chronos triumphed and cast his foes into the sea (D 7 B 4; 5). In the course of time, we may say, order triumphed over brute force.

Thus Aristotle was justified in his comment on the system of Pherecydes and other "theologians," that he put at the first the best, which is the begetting power, namely Zeus.[41] That is, the eclectic Pherecydes marks an advance over "Hesiod" both in his conception of Time and in his attempt to conceive of primary, almost spiritual, beings, from which are derived material elements. At least Zeus-Eros is more spiritual than Chaos, so far as soul precedes body. Yet order finally asserts itself only after triumphing over disorder. It may be from this source, and from Empedocles, that Apollonius of Rhodes, in the late third century, derived the ideas contained in the *Argonautica* (I, 494–511) on the origin of the World and the separation of earth, sky, and sea under the stress of discord (*νεῖκος*), and the emergence of stars, moon, and sun, of mountains, rivers, and animals, and finally his account of the wars of Ophion and Eurynome, daughter of Oceanus, against Cronos and Rhea, who hurled them into the Ocean, till they themselves suffered a similar fate at the hands of Zeus.[42]

Epimenides the Cretan was supposed to have helped the Athenians to cleanse their city of a plague (596–593 B.C.) by means of a sacrifice; he is described as a sort of sage or saint, experienced in all that pertains to mystical ritual.[43] According to one account he once slept for forty years (D 3 A 8; 3 B 1); according to another, he had the power of sending forth his soul at will from his body, to which it would return (D 3 A 2). In other words he was a mystic of the "ecstatic" type. His writings included a "Theogony" and works on ritual and politics. We are informed by Damascius (D 3 B 5) that Epimenides entertained two first causes (*ἀρχαί*), Air and Night, from which proceeded a third, Tartarus. From them came two Titans, parents of an Egg from which proceed the rest of generation. If the first part of this system seems to be an uninspired echo of part of "Hesiod," the introduction of the Egg by Epimenides (or an

---

thinks, too, of the φιλότης of Empedocles; the idea of Eros, as a procreative force, however, is clearly Orphic.

[40] Not Cronos; so Kern argues convincingly, *De Orphei Epimenidis Pherecydis Theogoniis*, 97 f.

[41] Aristotle, Met. N 1091 b1–10.

[42] With this passage contrast I, 419–430, which is truly Orphic and non-Empedoclean. Cf. Kern, *Orphicorum Fragmenta*, p. 100.

[43] Plutarch, *Solon* (= Diels, 3 A 4).

intermediate writer) is the earliest literary statement of this favorite Orphic idea, a symbol of the life-giving process.

Acusilaus in his prose adaptation of "Hesiod's" *Theogony* put Chaos first, "as altogether unknown" (ἄγνωστον); from its children, the (male) Erebus and (female) Night, proceeded Aether, Eros, Metis, and other divinities.

But it is Aristophanes who first provides us with a cosmogony that may fairly be described as Orphic, in the parabasis of the *Birds* (414 B.C.),—a cosmogony, it may be noted, offered as an orthodox [44] account of the *physis* of the birds and of the *genesis* of the gods and Erebus and Chaos,—an account that will eclipse that of the contemporary sophist Prodicus.[45] The part which is of special interest to us, translated by Swinburne, runs as follows:

It was Chaos and Night at the first, and the blackness of darkness, and Hell's broad border,
Earth was not, nor air, neither heaven; when in depths of the womb of the dark without order
First thing first-born of the black-plumed night was a wind-egg hatched in her bosom,
Whence timely with seasons revolving again sweet Love burst out as a blossom,
Gold wings gleaming forth of his back, like whirlwinds gustily turning.
He, after his wedlock with Chaos, whose wings are of darkness, in Hell broad-burning,
For his nestlings begot him the race of us first, and upraised us to light new-lighted.
And before this was not the race of the gods, until all things by Love were united:
And of kind united with kind in communion of nature the sky and the sea are
Brought forth, and the earth and the race of the gods everlasting and blest.
(693–702.)

Here again "Hesiod" provides a general frame, and the earlier powers, the Olympian gods being definitely post-poned; but both the Egg and the figure of Eros, the life-force in all its power, are entirely Orphic,—all, of course, except the comic ascription of priority and dignity to the birds.[46]

But the great Orphic cosmogony, which must have been fairly well developed as early as the sixth century, is contained chiefly in the accounts of the "Hieroi Logoi," or "Rhapsodies," composed at an unknown period,

[44] *Birds*, 690; 692: ὀρθῶς.

[45] For a reconstruction of the cosmogony of Prodicus, cf. A. W. Benn, *The Greek Philosophers*, p. 91, note.

[46] For a similar ridicule of a similar religious interpretation of nature, cf. Aristophanes, *Clouds*, 250 ff. On Eros and the Egg, cf. further J. Harrison, *Prolegomena to the Study of Greek Religion*, 624–658; Guthrie, *Orpheus*, 92–95.

and preserved in such later writers as Damascius.[47] From fragmentary accounts it is possible to reconstruct the main features of the system. In the beginning was Chronos, followed by Aether and Chaos, from whom proceeded a silvery Egg, half of which came to form the vault of Heaven, the other half the Sea and the Earth. From the Egg was born the first Orphic god, the golden-winged Phanes (The Shining One), with whom was identified also Eros, and Metis (Counsel), Ericapaeus (Life-giver); he is known also as Protogonus (first-born) and as Proteurhythmus (as awakener of rhythm in man). He produced Night, and in union with her brought forth Heaven and Earth, Cronos and Rhea, and Zeus and Hera, and other divinities. Finally, as in "Hesiod" Zeus swallowed Metis, so here he swallowed Phanes, and thus could be thought of as the primal creator of all things, something that Zeus had never been in the Olympian religion: "Zeus is the head, Zeus is the middle, in Zeus all things are completed."[48] With this Zeus, moreover, the somewhat spiritualized power of *Physis*, the Orphics closely associated, as a goddess both of vengeance and of justice, Dike, the primal "Way of Things."[49]

Thus once more the Orphics, like Pherecydes, "put the best first,"[50] by giving prominence to Zeus, who now stands both for intelligence and for love in the ordering of a world that he governs. He has become at once more abstract and more intimately concerned with the life and goodness of the world. And Pherecydes and the Orphics have added to the spatial conception of "Hesiod" the sense of a time-flow, in which great destinies are worked out. Though they necessarily succeed only imperfectly in reconciling imagination with reason, they nevertheless do attempt to moralize the notion of *physis*, of growth and purpose and intelligence in the universe; this is more than pantheism. On the other hand, these cosmogonies and theogonies fail to provide any theory, whether theological or scientific, of the way in which divine power may be supposed to unfold itself for good or for ill in the details of the world; they provide a bare symbol of a life-force, or of intelligence, without any content. Zeus-Phanes-Eros is not yet ready, like the Demiurge of Plato's *Timaeus*, to embody his own goodness in the created world;[51] yet the germ of Plato's thought here may be said to be partly Orphic, and indeed it is in commenting on *Timaeus* 32C that Proclus preserves for us the idea of Pherecydes that Zeus transformed himself into Eros.[52] Still less is the

[47] See Appendix 10: Orphic Cosmogony.

[48] Kern, *Orph. Frag.*, p. 91; cf. pp. 90–93.

[49] Plato, *Laws*, 715e; [Demosthenes], XXV, 11; Kern, *Orph. Frag.*, pp. 90 and 94; cf. J. Harrison, *Prolegomena*, pp. 506; 611; J. Harrison, *Themis*, pp. 517–535.

[50] See above, p. 56.

[51] Plato, *Timaeus*, 27d–32; see below, pp. 293–295.

[52] See above, p. 55.

Orphic capable of envisaging Aristotle's "unmoved mover," the goodness of the universe whose mere being moves all else because he is the object of the world's desire,[53] or the Christian God who "so loved the world" that He sacrificed Himself for it. Yet the Orphic God is alive, and has in him the seeds of the goodness in the world.

For an explanation of the evil in the world the Orphics refer to the transformed myth of Dionysus. The infant Dionysus (Zagreus), child of Zeus and Persephone, so the myth now runs, was tricked by the wicked Titans, enemies of Zeus, by means of a mirror and other playthings, and though he changed himself into various forms, and finally into a bull, they tore him to pieces and devoured him, all except his heart. The heart was rescued by Athena, who brought it to Zeus, who after swallowing it wedded Semele, who bore him the "new Dionysus." The wicked Titans (who, it must be remembered, had devoured the first god Dionysus) were destroyed by Zeus with a flash of lightning; from their ashes sprang the human race, which is partly evil and partly good, for it includes both Titanic and Dionysiac elements.

In the myth as thus interpreted by the adherents of the Orphic mysteries, not only has the death of Dionysus become a crime perpetrated by the Titans, who are therefore conceived as wicked, but the ritual of the Omophagia itself also appears to be criminal. No wonder, then, that "Orpheus" was later represented as having been torn to pieces by the Maenads, devotees of Dionysus.[54]

The Orphic version of the myth also suggests why the individual human soul, though imprisoned here in its tomb of flesh, craves reunion with Dionysus. It would be difficult to overestimate the importance of this group of ideas for the subsequent development of Greek mysticism and philosophy.[55] For better or for worse, it stamps once and for all man's nature as dual, spiritual and physical, good and evil. It dooms the individual to a sad lot and to suffering, not merely for his own sins (by reason of his freedom of the will), but for the original sin of the Titans, which is now ingrained in his own half-Titan nature. There is no release save by the mediation of a *daimon* and his cult.[56] Here is the beginning of the idea that this life is evil, compared with the life to come; that death may be a blessed release, and that asceticism is the best preparation for such a release. Here is the root of Puritanism and of the subjugation of the body. If this solution of the problem of evil is pessimistic, in that it takes a low

[53] See below, p. 318.

[54] Cf. M. Nilsson, *Harv. Theol. Rev.* 28 (1935), pp. 202–204. See further Guthrie, *Orpheus*, pp. 41–55; I. M. Linforth, *The Arts of Orpheus*, pp. 307–364, with searching criticism of the myth and of the importance given to it by modern scholars.

[55] See the long comment of Olympiodorus, *ad Phaed.* 61c (pp. 1–5 Norvin).

[56] Cf. J. A. Hild, *Étude sur le Démons*, pp. 118–151.

view of the "natural" man and his material environment, it is at least optimistic in the hope that it holds out to him of winning a better lot through his own effort, by initiation and a particular kind of life; these matters do not rest wholly with arbitrary gods or with chance or fate.

The pre-Orphic world was acquainted with evil and misfortune; but among the Greeks it was only those who came in some way under the influence of the Orphic cults who had what may be called "the sense of sin." In particular the feeling grew, partly through Plato's influence, and was handed on to early Christianity, that in the partnership between soul and body all the good comes from the soul, which is divine and immortal, and all the evil comes from the body and the senses, which are mortal; or, as the Orphics phrased it, the body (σῶμα) is the tomb (σῆμα) of the soul which is its temporary tenant;[57] the soul came from Heaven and by its incarnation in the body has entered upon the "Circle (or Wheel) of Generation."[58]

The Orphics, like some other mystics, believe in metempsychosis, the reincarnation of a single soul in a series of bodies.[59] The taint of evil to which the flesh is heir, or which the soul perversely acquires in this life, the soul, like a fallen angel, must expiate in order ultimately to regain its pristine purity and escape from the "Circle of Generation." By the observance of certain taboos, by the use of certain symbolic objects, above all by being initiated into the Orphic brotherhood and practising an "ascetic" life, it was believed that one might win such a purity and such an escape. A special method of life, as well as a special set of beliefs, thus distinguished the protestant Orphic from his more orthodox fellows. Much of the *askesis* and of the ritual was doubtless external enough: such was abstention from the eating of beans and from the wearing of woolen clothing, or the daubing of clay on the body to absorb its evil, or abstention from the eating of flesh. The Orphics held that man had not eaten flesh in the Golden Age, the age of innocence before the fall of man. It was also regarded as sinful because the soul of a man, freed from its body, might have come to inhabit an animal; flesh-eating would in that case be cannibalism.[60]

The brotherhood was sometimes exclusive and intolerant.[61] And there were Orphic charlatans who peddled indulgences and crude magic, if we

[57] Plato, *Gorgias* 493a; see below, p. 261.

[58] κύκλος γενέσεως, Proclus *in Plat. Tim.* 42cd (Kern, *Orph. Frag.* p. 244); for the idea, see also below, pp. 61 f.; 62; 314; for the Pythagorean κύκλος ἀνάγκης, Diog. Laert. VIII, 14.

[59] Somewhat similar is the Buddhist idea of *Karma*.

[60] Empedocles, D 31 B 135–137; Plato, *Laws*, 782cd; Virgil, *Georg.* III, 536–538; J. Haussleiter, *Der Vegetarismus in der Antike* (Berlin, 1935), especially pp. 54–96; A. O. Lovejoy and G. Boas, *Primitivism and Related Ideas in Antiquity*, p. 32.

[61] Cf. the picture of Hippolytus in the play of Euripides; see below, pp. 180 f.

may believe Plato.[62] But there was a better side to the Orphic religion. The more devout worshipers who partook of the ritual meal felt that in a mystical union they were actually becoming one wtih the *daimon* who was a mediator between man and god.[63] The ceremonial purity often became the symbol of a moral purity, and the *askesis* was a training of the character, as in the educational system set forth by Plato.[64]

The Orphics naturally were deeply interested in the fortunes of the soul in the next life. The initiated, even if unhappy here, might hope for happiness there, perhaps an unending and more or less refined carousal, while the uninitiated must suffer retribution, buried in mud, terrified and tormented.[65] Most, in fact, of the popular notions of the terrors of Hades as a place of purification and punishment, may be traced to Orphic sources.[66] But some of the Orphics, who shared with the Eleusinian initiates a fair hope for the future life, came in time to stress not mere initiation, as the condition of future happiness, but a pure life. Only the souls of the pure, they held, might hope after a period of further purgation, perhaps after probationary incarnations in a long period of time, to win a final escape from the "Circle of Generation" and reunion with divinity. This more ethical idea will meet us again in Plato, where the belief in immortality is a foundation stone for morality. It is in Plato too that we first meet the figure of Minos dealing out judgment to men in the Lower World on the basis of their past lives. Orphism, unlike the orthodox tradition, regards a man's deeds from an individualistic point of view; he will ultimately, in the next life if not here, prosper or suffer for his own deeds, and cannot leave a crime or a curse, as a social inheritance to be atoned for by his innocent descendants.[67] Thus the solution of the old problem which troubled Theognis [68] and which tragedy was ordinarily to handle conventionally [69] was pushed by the Orphics into the realm of the unseen, faith in the ultimate justice of the universe triumphing over the evidence of this world, in which justice obviously often miscarries. Orphic faith, like Messianic and apocalyptic literature, represents an attempt to explain present evil not as a falling away from an imagined

[62] *Republic*, 364b.

[63] Hild, *Démons*, pp. 118–151.

[64] Cf. C. H. Moore, "Greek and Roman Ascetic Tendencies," in *Harvard Essays on Classical Subjects* (Boston, 1912), pp. 109–117.

[65] Cf. Plato, *Republic*, 363cd.

[66] Cf. the painting by Polygnotus, in the Hall of the Cnidians at Delphi, of the visit of Odysseus to the world of the dead, as described by Pausanias, and cf. Greek and Latin poetry, *passim*.

[67] On Orphism in Plato, see F. M. Cornford, "Plato and Orpheus," *Classical Review*, 17 (1903), pp. 433–445; J. Dörfler, "Die Orphik in Platons Gorgias," *Wiener Studien*, 33 (1911), pp. 177–212.

[68] See above, pp. 40–42.

[69] See below, pp. 89 f.; 98.

Golden Age but as a preparation for a better life. Even for this life, however, the better Orphic would hold with Plato that man's true good consists not in external prosperity but in the condition of his soul. "Evil have I fled, better have I found," — so the mystic expressed his religious experience;[70] the same phrase was later used of marriage, another form of initiation.

The Orphic eschatology pictured in some detail the landscape which the initiate might hope to behold in the next life. Some of the landmarks appear, together with the hopes of the initiates, in the thin gold tablets found in graves in southern Italy and in Crete, giving guidance to the dead.[71] One of them, of the fourth or the third century B.C., begins as follows:

> Thou shalt find to the left of the House of Hades a Well-spring,[72]
> And by the side thereof standing a white cypress.
> To this Well-spring approach not near,
> But thou shalt find another, from the Lake of Memory
> Cold water flowing forth, and there are Guardians before it.
> Say: "I am a child of Earth and of Starry Heaven;
> But my race is of Heaven (alone). This ye know yourselves.
> And lo, I am parched with thirst and I perish. Give me quickly
> The cold water flowing forth from the Lake of Memory.
> And of themselves they will give thee to drink from the Well-spring.
> And thereafter among the other Heroes thou shalt have lordship." [73]

From other tablets it must suffice to quote only a few phrases:

> Out of the Pure [74] I come . . .
> I have paid the penalty for deeds unrighteous. . . .
> I have flown out of the sorrowful, weary Wheel;
> I have passed with eager feet to the Circle desired.
>
> Thou art become god from man.

Such phrases indicate clearly enough that for the Orphic initiates death is "swallowed up in victory." And for still more eloquent expression of their hopes we need only turn to Pindar.[75]

To the perplexities of the Greek world, baffled by the moral bankruptcy

[70] Quoted contemptuously by Demosthenes, *De Corona*, 259.

[71] D I B 17–20; discussed, with kindred matters, by J. Harrison, *Prolegomena*, pp. 572–595; the text also, by G. Murray, in pp. 659–673; cf. Guthrie, *Orpheus*, pp. 171–182.

[72] I.e. the Spring of Lethe, Forgetfulness.

[73] Trans. G. Murray, with slight changes made by F. M. Cornford to fit the text of D I B 17.

[74] I.e. the Orphically initiated.

[75] E.g. Pindar *Ol.* II, 53 ff.; *Dirges*, Frag. 114 (Bowra); see below, pp. 78–81. Cf. also the pseudo-Platonic *Axiochus*.

of the orthodox religion, the answer of all the "mystery religions" is one: if men's eyes are turned solely to the external things of this life, there are indeed grounds for holding that the world is evil and that Fate and the gods are cruel or indifferent, being external and aloof from man, whose duty is to refrain from presumption: "Seek not to become a god."[76] But if one's eyes are turned to what is divine in oneself, or to the life that lies beyond this life, in union with divinity, there are grounds for good cheer with regard both to the future and to this life. This is something beyond the *τλημοσύνη* of the poets, from Homer to Theognis;[77] it rests not merely on the endurance of evil but on the escape of the soul from an alien world to the divinity to which it is naturally akin. Fate, then, is for the mystic the evil "Circle of Generation," within which man, so far as he is the creature of *Physis*, must remain; but it is possible for him to obey the promptings of his other self and to find an immaterial good. Such an unorthodox attitude meets us sometimes in tragedy[78] and often in philosophy. To these departments of literature we shall presently turn. But first we must notice how far certain of the predramatic poets, partly epic and partly lyric, depart from the Homeric tradition.

Only one passage from the Epic Cycle need detain us; but this is one of singular interest, in that it shows that men were attempting to explain the responsibility of Zeus for the calamity of the Trojan War. A scholiast commenting on the "plan of Zeus" which was fulfilled in the carnage of the war,[79] remarks that among other explanations (one being an identification of the "plan" with Fate, *ἡ εἱμαρμένη*) there is the story that Zeus deliberately caused the war in order to relieve the encumbered earth of an excess of population; and the scholiast cites seven lines from the Cyclic epic, the *Cypria*. "There was a time when the countless tribes of men though widely dispersed over the earth oppressed the surface of the deep-bosomed earth; and Zeus saw it and had pity, and in his wise heart resolved to relieve the all-nurturing earth of men by causing the great struggle of the Trojan War, that the load of death might empty the world. And so the heroes were slain in Troy, and the plan of Zeus came to pass."[80] What is surprising about the Malthusian view of this poet (Stasinus), who recognizes in war a means of reducing overpopulation, is that he assigns it not to the blind forces of nature (*Physis*) but to a wise and pitying Zeus. If one could take a purely objective view of the world and its human inhabitants, one might easily admit that a less populous world of superior persons would constitute a better order; so far the "plan of

[76] Pindar, *Ol.* V, 27.
[77] See above, pp. 26–28; 35; 45.
[78] See below, pp. 89; 99.
[79] *Il.* I, 5.
[80] *Cypria*, II (T. W. Allen).

Zeus" might be regarded as wise. But that war would necessarily eliminate especially the inferior persons, however those might be defined, is just what can never be shown, nor is it apparently part of the "plan of Zeus" to discriminate. From the point of view of those whom war eliminates, moreover, the plan is not one of "pity," but one of cold, intellectual planning. It is not Stasinus, however, but rather Aeschylus, who will make the issue clear; for whereas the Zeus of the *Prometheus Bound* had intended to annihilate the present human race and to bring forth a new and possibly better one, Prometheus through sympathy with the plight of the existing race interfered to save it, and by bestowing on it fire and the arts strove to lighten its disabilities.[81] It was for this well-meaning but presumptuous interference that he was punished. Here are all the elements of Tragedy.[82] A superficial resemblance to the lines of the *Cypria*, and a deeper difference, is to be noted in the suggestion in Plato's *Critias* (121bc) that Zeus contrived the war between the Athenians and the inhabitants of Atlantis not merely to reduce overpopulation but to discipline by defeat the men of Atlantis for their moral decline.

The spirit of the Homeric Hymns, except the Hymn to Demeter, is light and buoyant; the rhapsodes who composed them were more moved by the external beauties of myth and ritual than by religious feeling. Quite detached if not unsympathetic, are the gods, and indeed the Muses, who, like the rhapsodes themselves or like the minstrels of the Homeric poem, "Sing one to another, sweet voice answering voice, of the imperishable gifts of the gods, and the endurance of men and of all that they suffer at the hands of the immortal gods, living witless and helpless, nor can they find any remedy against death, nor any defence against old age."[83]

Yet the primeval power of Mother Earth, the Physis that is older than Themis, is still conceived of as mighty and kindly and not beyond the entreaty of gods and men who may crave her gifts. Hera, who is clearly a power closely associated with the early chthonian religion and the Titans, when offended by Zeus "struck with her hand on the ground, and prayed: 'Hear now, Earth (*Gaia*) and wide Heaven above, and ye Titan gods who dwell beneath great Tartarus, from whom are sprung both gods and men, and grant that I may bear a child apart from Zeus'. . . . So she spoke, and smote the earth with her stout hand, and the life-giving earth was shaken." And in due course her prayer, we learn, was answered.[84]

One of the later Homeric Hymns to Earth, Mother of All, reverts to

[81] Aeschylus, *P. V.*, pp. 228–236; 442–506.

[82] See further below, pp. 119–122; and Euripides, *Or.* 1639–1642 (below, p. 205, n. 133).

[83] Hom. Hymn III, to Apollo (one of the earliest of the Hymns), 189–193.

[84] Hom. Hymn III, 331–352; see above, p. 11. But Hera "is not here a chthonian deity," according to Allen, Halliday, and Sikes (on l. 306).

primitive cult, in a somewhat developed form of expression. "I will sing of well-founded Earth, mother of all, eldest of all beings. She feeds all creatures. . . . Through you, O queen, men are blessed in their children and blessed in their harvests, and to you it belongs to give means of life to mortal men and to take it away. Happy is the man whom you delight to honor! He has all things abundantly. . . ."[85] There is no suggestion here that the power of *Physis* embodied in Mother Earth is anything but kindly. Yet in the Hymn to Aphrodite (V), the goddess of love, whose power is felt by all nature, by beasts and men and all the immortals except the three maiden goddesses, becomes herself the unwilling victim of love, and that, too, not through "natural" causes but through the mischievous devices of Zeus.

The Homeric Hymn to Demeter (II), composed perhaps late in the seventh century, contains both traditional ideas and the new spirit of the mysteries. Quite Homeric is the spirit of resignation in which the maiden Callidice addresses Demeter, whom she supposes to be a mortal in distress. "Mother, what the gods send us, we mortals bear perforce (ἀνάγκῃ τέτλαμεν), although we suffer; for they are much stronger than we."[86] What, then, beyond sheer endurance does the author of this Hymn suppose that mortals could do in the face of such adverse powers? They can at least not interfere with the possibly kindly designs of the gods, as Metaneira by her interference foolishly deprived her child of the immortality that Demeter had intended to confer on him (256–262). And the aim of the hymn is to suggest how it was that Demeter came to put at the disposal of the mortals of Eleusis those rites by which they might win blessedness both here and hereafter.[87] Thus that one of the Homeric Hymns which is full of the gravest matter is also suffused at its close by a radiant hope.

The lyric poets from the seventh to the fifth century, both choral and monodic, for the most part reflect but slightly the thought of the Greeks about fate, good, and evil. The notable exceptions to this statement are Simonides, Pindar, and Bacchylides; their interest in the problem will be

[85] Hom. Hymn XXX, 1–8; cf. Kern, *Orph. Frag.* 47 (= D 1 B 21), from one of the Orphic gold tablets (see above, p. 62): Earth "the first mother of all" is invoked with, or possibly identified with, other divinities, — Victory, Chance, Fate (Moira), and possibly Phanes (so Murray, not Diels). Cf. also the anonymous lyric fragment preserved in Hippolytus *adv. Haer.* (J. M. Edmonds, *Lyra Graeca*, III, p. 484): "Twas earth that at the first had the noble privilege of giving forth our human kind," etc.

[86] Hom. Hymn (II) to Demeter, 147 f.; cf. the "Homeric" Epigram IV (the work of a rhapsode, preserved in the pseudo-Herodotean *Life of Homer*), 1; 13 f. (pp. 200 f., ed. Allen): "To what a fate did Zeus the Father give me a prey. . . . Yet I will endure (τλήσομαι) the lot which heaven gave me even at my birth, bearing my disappointment with a patient heart." (See above, p. 26.)

[87] Hom. Hymn (II) to Demeter, especially 474–489; see above, p. 51.

the more apparent to us if we first note the meager interest of the other lyric poets of this period. The melancholy philosophy of Alcaeus is summed up in his advice to Melanippus to drink, since when we are dead we shall see the light of the sun no more.[88] Faith in Zeus, who "holds the ends of life and death," is the burden of an anonymous line that may possibly be Sappho's.[89] Yet the trend of these centuries is from personal gods to vaguer powers. For Alcman the master of all beings is Destiny (*Aisa*) along with Device (*Poros*), and man had best not seek to soar heavenwards; vengeance comes from the gods.[90] He traces the genealogy of *Tyche*, sister of Good Order (*Eunomia*) and Persuasion, and daughter of Forethought (*Prometheia*).[91] *Tyche*, indeed, becomes of increasing importance in the lyric, as in drama. "Fortune, beginning and end of men," sings an anonymous poet, "thou sittest in the seats of wisdom, and grantest honor to human deeds . . . thou most excellent of gods."[92] And another poet, of whom a fragment is preserved in a fourth century papyrus,[93] praises the power and excellence of *Tyche* and her frequent reversal of the proud and the lowly; "shall we call thee black Clotho or swift-fated Necessity (*Ananke*), or art thou Iris, the messenger 'twixt gods and men? For thou holdest the beginning and the last end of everything that is." Here Tyche, though almost identified with Fate, remains personal and is man's "housemate." In another hymn, the *Moirai*, the weavers of "numberless and inevitable devices of all manner of counsels," are besought to send men Good Order and Justice and Peace.[94] Ion of Chios, we learn from Pausanias,[95] composed a hymn to *Kairos* (Opportunity), whom he described as "the youngest of the children of Zeus." Hope and faith amid darkness are sustained by Hermolochus: "All life is inscrutable, wandering amid events with nothing sure. 'Tis hope that cheers the heart; no man knoweth certainly whither he goes; and often there bloweth a dread wind contrary to success. Yet in danger and calamity God is ever at the helm."[96] In these few passages we have surveyed practically all that especially concerns our problem in the lyric poets, apart from Simonides, Pindar, and Bacchylides, until we reach the poets of the Greek Anthology.

Simonides of Ceos (556–467 B.C.), who wrote his flawless songs with equal facility for the courts of tyrants and for the Athenian democracy,

[88] Alcaeus, 73 Diehl; cf. 91 D; Mimnermus 2 D; Theognis 567–570.

[89] Quoted by Stobaeus, *Ecl.* 1.2.9; J. M. Edmonds, *Lyra Graeca*, III, p. 438.

[90] Alcman, 1, ll. 13–16, and l. 36 Diehl.

[91] Alcman 44 D.

[92] Diehl, Frag. Mel. Chor. Adesp. 4.

[93] Anonymi Hymnus (Diehl, Vol. II, p. 313).

[94] Diehl, Frag. Mel. Chor. Adesp. 5.

[95] Pausanias, V, 14, 9.

[96] J. M. Edmonds, *Lyra Graeca*, III, p. 412.

and who could as easily compose songs of victory as dirges, is a puzzling figure. Regarded as a hireling poet, yet preferred by his Athenian contemporaries, perhaps understandably, even to the more conservative Pindar, he touched deep issues now with the curiosity of a cold intellectual, now with tenderness and eloquence. In his interest in the nature of Virtue (*Arete*) he is the forerunner of the Sophists.

All things, he holds, come ultimately from the gods. "No man winneth goodness (ἀρετά) without the gods, nay, nor any city; 'tis God who contrives all things; and nothing is there among men without toil."[97] A conventional religiosity appears in the Hymn to the Fates (*Moirai*) which prays, on behalf of some city, for peace and order.[98] So far, all this is neutral, as regards good and evil; but Simonides also holds that "easily do the gods steal men's senses,"[99] and he has forebodings about the uncertainty of life. "Man that thou art, say not what the Morrow shall be; nor, when thou seest a man in prosperity, say how long he shall be so; for change cometh more swiftly than the flight of a long-winged fly."[100] "Little is man's strength, and his cares are unavailing, and 'tis toil upon toil for him in a life that is short; for all he can do, there's a death that hangs over him and cannot be escaped, in which both noble men and base must share alike."[101] The words "noble" (ἀγαθός, or ἐσθλός) and "base" (κακός), earlier poets, from Homer to Theognis, have tended to use of a man's place in the social scale; but even Theognis recognizes that "every man is good, if he be just";[102] Simonides here perhaps uses the terms in an equivocal sense, both social and ethical.

But in his more heroic moods Simonides expresses the new conceptions of human virtue and responsibility which the fifth century are to develop. Hesiod has already complained of the hardships of life: "In front of Virtue (ἀρετή) have the deathless gods set sweat; long is the way to her, and steep and rough at first. But when one hath reached the height, easy is it thereafter, hard though it was."[103] This theme Simonides embroiders: "There is a tale that Virtue dwells on crags that are hard to reach, and that a company of swift nymphs attend her, nor may she be seen by the eyes of all mortal men, but only by him from whose body comes heart-devouring sweat, and who attains unto the height by manliness."[104]

Among the most famous of the poems of Simonides, and one that is

[97] Simonides, 10 Diehl; cf. 66: Ζεὺς πάντων αὐτὸς φάρμακα μοῦνος ἔχει.

[98] Anonymous fragment, ascribed to Simonides by Wilamowitz, *Isyllos von Epidaurus* (Berlin, 1886), p. 16; C. M. Bowra, *Greek Lyric Poetry* (Oxford, 1936), pp. 397 f.

[99] Simonides, 42 (Bergk).

[100] Simonides, 6 Diehl.

[101] Simonides, 9 Diehl.

[102] Theognis 148; see above, p. 43.

[103] Hesiod, *Works and Days*, 289–292; see above, p. 33.

[104] Simonides, 37 Diehl.

generally misunderstood, is the scolion to the Thessalian tyrant Scopas.[105] To the tyrant's inquiry as to his opinion of the saying of the wise man, Pittacus, that it is hard to be good (ἐσθλός), Simonides responds unexpectedly with an analysis of the nature of goodness quite in keeping with the spirit of the new Athenian democracy. It is hard to be truly good in the aristocratic meaning of the word, good in hand and feet and mind, foursquare and without blame: in fact only a God can fully realize such an ideal, and of men only those whom the gods favor. And since misfortune can alter man's estate, Pittacus is wrong: the aristocrat's goodness is beyond man's control. Simonides, in fact, despairs of ever finding such a paragon of virtue. But he will give his admiration to every man who does not willingly do anything base. Note both the inclusiveness of this code and its emphasis on the deed, freely chosen, as the criterion of excellence. This is a democratic code; and it looks into the heart, rather than at what fortune or the gods have sent. But what if the struggle naught availeth? Simonides will excuse the failure: "against Necessity (*Ananke*) not even the gods fight." [106] Finally the poet further defines this new conception of excellence in terms of civic virtue, and "soundness," and good sense: "All things are fair in which shameful things are not mingled." So the ideals of fifth century Athens are thus early asserted against the older code.[107] But evil remains, in the form of Necessity, something external to man, yet something which the gods, for all their perfection, cannot, or at least do not, avert. Nor does Simonides himself seem greatly concerned; for his interest is concentrated in the fortunes of men, not in the source from which they come.

It is hardly surprising that the poetry of Pindar should manifest a certain worldliness. "Nothing suceeds like success"; and a large part of Pindar's task was to shed the additional glory of poetry on those whose wealth or nobility or personal prowess had already received the accolade of victory. The cult of success is a cornerstone of his art, at least in the *Epinicia*; and if his brooding on the ultimate sources and conditions of success discloses even in these poems a philosophy or religion of circumspection and piety,

[105] Simonides 4 Diehl. The poem is reconstructed from portions quoted in Plato's *Protagoras*, 339a–346c, where it is the subject of captious criticisms by "Socrates." For interpretations of the poem, see J. T. Sheppard, ed., *Oedipus Tyrannus* (Cambridge, 1920), pp. xxx–xxxiv; C. M. Bowra, "Simonides and Scopas," in *Classical Philology*, 29 (1934), pp. 230–239; C. M. Bowra, *Greek Lyric Poetry* (Oxford, 1936, pp. 340–351); W. Jaeger, *Paideia*, pp. 212 f.; 280.

[106] Simonides 4, 21 (Diehl); see also below, p. 161, and n. 90 (for Sophocles); and, for Euripides' criticism, *Hecuba* 597 f. (and below, p. 188). A. S. Pease, ed. Cic. *de Div.*, pp. 390 f., has many examples of the commonplace.

[107] Cf. Sophocles, *Antigone*, 367–371; *O. T.* 873–881, a still more developed thought, in that it is *hybris* that leads to *ananke*.

or if his thought in quite different kinds of poetry seems otherworldly, that is the more remarkable fact.

Yet Pindar is seldom original in his religious thought; his mind is well stored with traditional myths and with aphorisms which readily spring to the surface as he forges his marvels of cunningly wrought verse. One must range widely among the odes and the fragments in order to gather a fair conception of all that Pindar believed or felt about a given matter, and his art is so intricate that there is always a special danger in wresting a passage from its context.[108] Nevertheless, though each ode has its unity and purpose, no one of the odes exhausts Pindar's thought about our problem. It is therefore necessary in dealing with this most elusive of poets to pass rapidly from poem to poem, seeking in each case to understand, if one may, how his turn of thought grows out of his general scheme.

The cult of success is prominent in the first Olympian ode. "For every one of all mortal men, the brightest boon is the blessing that cometh day by day. . . . Some men are great in one thing, others in another; but the crowning summit is for kings; refrain from peering further. May it be granted for thee to plant thy feet on high, so long as thou livest, and for me to consort with victors for all my days, and be foremost in the lore of song among Hellenes in every land."[109] Even more plain-spoken, not to say cynical, is Pindar in the fifth Olympian: "Evermore amid deeds of prowess must toil and expense strive for the victory that is veiled in peril; and it is those who prosper who are deemed wise even by their fellow-citizens."[110] Yet Pindar seldom speaks of success in any form without somehow suggesting that it bears a relation to powers higher than man. Wealth wedded to honor, he proclaims (*Pyth.* 5, 1–4), is a mighty thing, if one receive it at the hands of Fate (πότμος). And although he continues in this ode to ring changes on the note of wealth (lines 14, 55, 102) and blessedness (11, 20, 46, 94) and honor (8, 18, 31, 48, 98), he is quite as insistent that these blessings all proceed from God,[111] and to God must be given the glory.[112] Indeed much of the poem may be read as counsel to

[108] Cf. B. L. Gildersleeve's remark (*Pindar, the Olympian and Pythian Odes*, New York, 1885), pp. xxvii f., about the danger of translating Pindar, and his warning against "the attempt to form an image of the poet's world of thought and feeling by the simple process of cataloguing translations of his most striking thoughts under convenient rubrics." But Gildersleeve perhaps does less than justice to the value of such a work as E. Buchholz, *Die sittliche Weltanschauung des Pindaros und Aeschylos* (Leipzig, 1869).

[109] *Ol.* 1, 97 f.; 113–116. All references to Pindar, including the fragments, are to the edition of C. M. Bowra (Oxford, 1935).

[110] *Ol.* 5, 16–18. "The successful are the wise — an old sneer," Gildersleeve, note *ad loc.* One might compare the remark of Napoleon (and others), that God is on the side of the strongest battalions.

[111] θεός or πότμος or μοῖρα; 3, 5, 13, 60, 76, 117.

[112] 25: παντὶ μὲν θεὸν αἴτιον ὑπερτιθέμεν.

noble Arcesilas, its hero, to walk warily through life. "They that are wise (σοφοί) bear with a fairer grace even the power that is given of God; and thou, while thou walkest in the path of justice, hast prosperity in abundance around thee. First, for that thou art king of great cities, the eye of thy ancestry looketh on this as a meed most fit for reverence when wedded to a soul like thine" (12–19). This "eye," though not jealous like the "evil eye," nevertheless is a critical eye ever holding a noble man to the mark, and reminding him that *noblesse oblige*, that the highest have most cause to fear a fall, and must "walk delicately before the Lord." If Pindar once doubts "whether it is by justice or by crooked wiles that the race of men mounteth a loftier tower,"[113] other good men have been similarly perplexed, and with good reason; nevertheless his general conclusion is plain: "Out of labors undertaken with the aid of youth and right (σὺν δίκᾳ) there cometh a gentle life even unto old age. Let him know full well that he hath had wondrous bliss allotted him by the gods."[114] Here Pindar seems to be "on the side of the angels," though the lines that immediately follow[115] show that what he has in mind is still worldly success: "if a man winneth famous glory, as well as goodly store of wealth, further than this it is no longer possible for a mortal to plant his feet on any higher eminence."

A comfortable, unquestioning piety is therefore a part of Pindar's attitude; Zeus is in his heaven, all's right with the world, or at least with those whom he favors and who walk circumspectly. These are the two necessary conditions of human happiness: the good will of the divine power that bestows prosperity, and (as we shall see presently) the piety of the recipient. "Prosperity is all the more abiding if it be planted with the blessing of a god."[116] On the other hand, "various men excel in various ways, but it is meet that a man should walk in straight paths and strive according to his powers of Nature (φυᾷ)," powers both of body and of mind (*Nem.* 1, 25 f.). For himself he prays, not for gold or land, but only that he may find favor with his fellow-citizens, "praising what merits praise and casting blame on sinners" (*Nem.* 8, 35–39). Of the gods he will speak no ill;[117] but he does not seem to feel called upon to make a thorough-going arraignment of the Homeric mythology, in the spirit of Xenophanes and Plato. Still less does he raise the philosophic questions that are posed by the Book of Job and by the Greek tragic poets about the origin and meaning of evil and suffering.[118]

[113] Frag. 201; cf. Plato, *Rep.* 365b.

[114] *Nem.* 9, 44 f. Cf. frag. 145: ἀνδρῶν δικαίων χρόνος σωτὴρ ἄριστος. See also below, p. 75, n. 156.

[115] *Nem.* 9, 46 f.

[116] *Nem.* 8, 17: σὺν θεῷ γάρ τοι φυτευθεὶς ὄλβος ἀνθρώποισι παρμονώτερος.

[117] *Ol.* 1, 35; 1, 52; cf. *Ol.* 9, 35–39.

[118] Cf. L. Farnell, *The Works of Pindar* (London, 1932), II, 471.

Let us trace further in Pindar the various ways in which he expresses that which is "given" to man, and with which willy-nilly he must reckon. That it is something akin to Nature has just been suggested;[119] happiness may be "planted" in man by the gods, and his efforts are in accordance with his "nature." Most often, however, it is Zeus, or "a god" (θεός, or δαίμων), or "the gods" who bestow gifts on men. "Zeus giveth this and giveth that, Zeus, the lord of all";[120] "Lo, it is the mighty mind of Zeus that guideth the fate of men whom he loveth."[121] Or again, "by the gift of a god (ἐκ θεοῦ) alone doth a man flourish (ἀνθεῖ) with wisdom of heart."[122] And God (θεός) bends proud mortals or gives them glory as he desires.[123] "If there be any bliss among mortal men, it doth not reveal itself without toil; yet a god (δαίμων) may bring that bliss to an end, verily, even to-day. That which is fated cannot be fled; but a time shall come which, smiting with a stroke that is unforeseen, shall grant one boon beyond all hope, but shall withhold another."[124] In the prominence given to Zeus, and in the use of θεός alone, Pindar seems to be well along on the road to henotheism, if not monotheism, despite his conventional polytheism.[125]

Elsewhere it is *Moira*, or the *Moirai*, who bestow on men the "given," as birth-goddesses enthroned beside Eleithyia, who fetter men to diverse destinies,[126] so that we differ in our nature (φυά), and none of us are wholly happy.[127] Moreover, being still birth-spirits they watch over the ties of kinship; "if any feud befall men of the same kin, the *Moirai* withdraw to hide their shame."[128]

Pindar thus uses without any essential distinction the more and the less personal powers to express what befalls man without his own effort. Though the gods and *Moira* are occasionally antithetical,[129] they are far

[119] See above, p. 70.

[120] *Isth.* 5, 52 f.; cf. *Ol.* 13, 115; *Pyth.* 1, 67: Ζεὺς τέλειος, "giver of perfection."

[121] *Pyth.* 5, 122; for Zeus as "helmsman," cf. *Pyth.* 4, 273.

[122] *Ol.* 11, 10; cf. *Ol.* 9, 28 f.: ἀγαθοὶ δὲ καὶ σοφοὶ κατὰ δαίμον' ἄνδρες | ἐγένοντ'; cf. Frag. 98a.

[123] *Pyth.* 2, 49–52; cf. 88–96; in view of the arbitrary power of God, it is wise not to fight against him, for it is "a slippery course to kick against the goads."

[124] *Pyth.* 12, 28–32. Of line 30 (τὸ δὲ μόρσιμον οὐ παρφυκτόν) St. G. Stock remarks (Hastings, *Enc. Rel. Eth.*, V, p. 788) that it is "the key note of Greek tragedy," — which is only half the truth. See further below, p. 77.

[125] Cf. Buchholz, pp. 80 f.

[126] *Nem.* 7, 1–6.

[127] *Nem.* 7, 54–58; cf. *Ol.* 2, 33–37.

[128] *Pyth.* 4, 145 f.; for another example of Nature resenting what is "against nature," cf. the sun turning his course in horror at the Thyestean banquet; Euripides, *I. T.* 192–195.

[129] *Paian* 2, 40 f.: an evil *moira* fell upon the people of Abdera, but they endured, and the gods at last joined them in fulfilling their desires; *Paian* 6, 89–98: Troy would have fallen sooner, if Apollo had not defended it, but Zeus dared not relax the decrees of destiny (μόρσιμα), and it was fated (χρῆν) that Troy should fall; *Isth.* 8, 29–52: the oracle, set

more frequently joined or treated interchangeably.[130] Fatalism of the cruder sort is rare in Pindar.

Both in the earliest and in the latest of the extant epinician odes Pindar stresses the good fortune that comes through the dispensation of heaven and through noble birth, a manifestation of Nature which is itself god-given. Thus in the earliest ode, "an arrangement in God and Blood," [131] he sings: "Sweet, Apollo, is the end and the beginning of man's work, when it is sped by Heaven (δαίμονος ὀρνύντος), and haply it was even by thy counsels that [Hippocleas] won this prize. And his inborn valor (τὸ συγγενές) hath trodden in the foot-prints of his father" (*Pyth.* 10, 10–12). And in the latest ode Amphiaraus speaks of the Epigoni: "It is by the gift of Nature (φυᾷ) that there stands forth the noble spirit that passes from sires to sons" (*Pyth.* 8, 44 f.). In other words, "Blood will tell"; and if we ask what is the source of this superiority, we need only turn to the ninth Olympian ode, in which Pindar contrasts natural genius, the gift of God, with mere training: "That which cometh of Nature (φυᾷ) is ever best; but many men have striven to win fame by means of merit that cometh from mere training (διδακταῖς ἀρεταῖς); but anything in which God has no part is none the worse for being silenced. Yet some roads lead farther than others, and it is not all of us that a single kind of practise (μελέτα) will prosper." [132]

Fortune (*Tyche*) is for Pindar not the fickle goddess of later times who takes delight in the rolling of her wheel but the kindly power who may crown the efforts of man. Alcimedon won his victory by heaven-sent good-fortune (τύχᾳ μὲν δαίμονος) but with no slackness in his own prowess.[133] Yet there is no counting on her help. "Those who make no trial have an inglorious obscurity, but even when men strive indeed, fortune doth not show herself until they reach the final goal. For she giveth of this and of that, and ere now hath the skill of weaker men over-taken and overturned a stronger than they" (*Isth.* 4, 32–37). Quite

---

forth by Themis, about the son of Thetis, knowledge of which saved Zeus from being dethroned.

[130] *Isth.* 6, 10–18: Pindar prays to the *Moirai* in support of a prayer to the gods; Frag. 234: καλῶν . . . μοῖραν, coördinate with θεόσδοτος ἀτλάτα κακότας; *Pyth.* 5, 76: οὐ θεῶν ἄτερ, ἀλλὰ μοῖρα τις ἄγεν; *Ol.* 9, 26: σύν τινι μοιριδίῳ παλάμᾳ; *Ol.* 10, 21, θεοῦ σὺν παλάμᾳ; *Pyth.* 1, 48: θεῶν παλάμαις; Frag. 1, 1: σὺν θεῶν . . . αἴσᾳ; *Ol.* 2, 21 f.: θεοῦ μοῖρα; Frag. 124: ὅτε Λαομέδοντι πεπρωμένοι' ἤρχετο μόροιο κᾶρυξ.

[131] Gildersleeve, xxxiii.

[132] *Ol.* 9, 100–107; cf. *Ol.* 2, 86: σοφὸς ὁ πολλὰ εἰδὼς φυᾷ; *Nem.* 5, 40 f.: πότμος δὲ κρίνει συγγενὴς ἔργων περὶ | πάντων; also *Nem.* 3, 40–42; Euripides, *Hipp.* 79–81. On the rival claims of Nature, Practise, and Theory, to which may be added Wisdom (σοφία) and Art (τέχνη), a favorite subject of discussion in the fifth and later centuries, especially among the Sophists (see below, p. 251), cf. P. Shorey, Φύσις, Μελέτη, 'Επιστήμη.

[133] *Ol.* 8, 67; cf. *Nem.* 5, 48, of the boy who won through the τύχα of his trainer; *Nem.* 6, 24: σὺν θεοῦ τύχᾳ; *Pyth.* 8, 53: τύχᾳ θεῶν.

naturally, then, Pindar prays to Fortune the Savior (σώτειρα Τύχα), daughter of Zeus the Deliverer, to keep watch over Himera, for she is powerful over ships, and war, and the counsels of men, — all matters veiled in deep obscurity and subject to violent fluctuations.[134] *Tyche* has been in earlier poetry a Nereid,[135] or an Oceanid;[136] Pindar apparently considers her to be one of the *Moirai* (frag. 21). Yet in spite of her general amiability in Pindar, she is hard to entreat, and holds a "double rudder."[137]

A poet whose theme is so largely bound up with the fortunes of athletic contestants and of noble houses must necessarily reckon much with the vicissitudes of life. Not all the contestants can be victors, nor can this year's victor hope to win in his next contest; great families, even if favored, must have their ups and downs in a world of change. Youth must pass, and wealth, and fame. This universal theme Pindar sets forth many times, now in a spirit of melancholy, now finding in man's uncertain lot all the greater challenge to vigorous action.

"At divers times divers minds rushing down drive all men before them."[138] There is the key-note. In view of this uncertainty, Pindar counsels neither timidity nor rashness, but tact[139] and resolution and a reasonable ambition. The heroic virtues appear in families, as in the crops of the fields and in fruit-trees, only periodically; and in the absence of any clear token from Zeus, one must pursue due measure.[140] Familiar is the saying of men of old[141] that "the immortals mete out to men two trials for every boon," — trials which the foolish cannot bear with good grace, but the noble (ἀγαθοί) can, by turning to view the fairer side of things; life free from reverses has never been found; but if any man has in mind the true course of things, he should enjoy while he may what the gods give him, since the breezes veer fitfully.[142] Yet even Pindar's most sceptical utterance dissolves in a sudden radiance of hope. The divine power treats man as its foot-ball: success "does not lie within the control of men; it is a god (δαίμων) that gives it, tossing now one man now another on high, and then bringing him below the level of his hands" (*Pyth.* 8, 76 f.). "Short is the space of time in which the happiness of mortal man blossometh, and even so doth it fall, when stricken by some baffling will. Creatures of a day, what thing is man, or what is he not?

[134] *Ol.* 12, 2–12. It is likely that *Tyche* had a cult in Himera at this time, though elsewhere only in later centuries.

[135] Hom. Hymn (II) to Demeter, 420.

[136] Hesiod, *Theog.* 360.

[137] Frag. 20; cf. Wehrli, pp. 74 f.

[138] *Isth.* 4, 5 f.; cf. *Nem.* 8, 1–3.

[139] Cf. Frags. 234; 235; 170.

[140] *Nem.* 11, 37–48.

[141] *Il.* 24, 527–533; see above, pp. 26 f.

[142] *Pyth.* 3, 80–106. This is a mild form of *tlemosyne.*

Man is but a dream of a shadow; but when a gleam of sunshine cometh as the gift of heaven (διόσδοτος), a radiant light resteth on men, and a gentle life."[143] Indeed Pindar will go further; his Pelops, praying to Poseidon, cries, "High adventure calleth not for a coward. And of us men who must needs die why should any sit idly in the darkness and nurse an inglorious old age, with no share of all that is noble? As for me, I will abide the hazard of this contest, and do thou grant a welcome success."[144]

Pindar's conception of the ills of human life goes deeper than a mere observation of life's vicissitudes; it is not mere luck, or inequality in the dispensation of blessings; it involves a theory of prosperity itself, and of a man's behavior in prosperity, — in brief, the idea of the "envy of the gods."[145] Clearly the divine envy is a projection of the human envy that is only too palpable a fact, a fact which Pindar also recognizes. All that is exalted above the common lot excites man's jealousy. "For prosperity is envied to its full height, while the man of humble aspirations murmureth unobserved."[146] Praise is especially apt to arouse envy, often quite unjustly;[147] "tales are a dainty morsel to the envious, and envy ever fasteneth on the noble and striveth not with the mean."[148] Only the dead have passed beyond the tongue of malice.[149] Still it is better to be envied than pitied, to risk the jealousy of a sated audience than to forego the chance of a fair reputation,[150] — unless one risks the graver danger of provoking the envy of the gods. "I rejoice at thy good fortune, [Megacles]; but it is a grief to me that envy should be the requital of noble deeds. Yet they say that thus prosperity which abideth in bloom for a man bringeth now good now evil."[151] The condition of lasting prosperity on the grand scale, Pindar suggests, is occasional mischance; in the present case it happens to be a recent ostracism.

Such envy as men may feel at the spectacle of unabated prosperity the

[143] *Pyth.* 8, 92–98; an ode which, according to a scholiast, was blamed by some because, though in form an encomium, it is actually a lamentation on human life; "the Ecclesiastes of the Odes," Gildersleeve, p. xxx; cf. *Pyth.* 3, 34–37: a hostile *daimon* brought about the destruction of sinful Coronis, and with her of many innocent neighbors, as a forest fire spreads from a spark. Pindar finds no injustice hers; and the analogy with *Physis* suggests merely the inexorability of Nature, not a pattern of justice.

[144] *Ol.* 1, 81–85; cf. *Nem.* 7, 74: "If toil there was, greater is the delight that followeth"; *Il.* 12, 322–328 (Sarpedon, on the eve of battle); see above, p. 25.

[145] See also above, pp. 20 f.

[146] *Pyth.* 11, 29 f.; cf. 49–58.

[147] *Ol.* 2, 95–98; see below, p. 76, n. 157; cf. *Isth.* 2, 43.

[148] *Nem.* 8, 21; cf. *Nem.* 10, 20; *Ol.* 8, 54 f.: "if I have praised Melesias highly, let not envy cast a rough stone at me."

[149] *Paean* 2, 35 f.; cf. "*de mortuis nil nisi bonum.*"

[150] *Pyth.* 1, 81–100.

[151] *Pyth.* 7, 13–18.

gods, too, may feel, fears Pindar, in common with many other Greeks.[152] But the gods are in a better position than most men to translate their envy into positive vindictiveness, casting down what is exalted not necessarily because prosperity has led to sin but merely because it is exalted. This is the jealousy of rivalry. In the earliest of the epinician odes Pindar prays that the family of the victor "may suffer no envious reversal at the hands of the gods" (*Pyth.* 10, 20 f.). In the latest of the epinician odes Pindar returns to the point, praying that the gods may regard with no envy the fortunes of the house of Xenarces.[153]

That the gods are not merely, like many mortals, prone to look with envy on prosperity but to punish *hybris*, is Pindar's warrant for many counsels against presumption. For *hybris*, pride and sinfulness, is the fault to which man is most prone when most prosperous. Pindar is familiar with the Delphic warning, "Nothing in excess."[154] For himself he prays: "I shall sing with my hair entwined with garlands, while I pray that the envy of the immortals may not confound whatever pleasure I pursue, day by day, as I serenely pass to old age and come to the appointed term of life. For we all die alike, although our doom (δαίμων) is diverse. But if any man lift up his eye to things afar, he is too weak to attain unto the bronze-paved seat of the gods. . . . Most bitter is the end that awaits sweets unjustly won."[155] For others he has like counsel: "If any one among men hath good fortune (εὐτυχήσαις) by the winning of glorious prizes or by might of wealth, yet in his heart restraineth insatiate insolence (κατέχει φρασὶν αἰανῆ κόρον), such a man is worthy to be blended with his townsmen's praises. For from thee, O Zeus, doth great excellence (μεγαλαὶ ἀρεταί) attend upon mortals; and the weal of men who fear the gods hath a longer life (ζώει δὲ μάσσων ὄλβος ὀπιζομένων); but with the crooked-minded it liveth not blooming for all time alike" (*Isth.* 3, 1–6).

Like Solon and Theognis, Pindar personifies *Hybris*, the spirit of arrogance, and *Koros*, the feeling of weary surfeit that prompts lawlessness, yet without determining definitely their relationship. The house of Xenophon of Corinth, he says, "is resolute in repelling *Hybris*, the bold-mouthed mother of *Koros*";[156] In the earlier poets, however, it was *Koros*,

[152] See above, pp. 19–20; what may be called the classic expression of the doctrine will meet us in Herodotus, writing about a generation later than Pindar; see below, pp. 84–88.

[153] *Pyth.* 8, 71 f.; cf. *Ol.* 8, 86, a prayer that Zeus may not cause Nemesis to be "divided in counsel," but may bless his friends; *Ol.* 13, 24, a prayer to Zeus not to be envious of his praise of the athlete Xenophon.

[154] Frag. 204: σοφοὶ δὲ καὶ τὸ μηδὲν ἄγαν ἔπος αἴνησαν περισσῶς; cf. *Pyth.* 2, 34: χρὴ δὲ κατ' αὐτὸν αἰεὶ παντὸς ὁρᾶν μέτρον.

[155] *Isth.* 7, 39b–48; the warning against overweening ambition is enforced by the story of the fall of Bellerophon from Pegasus, here told for the first time with such a moral; in Homer and Hesiod, Bellerophon is not guilty.

[156] *Ol.* 13, 9 f.; cf. also the reference, a few lines earlier, to Eunomia, Dike, and Eirene,

bred of *olbos*, that led to *hybris* and so to *ate*; and this surely seems to be the more natural account of human conduct.[157]

Of *hybris* and its consequences, Pindar has examples ready to hand. The brief reference to Bellerophon has already been mentioned;[158] and there is Tantalus, too, who though honored by the gods "could not brook his great *olbos*, and because of his *koros* got himself an overpowering *ate*, which the Father hung over him in the semblance of a monstrous stone. . . . And if any man hopeth in anything that he doeth to escape the eye of God, he erreth" (*Ol.* 1, 55 f.). Such, too, was the fate, and such the moral of Ixion, that ungrateful man who, though befriended by the gods, "could not be content with his great *olbos*,—but his *hybris* drove him into overweening infatuation (εἰς αὐάταν ὑπεράφανον); and soon did the man, suffering what was fit, meet with a wondrous doom."[159] It does not detract from Pindar's general thought to remember that Ixion's fate here serves to illustrate the folly of those who rise enviously and ungratefully against Hiero, the noble vice-regent of Zeus.

Part, at least, of the evil in men's lives thus seems to come, in Pindar's view, not from the envy of the gods but from sin, and for this sin he holds man accountable. If *olbos* is God-given, and if it is a grave temptation to *hybris*, with its inevitable consequences (god-sent *ate*, further sin, and ultimate ruin), there is nevertheless no reason to suppose that Pindar believes that man cannot resist temptation. "They that are wise (σοφοί) bear with a fairer grace even the power that is given of God."[160] True it is that choice is difficult. "Countless are the snares that hang around the minds of men, and there is no way of finding out what is best for a man

---

the "golden daughters of Themis," who dwell in Corinth; as in Hesiod (*Theog.* 901) they are *Horai*, seasons, and regulate all that grows and ripens duly in the passing of time (cf. *Ol.* 4, 2), therefore wealth, within due measure, not gained by *hybris*. Thus *Physis* once more is brought under the control of *Nomos* and as Gildersleeve remarks "the central thought of the poem is ἕπεται δ' ἐν ἑκάστῳ μέτρον· νοῆσαι δὲ καιρὸς ἄριστος" (47 f.). Cf. further Lehrs, *Pop. Aufs.*, pp. 71 ff.; Buchholz, pp. 62 f., and (on χρόνος in Pindar as not a mere abstraction but a *daimonic* power), p. 10; on the latter point, see above, p. 70, n. 114, and for Sophocles, below, p. 142.

[157] Both Gildersleeve, *ad. loc.* and Farnell, II, 90, speak of Solon and Theognis as "reversing" the order: but their priority would seem to make Pindar, in this passage, at least, the innovator. Gildersleeve ingeniously suggests that there is little difference in that "according to Greek custom, grandmother and granddaughter often have the same name. It is a mere matter of "Ὕβρις — Κόρος — "Ὕβρις." It might be added that there is so strong a family resemblance between *Hybris* and *Koros* that they are almost interchangeable; cf. *Ol.* 2, 95: ἀλλ' αἶνον ἔβα κόρος κτλ., in which κόρος means the malignant envy of those who have heard too much praise of the good, and is almost equivalent of *hybris*; cf. Wehrli, p. 80, n. 2; also "Aristeides the Just"; and the remark of Pericles, Thuc. II, 35, §2.

[158] *Isth.* 7, 44–47; see above, p. 75, and n. 155; cf. also *Pyth.* 3, 34–37 (cited above, p. 74, n. 143); a *daimon* punished the *hybris* of Coronis with what amounts to *ate*.

[159] *Pyth.* 2, 25–30; cf. also lines 49–52; 88–96; and see above, p. 71, and n. 123.

[160] *Pyth.* 5, 12 f., cited above, pp. 69 f.; cf. *Isth.* 3, 1–6, cited above, p. 75, for temptation to *Koros* successfully resisted.

to light on, not only now but also in the end." The tale of Tlepolemus, son of Heracles, who in anger struck another, enforces the point: "tumult of mind (*φρενῶν ταραχαί*) hath ere now caused even the wise man to go astray." But Diagoras, the great athlete glorified in the ode, though he, too, has had his share of misfortune, "walketh along the straight path that hateth *hybris*."[161] Even so, noble purposes may fail of their fulfillment through the opposition of circumstances. "In the hands of man the fitting moment (*καιρός*) hath but a brief limit of time. Well hath [Damophilos] taken note of it, and followeth it as a willing helper, not as a drudge. But they say that the bitterest lot of all is to know the good and yet perforce (*ἀνάγκᾳ*) to be debarred therefrom" (*Pyth.* 4, 286–289). This "sorrow's crown of sorrow" is the fate of Damophilos, now exiled from Cyrene; nobility and intelligence are frustrated by circumstance so that opportunity (*καιρός*) cannot be seized; this is indeed tragedy. Yet it is not so profound tragedy as noble action confounded in the event; the full significance of the fate of Prometheus or of Oedipus lies beyond Pindar's contemplation.[162]

The limits imposed by our mortal nature are thus ever present to Pindar's thought; man is doomed to die, and man must remember the gulf that divides him from divinity. "If any man who hath riches (ὄλβος) excelleth others in beauty of form, and is wont to display prowess by his courage in the games, let him remember that the limbs he is robing are mortal, and that in the end of all he will be clad in a vesture of clay" (*Nem.* 11, 13–16). *Memento mori*: because he was seduced by gold to bring back from death one who was already its lawful prey Asclepius and his patient were both stricken by the thunder-bolt of Zeus. "We must seek from the gods," continues Pindar, "such boons as best befit mortal minds, knowing what lies at our feet, and of what destiny (*aisa*) we are. Seek not, my soul, the life of the immortals, but enjoy to the full the resources that are within thy power" (*Pyth.* 3, 59–62). Again and again, like hammer-strokes on the anvil, falls the counsel against cravings for what is beyond man's reach. "Two things there are alone that amid the fair flowers of wealth cherish the hoped-for bloom of life, if a man have good fortune and a goodly reputation. Strive not to become a Zeus; all things are thine if a share (*moira*) of these fair boons fall to thy lot; mortal aims befit mortal men."[163] Only a god has a heart free from sorrow; happy among men is he who wins fame by victories and sees his son also victorious. "Brazen Heaven he cannot climb"; but he reaches

[161] *Ol.* 7, 24–26; 30 f.; 90 f.

[162] See above, p. 71, n. 124, and Stock's comment on *Pyth.* 12, 30.

[163] *Isth.* 5, 12–16; cf. *Ol.* 5, 25–27, counselling him who is prosperous and generous: "Seek not vainly to become a god."

the utmost limit attainable by mortals, though only a hero like Perseus could find the way to the land of the Hyperboreans, that Earthly Paradise.[164] As for any real knowledge of the gods, that is forever impossible for man, since he is of a different race. "Why dost thou deem that to be wisdom wherein one man availeth little more than another? For he cannot with human mind search out the counsels of the gods" (frag. 50). In all this Pindar speaks like other orthodox Greeks. Yet once he allows himself the bold privilege of claiming for man not only kinship but a sort of approach to the nature of the gods: "One is the race of men, one is the race of gods, but from one mother [Earth] do we both draw our breath. Yet a power wholly sundered holdeth us aloof, in that the one is a thing of naught, while for the other the brazen heaven abideth as a sure abode forever. Nevertheless, we have some likeness, either in might of mind or in our outward form (*physis*) to the immortals, even though we know not what courses, day by day nor in the night seasons, fate (*potmos*) hath drawn for us to run."[165] If Pindar had followed up this striking thought in other odes one might be inclined to wonder whether he had not made his own the Orphic belief in man's divine origin and destiny; but such is apparently not the case. Pindar ventures the thought but once, prompted perhaps merely by the beautiful spectacle of a sound mind in the sound body of a boy athlete; elsewhere he recurs to the orthodox severance between men and gods. He never bids us, like the Orphics, to seek reunion with the divine.

Yet Pindar does at times seem to share with the Orphics and Pythagoreans a belief in immortality, and that, too, because he believes like them that the soul is divine, and is the temporary inhabitant of the body. Naturally it is chiefly in his *Dirges*, rather than in the *Epinicia*, that he touches upon this matter; and it may be doubted whether he was ever thoroughly imbued with Orphic thought.[166] Even when affirming that "the days of mortals are deathless, though the body die," he rests his argument on the immortality that consists in leaving children behind one.[167] So far Pindar expresses the average orthodox faith of his day.

[164] *Pyth.* 10, 21–50. The Hyperboreans live virtuously (43 f.) and amid revelry, in a world reminiscent of the Golden Age. See above, pp. 31; 60; Lovejoy and Boas, *Primitivism*, pp. 32 f.

[165] *Nem.* 6, 1–7. Cf. J. B. Bury, *Nemean Odes* (London, 1890), pp. 96 f., and *ad loc.* Bury takes the first words to mean that the race of men and of gods is one: so also Adam, *Religious Teachers of Greece*, p. 116; not so Jaeger, *Paideia*, p. 214.

[166] Guthrie, *Orpheus*, pp. 236 f., finds Pindar a "staunch defender of the traditional Olympian religion," whose occasional Orphic or Eleusinian coloring is sufficiently explained by its poetic possibilities and by the special interests of the individuals who have commissioned the writing of certain poems.

[167] Frag. 83, from a *Partheneion.* Cf. also *Pyth.* 5, 94–103; *Ol.* 8, 77–80; *Nem.* 4, 85–88, for the delight of the dead in the success of their descendants and in honor paid to themselves.

But in writing for the dead, or perhaps only for those who have been initiated into the Orphic or the Eleusinian cults, he allows himself to express a bolder hope. It is of the Eleusinian mysteries[168] that Pindar proclaims: "Blessed is he who hath seen these things before he shall pass beneath the ground. He knoweth the end of life, and he knoweth its god-given origin (ἀρχάν)."[169] He sings of those who have "by good fortune culled the fruit of the rite that releaseth man from toil. And though the body of all men is subject to almighty death, there remaineth alive an image of life [the soul], for it alone cometh from the gods. But it sleepeth while the limbs are astir; yet for them that sleep it showeth in many a dream the coming judgment whether of joy or of pain."[170] The idea that the soul is the "image" of a man, and survives him, is Homeric;[171] but the conception of the soul as divine, and the idea that it comes into its rights only in sleep or after death, are Orphic, and meet us here for the first time in Greek poetry.[172]

This faith in immortality is bound up with ethical conceptions; not only does the soul experience successive incarnations or rebirths but it is undergoing a probation the result of which, as it chooses well or ill, is to be everlasting bliss or everlasting punishment. Thus Pindar's world includes the equivalent of a Purgatory (both in this life and in other alternating lives lived out of the body, before or after this life), an Inferno, and a Paradiso which are based for the first time wholly on vice or virtue. It anticipates the Platonic eschatology and the great tradition, both pagan and Christian, in which the fortunes of the soul are imaginatively set forth in the light of man's moral responsibility and his deliberate choice.[173] Good and evil, both in this life and in the world to come, are no longer the simple gift of Fate or the sport of chance; they are rooted partly in man's nature, partly in the will of man.

The picture of the soul's destiny that Pindar paints is colored by prevailing myths and ideas of happiness or unhappiness. Judgment in Hades, successive incarnations, in Hades and on earth, and a final release for the just to the Islands of the Blest, or, for the wicked, an eternity of woe,—such appears to be Pindar's conception. "Of those from whom Persephone

[168] So Clem. Al. states specifically, *Strom.* III, 518, in quoting the lines.

[169] Frag. 121, from a dirge.

[170] Fragments 115 and 116, from a dirge.

[171] Cf. *Od.* 23, 104.

[172] Cf. further J. Adam, "The Doctrine of the Celestial Origin of the Soul from Pindar to Plato," in *The Vitality of Platonism*, pp. 35–76; more briefly in his *Religious Teachers of Greece*, pp. 131–137; Rohde, *Psyche*, Eng. Trans., pp. 411–421; Farnell, *Works of Pindar*, I, pp. 335–338.

[173] Cf. Nock, *Conversion*, p. 27, on Pindar's "picture of the after life which is in the main Orphic, though like Plato [Pindar] has substituted righteous conduct for initiation as a qualification for happiness."

shall have received due retribution for ancient grief (ποινὰν παλαιοῦ πένθεος) in the ninth year she sendeth back the souls to the upper sunlight; and from them come into being revered kings and men mighty in strength and surpassing in wisdom; and for all future time men call them holy heroes."[174]

The Elysium of Hades is enjoyed during the probationary stage by those who have thus far been righteous; but it is not the final goal, nor is it, for all the beauty of Pindar's description, a spiritual heaven. "For them in the world below the sun shineth in his strength, while here it is night; and in meadows red with roses the space before their city is shaded with trees of frankincense, and is laden with fruits of gold. Some of them take delight in horses and in sports, and some with games of draughts and with lyres: and among them bloometh in perfection the flower of bliss. Over the lovely land fragrance is ever shed, as they mingle all manner of incense with the far-shining fire on the altars of the gods. From the other side sluggish rivers of murky night belch forth endless gloom."[175] Strangely enough, it is not in the *Dirges* but in the second Olympian ode that Pindar paints his picture of the last judgment.[176] "The guilty souls of the dead straightway pay the penalty here on earth; and the sins committed in this kingdom of Zeus are judged by One beneath the ground, hateful Necessity[177] enforcing the doom he speaks. But ever through nights and ever through days the good receive an unlaborious life beneath the sunshine. They vex not with might of hand the earth or the waters of the sea for food that satisfieth not, but among the honored gods, such as had pleasure in keeping of oaths enjoy a tearless life; but the others have pain too fearful to behold. Howbeit they who thrice on either side of death have stood fast and wholly refrained their souls from deeds unjust, journey on the road of Zeus to the tower of Cronus, where the ocean breezes blow around the Island of the Blest, and flowers gleam bright with gold, some from glorious trees on the land, while others the water feeds, with wreaths whereof they entwine their arms and crown their heads."[178] Though the delights of this Island of the Blest may seem about as material as those of Jerusalem the Golden, or most other pictures,

[174] Frag. 127, from a dirge; quoted by Plato, *Meno* 81b. On the "ancient grief," see H. J. Rose, in *Greek Poetry and Life* (Essays presented to Gilbert Murray, Oxford, 1936), pp. 79–96; the "grief" is traced to man's original sin, the result of his Titan heritage. But cf. also I. M. Linforth, *The Arts of Orpheus*, pp. 345–350.

[175] Frag. 114, from a dirge; cf. frag. 117.

[176] It is written, however, for a Sicilian audience, who may be supposed to have Orphic interests.

[177] ἀνάγκᾳ. Cf. Ἀνάγκη, and the choice at the throne of Necessity, Plato, *Rep.* 617d; 620e; and see below, pp. 314–316.

[178] *Ol.* 2, 59–74, Tr. Adam. For the interpretation of certain difficulties in this passage, see Nilsson, *Harv. Theol. Rev.* 28 (1935), pp. 214 f.

pagan or Christian, of a Paradise, it is at least clear that they are won by a virtuous life; and Pindar enumerates among the heroes to be found there Peleus, Cadmus, and Achilles, — heroes, be it noted, and not ordinary mortals, and not merely a single favorite of Zeus, as in Homer.[179]

The lyric tradition of Simonides and Pindar is carried on by Bacchylides. Less varied in his range than either of his predecessors, if we may judge from the extant fragments even as they have been augmented in the past generation, less endowed than Pindar with the force and the fire of poetry that burns all before it,[180] Bacchylides has the Ionian sweetness, the Ionian tendency to melancholy, the Ionian fondness for gnomic utterance. His *gnomai* indeed are not always the inevitable outgrowth of his theme, and are sometimes introduced almost at random.[181] On the other hand he can introduce a moral reflection with subtle reticence; thus, in order to remind Hiero that even the greatest and most successful cannot expect to be forever free from suffering he introduces, without expressly pointing the connection, the moving story of the meeting of Heracles and Meleager in the world of shades (V, 53 ff.). His occasional melancholy and his reflections on the evils in human life sent by the gods or Fate are balanced by a conventional piety and warnings against *ὕβρις*, and by the conventional exhortation to *τλημοσύνη*.[182] One gathers that he is a conservative Greek of his age, a gentleman whose personal fortunes have never tried him sorely, and who is not seriously troubled by the spectacle of evil. He wears easily a cloak of inherited philosophy that he never makes his own.

At times Bacchylides might seem to be a fatalist of the crudest sort. "Neither prosperity," he sings, "nor stubborn war, nor all-destroying strife, cometh to us of our choice, but *Aisa* who giveth all bringeth a cloud now upon one hand and now upon another" (frag. 20). More often he connects a *daimon* with our lot,[183] though he reckons also, albeit somewhat confusedly, with chance and with human virtue. "A happy destiny is God's best gift to man (*εὖ μὲν εἱμάρθαι παρὰ δαίμονος ἀνθρώποις ἄριστον*); but even as Chance (*Συμφορά*) crusheth the good if she come with a load of woe, so she maketh a man eminent if she win her way. Honor hath various forms, and myriad are the kinds of human excellence; yet one outstandeth all, and it is his whom a just mind guides in what lieth at hand. . . . In every act of man the fitting season lends the

[179] *Od.* IV, 561–569; see above, p. 83; and Appendix 2: Afterlife in Homer.

[180] Even in his relations with Hiero there is less of strength and independence than in Pindar's attitude. Cf. Sir R. C. Jebb, Bacchylides, *The Poems and Fragments* (Cambridge, 1905), pp. 200–203.

[181] E.g. Bacchylides I, 49–74. References to B. are to Jebb's edition. Roman numerals refer to the *Epinicia* and *Dithyrambs*, Arabic numerals to the Fragments. Sometimes they are paraphrases of earlier poets. E.g. IX, 38–45; cf. Solon 1 Diehl, 43–54.

[182] E.g. XIV, 57–63; see below, p. 83.

[183] Frag. 9: *πάντεσσι θνατοῖσι δαίμων ἐπέταξε πόνους ἀλλοισιν ἄλλους.*

fairest grace, and God prospereth him that doeth a thing well." [184] The divine dispensation is often evil; so the brief story of Heracles and Deianira concludes on an ominous note: "Then it was that an irresistible *daimon* wove for Deianira a shrewd device, fraught with sorrow, when she learned the bitter tidings that the dauntless son of Zeus was sending to his goodly house the white-armed Iole, his bride. Ill-fated (δύσμορος), hapless one, what a plan did she conceive! Potent jealousy (φθόνος εὐρυβίας) was her bane and that dark veil which hid the future, when . . . she received from Nessus his fateful gift of wondrous power (δαιμόνιον τέρας)." [185]

Moreover the divine dispensation, even if good, is seldom unmarred to the end. "Few are the mortal men whom God (δαίμων) hath granted to be so fortunate all their days as to reach the time of grey temples without meeting woe" (frag. 21). And for Bacchylides the word *moira* sometimes retains some of its old force as a "portion," not as a "decree." "Happy the man on whom God (θεός) hath bestowed a portion of honors (μοῖραν . . . καλῶν), and with that enviable lot (τύχα) life-long riches too. For no man on earth is fortunate in all things," [186] — witness the tale of Heracles meeting Meleager in the world of the dead, and the touching words of the former, whose eyes were moist for the first and only time, "because he pitied the fate (πότμος) of that suffering wight": "Best were it for mortals never to be born, nor to look upon the sunlight." [187] The thought is echoed from Theognis,[188] but Heracles proceeds to the matter in hand in a more heroic and characteristic manner: "seeing that no good cometh of these laments, a man should speak of that which he is like to accomplish" (162–164). As resolutely does Theseus, in another poem, confronting the wanton Minos, temper resignation before the inevitable with determination: "Whatever the almighty Fate that cometh from the gods (ἐκ θεῶν μοῖρα) hath decreed for us and the scale of *Dike* inclineth to, we shall fulfil our destiny (πεπρωμέναν αἶσαν ἐκπλήσομεν) when it comes; but restrain thy fell intent. . . . Check the presumption (*hybris*) that would bring much woe, [or else] I will show the strength of my arms beside thine, and God shall decide the rest (τὰ δ' ἐπιόντα δαίμων κρινεῖ)." [189] Supernatural forces continue to operate through the rest of

[184] εὖ ἔρδοντα δὲ καὶ θεὸς ὀρθοῖ, XIII, 1–11; 16–18; cf. another very corrupt passage (VIII, 88–96) apparently about the inscrutability of our lot, in which one phrase can be read with certainty: διακρίνει δὲ θεῶν βουλά (89 f.).

[185] XV, 23–35; the δαίμων is Destiny (Jebb), rather than Jealousy (Jurenka); yet Jealousy is the agency used by the δαίμων, as *Ate* is sometimes sent by the gods.

[186] V, 50–55; cf. B. 28: ὄλβιος δ' οὐδεὶς βροτῶν πάντα χρόνον; and Horace, *Odes* II, 16, 27 f.

[187] V, 155–162; cf. also 94 f.

[188] Theognis, 425 ff.; cf. above, p. 42.

[189] XVI, 24–46. Minos was involuntarily stricken with desire through "the baneful gifts of the goddess Cypris" (9 f.).

the poem. The cunning of Minos is frustrated: "Moira was preparing another issue."[190] And the marvellous feat of Theseus evokes the reflection: "Nothing that the gods (*δαίμονες*) ordain is past belief to men of sound wit."[191]

Heracles and Theseus are heroes; yet their attitude and counsel represent what Bacchylides regards as the best hope for ordinary mortals. "One goal there is, one path of happiness for mortals, the power to keep a heart ungrieving to life's end. Whoso busieth his wits with ten thousand cares and afflicteth his spirit night and day for the sake of things to come, the labor of such an one beareth no fruit. For what ease is there left us if we keep the heart astir with vain lament?" (frags. 7 and 8). These lines express once more the philosophy of *τλημοσύνη*, and find a place naturally in the chapter of Stobaeus, "Of the need of bearing one's lot like a gentleman because we are human and ought to live according to virtue."[192] Still more explicit, and quite Homeric[193] are the "righteous words" that Bacchylides makes Menelaus address to the Trojans, who have just prayed to the immortal gods for respite from their sufferings. He begins: "Ye warriors of Troy, it is not Zeus, who ruleth on high and beholdeth all things, who is the author of grievous woes for mortals. Nay, open before all men is the path that leadeth to unswerving Justice (*Δίκα*), attendant of holy Orderliness (*Eunomia*) and wise *Themis*; happy the land whose sons take her to dwell with them." And he concludes with a warning against *hybris* and the wealth that it bestows only to involve the possessor in ruin (XIV, 51–63). This last counsel, growing naturally out of the situation (for Paris had been guilty of *hybris* in stealing Helen), reminds one of the more generalized thoughts of Solon on injustice and retribution in his "Prayer to the Muses." Elsewhere in an *epinicion*, Bacchylides paraphrases, without any special appropriateness, Solon's brooding on the divers paths that lead to success, and on the uncertainty of the future and of fortune's scales (IX, 35–47). But he continues with the remark: "The noblest lot for a man is that his own worth should make him widely admired among his fellows."[194] Here the idea of envy differs from the usual notion, for it is clearly admiration of moral worth, untainted with malice. It is here only a passing thought, and in the next breath our easy-going poet is recognizing the advantages of wealth, "which turneth to account even the unprofitable" (49–51). But in another considerably longer passage, in celebrating the victory of the young son of a virtuous

[190] Line 89.

[191] Lines 117 f.; cf. III, 57; Archilochus 74 Diehl; see above, p. 35.

[192] Stob. *Anth.* (ed. Wachsmuth and Hense, Vol. V, pp. 962; 969).

[193] See above, pp. 22 f.

[194] Lines 47 f.: *τὸ μὲν κάλλιστον, ἐσθλὸν | ἄνδρα πολλῶν ὑπ' ἀνθρώπων πολυζήλωτον εἶμεν.*

father, Bacchylides weighs the respective advantages of manly virtue (ἀρετά) and of wealth (πλοῦτος), and decides in favor of the former.[195] Virtue, he feels, is rewarded by the gods; and this is distinctly the point of the story of Croesus as he tells it, the tale of one in distress who is saved by the gods because of his piety and the greatness of his gifts to the gods;[196] — counsel for Hiero mingled with flattery of Hiero, whose gifts have indeed been great.[197]

Our study of orthodoxy and mysticism may well be concluded by a consideration of Herodotus. Born a full generation later than Aeschylus, and doubtless familiar with many of his tragedies, he is in some ways the representative of an earlier, more popular conception of the dealings of gods with men. Thus he exhibits the classic expression of the "jealousy of the gods" in its primitive form, before Pindar and Aeschylus purified the doctrine by connecting it with the ethical notion of *hybris* and *nemesis*.[198]

An undercurrent of pessimism pervades the vivacious story of Herodotus, chronicler of the instability of human affairs (I, 5; VI, 98). Indeed there is imbedded in his tale no little portion of the authentic matter of tragedy. Doubtless the interview between Solon and Croesus (I, 29–34) is an anachronism, and is not wholly consistent with the main burden of the extant poetry of Solon;[199] it is to be read as the dramatic expression of the philosophy of Herodotus himself. Moreover the question propounded by the wealthy Croesus, "Who is the happiest (ὀλβιώτατος) of all men?" is only one of many examples of similar questions preserved in the Greek tradition and thus belongs to folk-lore.[200] The surprising reply of Solon turns on the conviction that wealth in excess of daily needs is not in itself a sure guarantee of happiness (*eudaimonia*, or *olbos*); in fact the examples of happiness that he propounds are of men who died in the moment of triumph, whether of battle or of acts of piety. Thus it appears that death is no evil; it is better than life, and is God's best gift to man,

[195] I, 49–74; see also above, p. 81.

[196] III, 21–62; cf. XVII, 41–45.

[197] III, 63–98. For the interpretation of this poem, Jebb's comments (see above, p. 81, n. 180) should be supplemented by the discussion of J. T. Sheppard, ed. *Oed. Tyrannus* of Sophocles (Cambridge, 1920), pp. lxvii–lxxi.

[198] For the earlier conception as found in Homer, see above, pp. 19 f.; for Pindar, 74–76; for Bacchylides, 81; for Aeschylus below, p. 107. See also, on the relation of *phthonos* to *nemesis*, C. F. von Nägelsbach, *Nachhomerische Theologie*, pp. 46–57; E. Tournier, *Némésis*, *passim*; K. Lehrs, *Populäre Aufsätze*, pp. 33–74.

[199] For Solon, see above, pp. 36–38, noting certain variations in Solon's treatment of the theme; also I. Linforth, *Solon the Athenian*, p. 119: Herodotus "imported into his paraphrase of Solon's thought the idea which is so characteristic of his own philosophy"; similarly, E. Tournier, *Némésis*, p. 282 (Appendix IV).

[200] For the earlier tradition (preserved in later accounts) of the reply of the Delphic oracle to Gyges, Croesus, and others, and for the whole subject, cf. F. Wehrli, ΛΑΘΕ ΒΙΩΣΑΣ, pp. 30–60.

since continuance of life is always fraught with the possibility of a reversal of fortune.[201] The moral that Solon draws is that "the divine power is utterly jealous and fond of troubling man's estate; for in length of days there are many things to behold which one would not behold, and many things to suffer." [202] Therefore he reserves judgment and refuses to count any man happy (ὄλβιος) unless he reaches his end happily; before such an end, he may be counted "fortunate" (εὐτυχής) in the possession of a maximum of good luck, health, children, and personal comeliness (a rare approximation to the ideal of self-sufficiency). Only if these blessings remain to the end and are crowned by a peaceful death may one be deemed really "happy"; but often God bestows felicity (ὄλβος) only to uproot it utterly.[203]

There is just a hint in the end of the story of Solon and Croesus that Herodotus sees something more than divine jealousy in the outcome. "Great retribution from God (ἐκ θεοῦ νέμεσις μεγάλη)," he writes, "overtook Croesus, as it seems, because he regarded himself as the happiest of all men." [204] Though the word *hybris* does not appear in the context, Herodotus seems to regard this retribution, the accidental death of Croesus' son, as divine punishment for pride; so Croesus himself presently considers it.[205] Still later, poor bewildered Croesus, defeated and captured by Cyrus, bethinks himself of Solon's advice; and Cyrus, on hearing of Solon's advice to Croesus, relents in the very act of burning Croesus alive, "bethinking himself that he too was a man, and that it was a fellow-man, and one who had once been as blessed by fortune as himself, whom he was burning alive; afraid, moreover, of retribution (τίσις), and full of the thought that whatever is human is insecure." But only Apollo's intervention actually saves the life of Croesus from the flames. Nevertheless Croesus blames the god for his downfall, till the priestess of Apollo explains not only how perversely Croesus has misunderstood the god's oracles but also how far Apollo, though "unable to escape from destiny (τὴν πεπρωμένην μοῖραν . . . ἀποφυγεῖν)" has contrived to delay the fall of Croesus (the consequence of inherited guilt) for three years, and

[201] Herodotus I, 31: the prayer of the mother of Cleobis and Biton that they might receive τὸ ἀνθρώπῳ . . . ἄριστον was answered by their death, by which God (ὁ θεός) showed that ἄμεινον εἴη ἀνθρώπῳ τεθνάναι μᾶλλον ἢ ζώειν. Cf. Cic. *T.D.* I, 113; and, for the doctrine of μὴ φῦναι, see above, pp. 38; 42.

[202] Herodotus I, 32: τὸ θεῖον πᾶν ἐὸν φθονερόν τε καὶ ταραχῶδες . . . ἀνθρωπήιων πρηγμάτων πέρι, κτλ.

[203] I, 32: ἐκεῖνο . . . οὔ κω . . . λέγω, πρὶν τελευτήσαντα καλῶς τὸν αἰῶνα πύθωμαι . . . πρὶν δ' ἂν τελευτήσῃ ἐπισχεῖν μηδὲ καλέειν κω ὄλβιον, ἀλλ' εὐτυχέα . . . σκοπέειν δὲ χρὴ παντὸς χρήματος τὴν τελευτὴν κῇ ἀποβήσεται· πολλοῖσι γὰρ δὴ ὑποδέξας ὄλβον ὁ θεὸς προρρίζους ἀνέτρεψε. Cf. the close paraphrase of this passage in Sophocles, *O.T.* 1528–30, and see below, p. 161; for Aristotle's criticism, *E.N.* 1100b4–1101b13, see below, p. 326.

[204] Herodotus I, 34; this is the only occurrence of the word νέμεσις in Herodotus.

[205] I, 45: θεῶν κού τις.

has now saved his life. Croesus at last admits that the fault is not the god's, but his own (I, 86–91). In the advice that Croesus here gives to Cyrus, Croesus, like the aged Oedipus, seems to have learned by experience something about the dangerous consequences of *hybris*. Ironical is the fact, however, that it is Croesus who later counsels Cyrus that "there is a wheel (κύκλος) of human affairs whose movement suffers not the same men always to be fortunate"; and that he then gives the fatal advice about strategy which leads to the death of Cyrus, victim also of *hybris* and *koros* (I, 206–214; esp. 207 and 212).

Elsewhere in the *History*, moreover, it is mere prosperity and outstanding power, rather than arrogant pride, which incites the divine jealousy. The tyrant Polycrates was so uniformly prosperous that when he strove to break the continuity of his good fortune by throwing a precious ring into the sea it came back to him in the belly of a fish. His friend King Amasis of Egypt summed up the situation prospectively: "The gods are jealous (τὸ θεῖον . . . φθονερόν). I would have those whom I love now be successful, and now suffer a reverse, and thus vary their lives rather than be fortunate in all things; for never have I heard of any man who prospered in all things who did not at last come to an utterly evil end." Thus Polycrates was marked for calamity, and the event justified the fears of Amasis.[206] So far the philosophy of Herodotus is one of quietism, to avoid the eye of possibly jealous gods.

The defeat of the Persians by the Greeks illustrates a moral that is more implicit in Herodotus than explicit; nowhere does he say in so many words that it exemplifies the punishment of *hybris*. Yet he contrives by many little touches to suggest the impiety of Cambyses,[207] the pride of Darius,[208] and, above all, the arrogance of Xerxes;[209] and against these traits are set the *sophrosyne*, the rugged courage, and the love of freedom of the Greeks.[210] As Solon served as the foil of Croesus, and Croesus in turn of Cyrus, and Amasis of Polycrates, so the foil of Xerxes is his uncle Artabanus, whose utterances have the effect of a warning tragic chorus. "Seest thou how God with his lightning smites always the larger animals, and will not suffer them to wax insolent, while the smaller ones do not chafe him? Dost thou see how 'tis always the greatest houses and the tallest trees that his bolts smite? For God (ὁ θεός) loves to strike all that

[206] Herodotus I, 40–43; 120–125, for the sequel. Yet Polycrates was avenged, 126–128, if that will improve the moral.

[207] Herodotus III, 25; 29; 33; 64; 80 (the disquisition of Otanes on the *hybris* of the tyrant Cambyses).

[208] IV, 83; 85; 87; 91 f.

[209] VII, 24; 35; 38 f.; 45–52; 57 f.

[210] The speech of Themistocles, VIII, 109, thanking the jealousy of the gods for the punishment of Persian impiety, may be taken to represent the view of Herodotus himself.

is exalted. Thus a mighty host is destroyed by a small one, when God in his jealousy sends fear or a thunderbolt against them, wherefore they perish in a way unworthy of them. For God suffers no one to have high thoughts but himself."[211] Presently a delusive dream warns Xerxes that unless he undertakes the war, he shall be brought low as swiftly as he has waxed great; and when a like dream appears also to Artabanus, warning him against opposing "what must be (*τὸ χρεὸν γενέσθαι*)," he is convinced that it is a divine warning (VII, 14; 18). At the Hellespont Xerxes first counts himself blessed, then weeps to think of the shortness of human life, "Yet there are sadder things in life than that," replies Artabanus. "Short though our life is, there is no man . . . so happy as not to have felt the wish, I will not say once, but many times, that he were dead rather than alive. Calamities befall us; sicknesses harass us, and make life, short though it be, to seem long. So death, through the wretchedness of our life, is man's beloved refuge (*καταφυγὴ αἱρετωτάτη*); and God, who gives us a sweet taste of life, is found in this very gift to be jealous" (VII, 45 f.). In the rest of the conversation, as in the later conversation between Xerxes and the exiled Spartan King Demaratus, one feels the contrast between folly and the pride of imperial power and sober prudence and the quiet confidence bred by Greek love of freedom (VII, 47–52; 101–104). And Herodotus does not close his story without pointing to the further disasters of Xerxes after he has been driven home.

We need not pursue further the narrative of Herodotus. But we may ask how far his history, for all its theological bent, may be described as a moral interpretation of events. Certainly Herodotus was a pious man, and saw in the victory of the Greeks, those defenders of freedom, the hand of the gods.[212] But the gods themselves lack something of moral grandeur; if there is anything that impresses Herodotus as especially "divine," it is an extraordinary intervention that actually exceeds the demands of justice, such as the wrath that fell not on those who in a sense deserved it but, two generations later, on innocent men.[213]

The jealousy of the gods, as Herodotus understands it, therefore, has little in common with the conception of divine justice. Only as he applies the notion to his larger scheme, the conflict of Greece with Persia, does he begin to find in it the germ of a really ethical idea. But it is only a beginning. If the gods strike in their anger not prosperity, but the wanton pride that prosperity engenders, it is because the old idea of jealousy has been

[211] Herodotus VII, 10: *φιλέει ὁ θεὸς τὰ ὑπερέχοντα πάντα κολούειν . . . φθονήσας . . . οὐ γὰρ ἐᾷ φρονέειν μέγα ὁ θεὸς ἄλλον ἢ ἑωυτόν.*

[212] VII, 139: the Athenians, *next to the gods*, repulsed the invader; cf. VIII, 109.

[213] VII, 134–137; n.b. 137: *θειότατον . . . θεῖον . . . τὸ πρῆγμα.* Cf. Solon 1 (see above p. 36); and contrast Theognis, 731–752 (see above, pp. 41 f.).

purified and deepened. And that will be chiefly the task of other thinkers than Herodotus. A century later, Aristotle will distinguish between malice (ἐπιχαιρεκακία), jealousy (φθόνος), and righteous indignation (νέμεσις).[214] But already the tragedies of Aeschylus will have drawn men's minds from the thought of jealousy to that of retribution, and from justice to mercy. To tragedy we must now turn.

[214] Aristotle, *E.N.*, 1108a35–b6; better, as well as more fully, discussed in *Rhet.* 1386b9–1388a28; cf. *Magna Moralia*, 1192b18–29.

# CHAPTER IV

## THE IDEA OF TRAGEDY

IT IS above all in Greek tragedy that one moves most constantly amid the flickering lights and shadows of fate, good, and evil. One has not left the world of primitive superstition; yet one is already wrestling with the problems of philosophy, though still largely in terms of gnomic wisdom.[1] The ritual origin of drama and the ritual survivals in fully developed tragedy kept in the foreground man's sense of a relationship with greater powers, for better or for worse. The persistently recurring myths, at first of Dionysus, and later of local heroes or of heroes from epic saga, focussed attention on suffering, on falls from high estate, on triumph over circumstances. The development of tragedy as it approached its natural limits, as Aristotle would say,[2] and achieved its ideal potentialities, its "idea," as Plato might have conceived it in his more lenient moods,[3] no less than the propensity of serious poets, drew attention from the mere sequence of events to some conception of their relationship, raising questions as to the nature of tragic experience and as to the kind of causality that might explain it.[4]

The very fixity of the myths in their broad outlines had important consequences. In the first place, since all the world knew that a certain catastrophe had once taken place, it was natural for a poet to suppose that it *had to be*, — that it was fated to be, that it was the outcome of an oracle, that a god had willed it. Sometimes, indeed, we are able to detect a tragic poet introducing such agencies into what had hitherto been simply a

[1] On this matter, cf. J. T. Stickney, *Les Sentences dans la Poésie Grecque*, pp. 159–244; and for a collection of gnomic passages from the three major tragic poets, with English translations, D. W. Thompson, *Sales Attici, or The Maxims Witty and Wise of Athenian Tragic Drama* (Edinburgh, 1867).

[2] Aristotle, *Poetics* 1449a14 f., after mentioning the origins of tragedy and comedy, remarks: *πολλὰς μεταβολὰς μεταβαλοῦσα ἡ τραγῳδία ἐπαύσατο, ἐπεὶ ἔσχε τὴν αὑτῆς φύσιν.* It is well to recognize clearly that Aristotle's remarks on tragedy apply only slightly to Aeschylus, and are directed chiefly toward Sophocles, but not to all even of his plays; it is pedantic, for example, to insist on the ἁμαρτία of Antigone. Cf. H. D. F. Kitto, *Greek Tragedy*, pp. 104–114; 123–128.

[3] Cf. W. C. Greene, "Plato's View of Poetry," *H.S.C.P.* 29 (1918), pp. 34–38; 50–56.

[4] Cf. G. Freytag, *Technik des Dramas*, p. 18: "das Werden einer Aktion und ihre Folgen auf das Gemüth"; and W. Jaeger, *Paideia*, pp. 248–252, on the selection of myths by the poets to illustrate ideas such as "the inevitable rise and fall of human destiny with its sudden reversals and its final catastrophe."

sequence of events, thus imposing his own design on the traditional background. Divine interventions, oracles, and family curses, accepted phenomena lying beyond human control, are powers available to instigate or direct the action. Moreover the characters or the chorus, often though not necessarily always speaking for the poet, may proclaim their conviction that what is occurring is the result of fate, of necessity, or of chance; that is, of irresistible external forces, with no moral implication. Or they may suggest that the suffering of a personage is the consequence of divine jealousy (*phthonos*); or again that it arises from some human fault of character, from *hybris* or *ate*, and that they see in operation the retribution (*nemesis*) of the gods or of fate toward man, or of what has since been called "poetic justice." Thus it was within the discretion of each poet to manipulate the myth in such fashion as to bring out what most interested him; the rôle of the gods or of human character, the relentless power of fate or the tricks of chance, the just rewards of guilt or the ironical contrast between deserts and actual receipts, or even such supervening interests as the glorification of Athens or the origin of certain institutions (in "aetiological" myths).

Part of this result is achieved by a poet's decision as to the exact section of a long series of events which he is to present. All history, all human life, is continuous; all periods are in a sense transitional. Nevertheless it is possible to recognize historic "periods" that have a special unity, with "a beginning, a middle and an end." The same is even more true of the lesser slices of life that constitute a drama. Most Greek tragedies open at an advanced stage in the action, corresponding to the fourth or fifth act of a Shaksperian tragedy and representing the results of a *fait accompli*; the poets "set the audience, as it were," in Dryden's language,[5] "at the post where the race is to be concluded." Most of the race therefore lies in the past; and the past has well been termed "the tragic tense"; for the past is beyond recall.

Now the same event will appear variously as cause, as incident, or as result, according to the place which it occupies at the beginning, middle, or end. Thus the substance of the *Electra* of Sophocles, and that of Euripides, each a single compact and complete play, is the central member of Aeschylus' trilogy, and looks both backward and forward; accordingly where Aeschylus stresses the long working out of a family curse and retribution for sin, Sophocles concentrates on the human motives which make intelligible the immediate action, and Euripides on the pathos of misfortune. Again, the poet may shift the emphasis from one character to another; as Sophocles enhances Electra at the expense of Orestes, or in the *Philoctetes* allows Neoptolemus (whom he introduces into his play) to

[5] J. Dryden, *An Essay of Dramatic Poesy.*

steal our interest away even from his hero, or creates a secondary tragedy of Creon while working out the tragedy of Antigone. By pointing his camera, as it were, at a selected subject, the dramatist may suggest in the very development of his plot that fate is at work. This is the plot (*μῦθος*), which Aristotle calls the "end" (*τέλος*) or "first principle and, as it were, the soul of a tragedy" (1450a22; 37); and the structure of the incidents (*ἡ τῶν πραγμάτων σύστασις*) is the most important part of the play (1450a15). Certainly the dramatist's outlook on life must be sought even more in the plot than in any sentiments which his characters may express.[6]

It is often asserted that Greek tragedy is fatalistic, — that all the events are predestined, that the characters are helpless in the grip of fate, that they await the call of fate.[7] We shall see that any sweeping statement of this sort is fallacious;[8] even for Aeschylus, fate is not even the most important element in tragedy. What is true is that a part, great or small, of the action in most of the plays is considered to proceed from causes beyond the control of the characters. So much we should admit with regard to our own lives, though we act as if we were free. Conversely, as fate sinks into the background, human character emerges and controls, or seems to control, the situation; in such a case, the struggle of a will to overcome obstacles, or a struggle between two or more wills, provides the chief interest.[9] But the finest and most profound tragic effect comes when the poet is not content merely to set forth external events, nor even the fact of guilt, but exhibits also the moral attitude of his protagonist toward events and toward his own action. He answers the call of honor, come what may; he endures what fate or the gods send.[10] His act may have caused his downfall, but his will remains noble; he learns by suffering; and there may be a final vindication of the sufferer, though of an unexpected kind. Such tragedy, though lapsing now and again into traditional lament and

[6] E. Howald, *Die Griechische Tragödie* (München and Berlin, 1930), pp. 14–22, enters a plea for considering *all* phases of a play: not merely myth, or fate, or a single character or scene, but the whole.

[7] Cf. the playful phrase of Socrates, on the day of his death, as reported by Plato (*Phaedo* 115a): "And now Fate (*ἡ εἱμαρμένη*) calls me, as a tragic poet would say."

[8] For brief refutations of this fallacy, see T. D. Goodell, *Athenian Tragedy* (New Haven, 1923), pp. 134–138; H. W. Smyth, *Aeschylean Tragedy*, pp. 143–150; at greater length, with a more general bearing, A. Leach, "Fatalism of the Greeks," *A.J.P.* 36 (1915), pp. 373–401, reprinted in abridged form, under title "Fate and Free Will in Greek Literature," in *The Greek Genius and its Influence*, ed. L. Cooper (New Haven, 1917), pp. 132–155.

[9] Cf. C. R. Post, "The Dramatic Art of Sophocles," *H.S.C.P.* 23 (1912), pp. 71–127; F. Brunetière, "The Law of the Drama," summarized by T. D. Goodell, *Athenian Tragedy*, pp. 122–128.

[10] This is again the philosophy of *τλημοσύνη* (see *Indices* s.vv. *τλημοσύνη*, *tlemosyne*). Hamlet, just before his death, remarks: "The readiness is all" (*Hamlet*, V, 2); a sentiment which Edgar seems to echo: "Men must endure
Their going hence, even as their coming hither;
Ripeness is all." (*King Lear*, V, 2.)

pessimism, is penetrated by the feeling of fifth century Greece that life is a game played for high stakes, in which man may nobly win, or at worst, may nobly lose. The greatest Greek drama, in other words, rests on the interplay between fate and character, between what man can not change and what remains within his power.

It is a curious fact that the most famous ancient critic of Greek drama neglects the part played by character, and says nothing, in so many words, about either fate or tragic irony. This is the more surprising when we recall that the dramatist to whom Aristotle looks with greatest admiration is Sophocles, the poet of character, and that the play which he most admires is the *Oedipus the King*, the play which is most deeply saturated with fatalism and with irony.

The reticence of Aristotle with regard to fate seems to indicate that Aristotle did not believe that fate is the dominating motive in tragedy; if so, he was doubtless right.[11] Not that the dramatists, taking advantage of traditional beliefs about fate and oracles and curses, as about the gods, did not allow their characters "probably" (that is, naturally and plausibly) to allege fate as an excuse for their own or others' failings; but the inevitable conclusion of the dramas may still be the result not of arbitrary destiny, but of character. Such is the case particularly with Sophocles, who has planned his tragic effects in advance. Iocasta and Antigone die, not of necessity but because Sophocles intends them to die: Iocasta, the fatalist, who disregards oracles, because she hangs herself; Antigone, likewise a fatalist, because of her own act, though she could have been saved at the last minute but for Creon's misguided bungling.[12]

For his apparent reticence with regard to irony Aristotle compensates by his remarks about "*peripeteia*." This term, ordinarily translated as "reversal of fortune" or "reversal of situation" really conveys a more precise meaning: it is the outcome of an action which is the opposite of what was intended. "Thus in the *Oedipus* the messenger comes to cheer Oedipus and free him from his alarms about his mother; but by revealing who he is, he produces the opposite effect." [13] One might add many other examples from Sophocles and Shakspere. These consummations, being not the results of chance but the "inevitable and probable" result of good intentions and human blindness, are the more tragic. "Whosoever will save his life shall lose it." And, as Aristotle realizes, the *peripeteia* may be intimately related to the *anagnorisis*, that moment in a tragedy in which a

[11] Moreover, Aristotle wrote before Stoic dogmatism about fate had grown up; for later Peripatetic discussion of fatalism in connection with tragedy, see below, pp. 373; 375 f.; also cf. R. A. Pack, "Fate, Chance, and Tragic Error," *A.J.P.* 60 (1939), pp. 350–356.

[12] See below, p. 147.

[13] *Poetics* 1452a24–26; and see below, pp. 101–104, on tragic "irony."

sudden realization of the truth flashes upon a character, as to the identity of some individual or as to some other essential fact, — for example, the discovery by Oedipus of his own past.[14]

Since a tragedy should, in Aristotle's opinion, imitate actions which excite pity and fear, certain kinds of plot and of character are to be preferred. "In the first place, the change of fortune presented must not be the spectacle of a virtuous man brought from prosperity to adversity, for this moves neither pity nor fear, but is merely shocking; nor again that of a bad man passing from adversity to prosperity; for nothing can be more alien to the spirit of tragedy; it possesses no single tragic quality; it neither satisfies the moral sense (τὸ φιλάνθρωπον) nor calls forth pity or fear.[15] Nor again should the downfall of the utter villain be exhibited.[16] A plot of this kind would doubtless satisfy the moral sense, but it would inspire neither pity nor fear, for pity is aroused by unmerited misfortune, fear by the misfortune of a man like ourselves. . . . There remains then the character between these two extremes, that of a man who is not eminently good and just, yet whose misfortune is brought about not by vice or depravity but by some error or frailty (ἁμαρτία)." [17] Another kind of tragedy, which Aristotle ranks as distinctly inferior (though others, influenced by popular taste, rank it first), has "an opposite catastrophe for the good and for the bad," — that is, one must suppose, the virtuous are rewarded and the wicked are punished. But "the pleasure thence derived is not the true tragic pleasure, but is proper rather to comedy." [18]

Aristotle's ideal tragic hero thus comes to grief through his tragic fault (ἁμαρτία). This is more often a mistake of judgment than a moral flaw;[19] it is the artistic device by which the action is brought to a crisis, rather

[14] *Poetics* 1452a32–b8; see further F. L. Lucas, *Tragedy* (London, 1927), pp. 91–96; Lucas, "Reversal in Aristotle," *C.R.* 37 (1923), pp. 98–104.

[15] For τὸ φιλάνθρωπον and its close relation in Aristotle to "pity," cf. U. Galli, *Atene e Roma*, N.S. 12 (1931), pp. 243–253.

[16] Aristotle's principle would rule out Shakspere's *Richard III.* Furthermore even the faults and the suffering of a Greek hero are apt to arise from an exclusive or excessive devotion to some recognized duty, whereas those of a Shaksperean character come from self-indulgence. See also below, pp. 94, n. 22; 98 f. For the background of Shakspere, and the transition from the medieval emphasis on the fall of princes through Fortune to the emphasis on character, see W. Farnham, *The Medieval Heritage of Elizabethan Tragedy* (Berkeley, 1936) a valuable study, though I think it exaggerates the "Greco-Roman surrender."

[17] *Poetics*, 1452b34–1453a10, tr. S. H. Butcher.

[18] *Ibid.*, 1453a30–36. On the οἰκεία ἡδονή of tragedy, the pleasure peculiar to tragedy not as tragedy but as serious art, cf. G. F. Else, "Aristotle on the Beauty of Tragedy," *H.S.C.P.* 49 (1938), esp. pp. 193–199; on the "ethic" or "moral" plot, which edifies the spectator by exhibiting the good man passing from bad fortune to good, and on the tragic or "pathetic" plot, which provides not edification but *katharsis* of the emotions, see L. A. Post, "Aristotle and Menander," *T.A.P.A.* 69 (1938), esp. pp. 8–12.

[19] But see H. Phillips, Jr. in *H.S.C.P.* 44 (1933), pp. 244–246, whose study distinguishes both moral and intellectual meanings of ἁμαρτία throughout Greek literature.

than an explanation in moral terms of the suffering. Indeed it is sometimes the blunderer, sometimes another who suffers. In fact Aristotle, as we have seen, does not favor the play in which virtue is rewarded and vice punished. The pity which is proper to tragedy "is aroused by unmerited misfortune"; and Aristotle goes out of his way to praise Euripides, "most tragic of the poets," for his unhappy endings (1453a23–30). Yet the problem of "poetic justice" is implicit, and is all the more acute since Aristotle also holds that poetry is superior to history in its universality and truthfulness and in the degree to which it exhibits events as probable or inevitable, and not as merely fortuitous.[20] If Aristotle has taken pains to disavow his belief in poetic justice, the French and English critics of the seventeenth and eighteenth centuries, with few exceptions, went to the other extreme.[21] So Thomas Rymer, appealing to Aristotle as well as to the Greek tragedians, attributes to the latter the intention of improving on history: "Finding in history the same end happen to the righteous and to the unjust, virtue often oppressed and wickedness on the throne, they saw these particular yesterday-truths were imperfect and improper to illustrate the universal and eternal truths by them intended. Finding also that this unequal distribution of rewards and punishments did perplex the wisest, and by the atheist was made a scandal to the Divine Providence, they concluded that a poet must of necessity see justice exactly administered, if he intended to please."[22] John Dryden, in his "Essay of Dramatic Poesy" (1668) had blamed the ancients for often showing "a prosperous wickedness and an unhappy piety." But in the Prefaces to *All for Love* (1678), and to *Troilus and Cressida* (1679) Dryden revised his interpretation of the ancients. Thus, in the latter essay, he wrote of the "wicked man" in tragedy: "We are glad when we behold his crimes are punished, and that poetical justice is done upon him."[23] A few years later, John Dennis proclaimed: "Every Tragedy ought to be a very Solemn Lecture, inculcating a particular Providence, and shewing it plainly protecting the Good, and chastizing the Bad."[24]

[20] Cf. L. E. Matthaei, *Studies in Greek Tragedy*, Chap. V, pp. 148–216, "Accident," a penetrating analysis of the rôle in literature of the inexplicable, of surprise, and of the likely accident; R. Pack, "Fate, Chance, and Tragic Error," *A.J.P.* 60 (1939), pp. 350–356, emphasizing fate, minimizing chance (and *ἁμαρτία* in modern criticism). See also below, pp. 320 f.; 324–328; 373–376.

[21] Cf. the unpublished Harvard dissertation by J. L. Rudé, *Poetic Justice*, 1934.

[22] T. Rymer, *Tragedies of the Last Age*, 1678; cf. his *A Short View of Tragedy*, 1693, in which Rymer argues that poetic justice is more severe than history or law, in that the poets make men "suffer more than their fault deserved." He attacks Shakspere for the sufferings of innocent characters, asking with regard to Desdemona, "If this be our end, what boots it to be virtuous?" (Cf. Sophocles, *O.T.* 895 f.; see below, p. 160.) But in such criticisms, Rymer was anticipated by Shakspere himself; cf. the servants in *King Lear*, III, 7.

[23] Cf. Dryden's projected "*Answer*" to Rymer.

[24] J. Dennis, Epistle Dedicatory to his *Advancement and Reformation of Modern Poetry*,

It was Joseph Addison who first challenged the whole conception of "poetic justice"; and his words must be quoted at length. "The English writers of tragedy are possessed with a notion, that when they represent a virtuous or innocent person in distress, they ought not to leave him till they have delivered him out of his troubles or made him triumph over his enemies. This error they have been led into by a ridiculous doctrine in modern criticism, that they are obliged to an equal distribution of rewards and punishments, and an impartial execution of poetical justice. Who were the first that established this rule I know not; but I am sure that it has no foundation in nature, in reason, or in the practise of the ancients. We find that good and evil happen alike to all men on this side the grave; and as the principal design of tragedy is to raise commiseration and terror in the minds of the audience, we shall defeat this great end if we always make virtue and innocence happy and successful. . . . For this reason the ancient writers of tragedy treated men in their plays, as they are dealt with in the world, by making virtue sometimes happy and sometimes miserable, as they found it in the fable which they made choice of, or as it might affect their audience in the most agreeable manner."[25] On the whole Addison's point is well taken, though he deals more adequately with innocent suffering in Greek tragedy than with retribution on the guilty. Samuel Johnson likewise attacked with sturdy common sense the doctrine of "poetic justice." "Whatever pleasure there may be in seeing crimes punished and virtue rewarded, yet, since wickedness often prospers in real life, the poet is certainly at liberty to give it prosperity on the stage."[26]

Many critics have taken Shakspere to task for his various failures to illustrate "poetic justice." Macbeth, to be sure, a brave but too ambitious soldier, suffers his just deserts. Even Lear, a foolish old man, though more sinned against than sinning, deserves a little, a very little, of what he suffers. But the noble Hamlet's hesitation, and the philosophic rebellion of Brutus both lead to frustration and death, while the innocent Cordelia and the innocent Desdemona die through the caprice of events. Therefore, it is objected, Shakspere fails to observe justice. A similar case could be made against Sophocles. Ajax might be considered to suffer retribution for *hybris*. But the calamities of Oedipus and Deianira are caused by mistakes, rather than by sins.[27] Tragedy thus arouses in us a sense of

*Epistle Dedicatory*, 1701 (ed. Hooker, Baltimore, 1939, Vol. I, p. 200); cf. his *The Usefulness of the Stage*, 1698, p. 183 Hooker, on "poetick justice" as the manifestation of God and "a particular Providence."

[25] *Spectator* No. 40, April 16, 1711.

[26] S. Johnson, *Lives of the Poets* (1779–1781), "Addison." In the *Rambler* No. 93 (1751) Johnson had remarked: "Addison is suspected to have denied the expediency of poetical justice because his own Cato was condemned to perish in a good cause."

[27] Thus a character in Sophocles protests (frag. 107 Pearson): "Strange, that impious men

incongruity, a *malaise*, a "qualm," as it has been called.[28] And many critics feel that in such cases our moral sense has been challenged, not to say outraged.

Now the simplest answer to such criticism is to admit that tragedy, like life, often shows the suffering of innocent, or comparatively innocent persons, through what may be called natural causes. Nature may show signs of intelligence, even of a design; but it would be hard to prove that her purpose is our purpose. She tolerates evil, as well as fosters good, from any point of view.[29] Strictly speaking, there would be no tragedy if virtue were always rewarded and vice always punished. But we may go further and urge that the whole doctrine of "poetic justice" is immoral. It is the doctrine of Satan and the friends of Job. "Be good and you will prosper," it whispers. Plato again and again attacks the notion, urging that virtue leads to happiness, as an inward state of the soul, but not necessarily to outward material success; and here he is at one with Christian doctrine. Even the tragic fault on which Aristotle insists is, as we have seen, less a moral explanation of the catastrophe than the artistic device which precipitates it. Retribution of a sort there will be, but not necessarily in proportion to the moral deserts of the characters. The attitude of the judge, which is what is involved in the conception of "justice," is really out of place in tragedy. No one wishes to sit in judgment on the sufferer; one rather feels instinctive pity, or fear, or even indignation. The most that can be said as to justice, many a time, is that what has happened had to be. The ancients would say that it was fated; we may say that it occurred through "natural causes"; so far our logical demand that every fact have its cause is satisfied. But the data of life, at any given moment, warrant as little the optimism of a Hegel (who, like Voltaire's Doctor Pangloss sees only the harmony of all things) as it does the pessimism of Schopenhauer (who dwells wholly on the futility exhibited in tragedy).

All tragedy is sad. But whereas the spectacle of mere accident would be merely painful, tragedy presents a spectacle of suffering that is explained, though not necessarily justified. Moreover the members of the audience, who would feel nothing but pain if they were themselves sev-

---

sprung from wicked parents, should prosper, while good men of generous breed should be unfortunate! It is not right that heaven should deal so with men. The gods should manifestly reward the pious, and the unrighteous should suffer some manifest punishment for their wickedness. Then the wicked man would not flourish." With this commonplace, cf. Theognis (see above, pp. 40 f.); Ennius (see below, p. 334); *Job* 21; *Psalm* 73 (first half).

[28] P. H. Frye, *Romance and Tragedy*, esp. pp. 146; 141–157; 163 ff. The Romans use the verb *indignor* to express this sense of discrepancy with one's just deserts; Lucretius III, 1045: *tu . . . indignabere obire?* Virgil, *Aen.* XI, 831; XII, 952 (of the deaths of Camilla and Turnus); in more whimsical vein, cf. Martial, II, 90, 7 f.: *non indignantia fumos tecta.*

[29] Cf. W. M. Dixon, *Tragedy* (an admirable work, bearing on many phases of our whole subject), pp. 170–178; 185–204; M. Adler, *Art and Prudence* (New York, 1937), pp. 67 f.

erally to experience personally the sufferings of a tragic hero, or even to behold such suffering "in real life," feel a collective sympathy with the ideal suffering represented to them; their emotions and their moral sense alike are aroused and enlarged and in some degree satisfied; the experience of the individual hero is felt to be a type of universal experience, particularly as seen through the eyes of the tragic chorus. What's Hecuba to us? Nothing, or everything, according as the poet fails or succeeds. This is the paradox of tragedy: that the spectacle of pain and evil arouses in us a strange delight and a new admiration for man's powers; it is what Aristotle calls the *katharsis* or purging of our pity and fear, as these emotions are aroused, and allayed, by fitting objects. There is of course an extensive literature on the Aristotelian theory of *katharsis* and on the psychological effects of tragedy, which I refrain from discussing here.[30] It is enough for our purpose to observe that Aristotle seems to be exploiting the artistic counterpart of conceptions familiar to the Dionysiac and other "mystery religions"; that is, the physical or medical effect of "enthusiasm," which Pythagoreanism and Platonism philosophized. Music purges the soul, as medicine the body.[31] Plato is suspicious, however, of such drama as "feeds and waters" the emotions which should be starved,[32] while Aristotle finds in tragedy a positive psychological value.[33]

That the experience of witnessing a tragedy will be for the audience inspiriting rather than merely painful will depend on various further considerations, which are to be reckoned as among the chief resources of Greek tragedy. Chief will be the human dignity which the sufferers will in most cases maintain, the fortitude (τλημοσύνη) with which they will meet their lot. Although, like Ajax or Philoctetes or even Antigone, they may represent incompletely the right or the wise course of action,[34] we are proud to be their fellowmen. Next, perhaps, will be the suggestion

[30] Mention may be made, however, of A. W. Benn, *Greek Philosophers*, pp. 594–599; W. F. Trench, "The Function of Poetry according to Aristotle," *Studies* 19 (Dublin, 1930), pp. 549–563; N. W. DeWitt, "The Meaning of Katharsis in Aristotle's Definition of Tragedy," *Trans. Royal Society of Canada*, 1934, pp. 109–115 (proposing an interpretation based not on medicine but on viticulture, in which "purging" or "pruning" is essential); G. F. Else, "Aristotle on the Beauty of Tragedy," *H.S.C.P.* 49 (1938), pp. 179–204. See also below, p. 397.

[31] E. Rohde, *Psyche* (1894), p. 336 and n. 2; P. Boyancé, *Le Culte des Muses chez les Philosophes Grecs* (Paris, 1936), pp. 103–131; 185–199; Diels 58 D1 (I, p. 468, lines 19 f.): οἱ Πυθαγορικοί, ὡς ἔφη Ἀριστόξενος, καθάρσει ἐχρῶντο τοῦ μὲν σώματος διὰ τῆς ἰατρικῆς, τῆς δὲ ψυχῆς διὰ τῆς μουσικῆς. Cf. Plato, *Laws* 790c–e; Aristotle, *Politics* 1342a7–16; *Poetics* 1449b27 f.: δι' ἐλέου καὶ φόβου περαίνουσα τὴν τῶν τοιούτων παθημάτων κάθαρσιν.

[32] Plato, *Rep.* 606 d.

[33] For the paradox of the pleasure afforded by the spectacle of pain in tragedy, cf. St. Augustine, *Confessions* III, 2; Milton, Preface to *Samson* (see below, p. 397).

[34] Cf. W. Schadewaldt, "Sophokles, Aias und Antigone," *Neue Wege zur Antike* 8 (1928), pp. 61–117, esp. pp. 99–109.

that man is, for better or for worse, very largely the master of his destiny.[35] Some poets, like Sophocles, and to a lesser degree Shakspere, may further suggest, directly or indirectly, that the same forces that have tolerated the suffering and the evil have also brought into being the moral grandeur with which they are faced, and show a sunlight playing on the wreckage of the storm, with some promise of fair weather to come.[36] For a Christian martyr there may be the hope that amends will be made in a future life. In Greek tragedy all must be contained in the action, and the nearest to such posthumous amends that can be contrived is in the apotheosis or vindication of a suffering hero at the end of the play,[37] or the faint hopes of Antigone that she may be vindicated in another world.[38]

In Greek tragedy there are also several special considerations, one or more of which may affect our understanding of a given play. These may be listed somewhat as follows. (1) The poet is usually handing on a primitive tradition that his hero suffered in a certain manner; that is in itself a spectacle inspiring pity and fear, feelings which Aristotle holds to be proper to tragedy, apart from any question of moral blame. (2) Furthermore, the story of the suffering may preserve or even utilize the tradition of divine vindictiveness or jealousy (φθόνος), which a later age would repudiate.[39] (3) Or the idea of the hereditary curse may be at work, the idea that innocent children may suffer for the sins of their fathers. But this view is purified by the tragic poets, as Aeschylus and Sophocles perceive the difference between suffering for another's guilt (a natural, physical fact, verified by all experience) and punishment for another's guilt (the result of an immoral vindictiveness). The latter Aeschylus repudiates, and the hereditary curse now appears as an inherited though not insuperable tendency toward guilt. (4) The poet may also hold the primitive view that the hero's sinful act, regardless of his motives, is a pollution, and must, like any physical taint, be washed away. The outward act requires ritual expiation; the "doer" must also suffer.[40] (5) The poet may feel, with later Greeks, that the intention of the doer must be taken into account, and a distinction made between voluntary and involuntary

[35] *Julius Caesar*, I, 2: "The fault, dear Brutus, is not in our stars
But in ourselves, that we are underlings."

[36] Cf. A. C. Bradley, *Shakespearean Tragedy*, Lecture I, "The Substance of Tragedy," pp. 31–39. Bradley goes farther than Frye (*op. cit.*, pp. 151–152) in claiming such a moral reconciliation, an alleviation of the "qualm," a purgation of pity and fear, for Shakspere as well as for Greek tragedy. Cf. also W. M. Dixon, *Tragedy*, pp. 197–204.

[37] Cf. Sophocles, *Ajax*, *Philoctetes*, *O.C.*

[38] *Antigone*, 74 ff.; 451; 521; 897 ff.

[39] See below, pp. 103; 107; but also 139; and cf. also Gloucester, in *King Lear*, IV, 1, 38: "As flies to wanton boys, are we to the Gods: They kill us for their sport." Greek theology has no separate Devil or Satan; any god may therefore at times be used at times to explain evil.

[40] Aeschylus *Choeph.* 313: δράσαντι παθεῖν; cf. the orator Antiphon, *Tetral.* 2, 2, the imaginary case of a young man accidentally killed by a lance.

error, between deeds done with open eyes and deeds done in ignorance; only for the former is one responsible, and should be rewarded or punished. So Aristotle argues in the *Ethics*, though in the *Poetics* he does not make it clear just how much he understands by the term fault (ἁμαρτία), how far it is a moral lapse, how far only an intellectual error.[41] In the case of the *Oedipus* of Sophocles, both are involved, as we shall see.[42]

Finally, as we have observed, in tragedy and in life suffering often exceeds deserts. So far as suffering can be ascribed to "natural causes" or to chance, no moral values need be imputed. The righteous are as liable to painful diseases or to accidents as are the wicked; power and justice are not always united in the scheme of things. But the poet may suggest that the individual personage is only incidental to some majestic and inscrutable divine purpose. So in Sophocles the tragic error of Deianira is the means by which Heracles wins release from his toils; suffering Philoctetes is the instrument by which, in due time, Troy is to fall; Ajax and Antigone seem crushed, but are vindicated; and Oedipus is preserved by the gods for a special destiny. The part is subordinate to the whole. Such an interpretation of suffering, to be sure, puts a severe strain on the individual's ability to surrender personal happiness to an end that is not his, unless he makes it his: "Not my will, but Thine be done." Even disaster thus appears in Sophocles to result from the violation of a moral law which is upheld by some cosmic will or force or fate, and which, though not intervening to save the offender from the consequences of his deeds or from the deeds of another, will in the end reveal him as reconciled. This conception of Sophocles, more profound than the kaleidoscopic glimpses of Shakspere, impelled Arnold to say that Sophocles "saw life steadily and saw it whole." Aeschylus and Sophocles even held that from suffering, whether deserved or not, positive gain may be derived by an educative or disciplinary process.[43] So the Heracles of the *Philoctetes* and the Oedipus and the Theseus of the *Oedipus at Colonus* are the nobler for the hardships that they have surmounted.[44] The question still remains whether in

[41] See above, pp. 93 f.; below, pp. 327 f.

[42] See below, pp. 154–162. If calamity clearly springs from character, "justice" may be affirmed; so Edgar perceives (in *King Lear*, V, 3):

> "The gods are just, and of our pleasant vices
> Make instruments to plague us."

Macbeth does not perceive the justice of his fall, and it is he who cries out that life

> "is a tale told by an idiot, full of sound and fury,
> Signifying nothing." (*Macbeth*, V, 5.)

[43] Aeschylus, *Ag.* 177: πάθει μάθος (and see below p. 108); Sophocles, *Antigone* 1272 (Creon): ἔχω μαθὼν δείλαιος; *Tyro*, fr. 661 Pearson: πόλλ' ἐν κακοῖσι θυμὸς εὐνηθεὶς ὁρᾷ (note Pearson's comment).

[44] Sophocles, *Philoctetes* 1418–1422; *O.C.* 7 f.: στέργειν γὰρ αἱ πάθαι με χὠ χρόνος ξυνὼν | μακρὸς διδάσκει καὶ τὸ γενναῖον τρίτον; 560–568.

such cases this gain was "fated," a part of the divine plan, as Sophocles urged in the latter play, or whether it is merely a human attribute occasionally to make a virtue of necessity, as the oyster is said to secrete a pearl when irritated by a grain of sand. This uncertainty may dispose the poet to suspend judgment, and to rest content with the honest presentation of the ancient myth, or the ordinary man to cling to the facts in his own experience: "So the affair turned out."[45]

The ending of many a Greek tragedy, ordinarily expressed in a choral *clausula* or recessional or "doxology," represents a tapering off of the tragic tension and thus assists the *katharsis*. This is partly an artistic device, "classic" calm succeeding storm and stress, as in many a modern musical composition; but it is also a philosophic summation of tragic experience from the point of view of all time and all experience. "Passion in suffering lulled to rest sees much."[46] The recessional may merely express commiseration with the suffering. Or it may take the form of benediction and felicitation on the unexpectedly happy outcome of suffering,[47] or of calm resignation.[48] Or again it may suggest that wisdom comes through suffering.[49] It may review the past action, with a reflection on the inscrutability of human fortune, save to the divine understanding.[50] Five almost liturgical Euripidean *clausulae* run in identical words (except for the first line in the *Medea*), though the dramas vary widely in their outcomes:[51]

> There be many shapes of mystery,
> And many things God makes to be,
> Past hope or fear.
> And the end men looked for cometh not,
> And a path there is where no man sought.
> So hath it fallen here.[52]

Once more, the recessional may survey the catastrophe and revive the commonplace: "Count no man happy before his final day is seen to be without calamity."[53]

[45] Cf. Euripides, *Alcestis* 1163: τοιόνδ' ἀπέβη τόδε πρᾶγμα.

[46] Sophocles, *Tyro*, frag. 661 Pearson; see above, n. 43.

[47] Aeschylus, *Eum.* 881–1047 (see below pp. 135–137); Sophocles, *El.* 1508–1510; Euripides, *I.T.* 1490–1496.

[48] Sophocles, *O.C.* 1777–1779.

[49] Sophocles, *Ant.* 1348–1353.

[50] Sophocles, *Ajax* 1418–1420 (see below, p. 151); cf. *Trach.* 1270–1278; *Tereus* frag. 590 Pearson.

[51] Euripides, *Alc.* 1159–1163; *Med.* 1415–1419; *And.* 1284–1288; *Hel.* 1688–1692; *Bacch.* 1388–1392. These *clausulae* are dismissed by A. W. Verrall, *Euripides the Rationalist*, pp. 77, 112, 196, as mere Euripidean "tags" that point the irony of the plays.

[52] Trans. G. Murray.

[53] See Appendix 11: "Count no man happy."

These matters remain a mystery. Aeschylus has boldly adapted the myths in order to exhibit the increasing justice of Zeus, and the replacing of chaos by cosmos. Determined to show that suffering is due to sin, he upholds the justice of God, as it has been said, "at the expense of facts."[54] Sophocles, less revolutionary, less concerned to construct a theodicy in which fate corresponds to guilt, is no less pious in seeing an ultimate goodness and an "unwritten law" even amid the cruelties of the old myths. The cruelties and ironies of man's lot he views with no pessimism; rather they are what save man from any easy optimism, for they show that it is possible to face even undeserved misfortune with heroism. And this is the pleasure proper to tragedy, as Aristotle would say. Blind destiny is supplanted for Sophocles by irony, the spectacle of man's blindness or ignorance of whatever truth is unknown to him. For Euripides, sceptical of the myths, if not of religion, *pathos*, the tragic sense, will be the last resort of the poet; he thus marks a return to the earliest phase of tragedy, while experimenting with the moral ideals of his day in the spirit of the sophists and of Thucydides. Shakspere's tragedies arouse in us a sense of the pitiful waste of human excellence in a world which neither protects nor persecutes nobility but lets it fall, now (like Cordelia) through the operation of some evil force or some mischance, now like Hamlet or Othello through the terrible and unexpected recoil of well-meaning efforts.[55] This is not fatalism, but once more a sense of the ironical.

Irony (εἰρωνεία) is the characteristic of a certain kind of man, the dissembler (εἴρων) who says less than he knows, unlike the merely truthful man, and of course still more unlike his opposite the boaster (ἀλαζών).[56] A comic poet remarks that the fox is by nature εἴρων;[57] conversely, we call some people "foxy." Aware of the dangers to which one is exposed in life from envious men, possibly even from jealous gods, the ironical man lies low and plays safe, tempting neither providence nor his fellowmen.[58]

Irony is indeed one of the most universal and characteristic traits of

[54] E. Abbott, in *Hellenica* (London, 1880), p. 65.

[55] Cf. A. C. Bradley, *Shakespearean Tragedy*, pp. 23–31; P. H. Frye, *Romance and Tragedy*, pp. 151–154; T. Spencer, "Hamlet and the Nature of Reality," *Journal of English Literary History* 5 (1938), pp. 253–277, which bears also on the problem of appearance and reality.

[56] Aristotle, *E.N.* 1108a19–23; 1127a20–26; cf. Theophrastus, Characters I and XXIII. The two extremes become stock characters in the New Comedy.

[57] Philemon 89, 6–9 Kock. The Attic εἰρωνεία, it has been remarked, is "that shrewd, non-committal spirit, natural to a people of farmers and tradesmen, which Aristophanes has depicted for us in his typical Athenian figures, and which Demosthenes denounced," J. Burnet, ed. Plato, *Phaedo* (Oxford, 1911), p. lv. In his footnote Burnet adds that εἴρων "means 'sly,' 'cunning,' *malin*, and εἰρωνεία is not regarded as exactly a good quality." He compares the Scots words "canny," and "pawky"; New England Yankees sometimes relish, sometimes find exasperating, their local irony. (For Demosthenes, cf. *Phil.* I, 7, 37.)

[58] Cf. F. Wehrli, ΛΑΘΕ ΒΙΩΣΑΣ, *passim*.

Greek temperament and style from Homer to Lucian.[59] It lends itself particularly to dialogue in which one speaker deliberately practises dissimulation, either feigning ignorance in order to provoke or confound an antagonist, or feigning respectful agreement with his views as a preliminary to demolishing them. Such is the famous "Socratic irony," though it is to be noted that in Plato it is always the opponents of Socrates who impute it to him as a lack of candor, whereas he protests a sincere perplexity about certain matters.[60]

Bishop Thirlwall was perhaps the first to use the term "irony" of the tragic effect obtained by the contrast between varying states of knowledge.[61] The effect may be of various kinds. One character may innocently say something which another character takes in another sense than what was intended. Or he may deliberately, by equivocal utterances, mislead another, as the ambiguous oracles of Delphi to Croesus "palter with [the inquirer] in a double sense." But a deeper irony is to be found where all the characters fail to perceive the significance of a saying, or the inevitable outcome of a course of action which is apparent to the spectators, who share the privileged position of the poet and of the gods, and who moreover already know the essentials of the myth. We and the gods, as it were, are omniscient, and share the intimacy of a secret knowledge; we see all and hear all that goes on, and behold men inadvertently and blindly walking toward their doom. Nor need there be any malice in our pleasure at the spectacle; rather, like Lucretius, we feel it sweet to behold from our safe vantage-point sailors in distress on the vexed sea, not because there is any pleasure in the distress of others, but because their distress is the measure of our security.[62] So far our attitude is wholly detached and impersonal, like that of the spectator of a comedy or the reader of a detective story, whose satisfaction is purely intellectual because he does not allow his sympathies to become involved; and no doubt there are scenes in tragedy which appeal to a sense closely akin to that of the comic.[63] Sophocles in several plays uses a hyporcheme, a lively and cheerful dance-song of the chorus, just before a great calamity. And the beauty of many other choral odes depends on the refreshing contrast between the thought of the

[59] For a fascinating and wide-reaching study, cf. J. A. K. Thomson, *Irony*; on tragic irony, pp. 34–92.

[60] Cf. *Meno* 79e, where Meno compares his condition, paralyzed by the Socratic method, to that of one benumbed by a "torpedo-fish"; also *Rep.* 337a. Socrates doubts many things, and confutes many traditional views, often by an engaging naïveté; but he knows what he knows. On Socratic irony, see further the excellent remarks of Sir A. Grant, ed. Aristotle, *Ethics*, Vol. I, pp. 157 f.

[61] "On the Irony of Sophocles," *Philological Museum* 2 (1833), pp. 483–537; also, in German, in *Philologus* 6 (1841), pp. 81–104; 254–277.

[62] Lucretius II, 1–4.

[63] E.g. Eur., *Hippolytus* 732–751.

chorus, soaring into brighter regions, and the grim march of the events before our eyes.[64] *Per contra*, it may be the chorus, or its equivalent, who understand the dire realities which are mercifully veiled, till now, from the characters of a drama. Such is the effect of Maeterlinck's little play, *Intérieur*.

The sense of security given by wealth or intelligence or power may in itself be the beginning of disaster; for the semblance may be mistaken for the reality, δόξα for ἀλήθεια.[65] The ripest fruit is the readiest to fall; and all history is full of persons and nations who advanced confidently but blindly toward their doom. So Philoctetes reasons, in the play of Sophocles; "All human destiny is full of the fear and the peril that good fortune may be followed by evil. He who stands clear of trouble should beware of dangers; and when a man lives at ease, then it is that he should look most closely to his life, lest ruin come on it by stealth."[66] And Shakspere's Wolsey echoes the thought:

> This is the state of man: to-day he puts forth
> The tender leaves of hopes; to-morrow blossoms,
> And bears his blushing honors thick upon him;
> The third day comes a frost, a killing frost;
> And, when he thinks, good easy man, full surely
> His greatness is a-ripening, nips his root,
> And then he falls, as I do.[67]

Against such peril the only recourse is to moderation, or to obscurity.[68]

If one thinks of that state of superior knowledge or power to which the tragic character's ignorance is opposed as something objective, as fate or fortune, perhaps as a personal force that deliberately encompasses his ruin, then one is led to speak of "the irony of fate." The mere contrast between the apparent situation and the actuality, however, need not imply malice on the part of any superior power: and in fact neither Aeschylus nor Sophocles believed in the "jealousy of the gods" as some of their predecessors had believed in it, save as they believed in just gods who avenge wrong-doing, whether deliberate or involuntary.[69] What is more, the spectator

[64] Cf. the often quoted remark of Horace Walpole: "The world is a comedy to those that think, a tragedy to those who feel."

[65] Oedipus the King immediately suggests himself as the type of such illusory security (see below, pp. 155 f.; 156; 158; and cf. H. Kuhn, "The True Tragedy" (1941), pp. 24 f.); among philosophers, it is Parmenides (see Appendix 28), and Plato (see below, pp. 311–316) who most deliberately seek to pass from the world of δόξα to the world of ἀλήθεια.

[66] Sophocles, *Philoctetes*, 501–506; for the comic use of the sentiment, cf. Terence, *Phormio*, 241–246.

[67] *Henry VIII*, III, 2, 352–358.

[68] Cf. Horace, *Odes*, II, 10; again cf. F. Wehrli, ΛΑΘΕ ΒΙΩΣΑΣ.

[69] Cf. *Exodus* 20, 5; "For I Jehovah thy God am a jealous God," etc. For earlier Greek notions of divine "jealousy," see *Indices*, s.vv. Jealousy, *Phthonos*, *φθόνος θεῶν*.

of a Greek tragedy cannot view with detached calm the spectacle of Agamemnon or of Oedipus unwittingly marching to their destruction, of Oedipus even moving heaven and earth in order to bring to light precisely what as a matter of fact he most dreads; the spectator feels pity for the victim of circumstance, and fear of the power that so marvellously trips him up, together with some tendency to surmise how far the fall was deserved. He may further, knowing in advance the outcome, enjoy the suspense maintained by linguistic subtleties and *double entente*, while he watches the action that goes amiss.[70] For these reasons Lewis Campbell, in criticizing Bishop Thirlwall's essay "On the Irony of Sophocles," suggested that a more appropriate term than "irony," — a term at once too comprehensive and too narrow to be exact, — would be "pathetic contrast."[71] The point is well taken, even though the phrase "Irony of Fate" has gained such currency that it may be displaced with difficulty. At any rate, Campbell is right in protesting that "it injures the profound pathos of Greek tragedy by suggesting the suspicion of an *arrière pensée*, of the poet's face behind the mask, surveying his own creations with a sardonic smile." There is nothing sardonic, though there may be much ruthlessness, in Aeschylus and Sophocles: Euripides may play with the sardonic, as Hardy pulls the strings in his novels and tales and pretends that it is Fate. For Euripides has lost most of his illusions about the gods and the heroes, for which very reason he contrasts the more bitterly, as one betrayed, the shabbiness of the traditional Apollo with the decency of ordinary humanity (in the *Ion*), or the pretensions of military glory with the harsh realities of war (as in the *Trojan Women*).

So far we have been concerned with the general idea and trend of tragedy, the successive phases of which we may now survey in the work of the several poets.

[70] J. A. K. Thomson, *Irony*, p. 35: "There are scholars who write as if, in mentioning this verbal form of Irony, they had exhausted the subject. Why, a Greek tragedy is all ironical; it is ironical in its very nature."

[71] L. Campbell, ed. Sophocles (Oxford, 1879), Vol. I, pp. 126–133, "Note on the so-called Irony of Sophocles."

# CHAPTER V

## AESCHYLUS

FOUNDER though he was of Greek tragedy, Aeschylus was already heir to traditions which he mastered and adapted to new purposes. The conventions of the primitive Attic dramatic festival, traditional myths (mostly "slices from the great banquet of Homer," as he himself put it, referring to the epic cycle generally [1]), crude divinities both chthonian and Olympic, and religious conceptions that corresponded to them, these were his materials.[2] Even the great gods of tradition are of a grudging, if not malevolent, disposition, jealous of their newly-won prerogatives, and capable of blinding men to their hurt. Here are already the seeds of tragic conflict. More baleful still are the lesser *daimones* of the dimmer and more remote past. There is *Ate*, "Hurt," or ruinous folly, whom Homer has made the very daughter of Zeus, and who can be used to destroy men.[3] There is *Alastor*, the spirit of a murdered man calling for vengeance or expiation, personified or even incarnate in some survivor.[4] There are the Erinyes, also avengers of the murdered (especially of parents), and vindicators of curses, and indeed of law in general in an age before the gods or the *polis* have assumed responsibility for a consistent code dealing with murder.[5] There are the familiar means of communication between the gods and men, or between the dead and the living; oracles, dreams, and apparitions.[6] Ready for the explanation of human vicissitudes are the ideas of chance (τύχη),[7] and of

[1] Athenaeus 347e. For the traditional character of the materials of Aeschylus, cf. H. W. Smyth, *Aeschylean Tragedy*, pp. 1–32; F. Wehrli, ΛΑΘΕ ΒΙΩΣΑΣ, pp. 83–97.

[2] For the religious background of Aeschylus, and especially for the absence of a conception of divine love for man, much may be culled from C. F. von Nägelsbach, *Nachhomerische Theologie*, pp. 58 ff., even though these pages deal with later periods as well.

[3] See above, pp. 20–22; 36 f.; 43 f.; and cf. *Pers.* 107–116.

[4] *Alastor* is unknown to Homer, and is first named by Aeschylus, as the son of *Ate* (*Pers.* 821; cf. 353); Clytaemnestra claims to be herself the *Alastor* of past crimes (*Ag.* 1500–1504; cf. 1475–1480), but the chorus regard this as an evasion of responsibility (*Ag.* 1505–1508; see below, p. 128). *Alastor* has been compared with the Devil, but seems to be more specialized or functional, as blood calling for blood; he is the δαίμων γέννας of *Ag.* 1476 (cf. 1481 f.).

[5] See above, p. 17; below, pp. 133; 135; see J. C. Hild, *Démons*, pp. 153–191; see further H. J. Treston, *Poine*, cited below, Appendix 14.

[6] Cf. J. Girard, *Sentiment Religieux*, pp. 372–407.

[7] Τύχη is seldom personified in Aeschylus, and means ordinarily luck (the outcome of events that can be neither foreseen nor controlled by man) rather than fate; it may be

divine jealousy (φθόνος),[8] or of the *nemesis* that attends *hybris*;[9] and there are the many ancient forms of Fate, among them one not to be found in Homer, that of the family curse and hereditary guilt, a doom which may impose even on the innocent, like Oedipus or Orestes, the necessity of committing fresh crimes in expiation of old crimes. In all this inherited material there is little that can be ascribed to the mystical religions, even though Aeschylus, native of Eleusis, must have known something of their teaching;[10] Delphic Apollo has hardly succeeded in teaching men that murder may be expiated by the purifying of the murderer, without recourse being had to endless new murders; there is scanty suggestion in earlier literature, or indeed in Aeschylus himself, of any faith in human immortality.

At every point Aeschylus has transformed his inherited materials, pouring new wine into these old bottles.[11] Of the traditional myths he chooses only those that are fitted to express the ideas that interest him, in particular, his conception of human destiny; to these myths he adds the defeat of the Persians at Salamis. Whatever is mean or grotesque or casual in the myths that he utilizes, he transfigures into something sublime both by the loftiness of his style and by his exhibition of the action as the vehicle of a universal law; at the same time the characters, even though they are primeval gods or the heroes of the dawn of Greek legend, are presented in terms of almost contemporary Greek political and religious life. Of the innovations of Aeschylus in the technique of the stage none is more important than the addition of the second actor, which makes possible clashes of principle, even though it is only in the later plays that opposing characters actually confront one another. To his conviction that the doom of an individual is only a moment in a longer process, his frequent if not invariable custom of presenting trilogies contributes powerfully; the emphasis of Sophocles, in single concentrated tragedies, will be on the character and consequent fortunes of their protagonists. And Aeschylus has mastered the art of creating a foreboding atmosphere, of creating suspense, and of leading his characters step by step to the inevitable doom that awaits them.

All this, however, is but the means by which Aeschylus achieves the

either good or evil, and may occasionally be associated with divinities. (*Ag.* 661 f.; but hardly *Suppl.* 523.) See further H. Meuss, *Tyche bei den attischen Tragikern*, pp. 4–7; E. G. Berry, ΘΕΙΑ ΜΟΙΡΑ, pp. 19–21.

[8] *Ag.* 904; cf. 1008 ff.

[9] *Pers.* 345; 354; 362; 514; 818 ff.; *Ag.* 370 ff.; 468 ff.; cf. E. Tournier, *Némésis*, pp. 127–142.

[10] For resemblances and differences between Orphic teaching and the thought of Aeschylus with regard to sin and the family curse, cf. W. K. C. Guthrie, *Orpheus*, pp. 234 f.

[11] G. Murray, *Aeschylus, the Creator of Tragedy* (Oxford, 1940), pp. 205 f., and *passim*, defines the originality of the poet as consisting in (1) the transfiguration of the inherited myths, (2) innovations in stage technique, and (3) transformation of ideas.

transformation of traditional ideas.[12] The grossness of the older conceptions of the gods he refines, as in dealing with the passion of Zeus for Io,[13] and in showing the violence of the "new tyrant" Zeus toward Prometheus at last stooping to reconciliation with the rebel. The old belief in the jealousy of the gods toward mere prosperity he is one of the first to reject, as he protests that it is only impiety that begets ruin.[14] Thus *phthonos* is replaced by *nemesis*, just retribution. That "the sinner must suffer" is a "thrice-aged precept," doubtless older than the coming of Zeus.[15] Yet it is not only the sinner who suffers; Io is wholly innocent, Prometheus though defiant at least defies Zeus for the noblest reasons, and Orestes does not commit murder because he is of a murderous disposition. How are their sufferings to be reconciled with divine justice? Io's sufferings are conceived to be the means by which ultimately beneficent results are to be brought to pass;[16] and the sufferings of Prometheus, too, which are inevitable under the old reign of violence, will cease in the enlightened new era of reconciliation, and he will receive divine honors.[17] Orestes suffers because of the weight of an inherited curse; but whereas Eteocles has regarded his family curse as irresistible, and himself as helpless,[18] Orestes commits his terrible deed of vengeance voluntarily, and for pure motives, at the express command of a god; what is more, the gods will presently be found to sanction a termination of the vicious circle of blood-vengeance, as justice is crowned by mercy; so the curse will at last be laid to rest.[19] For the curse is now conceived by Aeschylus to be nothing absolute, but rather a terrible hereditary propensity that reappears in successive generations; but each individual is free to yield to it or to resist. God offers man the occasion of sinning;[20] and, if he yields, and commits the initial sin (πρώταρχος ἄτη, *Ag.* 1192) God helps him to his ruin.[21] From now on, he is no longer free, but is doomed.[22]

[12] It is somewhat surprising that M. Croiset should have found in Aeschylus no original or profound philosophic ideas, but merely thought drawn from the myths and the powerful statement of commonplaces (*Hist. de la Litt. Grecque*, III, pp. 192–200).

[13] *Suppl.* 571–599.

[14] *Ag.* 750–762; see below, p. 294.

[15] *Choeph.* 313 f.; cf. *Pers.* 813 f.; *Ag.* 1564.

[16] See below, p. 111.

[17] See below, pp. 118 f.; 123–125.

[18] *Sept.* 689–691; see below, pp. 115 f.

[19] *Choeph.* 1075 f.; *Eum.* 1045 f. cf. further L. E. Matthaei, *Studies in Greek Tragedy*, pp. 180–182: Aeschylean tragedy "first emphasises the idea of a pursuing destiny, only in order eventually to deny it. . . . It is possible to escape the family curse by perfect purity of motive. . . . The whole force of the Aeschylean plays lies in the reaffirmation of the strength of the human will."

[20] Aeschylus, frag. 156 (Niobe): *θεὸς μὲν αἰτίαν φύει βροτοῖς, | ὅταν κακῶσαι δῶμα παμπήδην θέλῃ.*

[21] *Pers.* 742: *ἀλλ' ὅταν σπεύδῃ τις αὐτός, χὼ θεὸς συνάπτεται.* "Heaven helps him who helps himself," for worse, as well as for better.

[22] Cf. Aristotle's distinction between original free acts and habits, good or bad, which are no longer free, *E.N.* 1114a16–21; see below, pp. 327 f.; and J. Adam, *Religious Teachers*, pp. 147 f.

What is true of the hereditary curse in the scheme of Aeschylus is true also of his conception of fate in general.[23] Firm believer in the inevitable rule of retribution for sin and of ultimate justice, he is not a believer in predestination in any mechanical sense. Prometheus defied Zeus voluntarily,[24] and looks forward to the day when Zeus will voluntarily [25] come to terms with him. But is Zeus, in turn, himself entirely free? Behind him stand the Moirai and the Erinyes, whom not even Zeus may escape.[26] But not even this is predestination; the fatality to which Zeus is subject is not mere mechanical necessity but is the moral nature which he must in time assume, and which therefore defines his freedom of action. To this moral law, Zeus approximates himself through the long perspective of time; the power in the universe at last becomes good; justice is done; and mercy seeks out the pure in heart. Human suffering, to be sure, remains; but it is no longer the result of divine jealousy or vindictiveness. Sometimes it is the deserved punishment of sin. But sometimes it is that mysterious and ruinous recoil of misfortune from good fortune which is inevitable in the changing realm of *physis* or *tyche*, an unexplained residuum of evil or *ate* in the universe which can not be explained on moral grounds, but which may be viewed objectively with the eye of tragic irony, or felt sympathetically in pity or fear.[27] And always, Zeus has decreed, the personal experience of suffering leads to enlightenment: "we learn by suffering"; "wisdom cometh by constraint." [28] This enlightenment the sympathetic chorus and, by the same token, the audience may share; "this I have learned from gazing on thy ruinous fortune, Prometheus." [29]

What is this hard-won wisdom, this discipline of adversity? Is it merely that of "a sadder and a wiser man," bruised but fore-armed for the next encounter, and taught by very fear to be cautious and restrained? [30] Is it the wisdom that comes not through another's precept, but only through bitter experience, a wisdom not only of the mind but of the moral fibre? "In sleep the anguish of remembering suffering flows into the heart, and health of mind comes to mortals in their own despite." [31] Is it the wisdom

[23] On fate in Aeschylus, or in Greek tragedy generally, some useful material may still be gleaned from such treatises as those of H. Blumner, *Ueber die Idee des Schicksals in den Tragoedien des Aischylos* (Leipzig, 1814); J. Wieberg, *De Fato Graecorum Quid maxime probabile sit Quaeritur* (Iena, 1869); cf. also below, Appendix 16: Fate and Character in Sophocles.

[24] *P.V.* 268: ἑκὼν ἑκὼν ἥμαρτον; K. Lehrs, *Populäre Aufzätze*, pp. 206–212, argues that μοῖρα is supreme, and that man's freedom of will is the source of tragedy.

[25] *P.V.* 177–179, 194; 260; cf. 220, of the past.

[26] *P.V.* 511–520; see below, pp. 124 f.

[27] Cf. Solon on *ate* (see above, pp. 36 f.); W. Jaeger, *Paideia*, pp. 253 f., emphasizing *ate*.

[28] *Ag.* 173–178; *Eum.* 520 f.

[29] *P.V.* 553 f.

[30] Cf. *Eum.* 522: ἐν δέει; see below, p. 133.

[31] *Ag.* 179–181; cf. *Job* 33, 14 ff.

that discovers through no royal road, but in hardship, even in defeat, new moral resources, of resolution and independence? [32] It is all this and something more. It is the tolerance and sympathy and forgiveness which only suffering can discover in a universe of fellow-sufferers. It is the lesson that Achilles learns in the presence of Priam.[33] Zeus it is who decrees it, because even he is capable of learning by suffering and surrender and forgiveness, in his dealings with Prometheus and Io and Orestes; mere retribution was the law of the older order.[34] Nor is the wisdom of suffering any longer the isolated fortitude of the individual, a humanistic *tlemosyne*; it springs from the heart of a *cosmos* that is close-knit and sensitive in every part. All nature groans and travails in sympathy with the suffering Prometheus.[35]

What is pathetic or tragic in the lot of a single character, viewed apart, thus becomes a matter of far-reaching justice when viewed as an example of the tremendous sway of the moral law, or even of universal physical laws. Aeschylus is not concerned merely to trace the harrowing experiences of Agamemnon or of Clytaemnestra or of Orestes, but to show what must befall them because they are links in an everlasting chain; hence the value of the trilogy form, which Sophocles, intent on the problem of the individual, discards. Aeschylus boldly addresses himself to no less a task than the reconciliation of timeless conflicting principles or duties; fate and freedom, justice and mercy, the individual and the universal order, suffering and happiness. All this he achieves by imagining the conflict of Zeus and Prometheus, of Orestes with his moral dilemma, to have been settled once and for all, and in the only possible way, by a miracle of divine grace and "persuasion" in the deepening of the character of Zeus, a miracle moreover perpetuated in the august court of the Areopagus, whose code is at once just and merciful.[36]

[32] Cf. Herodotus VII, 101–104.

[33] *Il.* 24; see above, pp. 26 f.

[34] See above, p. 107. It was on the cross that a Sufferer said, "Forgive them, for they know not what they do."

[35] *P.V.* 406–414; 431–435. The anthropomorphism, or should we rather say, the vivid imagination of the poet which sees the whole *cosmos* as alive and morally conscious, redeems these lines from the imputation of the "pathetic fallacy." With them, cf. the Stoic conception of Nature and *συμπάθεια*; see below, pp. 340; 352; 357; 362.

[36] The dénouement of the *Oedipus at Colonus* of Sophocles likewise turns on purification by suffering and deliverance from a rigid fate by a change in attitude of the Eumenides; but Sophocles does not so clearly make of the event a universal principle; see below, pp. 168–171; and cf. J. Girard, *Sentiment Religieux*, pp. 445 f.; W. Jaeger, *Paideia*, pp. 252; 256; 258. J. Adam, *Religious Teachers*, pp. 151–154, holds that Aeschylus raises, rather than succeeds in solving those mighty problems. A. W. Verrall, *Euripides the Rationalist*, pp. 220–224, dealing with the prologue of the *Eumenides*, shows how evasively Aeschylus reckons with the claims of Bacchus to the Pythian shrine in his attempt to bring it, and Apollo, under the overlordship of Zeus; see also above, p. 51 and n. 19; for "persuasion," see below, pp. 135–137.

The result of these daring undertakings is that Aeschylus purifies the conception of the Olympian gods, subordinating them to Zeus, who is, or becomes, all-wise and all-powerful, the embodiment of justice; his will is fused with Fate, which now is seen to be not only irresistible, but good; the Erinyes, once the chthonian powers of relentless vengeance, are persuaded to accept the beneficent rôle of spirits of fertility; and the sense of human guilt is appeased by the discovery that only wilful sin knows no forgiveness. The last lines of the *Oresteia* trilogy present in festal song the union of all-seeing Zeus and the rule of *Moira*.[37]

The *Suppliants*, the first part of a trilogy, and the most ancient European drama that has been preserved, deals with the arrival in Argos of the fifty daughters of Danaus and their father, descendants of Zeus and the Argive princess Io, who have fled from Egypt to avoid a loveless marriage with their fifty cousins; their appeal for protection to the king of Argos; and his decision, with the consent of his people, to defend them against the impending raid of the cousins. The rest of the trilogy included the conflict and a pretended reconciliation in which the marriages were to take place, followed by the murder of all the husbands by the brides, at their father's behest, — of all, that is, save one, whose bride Hypermestra truly loved him. (Their remote descendant Heracles was in due time to be the deliverer of Prometheus.) We need not here consider the reasons that have been suggested by modern scholars for their avoidance of the marriage. It seems clear that the reason is not consanguinity nor again the reflection of a changed social system from gynocracy (or "mother-right") to a patriarchal system and endogamy, nor any Amazonian hatred of marriage; it is rather the protest of the maidens against a forced marriage without love.[38]

The *Suppliants* thus represents a conflict of principles. On the one side stands the desire of the fifty sons of Aegyptus, and their resort to violence. On the other side stands the freedom of the individual maidens, speaking collectively as the Chorus, and their claim to wed, if at all, only as they may be persuaded by love. In the end it is love that wins Hypermestra;[39]

[37] *Eum.* 1045 f.: Ζεὺς ὁ πανόπτας | οὕτω Μοῖρά τε συγκατέβα.

[38] For brief refutations of the rejected suggestions, cf. H. W. Smyth, *Aeschylean Tragedy*, pp. 55–58; H. J. Rose, in *Folk-Lore* 22 (1911), pp. 277–291; 37 (1926), pp. 226–230; p. 229: "I am convinced that the plot of the trilogy turned on a moral question, the conflict between a woman's rights over her own person and her duty of becoming a mother." For the interpretation of the myth of the Danaids, cf. C. Bonner, *H.S.C.P.* 13 (1902), pp. 129–173; for many aspects of the *Suppliants*, reference may be made to the edition of J. Vürtheim, (Amsterdam, 1928), and to H. D. F. Kitto, *Greek Tragedy*, pp. 15–22.

[39] Aeschylus, *P.V.* 865: ἵμερος; and 858–869; frag. 44, a splendid tribute by Aphrodite to the cosmic power of love, for which she is responsible; on the mystic marriage of Heaven and Earth, cf. Pacuvius, 87–93 Ribbeck: Lucretius I, 250 f.; II, 992–1001; Virgil, *Georg.* II, 223–345; III, 242–279; *Pervigilium Veneris* 2–4; 59–67; J. Thomson, *The Seasons*, the latter

nor are her sisters averse to love.[40] But in the present emergency they invoke the right of fugitives to receive asylum and hospitality. Though they also advance claims on Argos based on their descent from the Argive Io, it is not these but rather the more universal claims of all suppliants and a more far-reaching humanitarian scruple that move the king of Argos to protect them.[41] And in their plea the maidens and their father invoke from beginning to end the mighty name of the defender of all suppliants, Zeus.

Now it must be accounted as no small difficulty for Aeschylus that the god whom he must exalt as the protector of suppliants is none other than the god who in the myth which he is unfolding has already made Io the victim of his passion. In the *Prometheus Bound*, for dramatic reasons, this aspect of the story will be even more sharply emphasized, in order to accentuate the ruthlessness of the Zeus against whom the humanitarian Titan is in rebellion. But in both plays we are invited to take a long-range view of the story, seeing what may have appeared to be mere brutal passion justified at long last as the necessary means by which a beneficent purpose is to be fulfilled in the return to Argos of the Danaids and the freeing of Prometheus. Aeschylus does not disown the brutal aspects of the myth that he has received; these aspects may be derived from the grafting of anthropomorphic on theriomorphic cult, or from the representation of astronomical phenomena. But in the *Suppliants*, at least, he minimizes them, for Zeus becomes the champion of the descendants of Io; and in the *Prometheus* he forecasts the mystical union of Zeus with Io, her release from suffering, and her glorious progeny (*P. V.* 848–873).

The *Suppliants* thus becomes a glorification of the god whose merciful regard for the weak and needy is sure. His ways are dark, but are revealed at last in splendor;[42] he is altogether just in his dealings with men (402–406). The divine law is far above the customs of men;[43] even in Hades there is the "other Zeus, who judges the sins of men" (230 f.; cf. 413–416); throughout the universe the will of Zeus is Fate.[44] The Zeus of myth is

part of *Spring*; similarly, with emphasis on human love, Sophocles, *Ant.* 781–799; Euripides, *Hipp.* 525–544; for Hypermestra, the only one of the Danaids to have illustrious offspring, since she alone had discovered that " 'tis love that makes the world go round," cf. the sly verses of Horace, *Odes*, III, 11, 25–52.

[40] *Suppl.* 1034–1042, in praise of Aphrodite and her attendants.

[41] *Suppl.* 455–499, a *locus classicus* for the rights of suppliants; cf. 940–944; the king of Argos, who has already had recourse to "Persuasion and the happy event that prevails" (523), urges that persuasion, not force, alone is valid.

[42] *Suppl.* 86–95, a magnificent passage, which ignores the woes of Io, dealt with a little before; cf. 574–599.

[43] For the divine law, *θέμις*, cf. 37; 336; contrast *νόμος*, 388; 390.

[44] 673: *ὃς πολιῷ νόμῳ αἶσαν ὀρθοῖ*; 1047–1049: *ὅ τί τοι μόρσιμόν ἐστιν, τὸ γένοιτ' ἄν.| Διὸς οὐ παρβατός ἐστιν | μεγάλα φρὴν ἀπέραντος*; and again 86–95.

becoming the symbol of a purer religion. Even if Aeschylus has no answer to the problem of the origin of evil, it is clear that he is convinced that the power in the universe is struggling toward goodness and mercy.

As the *Suppliants* shows the characters of a single myth acting in the light of an eternal principle, so the *Persians* (alone among extant Greek tragedies) interprets a great historical event in the light of a religious idea, the vengeance of God on arrogance.[45] Nothing could be more dramatic, or in a sense tragic, than the sudden reversal of fortune and humiliation of Xerxes at Salamis.[46] Yet in order to realize the full tragic possibilities of his theme Aeschylus has taken liberties with history. To enhance our sense of the arrogance of Xerxes, he idealizes his father Darius, whose equal arrogance and cruelty is recorded by Herodotus.[47] What is more, Aeschylus, like his predecessor Phrynichus, sets the scene not in Greece but in Persia, at Susa, before the tomb of Darius.[48] Aeschylus, too, not only by the remoteness of the scene confers on a recent event the necessary feeling of "old unhappy far-off things and battles long ago," but avoids the *nemesis* of the gods which would have attended any merely patriotic glorification of Greek victory. Mere victory, indeed, is not tragic; what does evoke pity and fear is the spectacle of defeat, or the sense that victory has indeed at last been won, but only by the aid of divine powers. The *Persians*, by exhibiting the impact of Salamis on the defeated people, excites pity and fear at the same time that it awakens in a Greek audience a sense of grateful relief for deliverance.

The shift of the scene has further consequences. It enables the poet to dilate on the *hybris* of the Persians; cruelty to men, arrogance against the powers of nature,[49] sacrilege against gods.[50] Yet the Persians are not mean, nor is Xerxes contemptible in defeat; rather does he inspire, like Shakspere's foolish King, Richard II, a real pity, once he has fallen; perhaps more pity, since we never see him till his disaster is complete. But above all the *Persians* is an indirect warning to the Greeks themselves, in their new confidence and power, that they must walk warily and humbly if

[45] W. Jaeger, *Paideia*, p. 254: "Here history actually becomes a tragic myth, because it has the magnitude of myth, and because the catastrophe of war so clearly displays the power of God."

[46] Cf. Seneca, *Thyestes* 614 f.: *Quem dies veniens vidit superbum, | Hunc dies fugiens vidit iacentem;* see also below, p. 368.

[47] See above, p. 86; and for Herodotus' moral interpretation of the Persian war, pp. 86–88.

[48] Phrynichus had learned from the grief and anger that met his *Capture of Miletus* not to dramatize again a Greek defeat; but in his *Women of Phoenicia* he avoided the opposite temptation, to gloat over Greek victory, by presenting Salamis from the Persian point of view.

[49] Such is the significance of the bridging of the Hellespont (*Persians* 68–72; 721–726; 744–751), τέχνη defying φύσις; cf. Prometheus, and see above, p. 31; below, p. 120.

[50] *Persians* 807–815; cf. 806, the chorus referring to Darius and Xerxes as gods.

they are to shun the *nemesis* that has prostrated Persian *hybris*. Not the Greeks, but the gods, achieved this victory.[51] Whereas Aeschylus with more than Miltonic grandiloquence piles up the great names of the Persians who were lost in the battle, not a single Greek is named, not even Themistocles. Greece, and in particular Athens, was at Salamis the instrument of God's will in chastising insolence.[52]

The battle having already taken place before the play begins, though the news has not yet arrived, there is no conflict of personalities; the drama consists rather in the gradual revelation of what has occurred, its effect on individuals, and the realization of its deeper meaning. The Chorus of Persian elders are filled with foreboding because no news of the Persian armament has come (10 f.; 64 f.; 115–139); yet there is irony in their reference to the divine deception, the *Ate*, the god-sped doom that has ever bidden the Persians to war (93–107). The queen-mother, Atossa, is likewise anxious (161). Her dream of last night, if she but knew how to read it, holds the kernel of the play; but neither she nor the elders appreciate its full weight (181–199; cf. 518–520). The Messenger brings sudden tidings; all the armament is lost. Atossa is stunned, and lamentation is left to the elders. Presently it transpires that Xerxes still lives, albeit crushed. For the disaster, and the details of the battle which the Messenger unfolds, he holds responsible "*Alastor*, or some evil *daimon*"; this sentiment every character and the Chorus will echo.[53] So it was that Xerxes did not perceive the guile of "the Greek" (Themistocles) or the *phthonos* of the gods but "spoke from an over-confident mind, nor did he understand what the gods would send."[54] The elders see in the catastrophe the hand of Zeus; with the plight of Xerxes they contrast the peaceful might of that Darius[55] whom Atossa counts happy in having died before this calamity.[56] Atossa is indeed learning by suffering to be on her guard (598–602); she offers libations, and bids the elders to invoke the shade of Darius, who now rises from his tomb.

Though unaware, in his abode below, of what has befallen his son, and having to be enlightened, Darius is nevertheless endowed with more than mortal wisdom, and preaches a sermon on the inevitable consequences of *hybris*. Salamis is the swift fulfilment by Zeus of prophecies that Darius had hoped would be long delayed, but that the folly of Xerxes has pre-

[51] *Persians* 101: θεόθεν . . . Μοῖρα (the chorus, before the news has come, of Persia's ancient propensity for war); 454: θεός (the messenger, of the battle); and *passim*.

[52] For incidental tributes to Athens, cf. *Pers*. 242; 347–349; 402–405; 792.

[53] *Pers*. 353 f. (Messenger); 472 (Atossa); 515 (Chorus); 725 (Darius); 911; 942 (Xerxes).

[54] *Pers*. 359 f.; 372 f. The messenger's suggestion of the *phthonos* of the gods is refuted by Darius, who attributes the disaster simply to the *hybris* of Xerxes (821 f.).

[55] *Pers*. 555: ἀβλαβής is an exaggeration.

[56] *Pers*. 709–712; see also above, p. 87.

cipitated; and God adds to the ruin that man begins (739–744). The *hybris* of Xerxes is contrasted with the virtues of previous Persians (who are greatly idealized, as is Darius himself); he heeds not his father's advice, not to attack Greece (790); more disasters are in store for Persia. All this comes from *hybris*, which, "when it has flowered, brings to fruit *ate*, whence is reaped a lamentable harvest."[57]

Now that the shade of Darius has returned to his tomb, the Elders contrast the peaceful power that he enjoyed (or so they are allowed to imagine) with the present disaster (852–908). Finally, in deep humiliation, Xerxes enters, and laments his hateful *Moira*, brought by a bitter *daimon*;[58] and the rest of the tragedy consists of alternate sorrowing by the King and his Elders, an Oriental keening of the dead. All this escapes making Xerxes ridiculous, because his plight, though pitiful and terrible, has been bound fast to the moral law of retribution. Let Athens, let the generations of men, give heed.

The story of Oedipus and his family is an old folk-tale which accumulated incidents and came to be variously interpreted by the poets. How much of the story was supposed to have been foretold by oracles, and therefore in a sense to have been predestined, was a matter of doubt.[59]

Unlike Sophocles and Euripides, who touch on the story of the Seven against Thebes in single plays, Aeschylus makes a trilogy of the Theban legend, tracing successive stages in the evil destiny of a royal house. His *Laius* must have mentioned the sin of Laius in carrying off Chrysippus, son of Pelops, a sin which brought on him the curse of Pelops,[60] a curse reinforced by the triple warning of Apollo that only if Laius died without child should he avoid ruining his city; this warning he ignored, and begot Oedipus, who in time slew his father and wedded his mother.[61] The *Oedipus* of Aeschylus may have included the victory over the Sphinx, the marriage with Iocasta, and the revelation of the past deeds of Oedipus, and must have included also the curse of Oedipus on his sons, called forth by some obscure motive, a curse which doomed them to fall in strife at

[57] *Pers.* 821 f. Cf. 813 f.: κακῶς δράσαντες . . . πάσχουσι (similarly *Choeph.* 313 f.); and the Pindaric advice that mortals should not be proud (*Pers.* 820; see above, pp. 76 f.). There is a curious pathos in the Epicurean parting advice of Darius to the Elders to enjoy the present while they may, since wealth helps not the dead (*Pers.* 840–842; contrast 709–712, cited above, p. 113).

[58] *Pers.* 909–912; cf. 1005–1007, *daimones* and *Ate* (chorus).

[59] See below, pp. 154 f.; 207 f.

[60] Athenaeus 602 f.

[61] *Septem* 745–758; 800–802; for the oracle to Laius, cf. Hypothesis to Sophocles, *O. T.* in the Laurentian Ms; also Euripides, *Phoenissae*, Hypothesis, and lines 13–20 (see below, p. 207); *Anthol. Graec.* XIV, 67; C. Robert, *Oedipus* (Berlin, 1915), Vol. I, pp. 66–68, distinguishing different stages in the growth of this oracle; and H. W. Parke, *History of the Delphic Oracle* (Oxford, 1939), pp. 303–305. It is important to note that the oracle of Apollo is of the conditional, or warning, kind; see below, pp. 121; 159; 402; Appendix 6.

each other's hands. This curse, like the earlier curse, is in the background of the third play of the trilogy, the *Septem*; but it is only in the last part that it assumes a preponderant rôle.

The sons of Oedipus, Eteocles and Polynices, were to rule equally: but Eteocles, for reasons that are not clear,[62] has exiled his brother, who with six other champions is coming against the seven gates of Thebes. At the news, Eteocles immediately recognizes the working, along with Zeus and Earth and the gods of the city, of "curse, the potent spirit of the vengeance of my sire."[63] Amid the military exigencies (and for sound dramatic reasons), the curse is then for some time all but forgotten. But later, after scenes charged with tragic suspense and irony, in which the successive attackers and defenders of the gates are named and described, and it at last appears that the two brothers are to confront one another — inevitably, one would say, yet Eteocles seems not to have anticipated this contingency,[64] — then it comes over him again that the curse of his whole house,[65] and especially his father's curse, have found him out (655; 695–720). Whatever may have been his power hitherto to act of his own accord, from now on he abandons himself to the power of the curse (689–691). And from now on the *motiv* of the curse is heard again and again in quickening tempo; before the battle, from the chorus of Theban maidens; after the catastrophe, from the messenger and the chorus alike; and finally in the lament for the dead brothers by their sisters and the maidens.[66]

For all that, the Theban trilogy is not a mere pageant of inexorable fate working through a curse.[67] Laius need not have carried off Chrysippus; later, he need not have disregarded the warning of Apollo. These offences seem to grow from some ruthlessness of character which Oedipus to some extent inherits, as we should say; or, as the Greek puts it, the curse of Laius condemns Oedipus to sin. Yet each of the crimes of Oedipus, his

[62] The relative ages of the brothers are not mentioned by Aeschylus; in *Septem* 1054 Antigone blames both brothers; but this last scene, 1010–1084, is possibly spurious, having been added after the composition of the *Antigone* of Sophocles; see below, p. 144 (for Ant.); p. 168 (for *O.C.*); p. 207 (for Euripides).

[63] Sept. 70: 'Αρά τ' 'Ερινὺς πατρὸς ἡ μεγασθενής.

[64] So, in the *Iliad*, Achilles and Hector, and in the *Aeneid*, Aeneas and Turnus, are kept apart till the last.

[65] *Sept.* 653 f., 689–691.

[66] *Sept.* 741–791, the chorus on the oracle given to Laius, and his futile evasion of it; 801 f., the messenger; 833 f., the chorus on the "dark curse of the house of Oedipus now fulfilled," 840 f., on the "father's curse," and 841–847, once more on the failure of the attempt of Laius to evade his oracle; finally in the lament of the sisters and the maidens, 886 f.; 893 f.; 898; 943 f.; 952; 977–979 (= 991–993, a refrain). [Also 1059–1061, if genuine; but see above, n. 62.]

[67] On this subject, see further H. W. Smyth, *Aeschylean Tragedy*, pp. 143–150, pages of great value for the whole subject of Fate in Greek thought.

murder of Laius, his marriage with Iocasta, and his curse of his sons, is the reckless working of something in his character. And now, in the *Septem*, Eteocles need not have driven his brother out. But there the matter stops; once there breaks on him the realization that the lot and his own marshalling of defenders have conspired to bring into conflict at the seventh gate himself and Polynices, whose claims to be a just assailant he repudiates, Eteocles sees himself caught in the meshes of a net; from now on he is a fatalist.[68]

The *Persians* showed *hybris* justly punished; the *Oresteia* will show the crime of Orestes justified and forgiven. Between the *Persians* and the *Eumenides*, stands the *Septem*, a stark tragedy unrelieved by any attempt at moral justification; for Eteocles, one feels, deserves a better lot than befalls him. Whatever may have been the rights of the quarrel between the brothers, Aeschylus is at pains to emphasize the patriotism of the defender of Thebes as contrasted with its arrogant assailants. Five of the seven assailants are characterized by their words and by the devices on their shields as guilty of *hybris*, as boastful, as defiant of the gods.[69] A partial exception seems to be the good seer Amphiaraus, wise and no boaster, who even denounces his accomplices Tydeus and Polynices; but he is cursed by his evil companionship; "the crop of infatuation (*ate*) yields as its harvest death" (597–614). As for Polynices, his curses, his vows of ruin or exile, and above all his pretensions to a just cause, are what steel Eteocles to his purpose; and it is noteworthy that it is Eteocles whose comments on the assailants, phrased in high moral terms, define the issue.

Eteocles himself is the earliest clearly drawn tragic hero in Greek drama, one whose character, on the whole good yet vitiated by the *hamartia* of fierceness and vengefulness and concentrated will to power, conforms to Aristotle's demands. Not irreligious, he is impatient with the panic of the Theban maidens and their helpless appeals to the gods; resolute and practical, he believes that the gods help those who help themselves. In the end he fails, but by sacrificing his own life he saves Thebes; his valor and his heroic endurance of a tragic doom ennoble a distressing tale of crime.[70]

In the Prometheus trilogy, Aeschylus returns to the theme of strife and reconciliation, and develops it on a cosmic scale. Hardly shall we find

[68] So in the *O. C.* of Sophocles, Polynices after his father's curse is revealed as a fatalist; see below, p. 168.

[69] Tydeus, ὕβρις, *Sept.* 406 (contrast the δίκη of Melanippus, 409; 415); Kapaneus, vain boasting (κόμπος) 425, and defying of the gods, 427–429; Eteoclus, defying Ares, 469; Hippomedon, ὕβρις, 502; Parthenopaeus, boasting, 529 f., 551. With their devices, beasts or other emblems of destruction, cf. again the Parthenon sculptures.

[70] On the isolation of Eteocles, alone with his destiny, and the deliberate omission of Polynices from the play, cf. H. D. F. Kitto, *Greek Tragedy*, pp. 46–49.

elsewhere in Greek literature, or even in the Bible, so daring a conception, spanning aeons of time and the vastness of space, of material power at first in conflict with moral ideals and then at last interpenetrated by them; but throughout the agonizing process the various members of the natural order vibrate with human sympathy for the suffering Titan in whom the struggle is chiefly incarnate. I say "chiefly," for the trilogy is unintelligible if we may not believe that his rival, Zeus, also embodies to some extent the tragic experience of suffering and enlightenment.

The *Prometheus Bound*, probably the first part of the trilogy, shows the punishment of Prometheus for having raised man from brutishness to civilization by the gift of fire and the arts, in defiance of Zeus. The *Prometheus Unbound*, of which scanty fragments remain, must have shown the ultimate reconciliation of Prometheus and Zeus and the setting free of the Titan. In the *Prometheus the Firebringer*, of which hardly more than the title is preserved, and which probably came last, it is likely that the poet dealt with the introduction into Attic cult of the festival of Prometheus, as a fire-god, somewhat as the *Eumenides*, after dealing with profound moral issues, foreshadows the later prerogatives of the Areopagus and the worship of the *Semnai Theai*.

The *Prometheus Bound*, though one of the most impressive and moving dramas ever composed, is very disquieting and very difficult to interpret if we look no further than its closing scene. The spectacle of the humanitarian Titan defying the authority of the cruel tyrant Zeus has awakened the instinctive sympathies of every spectator and reader, especially since the French revolution sanctioned the revolt of oppressed humanity against despotism. Yet we cannot fail to ask how the poet himself reconciled in his own mind the conception of Zeus that is set forth in this play not, to be sure, with the Zeus of popular Greek religion, but with the Zeus of his own *Suppliants* and with the Zeus of the *Oresteia* trilogy. Small wonder that the figure of Prometheus has been compared both with the crucified Christ and with Milton's Satan.[71]

A simple way of dealing with this perplexity is to hold that there is no solution; that in this play Aeschylus was inconsistent with his other plays; that he was satisfied here to represent a dramatic conflict, the *tlemosyne*[72] of a protagonist whose lack of *sophrosyne* has inevitably brought him into conflict with power; that he "threw his whole soul into the delineation of the heroic Titan, and for the purpose of effective contrast left Zeus as he found him in the legend."[73] But merely on the ground of art it may be

[71] See Appendix 12: Interpretations of *P.V.*

[72] Cf. *P.V.* 103–105.

[73] A. E. Haigh, *Tragic Drama of the Greeks* (Oxford, 1896), p. 112; Haigh compares Virgil's treatment of Dido, on which see also H. W. Garrod, "Vergil," in G. S. Gordon,

objected that an uneven contest between an evil Zeus and a righteous Prometheus would be no tragedy, but as Aristotle would urge, would be "merely shocking."[74] Nor may we ignore either what is known of the sequel in the rest of the trilogy or the mind of Aeschylus in general. Perplexed he may have been, but not inconsistent; rather his struggle, like that of the generations of man and of the *cosmos* that he depicts, was from primal *chaos* toward reconciliation and harmony. Even the crude ingredients of primitive myth and cult must serve his masterful mind.

The legend of Prometheus was a heritage from the past. In the Hesiodic *Theogony*, the myth of the sacrifice in which Prometheus tricked Zeus is partly aetiological.[75] In Hesiod's *Works and Days* the myth of the theft of fire by Prometheus and the vengeance of Zeus is intended to account for the origin of toil, which is there considered to be an evil.[76] So far, Prometheus is a clever meddler in the divine dispensation, and is so far evil. On the other hand, Aeschylus has inherited with his fellow-Athenians the ancient Attic cult of Prometheus, a fire-god, a culture-hero whose gift to man of *techne* is a blessing. But so far as he is a Titan Prometheus is hostile to the Olympian gods; in particular, he is the rival of another fire-god and patron of the arts, Hephaestus.[77]

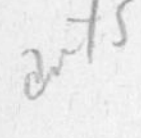

The innovations which Aeschylus has introduced into the myth all enhance the moral grandeur of Prometheus and correspondingly disparage the character of Zeus, so that in the extant play, at least, our sympathies are bound to be with the rebel. Aeschylus ignores the tricky sacrifice of Prometheus (and the jar of Pandora); he stresses the prophetic wisdom that Prometheus has gained from his mother, the Titan Themis-Ge.[78] In particular, he utilizes the tradition that Prometheus possesses a moral weapon in having learned from his mother a secret about the son, destined to be mightier than his father, who will be born to Thetis; for ignorance of this secret imperils the safety of Zeus, who may wed Thetis.[79] Zeus is furthermore in danger because at the time when he dethroned his father Cronos he laid guilty hands on him and received his father's curse. Finally, the ruthlessness of Zeus is exhibited by the introduction of Io, a recent victim of his passion. In the sequel of this play,

*English Literature and the Classics* (Oxford, 1912), pp. 150–156. L. R. Farnell, "The Paradox of the *Prometheus Vinctus*," *J.H.S.* 53 (1933), pp. 40–50, similarly suggests that Aeschylus let his (and the Athenians') admiration of Prometheus run away with him in this play, but escaped any change of ἀσέβεια by patching up the ending of the play. For a reply to Farnell, cf. H. D. F. Kitto, cited below, p. 124, n. 103.

[74] See above, p. 93.

[75] See above, p. 29.

[76] See above, pp. 30–32.

[77] See above, p. 30, n. 100.

[78] *P.V.* 211–213; 873 f.; the *Theogony*, 507–510, makes Prometheus the son of Clymene.

[79] Cf. Pindar, *Isth.* 8, 30–52; but Pindar does not connect the secret with Prometheus.

however, the liberation of Prometheus is effected not merely, as in the Theogony, because Heracles, at the behest of Zeus, shoots the eagle that has been gnawing his vitals and then sets him free; for there are new motives, indeed so many tokens of reconciliation that some of them seem superfluous. The centaur Chiron, wounded by Heracles, craves release from his immortality of suffering, and is allowed to become a voluntary, expiatory offering for the suffering of Prometheus.[80] Zeus has already given up his hostility to all the Titans, and liberated them; the curse of his father Cronos is thus no longer to be feared. There is further proof of the relenting attitude of Zeus in the fact that the liberator Heracles is a descendant of the once persecuted Io. And Prometheus himself has at some point in the action given utterance to his secret, and thus saved Zeus. Doubtless we shall never know in what order these motives were introduced by the poet; but there can be no doubt as to his chief intention, which is to represent the outcome of the conflict as a harmony won by mutual concessions.

We may now examine a little more closely the character and treatment in our play first of Prometheus, and then of Zeus. In the struggle with Zeus of the brutal Titans, creatures who rely solely on force, shrewd Prometheus has on the whole rightly disowned his fellows, and sided with Zeus and helped him to victory. Then, finding that Zeus in his hour of triumph proposes to act with no regard for feeble humanity, but to "destroy the whole race and create another new race" (234 f.), Prometheus has rebelled and frustrated the intention of Zeus. This is perhaps his first real offense; and his motive is pity and "philanthropy." [81] A good motive, no doubt; but primitive gods, and for that matter primitive human justice, give little heed to motives; we know, too, the proverbial reward of "good intentions." Whether the plan of Zeus was a magnificent scheme for a better world, we have no means of judging; if it was, then Prometheus rashly thwarted progress, and proceeded to perpetuate the pre-moral world of humanity, endowing it with the means of survival, but not necessarily of moral advance. If, as seems more likely, Zeus was merely indifferent to man, of whom he "took no account," [82] then Prometheus for better or for worse at least is rescuing man from annihilation. His offense is rebelliousness; but it can be counted an offense only as measured by the standards of Zeus, which are on this hypothesis not moral standards.

The means by which Prometheus saves man are of two kinds. First, he

[80] Cf. *P.V.* 1027–1029; Apollodorus, II, 5, 4, 5; II, 5, 11, 10.

[81] *P.V.* 241; 445 f.; cf. 10; 28; 123.

[82] *P.V.* 233 f. For a Malthusian view of the "plan of Zeus" in relieving the earth of surplus population by the Trojan War, cf. the *Cypria* of Stasinus, II (see above, pp. 63 f.); there the motive suggested is pity.

has prevented men from foreseeing their death, by planting in them "blind hopes" (250–252); blind, because deceptive, since no mortal can live forever, yet in a sense necessary, since ordinary men will hardly undertake activities that look to ends beyond the immediate future if they must expect to die forthwith.[83] So Prometheus at first (624 f.) would spare Io the knowledge of the toils that await her. This is the one grain of truth that Aeschylus chooses to preserve from Hesiod's myth of Pandora, in which man is allowed to retain Hope in an evil world.[84] In the second place, Prometheus steals fire for man, fire which is "man's teacher of every art and his mighty resource."[85] The various arts and sciences that he bestowed on man, and that he recounts, are not all derived from the use of fire; but they all in some way illustrate the use of reason, of skill and inventiveness (442–471; 476–506). They are all forms of *techne*, that intellectual mastery which the Greeks distinguished from the gifts of *physis*;[86] they represent the power that the Ionians sought through knowledge; as its teacher, Prometheus is termed, by the hostile agents of Zeus, "sophist," or "wiseacre" (62; 944); as its practitioner, he will at last become the recipient of a local Attic cult (here only as a fire-god, rival of Hephaestus). *Techne*, in a word, is the means by which man is to achieve civilization, something higher than the primitive *dolce far niente* of Hesiod's picture of the Golden Age.[87] Yet there is something lacking in *techne*. It can by medical science find remedies for disease and suffering, but not from death; to this effect is a significant addition of Sophocles, in the magnificent stasimon of the *Antigone* that glorifies man's achievements.[88] Even more significant is the inclusion by Sophocles of "the moods that mould a state," and the veiled dismay of his chorus that any one should have challenged the authority of the state. Lacking in the vision of Prometheus is any recognition of social and political ways and means or ideals; quite naturally and pardonably it goes no further than instinctive humanitarianism and provision for elementary human needs. When Protagoras in his turn makes use of the myth of Prometheus, as he is reported (or used as a mouth piece) by Plato, he takes pains to supply the deficiency.[89]

[83] This is what G. Santayana calls "animal faith," as opposed to "scepticism"; it is the will to live. Cf. also F. Wehrli, ΛΑΘΕ ΒΙΩΣΑΣ, pp. 6–10. For a slightly different interpretation of the present passage, cf. H. Kuhn, "The True Tragedy" (1942), pp. 55 f.

[84] See above, p. 30.

[85] *P.V.* 109–111; 254–256; Aeschylus does not imply, as does Hesiod, *Works and Days* 50, that man originally possessed fire, but had lost it through the reprisal of Zeus for the trick of the sacrifice; see above, p. 30, and n. 104.

[86] See above, p. 31; below, p. 289.

[87] See above, pp. 31–33.

[88] *P.V.* 478–483; cf. Sophocles, *Ant.* 332–375, and see below, p. 146.

[89] See below, pp. 244–246.

In challenging the authority of Zeus and its ruthlessness, Prometheus has committed an act of *lèse-majesté*, what Aristotle would consider a *hamartia*, and has done so voluntarily, expecting to suffer the consequences, though not, to be sure, to suffer so terribly.[90] Being a "lover of man," he suffers like a man, arousing pity and fear; being immortal, a God-man, his suffering is eternal, unless some unforeseen contingency shall set him free. His initial *hamartia*, then, is the deliberate theft of fire, a theft which Hephaestus in particular may be expected to resent; the corollary of the theft is the thwarting of the plan of Zeus to destroy the human race. But the theft is also an offence against the new order of gods in general.[91] It is an individualistic challenge[92] to the discipline and security of a system, the system for which he has helped to win power, and to which through impatience of its purposes he has now turned traitor. To be sure, as in all such cases, we shall reserve judgment with regard to the rightness of his conduct till we have seen whether the system that he has challenged is itself righteous, and whether his own course contains the seeds of ultimate blessing. But all that must lie in the future; for the present confronted by a choice between evils, connivance with Zeus or rebellion, he has chosen the course that his conscience and ours must approve.[93]

But the *hamartia* of Prometheus goes further than the initial theft. That was the result of pity. To the theft is added an attitude of obstinate pride and defiance that is nothing less than *hybris*. After all, as Prometheus himself knows, and as the friendly chorus of Ocean nymphs remind him, neither he by his defiant suffering nor mortals by their *techne* can prevail over Zeus (508–514; 545–552). Nevertheless, he refuses to betray to Zeus that secret which would win his own release; he seems to think of the prophecy that it contains, and which is conditional (*if* Zeus weds Thetis, he shall be overthrown by her son), as something that actually is sure to be fulfilled.[94] It will indeed be fulfilled, if Prometheus does not reveal the secret to Zeus, and thus enable him to avoid his fall by not wedding Thetis; and by refusing to betray it to Zeus within the present play, he invites the catastrophe, his engulfment in the bowels of the earth for thirty thousand years. The present play shows him curiously toying with his secret; he gloats over his private possession of it as his power over Zeus and final means of escape (522–525); then, moved by pity for Io, he reveals

[90] 268–272: *ἑκὼν ἑκὼν ἥμαρτον, κτλ.*

[91] 7–11; 82 f.; 945 f.; cf. 110; note the emphasis both on thievery and on the offense against the gods.

[92] 542–544: *Ζῆνα γὰρ οὐ τρομέων | ἰδίᾳ γνώμᾳ σέβει | θνατοὺς ἄγαν.*

[93] Cf. H. W. Smyth, *Aeschylean Tragedy*, pp. 107–113; L. E. Matthaei, *Studies in Greek Tragedy*, pp. 6–8.

[94] On conditional prophecies and oracles, see above, p. 114, n. 61.

to her all except the name of the bride whom Zeus must shun (755–770); at this point he hints that Zeus could escape his fall only by setting Prometheus free, but that this act of liberation (through a descendant of Io) will occur "despite the will of Zeus." But what actually leads to the liberation and the revelation of the secret, in the sequel, is the voluntary act of Chiron, ironically foretold in the present play by Hermes as something utterly inconceivable.[95] In the end, as we know, Prometheus, who has learned through suffering, lays aside his *hybris* and comes to terms with Zeus, and Zeus meets him halfway; only such a consummation of the struggle could break the deadlock.[96]

The rivetting of Prometheus to the crag in the first scene makes our play of necessity somewhat static; it can only exhibit the successive moods of the sufferer as he is visited by other characters. Each of them is in some way a foil, and brings out a side of his personality, for each, on the other hand, "has some touch of Prometheus."[97]

Zeus, never visible as a character in the Prometheus trilogy, nevertheless is felt throughout in the acts of his agents, in what is said of him by others (chiefly in the *ex parte* utterances of his foe, Prometheus), and in the majestic powers of nature which he did not create but which are now his servants. That he is harsh strength without love or wisdom, is attested by the words and deeds of his henchmen, Kratos and Bia, Hermes, and even Hephaestus. His arbitrary treatment of man we have already considered. In fact the character of Zeus in the *Prometheus Bound* is above all political. As Cronos dethroned his father Uranus, and was in turn dethroned by his own son Zeus, so the regime of Zeus, the "new tyrant,"[98] must fear some future revolution. Now the first duty of any political regime is to secure its own power and continuance in office; especially is this true of a "tyranny" that has won its power by force, and above all of the early stages of its rule, before its authority has been established beyond question. The word "tyrant," associated in certain phases of Greek history with

[95] 1026–1033; cf. 27. On the steps in this transformation cf. L. E. Matthaei, *Studies in Greek Tragedy*, pp. 27–33.

[96] Cf. G. Thomson, ed. *Prometheus Bound* (Cambridge, 1932), pp. 3 and 10, comparing the pride and enlightenment through suffering, in the *Iliad*, of Achilles and of Agamemnon.

[97] G. Norwood, *Greek Tragedy* (London, 1920), p. 96: "Hephaestus, pity without self-sacrifice; Cratos, strength without reflection; the Nymphs, tenderness without force; Oceanus, common-sense without dignity; Io, sensibility to suffering without the vision which learns the lesson of pain; Hermes, the power to serve without perception of the secret of sovereignty." Most essential of all, continues Norwood, is Io, both for motive and for linking the parts of the trilogy; on her, as the expression of *tlemosyne* (n.b. 704: τλῆναι), the weakness out of which shall come strength, cf. L. E. Matthaei, *Studies in Greek Tragedy*, pp. 22; 33; for the rôle of the chorus and its varying attitudes, pitying, questioning, challenging, counselling submission, but at last sharing the lot of Prometheus, cf. Matthaei, pp. 15–22; W. Jaeger, *Paideia*, p. 263, emphasizing the purified emotion and tragic knowledge of the chorus.

[98] 312; cf. 96; 224; 326; 736; 761; 955 f.; 996.

force, arbitrary acts, and cruelty if not lust, was not idly chosen by Aeschylus to characterize the regime of Zeus.[99] Ironical is the title given him by Prometheus, "chief of the blessed gods."[100] Enough has been said already of the indifference of Zeus to man, and of his persecution of Io.

Despite his harsh measures designed at securing his position, Zeus is far from secure. Not only is he subject to the curse of his father Cronos (910–912), but he is at the mercy of the secret in the possession of Prometheus. All this Prometheus knows, armed by the wisdom of his mother, Themis-Ge. Even the Ocean nymphs darkly hint that Zeus may be dethroned by some stroke of force, even if he does not relent in his purposes (166 f.); and Prometheus boldly prophesies his fall: "Have I not seen two tyrants [Ouranus and Cronos] fallen from these citadels? And third shall I behold him who is now lord fall most shamefully and speedily."[101] That, at any rate, is what the future holds if Zeus (and Prometheus) do not somehow yield. But they do yield, in the sequel; and Zeus no less than Prometheus learns by suffering. Zeus heals Io; he allows Chiron to take the place of Prometheus; he liberates the Titans; he bids Heracles to set Prometheus free. Though we do not know who began the reconciliation, we are allowed to believe that the *Prometheus Bound* fulfills the prophecy of Prometheus, that even Zeus is somewhat humbled, and is taught by time as it grows old.[102]

Aeschylus invites us to take a long view of Zeus. In the *Prometheus Bound* he shows us not God, not even the Zeus of the *Suppliants* and the *Oresteia*, not even the Zeus of the Homeric poems, but the most powerful god of a still earlier antiquity in conflict with new civilizing and humanitarian ideas. At first, Zeus had power, but not intelligence; Prometheus had intelligence, but not power; man had neither; only a coalition of power and intelligence could result in goodness. The poet is not writing a study in comparative religion, but a drama in which the myth is the

[99] 35: ἅπας δὲ τραχὺς ὅστις ἂν νέον κρατῇ; cf. 149–151; 163–167; 187–189; 224–226; 326; 391; 403–406; 649–651 (the lust of the tyrant); 735–740. So Sophocles in the *Oedipus Tyrannus* plays on the associations of the word, raising in the minds of the audience a disturbing surmise; what if Oedipus, so wise but so vehement, may prove to be not only a "king" but a "tyrant"? See below, p. 307, and n. 86.

[100] *P.V.* 170: μακάρων πρύτανις; cf. 96: ὁ νέος ταγὸς ("prince") μακάρων. So T. Hardy, on the last page of *Tess of the D'Urbervilles*: "'Justice' was done, and the President of the Immortals, in Aeschylean phrase, had ended his sport with Tess."

[101] 956–959; cf. *Ag.* 168–175. On the whole theme of "old king," "young king," and related matters in folk-lore, cf. J. A. K. Thomson, "The Religious Background of the *Prometheus Vinctus*," *H.S.C.P.* 31 (1920), pp. 1–37; summary on pp. 31–37.

[102] 908: ταπεινός; 926: μαθήσεται; 981: ἀλλ' ἐκδιδάσκει πάνθ' ὁ γηράσκων χρόνος. These phrases are spoken, to be sure, while Prometheus (though supposedly endowed with prophetic knowledge of the future) still believes that Zeus will actually fall. But they apply to the changed attitude of the Zeus who does not fall; the Zeus whose will leads to the pardon of Orestes (see below, pp. 134–137). G. Murray, *Aeschylus*, p. 99, goes so far as to say that "Zeus repents more than Prometheus."

important thing. Rather than deny the existence of the crude, primitive Zeus, he accepts him, but urges that he was capable of growth and moral advance; that force and intelligence and goodness could be (or, to speak as a dramatist, once upon a time actually were) fused at a given moment in pre-history. It is hardly too much to say that Aeschylus is the creator of this new Zeus.[103]

If Zeus appears, then, to have been in the mind of Aeschylus a progressive being, we may ask whether the poet conceived of anything still more ancient, more inclusive, more powerful, more righteous, a frame of reference to which this tremendous development may be related. And Aeschylus does not disappoint us. To the suggestion of the leader of the Chorus that Prometheus may some day be not less mighty than Zeus, he makes answer:

"Not in this way hath all-ordaining *Moira* decreed that these things shall be fulfilled, yet after being racked by countless woes and sufferings I am to escape these bonds; but craft (*techne*) is far weaker than necessity (ἀνάγκη)."
"Who then holds the helm of necessity?"
"The triformed Moirai and the ever-mindful Erinyes."
"And Zeus, is he weaker than those?"
"He may not avoid what is destined (τὴν πεπρωμένην)."
"What is destined for Zeus but endless rule?"
"Ask not, neither set thy heart on knowing."

And Prometheus "veils in mystery" his secret for the present (511–525). But he has already given us the most precise indication that is to be found in Aeschylus of the relations of Zeus and Fate. Behind the upstart god, stronger than he, armed with (or identified with) a necessity that defies *Techne*, and in partnership with the Erinyes, the earliest guardians of moral and physical law, stands *Moira*, Fate.[104] She guides all things; she is the moral law that Zeus violated when he laid hands on his father, and thus came under the sway of the Erinyes; she represents even the pattern

[103] Cf. H. D. F. Kitto, "The Prometheus," *J.H.S.* 54 (1934), pp. 14–20; H. W. Smyth, *Aeschylean Tragedy*, p. 120: "Aeschylus is an evolutionist as regards both gods and men."

[104] In *Il.* 19, 86 f. (cited above, p. 21), Agamemnon groups Zeus, *Moira*, and Erinys together, as responsible for his *ate*; cf. Pindar, *Paian* 6, 94 (see above, p. 71, n. 129); and *Mel. fr. adesp.* 5 Diehl (*Moirai* associated with Zeus), cited also below, p. 383. But in *Il.* 16, 433–458, Zeus dares not transgress the ruling of *Moira* to save the life of Sarpedon (see above, p. 15). On ἀνάγκη (*P.V.* 514 f.; cf. 105), here conceived both as impulse to cosmic action and as obstacle to interference, cf. Simonides 4, 21 Diehl (see above, p. 68), and W. Gundel, *Ananke und Heimarmene*, pp. 26–29; elsewhere in the play note ἡ πεπρωμένη αἶσα (103 f.; cf. Herodotus I, 91, cited above, p. 86) and Ἀδράστεια (936), equivalent to Νέμεσις, and an innovation of Aeschylus (cf. St. G. Stocks, in Hastings, *Enc. Rel. Eth.*, V, p. 788). These and other terms (εἱμαρμένη, δαίμων, δίκη, θέμις, ἄτη, ἀλάστωρ, etc.) are often identified by Aeschylus with the will of Zeus; the significant point is that here *Moira* is opposed to him.

to which the developing character of Zeus must conform; she is the law of progress, the philosophy of history in its successive stages;[105] of her law, far better than of the rule of Zeus, may be used the term "harmony."[106]

Yet *Moira* plans only in the most general terms, allowing temporary aberrations and the sufferings of individuals that are the stuff of tragedy. In many a concrete case there is no absolute good, but only a conflict of goods and duties in which man must choose his course in the light of conscience. So Antigone chose; so Prometheus, caught between the power of Zeus and his pity for man, made his choice, but by his suffering helped to close the gap between Zeus and man, between power and right. And so Orestes was caught in the terrible dilemma of duties that brought men crime and suffering, but that in the end discovered the way to peace. The study of the Prometheus trilogy leads us straight on to the *Oresteia*.

The *Agamemnon* presents the return to his home, after the fall of Troy, of the Greek commander-in-chief, and his murder at the hands of his wife, Clytaemnestra. The *Choephoroi* shows the murder of Clytaemnestra by her son Orestes, in vengeance of his father's death. In the *Eumenides* we see Orestes first pursued by the Erinyes, then tried and acquitted at Athens by the Areopagus; and the avenging Erinyes transformed into august guardian spirits. Each play, of course, has its internal unity and consistency; but it is utterly impossible to appreciate any one of the three without considering its relation to the rest of the trilogy, to the preceding and the consequent course of events. For the *Oresteia* contains two dramas: first, the external fortunes of Agamemnon and his family; and, behind this drama, the vindication of the moral law of fate, exhibited in the action and interpreted by the chorus.[107] In this sense, the action of the Agamemnon originates in the "primal *ate*,"[108] the curse of Thyestes, who had been tricked by his brother Atreus into feasting on his own children. But the curse cannot be allowed to rest with the murder of Agamemnon; he must be avenged; hence the *Choephoroi*. But Clytaemnestra, too, must be avenged; hence the pursuit of Orestes by the Erinyes, in the *Eumenides*, till at last the vicious circle of blood-vengeance is broken by the appearance of a new moral order. Beyond this moral thread of terrible obligations that links the parts of the trilogy, the poet contrives various reminders

[105] On the "succession of orders" and the progress of Zeus, cf. L. A. Matthaei, *Studies in Greek Tragedy*, pp. 33 and n. 4; 36–41.

[106] *P.V.* 551 f.: οὔπως τὰν Διὸς ἁρμονίαν | θνατῶν παρεξίασι βουλαί (the chorus, with a view only to the present situation). On "harmony" as the goal of Greek religious thought, especially of Aeschylus, cf. J. Girard, *Sentiment Religieux*, pp. 353–371, and *passim*.

[107] Cf. J. Girard, *Sentiment Religieux*, pp. 428–439; H. W. Smyth, *Aeschylean Tragedy*, pp. 151–153; 160 f.; W. Jaeger, *Paideia*, p. 257; G. Murray, *Spectator*, June 22, 1934, p. 962.

[108] *Ag.* 1192: πρώταρχος ἄτη. Aeschylus does not take the blame back, like some other poets, to Tantalus, still earlier in the history of the house.

or anticipations of earlier or later action: thus, toward the end of the *Agamemnon*, the dismayed chorus cry, "Who may cast forth from the house the curse of the race?"[109] When Clytaemnestra, years after, is told that "the dead are slaying the living," and realizes that her own death is at hand, she calls defiantly, "Give me the murdering axe!"[110] After the death of Clytaemnestra, Orestes brings forth the very robe, blood-stained, in which his father was entangled and slain;[111] the sight of it arouses the onset of his madness and his vision of the Erinyes which closes the *Choephoroi* and which leads directly to the opening of the *Eumenides*.[112] And the constant allusions of the chorus, as of the characters, to the curse of the house and the inexorable power of Fate provide a recurrent motive that recalls us again and again to the single theme of the trilogy.[113] The major theme is enforced by many minor motives (such as the robe or "net" that caught Agamemnon), and by constant touches of irony (such as the prayer of Clytaemnestra that the Greeks at Troy may not have been guilty of *hybris*, followed almost immediately by the herald's account of the *hybris* of "happy" Agamemnon, whose death in turn follows.[114] Nor can Aeschylus escape the Greek fondness for punning (by the use of popular etymologies) on proper names: well was Helen named, for a "Hell" she proved to ships and men and cities (*Ag.* 681–698); and Cassandra found Apollo indeed her "Destroyer" (*Ag.* 1080–1082).

Yet the trilogy, so closely knit together by the theme of guilt and inevitable retribution, moves through the wills of human agents who are at least partly, or at first, free to choose their courses. We do not behold them developing within the limits of a single play; nor does Aeschylus, like Sophocles, seem to be asking "What kind of characters would have been likely to act thus and so?" Rather does he seek to show what sort of temptations and motives could have sufficed to warp the wills of noble characters so that they sinned and suffered as the myth reports them to have done. In motivation, the trilogy is rich.

In the *Odyssey* the questions are asked: "How was Agamemnon

[109] *Ag.* 1565; and see 1560–1566. Cf. *Choeph.* 1063–1076; see below, p. 132.

[110] *Choeph.* 885–889. The "dead" probably means Orestes, whose pretended death has been reported; but it applies as well to Agamemnon, who, though dead, is mighty yet. And by referring to the ἀνδροκμῆτα πέλεκυν Clytaemnestra may mean the very axe with which she once slew Agamemnon.

[111] *Choeph.* 980–990.

[112] *Choeph.* 991–1075.

[113] Cf. J. W. Pugsley, "The Fate Motive and Its Echoes in the *Oresteia*," *T.A.P.A.* 60 (1929), pp. 38–47, calling attention to the dactylic phrases employed to express the motive. I have developed my discussion of the dramatic and ethical motives in the *Agamemnon*, with an analysis of the play, in *H.S.C.P.* 54 (1943), pp. 25–33.

[114] *Ag.* 338–348; 524–537. The audience, hearing the latter lines, might well recall *Pers.* 811–815.

slain? By what cunning did Aegisthus contrive the death of one far mightier than himself?" And the answer is simply that Clytaemnestra had joined Aegisthus in his domain, and that Agamemnon was wrecked near it and slain at a feast.[115] Aeschylus in the first play of his trilogy not only contrives the details of the action but convinces us that Agamemnon deserved to be slain, and that Clytaemnestra had what she regarded as ample motives for slaying him, motives that are introduced and emphasized in due order.

Agamemnon has little of the nobility that he sometimes displays in Homer. We do not see him in person till the play is half over; and what we have heard of him has done little to predispose us in his favor. His torment of heart when bidden to kill his daughter Iphigenia at Aulis, for the good of the fleet, is indeed powerfully pictured by the chorus (214–227), but so long before his entry that any sympathy for him that it may have aroused is all but forgotten. We remember only that he slew his daughter (or so he believed), that he is blamed for the deaths of countless Greek warriors, and that he has dealt arrogantly and sacrilegiously with Troy. When we see him, he is cold and proud. He counts the gods as merely his helpers in the sack of Troy.[116] He inveighs against pride in Solonian fashion;[117] yet he asks his wife's consideration for his captive Cassandra, victim of his own *hybris* (950–955). He shuns arousing the envy of the gods by treading on crimson tapestries (916–944), yet after a moment of vacillation, in which he is duped by his wife, he vehemently yields with a conventional word deprecating *phthonos*,[118] and goes in to his doom, which we hardly regret.

What Agamemnon loses in impressiveness and in our sympathy, Clytaemnestra gains; moreover Aegisthus, who in Homer is the arch-assassin, is kept by Aeschylus in the background till the end, when he claims the credit. What motives brought Clytaemnestra to kill her husband? Not merely, as in the epic story, was she enamored of Aegisthus (a motive here suppressed till the latter scenes of the *Agamemnon* and till the *Choephoroi*), but, as in Pindar,[119] she grieved for the sacrifice of her daughter Iphigenia; her she must avenge. There may be a grain of sincerity in her specious protestation of grief at her long separation from her

[115] *Od.* 1, 35–43; 3, 248–310; 4, 512–537; 11, 397–434.
[116] 811: μεταιτίους.
[117] 928 f.; see above, p. 36.
[118] 947–949; cf. 921. So Hamlet's father was slain when "unhousel'd, . . . unaneled;" and Hamlet refrained from killing the king when at prayer, in order to slay him when "about some act / That has no relish of salvation in't." (*Hamlet* I, 5, 76–79; III, 3, 73–95.) We may recall, too, that Shakspere deliberately presents the weaker side of Julius Caesar in his play; only after his death is he "mighty," and slays the living.
[119] Pindar, *Pyth.* 11, 22–25.

husband (858–904); that is, she resented it, and consoled herself with Aegisthus, so that love for her husband was turned into hatred. After Agamemnon's death, what she stressed in self-justification was the ancient curse of the house that constrained her to become its grim incarnation;[120] a claim, be it noted, which the chorus will accept only in part, since the ancestral *alastor* could at most be the abettor of her guilt.[121] Finally, it is significant that nowhere before her crime is perpetrated does Clytaemnestra show any vacillation of purpose; and afterwards there is no sign of remorse; indeed she mistakenly supposes that her own crime has brought matters to a conclusion (1567–1576). There is something magnificent in such determined and resourceful wickedness that claims, in the *Agamemnon*, our admiration, if not our sympathy. Only in the *Choephoroi* does Clytaemnestra forfeit every shred of claim on our feelings.

Of less importance for the action is the characterization of the other personages in the trilogy. Like Io in the *Prometheus*, Cassandra in the *Agamemnon* is the symbol of *tlemosyne*, of noble suffering[122] and the victim of *hybris*; like her, she provides a link between the immediate action and the past and the future. But whereas Io's rôle is wholly passive, Cassandra's unique gift of true but unbelieved prophecy enables her to visualize and to realize emotionally the horrors of the earlier crimes of the house of Atreus (1090–1099) and those afoot (1100–1135), including her own (1136–1177); then in a moment of collected vision to perceive the ethical unity of the whole story from the banquet of Thyestes to the appearance of an avenger of Agamemnon and herself (1178–1330). What is more, her suffering has given her a wisdom and a sympathy with suffering mortality beyond the mere fore-knowledge of the future vouchsafed to her by Apollo.[123]

Aegisthus embodies, even more than Clytaemnestra, the family curse, and wins our sympathy, if anything, even less than does Clytaemnestra. There is nothing heroic in his villainy; he appears only after Agamemnon is dead. This is a sign partly of his cowardice, partly of the poet's desire to keep some measure of sympathy for Clytaemnestra by not stressing her adultery till after the murder of Agamemnon; then, and only then, is he ready to prepare us for the revenge on the guilty pair that must follow.

The *Choephoroi* is still less a tragedy of character than is the *Agamem-*

[120] 1501: *ὁ παλαιὸς δριμὺς ἀλάστωρ.* Cf. 1468–1480, on the *δαίμων γέννης*; and *Choeph.* 910 f.: *Μοῖρα*; 924.

[121] *Ag.* 1505–1512; n.b. 1507 f.: *πατρόθεν δὲ συλλήπτωρ γένοιτ' ἂν ἀλάστωρ.*

[122] 1290: *τλήσομαι τὸ κατθανεῖν*; 1295: *τάλαινα*; 1298: *εὐτόλμως*; cf. 1302; 1304; 1316 f.; 1321–1323.

[123] With *Ag.* 1327–1330 (*ἰὼ βρότεια πράγματα, κτλ.*) cf. Sophocles, *O. T.* 1186–1212: *ἰὼ γενεαὶ βροτῶν, κτλ.* (see below, p. 158), and the theme of *μὴ φῦναι* (see above, p. 42); *Ajax* 125 f.; Pindar, *Pyth.* 8, 88–96; *Henry VIII*, III, 2, 352–358 (quoted above, p. 103).

*non*; supernatural agencies both control the action and dominate the imagination. Orestes slays his mother through no evil propensity of his nature, but simply because he falls heir to the horrible duty of vengeance which obligates him to set right one wrong by perpetrating another equally terrible wrong.[124] The counterpoise of filial duties has reached a deadlock; for Orestes to act is as wrong as for him to refuse to act, but not more wrong. Unlike Clytaemnestra, whose purpose was fully formed at the beginning of the trilogy, and who hardly needed to explain her motives, Orestes enumerates his motives: the command of Apollo, and the religious penalties that would attend his refusal to obey and thus to leave his father unavenged.[125] The chorus invoke on his behalf the divine powers of vengeance, the *Moirai* and *Dike*, and cite the ancient saying that "the sinner must suffer" (306–314). Just before he strikes down his mother, he resumes his case more briefly in rapid parley with her; if, as she pleads, *Moira* shared with her the blame for the murder of Agamemnon, *Moira* is equally to blame for her impending death.[126] After the slaying of Aegisthus and Clytaemnestra, he once more protests that his deed was just and was enjoined by Apollo (1026–1043), to whom the chorus commend him (1059–1064). All that might have been urged in defence of Clytaemnestra (the slaying of Iphigenia) is in this play passed over; in fact all the motives dissuading Orestes from his purpose are forgotten, till they appear to him in his madness in this last scene as avenging Erinyes. For the issue has come to an impasse, a battle of divine powers, and must be settled, if at all, in some new fashion. Electra, it may be said in passing, has played but a slight part in the action, and is hardly endowed with any vivid traits of personality; it was for Sophocles to concentrate interest in her character, leaving Orestes still the agent of destiny.[127]

In the *Eumenides* the conflict of moral obligations has become the paramount interest; the human interest is abated. Orestes is but the bone of contention between rival divinities: on the one hand, the blood-thirsty Erinyes; on the other hand Apollo, the blustering agent of Zeus and the exponent of the primitive *lex talionis*, but at the same time the sponsor of a ritual of purification that can purchase some measure of peace for the guilty. Athena, like a humane and resourceful chairman, guides the stormy proceedings to their conclusion. The moral outcome we shall consider presently.

[124] For the comparative absence of characterization of Orestes, cf. W. Jaeger, *Paideia*, p. 258; H. W. Smyth, *Aeschylean Tragedy*, p. 206: "Orestes is the *corpus vile* in the contest of moral forces that struggle for mastery."

[125] *Choeph.* 269–305; cf. *Eum.* 465–467. Of distinctly less weight is the fact that he has been deprived of his patrimony (135 f., Electra speaking; 301, Orestes; 864 f., chorus); cf. *Eum.* 757 f.

[126] *Choeph.* 910 f.; cf. 927, *αἶσα*.

[127] See below, pp. 162 f.

Apart from the characters in the *Oresteia*, we must note certain other dramatic devices that serve to link the thought and action with the central theme. Such, in the *Choephoroi*, is the dream that visits Clytaemnestra in the night before she is to be murdered, the vision of a serpent that she has borne and suckled and that bites her, sure token of some angry soul craving vengeance. Her conscience tells her whose soul it is, but not whom to fear; and it is Orestes who reads the dream aright.[128] She orders libations to be offered to appease the angry spirit (14–16; 22–59); but these libations are turned by Electra and the chorus, joined by Orestes, to another purpose: the evocation of the ghost of murdered Agamemnon from his tomb, and a communing with him, with prayers for vengeance. The remarkable scene that follows (84–163; 306–509) does not indeed culminate in the visible appearance of the dead, as in the *Persians*, where dead Darius rises and speaks; nor, as in *Hamlet*, does the ghost of the murdered king, uninvited, cry for vengeance. Rather does the scene, making use of pre-Homeric Greek belief, suggest that the dead not only dwell in the lower world but hover near their place of burial, dimly conscious of earthly things, with power to bless or to harm the living, and, if they have been foully murdered, craving vengeance. The ghost of Agamemnon, conjured up by affection, though unseen and though not speaking, makes palpable to the imagination the moral claims of the dead king.[129]

In the *Choephoroi*, Orestes arrives with his purpose fully formed to avenge his father; and the outcome is not in doubt. But the poet contrives to keep the emotional and moral tension high, chiefly by his use of the chorus, whose moods vary from despondency to triumph, from dismay to devout prayer and affirmation. Thus, after the brief Prologue, in which Orestes and Pylades make their reconnaissance (1–21), the Chorus of slave women, bidden by Clytaemnestra to offer libations to appease the angry spirit of Agamemnon, express in their entering song their doubts as to the efficacy of lustral rites to wash away bloodshed.[130] Moreover, fear has replaced security (54–60; 75–87); yet *Dike* holds her scale poised (61–65). The tone is on the whole despondent, yet pious. In the first episode (84–305) the purpose of the libations is changed by the advice of the Chorus to Electra; let vengeance for Agamemnon and justice be sought (106–163). Rising confidence, newly inspired by the recognition by Electra of her brother, culminates in a prayer to *Kratos* and *Dike*, and

[128] *Choeph.* 523–550; cf. 928 f. In the *Agamemnon* (279 f.) Clytaemnestra is scornful of dreams. In the *Eumenides* (94–139) it will be the turn of the ghost of Clytaemnestra to trouble the sleep of the Erinyes.

[129] See further C. E. Whitmore, *The Supernatural in Tragedy*, pp. 35–40.

[130] *Choeph.* 48; cf. 66–74; *Ag.* 1019–1021; *Eum.* 647–651; and *Macbeth*, II, 2, 60–63; V, 1.

above all to Zeus (244 f.; 246–254); religion is discredited, urges Orestes, if Zeus does not help the act of vengeance,[131] for Orestes is acting under the command of Apollo (269–305). The rite continues in a *kommos*, with alternate songs of the Chorus and of Orestes (or Electra). They invoke the gods; the *Moirai*,[132] Zeus,[133] the vengeful powers of the earth,[134] and Agamemnon himself,[135] who had better been slain at Troy than done to death at home (345–374). But the plea is not merely for vengeance; it is for vengeance under the guidance of *Dike*;[136] for hers is the ancient law that blood calls for blood, that "the doer must suffer."[137] Yet this means that every blow deserves a counter-blow (400–405; 461); not yet have we any glimpse of a final surcease of guilt, or any moral equilibrium. What justice can be done must be done by human hands, with the help of the nether powers (471–478). The mood is one of suspense.

The second episode (479–584) concludes the plea to Agamemnon, and initiates the plan of Orestes, which involves his bringing in disguise the report of his own death (554–584). While he prepares himself, the first *stasimon* of the chorus (585–651) expresses their wonder at the shameless audacities to which Eros has prompted women of legend;[138] but ever does *Dike* and *Aisa* (or Hermes, or Erinys) bring vengeance (635–651; cf. 622). The suspense is heightened. In the third episode (653–782) the false tidings of the death of Orestes arouses the well-concealed joy of Clytaemnestra, and the sorrow of the Nurse; Aegisthus is summoned, but (at the prompting of the Coryphaeus) without his guard. The second *stasimon* (783–837) is a prayer to the friendly gods for deliverance; it is full of hope that in a final act of bloodshed the old guilt of the house may at last be appeased; there is no hint of further ills to come. And now, in the fourth episode (838–934), after brief parley, Aegisthus goes to his doom. The moment before his death-cry is heard is filled by a tense song of the Coryphaeus; is it to be victory? The news comes quickly; and Orestes confronts Clytaemnestra, the guilty son his guilty mother. For his guilt now begins to appear, though at first momentarily, in the rapid charge and countercharge of the pair. Of her warning against her "vengeful hounds" we shall have an echo in the last scene from Orestes himself.[139] And the last words that he utters before driving her into the

[131] 255–263; cf. 483–488; and Soph. *O. T.* 895 f.; see below, p. 160.

[132] 306; cf. 464: *τὸ μόρσιμον.*

[133] 306, 382, 395, 409.

[134] 377; 399; 476–478.

[135] 315 ff., and *passim.*

[136] 308; cf. 461 f.

[137] 310–314; 313: *δράσαντι παθεῖν.*

[138] With *Choeph.* 585 f.: *πολλὰ μὲν γᾶ τρέφει δεινά, κτλ.* cf. Soph. *Ant.* 332–375: *πολλὰ τὰ δεινά, κτλ.*, with its similar note of misgiving; see below, p. 146.

[139] 924: *μητρὸς ἐγκότους κύνας*; cf. 1054.

palace to be dispatched are an admission that evil is to be met by evil.[140] But such misgivings are drowned in the third *stasimon* (935–972), a song of triumph. *Dike*, daughter of Zeus, has vindicated herself, first on Troy, then on the house of Agamemnon, and now on Clytaemnestra;[141] there has come Retribution (*Poine*), crafty but guileless,[142] slow but at last bringing all things to fulfilment;[143] and now is there light to behold.[144] Central in the song is homage to the heavenly law: "serve not the evil" (957–960). Yet in the *Exodos* (973–1076), when Orestes displays the bodies of the guilty pair and the robe in which Agamemnon was "netted," and once more justifies himself, the horrified Coryphaeus cries out that "for the survivor suffering bloometh" (1009); and Orestes in the midst of his self-justification betrays mingled feelings (1010–1017) and the first onset of madness (1021–1025; cf. 1048–1062). He sees indeed, or thinks he sees, the "vengeful hounds of his mother" (1054; cf. 924); and despite the exhortations of the Coryphaeus (1044–1047) he has no refuge but to throw himself as a suppliant on the protection of Apollo (1034–1043; cf. 1059 f.). Good wishes speed him; yet the last words of the play express the mingled relief and anxiety of the Coryphaeus, who reviews the three stages of the guilty house: the Thyestean banquet, the murder of Agamemnon, and this new deed. Is Orestes savior or destroyer? How can the wind of *ate* be lulled to sleep and stilled?[145]

The unanswered question that closes the *Choephoroi* finds its answer in the *Eumenides*. Both the murder of Agamemnon and the murder of Clytaemnestra can allege some moral justification, but each is also a crime; yet the two wrongs, representing two different levels of moral feeling, do not together comprise a right, but rather an *impasse*, a moral dead center. On the purely human level, no solution seems likely; the *Eumenides* therefore shows the moral dilemma taken under the charge of gods, the Erinyes pursuing, Apollo defending, Orestes. The case is then entrusted to Athena, who, after a preliminary inquiry, determines to leave the decision to the Athenian court of the Areopagus, now for the first time charged with such responsibility, but henceforth forever to be so charged. The curious fact that Athena after all leaves the decision to a human court, but intervenes to the extent of breaking the tie vote of the court by casting her own white pebble, is in part the poet's aetiological explanation of the court's prerogatives and its method of dealing with such a vote; but it also contrives, by associating divine sanctions with a human court, to suggest

[140] 930: *ἔκανες ὃν οὐ χρῆν, καὶ τὸ μὴ χρεὼν πάθε.*
[141] 935: *δίκα*; cf. 949.
[142] 936, 947: *ποίνα*; 947; 955.
[143] 935: *χρόνῳ*; cf. 955; 963; 965.
[144] 961 = 972.
[145] 1063–1076; there is a breath of hope in the word *μετακοιμισθέν*.

in more general terms that human justice is hereafter to proceed on the lines here followed. The tie vote of the just jurors duly recognizes the moral claims both of Orestes and of his prosecutors; the humane vote of Athena, followed by her appeals to the angry Erinyes to be "persuaded" to change their characters and to become kindly and honored spirits, symbolizes the only possible solution of the dilemma: pity, "the quality of mercy," divine grace added to the voice of reason. So in the "Disputa" of Raphael, the human agents gathered below have their counterpart in the glorious company of heaven.

The Orestes of Homeric legend was honored for having avenged his father; not before Stesichorus, earlier by only a hundred years than Aeschylus, was it suggested that he was pursued by the Erinyes. They are described for the first time in literature, and with almost archaeological detail, by the Pythian priestess in the present play.[146] Foul, wingless harpies, mere spirits of vengeance or "curses" (417) who dwell apart from the newer gods and clamor for blood, they naturally appear to Apollo, the defender of Orestes, as evil (71–73). Roused at the shrine of Apollo at Delphi by the unappeased ghost of Clytaemnestra, and angry at the escape of Orestes, they vent their spite. Yet it would be a serious mistake to overlook their ancient claims to represent a sort of *dike*,[147] a *dike* that has been challenged by Orestes aided by the "newer gods"; and they claim kinship with their sisters the *Moirai*.[148] But theirs is a limited sort of *dike*, that dogs a matricide (who spills kindred blood) but not the murderer of a husband; Athena shrewdly remarks that they care more for the name of *dike* than for its essence (430). Theirs is the letter that killeth, not the spirit that giveth life. Nevertheless the poet puts in their mouth not merely the "Binding Song," in which they assert their rôle as just, unforgetting spirits of vengeance (307–395), but in the second *stasimon* an even more extraordinary expression of the universal need of law and order, reverence, *sophrosyne*, *aidos*, and *dike*, and the contrast between the happiness of him who is just by free choice and the stormy way of the transgressor.[149] And the most amazing potentiality of the Erinyes remains: their transformation by Athena into *Eumenides* and *Semnai Theai*.[150]

If the case of the Erinyes against Orestes at the beginning of the play

[146] *Eum.* 46–59; cf. J. Harrison, *Prolegomena*, pp. 228–231. For the Erinyes in Homer, see above, p. 17; for the Erinyes and *Dike* in Heraclitus, see below, p. 225; for the development of the Erinyes in tragedy and in art, J. Toutain, "L'Evolution de la Conception des Erinyes dans le Mythe d'Oreste d'Eschyle à Euripide," *Melanges F. Cumont* (Bruxelles, 1936), pp. 449–453.

[147] N.b. *Eum.* 150; 154; 272 f.; 312; 511; 516; 525; 539; 550–564.

[148] *Eum.* 961–967; cf. 172; 334–340; 724.

[149] See Appendix 13: Second *stasimon* of *Eumenides*.

[150] See below, pp. 135 f.

represents a one-sided and partial conception of *dike*, so also does the defense of Orestes by Apollo both in the first scene and in the trial. Yet Apollo, prophet and interpreter of religious lore, is distinctly conceived as speaking not only for himself but for his father Zeus; and Athena is no less the spokesman of Zeus.[151] Thus the issue at stake is not merely the personal fortunes of Orestes but the conflict between the elder *Moirai*, with whom the Erinyes are associated, and the newer rule of Zeus, who guards the claims of suppliants and outlaws.[152] The conscience of the audience, and of mankind, cannot believe that Orestes, acting from no evil propensity but from a sense of duty, can be forever doomed to suffer; therefore he is conceived to have slain Clytaemnestra by the express command of Apollo, who must further defend him. Yet the same conscience cannot easily accept the pardon of a matricide; therefore Apollo must allow him to be hounded for a time by the Erinyes, till he is at last saved not by Apollo alone but by suasion in a human court under divine guidance (74–84).

Apollo's defense of Orestes is curious and not wholly convincing. First, he assumes responsibility for having commanded the murder of Clytaemnestra; so far he stands merely for the claims of Agamemnon to be avenged, a claim as primitive as that of Clytaemnestra which the Erinyes defend.[153] But the murder of Clytaemnestra, a fact not to be denied (588; 611), was (unlike the murder of Agamemnon) "justly" committed; that is, the motive was good, and the circumstances extenuated the guilty act of Orestes.[154] It is for this reason that Apollo has already "purified" Orestes by rites of cleansing, so that he is no longer a tainted person even if blood was once on his hands.[155] This Apolline ritual, symbolizing the attempt of the seventh century to go behind mere acts and to take into account motives, is a token of real moral progress; Athena recognizes it, for the fact that Orestes has been "purified" is given as one of her reasons for entrusting his case to the Areopagus (470–475). But Apollo goes further; he discriminates between the murder of Clytaemnestra, a just act of vengeance (203), and the wholly unjustified murder of Agamemnon, which was an attack on matrimony itself, a sacred bond instituted by Hera and Zeus and Kypris; this the Erinyes, so zealous to avenge bloodshed, have forgotten.[156] Here again we find traces of the newer moral code of

[151] For Apollo, *Eum.* 19; 616–621; 797–799; cf. 17 f.; 214; 229; for Athena, 663–666; 734–738; 826–828; 850; cf. 415.

[152] 90–93; cf. 232–234; 205.

[153] *Eum.* 84; 202 f.; 465–467; 579 f.; 594.

[154] 610: σὺν δίκῃ κατέκτανον; cf. 468.

[155] 237–239; 277; 281; 283; 287; cf. 232–234; 471–474; 576–578; see also below, Appendix 14; and for Oedipus and his motives, in Sophocles, pp. 160 f.; 169 f.

[156] 213–224. Apollo has nothing to say of Clytaemnestra's motives; Iphigenia is forgotten in this play.

the *polis*, which enhances the dignity of matrimony by extending the fellowship of the clan to include connections by marriage, so that murder of a husband is at least as wicked as murder of a father or a mother.[157] But it is when Apollo, in the Trial at Athens, and unfolding the decree or will of Zeus (618; 620), presents the formal defense, that his arguments are least convincing. He urges, first, that Agamemnon was a great king, therefore under the special protection of Zeus (626), and not to be slain by a woman, and treacherously.[158] And to the protest of the Erinyes that Clytaemnestra did not shed kindred blood, whereas Orestes did,[159] Apollo advances the astonishing argument, widely held in ancient Greece, that the mother is not the child's true parent, but only the nurse of the father's seed;[160] nay, even Athena herself was born of her father Zeus without a mother, — an argument which she herself presently accepts as a ground for casting her vote in favor of the male, Orestes (663–666; 736–740). It almost seems as if the poet must have written with tongue in cheek, meeting the bad and partial argument of the Erinyes with one as bad and as partial. But hard cases make bad law. The tie vote of the Areopagus sufficiently dramatizes the impossibility of deciding the issue on such grounds as either the Erinyes or Apollo have taken; while the acquiescence of the impartial Athena with the principle put forward by Apollo at least provides a motive, however absurd, for her breaking the tie, though it also evades the moral issue. Apollo and Orestes depart, the latter with gratitude to Athens and promises of Argive friendship foreshadowing the alliance of 458 B.C. (762–774; cf. 667–673).

The real solution of the deadlock, however, is achieved by Athena, goddess of reason. The Erinyes are infuriated by the acquittal of Orestes, and threaten to blight the land; Athena could rely on Zeus and his thunderbolt (826–828), but rather than resort to force she appeals to reason and to the majesty of Persuasion.[161] The Erinyes are not dishonored, as they suppose; the tie vote is evidence of that. But the will of Zeus, proclaimed by his prophet-son, has prevailed (795–799). Patiently she repeats her plea to these elder gods, "saving their face" as an Oriental might say: do not blight the land, but remain and receive a sanctuary and a cult, joining in the fortunes of the rising state. At last the plea moves the Erinyes;[162] they

[157] See Appendix 14: Blood-vengeance.

[158] 625–639. To the retort of the Coryphaeus, that as Clytaemnestra "bound" her husband in the fatal robe so Zeus "bound" his father Cronos, Apollo replies with a *distinguo*: the bonds of Cronos could be loosed; not so spilled life-blood, which can never be recovered (*Eum.* 640–650; cf. *Ag.* 1019–1021; *Choeph.* 48; 66–74); the thought is central for the *Oresteia*.

[159] *Eum.* 652–656; cf. 212; 605.

[160] 658–661. But Greek mythology also knew of Typhon, born of Hera without a father.

[161] *Eum.* 885: Πειθοῦς σέβας; cf. 794; 829; 970–972; 973: Ζεὺς ἀγοραῖος; *Suppl.* 523; 940–944.

[162] Note the shift from their lyric outcries to the iambics of the Coryphaeus at line 892,

sing a hymn of victory, pledging fair breezes, sunlight, fruitfulness, and piety for Athens; their own prerogatives remain (930 f.; cf. 950–955), associated with those of their sisters the *Moirai* (961–967); but thanks to Persuasion, and to Zeus, god of speech (970–972; cf. 988), good is to replace evil (974–978; 1012 f.). Though we are not so informed in as many words, Athena hints that the Erinyes, to whom will be given a sanctuary and a cult on the slope of the Areopagus, will be to the Athenians what the "Reverend Goddesses" (*Semnai Theai*) have been,[163] or what the "Kindly Ones," the *Eumenides*, have meant to Colonus and other regions of Greece.[164] And the play ends with a solemn joyous procession of Athenian citizens escorting the goddesses to their new home (a few hundred yards northwest of the theatre) — a procession that must have moved the Athenian audience to an equal religious joy and pride and patriotism.

"So to Pallas' citizens all-seeing Zeus and Moira bring their joint aid" (1045 f.), and the powers that have struggled for possession of the fortunes of Orestes are reconciled not only in his case but forever in a new conception of the social order and of the universe. The Erinyes even at first are not devils or incarnations of evil; they represent one aspect of *Moira* and of *Dike*, but only one aspect, vengeance inexorable and absolute, without regard either for the motives of the offender or for the outcome of their action. Whatever in their claims is just must not be defeated; the Erinyes must be appeased and honored and made the sanctions of the new code of justice embodied in the court of the Areopagus. Thus assimilated and feared they bring blessing to the land. This process of assimilation cannot be accomplished by the Zeus of the *Prometheus Bound*, the ruthless "new tyrant," who stands morally lower than *Moira*;[165] but it is within the scope of the Zeus of the *Suppliants* and of the end of the Prometheus trilogy, the Zeus who has learned by suffering to be wise and to feel pity, to relax the

---

and 900: *θέλξειν μ' ἔοικας*. A. W. Verrall, ed. *Eumenides*, pp. xxxii f., finds a "hiatus" between the refusal and the acceptance of Athena's invitation, and imagines that the lines expressing the reason that persuades them may have been lost, or may never have been written; or that some act or gesture takes the place of words. He compares the song sung on the Mount of Purgatory, hailing the forgiveness of sin, which Dante "could not understand" (*Purg.* xxxii, 61). The transition from vengeance to mercy and blessing accomplished by "persuasion" indeed demands the faith of the mystic.

[163] The benign *Semnai Theai* were already possessed of a cave beneath the hill of Ares. Of the name, there are hints in *Eum.* 1006; 1041: *σεμναί*. Not far below the Areopagus were found in 1932, among other Proto-Attic votive offerings, some terracotta plaques depicting a goddess (probably one of the Semnai Theai) and Serpents: cf. D. Burr, *Hesperia* II, 4 (1933), pp. 604–609; 636–640.

[164] See below, pp. 168; 170, for the setting of the *Oedipus at Colonus*. It should be noted that the name "Eumenides" does not occur in the text of our play, though ancient scholars used it in summarizing the content (cf. the *Hypothesis* of Aristophanes of Byzantium); and n.b. *Eum.* 992: *εὔφρονες*; cf. 1030; 1034; 1035; 1040; 868 f.

[165] See above, pp. 122–125.

letter of the law and to forgive in order that real justice may be done, to conceive of goodness not as something external and objective but as the will that moves from within. In the *Eumenides* it is his daughter Athena who speaks for him and who brings about the miracle that transforms vengeance into grace, not by force, for it is force that is being opposed, but by "persuasion."

A miracle it is, which we may the better understand, but not explain away, if we ponder the fable of the sun and the wind; the far beam thrown by a little candle, or by a good deed, in "this naughty world"; "the quality of mercy"; the "still small voice" that spoke after the wind and the earthquake, and the fire, and was the voice of God; the mystery of language itself, most Greek of all human discoveries and arts; by which thought is translated into action, and even hostile persons find a way to agree. The Greeks, who began by seeing in Persuasion (Peitho) only the handmaid of Aphrodite, ended by building altars to her as to the means of political harmony. Plato was pondering this cosmic mystery when he described the process by which "Reason persuaded Necessity," or again when he set forth the advantages of personal rule over impersonal law; Aristotle, when he discoursed on the superiority of *epieikeia*, equity, to law, because it is law "corrected" by a wise man with a regard for real justice. And the supreme doctrine of Christian theology, the incarnation, likewise mediates between the world of ideas and the world of phenomena; "The Word was made flesh, and dwelt among us." [166]

[166] See Appendix 15: References for *Eumenides*.

# CHAPTER VI

## SOPHOCLES

IT IS important for the understanding of Sophocles to remember that during his earlier years he was the younger contemporary and for a decade the rival of Aeschylus, drawing for the most part on the same store of legends, familiar with the same religious and moral ideas, and exploiting, or developing further, similar dramatic resources. It is even more important to realize that Sophocles, more fully than Aeschylus, came to express the currents of thought of his own age, an age in which Athenian national life reached its height, and in which the individual was learning to become himself, sometimes as citizen, sometimes at the expense of ancient traditions of social and family life; an age, moreover, in which the sophists were helping men to turn their minds from the world of external nature and of social controls toward the world of their personal problems.[1] The tragedies of Sophocles reflect the trends of this age. Instead of systematically justifying the divine order, or tracing the operation of fate or of a family curse through successive generations in trilogies of tragedies, he concentrates his attention in single dramas on the effect of tremendous forces on individual persons; he shows them battling with circumstance or with opposing persons; he reveals their motives. In a word, he creates the tragedy of character.

So much is commonplace; and we shall have to consider presently, in dealing with the several plays, how far Sophocles, working within this new field, has reckoned with fate. But we must not fail to appreciate at once how thoroughly the plays are impregnated with traditional ideas and forms of expression. The familiar religious and moral forces, for example, are constantly on the lips of the characters: the will of Zeus,[2] of other gods (sometimes vaguely designated as *θεός*, *ὁ θεός*, *θεοί*, or *δαίμων*); the moral laws guarded by the Erinyes; such divine agencies as prophecies and (more specially) oracles; and of course such traditional conceptions as *Moira*, *Themis*, *Tyche*, and *Chronos*.[3]

[1] See below, pp. 221–228.

[2] For the subordination of all other gods to Zeus, amounting to henotheism, cf. frag. 1129 Pearson: *οὐδὲ θεοῖς αὐθαίρετα πάντα πέλονται | νόσφι Διός· κεῖνος γὰρ ἔχει τέλος ἠδὲ καὶ ἀρχήν.*

[3] Cf. E. Abbott, "The Theology and Ethics of Sophocles," *Hellenica*, pp. 33–44; M. B. O'Connor, *Religion in the Plays of Sophocles* (Univ. of Chicago dissertation, 1923), pp. 109–

The thought of Sophocles is not to be discovered, any more than his style is to be discovered, merely in separate, detachable passages, in *gnomai* and set speeches;[4] it is ingrained in plot and character and the whole texture of his work. Moreover his thought, like his style, does not strain for novelty; it is plain, almost austere, in its truthfulness. Such originality as it may claim is in its probing of the familiar and the universal. Sophocles is for the most part orthodox, and in his practise illustrates the piety and restraint which his characters so often commend, and the violation of which leads to suffering.[5] Less inclined than either Aeschylus or Euripides to challenge the harshness of the old epic legends, he emends them, if at all, only tacitly. Unflinchingly he allows his characters to declare that evil, as well as good, comes from the gods; to refer to divine jealousy; or in momentary despair to revive the old pessimistic sayings that "God makes evil seem good to one whose mind he draws to mischief," or even that "never to have been born is best."[6] It would be rash to suppose that such sentiments are part of the essential thought of Sophocles. But it seems to be something more than the convenience of the dramatic poet that prompts the importance given to oracles; they are actually expressions of the divine will, and those who defy them (Laius and Iocasta, Oedipus and Creon) are confuted. The preoccupation of the poet with the problem of due burial (in the *Antigone* and the *Ajax* and the *Oedipus at Colonus*) also reflects a conservative and almost mystical attitude.

With the inquiries into the normal behavior and motives of human nature, initiated by the medical writers and continued by the sophists and by Thucydides, Sophocles is in full sympathy.[7] His speeches and dramatic debates show the influence of the sophistic rhetoric; he even provides a parallel for the contention of Protagoras that opposing arguments may be found on every topic.[8] But the profound admiration for the enterprise and resourcefulness of man which he shares with Protagoras is mingled

---

114, "Deified Abstractions and other Personifications"; pp. 115–128, "Expressions of Fatalism, Nemesis, and Pessimism."

[4] Sophocles, like the other tragic poets, makes use of *gnomai*, but is more apt to place them in the speeches and debates, above all in the *stichomythiai*; in the choruses, gnomic wisdom is absorbed in imaginative expression and in feeling. See above, p. 89, and n. 1; and cf. J. T. Stickney, *Les Sentences dans la Poésie Grecque*, pp. 193–213.

[5] Cf. Sophocles, *Phil.* 1441–1444, for εὐσέβεια; *Ant.* 1347–1353, for τὸ φρονεῖν, and cf. H. D. F. Kitto, *Greek Tragedy*, pp. 145–147; *Ant.* 1050, for εὐβουλία; *Ai.* 132 f. for the σώφρων; and for Sophocles himself, as εὔκολος, Aristophanes, *Frogs*, 82.

[6] Sophocles, *Phil.* 776: τὸν φθόνον πρόσκυσον; *Ant.* 620–624, on which see below, p. 146; *O.C.* 1225–1229, and below, pp. 170 f.; also E. Abbott, *op. cit.*, pp. 47–51.

[7] For the medical writers and Thucydides, see below, pp. 268–271. The phrase τὸ εἰκός used by them of the normal, reasonable, natural motive or action, is common also in Sophocles.

[8] Sophocles, *Ant.* 687; for Protagoras, D80 B6a, and below, p. 249.

with misgivings at human presumption.[9] Still more, Sophocles stands opposed to those warped conceptions of human conduct that find their ultimate sanctions either in man-made convention (*nomos*) or in the momentary advantage of the stronger or more shrewd (a common deduction from *physis*).[10] The *hybris* of an Ajax, the sophistic political creed of Creon in the *Antigone* and in the *Oedipus at Colonus*, the intellectual adroitness and selfishness of Odysseus in the *Philoctetes*, even the intellectual pride of Oedipus while king, are all obviously condemned by the poet. It is the straightforward Neoptolemus who serves as foil to Odysseus, while in the *Ajax* it is Odysseus himself who supplies the *sophrosyne* that the protagonist lacks, as Creon supplements Oedipus the king. But from Creon grown older and tyrannical, and upholding his arbitrary personal decrees, Antigone appeals to "the unwritten and steadfast laws of the gods, whose life is not of to-day or yesterday but of all time"; in other words, she appeals in a profound sense from human law to the law of nature which the gods themselves express and uphold, from *nomos* to *physis*.[11]

The fundamental piety of Sophocles need not be further illustrated at this point. The ultimate justice of the divine order he does not so much argue as assume, perhaps too easily.[12] But if the gods are just, they nevertheless tolerate or even cause great human suffering, as the characters of Sophocles again and again declare, now in moments of temporary discouragement, now because of a more lasting melancholy and a sense of man's feebleness.[13] Sometimes, to be sure, the suffering is the inevitable consequence of *hybris*, as in the cases of Ajax and of Clytaemnestra and of Creon in the *Antigone*; or comes, as in the cases of Oedipus and Antigone, through the defect of some noble quality of mind or heart. Even in these cases, however, except for Clytaemnestra, the suffering might have been avoided, or mitigated, but for the unexpected part played by *tyche*. Philoctetes is the victim of a special kind of *tyche*, both cruel and kind, a suffering actually sent by heaven for ulterior divine purposes, though he seeks to prolong his suffering unnecessarily through stubbornness.[14] We may see a similar mingling of forces in the lot of Oedipus, as it is at last revealed.[15] That is not to say that Sophocles exhibits what has

[9] Sophocles, *Ant.* 332–375; see below, p. 146.

[10] For *nomos*, see below, pp. 226–228; 244–252; for *physis*, pp. 258–264; 268–271; cf. 266 f.: and on the attitude of Sophocles, W. Nestle, "Sophokles und die Sophistik," *C.P.* 5 (1910), pp. 129–157.

[11] *Ant.* 447–457; cf. *O.T.* 863–872; and see below, pp. 144; 226–228; and J. Adam, *Rel. Teachers*, pp. 165–169.

[12] See below, pp. 162 f., on the *Electra*. But see Sophocles, frag. 107 (above, p. 95, n. 27).

[13] *Ant.* 621–624; *O.C.* 1225–1229, both cited above, p. 139, n. 6; *Ai.* 278; *O.T.* 1186–1196; *O.C.* 567; *Ai.* 125 f.; *Phil.* 436–452 (see below, p. 166); E. Abbott, *op. cit.*, pp. 47–49.

[14] See below, pp. 143; 164 f.

[15] See below, pp. 161; 168–171.

been called "poetic justice";[16] for there remains a discrepancy between the deserts of these tragic heroes and their fortunes which provides matter for the poet's irony and for pity. But what is more important to observe here is that for Sophocles suffering is by no means always the punishment of moral guilt; quite as often it is the noble but rash, or even the innocent of heart, who suffer, or who cause suffering, both in the plays of Sophocles and in life as we know it. Piety and wariness are not always enough; power and chance, *ananke* and *tyche*, do not always rest in the hands of justice.

If, then, the ultimate justice of the gods is to be upheld, it is not because they always prevent the suffering of noble heroes and give them material success but rather because they somehow provide that undeserved suffering be crowned by compensations of another order, compensations which vary with circumstances. Thus Sophocles sometimes invites us to consider such suffering not merely from the personal point of view of the sufferer, but in the light of the whole, or perhaps of some divine, far-off event. It is something like a vicarious atonement. The suffering of Antigone assists in the vindication of the moral order; that of Philoctetes in the divinely ordained fall of Troy; that of Ajax and of Oedipus in the blessings which they will bestow after their death on the land of Attica. Moreover even the personal glory which these sufferers win by assisting in such divine consummations may be held to outshine and outlast any more immediate and material success which they might have won.[17] As Plato will affirm, when a man is beloved by the gods, even suffering and other supposed evils will finally prove good, both in life and in death.[18] In death, yes; so Sophocles has shown. But in life? That is not so clear; yet even here Sophocles suggests how suffering may become victorious.

For the supreme compensation for suffering lies in its educative power. Man learns, first, that he has unsuspected powers of passive endurance, of *tlemosyne*.[19] He learns, too, that his will is free; his motives may still be pure, whatever the fell hand of circumstance may bring. Deianira "erred, intending well"; Oedipus was more sinned against than sinning.[20] Finally, over and above the potentialities of a noble nature, the product of inheritance (*physis*) and aristocratic training, there is the personal code of

[16] See above, pp. 93–96.

[17] Cf. E. Abbott, *op. cit.*, pp. 59; 65; J. Adam, *Rel. Teachers*, pp. 173–175; S. H. Butcher, "Sophocles," in *Some Aspects*, pp. 127 f.

[18] Plato, *Rep.* 613a; see below, p. 312. Once more the contrast is between seeming and reality.

[19] The *Philoctetes* best illustrates this point; e.g. 536–538: Philoctetes thinks no other man could have endured (τλῆναι) his experience; "but I have been slowly schooled by necessity (ἀνάγκῃ) to brook evils." (Cf. *O.C.* 8 f.) For the verbs τλῆναι and τολμᾶν, of bringing oneself to doing a courageous deed, cf. *Phil.* 82, 110, 481, 634.

[20] *Trach.* 1136; *O.C.* 266 f.; cf. frag. 665 Pearson: ἄκων δ' ἁμαρτὼν οὔτις ἀνθρώπων κακός.

the hero, his sense of honor or *arete*, which gains strength with the demands that are made on it, and which knows no compromise with lesser loyalties, or even with fate. Such is the faith of Plato's Socrates.[21] The characters of Sophocles "are the first who, by suffering by the absolute abandonment of their earthly happiness or of their social and physical life, reach the truest greatness attainable by man. . . . Dramatic action is for Sophocles the process by which the true nature of a suffering human being is unfolded, by which he fulfils his destiny and through it fulfils himself." [22] This is the essence of the humanism of Sophocles, and it brings us to our chief problem: the relation, in his tragedies, between character and fate.

That Sophocles recognizes, like all Greeks, the existence of what may be called fate, needs no demonstration. Nor is his conception of fate original, unless in the special prominence given to oracles; these we shall consider in dealing with the several plays. But we should note also the rather unusual, almost mystical way in which Sophocles regards *Chronos* and *Tyche*.[23] For Sophocles, time (χρόνος) is not merely the duration of successive events; it is frequently conceived as almighty (παγκρατής), alive and active and personal, with moral powers. Time "beholds all things";[24] it "soothes," [25] or "confounds" and "destroys." [26] Time, like suffering and nobility, teaches patience;[27] time alone reveals the just man, and finds out the culprit, sitting in judgment on him.[28] The vicissitudes of nature's cycle and of man's life are alike both made and marred by time.[29] So, too, the children of time, the months and the nights and days, preside over men's affairs,[30] and mighty is the opportune moment (καιρός).[31]

No less powerful in the affairs of men, and even less predictable, is

[21] See below, pp. 257–264; 274–276.

[22] W. Jaeger, *Paideia*, pp. 280 f. Homer's Achilles and the Aeschylean Prometheus in some ways anticipate the type. For the inherited *physis* of Neoptolemus as the source of his nobility (the best example in the seven plays), see *Philoctetes* 88–95; 874; 902–906; 971–973; 1013–1015; 1074; 1244; 1284; 1310–1313; cf. Pindar on φυά (above, p. 72); T. B. L. Webster, *Sophocles* (Oxford, 1936), pp. 35–49, who however overemphasizes this theme. For the power of Sophocles to live in his characters, and his "faith in the ultimate value of noble conduct to prevail, in some mysterious manner, against the destructiveness of things," see J. A. Moore, *Sophocles and Arete* (Cambridge, Mass., 1939), p. 74, and *passim*.

[23] For *Chronos* as a living, daemonic power in Orphic thought, see above, pp. 54; 56; for Pindar, p. 75, n. 156.

[24] Sophocles, *O.C.* 1453 f.

[25] *El.* 179.

[26] *O.C.* 609 ff.: συγχεῖ; *Ai.* 713: μαραίνει; *El.* 780: προστατῶν ("lowering").

[27] *O.C.* 7 f.: στέργειν . . . διδάσκει.

[28] *O.T.* 613–615; 1214 f.; see below, p. 158.

[29] *Ai.* 646–683; *O.C.* 607–623. (Two passages of supreme beauty and importance; cf. also *Phil.* 502–506.)

[30] *O.C.* 617–620; *El.* 1364–1366; *Ant.* 607 f.; cf. *Ai.* 131 f.; *O.T.* 1082 f.

[31] *Phil.* 837 f.

*Tyche*. Since there is no sure knowledge of the future and *Tyche* rules, argues Iocasta, 'tis best to live at random; and Oedipus, whose career has already been checkered, presently avows himself the son of *Tyche*, who will not dishonor him, and whose children, his kinsmen the months, have marked him now as lowly, now as great; a delusive reliance on a fickle power, as the event immediately proves.[32] Elsewhere *Tyche* often amounts to little more than luck, or its result, one's personal fortune, whether good or evil.[33] But when Philoctetes is told that his suffering has come "by a divine dispensation" (ἐκ θείας τύχης), he is to understand that what for him has hitherto appeared to be *tyche*, an unaccountable mischance, is now to be accepted as the expression of the divine will,[34] just as Oedipus finds necessity (ἀνάγκη) to be the expression of the divine mouth.[35] Finally, *tyche* itself may be viewed in terms of *ananke*. As it is "necessary to bear the fortune that the gods send," [36] so death itself is the gift of "necessary fortune," [37] while Tecmessa complains that "there is no harder evil among men than the fortune given by necessity (τῆς ἀναγκαίας τύχης)," by which she means her personal lot, the captivity forced on her by circumstance;[38] and she appeals for help against the "fortune threatened by necessity," thinking of the lot indicated by the prophecy of Calchas.[39] Thus for Sophocles both time and chance are symbols of living forces.

The humanism of Sophocles means above all the insistence of the poet on the dignity and importance of the individual character in his conflicts with opposing characters and with circumstance. Since he nevertheless continues to reckon with the traditional agencies of fate, it inevitably follows that many apparent or real discrepancies should emerge between the wills of his characters and the external forces that are still supposed to be absolute. The critics who have been concerned most either with character alone or with fate alone have been least troubled by the discrepancies; those who have tried to hold the balance even have drawn attention to tragic irony, or the pathetic contrast between appearance and reality, with perhaps some attempt to see in Sophocles as in Aeschylus a

[32] *O.T.* 977–979; 1080–1083 (see further below, p. 158); for other examples of *tyche* in *O.T.* see p. 154 and n. 78; in *Ant.*, pp. 145 f.

[33] Similarly δαίμων may be used of one's personal fortune, whether as a *fait accompli*, as in *Ai.* 534; *O.C.* 76, or as still to be realized, as in *O.C.* 1443 (see below, p. 168).

[34] *Phil.* 1326; cf. 1316 f. ἀνθρώποισι τὰς μὲν ἐκ θεῶν | τύχας δοθείσας ἔστ' ἀναγκαῖον φέρειν, on which see below, p. 165; *O.C.* 1585; E. G. Berry, ΘΕΙΑ ΜΟΙΡΑ *and* ΘΕΙΑ ΤΥΧΗ, pp. 22–26; and on the conception in Plato, below, pp. 299 f.

[35] *O.C.* 603: τὸ θεῖον αὐτοὺς ἐξαναγκάσει στόμα; 605: ἀνάγκη.

[36] *Phil.* 1326, cited above, n. 34.

[37] *El.* 48: τέθνηκ' 'Ορέστης ἐξ ἀναγκαίας τύχης. This, in Stoic terminology, is *fatalis necessitas*.

[38] *Ai.* 485 f.

[39] *Ai.* 803: πρόστητ' ἀναγκαίας τύχης.

tendency to moralize the conception of fate.[40] In considering the successive tragedies we must at least attempt, as Sophocles himself attempted, to see the workings of both fate and character.

The theme of the *Antigone* is the heroic resolution of the maiden to bury her brother Polynices, slain in the attempt to recover, as leader of the "Seven," the throne of Thebes from his brother Eteocles. Her attempt succeeds, in that Creon is at the last compelled to bury Polynices; but Antigone has meanwhile paid for her heroism with her life. Sophocles was free to invent the details of his play; the cyclic poem, the *Oedipodia*, had no mention of any decree against burying Polynices, nor of the defiance of Antigone.[41] Sophocles has probably invented this part of the story, attributing the interdict to the arbitrary, tyrannical Creon, and has done something to create sympathy for Polynices; Antigone he has isolated by creating a chorus of the opposite sex, and by avoiding any scene in which she and her lover Haemon meet. Thus the issue is drawn between the heroine, who upholds the sanctity of the family and the cult of the dead, and Creon, who asserts the sovereignty of the state and of his personal rule. In more abstract terms, the conflict is between the ancient religious ties of kinship and the dues of earth and the newer claims of the *polis* and its ruler. Each side states its case with the completeness of a sophistic debate, Creon arguing like any Thucydidean personage the reasons of state which justify his decree and the punishing of its transgressor,[42] Antigone appealing to the eternal law of the gods, an unwritten law, the quality of mercy; it is the appeal from *nomos* to *physis*, or at least to an *agraphos nomos*.[43] Both Antigone and Creon meet with disaster, she with living entombment and suicide, he with the death of his son Haemon and of his wife Eurydice.

What does Sophocles think of the issues, and what is his explanation of the outcome? It can hardly be doubted that his sympathies are chiefly with Antigone, in spite of certain harsh traits, the defects of her qualities, which flash out under great stress. Yet he allows her to die, a virgin

[40] See Appendix 16: Fate and Character in Sophocles.

[41] The last scene of the *septem* of Aeschylus, 1010–1084, which is perhaps spurious (see above, p. 115, n. 62) refers to an interdict against the burial of Polynices proclaimed by a herald in the name of the city's councillors, as well as to the motive of Antigone's resistance to the decree (her loyalty to kinship), but not to her having died as the result of resisting. Aeschylus does not refer to the relative ages of the brothers, nor does Sophocles in the *Antigone*; for the *O.C.* see below, p. 168.

[42] *Ant.* 162–210; 639–680; cf. Thuc. III, 37–40.

[43] *Ant.* 450–470; cf. W. Nestle, "Sophocles und die Sophistik," *C. P.* 5 (1910), pp. 129–157, esp. 132–139; R. Hirzel, Ἄγραφος Νόμος; see below, pp. 226–228. Readers of Thucydides must feel the tragic irony of the wretched fall of Athens, the proud city whose master Pericles had appealed to the "unwritten law" (Thuc. II, 37); indeed there is not a little of the "tyrant" in Athens, as Pericles himself admitted (Thuc. II, 63; see below, Appendix 38); so easily are appeals to noble ideals confounded by circumstance.

martyr. Is she quite perfect, and is Creon utterly wrong?[44] If so, Aristotle will be right in feeling that the outcome is merely revolting.[45] And it is clear that the last part of the play is intended to develop the tragedy of Creon, for whom a certain measure of sympathy is aroused; wrong-headed, repentant too late, he atones for his *hybris*. So evenly does Sophocles hold the scales. Is the issue then a deadlock and are Antigone and Creon both right, and both wrong? Is the conflict between family and state, individual and society, feeling and law, *physis* and *nomos*, insoluble, and is ruin the inevitable outcome?[46] Both Antigone and Creon fail to observe the wisdom or *sophrosyne*, which the chorus, loyal to the laws both of the land and of the gods (369), hold supreme, and to which they refer in the final lines of the play (1347–1353). But it is to be observed that it is especially the laws of the gods that they have in mind in these last lines and their comment immediately follows Creon's calamity; Sophocles is writing as a religious conservative. Why then does he cause Antigone to die? For we cannot fail to notice that the sequence of events is manipulated so that Creon's tardy attempt to save her is just too late. Ismene, the prudent sister who would refrain from defying Creon, survives; is she the expression of the *sophrosyne* that is to be admired? Strictly speaking, even the repeated attempts of Antigone to bury her brother were futile, and could never fully succeed against the opposition of Creon. Is not Antigone's piety nullified,[47] even if the impiety of Creon is punished?

There was nothing in the fixed data of the legend that required either Antigone or Creon to die. Antigone, to be sure, like all her family, are under the family curse of the house of Labdacus: so Antigone herself realizes at the outset of the play (2 f.), and so the Chorus remark once in her absence (583–615) and again to her face with consequent anguish on her part (852–856; cf. 857–868). There are conventional references to Fate on the part of the Chorus: with Antigone, already on her way to her tomb, they compare the legends of Danaë and of Cleopatra, both victims of Fate;[48] to the stricken Creon, who would welcome death as the best fate of all, they piously counsel resignation in the face of destiny.[49] It may be added that whereas the guard humorously remarks that he can suffer nothing but what is his fate,[50] Antigone bewails her passing before her allotted life is spent.[51] Similar are the references to *Tyche*. Sometimes it

[44] So H. F. Müller, pp. 29–35.

[45] See above, p. 93.

[46] So Boeckh, and Hegel, *Religionsphilosophie*, II, 114.

[47] So she herself asks, 921–928.

[48] 951: *ἁ μοιριδία . . . δύνασις*; 986 f.: Μοῖραι.

[49] 1328–1338: *μόρων . . . πεπρωμένης . . . συμφορᾶς*.

[50] 235 f.: *τὸ μόρσιμον*.

[51] 896: *πρίν μοι μοῖραν ἐξήκειν βίον*.

means mere chance (so the guard, 328 and the Chorus, 1182). Sometimes it is the equivalent of man's self-determination, as when Tiresias warns Creon (996) that he stands on the fine edge of *Tyche*; in other words, Creon's decision, which is within his control, will determine the course of the future. But the same word, *Tyche*, is used by the Messenger of the unaccountable, external power that controls men's happiness and unhappiness, as in the case of Creon: "*Tyche* raises and *Tyche* humbles the lucky or the unlucky from day to day, and no man can prophesy to men concerning these things which are established" (1158–1160).

In these passages we have reckoned with every important allusion in the play to external causes;[52] they are far from establishing a case for fatalism, and indicate rather the readiness with which men refer to external causes all that is unhappy or unforeseen. But that is all. The main springs of the action are the characters of Antigone and Creon. Antigone does what she does because she is the kind of person that she is, brave as well as tender, unlike her sister Ismene, whose heredity and circumstances are the same as hers. Creon also acts in accordance with his nature, and his *hybris*, which receives scope in his new tyrant's power, is punished by the gods, logically if terribly; for the loss of his son, caused directly by the death of Antigone, affects him in his most vulnerable point.

This play of character on character is also what absorbs the interest of the spectator. The successive episodes shift the emphasis, which the choral interludes subtly gather up. The prologue gives Antigone's point of view, the first episode Creon's, and the revelation that the corpse has been mysteriously sprinkled with dust; the beautiful choral song that follows (332–375) mingles admiration of man's inventiveness (*techne* mastering *physis*, as it were), with misgivings at the thought of any who may break laws of gods or men.[53] The second episode exhibits the clash between the "law" of Creon and the "unwritten law" to which Antigone appeals; the brute force of the man crushes the human weakness of the woman, but not the principle for which she stands. The chorus see the working of the ancestral curse, and of the power of Zeus who causes evil to seem good to one whom he draws near to Ate;[54] Creon, though unnamed, is in their mind. In the third episode, Haemon's pleading, which represents *vox populi*, makes Creon only more stubborn. The chorus sing of the power of Eros (who has animated Haemon). Antigone has now done all that is in her

[52] Unless we are to include also the remark of the Chorus, 621–624; see below, and n. 54.

[53] See above, pp. 139 f.; cf. 120; 131.

[54] 620–625. This is the nearest to the "jealousy of the gods" that we have in Sophocles; and it is not the poet's own view. For the sentiment and its expression in Greek and Latin, see Jebb's note on *Ant.* 622, and his Appendix, p. 255; also schol. on *Ant.* 620; and Nägelsbach, *Nachh. Theol.*, p. 56, comparing Eur. *Hipp.* 241; *Orest.* 79; *Troad.* 1036; *Phoen.* 1614; *Herod.* VI, 134, 135.

power; the fourth episode, in which she takes her leave of the world, shows her most human side. She thinks of other imprisoned victims of fate, but receives little comfort from the Chorus, who also sing, after she has gone, of other royal sufferers of a like fate.

The fifth episode opens; it is still not too late for Creon to relent and save Antigone. Tiresias gives him first a kindly warning; then, angered by his impiety, the sternest and most direct kind of threat of divine retribution; but it is finally to the counsel of the chorus that Creon submits, convinced at last that "one must not wage war with necessity."[55] Even now Creon could save Antigone if he hastened to the tomb; and the hope of the chorus is expressed in a hyporcheme. But in his new good intention Creon delays to perform rites for Polynices, and arrives at the tomb too late. Shall we say that this is mere luck, or is it again the character of a man who once more goes to extremes, inopportunely stopping to do what he lately forbade another do, and thus ironically missing the business in hand? In any case, Antigone could have lived, if the poet had wished her to live; she died because the poet intended her to die.[56] Creon himself puts various interpretations on the deaths of Haemon and Eurydice; of Antigone's death he has not a word to say, except in the most general terms: "all is amiss with that which is in my hands" (1344 f.). Haemon's death, he says, occurred not through his folly but by Creon's own folly (1269; cf. 1340); yet it was some god who cruelly smote him (1272–1275). For Eurydice's suicide, too, he accepts full blame (1319 f.; 1341), though he has acted unwittingly; yet he refers to it also as a new leap of doom (1346). These expressions, in his distraught condition, amount only to a confession that his own deeds have brought upon him the blows of retribution. And with that we must leave Creon, who has received rude but not undeserved justice.

There remains Antigone. The flaws in her character cannot be said to justify her terrible end, or anything like it. Yet she did what she did with full knowledge of the nature of the consequences. She fails to be rescued, as we have just observed, by a very narrow margin, and through something very near to accident; but there is a grim tang of reality about that. People do suffer through forces beyond their control and beyond their deserts. They are sometimes faced by intolerable moral alternatives. What matters for Antigone is that she went to her death believing that it was the result of her own free act, and that Creon meant her to die. That being the case, we would not have had her choose otherwise; she is nobler and more to be envied in her death than Creon after his empty triumph, living on without wife and son.

[55] *Ant.* 1106: ἀνάγκῃ.

[56] See above, p. 92.

The *Ajax*, next in order after the *Antigone* if it does not actually precede it, likewise has much to do with the question of the right of a dead warrior to burial, and likewise contains a debate on the merits of the question. But this is in the last part of the play, which shows how the great Ajax, though guilty of *hybris*, though humiliated and a suicide, won such vindication that he could become in later days one of the Attic heroes; doubtless an Attic audience was conscious of no slackening of dramatic interest even though the hero falls on his sword when the play is not much more than half over.

The suicide of Ajax, the expression of his wounded pride because the arms of dead Achilles had been awarded not to himself but to Odysseus, was part of the all but universal tradition; that Sophocles could not change, though he could glance with good effect at another tradition, namely that Ajax had died madly battling the Trojans; Ajax in our play thinks of such an end only to dismiss it as too gratifying to the Atridae (466–470). A deeply offended soul, Homer makes him turn aloof from Odysseus in silence in the world of the dead.[57] He is the type of unrewarded *arete*.[58] In Sophocles, too, Ajax is a warrior second only to Achilles, great-hearted, prudent at his best (119 f.), though not shrewd like Odysseus, and lacking in *sophrosyne*. In the past he has boasted that he needs no help from the gods (758–777); on being denied the hoped-for arms he loses self-control, and plans to kill the Greek leaders. This is *hybris*, as both Athena (127–133) and later Menelaus (1073–1083) rightly declare. There is a tragic fault, then, in Ajax, which if unchecked would work terrible mischief. It is checked by no less a being than Athena herself, who intervenes by afflicting Ajax with a temporary madness, during which he kills sheep and oxen instead of the men whom he takes them to be. It is his feeling of humiliation when he comes to his senses, and not merely his offended pride at losing the arms, that gives rise to his invincible decision to take his life. This is probably one of the innovations of Sophocles: the death of Ajax is still the direct outcome of his character, but as Sophocles has manipulated the story Ajax need not have died if Athena had not intervened and changed the effect of his murderous actions. But in that case he could never be revered by posterity as a hero. Athena therefore plays the part of fate,[59] not in willing his death, but in diverting his actions in such a way that the outcome, his character being what it is, will inevitably be his death, but may be followed by a sort of apotheosis. And her deed, it should be noted, is a *fait accompli* at the opening of the play.

[57] *Od.* 11, 543–551.

[58] W. Headlam, *C.R.* 17 (1903), p. 288.

[59] The divine origin, and therefore the inevitability of the madness is emphasized by the Chorus (186; 278 f.) and by Ajax himself (455 f.).

There has been difference of opinion as to Athena's motives. Clearly her first aim is to save her favorite Odysseus and the other chieftains, and through them the Greek host. So far her motive is wholly kindly and good. From the point of view of Ajax's immediate interests, however, it is disastrous; no wonder that Ajax complains that Athena has foiled him (450–453; cf. 401 f.), or that his wife Tecmessa protests that her woes would not have been sent save by the will of the gods, woes engendered by Athena for Odysseus' sake.[60] Yet Athena has no lasting spite against Ajax. She allows him to suffer the necessary consequences of his *hybris,* since only thus can the other Greeks be saved; but it is she who reminds Odysseus of the bravery and prudence of Ajax in better days (119 f.), and warns him against pride (127–133). Nor does she vindictively pursue Ajax after his death: "this day alone will the wrath of Athena vex him"; so ran the warning that came through Calchas (756 f.). The way is left clear, not indeed for his longer life, but for the vindication of Ajax to posterity; something which would have been quite impossible if she had allowed him to kill the chieftains. Here is an ultimate kindness. Moreover whereas Calchas explains the wrath of Athena that pursues Ajax this one day as caused by his pride in boasting in battle that he had no need of her help (758–777), a natural enough interpretation to come from the lips of a seer, Athena herself in the prologue, though warning against *hybris,* says nothing of any wrath on her part against Ajax.

Once Ajax comes to his senses, his mind is quite clear, and his mind is immediately made up to take his life: this purpose holds, though he deceives others about it, and shows little enough affection for the loyal Tecmessa. His death follows from his own will, not from any external fate, or even from Athena's will. To be sure the warning of Calchas stipulates that he may yet be saved if he does not go forth this day from his tent. As a matter of fact we know that he has already gone forth, so that this warning has no effect on the action; once more the death of Ajax is already, as it were, a *fait accompli.* That is the external counterpart of the fact that Ajax himself says nothing of the reasons that might move him to wish to live, and is deaf to them when Tecmessa supplies them.

Now that Ajax is dead, and has paid the full penalty for his *hybris,* it is his reputation that is at stake. Teucer, who represents his continuing interests, urges, against the decree of Menelaus, the right of Ajax to burial. But it is Odysseus, here the epic character rather than the contemptible Odysseus of the *Philoctetes,* yet even here moved by expediency and self-interest (121–196; 1365), who is at last successful in vindicating the honor of Ajax. After all, Ajax was a great warrior (1336–1345), and had been

[60] 950–953. H. F. Müller holds, pp. 54–56, that Ajax is the plaything of Athena, and that he is punished more than he deserves. As to the latter point, see below, pp. 150 f.

no traitor in the war (1132); though guilty in life of *hybris* he must not in death be the victim of the *hybris* of others (1091 f.). Athena no longer intervenes; but her very absence, leaving the field clear for Teucer and for her protégé Odysseus, is tantamount to her connivance in the rehabilitation of Ajax. From a dramatic point of view, too, it is more effective to allow mortals to bring to pass the change of sentiment about him.

So Ajax wins his vindication, and is made ready in time to become an Attic hero. But what justice can one see in the humiliation and suffering after which he wins this vindication? Has his *hybris* deserved such a *nemesis*? Several answers are possible. One may feel, with Teucer, that the gods bring such things to pass in a jesting mood, and observe the irony in Ajax having died on the sword given him by his foe, Hector, a fatal gift. "Was it not the Erinys who forged this blade? . . . I at least would deem that these things, and all things ever, are planned by gods for men" (1028–1039). Or one may see in the death of Ajax, as the Chorus do, the fatal result of his evil mood: "thou wast fated, hapless one, thou wast fated, then, with that unbending soul, at last to fulfil an evil doom of woes untold" (925–929; cf. 929–936). That is to say, as we might phrase it today, Ajax was an incurable paranoiac, and his humiliation and death were the necessary termination of his perverted mind. But one may look further, with Tecmessa. A fatalist herself, with regard to her own lot (485; 504; 516), she sees in the death of Ajax different aspects as it affects different persons: for the Atridae no gain, as they will later realize, for herself anguish, for himself the release that he longed for (961–974). He is the victim of the gods, not of the Greek chieftains.[61] If so, nothing is here for taunts on the part of the Greeks.

But we must note that there is not the least suggestion of forgiveness on his part, either of gods or of men; he seeks death merely as the best way out of a bad business. Even if good is to come after evil, it is not out of the evil that it comes; the apotheosis of Ajax is justified by his former heroism, not by the circumstances of his death, thus differing from the vindication of Jeanne d'Arc, or, to some extent from the vindications of Antigone and Philoctetes and Oedipus at Colonus. For the deeds which cause the deaths of Antigone and of Jeanne d'Arc are precisely their claim to our admiration. Philoctetes and Oedipus, though victims of circumstances beyond their control, and though not reconciled to their lots nor to their fellowmen who seek to profit by their lots, nevertheless become somehow the channels of divine power and grace. The humiliation and death of Ajax, however, though inseparable from the character which wins eventual apotheosis, are something apart from his glory; he becomes a hero not because of, but in spite of, the manner of his death. Both his

[61] 970; so A. C. Pearson interprets, *C.Q.* 16 (1922), p. 127, as against Jebb.

humiliation and his glory stem from his character because that character has two faces, that of the heroic warrior and that of the man who lacks *sophrosyne.*

If a moral must be drawn, it will be that which Agamemnon draws: "It is not the burly, broad-shouldered men that are safest, but the wise prevail in every field."[62] The "wise" Odysseus, patient and restrained, and even generous, certainly outlives the wilful, short-lived Achilles, and the boastful yet sensitive Ajax. Yet it is not always the wise and the successful to whom our hearts go out. Something more than a perverse sentimentality warrants our sympathy with the defeated, even when their defeat seems well deserved or at least logically explained. It may be irony or pathetic contrast, if the sufferer is generally worthy. Even if there be a moral and intellectual sense that the gods have done justly, there is a fellow feeling with the sufferer, and sorrow that he should have to suffer. And there is always wonder at the strangeness of fortune. This is of the essence of tragedy. "Many things shall mortals learn by seeing; but before he sees, no man may read the future, how he shall fare." So the Chorus sing at the very close of the *Ajax* (1418–1420); and the Chorus will sing, in similar strain, in many a play of Sophocles and Euripides.[63]

In the *Trachiniai* Sophocles shows the death agony of Heracles caused by the well-meaning attempt of his devoted wife Deianira to recapture his affection by a device (the robe anointed with the blood of the centaur Nessus, slain long before by Heracles) which she might have realized could bring no good to her husband. There is irony or pathetic contrast, then, between her good intentions (1123; 1136) and their appalling result; there is a further pathetic contrast between the heroic labors of Heracles in the past and his wretched end, an end not here relieved by any suggestion of his apotheosis. The contrast is enhanced by the difference between the triumphant entry of the herald Lichas (205 ff.) and the agonizing entry of Heracles (983 ff.). To be sure there was also a bestial side of Heracles, more commonly exploited in comedy or in such a quasi-satyr play as the *Alcestis* of Euripides, which Sophocles does not here stress; yet he allows us to realize that it was the infatuation of Heracles for the Euboean princess Iole that led him to destroy her father's city Oechalia; and moreover that it was the desire of Deianira not to be supplanted by Iole that led her to the rash step which proved to be her husband's ruin.

The two leading characters, husband and wife, never meet in the play, but are shown only as they confront minor characters. For that fact one reason may be that Sophocles wishes to have the same actor play both

[62] 1250–1252; but Agamemnon himself is here not possessed of *sophrosyne*, as the Chorus remark, 1264 f.

[63] See above, p. 100.

parts. A deeper reason may be that he intends to exhibit not the Dorian hero in action but rather the results of his own and Deianira's previous actions; so when we first see him, the play is three quarters over, and his suffering is already a *fait accompli*. Deianira accordingly holds our interest, and it must be added our sympathies, during most if not all of the play. As Virgil's Dido grows under the poet's hand possibly beyond his original plan, and as she captivates modern readers certainly more than Virgil's Roman readers, so Deianira transcends the limits of the traditional story.[64]

At several points in the play we are told that what befalls Heracles is fated. Deianira, whose lot has been unhappy and anxious, and who now feels special anxiety at the fifteen-month absence of Heracles, bethinks herself of the tablet that he left with her before his departure; a tablet in which, as she explains little by little, he has told her of an oracle, received by himself long before at Dodona, to the effect that he was fated either to die or to succeed in a final task and have rest thereafter. Furthermore he had himself fixed the time, fifteen months, at the end of which one of these alternatives was to be fulfilled (46 f.; 76–81; 156–174). The time has now elapsed. The fortunes of Heracles are thus understood from the outset of the play to be "the doom ordained by the gods";[65] what is more, this oracle, like that of Calchas in the *Ajax*,[66] though presenting alternatives, has already been fulfilled in one sense by the time that we hear of it. With this oracle agrees another prophecy given at a still earlier time by Zeus to Heracles, who recalls both prophecies in his agony: it is that he should perish through no living creature, but through one who was dead. So it was the dead centaur Nessus who had at length slain him, "the dead the living, even as the divine will was foretold"; and as for his expected release from toil, that too is fulfilled, for toil comes no more to the dead (1149 f.; 1159–1174). The beginning and the end of the play thus attribute the agony and death of Heracles to Fate.

So long as Deianira holds the centre of the stage, however, we are fascinated by the nobility and the tenderness of her character. Not jealous of Iole, in the ordinary sense, but grieved at her husband's errant mood, as any woman in her situation would be (545 f.), she sets about doing what she can to mend matters. All this part of the play thus turns on the character and the will of Deianira, who, rightly or wrongly, wisely or foolishly, sends the robe to Heracles because that is just what such a person as Deianira would do. Here she betrays no feeling that Fate is at work, unless it be in the excuses that she makes for Heracles and Iole, victims of Eros, whose power she herself also knows.[67] Yet the Chorus comment on

[64] See above, p. 117, n. 73.

[65] *Trach.* 169: πρὸς θεῶν εἱμαρμένα.

[66] See above, p. 149.

[67] 438–448; the theme is enlarged upon by the Chorus, 497–516; cf. 861 f.

the part that Fate has played in all this: "See, maidens, how suddenly the divine word of the old prophecy hath come upon us. . . . And that promise is wafted surely to its fulfilment. If a cloud of death is around him, and the doom wrought by the Centaur's craft is stinging his sides, . . . of such things this hapless lady had no foreboding; but she saw a great mischief swiftly coming on her home from the new marriage. Her own hand applied the remedy; but for the issues of a stranger's counsel, given at a fatal meeting, for these, I ween, she makes despairing lament, shedding the tender dew of plenteous tears. And the coming fate foreshadows a great misfortune, contrived by guile." [68] This mingling of fate with actions fully launched by purely human motives cannot be said to enhance either the power of fate or the portrait of Deianira.

The tragedy of Heracles, then, is a tragedy of fate. Although his end may be said to grow out of his character, which caused him to bring home Iole, and may even on that account be considered to be just, *nemesis* answering to *hybris*, and although the precise manner of his end may be said to grow out of the character of Deianira (as the tragedy of Creon depends on the tragedy of Antigone), the emphasis on fate in the early scenes and the fact that so much of the action has already taken place before the play opens has the effect of giving Heracles over to fate. That is the lesson summed up by his son, Hyllus, at the very end of the play: "Mark the great cruelty of the gods in the deeds that are being done. They beget children, they are hailed as fathers, and yet they can look upon such sufferings. No man foresees the future: but the present is fraught with mourning for us, and with shame for the powers above, and verily with anguish beyond compare for him who endures this doom. Maidens, come ye also, nor linger at the house, ye who have lately seen a dread death, with sorrows manifold and strange: and in all this there is nought but Zeus." [69]

It is the tragedy of Deianira, however, which occupies our minds and sympathies during a great part of the play, and which is made the more profound by the brutal failure of the dying Heracles to show the least affection for his devoted wife, or to utter a word of forgiveness now that he knows her act to have been innocent in intent. The tragedy of Deianira is a tragedy of character. Deianira is impetuous, as well as loving; that is her *hamartia*, or tragic fault. Faced by a situation forced upon her by fate, she acts fondly, but foolishly; her voluntary deed gives effect to the evil deed of Nessus; and when she realizes, too late, the effect of her impetuous act, she takes her life. If we are to consider only external acts, as nature does, she has sinned, and she pays the penalty of her fault;[70] if we may

[68] 821–851, trans. Jebb. [69] 1264–1278, trans. Jebb.

[70] The external resemblance between the deed of Deianira, who slays her husband (as her

consider also the motive, she is innocent, and does not deserve to die. But she thinks otherwise, and visits on herself the verdict of "guilty." That is the verdict not of justice but of a loving heart, appalled by the ironical and tragic contrast between what she intended and what she has done.

In the *Oedipus Tyrannus* Sophocles achieves his masterpiece of construction and of dramatic effect, and what many besides Aristotle have regarded as the typical Greek Tragedy. The gradual disclosure of antecedent circumstances, the clashes of the major personages, the converging of the characters whose revelations will accomplish at once the recognition and the reversal of fortune, the calculated suspense and the accumulated irony of situation, the catastrophe, and at last the appalling denouement through the act of Oedipus himself, all constitute a triumph of manipulation. But behind it all one feels, and it is intended that one shall feel, the relentless force of fate. Even the part of luck or coincidence in the meetings of the characters at particular moments in the action passes unchallenged by the spectator, and may well be regarded as phases of fate (as they appear in Hardy's novels and stories).[71] The play is concerned chiefly with the detection of a crime, but differs from a modern detective story in that the audience knows from the start who committed the crime, though the criminal does not; still more significantly, it arouses not only our curiosity but our deep emotions. And although each of the existing plays of Sophocles, being complete in itself, is highly concentrated, the *Oedipus Tyrannus* is the most concentrated of them all.

The theme of the play may be stated in a few words: the discovery by Oedipus, King of Thebes, that he has unwittingly long since murdered his father Laius and wedded his mother Iocasta, and his blinding of himself after the discovery.

The germ of the story was an old folk-tale,[72] of which traces appear in the *Odyssey*,[73] though the most characteristic elements of the Sophoclean drama are wanting. The legend of the Theban royal house grew, in the *Oedipodeia* and the *Thebais* and in Pindar,[74] notably by the introduction

---

very name, Δηάνειρα, indicates), and that of Clytaemnestra has often been remarked. Heracles corresponds to Agamemnon, Iole to Cassandra, also taken at the capture of a city; a garment is the means of death in both cases. But the spirit, of course, is utterly different. For further debts of the *Trachiniai* to the *Alcestis* and other plays of Euripides, cf. M. L. Earle, *T.A.P.A.* 33 (1902), pp. 1–21; to the *Andromache*, G. H. Macurdy, *C.R.* 25 (1911), pp. 97–101; and on the relation of this play, an example of "New Tragedy," to Euripides, cf. H. D. F. Kitto, *Greek Tragedy*, pp. 290–300. See also below, p. 176, and n. 14.

[71] The *O.T.* is full of actual allusions to *tyche*: cf. 52, 80, 263, 442, 469, 977, 1080, 1526.

[72] Cf. C. Robert, *Oidipus* (Berlin, 1915), Vol. I, esp. pp. 64–66; H. J. Rose, *Modern Methods in Classical Mythology* (St. Andrews, 1930), pp. 24–30.

[73] *Od.* 11, 271–280.

[74] *Ol.* 2, 42 ff.

of the curse of Oedipus on his sons, a curse which Aeschylus treated (in a trilogy of which only the *Seven against Thebes* has survived) as a phase of the continuing curse, or the pursuit of the Erinyes, that afflicted the whole royal house of Thebes.[75]

Sophocles interpolates into the story of Oedipus his Corinthian sojourn, which makes possible his successive phases of anxiety, dread, and hope, with regard to his parentage, — emotions ironically contrasted with the truth which the spectators know, — and which also opens the way for the convergence of the two herdsmen, Corinthian and Theban. More important still, Sophocles transfers the chief supernatural element in the story from the Erinyes to Apollo, whose oracles he makes dominate each critical moment of the action. The family curse drops into the background. What gives this play an especially fatalistic tinge is the fact that at the moment when it opens the warning oracle given to Laius and later to Oedipus about parricide and incest has already been fulfilled. Thus both the general outline of the story, fixed before Sophocles took it up, and the oracular interpretation of it which he emphasizes conspire to give us the impression that what has occurred could not have been otherwise, that it was all fated.

Granted, however, that Oedipus is already guilty of parricide and incest, there will be no tragedy if these facts do not transpire. But in that case, too, the old oracles and their god Apollo will be in disrepute, as the Chorus will protest.[76] Consistency demands therefore that the agencies of fate discover the facts which fate has already caused; the plague which is afflicting Thebes is the force which initiates the events leading to the discovery. The steps which Oedipus takes to deal with the plague caused, as he now learns from a new Delphic oracle, by the as yet unavenged murder of Laius, lead inevitably to the discovery of himself as the murderer, and what is more, as one guilty of incest. Here we enter the province of irony and feel the tragic contrast between the good intentions of Oedipus and the awful facts that they will reveal, between his quick resolution and intelligence and his abysmal ignorance of the truth, between *δόξα* and *ἀλήθεια*.

Fate, then, has provided the field of action, the conditions within which the will of Oedipus must work. His will provides the action itself, and at the end the denouement in his self-blinding. All his decisions and acts moreover proceed from a consistent character, the result of heredity and of his past acts. Nevertheless this character is not easy to define, for it is many-sided and shows different sides in different situations. At first Oedipus does not suspect that he is personally involved in the quest for the

[75] See above, pp. 114 f.

[76] *O.T.* 863–910; n.b. 895 f.: *εἰ γὰρ αἱ τοιαίδε πράξεις τίμιαι | τί δεῖ με χορεύειν*; and 910: *ἔρρει τὰ θεῖα.*

murderer of Laius. Then, when accused by the blind seer Tiresias of being the murderer, he is involved, but wrongly suspects his brother-in-law Creon, who brought the new oracle from Delphi, of having plotted with Tiresias to overthrow him. (Creon, it should be noted, is here drawn as honest though shrewd, not as the tyrant already drawn in the *Antigone*, or later drawn in the *Oedipus Coloneus*, both of which represent him as an older man corrupted by power.) Finally the successive revelations of Iocasta (intended to reassure him), of the Corinthian herdsman (calculated to remove him from the Theban milieu), and of the herdsman of Laius (intended to confirm the report that Laius had fallen at the hands of a number of assassins), conspire to bring out the whole truth; and his own hand inflicts the penalty. Fate has indeed contrived all, but has contrived the revelation through the character and the acts of Oedipus himself.

Let us consider in greater detail these successive phases in the interplay of fate and character. At the outset of the drama we see Oedipus as the type of the kingly personage (Oedipus has the βασιλικὸν ἦθος, as the scholiast remarks, on l. 93), a noble, admired, active, resourceful, but not yet a moving or tragic or individualized character, except as we begin to realize that he is ignorant of the truth. So far the tragedy is merely in the irony of situation, as when Oedipus pronounces, even as if on behalf of his own father (264; cf. 135–141; 258–268), a curse on the unknown murderer of Laius! In the scene with Tiresias, the anger of Oedipus against the reluctance of the seer to speak is at first impersonal, for Oedipus is still the champion of the state who resents the seer's apparent lack of patriotism, and who discounts his protest that he is acting for the interest of Oedipus as well as for himself. After the blunt accusation of Tiresias that Oedipus is the murderer of Laius, his anger turns to personal feeling; past achievement and pride of intellect in having foiled the Sphinx blind him to the loyalty and the superior knowledge of the seer. Oedipus is wrong, and the tragedy still lies in the ironical situation, the contrast between the semblance and the truth (between δόξα and ἀλήθεια). Oedipus is saying the very opposite of what he would say if he knew the truth. The revelation of Tiresias has been forced from him by the anger of Oedipus; and Oedipus in turn will not believe Tiresias because he thinks the accusation comes merely from the anger of Tiresias. Blind Tiresias, however, sees the truth, while seeing Oedipus is blind to it; yet he too shall soon be blind, — and then shall see! (369–375; 412–419; 454 f.).

In the first scene with Creon, Oedipus will not listen to reason. His mind is closed, because he will not believe himself guilty, and must find some other culprit. Not exactly his conscience but his sense of security has been troubled by the repeated accusations of Tiresias, which involve murder and incest and blindness to come and a hint that the murderer is after all Theban-born; thoughts which Oedipus can hardly fail to connect in his own heart with the terms of the similar oracle that he once received at Delphi after leaving Corinth, though it is only in the sequel that he refers to that oracle.[77] Hence the unjust accusation against Creon: Oedipus is not himself, but the victim of *ate*; his character is all but effaced by the trend of events. If we remember this scene when we witness the concluding scene of the play, in which the gentleness of Creon, here so unjustly treated, adds to the humiliation of Oedipus, and in which Creon *does* become king, after all, though not through the treachery of which he is here accused, we feel again how utterly Oedipus has been at cross purposes with reality. Creon in this play, like Odysseus in the *Ajax*, is endowed with *sophrosyne*; their vindication is contrasted with the excess of the two protagonists.

Then comes the scene with Iocasta, who seeks to allay his feelings at having been charged with the murder of Laius. Why, as to the lore of seers, which Oedipus believes Creon to have suborned for his nefarious designs, that is already discounted. Laius was supposed to be destined by an oracle to be slain by his son; but that son was exposed in infancy, and Laius was slain by robbers at a place where three roads meet. "Where three roads meet!" Again old memories flash into the mind of Oedipus. Can he indeed be the murderer? Is there any witness of the murder of Laius? Yes; a Theban, now a herdsman, and he can be sent for; meanwhile Oedipus tells his own tale of his youth at Corinth as son of King Polybus, of the doubts cast on his birth, his journey to Delphi, the oracle, and his slaying of an elderly stranger at the "triple ways." All points to his having slain Laius; but only the Theban herdsman can throw light on the matter.

From this point Oedipus ceases to be the king, acting for the good of the country, and becomes merely the individual seeking to learn his own status. Nor has he a detached curiosity to know the truth, to track down the murderer of Laius; rather he seeks to prove that the murderer is not himself. He is no longer the hunter but the hunted, trying to escape his fate.

Before the Theban herdsman arrives, a messenger from Corinth brings tidings of the death of old King Polybus, whose son Oedipus has supposed himself to be, tidings which Oedipus receives with unfilial joy (964–972; 988), for he is now convinced that though he may be the murderer of Laius and so has lost his place in Thebes, he at least cannot become the slayer of his father, since Polybus has died a natural death. But the Corinthian now confides to him that Oedipus is no son of Polybus, but a

[77] See below, next paragraph.

foundling delivered to him by someone of the household of Laius. Iocasta instantly foresees what will transpire, tries in vain to dissuade Oedipus from further investigation, and rushes to what we later learn is her suicide.

Oedipus, all the keener in his quest, suspects Iocasta of snobbishness in wishing to conceal his possibly lowly origin (1078 f.; cf. 1062 f.), whereas he recklessly avows himself the child of *Tyche*, who has given him in the passing months the ups and downs of fortune.[78] The Chorus joins in his hopeful mood in a hyporcheme that looks to see Oedipus saved not later than the morrow's full moon (that marks the new *month*).[79]

All hinges on the evidence of the Theban herdsman: will he adhere to his former story, that Laius was slain by a band of robbers, or will he say that it was a single wayfarer who slew him? [80] Not this point, however, comes out when the Corinthian messenger confronts the Theban herdsman, but the whole story of the birth and the disposal of the infant Oedipus. It is now the turn of Oedipus, convinced of what Iocasta saw before, to rush forth, not to death, but to the act of self-blinding and the long years of suffering which are to be his self-inflicted *nemesis*, and, in a sense, his penance. Pity is mingled with the sorrowful meditations of the Chorus on the vicissitudes of life and the contrast between the semblance and the reality: "Alas, ye generations of men, how mere a shadow do I count your life! Where, where is the mortal who wins more of happiness than just the seeming, and, after the semblance, a falling away? Thine is a fate that warns me,—thine, thine, unhappy Oedipus,—to call no earthly creature blest. . . . Time the all-seeing hath found thee out in thy despite" (1186–1196; 1212). In this line is summed up the burden of our drama of circumstance: Time, like a judge, brings all things to trial and sentence. (1212 f.; cf. 613 f.)

A noble character is Oedipus, but impulsive and passionate and violent, a character moreover that can be perverted by situations beyond his control until he acts blindly, like the victim of *ate*. To that extent the play is a tragedy of fate. Even in his attempt to kill Iocasta, just before he blinds himself, it was no mortal, says the messenger, but "some *daimon*" that was his guide; that is, some power beyond his control;[81] and blind Oedipus protests that it was Apollo that brought his woes to pass, though it was his own hand, and none other that struck his eyes (1329–1331). And the messenger expressly refers to the self-punishment of Iocasta and Oedipus

[78] 1080–1085. Τύχης, 1080, recalls Iocasta's appeal to τύχη, 977 (see below, p. 159), and also the warning of Tiresias, 442, that it was precisely the τύχη of Oedipus that had ruined him.

[79] 1086–1109; cf. J. T. Sheppard's notes on 1080–1090.

[80] On the irony and the suspense created by the references to one or to more assassins, see my paper "The Murderers of Laius," *T.A.P.A.* 60 (1929), 75–86.

[81] 1258 f.; cf. 828; 1300; 1310; *Ai.* 243 f.

as "ills voluntary, not unpurposed," and as therefore of the most grievous kind, clearly as contrasted with the involuntary evils already brought to light (1229–1231). The secondary characters exhibit also a certain fatalism. Tiresias, of course, is the mouthpiece of fate. Iocasta, sceptic about seers and oracles, yields or closes her eyes to fate rather than resist it; her philosophy is one of letting sleeping dogs lie. "What should mortals fear, for whom the decrees of Fortune (τύχη) are supreme, and who hath clear foresight (πρόνοια) of nothing? 'Tis best to live at random, as one may."[82] She does not disbelieve in fate, or even in divine governance, but she maintains that the future cannot be foreseen.

And now the question of good and evil: has Oedipus deserved his fate? Have the gods dealt justly with him? Or with Iocasta? Let us take her case first. She and Laius were warned by an oracle "that it was fated (*moira*) that he should be slain by a son who should be born to them" (713 f.). Unless one is to suppose either that the son was already begotten or that the utterance of the oracle made it necessary both that the child should be born and that he should kill his father, in which cases nothing that they could do could thwart a destiny already in process of being fulfilled, one must conclude that the oracle is of the warning or conditional type, and that it would have been prudent for Oedipus and Iocasta, thus warned, to have had no child. Both Aeschylus and Euripides[83] clearly mark the oracle as of the conditional or warning type:[84] *if* Laius and Iocasta had a child, certain dire results would follow; but they disregarded the warning. Sophocles leaves the point in obscurity, or even implies that Apollo prophesied the birth of the child. At any rate, the child was born, and the parents tried to circumvent the oracle by exposing the child three days after its birth. In vain, as it proved; and Iocasta, embittered by the loss of her child through the gods' intermediaries, oracles and seers (712; 946 f.; 952 f.; 977 f.), has not given up her faith in Apollo, to whom indeed she turns in distress (911–913; 918–921). But if it was ever possible for her to be saved, that was long ago; now she is swept along in the tragedy of Oedipus.

Oedipus is more reverent, though too self-confident. He also should have been fore-armed by the warning of Apollo that he received at Delphi after he left Corinth (788–793); he, of all men, should have been wary of killing any older man, or of marrying any woman. (As a matter of fact,

[82] 977–979; cf. 911–923; 971–973; and for the echo of τύχη by Oedipus, 1080 (and see above, p. 158, n. 78).

[83] But not Pindar, *Ol.* 2, 35–42.

[84] See above, pp. 23; 114; 121; cf. also Euripides, *Phoen.* 16–25; and for the oracle given to Laius as the typical problem for later philosophical discussions of oracles in relation to fate, see below pp. 347; 348; 364 (Chrysippus, and Cicero); 372 (Albinus); 375 (Alexander of Aphrodisias); cf. p. 350, n. 111; 385 (Oenomaus the Cynic); 385 (Chalcidius); also Appendix 6: Conditional Prophecy.

he *is* trying to act on the warning of Delphi by avoiding Corinth (794–797; 994–998), and there is irony in the result.) But his rash vengeance on the rude behavior that he met at the triple ways, and his lack of caution in marrying soon afterwards the widowed queen of Thebes were certainly *hybris*, and *nemesis* must as certainly follow. These events, to be sure, lie outside the action of the drama before us, and we are advised by Aristotle that we should not, therefore, inquire too curiously into their probability.[85] What we are entitled to observe, however, is that the same rashness appears again in the drama, and leads to the discovery of the plight of Oedipus. After the violent scenes with Tiresias, Creon, and Iocasta, the Chorus are disturbed: they hope that Oedipus is not, as some of his actions and words suggest, guilty of such deeds of *hybris* as are characteristic of the traditional tyrant; for if so, he must surely fall under a constraining doom (*ananke*), or religion will be discredited (863–910). The Chorus is mistaken in even suspecting Oedipus of baseness; yet he is capable at times of fits of *hybris* and therefore liable to suffer its consequences, which have little to do with man's motives.[86] And once more we must never forget that the ultimate revelation and the catastrophe are the *data* of the legend accepted by Sophocles, though he has chosen to represent them as having been willed from the beginning by Apollo.

It is Apollo, then, who must bear the responsibility for the good or evil in the fate of Oedipus. At first sight it may seem that Sophocles is not concerned to exhibit the goodness or evil of this fate, but only its inexorable nature. Such has Apollo willed; such must Oedipus suffer. The fact that Oedipus did not will or foresee the results of his actions has nothing to do with the matter. That is the consequence of the traditional association of Apollo and of the Delphic oracle with prophecy, which is primarily concerned with external facts and which ignores motives.[87] Apollo and his oracle, to be sure, come to have another aspect; for Apollo is the god particularly charged with the ceremonial purification of extenuated guilt. Thus Apollo, who bids Orestes to avenge his father, and thus to incur blood-guilt, is also the advocate of Orestes and the "cleanser of his mur-

[85] *Poetics* 1454b6.

[86] Cf. J. T. Sheppard, ed. *O.T.* pp. xiii, xxii, on the tragedy of "this innocent good man who behaves sometimes in the manner of the sinner who is justly ruined"; pp. xxiv–xl, on "the innocence of Oedipus"; pp. xli–lviii, on the traditional character of the "tyrant," which Oedipus seems at times, but only seems, to approximate.

[87] J. T. Sheppard, ed. *O.T.* pp. xxxv f.: "In some sense, the evil comes from the gods. It comes, however, not by miraculous intervention, but through the normal processes of human will and human act, of human ignorance and human failure. Sophocles justifies nothing. He accepts, for his tragic purpose, the story and the gods, simply treating them as if they were true. . . . He neither attempts, like Aeschylus, to justify the evil, nor presumes, like Euripides, to deny its divine origin. . . . His gods . . . stand for the universe of circumstance as it is."

der."[88] That is because Orestes, though technically guilty, is morally guiltless in that his motives are pure; his social status is finally cleared by the court of the Areopagus. Euripides adds a further deed of expiation in the exploit of Orestes in Tauris.[89] But Apollo could go even further. Herodotus tells the story of Glaucus who was reproved by Delphi for contemplated perjury (VI, 86); thus the motive becomes all-important, and goodness is in the state of the will, as the Stoics later hold.[90]

In the present play, Sophocles is not ready to go so far. Oedipus toward the end protests that he were better off had he perished when he was exposed in infancy (1349; cf. 1391–1393). As it is, he feels in the first torrent of his passion that his self-inflicted blindness is not enough; would that he could make himself deaf as well (1386–1390). Yet now that he can no longer act, but only suffer, a reaction sets in. The exodus of the play is still controlled by fate, but is softened by human sentiments of pity and tenderness. Presently Oedipus begins to feel himself set apart by fate: "Of this much am I sure,—that neither sickness nor aught else can destroy me; for never had I been snatched from death, but in reserve for some strange doom (μὴ 'πί τῳ δεινῷ κακῷ). Nay, let my fate (*moira*) go whither it will" (1455–1457). And he turns to thoughts of his children's lot. Here, indeed, Oedipus does not protest that his motives were pure; that he sinned unwittingly; that his blindness is too great a penalty for his deserts: all that will come in the *Oedipus Coloneus*, where we shall learn also of that strange doom for which his life has been spared and what goodness there may be in fate.[91] Yet the change of tone in this last scene of the present play prepares us for what Sophocles in his old age will make of the old, cruel tale of Oedipus.[92] For the present the poet prefers to end on the note of pathetic contrast, which enhances the lesson of *sophrosyne*, with a glance at the old Greek spirit of wariness, hardly to be divorced from the belief in the divine envy ascribed by Herodotus to Solon: "Dwellers in our native Thebes," sing the chorus of Theban elders as they march out, "behold, this is Oedipus, who knew the famed riddle, and was a man most mighty; on whose fortunes what citizen did not gaze with envy? Behold into what a stormy sea of dread troubles he hath come!

[88] Aesch. *Eum.*; see above, p. 134; and cf. H. W. Parke, *History of the Delphic Oracle*, pp. 308–310.

[89] Euripides, *I.T.*; see below, pp. 199–201.

[90] Cf. T. Dempsey, *The Delphic Oracle, Its Early History, Influence and Fall*, Oxford, 1918, pp. 133–138; H. J. Rose, *Modern Methods*, pp. 28 f.; J. T. Sheppard, ed. *O.T.* pp. xxx–xl, who compares Simonides' retort to Pittacus (see above, p. 68) for the current Greek idea (unlike the Stoic) that virtue is not immune to fortune and necessity and calamity; a man may be guilty through no fault of his own. See also below, p. 188, for Euripides.

[91] *O.C.* 265–267; 510–548; 962–996; 438 f.; see below, p. 169 f.

[92] Cf. further Sir R. W. Livingstone, "The Exodus of the *O.T.*," in *Greek Poetry and Life*, pp. 158–163.

Therefore, while our eyes wait to see the destined final day, we must call no one happy who is of mortal race, until he hath crossed life's border, free from pain."[93]

The story of the avenging of the death of Agamemnon by his son Orestes on Aegisthus, possibly on Clytaemnestra too, is as old as the *Odyssey*. No Greek of primitive times would have doubted that Orestes was justified in thus avenging his father, or indeed that it was his duty to avenge him. Yet this duty involved, as the story came to be told, the killing of his mother; and Orestes was therefore necessarily pursued by the Erinyes, who avenge the spilling of kindred blood.[94] The Epic cycle was familiar with Apollo's rôle as purifier of Orestes, as of others similarly defiled, and also as instigator of the vengeance.[95] Not till the choral lyric poets Xanthus and Stesichorus treated the story did Electra become an accomplice in the vengeance. The story was almost ready for dramatic treatment when Pindar speculated on the reasons that might have impelled Clytaemnestra to kill her husband.[96]

It was characteristic of Aeschylus that he regarded the act of Orestes not, as did the *Odyssey*, merely as a single righteous act of retribution, but as part of a complex chain of events, itself justified or indeed required by the guilt of Clytaemnestra, but also in turn requiring to be expiated.[97] The form of the trilogy was admirably suited to the exhibition of the three phases: in the *Agamemnon*, the hero's pride humbled by Clytaemnestra's guilt; in the *Choephoroi*, the vengeance of Orestes; in the *Eumenides*, the justification of Orestes and his salvation from the Erinyes by divine aid. Thus the motives in the trilogy are even more religious than human; and what has to be is regarded as in a sense fated. In particular, Orestes acts, but acts as the agent of destiny; the part of Electra is slight, and she disappears early in the *Choephoroi*.

Sophocles in his *Electra* returns to the epic version of the story. It was necessary for Orestes to kill his mother, it was fated, it was right; and that is all. He intends to act in accordance with the oracle of Apollo (32–37; cf. 1264–1270), and feels no remorse when the deed is done, but blandly and confidently proclaims: "All's well, if Apollo's oracle spake well" (1424 f.). The Erinyes do not pursue him afterwards in this play, nor is there any sequel to it. Even the motives and feelings of Orestes are slighted; he seems to be the tool of fate.

But it is only at the beginning and at the end of the play that Orestes,

[93] *O.T.* 1524–1530; see above, p. 100 f., and Appendix 11; for Solon, pp. 84 f.; for Aristotle's comment, below, pp. 325 f.; for the idea of *sophrosyne* in the final scene, cf. J. T. Sheppard, ed. *O.T.*, pp. lix–lxxix.

[94] See above, p. 133.

[95] Cf. above, pp. 134 f.; 160 f.; below, Appendix 14.

[96] Pindar, *Pyth.* 11, 22–25.

[97] See above, pp. 128 f.

and fate, are dominant; in all the intervening part, Sophocles has chosen to concentrate attention on Electra and her motives: loyalty to her dead father, resentment against the guilty couple, and anger at her own lot. Again and again she returns to the theme: "set amid evils, I too must needs (*ananke*) do evil" (308 f.; cf. 221 f.; 256; 619–621). The character and feelings of this heroic maiden, then, are the real subject of the play; only the actual deed of vengeance, which after all is fated, is reserved for Orestes. Hence the delay in the recognition of brother and sister, which lets us observe at length Electra's feelings in relation to Clytaemnestra, toward her dead father, and toward the brother whom, because of his ruse, she supposes to be dead. The motives of the Aeschylean Orestes are transferred to the Sophoclean Electra, but become even more personal. The whole action is envisaged from her point of view; her prayer is personal, and barely generalizes the moral problem (110–120; cf. 244–250); even the Chorus see the situation chiefly from her point of view, while affirming their faith that the Erinyes will do justice (472–515; 173–184). But Electra's appeal to the chthonian powers, including "Curse" and the Erinyes (110–120), and her interpretation of Clytaemnestra's dream as having been sent by Agamemnon (417–425; 459; cf. 484), find their response when the Chorus, at the very moment of Clytaemnestra's death, recognize the potency of the Curse and the flowering of Moira;[98] and Aegisthus just before his death feels the compulsion of *Ananke*.

The *Electra* of Sophocles has abandoned, it appears, all religious questioning: Orestes moves on the level of fate and a divinely ordained duty, Electra on the level of human, amoral emotion. It was left to Euripides, in his *Electra*, a play apparently later than that of Sophocles,[99] to show up the moral contradictions in the traditional story.[100]

In the earlier and in the later treatments of the story of Philoctetes, in the epic cycle, in Aeschylus and Euripides, the question at issue is whether or not the suffering hero, left behind with the bow of Heracles at Lemnos on the way to Troy, will now rejoin the Greeks; for without him Troy cannot be taken. Human persuasion or deception prevails, and the Greek cause triumphs. Sophocles lays stress on the character of Philoctetes, a stubborn but much wronged man; and in order to bring out his gentler and nobler side he shows him in relation not only with his worst enemy, the unscrupulous Odysseus, but with the ingenuous young son of Achilles, Neoptolemus, who consents at first to abet the guile of Odysseus. Their stratagem bids fair to succeed, till the suffering of Philoctetes softens the young man's heart, and he refuses to be a party any longer to the deceit;

[98] 1419–1421; 1413 f., where the sense is clear though the text is corrupt.
[99] So Jebb holds, ed. Sophocles, *Electra*, pp. liii–lvi, *pace* Wilamowitz.
[100] See below, pp. 203 f.

to no little degree Neoptolemus becomes the hero of the play. Yet Philoctetes will not yield to his entreaties and voluntarily go to Troy. Apparently the action has reached an impasse, and no human agency will bring Philoctetes to Troy, whereas it was the universally accepted story that he did go to Troy.

As a matter of fact, the denouement does not develop out of the human characters, but is accomplished by the apparition of a *deus ex machina*, the hero Heracles, whose bow Philoctetes possesses, and who bids him acquiesce and go to Troy. This intervention has been criticized by many readers, who have felt that a satisfactory denouement could have been contrived in the yielding of Philoctetes to the persuasion of Neoptolemus. Yet it is clear that Sophocles deliberately preferred the supernatural ending,[101] and in fact undid whatever headway Neoptolemus might have made in persuading Philoctetes by introducing the short scene (1293–1304) in which Odysseus, who is utterly antipathetic to Philoctetes, intervenes. It cannot be denied that the appearance of Heracles is of great dramatic effect; moreover it emphasizes, as perhaps no other device could so easily have done, the view of Sophocles that Philoctetes, though at every moment the master of his own decisions, is also an instrument in the hands of destiny. From this point of view the appeals of Neoptolemus and the resistance of Philoctetes are alike illusory and superfluous, since the outcome of the action is to be the same in any case. As a matter of fact, the denouement is ironical in that Philoctetes has to yield, but wins glory by yielding, while Odysseus, though his end is achieved, has not for all his cleverness reckoned with Neoptolemus, and is defeated and discredited in the means that he has used. And Sophocles has used several devices to remind us of the contrast between the real action (which is controlled by fate), and the apparent action, which Philoctetes supposes to rest within his own control.

Not only the outcome of the story but the earlier events in the life of Philoctetes and his long years of solitary suffering were fated, part of a divine plan. Such is the opinion of Neoptolemus;[102] so Odysseus proclaims (989–998); so the Chorus agree (1118–1120); so Heracles declares (1415; 1421–1444); and so Philoctetes himself at the last, beholding Heracles, is compelled to admit in words that associate Fate and the all-subduing power of his personal destiny with the advice of his friends.[103]

[101] As Euripides sometimes deliberately makes such an ending necessary, — e.g. in *I.T.* On the value of the *deus ex machina*, cf. P. Decharme, *Euripides*, pp. 262–273, and A. Leach, "Fate and Free Will," p. 144 in L. Cooper, *The Greek Genius*.

[102] *Phil.* 191–200; cf. 1326–1335; n.b. 1326: σὺ γὰρ νοσεῖς τόδ' ἄλγος ἐκ θείας τύχης, and E. G. Berry, ΘΕΙΑ ΜΟΙΡΑ, p. 23.

[103] 1466–1468: ἔνθ' ἡ μεγάλη Μοῖρα κομίζει | γνώμη τε φίλων χὠ πανδαμάτωρ | δαίμων, ὃς ταῦτ' ἐπέκρανεν.

The theophany therefore is not an overruling divine manifestation, but is only the last and most impressive exhibition of a divine power which has been at work throughout. Since it was the gods who involved Philoctetes in his plight, it is for them to extricate him (cf. 843) and not for any merely human agency. Their control is harped upon in every episode; even the bow of Heracles, that symbol of the action which passes from hand to hand, is addressed "as a god" (657). The change of the wind from adverse to fair is another divine intervention (464 f.; 639 f.; 855; 1450 f.).

Nevertheless it is not until toward the end of the play that we have positive assurance that Troy will fall "this present summer" (1337–1341). That is because Sophocles has delayed the full reporting of the oracle of the captive Trojan Helenus, and has allowed only parts of it to be cited,— parts which seem to have a conditional character, and therefore to leave the issue to human choice. Thus we learn that the fall of Troy depends on the presence both of Neoptolemus and also of the bow of Heracles (113–115; cf. 345–347); later we learn that the bow will not avail unless Philoctetes accompanies it and moreover comes willingly (611–613; cf. 839–841; 1332; 1443–1447). Surely we are inclined, and entitled, to suppose that the final outcome may depend on the success with which Odysseus and Neoptolemus play their parts. Possibly they may also feel some doubt as to the omniscience or the good will of Helenus, a Trojan captive, and are the less willing to leave the outcome wholly to fate. At any rate, the play proceeds on the human level, and human motives fully account for the deadlock of wills which is broken only by the appearance of Heracles. Philoctetes himself is so much absorbed in the immediate situation that he all but ignores, till the end, anything but human factors.

The greater part of the play, then, is a drama of character. Our interest is fixed not merely on the outcome but on the way in which Philoctetes rises above hard circumstances. His bitter experience has bred in him a deep distrust of the gods and their "jealousy";[104] yet he has been schooled by necessity to a philosophy of endurance.[105] Neoptolemus draws a distinction between the sufferings inflicted on him by the gods, which like all men he must bear,[106] and those further, self-inflicted sufferings, the result of his intractable temper, which deserve no pity (1316–1322); a distinction drawn also in the *Oedipus Tyrannus* between the condition of Oedipus for which he was only in part responsible and the blindness for which he was wholly responsible.[107] Philoctetes could end his sufferings

[104] 776–778; contrast 775.

[105] 536–538; n.b. 537: *τλῆναι*.

[106] 1316 f.: *τὰς μὲν ἐκ θεῶν | τύχας δοθείσας*; cf. 1326, cited above, p. 143, n. 34; *Od.* 6, 188–190, and see above, p. 26, and n. 81.

[107] *O.T.* 1229–1231; see above, p. 158.

at once and win glory if he would consent to forgive the Greeks and go to Troy; he prefers to suffer, or at least to forgo the glory.[108] To allow him to be persuaded by Neoptolemus, as we have seen, would mean settling the outcome of the play on human grounds, and would also dispense with the theophany which Sophocles particularly desired.

Nevertheless we cannot overlook the fact that the long years of suffering were fated, and that no fault of Philoctetes earned them (684–686). What case can be made for the justice of the gods toward Philoctetes? The sufferer himself, observing with jaundiced eye the fall in the Trojan War of some of the noblest Greeks and the survival of certain rascals, bitterly remarks that "war takes no evil man by choice, but good men always. . . . No evil thing has been known to perish; no, the gods take tender care of such, and have a strange joy in turning back from Hades all things villainous and knavish, while they are ever sending the just and the good out of life. What am I to think of these things, or wherein shall I praise them, when, praising the ways of the gods I find that the gods are evil?" (436 f.; 446–452). The complaint grows out of a particular moment and mood; yet it might seem at the time to be supported by the whole experience of Philoctetes himself. In the end, of course, the gods, who have made the innocent Philoctetes the instrument of far-reaching destinies, will bestow on him glory, even as Heracles has "after enduring many labors, won deathless glory" (1418–1422), and as Oedipus, another victim for the most part of external circumstances, is reserved by the gods to become the channel of divine grace.[109] These ultimate plans and compensations neither Oedipus nor Philoctetes can anticipate; yet their belated glory, the spiritual reward of vindicated honor, may be held to be real compensations. This is no "poetic justice" of the material sort, but rather the attempt of Sophocles to find room within the scope of the cruel old legends for human heroism and for divine goodness at last revealed.

The external action of the *Oedipus at Colonus* turns on the fulfilment of an oracle concerning the manner and place of the death of Oedipus; parallel with it is what may be called the internal action, the moral rehabilitation of Oedipus, from disgrace to blessedness. All this seems to be the expression of fate. Yet it would be surprising if Sophocles were to deal with his themes without allowing character to mould, or to seem to mould, a good deal of the action; and indeed he does not disappoint us. It is chiefly at the outset of the play, when Oedipus arrives at Colonus, and

[108] So urge also the Chorus, 1095–1100 (cf. 1165 f.), though admitting, 1116–1119, that the suffering comes from πότμος.

[109] See above, pp. 161 f.; below, pp. 168–171. H. D. F. Kitto, *Greek Tragedy*, pp. 300–307, treats the *Philoctetes* not as tragedy, but as a drama of intrigue. By concentrating attention on Neoptolemus he seems to me to miss the tragic (and universal) import of the play, though it admittedly is a tragedy with a "happy ending."

at the end, when he mysteriously passes to his doom, that the action appears to be controlled by the oracle. From time to time in the intervening episodes we are reminded of the oracle; and the arrival and the activity of Theseus, who befriends Oedipus, has something of the character of a *deus ex machina.* Yet the action of these episodes seems to spring chiefly from the characters of Oedipus, Creon, and Polynices. In particular, the fact that Oedipus already knows in general his destiny, and is eager to fulfil it, makes all that he does appear to be the result of his will. He has the illusion of freedom; or we may say, if we prefer, that fate works through his will. And when he learns from Ismene that his sons and Creon have discovered that there is a potency in the control of his person not only after his death but also during his lifetime,[110] a powerful motive is supplied for his resentment and for his resistance to their attempts to win his return to the Theban border. The moral interest perhaps declines for a time, and the human interest rises, in the scene in which Oedipus curses his unfilial sons and prophesies their death at each other's hands. It may be felt that the most appealing parts of the play are those in which Sophocles, native of Colonus, fondly rehearses the beauties of his birthplace, and those in which amid circumstances of great impressiveness Oedipus becomes an Attic hero.

Two opposing kinds of fate cross one another in the play, the baleful family curse, and the kindly oracle which controls the outcome. Oedipus is still a victim of the ancient curse, as he realizes (596); his sons know that it still blights the house (367–370); Polynices conveniently blames on it his exile (1299 f.); on the eve of the passing of Oedipus, the Chorus, elders of Colonus, pray that blessing and not evil may come to them who have looked upon a man accursed (1480–1484); even after his departure, his young daughter Antigone, still uncomprehending, and thinking of the loneliness before her, laments the family curse (1670–1672). With the family curse must be considered also the new and terrible curse against his kin uttered by Oedipus himself. It would perhaps not have been spoken if he had not been subject to the misfortunes brought about by the family curse; but it would also not have been spoken if the conduct of Creon and the sons of Oedipus had not provoked the anger of the sufferer. Flint strikes steel, and the curse flashes from the conflict of characters. It comes not all at once, but progressively, as Oedipus learns more of the situation: first it is vague (421–427; 450–452); then in round terms, on the land and on his sons (787–790); next on Creon and his sons (865–870); and last and most terribly on Polynices in particular (1370–1396). In spite of his father's prophecy and curse, Polynices persists in the war, partly because any other course would involve loss of "face," as an Oriental

[110] *O.C.* 389 f.; contrast 92–94.

might say (1414–1430); that is the expression of his character. His claim to the throne, we learn in this play (though not in Aeschylus nor in the *Antigone*, is based on the fact that he is the elder brother).[111] But the deeper reason for his persistence is his conviction that he is now the double victim of his father's and of the family curse (1424–1426; 1432–1434). If he must die, die he must; that or some other fate rests with fortune (ἐν τῷ δαίμονι: 1441–1444). And when Oedipus remarks to Theseus that the vengeance of the gods, though slow, is sure, he is thinking doubtless of the vengeance already stealing upon his sons (1536 f.). Already Ismene has remarked that in addition to the evil heritage of the house "now, moved by some god, and by their sinful minds, an evil rivalry hath seized them, thrice infatuate, to grasp at the rule and kingly power";[112] and this is the outcome. The Chorus, at first tempted to consider the doom of Polynices as a new evil issuing from Oedipus, then surmise that it may come from Fate (*moira*, 1450 f.); both these explanations are true, as well as Ismene's. The children of Oedipus bear a heavy load of destiny, as well as of personal responsibility. Their later fortunes fill two earlier plays of Aeschylus and Sophocles, the *Seven against Thebes* and the *Antigone*.

Crossing the path of the family curse is the beneficent oracle. After the first anguish of the blinding was over, Oedipus had begun to feel that his life must have been spared in childhood for some strange doom.[113] Earlier, after leaving Corinth, he had learned from Apollo something of the end that awaited him: not, indeed, the exact place where he was to die, but the tokens by which he might recognize it,—namely a place sacred to the dread goddesses (*Semnai Theai*) where he should find hospitality, and where moreover some sign, earthquake or thunder or lightning, should confirm the token. There his passing would bestow blessing on his hosts, ruin on those who had exiled him (84–95). The first tokens he recognizes on his arrival at Colonus; triple thunder later marks his passing. There must have been other oracles, for during his exile Ismene has reported them "all" to him (353–355). It is she who now reports the new oracle of Apollo that makes his sons eager to control his movements during his lifetime as well as to possess his tomb (389–392; 412–415). Polynices hears also from the Argive seer Amphiaraus that victory will befriend the side that Oedipus joins (1302; 1331 f.). By comparing this oracle with other earlier prophecies of Apollo, Oedipus is able to infer that his sons will never reign (450–454). Both they (604 f.) and he (619–623;

[111] *O.C.* 375; 1294; 1422; for Aeschylus, see above, p. 115, n. 62; for the *Antigone*, p. 144; for Euripides, below, p. 207, n. 146.

[112] *O.C.* 367–373; cf. *Ant.* 620–624; and see above, p. 146, and n. 54.

[113] *O.T.* 1455–1457; see above, p. 161.

cf. 793) have presentiments, derived from the new oracle, that they are to do battle at Colonus.

Such are the warnings of Apollo in our play. Apollo's will, which is the will of Zeus interpreted, has hitherto seemed to Oedipus, from his infancy to his discovery of his parentage, to have been irresistible but arbitrary; nor could we assign any more intelligible reason for the course of events up to this point than that they were part of the old folk-tale. Now it appears that Apollo's will for Oedipus is in the long run friendly; Oedipus is to become a sort of Attic hero, and this was planned all along.[114]

It is tempting to go further, and to see in our play not merely the social rehabilitation of the outcast (as in the *Ajax*, and in the *Philoctetes*) but a moral renaissance as well. Doubtless the years have done something to make of the violent, self-willed, arrogant Oedipus a venerable figure. His old taint, never of wilful sin, has been washed away by suffering. Pitiable at first in his weakness, he gains strength as the play goes forward, and he walks as if guided by an inner light. But before we accept him as a saintly figure, let us remember that the old fury flares up even now in that curse against his sons which is already at work even as he passes from this life. Though Sophocles believes more than most Greeks in the educative power of suffering,[115] Oedipus has not learned by his suffering to forgive; he does not even pity Polynices, as do Antigone and Theseus. The curse, though sufficiently explained by situation and character, and though an essential part of the folk-tale, is for all that no less shocking.

Indeed the glory in which Oedipus departs and the honor that is to live after him is not won through any superior moral quality, whether innate or acquired through suffering.[116] When the evidence pointed to his having killed Laius, but not yet to parricide and incest, he seemed to himself, as he would seem to any Greek, to have the gods against him, to be most wretched of men,[117] to be evil and unhallowed.[118] In the present play, he does not at first assert his innocence, but boldly appeals to the "dread goddesses" for pity on behalf of himself and of Apollo, who once foretold both his misadventures and the final rest.[119] Later he justifies himself to

[114] *O.C.* 87 f. (Apollo); contrast *O.T.* 738 (Zeus).

[115] See above, pp. 99 f.; 141 f.

[116] S. H. Butcher, in his essay on Sophocles, in *Some Aspects of the Greek Genius*, pp. 127–131, makes possibly too much of the change in the character of Oedipus and too little of the persecution by the gods. H. D. F. Kitto, *Greek Tragedy*, pp. 391–401, also finds the gods to be indifferent, but holds the theme of the play to be the growth of Oedipus from misery to greatness, through his innate dignity; thus the movement of the *O.T.* is reversed. The *O.C.* "is Sophocles' answer to the tragedy of life. He knows that he cannot justify God to man, but he can justify man to man."

[117] *O.T.* 816: ἐχθροδαίμων; cf. 815.

[118] *O.T.* 822 f.

[119] *O.C.* 86–98. Oedipus has already been told (42 f.) that the goddesses are known at Colonus as "the all-seeing Eumenides, though elsewhere they have other names." See also above, p. 136.

the Chorus, who need not fear any taint from his person, since his acts are more those of suffering than of doing (265–267); and, what is more, the killing of Laius was done in ignorance and was provoked by the older man's deeds, while his parents had deliberately sought his death; how then could he be called "evil in nature"? [120] A second time he protests to the Chorus that his motives were innocent, that he has acted in self-defence, and that he is "stainless before the law, void of malice." [121] All this and more he urges, finally, in reply to Creon: his deeds of murder and incest and his sufferings were no choice of his, but "such was the pleasure of the gods, angry perchance with the race of old" (962–965); such is the plight into which he came, "led by the gods" (997 f.); as an individual he is innocent (966–968); how indeed could he personally be guilty of deeds foretold by an oracle given before he was born (969–973)? It is the chorus who acquit him: "The stranger is a good man; his fate has been accursed, but it is worthy of succor" (1014 f.). So Theseus also feels; and the *Semnai Theai*, dwelling in Colonus, accept Oedipus, confirming the oracle of Apollo. He is in the hands of the gods, who may be supposed at the last to distinguish between the outward guilt of Oedipus and his innocence of intent, since they use him. But there has been no change of heart in Oedipus, except in his heroic endurance of suffering and in his discovery that he is an instrument of the gods.

Nor should we fall into the mistake of reading too much into the tardy reparation that the gods make to Oedipus. He is not the recipient of divine tenderness, an example to prove that "whom the Lord loveth he chasteneth"; he has suffered the consequences of certain acts committed rashly, but in ignorance, acts moreover which the gods planned even before his birth. If there be justice, then, in the gods' dealings with Oedipus, it is in their ceasing to punish him and in granting him a painless death and posthumous glory. They have always intended to use him for their purposes as a tutelary spirit of Attica, with a mysterious potency for good and for evil. The sense of the marvellous in the closing scene,[122] the confidence, the inner light, the domination of the whole situation by Oedipus, all make us forget the earlier persecution. Apparently Sophocles feels that all is now well, and does not share in the temporary pessimism of the chorus, who have echoed the familiar commonplace:

> Never to have lived is best, ancient writers say;
> Never to have drawn the breath of life,

[120] 268–275; 270: κακὸς φύσιν.

[121] 510–548; n.b. 539, 547 f. Such is the plea of a *mens conscia recti*.

[122] On the triple thunder, and related matters, see my "Note on *Georgics* IV, 491–493," in *Studies in Honor of E. K. Rand* (New York, 1938), pp. 113–122.

Never to have looked into the eye of day.
Second best's a gay good night and quickly turn away.[123]

Even the Chorus presently recover hope: Oedipus has been the victim of the arbitrary will of Apollo; "many were the sorrows that came to him without cause (*μάταν*); but in requital may a just god lift him up." So pray the Chorus before the word has come of his disappearance (1565–1657); and it is in a spirit of resignation that they finally accept the story of Theseus; "for verily these things stand fast."[124]

[123] O.C. 1225–1229. Trans. W. B. Yeats. For the commonplace, *μὴ φῦναι*, cf. above, p. 42, and n. 189.

[124] 1779, Jebb's interpretation.

# CHAPTER VII

## EURIPIDES

SUPERFICIALLY the easiest of the three Attic tragic poets for the modern spectator or reader to appreciate, Euripides is actually the most baffling. Admired in antiquity, at least after his death, he has in modern times been viewed now with enthusiasm, now with disparagement or even with scorn.[1] His beauties of detail in scenes and in lyrics and in *gnomai*, all will grant; his broad human sympathies and his sensitiveness to the gentler virtues are universally acknowledged.[2] He still uses the ancient myths, even if he (like many others who pass for conservatives in religion) freely adapts them, or uses the least familiar legends; and he retains most of the conventions of the theatre. On the other hand, he is familiar with the current social and intellectual trends of his own age. The more one considers especially the plots of his dramas, therefore, the more one may be inclined to set down the poet as a conservative; whereas if one gives heed to the poet's humanitarianism, or to the ideas expressed in particular scenes and speeches, one may be more impressed by his rebellious attitude, his "romanticism," or his scepticism.[3] Moreover Euripides has not been at pains, or perhaps it would be fairer to say that he has been unable, to achieve consistency of attitude or tone within his dramas; he is thus all things to all men, and is particularly liable to misinterpretation when single plays, still more when detached sentiments, are exhibited as specimens of "the Euripidean point of view."[4]

[1] A. W. Verrall, *Euripides the Rationalist*, pp. vii–ix; P. Masqueray, *Euripide et ses Idées*, pp. vii–x; G. Murray, *Euripides and his Age*, pp. 7–10; P. H. Frye, *Romance and Tragedy*, pp. 195–204.

[2] W. E. H. Lecky, *History of European Morals* (New York, 1929), I, pp. 228 f. cited by G. H. Macurdy, *The Quality of Mercy*, p. 1; cf. also J. Buchan (Lord Tweedsmuir), *Pilgrim's Way* (Boston, 1940), pp. 112 f., who found in the South African veld that his favorite poet Wordsworth, well suited to "a landscape instinct with human traditions," was here irrelevant, and indeed that he "did not want any sort of literature, with one curious exception. This was Euripides."

[3] For the former interpretation, cf. J. Burnet, "The Religious and Moral Ideas of Euripides," in *Essays and Addresses* (New York, 1930), pp. 46–63; for the latter, A. W. Verrall, *Euripides the Rationalist*, and *Four Plays*, and *The Bacchants of Euripides* (some account of Verrall's views is taken below, in connection with the several plays; see also below, Appendix 18); also, in quite different spirit, G. Murray, *Euripides and his Age*; E. R. Dodds, "Euripides the Irrationalist," *C.R.* 43 (1929), pp. 97–104.

[4] Cf. Decharme, *Euripides*, pp. 373–378; also, with a different interpretation, Verrall, *E. the R.*, pp. 231 f.

Even more a man of his times than is Sophocles, Euripides uses the ancient myths to interpret contemporary problems; war and peace, convention and reason, *nomos* and *physis*, the rights of individuals, the status of woman.[5] Sometimes he creates living men and women, and succeeds in setting forth ideas with a universal bearing; sometimes we feel that we are only catching echoes of contemporary debates, that "date" as do many of the plays of social significance of Ibsen and Shaw.[6] Moreover the thought of Euripides is not often original; he expresses now one, now another of the ideas that are in the air during the last four decades of the fifth century, ideas that have been given currency by the philosophers, the sophists, and the rhetoricians of the first half of the century.[7]

The dramatic form lends itself to conflicts of feeling and thought, and allows the poet to arouse sympathy for various types of character. In an age in which the individual is realizing a new importance, and is taught by the *rhetor* and the sophist how to vindicate his own point of view, it is natural that Euripides, like Sophocles, should develop the set speech, or *rhesis*, as a dramatic instrument; and quite as natural that he should transfer to the theatre the debates and the forms of argument of the assembly, the courts, and the philosophic groups, whether in pairs of long antithetical speeches or in more rapid dialogue, or even in line-for-line repartee (*stichomythy*).[8] But the poet's restless interest in general ideas of wide applicability often leads him to introduce commonplaces of argument, maxims and tirades, at the expense of dramatic appropriateness or of consistency.[9] From this fact one may be tempted to conclude not merely that Euripides has his lapses as a literary artist, which is true, but, what is less clear, that like many of the sophists, he is primarily a rhetorician, an orator interested in scoring intellectual points, and only secondarily an artist, or even a propagandist or reformer. Even so, the many inconsistencies, the dissolving phantasmagoria of ideas, prevent us from finding any single expression of his outlook on life, — for example, his conception of fate. It is possible to write a book on "Euripides and his Ideas," and indeed Masqueray has done precisely this; or one may discuss "The Critical Spirit

[5] W. Jaeger, *Paideia*, pp. 339–348; H. D. F. Kitto, *Greek Tragedy*, pp. 309–311.

[6] Cf. G. Norwood, *Euripides and Mr. Bernard Shaw* (London, 1913).

[7] W. Nestle, "Die philosophische Quellen des Euripides," *Philologus*, Suppl. 8 (1900), pp. 638 ff.; Nestle, *Euripides, der Dichter der Griechischen Aufklärung* (Stuttgart, 1901); A. W. Benn, *Greek Philosophers*, pp. 68 f.; 82; P. Decharme, *Euripides and the Spirit of his Dramas*, pp. 21–42; P. Masqueray, *Euripide et ses Idées* (1908), pp. 187–202; J. H. Finley, Jr., "Euripides and Thucydides," *H.S.C.P.* 49 (1938), pp. 23–68. On the sophistic movement, see below, pp. 221–228.

[8] Cf. Finley, *op. cit.*, pp. 55–58; 65 f. For the contradictory theses of Protagoras and others, see below, pp. 249 f.

[9] Masqueray, *op. cit.*, pp. 74–91; J. T. Stickney, *Les Sentences dans la Poésie Grecque*, pp. 215–244; n.b. pp. 216; 237–240, for the favorite Euripidean commonplaces.

in Euripides," as Decharme has done in the first part of his book. But one may hardly pretend to set forth "The Theology of Euripides." And the reason for the inconsistencies, both artistic and intellectual, may prove at last to be the sincere bewilderment of a poet who has honestly tried to use ancient forms (for example, the gods and other supernatural forces) to express the many-sided facets of life, but has found the task too great. Euripides is baffling because he is himself baffled.

Ancient legend, compassion for ordinary mankind, psychological insight into abnormal characters and situations, great rhetorical gifts, a sense of the theatre that easily passes from drama into melodrama, a sadness at the spectacle of the Athens and the Sparta of his own age, but a willingness to refashion tragedy into a new *genre* (the tragi-comedy with a happy ending), a weighing of religious and philosophical conceptions of man's destiny and his place in the *cosmos*; these elements contribute in varying degrees to form a series of dramas that never fail to interest us, but that seldom achieve the sense of mastery that we find in Aeschylus and Sophocles. Rather do we feel that Euripides is striving at different times (or even at the same time) to realize quite different objectives. It is therefore important to determine the general chronology of the extant plays, and to discover, if we can, the particular objective of each play or group of plays. We may then consider a few aspects of the several plays of Euripides and may finally inquire what general conclusions may be drawn with regard to his attitude toward fate, good, and evil.[10]

Of the more than ninety plays of Euripides of which we know, seventeen have survived;[11] most of these date from the poet's later years, and indeed all but the *Alcestis* (438 B.C.) fall within the last twenty-five years of his long life. The *Medea* (431), like the *Alcestis*, already shows a break with the Homeric cycle, and an interest in womanhood; also in unhappy love, as does the revised *Hippolytus* (428). The latter play, together with the *Heraclidae* (c. 431–430), the *Suppliant Women* (c. 420–419), the *Heracles* (c. 420–418), and the *Ion* (c. 418–413), comprise in their themes an "Attic" group, with occasional patriotic sallies. After the Peace of Nicias (421), the poet's disillusionment and hatred of war already apparent in the *Andromache* (early in the Peloponnesian War) and the *Hecuba* (c. 425), becomes even more marked in the *Trojan Women* (415). But another group comprising the earlier *Alcestis* and *Ion*, the *Iphigenia*

[10] For the chronology and grouping of the plays, cf. A. Dieterich, in *P.W.*, VI, 1248–1270, G. Macurdy, *The Chronology of the Extant Plays of Euripides* (Columbia Univ. dissertation, 1905); J. H. Finley, Jr., *H.S.C.P.* 49 (1938), pp. 28 f.; H. D. F. Kitto, *Greek Tragedy*, pp. 185–187; 312–317; 332 f.; 374–385 (dealing not so much with questions of chronology in the strict sense as with the groups of plays, falling generally in successive periods, which manifest similar conceptions of tragedy).

[11] See Appendix 17: *Rhesus.*

*among the Taurians* (414–412), and the *Helen* (412), borders on high comedy. Still other plays of this period are even more melodramatic: the *Electra* (413), the *Phoenician Women* (c. 409), the *Orestes* (408), and the *Iphigenia at Aulis* (c. 407). Finally the *Bacchae* (c. 407), like the last-named play composed after the poet's renunciation of Athens, signalizes at once a return to the conventions of tragedy and a surprising religious outlook.

More significant for our general subject than such a chronological survey of the plays is a classification, which will indeed also prove almost to correspond to this sequence, but which is based on the extent to which Euripides adheres to a "tragic way of thinking about life." [12] A common quality is to be found in one group, consisting of *Medea*, *Hippolytus*, *Heraclidae*, *Heracles*, *Andromache*, *Hecuba*, *Suppliant Women*, and *Trojan Women*; they all have a truly tragic point of view, exhibiting the calamitous consequences of the defects (*hamartiai*) of human nature, whether in the individual (*Medea* and *Heracles*), or in nature (*Hippolytus*), or in society under the conditions of warfare (the remaining five plays of this group). Sometimes the sinner, sometimes a victim, suffers; sometimes the suffering is the communal result of man's inhumanity to man. It is curious to observe that of this group all except the *Hippolytus* are by Aristotelian canons poorly constructed, and abound in oversimplified characters, inconsistent characters, sophistic debates or tirades, and episodic plots barely unified by their formal prologues.

In a second group of plays, Euripides shows a mastery of construction and of subtle character-drawing, together with a command of irony; but the point of view is no longer tragic. These are the earlier *Alcestis*, the *Ion*, and the *Iphigenia among the Taurians*, and the *Helen*, a group that mingles tragedy with comedy, and leads to happy endings; Menander would seem to stem from such plays almost as easily as from Aristophanes.[13] Effective though these plays are, they are full of artificialities and improbabilities of plot; and they seldom wring the heart.

The melodramatic group (*Electra*, *Orestes*, *Phoenician Women*, and *Iphigenia at Aulis*) are more sinister than the tragi-comedies, without being really tragic. The characters of Electra and Orestes are abnormal case-studies, lacking in universality, and so cannot arouse pity or fear. The *Phoenician Women*, crowded with theatrical action but devoid of convincing characterization and inner motivation, is more like an historical pageant than a tragedy of cause and effect; while in the *Iphigenia at Aulis* neither the irresolute Agamemnon (who indeed deserves what he suffers) nor his rather inconsistently portrayed daughter are truly tragic figures; rather are they the victims of an arbitrary blow of a divine power, and the

[12] H. D. F. Kitto, *Greek Tragedy*, p. 186.

[13] See Appendix 18: A. W. Verrall.

happy ending (the work of another hand than our poet's) does not afford the *katharsis* of true tragedy.

The final play, the *Bacchae*, on the other hand, is in the strict form of earlier tragedy, and exhibits the *hybris* of Pentheus leading to *nemesis*; it even returns to the theme of Dionysus himself, the god of tragedy, as well as to the more universal theme of two of the earlier plays of Euripides, the terrible power of elemental natural instincts, and the ironical results of opposing them (*Medea* and *Hippolytus*).

We may now consider rapidly the several plays of the successive groups. And first, passing over for the moment the *Alcestis*, we are confronted by the eight real tragedies (with which we shall later associate the *Bacchae*).

The story of the *Medea* consists in a sequel to the legend of Jason's winning of the Golden Fleece by the aid of the barbarian princess and sorceress, Medea, who has fallen in love with him and accompanied him back to Thessaly. Now a fugitive in Corinth, Jason has set her aside in favor of a new and more immediately advantageous marriage with the daughter of King Creon of Corinth. A familiar theme, with traits like those of the stories of Ariadne and Dido; and the present play reminds us that "Heaven has no rage like love to hatred turned, Nor hell a fury like a woman scorned." The jealousy, the duplicity, and the revenge of Medea provide the action. After feigning resignation and securing from King Aegeus of Athens a promise of asylum in his land, she destroys Creon and his daughter by the gift of a poisoned robe,[14] slays her two sons in order to crush their father Jason, and (dropping the thought of flight to Athens) escapes in a dragon-chariot through the skies.

The plight of Medea is at first pathetic, and is set forth in a famous speech on the hardships of woman's lot, aggravated by man's easy acceptance of a double standard of morality, while woman perforce is faithful; aggravated moreover in her case by her barbarian origin and forelorn condition (*Medea* 230–266). It ought to be unnecessary to disprove the silly but oft repeated allegation that Euripides was a misogynist. P. Decharme [15] has said more than enough in favor of it, and little enough of the poet's sympathetic treatment of Alcestis, Andromache, Creusa, Iphigenia, or even of Medea and Phaedra and Melanippe.[16] In the *Medea*, besides the great speech on woman's hard lot, suggested by Medea's plight, we have Jason's slighting remarks about womanhood [17] prompted by his

[14] The *Trachiniai* of Sophocles, which shows another heroine responsible for a similar but unintended act, has been interpreted as a rebuke to Euripides that suggests how differently an injured wife may behave. See above, pp. 151–154, esp. p. 153, n. 70.

[15] P. Decharme, *op. cit.*, pp. 93–112.

[16] To the fragments of the *Melanippe Bound* in Nauck may now be added the interesting papyrus fragment; cf. *Trag. Graec. Frag. Pap.*, ed. A. S. Hunt.

[17] *Medea* 573–575; 909; cf. *Hipp.* 616–650.

own uneasy conscience, and Medea's deceptive excuse of a woman's tears (928). More germane to the plot in hand than expressive of genuine universal condemnation is Medea's remark that woman is by nature not apt for virtuous deeds but expert in mischief (407–409); she is in revolt against oppressions like the Jael whose deeds are sung by Deborah. So the Chorus (of Corinthian women) respond with a song of triumph for womanhood that is thus turning the tables on man and disproving the ancient attacks of poets [such as Hesiod and Semonides] on woman, as if rivers were flowing backwards.[18] But the Chorus later (1081–1088) shyly introduce a sad reflection on the blessedness of the childless by remarking that few women are gifted with wisdom. All these sentiments, and such others in other plays, must be considered in the light of their contexts. No one has argued that the unfavorable delineation of individual men (such as Jason) or that detached sentiments directed against individual men or against the wickedness of the human race, prove Euripides a hater of the male sex. He condemns neither man nor woman, but seeks to understand them as individuals and the society in which they must live.

As Medea's plan of vengeance develops, it becomes increasingly clear that hers is a deeply passionate nature which has marked her out to love, to suffer, to hate, to strike back even at what she most loves. Instinct, the goddess Kypris, *physis*, is her whole life, even if her emotions are attended by intellectual cunning and the arts of the sorceress.[19] This terrible natural force, like the Aphrodite of the *Hippolytus* and the Dionysus of the *Bacchae*, may not be denied; yet to be possessed by it and to yield to it spells tragedy. Barbarian that she is, she cannot easily mould herself to *nomos* and the ways of the *polis* and the *sophrosyne* that others so easily commend.[20] Indeed, had Jason's recent conduct been more regular, had he not outrageously proposed a new "design for living" in the form of a *ménage à trois*, Medea would not have been put to such a test. As it is, the dramatic conflict is not, as Sophocles would have made it, between Medea and Jason, but within the divided soul of Medea herself, torn between vengeful rage and tender love of her children. In a great soliloquy (1021–1080) and in a later tormented speech on the verge of action (1236–1250) she battles with her resolution. Being what she is, the result is certain: "I am broken by evil, and I know what evil things I have to do, but

[18] *Medea* 410–430. For this rhetorical figure, the *ἀδύνατον*, see below, p. 220, n. 3.

[19] Note the emphasis on the *θυμός* of Medea, 106–110; 271; 879; 883; 1070 f.: *θυμὸς δὲ κρείσσων τῶν βουλευμάτων* | *ὅσπερ μεγίστων αἴτιος κακῶν βροτοῖς*; on *ὀργή*, 447; 615; 870; 909; on *αὐθαδία*, 103 f.: *ἄγριον ἦθος στυγεράν τε φύσιν* | *φρενὸς αὐθάδους*; 1028; and the ironic 223 f.; on *Κύπρις* and *Ἔρως*, 527; 530; cf. 330; 627–641; for *σοφία*, 285; 539; cf. 292–305; 580–583.

[20] 485; 635–641; 811–815; cf. 1121: *παρανόμως*; 119–130, of Jason's conduct, but gnomic; 214–224, of Medea's feigned surrender; 911–913, Jason's commendation of it.

passion (θυμός), the cause of direst woes to man, hath triumphed over my sober thoughts" (1077–1080).

Jason, the perfect egotist and opportunist, prepared to profit now by his new bride's help, as formerly by Medea's, thinks he has done enough for Medea in bringing her from her benighted barbarian home to civilized Greece (536–541; 1330–1332), where she may find an appreciative public for her cleverness, where her children may win reflected glory from prospective step-brothers, and where all this strange family may enjoy economic security (547–575; 595–597), if she will only be sensible. The *hybris* of such a Jason receives hardly more than just *nemesis* in the loss of his children.[21] Yet only a perverse sentimentality will really sympathize with Medea in these last terrible scenes and protest that "*tout comprendre, c'est tout excuser.*" For it is not justice that we behold but vengeance at the expense of Creon and his daughter and of Medea's own innocent children.[22] Here is a tragedy that transcends mere pathos. For Medea is not merely a noble woman to whom a flaw, a tragic *hamartia*, brings suffering; her passionate nature is the whole of her, for love and for hate, for better and for worse. "I did wrong (ἡμάρτανον) that hour I left my father's house, persuaded by a Hellene's words, who now shall pay the penalty, so help me God!" (800–802).

In this clear and honest insight Medea says all that need be said of her own responsibility in the story; Jason is not so honest. For the story, apart from Medea's supernatural powers, moves on the human level without recourse to fate,[23] or chance,[24] or divine interference.[25] Naturally there are conventional references to gods as powers or as moral agencies; but there is no suggestion that the course of the action was in any sense predestined. Pessimism there is; it is the Chorus who declare that the childless are far happier than those who have given hostages to fortune;[26] while

[21] 1366; cf. 1231 f. Creon's love of his children (329; cf. 344 f.) and the spectacle of the childless Aegeus perhaps suggest to Medea the surest means of wounding Creon and Jason, namely in the loss of their children.

[22] Cf. the plea of the Nurse, 116–118.

[23] Of the "ruin" of the various characters, ἄτη is used, 279; 979; 987; συμφορά, 1204; 1221; 1233; of death, μοῖρα θανάτου, 987; of murder, αὐτόχειρ μοῖρα, 1281; nowhere any tinge of fatalism.

[24] "Hapless" is all that is implied by 1250: δυστυχὴς δ' ἐγὼ γυνή; cf. 1264.

[25] The Chorus piously attribute Medea's plight to θεός, 362 f; as sorceress, Medea honors Hecate above all, 395–397; but appeals to *Themis*, to Zeus, to *Dike*, to Helios, and to θέσμια, as keepers of the moral order, 160; 169; 492–495; 764; 1352; Jason for his part also appeals to Zeus, 1405, and to the *daimones*, 1410. The Chorus see in Jason's fate the just act of a *daimon*, 1231 f.; but also see in Medea an *Erinys* and *Alastor*, 1259 f. (text doubtful); cf. 1333; Jason prays that his children's *Erinys* and *Dike* may destroy her, 1389. Of the imminent death of Jason's bride and her father, Medea remarks briefly in self-vindication, "The gods and I have devised these schemes with evil intent" (1013 f.).

[26] 1090–1115; cf. Antiphon, below, p. 233.

it is the Messenger who, after telling of the hideous deaths of Creon and his daughter, indulges in the pessimistic commonplace that human life is a shadow, that pretence to wisdom is vain, that wealth may bestow good luck, but that no mortal is happy (εὐδαίμων).[27]

The melodramatic dénouement, in which Medea makes her escape in the dragon-chariot, ignores, as we have seen, the contemplated asylum in Athens. There are therefore those who either regard the scene with Aegeus as a blemish or who find the miraculous finale an unfortunate afterthought.[28] It is true that Medea has hitherto been helpless, except for her wits, and the use of the "machine" is a startling conclusion, even if Medea is herself the "goddess" who has it at her command. The familiar closing lines of the Chorus that comment on the unexpected outcome of the story (here varied by the substitution of "Zeus" for the more generalized expression, πολλαὶ μορφαὶ τῶν δαιμονίων) do indeed suggest divine intervention in what has been up to the last moment a story of human wills, the ruin of lives, guilty and innocent, by passionate human nature.[29]

The *Hippolytus* is another drama of vengeance; but this time it is the goddess Aphrodite herself who, slighted by the refusal of young Hippolytus to think of love, uses Phaedra as a means of revenge, to the ruin of both Phaedra and Hippolytus. Her rôle is found in the Prologue, and is balanced by the appearance of Artemis, champion of Hippolytus, as *dea ex machina* in the Epilogue; all the intervening scenes appear to move on the human level, with Phaedra and Hippolytus acting respectively as the human counterparts of these goddesses of love and of purity.[30]

The means of vengeance devised by Aphrodite is the infatuation of Phaedra, the wife of Theseus in his later years, for his son by the Amazon Hippolyta. Phaedra strives to conceal her guilty passion, but is wasting away; her old Nurse elicits the secret from her, and in order to save her betrays it to Hippolytus, first pledging him not to divulge what she is to tell him. He is naturally outraged at the disclosure, and denounces Phaedra, who, fearing that he will expose her to Theseus, hangs herself, leaving a false accusation against Hippolytus. Theseus charges his son with having seduced his wife; Hippolytus denies the charge, but will not break his oath and expose Phaedra. He is therefore sent by Theseus into exile with a curse, which is promptly realized by a sea-monster frighten-

[27] 1224–1230; cf. Pindar, *Pyth.* 8, 92–98; above, pp. 73 f.

[28] Aristotle, *Poet.* 1454b1, condemning the use of the "machine" in the *Medea*; Verrall, *Four Plays*, pp. 127–130; G. Norwood, *Greek Tragedy*, pp. 196 f.

[29] *Medea* 1415–1419; see above, p. 100. Verrall takes the "tag" as ironical.

[30] There is a similar concentration of the divine machinery at the beginning of the *Ajax* of Sophocles (see above, p. 148); similarly at the beginning and the end of the *Trachiniai* (above, p. 152), of the *Electra* (above, pp. 162 f.), of the *Philoctetes* (above, pp. 164 f.), and of the *Oedipus at Colonus* (above, pp. 166 f.).

ing his horses so that he is dragged to death. Before he dies, however, Artemis vindicates his innocence, and father and son are reconciled. A cruel story, with elements that remind us of Joseph and Potiphar's wife, but a story that proceeds austerely rather than sensationally; a play moreover that is full of the haunting beauties of the natural world and full of insight into human hearts.

In its simplest terms, the *Hippolytus* represents a conflict between two powers, or attitudes toward life: passion (ἔρως) and chastity (σωφροσύνη). Aphrodite and Artemis cannot be dismissed as mere stage machinery. There is in the world an elemental, creative, non-intellectual, non-moral force, beautiful in its manifestations, but also terrible in its potentialities, which we call Love.[31] Symbolized by Aphrodite, or Kypris, it is both sweet and painful, both a beneficent power and a jealous spirit that will not be denied; Kypris is a goddess, and something more (359–361). On the other hand there is a way of life that shuns passion and personal indulgence, seeking moderation and self-control; this is the way of the ascetic, the celibate, the recluse; at times it has something in common with the Orphic, and of the devotee of Artemis.[32] Yet neither passion nor chastity alone is in itself a perfect good; passion, uncontrolled, leads to disaster, while chastity and self-control, however good, may lack positive and ulterior motive forces; and even moderation may become immoderate. So Phaedra, losing against her will her self-control, is both instigator and victim of disaster; and Hippolytus, whose way of life is wholly self-centred, is as ineffectual and negative as Artemis. Our play is therefore not a struggle between good and evil, but a conflict of two partial, relative goods.

In the earlier *Hippolytus*, which had shocked the public, Phaedra had openly avowed her love of Hippolytus; the present revised play shows her struggling against her passion, and in the first half concentrates the interest on her. Even if the sympathy of the spectator shifts in the second half to Hippolytus, for whom the play is still named, it may well be argued that she remains the more interesting and vital figure.[33] For however noble and in some ways appealing we may find the young Hippolytus, devoted only to Artemis and the woodlands and meadows, something is

[31] 347 f.; 443–476; 525–564; 1268–1281; Euripides frag. 890 Nauck. Euripides doubtless believes in Aphrodite as Lucretius believes in Venus Genetrix.

[32] Note the emphasis in the play on σωφροσύνη (358; 413; 431; 667; 731; 995; 1007; 1013; 1100; 1365; 1402), and especially the counsels of the Servant (88–107) and of the Nurse (253–266), and the praise of τὸ σῶφρον by the Chorus (431 f.). See also below, p. 216, on the *Bacchae*.

[33] For the shift of sympathy, cf. A. R. Bellinger, *Yale Classical Studies* 6 (1939), pp. 25 f.; for the primary rôle of Phaedra in the present play, D. Grene, *C. P.* 34 (1939), pp. 45–58. Seneca and Racine name their plays for Phaedra.

lacking in his nature; he is not a complete human being.[34] We may discount the imputation to him by Theseus of Orphic cult and whatever of fanaticism that may imply; [35] we may forgive him the partial breaking of his word (612) and his attack on womanhood (616–668), provoked by the shock and stress of the moment, and redeemed by his later gallantry in refusing to break his oath and tell the truth about Phaedra.[36] That (except his forgiveness of his father) is his most positive deed, a feat of reticence. Yet his *sophrosyne* is not the result of schooling amid the temptations of life, but the gift of *physis*; [37] in his avoidance of normal human ties he is an escapist. His friendly servant sees in him a bit of the prig; [38] and indeed in his attitude both toward the servant and still more toward Aphrodite he is guilty of *hybris*, a pride of superior virtue. One may ask, to be sure, what else he could have done within the limits of the action; certainly he was not to respond to Phaedra's passion. The damage was done, however, by his previous life of cold indifference to womankind; in our play he merely runs true to form. His outburst of angry denunciation made it impossible for Phaedra to believe that he would not go further and denounce her to Theseus, and so made her ruinous stratagem a natural means of vengeance. His touching forgiveness of his father is the final testimony to the integrity of this noble though one-sided character.

Phaedra is a more subtle character. Essentially chaste, and much concerned for her good name,[39] she nevertheless, unlike Hippolytus, has to struggle for self-control. But struggle she does, suffering in silence, preferring death to disgrace, and not deigning to reply to the denunciation of Hippolytus. The odds are against her: the bad blood of her notorious Cretan family (337–341; 372); her imprudence in allowing propinquity and passing fancy to draw her into intimacy with the young prince (24–40), idleness (384), the weakness of fasting, her roaming thoughts of the woodland haunts of Hippolytus (208–231), and the temporary absence of Theseus all conspire to undermine her resolution. No wonder that the Nurse (494) and that Hippolytus (1034 f., with oxymoron) cast doubt on the strength of her *sophrosyne*; for like many another, she sees the right course, but against her will she chooses ill.[40] Even so disaster might have

[34] Cf. I. M. Linforth, "Hippolytus and Humanism," *T.A.P.A.* 45 (1914), pp. 5–16.

[35] *Hipp.* 948–954, on which see I. M. Linforth, *The Arts of Orpheus*, pp. 50–59.

[36] 657 f.; 983–1035; 1060–1064; 1307–1309.

[37] Cf. 79 f.; and P. Shorey, "Φύσις, Μελέτη, 'Επιστήμη"; and see below, p. 218 and n. 206.

[38] 93: τὸ σεμνόν.

[39] 415–430; 489: εὐκλεής; 687 f.; 775: εὔδοξον . . . φήμαν; cf. 47.

[40] 375–390, on which see Ovid's comment, *Met.* VII, 20, and Aristotle on ἀκρασία (below, p. 328), and E. R. Dodds, "Euripides the Irrationalist," pp. 97–104, esp. p. 99; but Phaedra's remark, 380 f., is not to be taken as Euripidean justification of irrational weakness of will, but only of his understanding of human nature. Cf. also 1305 (Artemis): οὐχ ἑκοῦσα.

been averted had it not been for the machinations of Aphrodite,[41] and the meddling of the Nurse who, at first shocked by the discovery of the object of Phaedra's love (354–361), then on "sober second thought" (436) determined to save the life of her beloved mistress (496 f.), supplies, now subtly now crudely, the arguments for yielding to passion which Phaedra's finer nature could not voice.[42] The steps by which Phaedra hesitates, and presently yields (though in ignorance of what the Nurse intends), are developed with consummate skill.[43] The rest follows inevitably; and when Phaedra is convinced (wrongly, as it proves) that Hippolytus means to reveal her passion to Theseus, it is as certain that she will seek to clear her own reputation at the expense of his as it is certain that Medea, scorned, will seek vengeance on Jason.

As Hippolytus goes into exile under his father's curse, the Chorus (women of Trozen) sing a troubled song of sympathy (1102–1150); they would fain believe in the divine understanding (*ξύνεσις*), but are dismayed by the vicissitudes of man, and the disparity between deeds and fortunes (*τύχαι*); and when they behold blameless Hippolytus[44] in his stricken state, they feel anger at the gods (1146). Yet, as they know, there is no escape from what must be.[45] When dying Hippolytus is brought into his father's presence, he too protests his innocence and the injustice of his lot; he, the upright and the reverent, has come to this cruel end;[46] can it be that he, though innocent, is atoning for the guilt of ancestors?[47] The answer to the question comes from the lips of Artemis, defender of his innocence: "Thy nobility of soul hath been thy ruin" (1390). A hard saying, which touches the very root of the matter; for the *sophrosyne* of Hippolytus is not enough, as he has almost realized (1034 f.). Nor can Artemis herself save him, against the wills of Kypris (1327; 1400) and Zeus (1331) and his own *moira* (1436); this is not so much either diabolical machinery or predestination as the expression of the truth that such a character as Hippolytus, offender against the natural power represented by Aphrodite, must of necessity suffer, even if the means of bringing about his suffering seem to us capricious and the extent of his suffering out of

[41] 27 f.; cf. the rôle of Venus in *Aeneid* I.

[42] 439–461; 493–496; cf. the Servant to Hippolytus, 88–107. For the invincibility of Love, 439–444, cf. *Troad.* 948–950; 964 f. (see below, p. 193); Aristophanes, *Clouds* 1079–1082 (the argument of *Adikos Logos*). To the Protagorean maxim in a lost play of Euripides (frag. 19 Nauck): *τί δ' αἰσχρόν, ἢν μὴ τοῖσι χρωμένοις δοκῇ*; Plato is said to have retorted: *αἰσχρὸν τό γ' αἰσχρόν, κἢν δοκῇ κἢν μὴ δοκῇ.*

[43] 337–520; cf. L. E. Matthaei, *Studies in Greek Tragedy*, pp. 88–92; the whole essay, pp. 76–117, is full of understanding.

[44] 1150: *τὸν οὐδὲν ἄτας αἴτιον*; cf. 1382 f.

[45] 1256: *τοῦ χρεών.*

[46] 1363–1369; cf. 1415.

[47] 1379–1383. There is indeed a curse in the family, and Hippolytus himself is the scion of Theseus' earlier incontinence.

proportion to his offence. That is tragic justice, if not "poetic justice."[48] But that is not all. Just as she departs to her suicide, which is to be accompanied by the letter incriminating Hippolytus, Phaedra has exclaimed: "When he shares my plight, he shall learn to be wise" (731: σωφρονεῖν). Her prophecy is fulfilled, but not as she intended; for Hippolytus does indeed learn by suffering, and the fruit of his education is his forgiveness of his misguided father in the last scene, a scene which allays the tragic "qualm." The brutal Theseus may not seem to deserve such forgiveness; yet, as Artemis observes, he caused his son's death in ignorance (1334–1337), and involuntarily, and naturally, since the gods put error in his way (1434 f.). As it is, he remains, like Creon at the end of the *Antigone*, the chief sufferer (1338; 1407–1414), since he must live on in his state of tragic enlightenment.

Finally, we must return to Phaedra; is she justly treated by the gods? If Hippolytus, faultily faultless, deserves something of his fate, but is ennobled by it, may we say the same of her? No; she is the innocent victim, the pawn in Aphrodite's scheme of vengeance: "She shall die gloriously, but die she must; for I will not rate her suffering so high as to forgo retribution on my enemies" (47–50). Granted that there are in her nature the very elements that lend themselves to Aphrodite's scheme, her will, so long as it remains her own, is noble; and the irony of her fortune is precisely that she is forced by circumstance to become the very thing that she shrinks from being. Her hasty suicide prevents her from winning the tragic understanding that the survivors gain; it is only her reputation that is saved.

The story that Euripides presents in the *Mad Heracles* differs widely from the legend found elsewhere (for example in the *Trachiniai* of Sophocles). It falls into three clearly marked parts. At first Heracles (the son of Zeus by a mortal mother) is away from Thebes, on the last of his labors, and the royal power has been seized by a tyrant, Lycus, who is about to put to death the hero's supposed father, Amphitryon, his wife Megara, and his children. In the nick of time, Heracles appears and turns the tables on Lycus. So far (lines 1–814) we have a brief tragedy with a happy ending, exhibiting the power of Heracles. But now the goddess Iris, messenger of Hera, appears, and bids the reluctant divinity *Lyssa* (Madness) to drive Heracles into the frenzied murder of his wife and children; on recovering his senses he is horrified, and is on the point of suicide. Here, in ironical contrast with the former part, is made manifest the power of Hera (815–1152). From his purpose of suicide Heracles is rescued by his friend Theseus (who is here conceived quite otherwise than in the *Hip-*

[48] Cf. L. E. Matthaei, *Studies in Greek Tragedy*, pp. 97; 105; 111–113.

*polytus*); Theseus persuades him rather to undergo rites of expiation and to take up an honored abode in Athens (1153–1428).

The relation of the three parts of this triptych has been something of a problem for the critics. All agree that the last part, in which a kind of reconciliation is found, is of great importance; some would see in it the chief point of the play, the Athenian kindliness of Theseus receiving the unhappy victim of divine anger, a theme found elsewhere in Attic tragedy.[49] But the earlier scenes, and especially the attitude of Hera toward Heracles also demand explanation. Heracles protests that he deserves well of gods and men for his labors and benefactions, but that his life has been a series of persecutions by Hera, a fact which the action of the play and the comments of the characters require us to accept.[50]

Nevertheless there is an apparent inconsistency in the attitude of Heracles. To the kindly counsel of Theseus he responds in an impassioned *rhesis* (1255–1310), showing that life now, as well as of old, is for him unbearable: he has been dogged by the inheritance of a family curse; Zeus, "whoever this Zeus may be," begot him to annoy Hera, whose serpents attacked him in his cradle; then his labors, and now this last coping-stone of suffering, have laid him low; this is a "sorrow's crown of sorrow" in that he had once been counted happy.[51] Now let Hera rejoice; she has had her will. But "who would pray to such a goddess? Her jealousy of Zeus for his love of a woman hath destroyed me, the benefactor of Greece, who am innocent."[52] Yet Theseus goes on to plead (1313–1339) against suicide, since no man or even god is wholly happy, if the poets speak sooth;[53] let not Heracles be less rugged in enduring fortune (τὰς τύχας) than the gods who have sinned, but let him come to Athens, where Theseus will be a friend in need. All that, replies Heracles, is beside the point (πάρεργα); for he cannot believe those wretched tales of the poets about unholy deeds of the gods, for God (ὁ θεός), if he be truly god, hath need of naught.[54]

[49] Euripides, *Heraclidae* and *Suppliants*; Sophocles, *O.C.* (considerably later than *Heracles*); cf. Aeschylus, *Eumenides*. G. H. Macurdy, *The Quality of Mercy*, pp. 126–129, stresses this interpretation, and also the implicit criticism of the *O.T.* of Sophocles; the merely ritual pollution, without moral guilt, of an involuntary criminal like Oedipus or Heracles, deserves ritual expiation rather than persecution.

[50] For the persecution by Hera, *Heracles* 831–842; 855; 857 (Iris, with whom compare the Kratos of *P.V.* and see above, p. 122, n. 97; and with the reluctant *Lyssa* (*Her.* 843–854; 856; 858) compare the Hephaestus of *P.V.*); *Her.* 1127; 1135 (Amphitryon); 1253; 1266–1268; 1303–1310; 1392 f. (Heracles); 1191 (Theseus); 1311 f. (Chorus; cf. 885: δαίμων; 919: θεόθεν); for man's ingratitude or impotence, 1253 f. (Heracles, to Theseus).

[51] 1291 f.; cf. 1299 f.; Dante, *Inf.* V, 121; Tennyson, "Locksley Hall," 76.

[52] 1310: οὐδὲν ὄντας αἰτίους; cf. *Hipp.* 1150; 1382 f.; and see above, p. 182.

[53] 1314 f.: οὐδεὶς δὲ θνητῶν ταῖς τύχαις ἀκήρατος, κτλ. Cf. Horace, *Odes* II, 16, 27 f.; and see above, p. 82.

[54] 1340–1346; cf. *I.T.* 380–392; Eur. frag. 292 Nauck (*Bellerophon*); Xenophanes, D21B11–17.

He agrees, however, that suicide would be cowardice; he will live, and go to Athens, since he must now be the slave of *Tyche* (1347–1357). He accepts, in other words, the counsel of *sophrosyne* and *tlemosyne* (1227 f.; 1242–1254; 1320 f.; cf. 1396), while rejecting the conception of divine immorality. But he still believes that his sufferings have been caused by Hera (1372 f.). How is this inconsistency to be interpreted?

A natural explanation is that Euripides is here, as elsewhere, expressing his rejection of the whole immoral tissue of traditional folk-religion, like Xenophanes before him, and like Plato a little later.[55] But it is to be noted that as the play stands, the action has been controlled by Hera, as by Aphrodite in the *Hippolytus*, or as by Athena in the *Ajax* of Sophocles. We have seen, however,[56] that Athena's motive, though apparently cruel, was ultimately beneficent; and Aphrodite, though partly the petulant woman of legend, is also a divine and elemental force with powers for good and for evil.[57] In the first part of the *Heracles*, before the intervention of Hera, we may observe the changing attitude of the characters and of the Chorus: while ruin threatens the family of Heracles, they are fatalistic, and accuse the gods; when the tables are turned, their religious faith returns.[58] Plainly Euripides accepts, at least for dramatic purposes, the familiar divine machinery and the familiar religious conceptions; the question remains whether he has in this play suggested within this framework an ethical interpretation of his story.

The answer to this question is perhaps to be found in the scene in which Iris instigates the madness of Heracles. "We have not come to do your city any hurt, but against one man only is our warfare, even against him whom they call the son of Zeus and Alcmena. For until he had finished his bitter labors, Fate preserved him (τὸ χρή νιν ἐξέσῳζεν), nor would father Zeus ever suffer me or Hera to harm him. But now that he hath accomplished the labors of Eurystheus, Hera is resolved to fasten on him

[55] See above, n. 54; for Plato, below, pp. 293 f.

[56] Above, pp. 149 f.

[57] Above, p. 180.

[58] *Her.* 282 f. (Megara): it is folly to struggle against τὸ ἀναγκαῖον or (309–311) against τὰς τῶν θεῶν τύχας; what must be (ὃ χρή) no one will ever avail to alter (311); 339–347 (Amphitryon blaming Zeus, as inferior to himself in ἀρετή; he is either ἀμαθής or not δίκαιος); 509 (Amphitryon was once great, but is now the victim of τύχη; no ὄλβος or δόξα is secure); 637–700 (the Chorus on old age; if the gods were wise, they would bestow youth twice over on the virtuous; as it is, there is no mark distinguishing the good from the wicked). Then, after the triumphant return of Heracles, 735–816 (the choral song on the μεταβολὰ κακῶν, 735); 738: δίκα καὶ θεῶν παλίρρους πότμος; *hybris* will meet retribution (740 f.; cf. 755 f.); the folly of those who assert the weakness of the gods (755; contrast 637 ff.); the gods *do* give heed to right and wrong (773 f.); the event has shown whether τὸ δίκαιον θεοῖς ἔτ' ἀρέσκει (809–814). A similar contrast in the attitude of the Chorus is to be noted in the *Heraclidae;* fatalism in 608–618; confidence in Zeus and Moira, 748–769; 892–900; cf. 934 (Messenger) on the reversal of fortune.

the guilt of slaying his own children" (824–832). The great Dorian hero, then, is under divine protection only so long as he is engaged in his humanitarian labors, but his value ceases there; under the normal conditions of peaceful life he is exposed to the enmity of the gods, and his very strength becomes dangerous.[59] In fact he has to be taken under the protection of the Attic hero, Theseus.

The "moral" of the *Heracles*, if we may use such a term, is the proneness of great and violent natures, subjected to the chances of life, to run amuck with consequences beyond their calculation or comprehension.[60] If it be objected that it is not chance but Hera's hatred that trips up Heracles, the answer is that Euripides has not chosen to dispense with the dramatic possibilities latent in the old myth of Hera's enmity, even if he personally disbelieves in such evil divinities. Call it a "fact of nature," if that is a better phrase; the fact happens to be that rugged strength and the will to power are very partial and unreliable resources for human happiness. And in his capitulation Heracles announces that he yields to "fortune," by which he means not the fickle goddess whom the Hellenistic world lifted to eminence, but the whole strange course of his life which only a more wary and subtle person could have foreseen.[61] From his tragic experience, however, he has learned the value of *sophrosyne* and *tlemosyne;* and he has learned one thing more. So strong and self-reliant before, in his last words he declares: "Whosoever prefereth wealth or might to the possession of good friends, he thinketh ill."[62] This very human discovery by Heracles of the value of friendship, and its embodiment in the person of the "philanthropic" Theseus, may help us to understand those war-tragedies of Euripides that show the inhumanity of man when he has allowed his normal instincts to be swept away by the passions of the herd.

The background for the war-tragedies of Euripides is, of course, provided for us by Thucydides, in whose pages we may trace the progressive degeneration of the Athenian character, from the enlightened idealism of Pericles and his imperialistic democracy, through the stages of the "good" and necessary Peloponnesian war that he accepted in defense of his country (which even he realized was now a "tyranny"[63]) against jealous neigh-

[59] See Appendix 19: Euripides, *Heracles*.

[60] To compare a lesser work with a greater, something of this "moral" may be seen in the helplessness of clumsy, muscular Lenny in J. Steinbeck's *Of Mice and Men* (New York, 1937).

[61] *Her.* 1357. Elsewhere in the play, also, τύχη means little more than personal misfortune; 310; 509; 1140; 1321; 1396; 1393, here to be sure connected with the agency of Hera. We have hardly reached as yet in Euripides the conception of chance either as a personality or as an irrational force; see further below, p. 218.

[62] *Her.* 1424 f.; cf. 1337–1339; 1404; contrast 550–561; and for remarks on the insecurity of wealth and reputation, 511 f.; 643–648.

[63] *Thuc.* II, 63.

bors, till Athens, too, hard pressed by defeats that could not have been foreseen, showed the same cruel traits that she had condemned in others. Euripides, at first the Athenian patriot, presented in the chivalrous Demophon (son of Theseus) of the *Heraclidae*, and in Theseus himself in the *Suppliant Women* and the *Heracles*, the hospitality of Periclean Athens to the oppressed of other cities, and the freedom of Athenian institutions;[64] in the *Andromache* he attacked the Spartan character as embodied in the diplomacy of the villain Menelaus.[65] As the war continued, however, he wes completely disillusioned; the *Hecuba* and the *Trojan Women* show the devastating effects of war on victims and on conquerors alike. Euripides rises above Athenian patriotism to the espousal of a more universal humanity.

The *Hecuba* shows the widow of Priam, after the fall of Troy, first the victim of Greek vengeance, in having to submit to the sacrifice of her daughter Polyxena in order that the shade of Achilles may receive due honor; and then, when the body of her son Polydorus has been discovered, treacherously slain by the Thracian ally of Troy, Polymestor, to whom he had been intrusted along with Trojan treasures, it shows Hecuba taking cruel vengeance on Polymestor by tricking him into a tent where his innocent children are slain before his eyes and he is himself blinded. Once more we have a play that falls into two distinct parts, so that the critics have generally failed to find in it a unity of action;[66] once more, as in the *Medea* and in the *Hippolytus*, the sympathy of the spectator is at first wholly with the heroine, but shifts toward the end, when, crazed by suffering and injustice she wreaks hideous vengeance. Indeed Hecuba is becoming a veritable "hound" (*Hec.* 1273); and it is Polymestor who now claims a little of our sympathy, and who prophesies her impending fate, and that of Cassandra and Agamemnon (1259–1284); so great is the reversal of fortune.

It can not be urged that all this strange transformation is implicit in the character of Hecuba, which is not portrayed with any special fulness. Nor is the fact that her suffering drives her into a betrayal of her own better

[64] *Heraclidae* 236–273; cf. 901–909; 957 f.; 965 f.; *Suppl.* 320–330; 349–353; 399–455; cf. *Heracles* 1163–1171; 1322–1339.

[65] *Andromache* 309–746; above all note the invective of Andromache (445–463) against the "citizens of Sparta, the bane of all the race of men, schemers of guile, masters in lying, devisers of evil plots," etc. (cf. *Suppl.* 187), with the summing up of the tragic situation: "not justly do ye fare well in Greece" (*And.* 449: ἀδίκως εὐτυχεῖτ' ἀν' 'Ελλάδα). For the construction of the play, much is to be learned from A. W. Verrall, *Four Plays*, pp. 1–42.

[66] Thus G. Hermann, in his second edition of the *Hecuba* (1831), could not justify the play on Aristotelian principles. L. E. Matthaei, *Studies in Greek Tragedy*, pp. 128–157, argues that its tragedy consists in the presentation of two conflicting conceptions of justice, social and personal, *nomos* and *physis* (p. 128); J. T. Sheppard, *Proc. of Eng. Class. Assoc.* 20 (1923), pp. 86–90, does not accept this view, but stresses the change in spirit of Hecuba.

nature the whole of the tragedy. The death of Polyxena (now by the fortunes of war a mere slave) was demanded by the traditional claims of society as a debt to its dead hero Achilles; this *nomos*, upholding at whatever grim cost the supposed good of the group, is urged, though for different reasons and not without dissent, by most of the Greek leaders (107–140; 301–331). And Polyxena herself, who now has nothing left to live for (349–378), accepts the inevitable, and becomes a willing sacrifice (like Macaria in the *Heraclidae*, and like Iphigenia at Aulis, though these innocent and heroic maidens think they are serving the interests of their own communities). Polyxena's nobility wins the admiration even of the Greeks (542–582); and, as her mother remarks, "The good are always good, nor suffer change of nature (*physis*) through what befalls them, but remain forever noble." [67] But this is not justice; and if Polyxena is reconciled to her fate, Hecuba is not, and the discovery of the corpse of Polydorus excites a fresh access of grief and her plan of revenge on his murderer. Now her vengeance springs from purely personal, instinctive sources, from the heart of *physis* itself. Thus it is that Dido struggles, but in vain, against the *Fatum Romanum*. It is striking, and ironical, that the very person whom she persuades to connive with her plan is her city's foe Agamemnon, who has taken as his prize her daughter Cassandra, and who has already spoken on behalf of Hecuba (120–122), and is well disposed toward her (745 f.; 850–853; 902–904). Strange is it, as the leader of the Chorus remarks, how *nomos* makes friends of foes, and foes of friends (846–849). Yet Hecuba's first appeals to Agamemnon in the name of *Nomos* and justice (800) fail, as she perceives (812); she therefore turns to Persuasion (*Peitho*, 816) and even stoops to invoke the name of that goddess, Kypris (whom Peitho often attends), and Agamemnon's relations with her own daughter Cassandra (824–835). Cautious Agamemnon, first guarding himself against responsibility for the actual deed of vengeance which some Greeks might resent, and not suspecting the full horror of what is to follow, yields. Later, after a scene in which the dissimulation of the fly, Polymestor, is exceeded by that of the spider, Hecuba (953–1020), and the vengeance is completed, "a fearful penalty for a shameful deed," as the leader of the Chorus exclaims (1086 f.), Agamemnon listens to Polymestor's specious self-justification (based on pretended reasons of state), and Hecuba's reply, and decides in her favor (1132–1251). But it is too

[67] 597 f.; apparently written in criticism of Simonides 4 Diehl (see above, pp. 67 f.); the whole passage, 592–603, speculates on the difference, as regards the contributions of φύσις and τροφή, between agriculture and humanity; good land brings good crops only with good fortune and care, while man, good or bad, runs true to his φύσις, though τροφή supplies moral standards. These "random speculations" (603) of Hecuba lack dramatic appropriateness, but are characteristic of fifth-century thought. Cf. P. Shorey, **Φύσις, Μελέτη, 'Επιστήμη**; also see Plato, *Rep.* 491d–492a, and below, p. 300.

late to save Hecuba and Cassandra and Agamemnon from the unhappy ends that Polymestor now foretells; and in a sense he has the last word (1284).

And justice? The fortunes of Hecuba were undeserved; she was the innocent victim of war and the cohesive power of society: *Le criminel, c'est la société*. But her vengeance, too, is unjust; and her deepest tragedy is not in what she suffers but in the hideousness of what she brings herself to do, when she defies society and takes matters into her own hands with diabolical cruelty, losing her own soul. The scales, weighted with wrongs on either side, even if they could hang even, could never weigh out justice. Yet Euripides has not in this play cried out against fate or the gods or chance, even if some of his characters resort to the conventional phrases.[68] The three choral songs[69] bring out the woes of the Trojan captive women and even of the Greek mothers through the guilt of Paris and Helen; as individuals they suffer, but they are the helpless victims of universal sinful, suffering humanity. Their songs will be heard again, with even greater power, in the *Trojan Women*.

After the battle of Delium (424 B.C.) the Boeotians refused to surrender the Athenian dead, "transgressing the accepted conventions of the Greek";[70] in 420, Alcibiades secured an alliance between Athens and Argos. Both events were in the mind of Euripides when he composed the *Suppliant Women*, a tragedy on the aftermath of the campaign of the Seven against Thebes. The Chorus, mothers of the slain chieftains, attended by Adrastus, beg Theseus for help in recovering the bodies from the Thebans, who have refused to surrender them; their cause is just, but only Theseus has the power and the good will to prevail over the insolence of the Thebans. (*Suppl.* 63; 65 f.; 124; 184–192.) At first Theseus refuses: Adrastus and his fellow warriors have preferred courage to discretion (**εὐψυχία** to **εὐβουλία**), and should accept the consequences (161). He himself believes that human good outweighs evil (195–200); and since the gods have bestowed on man the gifts that lift him above barbarism, —

[68] Thus 43: *ἡ πεπρωμένη*, and 58: *θεῶν τις* (the ghost of Polydorus speaking); cf. 722: *δαίμων* (Coryphaeus); 629: *χρῆν* (Chorus); 640: *ἀνάγκαι*, and 1295: *ἀνάγκη* (Chorus). For *τύχη* in the sense of one's personal "plight," 341; cf. 360; 628; but 786: *τύχη*, is "Fortune's self," the only being whom Hecuba could regard as comparable with her own *τύχη*. Later (864–867) she complains that no mortal is free; all are slaves of circumstance or of *tyche*. Finally the sympathetic herald Talthybius, who has seen the death of Polyxena, asks whether Zeus beholds men, or whether the gods are a delusion and it is *τύχη* that oversees all mortal things (488–491); the question is unanswered; see further below, pp. 217 f.

[69] 444–483; 629–656; 905–952; excellently discussed by L. E. Matthaei, *Studies*, pp. 140–144.

[70] Thuc. IV, 97: *παραβαίνοντες τὰ νόμιμα τῶν* Ἑλλήνων; cf. IV, 98: *τὸν δὲ νόμον τοῖς Ἕλλησιν εἶναι, κτλ.*; Eur. *Suppl.* 19: *νόμιμ' ἀτίζοντες θεῶν*; 526: *τὸν Πανελλήνων νόμον σῴζων*; cf. 301; 310; 537–541; 671.

intelligence (σύνεσις), and speech, and the arts, and divination,[71] — it is presumption not to be content with these gifts (214–218). Thus Adrastus, though warned by Phoebus, was not wise, but threw in his lot with the wicked, and the gods often destroy the good and the wicked together (219–238). Of the three classes in a state, it is neither the greedy rich nor the envious poor but rather the middle class that is wise and saves it;[72] since Adrastus has been ill-advised, let him bear the brunt of his *tyche* (246–249). Yes, agree the Chorus, Adrastus has erred (ἥμαρτεν, 250), like other young men; but he should be forgiven.

Yet it is not their supplication, nor that of Adrastus, that melts the resolution of Theseus, but the plea of Aethra, his own mother, who bids him honor the will of the gods (301) and "the custom of all Greece" and the *nomoi* that bind men together in cities (303–313). Here we must note that the right of the dead to receive burial, denied in the *Antigone* by the arbitrary *Nomos* of Creon, and upheld by Antigone's appeal to the "Heavenly Laws,"[73] is here based on universal Greek *nomos* which has also a divine sanction. Moreover, Aethra continues, Athens grows through toils, unlike the cautious states whose sight is darkened.[74] To this challenge Theseus rises; it is indeed his habit to run risks to punish the wicked, and he will now do so, but only, democratic monarch that he is, after getting the consent of his people (334–358); this anachronistic picture of Athenian democracy is presently enforced in the parley with the Theban herald (399–455) on the relative advantages of democracy and despotism. The herald's specious arguments in the sequel show that the Devil can quote scripture: he twists pacifism to his purpose (473–493), with a shrewd remark on the dangers of trusting Hope (*Elpis*, 479 f.; contrast 328–331); he urges that it was *hybris* that ruined the Seven (494–510). But their *hybris*, replies the leader of the Chorus, was avenged by Zeus; no reason now for Thebes to show *hybris* against the humbled (511 f.; cf. 528–530). And Theseus, first giving his resolute answer to the herald that he will uphold "the law of all Greeks" (526), adds a reflection on the struggles of human life and the fastidiousness of *Tyche*, drawing the moral of moderation even in retaliation for injustice.[75]

The herald withdraws, and Theseus follows with his troops, confident that the justice of his cause will bring divine help and therefore victory (592–597). During the suspense of waiting, the Chorus, a moment ago

[71] 201–213; cf. Aesch. *P.V.* 439–506 (see above, pp. 119 f.); Soph. *Ant.* 332–375 (see above, p. 146); here it is not Prometheus, nor man himself, but the gods who are given credit for these gifts.

[72] 238–245; cf. Solon, 4; 5 (see above, p. 38), and Aristotle (see below, p. 330).

[73] See above, p. 144.

[74] 323–325; cf. 576 f.; Thuc. I, 70.

[75] 549–557. ὁ δαίμων, 552, in its context means *Tyche*.

likewise confident (564 f.), now waver between hope and fear: *Moira* does overturn the victor, but are the gods just? Yes, and they have the last word (608–616). But what fate (αἶσα, πότμος, 623) awaits Theseus? The answer comes when a Messenger reports the success of the upholder of "the *nomos* of all Hellas" (671), brave in danger, yet not tainted with *hybris*. But it is Adrastus who points the moral with the utmost force: the folly of man, who fails to realize his dependence on the will of Zeus; thus he himself had rejected a fair offer of Eteocles; then in turn the Thebans suffered the wages of their *hybris*; "and ye cities, though ye might by reason (*logos*) settle your ills, yet ye bring your disputes to a conclusion by bloodshed, not by reason."[76] The rest of the action is of less interest to us: the mourning of the dead; the account by Adrastus of the characters of most of the Seven (more sympathetic than the account in Aeschylus, or indeed than the conception earlier in the present play); the rather gratuitous self-immolation of Evadne, widow of Capaneus; and the pact of friendship between Theseus and Adrastus, sanctioned by Athena "from the machine," that foreshadows the Argive alliance of 420. But the chief impression conveyed by the *Suppliant Women* is the one that the poet doubtless intended: the futility of war, mitigated only by the clemency of Athens.

Athenian clemency, if it really existed, soon suffered a notable decline. Readers of Thucydides perceive a turning point in this degeneration in the year 416 B.C., when the Athenians sought to compel the neutral Melians to enter the war on their side, and, failing in this attempt, besieged them till they killed or enslaved the population of the little island. Thucydides sets forth the conflict of ideas, might against right, utility against justice, in the "Melian Dialogue," which he represents as having taken place between the Athenian envoys and the Melian leaders before the siege; and his narrative goes on to tell of the Sicilian Expedition of the next year, which ended in Athenian disaster. The suggestion is clearly that *hybris* was followed by *nemesis*.[77] Even before the Athenian fleet sailed for Sicily, Euripides threw his fierce indignation into the greatest of his war plays, the *Trojan Women*. Anti-Spartan before, the Athenian poet now appears to be anti-Athenian, as Bernard Shaw in his *St. Joan* sets forth the stupidity and futility of the English captors of the French heroine. The Athenians, who like all Greeks have been brought up on the Homeric tradition to see in the Trojan War a glorious triumph of Greece over barbarian arms

[76] 734–749. By λόγος we are to understand not merely the words that may pass in a parley but the powers of the human reason that make such parley possible. We have here an antithesis close to the familiar λόγος vs. ἔργον, with a suggestion of "fools rush in," etc.

[77] Thuc. V, 84–116; VI, 1 ff.; see below, pp. 268; 271; and for the relation of the "Melian Dialogue" to the *Trojan Women* and to other plays of Euripides, J. H. Finley, Jr., *H.S.C.P.* 49 (1938), pp. 55–58.

(though with respect for the nobility of the Trojans), are now invited to behold the reverse of the tapestry: the sufferings of the vanquished, and the judgement of Heaven on the victors. Yet the theme, drawn from the legendary past, reaches far beyond the audience of the poet's own day; we who have seen the play performed during the tragic wars of our own generation have felt in it the sorrows of innocent peoples of our day and the moral condemnation of armed tyranny. *De nobis fabula narratur.*

In the *Trojan Women* the poet takes up the story only a very little earlier than the moment chosen for the *Hecuba*. (The walls of Troy have not yet fallen; but Polyxena is already dead.) The *Troades* is the last play of a trilogy which included the lost *Alexander* (with a slave for hero) and the *Palamedes* (on the death of a hero falsely accused of treason). In the Prologue we learn that not only Poseidon, always a friend of Troy, but Athena, the friend of the Greeks, now offended by the *hybris* of Ajax and of other Greeks, are joined, with the approval of Zeus, in their purpose of vengeance by storm and death on the Greeks who will soon be setting out for their homes; thus shall every sacrilegious sacker of cities pay the penalty (*Troad.* 1–97). The ominous note here struck is enforced later by the prophecy by Cassandra of the deaths of Agamemnon and herself and of Odysseus (356–364; 427–450). But we are not to behold "poetic justice" done within the action; our interest is to be held by the pageant of suffering women, of Hecuba and Cassandra and Andromache and the other captives who are claimed as prizes by the victors. Of action in the strict sense there is little (as, for a similar reason, in the *Prometheus Bound*); of lamentation by the Chorus of captives and by the leading characters, there is much (as in the earliest Greek tragedy). What grows upon the spectator is realization that the spirit of these crushed figures rises with each fresh blow of misfortune; that the worst that can befall humanity is not the suffering but the doing of injustice (as Plato's Socrates will also hold);[78] and that pity reaches out to include not only the innocent victims of injustice but even its blind perpetrators.

Cassandra's scene (308–461) is full of ironical contrast: the marriage song that she sings for herself, this pure, frenzied maiden soon to be led away for Agamemnon; her prophecy of retribution that is to fall on the apparent victors; her thesis that fallen Troy, whose warriors fell nobly in self-defense, is happier than victorious Greece, whose myriads fall for Helen's sake;[79] any wise man will shun war, but if war comes, it is the city that nobly falls that deserves not pity but a crown (400–403); her own death shall be swallowed up in victory (ἥξω . . . νικηφόρος, 460). Even

[78] See below, pp. 257 f.

[79] 365–399; note the nettled tone of Talthybius, the Greek herald, at this contempt of "all that seems great and wise," 411 f.

after the Cassandra scene of the *Agamemnon*, this is a magnificent episode.

Andromache, Hector's widow who is now to become the slave of Pyrrhus, son of Achilles, is an even more tragic figure. With Hecuba, she keens the dead (568–629), and weighs her own best course. Polyxena is dead; she sleeps well, for death is only not to be, and freedom from sorrow;[80] while Andromache feels the irony of her own good name having become her ruin;[81] and her former good fortune makes her present plight the more grievous.[82] Were she not better dead? But Hecuba counsels her to yield to *tyche* (692; 697), as sailors yield to a storm; tears will not restore Hector; but tact and gentleness may win the heart of Pyrrhus and so save Andromache's little son Astyanax (685–705). The words are no sooner spoken than the herald comes and tells, though with a struggle, of the sentence of the Greeks; Astyanax must die, lest Troy rise again. The mother's anguish at the cruelty of these Greeks who out-Herod Herod in their barbarism (764), and the tenderness of her parting with the child, form the most tragic scene in Greek literature (712–779).

But the central figure is Hecuba, on whom falls the weight of all this woe. Far grander than the pitiful and vindictive Hecuba of the earlier play that bears her name, she rises from lamentation to consolation, from self-pity to a comprehension of the universal burden of humanity. Even though the gods have betrayed her, in her misfortune something bids her call on the gods (469–471); she will clutch at the memory of happier things, and make a song of them to contrast with her stricken state, only to realize that one must count no man happy ere he die.[83] She brings strength to Andromache, and then shares in her anguish. When Menelaus seeks vengeance on Helen, she claims the privilege of replying to Helen's self-defense. Helen has blamed her own lapse and the War not on herself but on Hecuba and Priam, for bearing and rearing Paris (919–921); on the Choice of Paris, abetted by Kypris (929; 931; 940), that goddess who is mightier even than Zeus (948); and on sheer force;[84] she protests that she has tried to escape from Troy (952–958). One by one, Hecuba scornfully refutes each of these defenses; as for Kypris, that is a euphemism for Helen's or for any man's desire (988–990); as Menelaus agrees, Helen left

[80] 630–642; 679 f.; Lucretius III, 931–977, and Hamlet's Soliloquy.

[81] 657 f.; cf. 742–744: Hector's heroism is the cause of Astyanax' ruin, as good is turned to evil; 935–937: Helen's beauty is her ruin (cf. 963 f.); 529 f.: κεχαρμένος . . . ἄταν, of the Trojan Horse.

[82] 639 f.; contrast 472 ff., and see below, and n. 83.

[83] 472–474: she thinks at first, not that "a sorrow's crown of sorrows is remembering happier things" (see above, p. 184), but that it will bring relief (φίλον, 472; cf. Tennyson, *In Memoriam* V, Stanza 2; contrast 639 f. (Andromache), cited in n. 82). For the gnomic conclusion, 509 f., see above, pp. 100; 161 f.

[84] 962; cf. the *Helen* of Gorgias; see below, p. 253.

Greece "willingly." [85] In the last scene, when the body of Astyanax is carried before Hecuba, who must perform the rites that his captive mother cannot, the aged queen shows a quiet dignity and exquisite compassion, together with contempt for the fear and stupidity of the Greeks (1156–1250). And now the herald proclaims that the city is to be set afire, and that Hecuba must go to Odysseus. She takes her leave of Troy; her sudden impulse of throwing herself into the flames is thwarted; she beats on the earth, and calls on Priam, but he cannot hear, for "holy Death" has closed his eyes (1260–1315). With the other lamenting women she goes forth.

A hopeless tragedy? Not quite hopeless. Granted that Hecuba and the other captive women are not aware of the plans of the gods for retribution on the Greeks, and that Cassandra's prophecies are never believed; granted that the gods have seemed to betray the piety of the Trojans, as the Chorus and Hecuba complain;[86] granted that the surrender to *tyche* that Hecuba counsels is cut off by *tyche*, so that she counts him a fool who thinks to be secure in prosperity, whereas *tyche* capers crazily, and no man of his own power is fortunate.[87] Even so, Hecuba calls instinctively on the gods (469–471), and praises the divine power in what Menelaus calls a "strange" prayer: "O thou base of the Earth, and thou that art enthroned above the Earth, whoever thou art, hard to know, Zeus, or Nature's Necessity (ἀνάγκη φύσεος) or Reason of Man, to thee do I pray; for all things mortal dost thou lead aright (κατὰ δίκην) along their silent path." [88] Whether this be Ionian science breaking in on tragedy, or a foretaste of the Stoic mingling of Reason (νοῦς) with *physis*, whether it be pantheism or agnosticism, it is an affirmation of Hecuba's faith in the existence of a power of justice. Her experience has given her little enough cause for such a faith; in her, as in other tragic heroes and heroines, such faith springs from her own unconquerable soul; even in her extremity, by reason of her *tlemosyne* she is more than a victor.

The plays of Euripides that we have considered up to this point are true tragedies, in which our hearts are wrung by the sufferings of those who are the victims of their own perverse characters or of the cruelty of others. We may now contrast with the tragedies the four tragi-comedies which antedate and overlap them: the *Alcestis* (438 B.C.), the *Ion*, the *Iphigenia*

[85] 1037–1039. How plastic is Greek myth, one may observe by contrasting this Helen with the Helen of the *Iliad;* still better with the scatheless Helen of the fourth book of the *Odyssey* and with Euripides' own *Helen.*

[86] For the Chorus, 821: μάταν, κτλ.; 859 f.: τὰ θεῶν δὲ | φίλτρα φροῦδα Τροίᾳ; for Hecuba, 612 f.; 1240–1245; 1280 f.

[87] 692; 697; 1203–1206, with which cf. 67 f. (Poseidon, of Athena's capriciousness).

[88] 884–888; for the influence here of Anaximenes, Diogenes of Apollonia, and Heraclitus, see J. Adam, *Religious Teachers*, pp. 299–304; and on the religious uncertainty of the period, W. Gundel, *Ananke*, pp. 37 ff.; with this "novel" prayer (889), cf. also the *Hymn* of Cleanthes (below, pp. 339; 345); and Wordsworth, *Tintern* Abbey, esp. lines 95–102.

*among the Taurians*, and the *Helen* (three plays composed probably between 418 and 412). Here we are in a world of miracles and artifice, of romantic and breathless escapade, of flippant attacks on Delphi and on the Olympic divinities, of mischievous irony, of chance events and surprising coincidences and happy consummations. Theatrical realism replaces the "probabilities" of tragic action, sentimental pathos the deeper note of tragic suffering. All is rapid and glittering and witty. Yet these are not contemptible dramas; the *Alcestis* and the *Iphigenia*, at least, are often performed to-day with great effect. But we must ask how far the poet intends us to understand the action to be the outcome of purely human factors, and how far he attributes it to the divine machinery (which is of course retained, whether in deference to tragic convention, or for the purpose of satire), or how far again he supposes the evil plight of his characters and their happy escape to be brought about by remote and blind forces, by fate or by *tyche*.[89]

Apollo, speaking the prologue of the *Alcestis*, tells us that in gratitude to the "righteous" Thessalian King Admetus, whom he has formerly served, he has saved him from immediate death by "tricking the *Moirai*" into agreeing to a postponement of his death, provided that a substitute can be found. The aged father and mother of Admetus have refused; only his wife, Alcestis, has consented, and "is fated this very day to die."[90] Thus we begin our play with a miracle of divine intervention. The god Death claims his due, though Apollo prophesies (64–71), what we shall presently witness, the arrival of Heracles, who will wrest Alcestis from Death and return her to her husband: another miracle.

We may not linger over many interesting aspects of the play: the nobility and pathos of Alcestis, loving life but loving her husband more, and going willingly down to Hades in his stead; Admetus, to us a far from appealing figure, but hospitable in his way, and noble in all but in accepting his wife's sacrifice, as he realizes too late (384; 935–961); his conventional father's greedy and "Epicurean" clinging to what remains of life (614–628; 681–733; n.b. 683; 703–705); Heracles, bluff and tactless and good-natured (*not* the Heracles of epic and tragic saga), whose drunkenness in what he learns to his dismay (and only because of his condition) to be a house of mourning leads directly to the rescue of Alcestis, and who then toys ironically with his host as he introduces her veiled figure. More to our purpose is it to observe the constant harping of the characters and of the Chorus on the theme of "fate" or "necessity," on what is "right," on

[89] On the tragi-comedies in general, cf. H. D. F. Kitto, *Greek Tragedy*, pp. 312–331.

[90] *Alc.* 1–21; 21: *θανεῖν πέπρωται*; cf. 107; 148; 158; 523; and 297 f.: "This is a god's doing." For the tradition of Apollo "tricking" the *Moirai* in this case (12; 33 f.), cf. Aesch. *Eum.* 721–728. The story of the *Alcestis* clearly derives from a folk-tale.

the "plight" of Alcestis and Admetus, and on the need of "endurance."[91] Yet these are mostly conventional phrases, as are the gnomic utterances: "Necessity (*Ananke*) is all-powerful, and accomplishes what Zeus intends" (962–990); "Death is common, the debt of nature" 418 f.; 527; 780–784; cf. *Hamlet,* I, 2, 72–106); "You were not the first to lose a wife" (417 f.; 892–894; 931–934); "Marriage is a burden" (238–243; 878–888); "Time will soften the blow" (381, Alcestis; 1085, Heracles, in identical words). Not to be overlooked is the sermon of the drunken Heracles "On the Nature of Mortal Affairs": All men must die; when, they know not, for *Tyche* is obscure to the arts and sciences; therefore drink, make merry, and honor Kypris; that is the way to rise superior to *Tyche.* Mortals must think mortal thoughts, but not be solemn about this business of life.[92] *In vino veritas*; yet the same Heracles, sobered by the discovery that it is Alcestis who has died, marches off to recover her. And it is chiefly in the action, rather than in *gnomai,* that we must find the poet's real opinion of fate, good, and evil.

Now the really important point is that although Admetus has fulfilled his "allotted length of days" (695: τὴν πεπρωμένην τύχην), and is "craving impossibilities" in begging Alcestis not to leave him (202: τἀμήχανα ζητῶν; cf. 250; 388), once she is pledged to die for him, and although nothing avails against *Ananke* to bring the dead back to life (962–990), Alcestis is nevertheless restored to him. He is allowed to eat his cake and have it, too. We have been prepared by Apollo in the prologue for what happens; the Chorus, who did not hear Apollo, can only comment in the lines of the familiar recessional[93] on the unexpectedness of this divine consummation.

On the face of the action, then, the *Alcestis* is a drama of providence, in which the Olympic divinities overrule the *Moirai* and *Ananke.* This looks like "poetic justice." Neither spouse has deserved to die (247); moreover the uprightness of Admetus and his hospitality to Heracles win him respectively a substitute for his death and a reprieve for the death of Alcestis. Is that too banal a conclusion? The character of Heracles (which Browning in *Balaustion's Adventure* thought it necessary to elevate), as well as the hasty burial of Alcestis and the inopportunely urgent hospitality of Admetus and other matters in the plot, convinced Verrall that Euripides, rationalist that he appears in other plays, does not intend the miraculous element to be taken seriously: Alcestis merely swooned, and Heracles found her alive at the tomb; his "struggle with Death" is only a deduction from his big talk; the prologue is for the edification of the pious.[94] In-

[91] See Appendix 20: Vocabulary of *Alcestis.*

[92] 780–802; for "mortal thoughts," cf. Pindar (above, pp. 77 f.).

[93] Here used for the first time, so far as we know; see above, p. 100.

[94] See Appendix 21: *Alcestis* and Verrall.

genious though Verrall's theory is, it seems a simpler explanation of the facts to suppose that Euripides in his tragi-comedies (and the *Alcestis* in particular took the place of a satyr-play, where comedy was expected) merely uses the traditional tragic divine machinery for something less than tragic ends, and is here more interested in startling dramatic effects than in probability. It is at least possible that in the *Alcestis* he actually suggests that virtue has been rewarded at the expense of Fate.

Some twenty years (or more) later, a sadder and a wiser man, Euripides again gave Apollo the chief place in his celestial machinery; but this time, in the *Ion*, he made Hermes deputize for Apollo in the prologue, and Athena at the end of the play. Hermes informs us that some years ago he brought hither to Delphi the child born to the Athenian princess Creusa, who had been ravished by Apollo; the child has grown up in the temple, where he is now an attendant. Meanwhile Creusa has married a soldier of fortune, Xuthus, with whom she will this day seek from the oracle a cure for their childlessness. Apollo will give to Xuthus this child, now to be called "Ion," who will also be recognized by Creusa as her own. So far prophecy, on Apollo's behalf.[95] As the action develops, Ion ("the Comer"), the first person whom Xuthus meets on coming forth from the oracle, is by its bidding claimed as his own, but with no knowledge of his maternity; and when Creusa learns from one of her handmaids that Xuthus now has a "son," while she is still childless (and embittered by the old loss of her child) she connives with an aged servant to poison Ion. Fortunately a dove, which happens to taste the poison first and to die immediately, gives Ion the needed warning; he is about to tear Creusa from the altar where she has taken refuge and to slay her, when the Pythian priestess produces the tokens, once found in his cradle and now identified by Creusa, that prove him to be her child, but not the son of Xuthus. Creusa, explaining that he is Apollo's child, is now content; not so Ion, who is determined to ask the god who is his father. He is forestalled by Athena's appearance and proclamation on behalf of Apollo (who "does not deign to appear himself, lest blame arise for deeds of yore"); Ion is indeed the child of Creusa and Apollo, and is to become the glorious ancestor of the "Ionian" Greeks; but the discovery to Creusa of Apollo's plan of letting Ion appear to be the son of Xuthus has led to such unfortunate consequences that the god now thinks it best that for the present Xuthus be kept in ignorance of the fact that Ion is Creusa's son. "In all things hath Apollo done well. . . . God's mill grinds slow but sure" (1595; 1614 f.).

This lame and impotent conclusion is somewhat different from what the prologue foretold; Apollo's plans have gone amiss because of human

[95] The prophetic powers of the god and his good will are stressed: *Ion* 5–7; 67 f.; cf. 1117 f.; 1582.

intervention; he has covered his tracks as best he can, but the result should be anything but reassuring to the faithful. Superficially a "drama of Providence,"[96] this is really a "travesty of Providence,"[97] a cry of "*écrasez l'infâme.*" If Apollo exists, he appears in the light of a seducer, deceiver, and bungler, and is indeed frankly attacked by Creusa and Ion in unanswerable terms.[98] But it is more than probable that the poet himself rejects the traditional Apollo altogether (while pretending not to do so), and sees the whole action as a purely human drama: long ago the seduction of Creusa at Athens by some Athenian (and the death of her infant); the seduction of some Delphian woman,[99] and the birth of Ion, who is now exploited by the temple authorities for the duping of Xuthus and Creusa; the rest is their self-deception, and the pious conclusion, with the suggestion of "poetic justice" (1619–1622) only the ultimate irony in a wholly ironical play.[100] It may be added that the rôle of *tyche* is considerable both in the action and in what is said of it. There is the coincidence of Creusa and Xuthus coming to Delphi, where Ion has been reared; the fortuitous meeting of Xuthus, coming from the oracle, with Ion; the dove, that happens to taste the poison; the recognition of the tokens by Creusa (if they are trumped up by the priestess). All this may be identified with the will of Apollo, if his existence be admitted;[101] but it is what men ordinarily call "chance." So Ion proclaims: "O *Tyche*, thou who hast brought change to myriads of men, causing them now to suffer misfortune, and now to fare well, by what a narrow margin have I escaped slaying my mother!"[102] In fact the struggle of mortals with *tyche* in this play is what brings to pass their enlightenment.

I have called the *Ion* a tragi-comedy; that does not mean that it is a

[96] Actually, according to R. G. Moulton, *The Ancient Classical Drama* (Oxford, 1890), p. 98; F. M. Wassermann, "Divine Violence and Providence in Euripides' Ion," *T.A.P.A.* 71 (1940), pp. 587–604.

[97] P. H. Frye, *Romance and Tragedy*, pp. 196–199.

[98] By Creusa, 252–254; 859–922; by Ion (who at first, 339–380, will believe no evil of Apollo), 436–451; 1312–1319. The pride of Greek aristocrats in tracing their descent from gods by human mothers may be illustrated from Pindar; but it is the ugly implications of such legends that Euripides is exploiting.

[99] Possibly the priestess herself, by Xuthus: n.b. 545–565; 1324–1379.

[100] This is in general the interpretation of A. W. Verrall, ed. *Ion* (Cambridge, 1890); *Euripides the Rationalist*, pp. 130–164. The *Ion*, of all the plays of Euripides, lends most support to Verrall's views. For a different interpretation, cf. A. S. Owen's edition (Oxford, 1939); G. Norwood's review of the latter, *A.J.P.* 43 (1942), pp. 109–113, avoids some of Verrall's excesses, while trenchantly reaffirming his chief points.

[101] Cf. 67 f.; 369–380; 554 and 569 f., of the same "discovery"; 1117 f.; 1343–1368; 1384–1388; 1456. That Apollo in the *Ion* is in part ("metaphysically") a synonym for Circumstances, but not for God, is the suggestion of L. E. Matthaei, *Greek Tragedy*, pp. 47–70. Cf. "Aphrodite" in the *Hippolytus*, a fact in human nature, as well as a personality.

[102] *Ion* 512–515. For τύχη, see also 661; 668; 748; 1461; 1501; cf. 381–383; 699; 753; 772; 775; 968; 971; 1045–1047; 1461; 1485; 1505; 1621; for δαίμων, 752; 1262; 1374 (contrasted with θεός); cf. 1604; 1620.

comedy, for all its apparently happy ending. Creusa thinks she has found her son, and gladly accepts the explanations and instructions of Athena. But for Ion the strange revelations of this day [103] have perhaps found a mother and a father; but they have taken from him his faith in the goodness of the gods. The young acolyte, in the early morning so happy in his sacred service (82–183; n.b. 151–153), has suddenly grown up; he has learned that Apollo can seduce and deceive (440–451); with a surprising maturity of social and political discernment he contrasts his former estate with the life in Athens that awaits him (582–647); he can even doubt the virtue of this new-found mother, as earlier of Xuthus (1520–1527; cf. 545–565); he is confused by Apollo's tactics in foisting him off on Xuthus; are the god's revelations true or false? (1532–1548; contrast 339–380.) And at the last, since this question is not answered by Athena, he accepts her statement that he is the son of Apollo and Creusa (1606–1608), but does not join in Creusa's joyous blessing of the god.[104] Why, indeed should he rejoice? Ion's coming of age has been for him a spiritual disillusionment.

The *Iphigenia among the Taurians*, a romantic drama of adventure, tense with thrilling escapes, a moving recognition scene, and a happy conclusion, is best understood not as a drama of Providence but as another attack on Delphi and the traditional Olympian gods. Iphigenia, daughter of Agamemnon, was not really sacrificed by him at Aulis, it appears, but was spirited away by Artemis to become her priestess in the barbarian land of the Taurians (the Crimea). Thither her brother Orestes is sent by Apollo to steal the magical image of Artemis; but he and his comrade Pylades are captured by the barbarians. Just as Iphigenia is on the point of sacrificing her brother to Artemis, she recognizes him; they outwit Thoas, the king of the land, and escape with the image to Athens by the aid of Athena, who appears once more "from the machine," somewhat as in the *Ion*.

Whereas Aeschylus in the last play of the *Oresteia* has represented the Erinyes as reconciled by Athena, and the troubles of Orestes as now ended, Euripides shows some of the Erinyes continuing, or at least seeming to continue, their persecution and Pythian Apollo sending him on this new and dangerous mission. I say "seeming," for the Erinyes who are so real in Aeschylus are for Euripides only the hallucinations of Orestes' crazed mind. Possibly the command of Delphi, too, is hallucination, and in that case the appearance of Athena will be also hallucination, though shared by Thoas; and the whole play must then be interpreted on the human level

[103] 1354: *ὦ μακαρίων μοι φασμάτων ἥδ' ἡμέρα.* Later revelations are less "blessed."

[104] 1618: *ἄξιον τὸ κτῆμά μοι* is assigned by the Mss. to Creusa, not, as by some modern editors, to Ion.

as the spectacle of a noble mind losing and recovering its grip on life.[105] More probably Euripides is accepting Apollo for dramatic purposes, but suggesting that he is cruel in sending Orestes on a perilous and useless errand (which conflicts with the interests of the god's even more cruel sister Artemis), so that the chestnuts have to be pulled out of the fire by Athena. If it be urged that these further sufferings of Orestes are less great than those of Ajax or of Philoctetes or of Oedipus in the tragedies of Sophocles, which have seen behind the veil the working of Providence, it must be replied that all these later sufferings of Orestes are gratuitous; he has already done ample penance. Euripides, retaining the conventional divine machinery and pretending to accept the popular belief in the traditional gods, uses them for contrast with the nobility of his human characters. The criticism by Iphigenia of the inconsistency in men's conception of Artemis, patroness of human sacrifice, is rational and unanswerable: the goddess has been conceived in the image of sinful men; "no god can be evil." [106] Even more bitter is the complaint against Apollo and his oracles by Orestes, the innocent victim of their persecution.[107] Against these deities, we are shown the tenderness and courage of Iphigenia, the beautiful devotion of Orestes and Pylades to each other, and the resourcefulness and daring of the Greeks in contriving their escape.[108]

In this drama of intrigue much is achieved by human resolution; but much also is the result of chance. Not only do the characters attribute their misfortunes and their successes as much to *tyche* as to the gods or to themselves,[109] but we must note several crucial instances in the action: the converging fortunes of brother and sister in remote Tauris, under the impulse of different divinities (also brother and sister), with quite different interests; the recognition scene, contrived to occur just in the nick of time, "natural" so far as Iphigenia's act in writing a letter is concerned, but less natural as regards Orestes' words;[110] and finally, when the fugitives' ship has all but cleared the harbor, the sudden wave that threatens to trap them after all, and makes the loosing of the knot depend solely on the "goddess

[105] So in general Verrall interprets the play, *Euripides the Rationalist*, pp. 166–216.

[106] *I. T.* 380–391; cf. 1082–1088; 463–466 (Chorus). I cannot share the misgivings of those critics who deplore the duplicity of the Greeks in outwitting the "pious" barbarian Thoas, — "pious," that is, in upholding a cult of human sacrifice. Yet the poet has his fun in contrasting the Greek legend of Orestes' matricide with "barbarian" scruples in such a case (1174; cf. *Troad.* 764, and see above, p. 193).

[107] *I. T.* 560; 570–575; 711–715; cf. 987 f. (Chorus). 1234–1282 is a delightfully mischievous choral song on the mercenary character of young Apollo and his oracle; cf. Verrall, *Euripides the Rationalist*, pp. 217–230.

[108] 102–115, with emphasis on τολμή; 597–612; 674–710. The piety of the herdsman who took Orestes and Pylades for gods is a handsome tribute, even if his sceptical fellow is nearer the facts (264–280).

[109] See Appendix 21 *bis*: Τύχη in *I.T.*

[110] Arist. *Poet.* 1454b 30–35: O. "says what the poet, not what the plot requires."

from the machine." Here, at least, the machine is deliberately chosen; for the wave need not have been introduced. It is to be justified, if at all, not by the need of saving Iphigenia and Orestes but by the need of a divinity to foretell what mortals cannot know, and also to win over Thoas and save the chorus of Greek women from his vengeance.[111] Athena in this scene sheds a certain glory on the action; but her aetiological disquisition connecting these far-off events with the institutions of classical Attica, and toning down the savagery of Artemis to a bit of archaic ritual (1446–1472; cf. 945–967), and her reference to an all-embracing Fate [112] is, and is doubtless intended to be, rather less convincing than is the last scene of the *Eumenides*.[113]

All readers of the *Helen* are struck by its resemblance in structure to the *Iphigenia among the Taurians*; but the material and tone are far more fantastic. The scene is in Egypt, where, according to the legend put forward by Stesichorus in his "Palinode," the real Helen has spent the ten years of the Trojan War and the seven ensuing years, thanks to divine interference, while only a phantom Helen has been at Troy. The real Helen corresponds, then, to Iphigenia; the Egyptian king Theoclymenus (who wishes to marry her) to Thoas; her shipwrecked husband Menelaus to Orestes; the successful escape of the reunited husband and wife, after the outwitting of Theoclymenus, is parallel to the escape of the brother and sister in the earlier play; the intended vengeance of the king on his sister, the prophetess Theonoe, who has helped the fugitives, is forbidden by the Dioscuri (brothers of Helen), who appear "from the machine," thus providing a counterpart to Athena's rôle in the *Iphigenia*. The even lighter touch of the later play has suggested to some critics that it was actually intended as parody of other tragic drama or even of the poet himself.[114]

For our purposes it must suffice to observe in the *Helen* (1) the large part played by divine interference, sometimes identified with fate;[115] (2) the large rôle of *tyche*, either as circumstance or personal fortune,[116] or more significantly as an active force in the plot; and (3) the gnomic

[111] Arist. *Poet.* 1454b 2–6: "The Machine should be employed only for events external to the drama, for antecedent or subsequent events which lie beyond the range of human knowledge, and which require to be reported or foretold; for to the gods we ascribe the power of seeing all things."

[112] *I.T.* 1486: *τὸ γὰρ χρεών σου* [sc. Thoas] *τε καὶ θεῶν κρατεῖ.*

[113] On the "machine" in Euripides, see further P. Decharme, *Euripides*, pp. 262–273; C. E. Whitmore, *The Supernatural in Tragedy*, pp. 66–81, with some criticism of Verrall.

[114] A. W. Verrall, *Four Plays*, pp. 43–133, supposing the play to have had a private performance; cf. G. Norwood, *Greek Tragedy*, pp. 260–264.

[115] See Appendix 22: Divine Interference in *Helen*.

[116] 264; 277; 345; 463; 1195; 1290; cf. also *μοῖρα, μόρσιμον, πότμος, δαίμων* (212 f.; 255; 613; 1286), and *εὐτυχής* (*δυστυχής*), (285; 304; 360; 565; 855; 1082; 1197; 1213; 1299; 1369).

utterances which associate the gods with *tyche* or *ananke*.[117] Superficially, all this suggests Providence;[118] but the whole tone of the play forbids such an interpretation, and the play lacks any moral basis for the action in character, unless it be in Theonoe's attitude. She indeed, on whose cooperation depends the escape of Helen and Menelaus, surprisingly announces that this day there is strife in Heaven about their destiny, but that she herself has the deciding voice;[119] to the appeal of Helen on the ground of the divine love of justice,[120] and of Menelaus on grounds of nobility of conduct (εὐψυχία, 953) and gratitude for past favors to her father, she assents, with a striking affirmation of the deathless consciousness of justice that is felt even by the dead who have returned to the "deathless aether" (1013–1016, lines which have been held to express the personal faith of the poet). Her righteous complicity, which saves the husband and wife, and which therefore provokes the anger of her brother the king, is approved by the Dioscuri, and thus saves her, too (1642–1686; cf. 1030 f., the affirmation by the Coryphaeus of "poetic justice"). This pious conclusion, let us not forget, allows us to see in Helen "the best and most chaste of women" (1685), and is perhaps a sufficient commentary on the seriousness of the poet's intentions.

From the tragi-comedies we may now turn to the melodramas of Euripides, plays that are as tense with situation and miraculous incident, and even more grim in tone, and sometimes more careful in their characterization. The *Electra* takes up once more the story, already treated by Aeschylus in the *Choephoroi*,[121] and probably treated already also by Sophocles in his *Electra*,[122] of the avenging on Aegisthus and Clytaemnestra, by Orestes and Electra, of Agamemnon's death. What Aeschylus has considered as a conflict of religious duties in a universal context (for the *Choephoroi* leads to the *Eumenides*), and what Sophocles has interpreted as a fact to be explained in terms of human motives, Euripides now exhibits as the unique crime of individuals with quite special antecedents; nor does he condone their crime. The two questions that he sets himself are: What kind of people could conceivably have perpetrated the crimes attributed to them by the accepted legend, and what moral justification could they, rightly or wrongly, have alleged?

[117] See Appendix 23: Τύχη in *Helen*.

[118] On the equivalent of θεία τύχη in Euripides, cf. E. G. Berry, ΘΕΙΑ ΜΟΙΡΑ, pp. 27–33, tracing the reflection in Euripides of a transition in Greek belief from providence to chance.

[119] 878–891; n.b. 887: τέλος δ' ἐφ' ἡμῖν (a phrase anticipating Peripatetic discussions); see below, pp. 327; 373 f.; cf. 968: κυρία; 996: ἐν σοί.

[120] 903–923; 940–944; cf. Solon 1, 1–32; see above, p. 36.

[211] See above, pp. 130–132.

[122] See above, pp. 162 f.; the question of priority is not absolutely settled. On the *Electra* of Euripides as criticism of Sophocles, cf. G. H. Macurdy, *The Quality of Mercy*, pp. 122–125.

The three major characters are all represented as conditioned by their past lives, on which they have brooded until their wills have been warped and hardened. Clytaemnestra, the frustrated mother who has lost Iphigenia at Aulis (*El.* 1011–1026), the false wife who has found no joy in her new life with her paramour Aegisthus (1105 f.), the vain woman (1071–1075) who was jealous of Agamemnon's captive Cassandra (1030–1040) and of the unpunished Helen (1027–1029), has vented all her spite on her remaining daughter Electra, treating her as a slave, and conniving with Aegisthus to marry her off to an obscure but honorable peasant (of good birth, but impoverished), lest any child of Electra should have the power to slay Aegisthus (19–42; 300–313). Electra, "the unwedded" (for her husband is a husband only in name), denied the normal fruition of a woman's life, starved and brutalized by her treatment and by years of waiting for the hour of vengeance, is utterly cold-blooded in planning her mother's death (647–698; 962–984), even pretending that she herself has become a mother in order the more plausibly to lure her own mother into her power (650–660; 1123–1133). Little though our sympathy with Aegisthus can be, Electra's gloating over his corpse is terrible to hear (907–956). Orestes, exiled in childhood, is the maddened incarnation of the intolerable duty imposed on him by the blood-feud and by Apollo's oracle. Devoted to the sister to whom he is now restored, but condescending toward her husband,[123] he is confident that *tyche* (which in this play more often means fate than chance) will accomplish the slaying of Aegisthus,[124] that right will prevail, else he cannot believe in the gods (583); but he slays Aegisthus while his guest at a feast (774–859), and proclaims that the gods are the authors of this *tyche*, and he is their servant.[125] Yet, unlike Electra, he has a lingering filial regard for his mother, and has doubts about the righteousness of killing her (969–984); the oracle of Phoebus was foolish; it was an avenging fiend (*alastor*) in the likeness of a god that enjoined vengeance; he cannot believe that the oracle was righteous; yet he will do the dread deed, *if* such is the will of the gods.[126] Both Electra and Orestes, once Aegisthus and Clytaemnestra have been struck down, are immediately overtaken by remorse (1177–

[123] 367–398, Orestes weighing *φύσις* (368; 390; cf. 941, Electra) and *εὐψυχία* (390) against *πλοῦτος* (374), and showing for the husband a grudging respect (380–385; tacit rebuke from the husband, 406 f.). The realistic delineation of the husband, a foil to the neurotic criminals of the legend, provides the touch-stone of common decency.

[124] 648; cf. 610 (the old man: O. has no friends, only his arm and *Tyche*); 403, 594 (Chorus).

[125] 890 f.; cf. 996 f. (Chorus), ironically of the *tyche* of Aegisthus.

[126] 971; 979; 981; 985–987; cf. 583; 737–745 (Chorus) on the use of "Tales of horror," which, though incredible, are profitable in making men worship the gods. Cf. "religion, the opiate of the people."

1232); and the stale protestations of justice [127] are called in question. Was justice done, after all?

The Dioscuri, twin brothers of Clytaemnestra, now appear from the machine to pronounce a most singular verdict (1238–1291; cf. 1296 f.). With their traditional, aetiological prophecies (linking Orestes with the institutions of the Areopagus) we are not concerned, nor with their forecast of the plot of the *Helen* (but not of the *Iphigenia among the Taurians*). But what of the moral import of their jumbled theological pronouncement in their speech and in the dialogue that follows? "Clytaemnestra hath received her just reward; but, Orestes, no just deed is thine. And Phoebus, — ah, but he is my lord, and my lips are sealed; but wise though he be, not wise was his oracle. Still, we must accept all that; and henceforth thou must do what Moira and Zeus ordain for thee. . . . We did not save our sister Clytaemnestra; for Moira's compulsion (*ananke*) led where it must (ᾗ τὸ χρεών, 1301), and the foolish oracle of Phoebus. And why should Phoebus make thee, too, Electra, thy mother's murderess? Thy deeds and thy brother's were done in common; common therefore is thy doom, and one ancestral curse (*ate*) is the ruin of you both." That is the substance; and like old Caspar in Southey's poem, the Dioscuri cannot tell "what good came of it at last . . . but 'twas a famous victory." But though in theology they are clearly beyond their depth, the barely veiled point intended by Euripides is clear enough: the murders done by Orestes with the help of his sister are not "just," but are cold-blooded crimes, and it is worse than useless to throw the responsibility for them on a god. If human justice can be done when blood has been shed, it must be done on other terms than these; perhaps by courts of justice replacing private vengeance,[128] perhaps by "Reason persuading Necessity," as Aeschylus hinted,[129] and as Plato affirmed.[130] The quality of mercy must temper fate, must temper even justice. These are knotty problems, far too difficult for the Dioscuri; but at least they feel a divine pity for Orestes and Electra, united for a brief and tragic moment only to part forever (1327–1330).

Five years after composing the *Electra*, Euripides brought forth his *Orestes*, not because he had any new moral insight into the tragic legend (for that Apollo's oracle was wrong is the premiss of both plays), but because he could see in the immediate sequel of Clytaemnestra's death the opportunity for contriving new melodramatic situations and for exploring

[127] 771; 952–956 (El. after the murder of Aeg., on *dike* and retribution); 957 f. (Chorus); 1051; 1093–1096 (Clyt. and El. both claiming *dike*); 1147–1155; 1169–1171, the Chorus, giving a verdict of *dike* on Clyt.'s death.

[128] In his *Orestes*, but not in his *Electra*, Euripides assumes the existence of such a court at Argos; both plays, and the *Eumenides*, point to the Athenian Areopagus in this connection.

[129] In the *Eumenides*; see above, pp. 135–137.

[130] In the *Timaeus*; see below, pp. 303–305.

new aspects of abnormal psychology. For six days since the murder, the mad Orestes has been nursed by Electra; this is the one tender trait in her otherwise harsh nature. Menelaus, who comes to help his nephew, proves too weak a reed to support him in his hour of danger; on learning that Orestes and Electra are about to be condemned to death by the court of Argive citizens he prudently refrains from interfering. But now the condemned pair, with Pylades, seek, if die they must, at least to wreak vengeance on Menelaus. One reckless coup follows another: they seize Helen, wife of Menelaus, and their daughter Hermione; Helen mysteriously vanishes at the moment when she is to be slaughtered; the palace is set on fire; and Orestes is holding the dagger over innocent Hermione when Apollo, appearing from the "machine" with Helen, stays both the hand of Orestes and the threats of Menelaus. Helen, he explains, saved by himself, is to enjoy immortality and worship; Menelaus is to return to Sparta and find another bride; Orestes is to be acquitted at Athens, and marry Hermione, and rule Argos, reconciled with its citizens. So "all's well that ends well."

The gulf between this jaunty disposition by the god of all problems, both physical and moral, and the agony of the human beings is disquieting, if it is not comic.[131] A little aetiology, to settle the cases of Orestes[132] and Helen,[133] a casual acceptance of the god's own responsibility for the murder of Clytaemnestra by Orestes (1665), a recommendation of peace and reconciliation (1678 f.; 1682 f.), and Apollo has done. It has been suggested that his appearance has been "sudden and terrific, striking all beholders into a trance from which they awaken changed men";[134] and indeed there is a contrast between the nightmare of the past and the promise of peace and forgiveness in the dawning future faintly suggestive of the even more pleasant awakening and reconciliation of the estranged lovers in the fourth act of *Midsummer Night's Dream.* Now peace and forgiveness are surely commendable; but there is not spoken by the god one word of apology or justification for the useless crimes and suffering

[131] Aristophanes of Byzantium, in his Hypothesis to the play, writes (l. 10): *τὸ δρᾶμα κωμικωτέραν ἔχει τὴν καταστροφήν.*

[132] *Orestes* 1643–1660. The trial at Argos, whose court is singularly like the Ecclesia of fifth-century Athens, is superseded, as it were, by an appeal to the higher court at Athens; and legend affirmed that Orestes married Hermione, whom he has just threatened with death. Similarly the traditional marriage to Electra and Pylades is here ordained, 1658 f. For the official, oracular tone, note the abrupt imperative, *παῦσαι*, 1625; also 1654: *πέπρωται*, and 1656: *μοῖρα.*

[133] That Helen was actually worshiped in later times is a fact here explained by the miracle of her rescue by Apollo at the behest of Zeus (1633 f.; 1683–1690); and the gods also deliberately caused her beauty to embroil Greeks and Trojans in order to rid the earth of superfluous population (1639–1640); cf. Stasinus, *Cypria* II Allen; see above, pp. 63 f.); and Menelaus, her long-suffering husband, is now well rid of her (1662 f.)!

[134] G. Murray, *Euripides and his Age*, p. 160.

imposed by the gods on these mortals. This "orthodox" epilogue may satisfy the faithful who will accept legend and traditional theology at the expense of their moral convictions; but it defies the mature thought of Aeschylus, and it cannot represent the real intent of Euripides. For his modern interpretation of the ancient legend we must turn back to the earlier part of the action, in which crazed and misguided mortals commit crimes which they think the gods have forced them to commit. Of them, indeed, some fifth-century Puck, a *fin-de-siècle* Puck, seems to cry, "Lord, what fools these mortals be!" [135]

For Orestes, whether his madness be conceived as the visitation of actual Erinyes,[136] or merely as the frenzy of over-wrought nerves,[137] we may feel a certain pity, but no sympathy, for the vengeance which he and Electra have visited on their mother, or for the attempts on Helen and Hermione. The case set forth by old Tyndareus for the rule of law in an organized society as against the primitive blood-feud, is unanswerable,[138] certainly it is not answered by the subtleties of the defense put forward by Orestes (544–604; 931–942), nor by his unnamed defender in the trial (917–930), nor by Pylades (1131–1152; 1241–1245). The common lot of Electra and Orestes is seen by Electra to come from the gods, and in particular from their unhappy inheritance;[139] the plight of Orestes they blame on the oracle of Apollo.[140] But the oracle is not mentioned in the trial (866–952). Orestes wavers between bad conscience (396), and faith that Apollo will at last save him,[141] and fatalism (1035), not without a resolute endurance [142] and what he regards as "nobility." [143]

The *Phoenician Women* treats in one long play, with great freedom, most of the legend of the house of Cadmus, with chief emphasis on the events treated by Aeschylus in the *Septem*. The earlier events are summarized chiefly in the choral songs and in one of the speeches of Tiresias

[135] On the treatment of this legend of the heroic age in terms of the late fifth century, cf. A. W. Verrall, *Four Plays*, pp. 199–264.

[136] *Or*. 316–327 (Chorus); 531 f. (Tyndareus, on this judgment from Heaven); 791 (Orestes); 1650 (Apollo).

[137] 37–45 (Electra); cf. 270; 400; 407; 845; there is possibly satire on Aeschylus in the reference to the Erinyes as "Eumenides" (37; 321; 1650); in this play they show no kindness.

[138] 491–525; n.b. 495; 523; and for the illogicality of the *lex talionis*, 507–517.

[139] So Electra, 1–26; 267; 960 ff. (n.b. 974: φθόνος . . . θεόθεν; 978: μοῖρα); similarly the Chorus, 807–843; 1547 f., almost in parody; cf. Orestes, 394: ὁ δαίμων; and Helen, 78 f.; 121.

[140] So Electra, 28–31; 162–165; 191–194; so Orestes, 275; 285–293; 416; 591–601; so Helen, 76; so Apollo himself admits, 1665.

[141] 416–420; 597–601; cf. 1667, Apollo vindicated. But 1179 f. (θεοῦ πρόνοια discarded in favor of human intelligence) is cynical.

[142] 1022–1024 is equivalent to *tlemosyne*; cf. 1–3, El.'s comment on the power of man's *physis* to endure anything; and 126–129, her shrewd comment on the ingrained quality of *physis*, for better or for worse, as seen in Helen's vanity.

[143] For εὐγένεια, 1060–1064; here suicide is contemplated. Cf. also 774–806.

(*Phoen.* 931–952); but Oedipus and Iocasta survive their sons Eteocles and Polynices, and the last scenes combine some of the matter both of the *Antigone* and of the *Oedipus at Colonus* of Sophocles. Parts of the play are certainly interpolations by later poets or by actors;[144] these, however, happen to affect but slightly the materials available for our subject. Whereas Aeschylus creates more sympathy for Eteocles than for Polynices, Euripides treats Polynices as the injured brother who has *dike* on his side,[145] while Eteocles, who is here the elder brother,[146] is guilty of *hybris* in refusing to allow Polynices his year of rule in due course; he is the full-fledged tyrant (506; 524 f.) who regards *dike* as a mere word, since might makes right (499–525). In general, however, characterization is not very full or significant in this play, and the linking of the great movements in the long action is not close save for two considerations: these are the part played by oracles (and by a curse and by a prophecy), and the recognition by the characters of these and other divine or fateful agencies.

Five oracles (or the equivalent) dominate the action. (1) We have in the *Phoenician Women* (17–20) a brief but classic version of the oracle given by Apollo to Laius, the oracle which became in later times a favorite theme for casuistical argument:[147] "O Lord of Thebes, land of goodly steeds, beget not children against the will of the gods; for if thou beget a son, that son shall slay thee, and thy whole house shall wade in blood." The oracle as here reported, we must note, is of the "conditional" type,[148] though preceded by a command, and is immediately followed[149] by the story of the fulfilment of the stated condition, and therefore of the killing of Laius by Oedipus and the troubles that sprang from this murder. (2) Because of this accursed inheritance from Laius (1608–1614; 1611: ἀρὰς παραλαβὼν Λαίου καὶ παισὶ δούς) and because of the unfilial acts of his sons, Oedipus utters the curse against them which condemns them to win rule over Thebes, if at all, only by the sword (63–70; 254 f.), indeed, to die at each other's hands.[150] (3) Of incidental interest is Apollo's oracle given to Adrastus, which linked his

[144] Cf. J. U. Powell, ed. *Phoen.* (London, 1911), pp. 1–31; D. L. Page, *Actors' Interpolations in Greek Tragedy* (Oxford, 1934), pp. 20–29; cf. also A. W. Verrall, *Euripides the Rationalist*, pp. 231–260.

[145] *Phoen.* 154 f.; 256–260; 452; 491–493; yet Capaneus still shows *hybris*, 179; 182–184.

[146] 71 f.; cf. 56; the relative ages of the brothers are not mentioned by Aeschylus (see above, p. 115), nor by Sophocles in the *Ant.* (above, p. 144); but in *O.C.* Polynices is the elder (above, p. 168).

[147] Cf. also *Phoen.* Hypothesis; Aesch. *Sept.* 745–758 (see above, p. 114; cf. p. 121); Soph. *O.T.* 711–714 (above, pp. 155; 159; and the reference to later discussions of the oracle, p. 159, n. 84.

[148] See above, p. 23.

[149] *Phoen.* 21–80; cf. 380 f.; 867–869 (Tiresias); 1595–1599 (Oedipus).

[150] 872–883; 880: ἐγγὺς δὲ θάνατος αὐτόχειρ αὐτοῖς; cf. 1426 (the curse fulfilled).

fortunes with those of Polynices (409–423). (4) The prophecy of Tiresias (884–952) about the *tyche* of Creon (892; 897; 914) and of the city (cf. 993) is announced with all the authority of an oracle,[151] and is linked with the ancient tale of the dragon slain by Cadmus, which must yet be avenged by the sacrifice of a scion of Cadmus (930–952). The prophecy is of the "conditional" type, and is again phrased with a command: "Creon, save either thy son or the city" (951 f.; cf. 913 f.). As Laius sought to evade his oracle, so does Creon; but his noble son voluntarily sacrifices himself, and so saves Thebes from capture.[152] Finally Oedipus refers to the oracle of Apollo foretelling his own death at Colonus (1703–1709; cf. 1687).

These are the external forces which link the destinies of the characters, and to which they refer their actions. Of minor importance are other suggestions of causality. Iocasta knows not (350–353) whether to blame the ruin of the house of Oedipus on sword or strife or on Oedipus himself, or again on the visitation of the gods (τὸ δαιμόνιον); presently she accuses "some one of the gods," but in the same breath blames her "unhallowed" marriage, and then with a sigh resigns herself to bearing what the gods send (379–382). Iocasta, the Messenger, and the Coryphaeus all associate *tyche* with the gods;[153] Antigone attributes the lot (δαίμων) of Polynices to *tyche* (1653). To the inquiry of Oedipus about the *moira* of his sons, Antigone replies that his own *alastor* has fallen upon them;[154] to his inquiry about Iocasta's *moira*, she replies with an account of her mother's suicide, the consummation of a god's deed.[155] A moment later, to Creon's kindly reference to the *alastores* of Oedipus, the reply of Oedipus is a lamentation on his *moira* (1593; 1595). But these manipulations of traditional conceptions (most of them in the interpolated last scene of the play) do not rival the profound analysis of tragic experience that we find in the *Septem* [156] and in the *Oedipus at Colonus*;[157] melodrama the *Phoenician Women* remains.

Of the two extant plays of Euripides that were first performed just after his death, the *Iphigenia at Aulis* may well be the later, for it bears evidences

[151] 907; 911: θεσφάτων ἐμῶν; 916: ἅπερ πέφυκε ταῦτα κἀνάγκη σὲ δρᾶν; cf. 999 f. (Menoecus, contrasting himself with those who are θεσφάτων ἐλεύθεροι | κοὐκ εἰς ἀνάγκην δαιμόνων ἀφιγμένοι); yet Tiresias intimates that the soothsayers' lot is not a happy one (878 f.: 953–959).

[152] 960–1018; 1090–1092; 1202–1207; 1310–1321. With the εὐψυχία of Menoecus we may compare the γενναιότης of Antigone (1680–1692); somewhat more negative is τὸ εὐγενές (1622–1624), the *tlemosyne* of Oedipus (1725 f.; 1762 f.), of Iocasta (382), and of Creon (705).

[153] Iocasta, 1202; Messenger, 1197–1199; Coryphaeus, 1200 f.

[154] 1552: ποίᾳ μοίρᾳ; 1556: σός ἀλάστωρ.

[155] 1566: τίνι . . . μοίρᾳ; 1580: θεός.

[156] See above, pp. 114–116.

[157] See above, pp. 166–171.

of having been left not quite completed by the hand of the poet, and of having been rounded out for performance by at least one other hand and then adapted or interpolated by other poets or actors in succeeding generations.[158] Even if it is by some months later than the *Bacchae*, we had best consider it first, since it belongs with the melodramas.

The Greek fleet is wind-bound at Aulis, and Calchas has announced that only by the sacrifice to Artemis of Agamemnon's eldest daughter, Iphigenia, can it be freed to capture Troy. Agamemnon has sent for his daughter, under pretence that she is to be married to Achilles, but without letting Achilles know of the ruse. He now repents, and writes a letter revoking the earlier message; but his letter falls into the hands of Menelaus, who demands that the plan be carried through. Word comes, to Agamemnon's dismay, that Clytaemnestra and Iphigenia have arrived at the camp; Menelaus now relents, but Agamemnon suddenly returns to his first purpose, which he seeks to conceal from his wife and daughter in an ironical scene. Achilles, learning of the scheme, is indignant that his name should have been compromised, but undertakes to defend Iphigenia. Yet after Clytaemnestra and Iphigenia have appealed in vain to Agamemnon, it appears doubtful whether Achilles can save the girl from the army's set purpose to sacrifice her. Iphigenia, however, now resolves of her own accord to allow herself to be sacrificed for the good of Greece, and takes her leave of her mother. And so the play may have ended. But in a final scene, by a later hand, a messenger reports the miraculous disappearance of Iphigenia just as she was to die, and the substitution of a hind in her place.

Though the setting and theme of the play belong to ancient saga, the characters are conceived with a fourth-century realism close to that of the New Comedy. Agamemnon is weak[159] when he should be strong, and strong when he might better be merciful,—or rational. Menelaus is the essence of narrow selfishness; Clytaemnestra, devoted to her daughter, is a weak and desperate creature; Achilles makes good intentions do duty for heroism. All are foils to Iphigenia, girlish at first, but rising suddenly to the heroism[160] of a Macaria or a Polyxena or an Antigone, and shutting her eyes to her father's faults. "Suddenly," indeed, as all the rapid discoveries of intention and reversals of attitude in this swift-moving play are sudden and theatrical. To these dramatic devices we may add the supernatural elements: the "windlessness" of the fleet (88; 351 f.); the oracle of Calchas (89–92; 358 f.; 1261–1263); and perhaps also the miracu-

[158] G. Murray, Oxford text of *I.A.*; D. L. Page, *Actors' Interpolations*, pp. 122–216.

[159] Ag. falls back on the philosophy of λάθε βιώσας, 446–453; cf. 16–34, and 161–163 (work of the younger Euripides?).

[160] 1402: *γενναίως*; contrast 1457: ἀγεννῶς.

lous rescue of Iphigenia by Artemis,[161] if this "happy ending" and suggestion of "poetic justice" was within the poet's original plan. And once more the association of *tyche* with the gods is incessant.[162] But of far greater significance than any of these trite comments is the central fact in the legend: the cruel, arbitrary demand of the goddess that an innocent maiden be sacrificed. Even if we suppose the play to end with the actual sacrifice, we have not real tragedy, for there is no real relation between the character of Iphigenia and what happens to her;[163] we have only the brutal blow of an external fatality. If, on the other hand, we accept the concluding scene as at least carrying out the intent of Euripides, we must admit that it is a frivolous dénouement,[164] compared with those plays of Aeschylus and Sophocles that see the divine will, however harsh, at last justified. There is, of course, one further possible interpretation, that of Lucretius: the story exhibits the fruits of superstition;[165] in that case the concluding scene will be rejected altogether.

There is no better proof of the amazing range and fertility of the genius of Euripides than the fact that in the same year, in his old age, in which he composed the *Iphigenia at Aulis*, a loosely constructed melodrama, he was able to compose also the *Bacchae*, a real tragedy of cause and effect in the strictest mould of earlier drama. Possibly the surroundings of his self-imposed exile in Macedonia, where primitive social and religious institutions still survived, suggested to him that he return to the original theme of tragedy, the god Dionysus, his myth and his ritual,[166] with the fullest use of the chorus (the original element from which tragedy evolved). In any case, tragedy in this play has come full circle in its career.

[161] 1578–1629; 1581: *θαῦμα*; 1610 f.: *ἀπροσδόκητα δὲ βροτοῖς τὰ τῶν θεῶν, | σώζουσί θ' οὓς φιλοῦσιν.*

[162] 351 f.: *ἐξεπλήσσου τῇ τύχῃ τῇ τῶν θεῶν | οὐρίας πομπῆς σπανίζων*; 411: *Ἑλλὰς δὲ σὺν σοὶ κατὰ θεὸν νοσεῖ τινα* (cf. 1403: *τὸ τῆς τύχης δὲ καὶ τὸ τῆς θεοῦ νοσεῖ*); 441–445: *ἰούσης τῆς τύχης . . . | δύστηνος . . . | ἐς οἷ' ἀνάγκης ζεύγματ' ἐμπεπτώκαμεν. | ὑπῆλθε δαίμων, ὥστε τῶν σοφισμάτων | πόλλῳ γενέσθαι τῶν ἐμῶν σοφώτερος* (with deep irony); 1136: *ὦ πότνια μοῖρα καὶ τύχη δαίμων τ' ἐμός* (cf. 1137); 1404 f.: *τίς θεῶν . . . εἰ | τύχοιμι*; 1408 f. (*θεομαχεῖν* contrasted with *τὰ χρηστὰ τἀναγκαῖά τε*). But in 864, *tyche* is associated with human *pronoia*: Some of these passages may be later than Euripides; certainly interpolated, but of interest, are the gnomic lines, 1319–1337, on the vicissitudes sent by the gods.

[163] The matter stands a little differently with Agamemnon, who according to a legend not mentioned in this play had offended Artemis by killing a deer; hence his wind-bound fleet. Here the kernel of old folk-religion underlies the plot, but is incapable of being moralized, as Sophocles, for example, moralized the legends of Oedipus and of Philoctetes.

[164] It may be explained, if not justified, by the need of saving Iphigenia alive for the episode in Tauris, which in turn has its aetiological use for Attic cults.

[165] Lucretius I, 84–101.

[166] See above, pp. 49; 51; 59 f. E. R. Dodds, "Maenadism in the *Bacchae*," *Harvard Theological Review* 33 (1940), pp. 155–176, suggests as an alternative to the "Macedonian hypothesis" the impact on fifth-century Athens of renewed invasions of Oriental cults, among them that of Sabazius (the Thracian or Phrygian Dionysus).

The theme of the *Bacchae* is the punishment by Dionysus of the *hybris* of those who oppose his worship, and his triumphant epiphany. It provides abundant opportunity for tragic irony, as the god draws his opponents unwittingly to their ruin; it exhibits a contrast between their varying attitudes, and between two utterly different conceptions of "wisdom"; and it at least raises, if it does not settle, the question of divine *dike*. We may note that the *Bacchae*, unlike the tragi-comedies and the melodramas, makes no use whatsoever of *tyche*, though the will of Zeus and *ananke* are invoked at the close as having played a leading part.

Dionysus himself speaks the Prologue, in which the theme and the action are clearly sketched. (1) He sets forth his own history and status as a god, and his plan of extending his cult to Greece; (2) he commends Cadmus, the former king of Thebes, who honors him (*Bacchae* 10), (3) but announces his hostility to the daughters of Cadmus (26–31) and to the present king, Pentheus, who oppose him;[167] (4) he is therefore punishing the women by driving them to revel madly as Bacchanals (32–42), and will punish more severely any serious opposition to this plan (50–52); and (5) will reveal himself as a god;[168] but (6) meanwhile, for the furtherance of his plans, he has temporarily assumed a human guise (54 f.; cf. 4). This last announcement prepares us for the irony of the scenes in which the "stranger" from Lydia deals with Pentheus, and should provide us with the necessary indications for understanding that the "stranger" is simply the god in disguise.

After the entering song of the Chorus, Bacchanals from the Orient, we behold the old seer Tiresias and the aged Cadmus preparing to join the Theban women who are already madly worshiping Dionysus on Mount Cithaeron, and the intervention of Pentheus, who becomes so far enraged as to command the arrest of the "stranger" whom he holds to blame. Another choral song, and a soldier enters with the fettered "stranger," or Dionysus, as we may well call him, though he does not yet reveal his divinity. His calm yet defiant bearing amid the insults of Pentheus causes him to be thrown into prison; but, after another hymn from the Chorus, a miracle occurs, or seems to occur: the palace is shaken, and Dionysus appears, free and confident, while baffled Pentheus blusters in vain. And now a messenger reports the miracles performed by the Theban bacchanals on the mountains: the flowing of milk and wine and honey at their will;

[167] 45: *θεομαχεῖ*; cf. 795; 1255; contrast 199 (Cadmus) and 325 (Tiresias): *οὐ θεομαχήσω*. The word *hybris* does not appear in the prologue to characterize the opposition of mortals to Dionysus (though it is used, line 9, of Hera's attitude to his mother Semele); but it appears constantly in this connection later in the play: 375 (Chorus); 516; 616; 1347 (in these cases, Dionysus); 1297 (Cadmus); and cf. 1377 f. (Dionysus).

[168] 22: *ἐμφανὴς δαίμων*; 42: *φανέντα . . . δαίμονα*; 47: *θεὸς γεγὼς ἐνδείξομαι*; 50: *δεικνὺς ἐμαυτον*; cf. 859–861; 1031.

their rending (*sparagmos*) of wild creatures; and their own scathelessness, — sure tokens that a god is with them. Pentheus still threatens, and heeds neither the warnings of Dionysus nor his offer to bring the Theban women home; but he falls into the "net" that Dionysus prepares by offering to take him, disguised in bacchanal attire, to spy on the revels. The plan goes forward, Pentheus falling utterly under the sway of his guide. Presently another messenger brings word that Pentheus is dead, rent apart (the victim of a *sparagmos*) by his mother Agave and her companions, who took him for a beast. Agave enters in triumph with the head of Pentheus, and Cadmus in grief with the rest of his dismembered body; he brings his daughter to her senses, and they mourn. Finally Dionysus appears from the "machine," prophesying the future fortunes of Cadmus and his family, and justifying this punishment of *hybris* as the will of Zeus. But Agave will have no more to do with Dionysus and his revels.

A story so revolting as this demands a special effort on our part if we are to understand its intent; even if we give ourselves up to the magic of the poetry (especially of the marvellous choruses), which our outline has ignored, the problem is no clearer. We may begin by observing what sort of persons accept or reject the new god. Tiresias, not the profound prophet with second sight that he elsewhere appears, is merely the religionist who accepts tradition and "will have no rationalizing about the gods" (200–209), yet who also argues like any sophist the social utility of Demeter, giver of grain, and of Dionysus, giver of the vine and of the mantic frenzy, and who relates with amusing etymological embellishment the myth of his birth (266–309); 'tis best not to oppose this new god (309–327). Old Cadmus, too, is a conformist, though even less certain of the god's existence (330–334); with a touch of family pride he champions the acceptance of Semele's son as at least the better risk;[169] and at the last his pity for Pentheus, justly dead (1249 f.; but contrast 1348), comes from the heart (1216–1250). Pentheus, the unimaginative rationalist, who is determined to uproot the new cult, suspecting that Dionysus masks Aphrodite,[170] is harsh toward Tiresias, whom he holds responsible for the new cult (255–266), and toward the "stranger," whom he holds responsible for the myth of Dionysus.[171] He is in fact the typical "tyrant,"[172] arbitrary and sure of

[169] 330–340. There is of course an incompatibility between the oriental origin of Dionysus and the myth of his Theban birth which must have arisen after his cult reached Greece.

[170] 222–225; 485–487; rebuked by 314–318 (Tiresias) and by 685–688 (Messenger). It is beside the point to admit that Dionysus and Aphrodite are traditional allies (cf. the Bacchanalian scandal in Italy, 185 B.C.); the point is that Euripides does not wish to press such charges against Dionysus in the present play. For lines 402–408, see below, p. 213, and n. 179.

[171] 242–245: the charge of Pentheus that this is *hybris*, 246 f., meets its retort from Dionysus, 516–518.

[172] 995: τὸν ἄθεον ἄνομον ἄδικον (Chorus); cf. 778–801.

himself, until he falls under the power of the god. Narrow in his sympathies, he has something of the "Puritan's" contempt for superstition and for whatever he cannot understand; and though he is partly right (for Dionysus proves terrible in his vindictiveness), Pentheus, unlike Hippolytus, has been too nearly the villain of the piece in the earlier scenes to win our complete pity even at the end.[173]

Of a haunting loveliness surpassing anything else of their kind in all literature are the songs of the Chorus, the Oriental followers of Dionysus, who voice the joy and the yearning of children of nature yielding themselves to the beauty, the peace, the wisdom of a life that is lived in closest communion with the elemental forces of the world and with their god.[174] Translation or paraphrase, still more analysis, fails to capture the fragrance of these songs; but we must set down in a few words their contribution to our inquiry. (1) The *Parodos* (64–169) glorifies the cult of Dionysus, with proclamation and hymn to the god and beatitude for his worshiper, with myth and invocation to Thebes (the god's birthplace) and to Crete (where his father Zeus was born), and with glad memories of Bacchanal revels and the marvels done by the god. The joyous picture of the *omophagia*,[175] and of the marvellous flow of milk and wine and honey (135–143) foreshadows the messenger's story of the miracles performed by the Theban bacchanals.[176] (2) In the *First Stasimon* (370–432) the maidens, who have witnessed the impiety (263) of Pentheus, call on Holiness[177] to give heed to his *hybris* (375) against Dionysus, the bringer of joy and healing. Their song is against lawlessness (388), and hymns the blessings of peace (389) and wisdom (390: τὸ φρονεῖν); not, indeed, wisdom as the world knows it, nor more than mortal thoughts;[178] not the cult of Aphrodite of Paphos;[179] but the haunts of the Muses and of merry, peace-loving Dionysus, who favors the simple more than the "wise."[180] (3) In the

[173] For a defense of Pentheus, cf. G. Norwood, *The Riddle of the Bacchae* (Manchester, 1908), pp. 58–67.

[174] A. E. Phoutrides, *H.S.C.P.* 27 (1916), pp. 122–130, sees in these choruses not the poet's own belief but his sympathetic treatment of popular religious belief.

[175] See above, pp. 51; 211 f.

[176] 699–711; 734–747.

[177] 370: 'Οσία, possibly the Orphic abstraction, half a goddess.

[178] 395 f.: τὸ σοφὸν δ' οὐ σοφία | τό τε μὴ θνητὰ φρονεῖν. The last an echo of Pindar? (See above, p. 77.) In this Dionysiac play there is no hint of Orphic immortality.

[179] 402–408; A. W. Verrall, *C. R.* 8 (1894), pp. 86 f., and *The Bacchants of Euripides*, pp. 152–157, though with varying interpretations.

[180] 397–399; 427–432. With this reversal of ordinary values and depreciation of "wisdom," cf. 480; 504; 655 f., all reminding us of the ironical scene in Sophocles, *O. T.* 316–462, between "blind" Tiresias and "seeing" Oedipus. For the retreat from "wisdom" and the discovery of a simpler faith, cf. Virgil's challenge to Lucretius and his acceptance of the religion of the country-side (and Bacchus), ironically described as a "second best," *Georg.* II, 475–494, esp. 485–489.

*Second Stasimon* (519–603), the Chorus sing of the mystical second birth of Dionysus, and call upon him to save their imprisoned "fellow-reveller" (548) within the palace. (4) The *Third Stasimon* (862–911) is an amazing song which glorifies what amounts to *physis* (the life of the wilderness); this is divine (883), and triumphs at long last over folly and irreverence and over thoughts and deeds that transcend law (891 f.); for what is divine is an eternal law rooted in *physis.*[181] As for "wisdom," what fairer gift from god to man is there than victory over foes? [182] Happy he who, though ambition may or may not succeed, finds true happiness in each passing day.[183] (5) Pentheus has gone to the mountains; and in the *Fourth Stasimon* (977–1023) the Chorus sing of the terrible vengeance that is afoot against this unjust man who relies on force.[184] Mere "wisdom" (1002: γνωμᾶν σωφρόνα; 1005: τὸ σοφόν) is death, compared with the "other great and shining things." [185] (6) When the death of Pentheus is reported, the Chorus rejoice (1153–1164); but when his mangled members are before our eyes, their Leader is torn between loyalty to the god (1172; 1193; cf. 1031), and horror (1184; 1200); her last word is that justice has been done, however pitiful the blow (1327 f.). And the play ends with the familiar choral recessional [186] on the unexpected dealings of the gods.

These devoted worshipers of Dionysus, then, along with their gentleness and love of the simple life according to nature, can feel the Bacchic frenzy and can share in the inexorable ruthlessness of their god. What now of the god himself? We have already noted in the Prologue his jealous regard for his own prerogatives and his determination to avenge, as *hybris,* any refusal to accept his divinity. The gentleness of the god and his benefactions to man are to be observed chiefly in the first half of the play, in what is said of him by others (notably by Tiresias and by the Chorus), and above all in the "stranger's" quiet deportment and counsel of quietness.[187] But the gentle behavior of the "stranger" masks a harden-

[181] 894–896: *ὅ τι ποτ' ἄρα τὸ δαιμόνιον, | τό τ' ἐν χρόνῳ νόμιμον | ἀεὶ φύσει τε πεφυκός.*

[182] 877–881 = 897–901. Here the hardness of Dionysus and his worshipers flashes through; G. Murray in his translation diffidently seeks by interpolation to save "the idealised Bacchic religion of Euripides" (see his note, pp. 91 f. of his Translation).

[183] 902–911; the Bacchic frenzy leads to depression, if it does not achieve what the philosophers will call *ἀταραξία.*

[184] 977: Λύσσας κύνες; 991: *δίκα* (cf. 1011); 995: *τὸν ἄθεον ἄνομον ἄδικον* (cf. 997; 1042); 1001: *ὡς κρατήσων βίᾳ.*

[185] 1006 f. Our text here is uncertain; and what the "other" things are must remain obscure, as perhaps the poet intended even in his own manuscript. Something however is suggested like "Except your righteousness shall exceed that of the Pharisees," or "The letter killeth, but the spirit giveth life." See also below, p. 218, n. 206.

[186] See above, p. 100.

[187] 641: *πρὸς σοφοῦ γὰρ ἀνδρὸς ἀσκεῖν σώφρον' εὐοργησίαν*; 621; 636: *ἥσυχος* (cf. 647; 790); 861: *ἀνθρώποισι δ' ἠπιώτατος.*

ing of purpose[188] when it is exposed to the *hybris* of Pentheus; and the ironical scenes that follow show him luring the King to destruction as a spider lures a fly. But who is the "stranger"? If we remember that in the Prologue the god has announced that he is to accomplish his purpose by taking a human guise, we shall be disposed to answer simply that the "stranger" is the god, even if (or, better, precisely because) he does not reveal his divinity in these scenes.[189] The case for the identity of the "stranger" and the god would seem to be strengthened by the miracle that the "stranger" performs "himself" in escaping from captivity, and that the god performs in shaking the palace and in assisting the escape (576–606; 622–636), miracles which are continued by the miracles performed by the "stranger" (or by the god) on the mountain (699–764; 1063; 1068–1083; 1088 f.; 1127 f.). The reality of the "Palace Miracle," to be sure, and the reliability of the messengers who report the strange happenings on the mountain, have been criticized by some scholars, who find in these phenomena merely some sort of hypnotic suggestion; the palace was only shaken, and perhaps a part of it thrown down, by an earthquake; Pentheus is not aware of any ruin, nor is any reference made to it later in the play, partly since even more portentous events are now reputed to have taken place (which may also admit of rationalistic explanations). This criticism may be accepted, but not, I think, the further inference that the "stranger" is not the god, but only a human hierophant. Everything is intelligible if we conclude that it is the god himself who hallucinates the Chorus into believing that a miracle has occurred, and who further hypnotizes Pentheus into his fatal adventure on the mountain.[190]

For although the god has been gentle (ἥσυχος), when Pentheus refuses to come to terms and be "saved" (806) the vindictiveness of the god proceeds to its inexorable end. Not even in his epiphany, which may be supposed to appeal to the pious in the audience, does the god show any of the pity that the mortals show in the last scene. Like Cadmus, he insists that *hybris* has been justly punished;[191] but whereas Cadmus urges that "gods ought not to show anger, as do mortals" (1348), the god's answer is merely: "My father Zeus willed all this long ago" (1349; cf. 1351: ἀναγκαίως). Here, for the first time in the play, there is a suggestion of fatality, a recourse to motives or forces transcending the personages of the action.

What, then, of the whole intention of the *Bacchae*? Is Euripides defend-

[188] Cf. 861: δεινότατος, in the line just cited.

[189] For the ambiguity, cf. 464 (Lydia is his πατρίς); 466 (he is sent by Dionysus); 493–503; 516–518; 648–656; 975 f.

[190] See Appendix 24: Palace Miracle in *Bacchae*.

[191] 1297, Cadmus; 1347, 1377 f., Dionysus.

ing, or attacking, Dionysus? Even to pose the question so simply is to risk misunderstanding the play. The poet is not so much concerned either to approve or to disapprove of the god as he is to present him as the symbol of something that undeniably exists. The religion of Dionysus corresponds to a fact in human nature no less ineluctable than the existence of certain elemental forces: among them, the vine, the power of wine, the life according to nature, with its mellowing or brutalizing of man. Deny such forces, and there is tragedy; give in to them utterly, and tragedy ensues no less. Not here for the first time is Euripides dealing with such a theme; for in almost the earliest of his extant dramas, the *Hippolytus* (also a tragedy in the strictest sense), we saw the inexorable fates alike of him who denied and of her who surrendered to the elemental powers that transcend reason, *nemesis* following *hybris*.[192] The *Bacchae* is no palinode, no recantation of a life-long rationalist who now takes refuge in mysticism; for Euripides has always seen the danger of thinking of Aphrodite, or of Dionysus, as sovereign divinities with human passions. Divinities so conceived are evil. Somewhere between complete surrender to instinct and complete denial of instinct lies the path of *sophrosyne*, a law of Zeus which man breaks at his own peril.[193] This is no easy path to find for us who are no longer innocent children but grown men who have tasted of the Tree of the Knowledge of Good and Evil; but only by threading warily the maze of instincts and repressions, Euripides would persuade us, can we walk as men who have attained to our full stature, as men who have learned the meaning of "wisdom."

The thought of Euripides as a whole, and his attitude toward the problem of fate, good, and evil, we have seen to be far from consistent. As humanist and as dramatist, he feels the action of his plays emotionally, from the point of view of the individual characters, whether they are normal or pathological. Yet these individuals must find their place in a larger setting in the external *physis*, in fact in a setting no less vast than the *cosmos* with its irresistible laws, whether in particular cases these laws prove friendly or destructive. Here the poet should make clear his intellectual attitude.

In a famous fragment (910 Nauck), a Euripidean character praises the guileless sage, happy in the study of ageless Nature and her immortal order. The sentiment, possibly suggested by the person of Anaxagoras,

[192] Cf. A. R. Bellinger, "The Bacchae and Hippolytus," *Yale Classical Studies*, 6 (1939), pp. 17–27; and see above, pp. 176–183.

[193] 1340–1345; 1341: σωφρονεῖν. But the *Bacchae* is neither a teetotalist tract nor an invitation to intoxication. It is almost incidental that this play, expressing alike the beauty and rightness of natural instincts and the ugliness and the negative character of the spirit that denies them, should use as its symbol the god of the vine; not accidental, however, for Dionysus is also the god of tragedy itself.

may have become a commonplace in the next century, for we find it also in Menander;[194] and it is close to the attitude of both Epicureans and Stoics toward the majesty of the *cosmos*. Other Euripidean characters provide us with cosmogonies that clearly derive from Ionian thinkers.[195] But whether the *cosmos* is providentially ordered is a question on which Epicureans and Stoics will be sharply divided; and Euripidean characters anticipate their divergencies. Does the *cosmos* exhibit reason, and does the good in it outweigh the evil, especially from the point of view of man's interests? Theseus in the *Suppliant Women* thinks so, and his speech, glorifying man's intelligence (σύνεσις), but acknowledging its divine origin, has been called the oldest theodicy of the Greeks.[196] And Hecuba, in her "strange prayer" in the *Trojan Women*,[197] expresses her troubled faith in the power of justice, however it may be named, that guides mortal affairs. Moreover the Chorus of the *Hippolytus* have already speculated on that divine understanding (ξύνεσις) in which they would fain believe, though men's vicissitudes make faith difficult.[198] Talthybius in the *Hecuba*, after witnessing the death of innocent Polyxena, goes further; he wonders whether the gods are a delusion, and whether it is *tyche* that oversees all mortal things.[199] Still another character echoes the sentiment: "Oft has the thought entered my mind: does Fortune or some divine power sway the life of man?"[200]

Between these extremes of faith and doubt it is the business of religion to mediate. But Euripides cannot be said to have found any reconciliation between the cosmic and the moral laws. The gods and the myths he has accepted for dramatic purposes, even to the extent of sometimes using gods in final scenes to give a pious conclusion to a story that offends the moral sense. Some divinities (Aphrodite and Artemis in the *Hippolytus*, and Dionysus in the *Bacchae*) correspond to facts in human nature; others he clearly attacks or rejects (Apollo in the *Ion*, Artemis in the *Iphigenia among the Taurians*).[201] We are therefore confronted by an ambiguity in Euripides; the gods are criticized or denied, or the myth is ridiculed, at the very time that the myth is being represented, or (as in the case of the *Ion*

[194] Frag. 481 Kock.

[195] Eur. frag. 839 (*Chrysippus*); 484 (*Melanippe the Wise*).

[196] Eur. *Suppl.* 195–218; see above, p. 189 f.; cf. W. Nestle, "Pessimismus," p. 92, comparing Heraclitus, and Nietzsche's "beyond good and evil."

[197] *Troad.* 884–888; see above, p. 194; cf. *Phoen.* 536–547, for the ethical application of an appeal to *physis*; it is parodied by Aristophanes, *Clouds* 1290–1295.

[198] *Hipp.* 1103–1110; see above, p. 182.

[199] *Hec.* 488–491; see above, p. 189, n. 68.

[200] Eur. frag. 901.

[201] Cf. *Heracles* 342; 1315–1319; 1341–1346; frag. 286 (*Bellerophontes*); frag. 506 (*Melanippe Bound*); Plato, *Gorg.* 470c ff.; F. Solmsen, "The Background of Plato's Theology," *T.A.P.A.* 67 (1936), pp. 210–212; and see below, pp. 295 f.

or the *Iphigenia among the Taurians*) is being partly invented by Euripides himself. Such criticism is not necessarily irreligious by Athenian standards, as infringement of ritual would have been; indeed the criticism of the traditional religion may be undertaken in the interest of a moral cause, such as peace. But the result is in any case a profound scepticism or even pessimism not only about the goodness of the gods of legend but even about any basis for morality to be found in *physis*; this is the product alike of the contemporary rationalizing of *physis* and of the poet's own sensitiveness to man's fortunes in relation to his environment.[202] The poet's dramas are "sicklied o'er with the pale cast of thought."

Yet the reader of Euripides who comes to his plays fresh from Aeschylus, or even from Sophocles, must feel that the later poet is less fatalistic than his predecessors. For in his real tragedies, the action develops chiefly on the human level, with only conventional allusions to the agencies of fate; it is in the tragi-comedies and in the melodramas that more is made of fate (and of chance), particularly in the utterances of the divinities who sometimes appear at the end.[203] The casual reader of Euripides will also be struck by the many allusions to *tyche*, allusions which almost amount to an Euripidean *cliché*; but he will be surprised to discover, on more careful study, how little of the action in the plays is actually due to chance. Again, most of the real tragedies are full of references to chance, or to an individual's "fortune," while the action shows man and woman acting or suffering under the stress of circumstance according to their several characters; but again the tragi-comedies and melodramas often actually turn on a chance event.[204]

Even those dramas of Euripides that most fully recognize the rôle of fate or of chance, however, and still more the real tragedies, turn on the characters of human beings who feel and think and endure.[205] Euripides, reckless borrower of the symbols of poetry and religion and earlier poetry, is first and last a humanist and a poet, nor shall we understand him if we seek to imprison him in any easily phrased formula. Neither rationalist, though he can outdo the sophists at their own business, nor mystic, though he has expressed with transcendent power the ecstasy and the enthusiasm of the mystic or irrationalist,[206] neither fatalist nor champion

[202] Cf. Eur. *Hipp.* 189 f.; 207; *Hel.* 1137–1143 (and see above, p. 202); frags. 37; 196; 332; 757.

[203] See Appendix 25: Fate in Euripides.

[204] See Appendix 26: Τύχη in Euripides.

[205] For *tlemosyne* in Euripides, and especially for εὐψυχία, καρτερία, or γενναιότης, cf. J. A. Symonds, *Studies of the Greek Poets*, II, pp. 38–54.

[206] *Medea* 1078–1080 (θυμός), above, p. 177, n. 19; *Hipp.* 79–81; 921 f. (φύσις superior to teaching); cf. *Suppl.* 911–917, on the need of ἄσκησις to overcome heredity, and see P. Shorey, Φύσις, Μελέτη, Ἐπιστήμη; *Hipp.* 375–387 (what amounts to weakness of will), and above, pp. 171–181; *Hipp.* 191–197 ("that Other (ἄλλο) that is more precious than

of absolute freedom in any strict philosophic sense, Euripides above all feels the stinging winds of the world about him. Anger he feels at the evil, wonder at the good in human life, and compassion with man's striving to rise above circumstance.

Euripides, like his predecessors in poetry, has used its ancient symbols of myth and metaphor, pouring into these old skins the new wine of his own age; more than most of his predecessors, he has also used the symbols of philosophy, which likewise began in poetry but which became more and more the tokens of abstract thought. In our remaining chapters, we must follow our problem through the course of Greek philosophy itself, from the earliest thinkers of Greece to those of the classical age and beyond into certain later periods that felt the impulse of Greek thought.

---

life"); *Bacch.* 1005–1010 ("The Other Things (τὰ δ' ἕτερα) are great and shining"), both times in contrast with mere "wisdom"; see above, p. 214; also J. Adam, *Religious Teachers*, pp. 316–318; E. R. Dodds, "Euripides the Irrationalist," pp. 97–104.

# CHAPTER VIII

## SOCRATES AND HIS PREDECESSORS

### I

IF WE recall the preoccupation of the Greek poets and of the mystics with the problem of Fate, Good, and Evil, it would be somewhat surprising if we were to find that their successors the philosophers had lost all interest in the question.[1] The pre-Socratic philosophers were still concerned with divine powers, however much these powers might doff their anthropomorphic guise. Moreover non-anthropomorphic divinities were older than Homer, and stood also in Homer, no less than did the individualized gods, as the causes of existence and of change, and often, though not consistently, of Good. If the divine and living cause of all things was henceforth to be defined as one or more divine substances or forces,[2] and was to be conceived no longer as being capricious or arbitrary but as being at least as regular in operation as human institutions,[3] it would be reasonable to inquire whether the fixed and regularly operating divine cause of things could be described as good and as productive of Good, and what origin was to be assigned to Evil.

Although the pre-Socratic Greek philosophers may not often have entitled their works "Περὶ Φύσεως" ("On Nature"), the title was often rightly given to them in later times; for *Physis*, alive and divine, was the subject of many of their inquiries. That "nature" is an appropriate translation of φύσις will hardly be denied, though the exact denotation of the word remains a matter of controversy. It seems clear to me that the term includes both the conception of the "stuff" of which anything is made and also the idea of origin and process, as well as the causal nexus of all things in a whole.[4] In the fifth century it acquires also an ethical coloring. Now it is a commonplace that both Plato, speaking through the mouth of

[1] The first two paragraphs of this chapter, together with parts of pp. 225 f. and Appendices 27 and 28, are condensed from the much fuller discussion in my article, "Fate, Good, and Evil in Pre-Socratic Philosophy," *H.S.C.P.* 47 (1936), pp. 85–129, to which I may refer the reader for details.

[2] Cf. R. K. Hack, *God in Greek Philosophy, passim.*

[3] See above, pp. 10 f.; and below, 224–226; for the converse, pp. 32 f.; 36; 125. For the concept of the regularity of Nature that is implied in the rhetorical figure **'Αδύνατον**, cf. H. V. Canter, *A.J.P.* 51 (1930), pp. 32–41; E. Dutoit, *Le Thème de l'Adynaton dans la Poésie Antique* (Paris, 1936), and my review of it, *A.J.P.* 59 (1938), pp. 244 f.

[4] See Appendix 27: *Physis.*

Socrates, and Aristotle went out of their way to declare that the pre-Socratics had no real idea of causality, and that in particular Anaxagoras, whose *Nous* ("Mind") seemed at first to promise better things, proved to have nothing better than a mechanical explanation.[5] What both Plato and Aristotle really mean (the latter thinking in terms of his own four types of cause),[6] is that the forerunners of Socrates did not conceive of Nature as teleological, as Socrates and as they themselves did, and moreover that without such a conception (Aristotle's final cause) there is no room in the world for ethical distinctions. In terms of our problem, they attribute to the pre-Socratics a conception of Fate, but not of Good and Evil. Yet although these critics fail more than once to recognize the importance of certain other ideas (especially the living, divine causality which is implicit in each of the pre-Socratic systems[7]) nevertheless they rightly perceive that even those pre-Socratic philosophers who most conspicuously emphasize the conception of a divine, cosmogenetic principle do not show that the supreme power in the world, — God, or *Physis*, or Fate, — has either the purpose or, except incidentally, the effect of causing Good or Evil.[8] Their science, to be sure, was not based upon a sufficient empirical foundation; but even though a thoroughly empirical science might indeed consider cosmic Good and Evil, it could not deal with human values. More significant, therefore, is the fact that the analysis of human values had not yet gone far beyond the naïf though often beautiful conceptions of the poets. What was needed next, therefore, was both the empirical pursuit of science and that criticism of human values on which a theory of Good and Evil must rest; and there remained the further question of man's relation to his environment.

## 2

That Socrates and his contemporaries "brought philosophy from heaven to earth" is a commonplace,[9] and the Sophistic movement is often described as a revolt against science.[10] Yet the change was not so sudden as is sometimes supposed. Not only was the word "sophist" itself frequently used both of artists and of pre-Socratic philosophers and even of Plato and his contemporaries,[11] but some, at least, of the thought of the pre-

[5] Plato, *Phaedo* 96a–99a; Aristotle, *Met.* 984b15; 985a18 (= D59A58; D59A45); see also below, Appendix 39; pp. 274; 285; 292 f.

[6] See below, pp. 286; 318 f.

[7] See Appendix 28: Pre-Socratic Philosophy.

[8] For a brief summary of such attempts to moralize *Physis* as are to be found among the pre-Socratics, see below, pp. 224–226.

[9] Cicero, *T. D.* V, 10, is speaking of Socrates; but his remark fits most of the Sophists about as well.

[10] E.g. by Burnet, *T.-P.*, p. 109.

[11] Among σοφισταί are counted, in popular speech, the Seven Wise Men, Solon, the Pythagoreans, Socrates, Plato, etc., as Aristides remarks (D 79, 1.).

Socratics appears, in changed form, in the new age. We may see the transition, if we wish, in the *physiologos* Archelaus, pupil of Anaxagoras and teacher of Socrates, who is said to have applied the antithesis of Nature and Law to the field of ethical ideas, proclaiming that justice and baseness exist not by nature but by convention.[12] Democritus, humanist as well as scientist, raised the issue between subjective sensation and objective reality, declaring that qualities exist by convention, atoms and the void by nature.[13] Moreover the Sophists Hippias and Antiphon and Prodicus, whose championship of *physis* against *nomos* we shall consider presently, were all still interested in *physis* in the older sense, as well as in ethics.

It is now realized that the Sophists were united more by a common profession, the training of pupils (chiefly well-to-do young men) for public life, than by any common doctrine; it is, therefore, fallacious to speak of "the sophistic point of view." [14] They no more deserve a universal condemnation, as perverters of morality, than they deserve undiscriminating eulogy, as educators. Probably many of them were more concerned with method than with ideas, with style than with content. The earlier Sophists well served literature, and even Athenian public life, by sharpening wits and developing style; the later eristics were a public nuisance. The Sophists also varied as individuals; Plato respects Protagoras and Gorgias far more than the rest, however much he may feel their inadequacy. Moreover the extent to which teachers should be held responsible for the vagaries of wayward or vicious pupils is always hard to calculate. Xenophon and others tried to clear Socrates from blame for the careers of Alcibiades and Critias (not disciples in any strict sense); Plato, though fair to Protagoras and Gorgias themselves, has not been at equal pains to defend Protagoras and Gorgias and Hippias against the suspicion that they unwittingly let loose a plague of evils in the persons of unworthy imitators.

Protagoras and Gorgias are a generation or so older than Hippias and Prodicus and Antiphon and Socrates, and still older than most of the other Sophists who concern us.[15] Yet they were busy during most of their earlier careers with training in rhetoric and in *arete*, and apparently did not bring forward the sceptical views for which they became famous, not to say notorious, till the dogmatic utterances of their juniors had become current; they then met dogmatism with scepticism. They wholly escape the notice of Xenophon in the *Memorabilia*, and are most familiar to us

[12] See below, p. 223, and n. 18.

[13] D.L. IX, 45 = D 68 A 1 (p. 84), reading with Zeller *ποιότητας δὲ νόμῳ εἶναι, φύσει δὲ ἄτομα καὶ κενόν* (Mss. *ποιητὰ δὲ νόμιμα*). Cf. D 68B 9: *νόμῳι . . . ἐτεῆι.*

[14] See Appendix 29: Sophists.

[15] Cf. Benn, p. 66; and his preface, pp. viii–xi; Burnet, *T.-P.*, p. 111; Taylor, *P.M.W.*, p. 236.

from the pages of Plato in which Socrates confronts them, and in which Plato's own thought is already taking form. The younger Sophists, on the other hand, are better represented in Xenophon; moreover they are nearer in many of their interests to the physical speculations of the previous age. As a matter of convenience, therefore, and perhaps also of logic, we may well begin with them and defer consideration of the elder sophists till later.[16] Moreover we shall notice that because our chief witnesses to the teaching of the major sophists are Xenophon and Plato, who represent them in conversation with Socrates, it will be difficult, and perhaps undesirable, to discuss the sophists without considering Socrates also to some extent.[17] But since the significance of Socrates consists largely in his reply to problems raised by the sophists, it will be convenient to consider him more fully after dealing with them.

Archelaus is described by Diogenes Laertius as having busied himself chiefly with physical speculation; but after mentioning the fact that "Socrates introduced ethics" Diogenes adds: "He (Archelaus), too, seems to have treated of ethics, for he philosophized on laws and goodness and justice; Socrates took the subject from him, carried it to its perfection, and was regarded as its inventor." Then, after stating two of the physical theories of Archelaus, Diogenes remarks casually, in the phrase already mentioned, that Archelaus said "that what is just and what is base depends not on *physis* but on *nomos*." [18] It is doubtless an accident that the remark has come down to us as if it were his discovery. But the antithesis between *Physis* and *Nomos*, between Nature and Law (Custom, or Convention), which the Callicles of Plato's *Gorgias* is represented as describing, a generation later, as a contrast between the "popular and vulgar" notion of right and the truer conception, as he regards it, of "natural right," [19] was doubtless commonplace in the youth of Socrates.[20] Just what *Physis* was supposed by her early champions to sanction is as yet obscure. Is Nature kindly or cruel? Does she sanction the brotherhood of man or a struggle for survival? What Archelaus understood by *physis* is not known to us; and in the case of Hippias, as will presently appear, we are left almost as completely to conjecture.

When men argue, they often find that the issue may be stated in terms of an antithesis between familiar terms, — society and the individual,

[16] Cf. further A. Chiapelli, *Sofistica Greca*, pp. 16–18.

[17] See Appendix 30: Socratic Problem, I.

[18] D. L. II, 16 = D 60A 1: *τὸ δίκαιον εἶναι καὶ τὸ αἶσχρον οὐ φύσει, ἀλλὰ νόμῳ*; see above, p. 222, and n. 13; and cf. D 60 A 2 (Suidas).

[19] Plato, *Gorgias* 482c–483a; see below, pp. 260 f.

[20] On the *τόπος*, and the discussion of it in the *Gorgias*, see Aristotle, *Soph. El.* 173a7–30. For examples of the antithesis in the "Hippocratean" writings, earlier than the sophistic period, cf. Chiapelli, pp. 6–11; Beardslee, *Use of Φύσις*, pp. 31–42. For similar doctrines held also in the fourth century, cf. Plato, *Laws* 888e–889e, and see below, pp. 295 f.; Appendix 41.

heredity and environment, stability and progress, freedom and discipline, nature and convention. Often, as in the present case, the terms themselves have had a long history, and have undergone great changes in meaning; words that began by describing facts have come to suggest norms of conduct. So it was with, *dike*, *nomos*, and *physis*. When men in argument finally differ, and agree to disagree, it is because they differ as to the relative values that they assign to the terms in the antithesis. Since the debate about *Physis* and *Nomos* pervades fifth century thought, and since it raises questions of perennial importance about the relations of Man to Nature and of the individual to society, it is well at this point, before we consider the views of the various sophists and of Socrates, to recall briefly the background in previous Greek thought.[21]

The idea of *Physis* (not the word) fills the pre-Homeric and the Homeric world and the world of Hesiod, so far as men recognize in diverse natural powers the sources from which all things, whether good or evil, proceed; against it stands the company of the anthropomorphic gods, also powerful, yet imperfectly endowed with moral excellence. The idea of *Moira* envelops both *Physis* and the gods.[22] The word *physis* at first means nothing more than the specific character of a thing, as of a plant.[23] *Dike* is used of the "way of things," in Homer of the behavior of old men, in later poets of a wolf, of a dog, of water, or of a colt,[24] with some suggestion of the regularity of Nature, at least in certain small observed areas;[25] yet *dike* is already used also of human acts with the suggestion of a "right way" of conduct, presently in rivalry with *themis*, a right decree or a taboo, human or divine.[26] Later, *nomos*, the usual manner of behavior,[27] gains prestige as the *polis* acquires stability.[28]

The relations of *Good* to *Physis* are the subject of endless speculation among the early Greeks. The Hesiodic *Theogony* at times seems to deal with a neutral *Physis*, at other times to suggest the triumph of *Themis*

[21] See Appendix 31: *Physis and Nomos*; bibliography.

[22] See above, pp. 14 f.

[23] *Od.* 10, 303 (the only use of the word *physis* in Homer); see above, p. 14.

[24] *Od.* 24, 254–5; Pind. *Pyth.* 2, 155; Aesch. *Ag.* 3; *Sept.* 84; Soph. Fr. 659 Pearson, l. 1.

[25] See above, p. 220, n. 3; cf. Aristophanes, *Clouds* 1292: it is οὐ δίκαιον ("not natural") for the sea in the course of time to become fuller.

[26] Cf. Harrison, *Themis*, pp. 516–518; 531–535, distinguishing *Dike*, Natural law, from *Themis*, moral right, the product of the social order; and Jaeger, *Paideia*, p. 100, showing that the fundamental meaning of *dike* is much the same as "due share," though there are also derivative meanings (law-suit, judgment, penalty). See also below, p. 225, n. 35.

[27] *Nómos*, custom, law, is akin to the more primitive *nomós*, a pasture, a usual haunt; for other possible cognates, such as *nemesis*, the power that "assigns" portions and resents trespasses or encroachments on them, cf. Cornford, *Rel.-Phil.*, pp. 31–35.

[28] *Nómos* is first found in Hesiod, *W. D.* 276, where it is used of the distinction arranged by Zeus between predatory beasts and men (to whom alone is assigned *dike*).

over *Physis*.[29] The Orphic theogonies sometimes represent an attempt to moralize the world of *Physis*.[30] For Pindar, the crown of all the gifts of heaven to man is his breed, or nature (*φυά*), something which his own deliberate efforts could not achieve, though his *arete* and prudence may foster it.[31] Solon, the champion of *eunomia* (the rule of law), uses the image of a wind clearing the clouds away to suggest the inevitability of the vengeance of Zeus; the moral law is as certain as natural law.[32] Conversely, Anaximander and Heraclitus use legal and moral concepts to express the inviolability of the physical order, Anaximander by seeing the processes of coming into being and passing out of being in terms of *dike* and *tisis*, "justice" and "reparation,"[33] (a sort of *lex talionis*), Heraclitus by speaking of the process as an "exchange," and by proclaiming that if the Sun were to overstep his measures, the Erinyes, the handmaids of justice (*Dike*) will find him out.[34] And in spite of his proud individualism, Heraclitus holds that the *logos* by which man is to penetrate the mysteries of Nature is no private possession but is "common" because it is nourished by the one divine law.[35] Thus the Ionian Greeks discovered the conception of a physical *cosmos* governed by law as binding as that of human society. Meanwhile in the western Greek colonies Pythagorean mathematics and astronomy and musical theory were dealing with the harmonies or proportions of the cosmos; these ideas provided for the Pythagoreans themselves, and for Plato and Aristotle, patterns for the building of human justice in actual or in ideal commonwealths. And Empedocles explained the cosmic process of change by appealing to a "law governing the mixture," or to a "broad oath."[36] The idea of the

[29] See above, pp. 28 f.; 53.

[30] See above, pp. 57 f.

[31] See above, pp. 70–72.

[32] See above, p. 36; cf. also Hesiod, above, p. 33; and Pindar, *Pyth.* 3, 34–37, and above, p. 74, n. 133.

[33] Anaximander, D 12 B 1.

[34] Heraclitus, D 22 B90 and 94.

[35] Heraclitus, D 22 B 113 and 114; Jaeger, *Paideia*, pp. 178–181; and pp. 303 f. (cited below, Appendix 27); Burnet, *T.-P.*, p. 106: "In early days the regularity of human life had been far more clearly apprehended than the even course of nature. Man lived in a charmed circle of law and custom, but the world around him still seemed lawless. So much was this the case that, when the regular course of nature began to be observed, no better name could be found for it than Right or Justice (*δίκη*), a word which properly meant the unchanging custom that guided human life." Jaeger, *Paideia*, p. 321, remarks that it is hard to determine whether the conception of regularity was derived first from nature and then applied to the world of men, or whether a view of human life was projected upon nature. For the interrelation of the idea of human law with the conception of cosmic law (and the application of the latter to the special case of medicine, the necessary consequences of man's place in the cosmos), see further R. Mondolfo, *Problemi*, pp. 21–85.

[36] D 31 A 78; D 31 B 30.

unity and regularity of the *cosmos* was furthered by the religious attitude of the mystics.[37] That there is a law in Nature is thus a belief widespread in early Greek thought; yet few, if any, of these conceptions of *Physis* include the belief that Nature has a purpose.

The age of the Sophists inherited all these conceptions, and talked familiarly of *Physis* and *Nomos*. But from about the middle of the fifth century the two ideas tended to become rival claimants for man's allegiance. Rapid internal political changes and contact with other Greek states and with foreign societies of very different *nomoi*, with tyrannies, democracies, oligarchies, and monarchies, as well as with backward tribal societies, undermined the notion that any given *nomos* was eternal. Many a Greek city could point to an actual "law-giver" who had established its *nomoi*. Furthermore, laws were now being changed before men's eyes. Not *nomos*, ancestral custom, but the latest *psephisma* of the assembly, was now sovereign.[38] Why, it could fairly be asked, should one assume that one's own *polis*, one's own social group, one's own age, represented the last word in political or ethical sanctions? "*Autres pays, autres moeurs*" is the moral of the well-known anecdote in which Herodotus records the ironical researches of Darius in comparative religion and culture, and the horror of his Greeks and his Indians when they learned about each other's burial customs.[39] The cynical contempt of Cambyses for ancient religious *nomoi* strikes Herodotus as being proof of his madness: "for if one were to offer men to choose out of all *nomoi* the best, they would after examination choose each his own; so convinced are they that their own *nomoi* are far the best." This truth he illustrates by the anecdote about Darius, which indeed discredits the notion that *nomoi* are anything but provincial; but he reasons, in his tolerant fashion, that there is no reason for interfering with other peoples' *nomoi*, just as he himself reports many stories that he does not believe.[40] Pindar is right, he concludes: "*Nomos* is king of all." [41] Other men will more bitterly protest that *Nomos*, the custom of the community, is no longer the King but the tyrant, and must be dethroned in favor of the older and legitimate sovereign, who is *Physis*. Here begins the revolt of the individual against the arbitrary ways of the social group, a revolt which can find no ultimate sanction, no absolute law, until it reaches an all-embracing society, or even *Physis* itself.

This is a critical moment in the history of thought. If mere *nomos*, mere precedent or custom or convention or arbitrary decree, is to be chal-

[37] Cf. K. Joel, *Naturphilosophie*, pp. 35–140.

[38] As an occasional variant of *νόμος*, we find also *θέσις*, in contrast with *φύσις*.

[39] Herodotus, III, 38; cf. [Plato], *Minos* 315 bc.

[40] Herodotus VII, 152.

[41] *Ibid.*, III, 38. The meaning of Pindar (frag. 152 Bowra) is twisted as usual; see below, pp. 232; 251; 260.

lenged, is there a more fundamental law to replace it? Many Greeks appeal to the "unwritten laws," which represent, it is supposed, something more universal than any particular law of any place or time.[42] Such is the "common law" of Heraclitus, which is rooted in nature.[43] Such, too, are the laws, infringement of which carries its own punishment, which Socrates persuades Hippias the gods have established;[44] such are the "unwritten laws" to which the Antigone of Sophocles appeals from Creon's decree,[45] and the "unwritten laws" the breaking of which Pericles says brings acknowledged shame;[46] and such are what Aristotle calls the "unwritten principles which may be said to be universally recognized," or the "universal law of Nature," which he distinguishes from the "particular law ordained by a particular people for its own purposes, and capable of subdivision into written and unwritten law."[47] The author of the *Rhetorica ad Alexandrum* appeals to "the unwritten custom of all or of the majority."[48] In later times, Roman jurists, imbued with the Stoic conception of natural law to be found in the *cosmos*, sought to identify it with the common element to be found in the laws of all peoples, *ius naturale* with *ius gentium*.[49]

What is the content of this "unwritten law" which is assumed to be the "law of nature"? It seems to include much that we recognize in one's personal sense of honor, in good manners, in conscience, in the intuitions of the mystic, in the unwritten code of the Spartan, or in the activity of the Athenian Areopagus (even in the fifth century). In time it may come

[42] On this whole subject, cf. Nägelsbach, *Nachhomerische Theologie*, pp. 80–84; Hirzel, Ἄγραφος Νόμος; Hirzel, *Themis*, pp. 359–410; Eckstein, *Naturrecht*.

[43] See above, p. 225.

[44] Xen. *Mem.* IV, 4, 5–25; see below, p. 229.

[45] Sophocles, *Ant.* 449–460; Antigone claims divine sanction for a law of nature (cf. *O.T.* 863–871; see above, pp. 155; 160), and natural law brings its violator inescapable punishment (*Ant.* 748 f.), as Creon finally admits (*Ant.* 1113 f.), fearing that it is best to respect τοὺς καθεστῶτας νόμους, by which he means not the laws of the state but those decreed by hallowed custom. See further above, pp. 140; 144.

[46] Thuc. II, 37.

[47] Aristotle, *Rhet.* 1368b7; 1373b4. The language of the two passages is only apparently discrepant. Cf. Hirzel Ἄγραφος Νόμος, pp. 1–14; V. Johnson, "Aristotle on *Nomos*," *C.J.* 33 (1938), pp. 351–356.

[48] Anaximenes (?), *Rhet. ad Alex.* 1421 b 35 ff.

[49] Cf. Cic. *de Rep.* III, 33: *est vera lex recta ratio naturae congruens, diffusa in omnes, constans, sempiterna . . . nec erit alia lex Romae, alia Athenis, alia nunc, alia posthac, sed et omnes gentes et omni tempore una lex et sempiterna et immutabilis continebit, unusque erit communis quasi magister et imperator omnium deus . . . cui qui non parebit, ipse se fugiet ac naturam hominis aspernatus hoc ipso luet maximas poenas, etiamsi cetera supplicia quae putantur effugerit.* Gaius, *Inst.* I, 1: "The law which natural reason has constituted for all men obtains equally among all nations, and is called *ius gentium*." It should be added that both *ius scriptum* and *ius non scriptum* are sub-classes of *ius civile*, and have nothing to do with either *ius naturale* or *ius gentium*; cf. Hirzel, Ἄγραφος Νόμος, pp. 14–19. See also below, p. 343.

to be custom, or "second nature," so that it would be foolish or unnecessary to enact it as written law; so Plato holds that if children are imbued by education with the spirit of law and order, legislation about manners and good taste becomes superfluous and silly.[50] Pity, the quality of mercy, gratitude, self-sacrifice, the virtues of the hero, the sage, and the saint, these can never be prescribed, and may indeed be actually impeded or frustrated by dead convention and the law of the state.

So much may be granted, and the inherent rightness of an appeal from parochial law to that universal law which may be supposed to exist in Nature. But the fact is that of those who in the fifth century so eagerly appealed to Nature few had any idea of just what Nature sanctions.[51] Still more ominous is the fact that political change and *stasis* and war came before men had time to work out patiently the implications of the new appeal to Nature. The naïf individualist, the super-patriot defending the state's right to exist, democrats justifying the *status quo*, aristocrats justifying a reactionary *coup*, the Athenian Empire crushing revolts and seeking to conscript the neutral Melians, all tended to find support in "Nature." Democrats held that men are "naturally" equal and alike; aristocrats believed that men are "naturally" unequal. In a realistic world of action, the doctrine that "might makes right," and that justice is merely "the interest of the strongest," was bound to assert itself. Heraclitus had declared that "War is the father of all"; but he had also recognized the law of the *cosmos* within which this ceaseless war goes on. Now the idea of a *cosmos* that included man was fading away; but the fact of war remained. The Sophists, creatures of the age, reflected both the new doctrines and the older faith in *Nomos*. To their various contributions to the discussion we may now turn.

## 3

Although many historians of philosophy state in a positive and off-hand manner that Hippias was the first great champion of *physis* against the claims of *nomos*,[52] the somewhat surprising fact is that the evidence for priority is hard to find; indeed, even his championship of *physis* as the basis of morals is not certain. Hippias the polymath, the Jack-of-all-trades,

[50] Plato, *Rep.* 425 a-e; *Laws* 773 c ff., 788 b; 793 b; 838 e; 839 a; Cicero, *Pro Milone*, 10: *haec non scripta sed nata lex . . . ex natura ipsa*; Propertius, IV, 11, 47 f.; *mi natura dedit leges a sanguine ductas, ne possem melior iudicis esse metu* (the proud boast of the individual in whom *physis* is felt to be nobler than *nomos*).

[51] On the difficulty, or impossibility, of deriving Ethics from Nature ("what ought to be" from "what is" or from "what certainly will be," or from "what commonly is" or from "what originally was"), see H. Sidgwick, *The Methods of Ethics*[7] (London, 1907), pp. 80–83.

[52] So, *inter alios*, Dümmler, Zeller, and Benn: but no evidence is given for the priority of Hippias beyond a reference to Plato, *Protag.* 337c. D. L. II, 16, cited above, p. 223, makes no claim of priority for Archelaus. Actual priority is probably beyond the possibility of proof.

the inventor of a system of mnemonics, the mathematician and popularizer of science, we know.[53] But Hippias the moralist, the champion of *physis*, the cosmopolitan, where is he to be found? His conversation with Socrates, which Xenophon "knows of," represents him as forcing Socrates to identify "the just" with *nomos*, an identification which Socrates proceeds to justify in orthodox Greek fashion.[54] That Socrates may have taken this position, no reader of Plato's *Crito* will care to deny categorically, though it is far from exhausting the thought of Socrates on this matter, and is inconsistent with the attitude of Socrates as Plato presents it in the *Gorgias*.[55] It is, in fact, merely the side of his teaching which Xenophon wishes to stress in meeting the accusation of Polycrates that Socrates "despised the established laws." *Nomos*, says Socrates, includes such laws as men agree to write down; even if they are subject to change, as Hippias objects, that is only like men's activities in other fields, such as making war and then making peace. Hippias concurs.[56] *Nomos* also include unwritten laws, continues Socrates; these Hippias recognizes: "You mean those which are in every land recognized as in force on the same points"; and since they cannot be the result of common action of men sundered by space and language, he suggests that they are imposed on man by the gods, "for among all men the first law (πρῶτον νομίζεται) is reverence for the gods."[57] The argument is simply "*quod ubique, quod semper, quod ab omnibus*";[58] there is no mention of *physis*. Hippias admits, as an example of such a universal law, honoring one's parents. He is not so sure about the feeling against incest, which, he points out, is sometimes violated; but he finally concurs when Socrates argues that incest is punished by the birth of an inferior progeny, a Spencerian sort of punishment.[59] Again, be it noted, it is the gods who are thought of as sustaining this moral law, and *physis* is not named; furthermore, the argument is advanced by Socrates, not by Hippias.

We have not progressed very far in our search for evidence of Hippias as champion of *physis*; and if we turn to the material admitted by Diels to the pages of his *Fragmente der Vorsokratiker* we shall find nothing under either "*Leben und Lehre*" or "Fragmente." One phrase catches the eye, the statement by Suidas that Hippias "defined his goal as self-sufficiency."[60]

[53] For a brief general account of Hippias, see D. Tarrant, ed. *Hippias Major* (Cambridge, 1928), Intro., pp. xvii–xxviii.

[54] Xen. *Mem.* IV, 4, 5–25.

[55] See below, pp. 262 f.; cf. also Xen. *Mem.* IV, 3, 16, and E. C. Marchant, Loeb ed., pp. xix f.

[56] Xen. *Mem.* IV, 4, 13–14.

[57] IV, 4, 19; cf. Hirzel, Ἄγραφος Νόμος, and see above, p. 227.

[58] The principle enunciated by St. Vincent of Lérins.

[59] Xen. *Mem.*, IV, 20–25.

[60] D 86 A 1.

This is a very natural inference from what is recorded of the appearance of Hippias, dressed in articles of his own making, and discoursing on every kind of literature, and even composing in all kinds.[61] This self-sufficiency and versatility may be interpreted as the result of a desire to free oneself, as an individual, from any dependence on a developed, differentiated society in which a division of labor and professionalism has grown up; it is a sophisticated return to the activities and virtues of the primitive world of pioneers; and it agrees with what is reported of the archaeological interests of Hippias.[62] Such a deliberate primitivism, a "return to nature," has its amiable side, and agrees with the general instinct of Greeks to find its Golden Age, the Age of Innocence, in the past, as well as with the love of modern men for "the simple life"; it is quite different from the versatility of the amateur which Pericles, according to Thucydides, believed that fifth century Athenians could enjoy, by the interdependence of men, in an imperialistic democracy.[63] The account, as regards Hippias, is found in the *Lesser Hippias*, a work attributed to Plato, and quite possibly correctly; the substance can hardly be an invention, in any case. And it is to the *Protagoras* of Plato that we must turn for the one passage in ancient literature in which Hippias appears as the defender of *physis*.

Protagoras is represented as having already made his defence of the value of social control, or *nomos*, which we must consider later; and Socrates, while analyzing the nature of *sophrosyne*, has brought to light certain fallacies. The discussion is now in danger of being abandoned prematurely, and Hippias, among others, tries to persuade Protagoras and Socrates to continue. "Gentlemen," he begins, "I regard you all as kinsmen and friends and fellow-citizens by *physis* and not by *nomos*. For the kinship of like with like comes by *physis*, but *nomos*, the tyrant of men, constrains us to do many unnatural deeds."[64] And he proceeds to tender his good offices as a mediator between the two momentarily estranged speakers. His speech, like the immediately preceding speech of Prodicus, is a bit of comic interlude; and it hardly advances the argument, for Protagoras is not to be seriously confronted either by Hippias or by Socrates with the claims of *physis* as a moral sanction. It serves as a reminder that there is another point of view, not to be pressed here, but not to be forgotten. The immediate question for us is whether we are entitled to regard the passage as serious evidence that Hippias actually held the view that men are by nature kindred, and therefore to consider him as the real founder of the idea,

[61] Plato, *Hipp. Min.* 368 b = D 86 A 12.

[62] Plato, *Hipp. Ma.* 285 d = D 86 A 11; cf. F. Dümmler, *Kleine Schriften*, I, p. 205; Lovejoy and Boas, *Primitivism*, pp. 113–116.

[63] *Thuc.* II, 41.

[64] Plato, *Protag.* 337c = D 86 C 1 ("Imitation").

developed by Cynics and Stoics, of a world society rooted in *physis*, of a kindly law of nature, and of slavery as unnatural. It has been argued that because the words of Hippias are not really relevant to the argument Plato must have been quoting a real saying of Hippias.[65] This conclusion seems to me to go beyond the evidence. Granted that some passing allusion to *physis* was in order, a spokesman must be found for it. Plato has prepared the way by introducing Hippias, one of the two conspicuous sophists of the age who still discoursed on *physis*, early in the *Protagoras*, and as there discoursing not on any of his many other interests but precisely on *physis*.[66] But a larger problem is involved, which is nothing less than Plato's literary method of dealing with his characters. This is part of what may be called the "Platonic problem," a counterpart of the "Socratic problem." Is Plato the faithful reporter of the actual words and opinions of his characters, or is he the masterful manipulator of the *dramatis personae*, putting in their mouths what the argument requires? I have already indicated my sympathy with those who hold that Plato exercised more and more freedom in this matter.[67] Yet even so Plato as a dramatic artist would select his characters with an eye to their appropriateness for the opinions that they were to express. If the myth given to Protagoras in this dialogue is Plato's, rather than the sophist's, it must at least be one that the real Protagoras could consistently have set forth. So it is with the comic relief of the speech of Prodicus, mentioned above; though its verbal distinctions do not advance the thought, it would miss the mark if it were out of character, for we are dealing with Plato, not with Aristophanes. And so, too, with the little disquisition of Hippias. It is quite possible that the remark that all men are kinsmen by *physis*, not by *nomos*, and all the important inferences that could be drawn from it, never fell from his lips. But what we are entitled to believe is that Plato felt it to be a reasonable remark for the real Hippias to have made, — the man who still took *physis* seriously, who was interested in primitive society, who tried to be self-sufficient, who in conversation with Socrates took issue with the idea that *nomos* is a reliable and a sufficient standard.[68] And perhaps that is all that we have any right to claim for Hippias and the appeal to *physis* as a moral standard. But before we leave him, let us note that no one has imputed to him any conception of *physis* as ruthless, or as sanctioning the rule of the stronger; that is to be a later development.[69] And we may note, too, that if the

[65] See H. E. Stier, "*Nomos Basileus*," p. 245.

[66] Plato, *Protag*. 315c.

[67] See above, p. 223, and below, Appendix 30.

[68] See Appendix 32: Xenophon on Socrates.

[69] Cf. H. Sidgwick, *Journ. of Philology* 5 (1873), p. 74: "The mere adoption or bringing into prominence of the distinction between the 'conventional' and the 'natural' as applied to the laws and usages of society is no evidence of egoistic antisocial dispositions or convictions."

words attributed to Hippias by Plato are at all authentic, he takes liberties with the phrase of Pindar which he quotes. For Pindar, as for most conservative Greeks, *nomos* is a legitimate monarch, a *basileus*; for Hippias, as he is represented, it is an unconstitutional ruler who has seized power, a *tyrannos*. The same passage of Pindar is fated, as we shall see, to suffer another perversion when it is quoted in Plato's *Gorgias*.[70]

Antiphon the sophist, who is probably though not certainly to be distinguished from Antiphon of Rhamnus, the orator, is ignored by Plato. The one conversation which Xenophon represents him as holding with Socrates[71] reveals little of his thought beyond a pity for Socrates' mean way of living and a contempt for his kind of philosophizing, which is futile and impractical. (Significant is the reply of Socrates, that it is a mark of the godlike to need as little as possible.) Probably apocryphal are the later intimations that Antiphon had at one time or another been an interpreter of dreams and prodigies; possibly also the tradition that he for a time practised the profession of "consolation" (τέχνη ἀλυπίας); in this case, he would have been practically the founder of a long line of consolers.[72] This suggestion may have come from a full knowledge of Antiphon's work "On Concord" (Περὶ Ὁμονοίας), of which only some twenty-five fragments have survived in quotations.[73] This work, which may now be dated close to 440 B.C.,[74] and which may therefore be recognized as the earliest surviving example of Attic prose, is full of poetic, gnomic, antithetical turns of style, like the pessimistic elegy of Theognis which in several ways it resembles.[75] Addressing some friend (this, too, like an elegiac poet), Antiphon dwells, in the fragments that have survived, chiefly on the wretchedness of human life, but suggests the direction in which salvation may lie. If this is not precisely "consolation," it is an attempt to warn himself and his friend against such a way of life as would make consolation necessary. The general trend of his thought may be briefly summarized, the fragments being gathered in sections.[76]

(1) Life is open to vituperation, my friend; nothing noble is it, but all

[70] See above, p. 226, and below, p. 260; also p. 251.

[71] Xen. *Mem.* I, 6 = D 87 A 3.

[72] D 87 A 6–9; cf. C. Buresch, *Consolationum Historia*, pp. 72–89; but on Democritus as prior in this field, cf. pp. 7 f.; also, for Homer, see above, pp. 26 f., and n. 83.

[73] D 87 B 44a–71.

[74] The date depends primarily on the presence in Antiphon's work of ideas or phrases which are echoed by Euripides in plays of known date; cf. G. Altwegg, *De Libro* ΠΕΡΙ ΟΜΟΝΟΙΑΣ *Scripto* (Basel, 1908), pp. 60–76; J. H. Finley, Jr., *Origins of Thucydides' Style*, *H.S.C.P.*, 50 (1939), pp. 65–68.

[75] D 87 B 44a (Philostratus); E. Jacoby, *De Antiphontis Sophistae* ΠΕΡΙ ΟΜΟΝΟΙΑΣ *Libro* (Berlin, 1908), pp. 48–69; Altwegg, pp. 77–79; Finley, pp. 74 f.

[76] I follow the ingenious order of arrangement which Altwegg worked out, pp. 20–55; cf. his attempted reconstruction of the text, pp. 95–98; some conjecture is required to fill *lacunae*.

mean, feeble, ephemeral, and full of pain, for beast and "godlike" men alike; a brief turn of sentry-duty, a bivouac. Every time of life has its burden; each day, each night begins a new doom.[77] Marriage is a gamble, at worst a sorrow, at best (and Ah! how sweet that is!) a mingling of joy and sorrow, the giving of a hostage to fortune, with a doubling of one's own stakes; if there are children, all's anxiety; and old age has its special burdens.[78] So far Antiphon shares the disillusionment of Hamlet, who finds civilized man so far less noble than he should be;[79] of Hobbes, who finds the life of the natural man "solitary, poor, nasty, brutish and short," and a "war of every man against every man";[80] of Schopenhauer's pessimistic estimate of men's lot in mere living.[81]

(2) Wretched though life is of necessity, some men make it even worse by not living in the present, but by busying themselves instead with preparations for living, hoarding, suffering for some future life; so time, the most precious of all things, goes to waste, and they miss the present life. But life cannot be lived over again, any more than one can take back a move in a game of draughts. There is a fable of a miser who refused to put his money out at interest, hid it, and had it stolen. When he complained of his lost opportunity, he was bidden to hide a stone and imagine it to be his money; he would thus be just as well off as if he still had his (unused) money.[82] All this is the challenge of the realist to the idealist, of the utilitarian to the mystic, with something of the commonsense of the Parable of the Talents.

(3) When it comes to action, Antiphon reserves his approval neither for the eager visionary nor for the hesitating coward, though hesitation (ὄκνος) has its uses when sober second thought saves one from a rash and evil intent; nor again for the man who thinks to inflict evil without suffering it, for many a victim of deceitful hopes (ἐλπίδες), has been hoist with his own petard; but rather for the man who is endowed with *sophrosyne*.

[77] Cf. *Macbeth,* V, 5: "To-morrow, and to-morrow, and to-morrow," etc.

[78] D 87 B 51, 48, 68, 50, 69, 49 (the longest and most interesting fragment in this section), 71, 66 (cf. Martial, XII, 34, 10: *nulli te facias nimis sodalem*). Altwegg is inclined to include with this group frags. 45–47, on fabulous, barbarian peoples, types of man's wretchedness; so also Diels. But antiquity was more apt to idealize outlandish and primitive races; H. Kramer, *Quid Valeat ὁμόνοια in litteris Graecis* (Göttingen, 1915), pp. 56–58; Lovejoy and Boas, *Primitivism*, Chap. XI, "The Noble Savage in Antiquity."

[79] *Hamlet*, II, 2: "What a piece of work is man! . . . And yet, to me, what is this quintessence of dust?" Cf. T. Spencer, "Hamlet and the Nature of Reality," *Journ. of Eng. Lit. Hist.* 5 (1938), pp. 253–277; and see also below, p. 358.

[80] Hobbes, *Leviathan*, Chap. XIII; see below, p. 252.

[81] Schopenhauer, *Die Welt als Wille und Vorstellung*, Book IV, §§57–58; cf. Altwegg, p. 55, and n. 3.

[82] D 87 B 53a, 77, 52, 53, 54. With this last frag., cf. Aesop. *Fab.* 412 Halm; Horace, *Odes* I, 11; III, 2, 1: *nullus argento color est avaris*: Martial, II, 90, 4: *properat vivere nemo satis*.

This quality is best defined as the power of self-control gained by resisting immediate pleasures; for to indulge one's immediate desires is to prefer the worse to the better. Yet he cannot be called self-controlled who has not known temptation; Antiphon cannot praise "a cloistered and fugitive virtue." [83] Here Antiphon reveals himself as a moralist, if not of great profundity, at least of some perception, and quite in the most characteristic Greek tradition; the medical and Pythagorean and Platonic conception of justice as harmony, and the Aristotelian conception of virtue as a mean, are suggested, as well as the claim of Pericles that the Athenian combines the virtues of caution and decision, which are generally considered incompatible.[84] No mention is made of *physis* or *nomos*; the virtue described is self-regarding rather than social, and is the product of voluntary action and self-interest, not of social pressure; yet it is striking that Antiphon, who in the previous section appeared as a utilitarian, rejects mere hedonism. There is no hint of any anti-social attitude.

(4) By way of contrast with *sophrosyne*, there is its opposite, *anarchy*, which is the worst evil among men; hence the time-honored custom of schooling boys in obedience, so that they may be stable when grown to man's estate. Education (παίδευσις) is indeed the foremost human concern; for as a farmer sows, thus he reaps; nor will a goodly education, implanted in the young, disappoint our hopes, rain or no rain. Friends, too, are a part of education, if they be well chosen; and old friends are closest.[85] Though there is no use here of the word *physis* the agricultural simile applied to education falls in with the stock debate of the period on the relative parts played by nature and by training.[86] It is to be noted that Antiphon thinks of education as the seed to be planted in the young (somewhat as in the Parable of the Sower), not as something burgeoning from the natural man, nor, again, as a turning of his eye toward the truth (as Plato will urge). The emphasis on obedience as a bulwark against anarchy suggests *nomos*.

Among all the fragments of the work "On Concord," there is not a single use of the word which unquestionably stands as the title.[87] Either the portions of the work which most specifically justified the title have been lost, or we must seek "concord" in the brief references to "obedience," to avoidance of "anarchy," to "education," and to "*sophrosyne*." These,

[83] D 87 B 56, 67, 55, 57, 56, 58, 59.

[84] *Thuc.* II, 40.

[85] D 87 B 61, 70, 60, 62, 64, 65.

[86] Jacoby, pp. 41–46; Shorey, Φύσις, Μελέτη, 'Επιστήμη; Jaeger, *Paideia*, pp. 303; 311; contrast Pindar (see above, p. 72); and see below, pp. 250 f. and n. 182.

[87] For the attempts of Sauppe, Croiset, Dümmler, Poehlmann, Nestle, and Wilamowitz, to find here at least the spirit of concord (altruism; or the social use of money) see Altwegg, pp. 56–58; and Jacoby, pp. 21–40; Kramer, 54–59.

indeed, though scanty, do give some idea of the way in which Antiphon may have supposed that some degree of order and happiness is to be retrieved from chaos and ruin; it is, in a word, the way of *nomos* controlling *physis*.

Whether Antiphon was thinking of social "Concord" or of an internal harmony within the personality of the individual has been a matter of dispute. The ordinary use of the word *ὁμόνοια*, both in the latter part of the fifth century and later, was related to society; it became a rallying cry in times of civil strife both in Greece and (as Concordia) in Rome.[88] "Obedience" and the avoidance of "anarchy," and "education" all have social implications. On the other hand, it was the Peloponnesian War and the *stasis* that followed, which caused the social value of concord to be much discussed; in the preceding decade the nature of the individual man and his problems were to the fore, at least in drama. Now if Antiphon's work "On Concord" is as early as 440 B.C., one would expect it to deal more with personal problems, as, indeed, does its brief discussion of *sophrosyne*, which is a kind of internal concord or harmony.[89] That is slight evidence, to be sure, for supposing the whole work to have dealt chiefly with a personal virtue.[90] And there are difficulties. Both Antiphon's remark about the evil of anarchy and the line in the *Antigone* of Sophocles, of which it is a close copy, certainly refer to civic anarchy, defiance of social law and order.[91] We may observe, moreover, that the word *ὁμόνοια*, which appears somewhat odd, if applied to the individual, is hardly to be found before Antiphon.[92] But the conception of personal virtue as an inner harmony of parts that mirrors the *eunomia* of the state, or the state's organization as merely "man writ large," will soon become familiar.[93] In any case, whether the work "On Concord" was devoted chiefly to civic or chiefly to personal harmony, there is nothing in what has been preserved of it that lends color to any suspicion of Antiphon's having taught anti-social doctrines.

Even more interesting and important than Antiphon's "On Concord" is his fragmentary work "On Truth" (Περὶ Ἀληθείας), the very title of

[88] Jacoby, pp. 9–25; Kramer, pp. 13–30.

[89] Altwegg, pp. 58–60; 77–79; Finley, p. 68; *contra*, Kramer, pp. 15; 54–59.

[90] The comments of Iamblichus on *ὁμόνοια* (D 87 B 44a) begin with the personal and go on to the civic virtue; whether he was dealing with Antiphon's work or not, however, there is no way of knowing (Blass, Diels, Finley, p. 68, believe so; *contra*, Altwegg, pp. 58 f.).

[91] Antiphon, fr. 61; Sophocles, *Antig.* 672; Kramer, p. 55; Finley, pp. 66 f.

[92] Kramer, p. 13; its occurrence in Democritus (D 68 B 250: *ὁμονοίης*; 255: *ὁμονόους*; both in the social sense) cannot be dated.

[93] Plato, *Rep.* 368 de: 432 a: *ὀρθότατ' ἂν φαῖμεν ταύτην τὴν ὁμόνοιαν σωφροσύνην εἶναι, χείρονός τε καὶ ἀμείνονος κατὰ φύσιν συμφωνίαν ὁπότερον δεῖ ἄρχειν καὶ ἐν πόλει καὶ ἐν ἑνὶ ἑκάστῳ*; 351e–352a: *εἴτε πόλει τινὶ εἴτε γένει . . . καὶ ἑνὶ . . . στασιάζοντα καὶ οὐχ ὁμονοοῦντα αὐτὸν ἑαυτῷ*; cf. *Laws* 960d.

which reminds one of the earlier Parmenides and of the contemporary Protagoras, and which may be dated toward 430 B.C.[94] The first book deals in eclectic (chiefly Eleatic) fashion with the theory of knowledge, and with mathematics; the second and possibly a third book with physics, anthropology, and ethics. By far the longest and most interesting of the fragments of this treatise are those which were discovered in 1906 in Egypt.[95] Here we have, in elaborately symmetrical and antithetical style,[96] a systematic exposition of the thesis that real justice is based not on *nomos* but on *physis*. I translate or paraphrase most of the text of these fragments, with brief comment, for convenience dividing and numbering the portions.

(1) "Justice consists in not transgressing the ordinances of the *polis* of which one is a citizen."[97] This is the ordinary definition of justice, not Antiphon's; it is what Socrates defends, in conversation with Hippias;[98] or what Protagoras holds.[99]

(2) "A man would practise justice most advantageously if he were to hold high the laws in the presence of witnesses, but, in the absence of witnesses, the precepts of nature; for the precepts of the laws are arbitrary, while those of nature are necessary; those of the laws are the product of agreement, not of natural growth, while those of nature are the product of natural growth, not of agreement. So the transgressor against ordinances, if not detected by those who made the agreement, is exempt from disgrace and punishment, but not if he is caught; while the man who violates any of the innate principles of nature meets with no less evil if he goes undetected by all men, and with no more if all men see him; for he is injured not by men's opinion (διὰ δόξαν) but by fact (δι' ἀλήθειαν)."[100] Here Antiphon challenges Protagoras; he argues that conventional justice, the justice of the "social contract," is wholly superficial; from this point of view what matters is not what one does, but what Mrs. Grundy thinks.[101] An offence against nature, on the other hand, is a serious matter, and brings its own punishment, whether or not one is observed; one who plays

[94] The date turns chiefly on Aly's analysis of the relation of Antiphon's mathematical activity to that of his contemporaries, and again on echoes of Antiphon's ethical dicta in drama (W. Aly, "Form-probleme der frühen Griechischen Prosa," *Philologus*, Suppl. 21 (1929), pp. 115–116; 141–147; cf. Finley, pp. 69–73); another argument of Aly (pp. 117–133), based on the place of Antiphon's discussion of *physis* and *nomos* among other such discussions reaches a similar conclusion (see below, p. 238, and n. 113).

[95] D 87 B 44 (= *Oxyrh. Pap.* XI (1913), No. 1364; XV (1922), No. 1797) with various supplements of *lacunae* by Diels.

[96] H. Diels, *Intern. Monatschrift*, 11 (1916), p. 99, compares Gorgias and Hippocrates; but cf. Finley, pp. 36–49; 59–63.

[97] D 87 B 44 Frag. A, Col. 1, ll. 1–11.

[98] Xen. *Mem.* IV, 4, 12 ff.; see above, p. 229.

[99] See below, pp. 244–248, also pp. 253 f. (Lycophron).

[100] D 87 B 44 Frag. A, Col. 1, l. 12, col. 2, l. 23.

[101] See below, pp. 254 f., on Critias; and p. 311, on the "Ring of Gyges."

with fire burns one's fingers. This corresponds to the second type of law cited by Socrates in the conversation with Hippias, the "unwritten laws," everywhere observed, and referred by Socrates, with the concurrence of Hippias, to the gods, though not, as we noted, to *physis*.[102] Here the antithesis is between opinion and fact (or truth), or, what amounts to the same thing, as the sequel will show, between law and nature. Not without significance is Antiphon's choice of his title, *On Truth* (fact, ἀλήθεια, "what cannot remain hidden"), nor his identification of truth with nature. Finally, Antiphon does not advocate breaking laws; he merely observes the weakness of the legalist's position: if the only reason for obeying a law is that it is the law, it doesn't matter if one breaks it (and is not caught). Such law would have lost the sanctions of *aidos* and *dike* with which Protagoras sought to invest it.[103]

(3) . . . "Most of the things that are legally just are at odds with nature. Laws are laid down for the eyes as to what they may see, and what not, for the ears what they may hear, and what not; . . . for the mind what it may desire, and what not. None of the things from which the laws deter man are dearer or nearer to nature than those toward which they direct them."[104] In other words, the restrictions of conventional law are not rooted in *physis*, but are mere taboos.

(4) "Life and death are both natural, and depend respectively on the profitable and the unprofitable. Now the profitable, so far as it is established by the laws, amounts to fetters on nature; so far as it is produced by nature, it is free."[105] This is a condensed statement of the utilitarian's creed; the good, the profitable, is measured by its survival value, something fixed by nature, by comparison with which conventional estimates of the profitable are irrelevant, are indeed impediments.

(5) "To speak the honest truth, the painful helps nature [i.e. life] no more than what gladdens; so what is painful would profit no more than what is pleasant; for what is truly profitable ought not to hurt but to be of advantage. . . ."[106] This is a clumsily antithetical way of saying that nature sanctions hedonism at least as readily as asceticism, if profit is our standard. There is, of course, an element of truth in the contention, though it does not concern all contingencies.[107]

[102] Xen. *Mem.* IV, 4, 19–25; see above p. 229; Eckstein, *Naturrecht*, p. 36, compares the *poenae naturales* of later thought; Menzel, *Kallikles*, pp. 60 f., remarks that Antiphon does not specify what is included among the decrees of nature, but that in any case Nature is regarded as normative.

[103] See below, pp. 245 f.

[104] D 87 B 44 Frag. A, Col. 2, l. 26 — Col. 3, l. 25.

[105] D 87 B 44 Frag. A, Col. 3, l. 25 — Col. 4, l. 8.

[106] D 87 B 44 Frag. A, Col. 4, ll. 8–22.

[107] Cf. Barker, *Pol. Theory*, p. 84, n. 3, who points out the fallacy of isolating the individual from society.

(6) Antiphon goes on to give examples of scrupulous behavior,—retaliation only after suffering injury, good treatment of harsh parents, waiving of opportunity to meet legal charges by counter-charges,—examples, shall we say, of observance of a Golden Rule,—and argues that they are "at odds with nature, for they involve more suffering when less is possible, less pleasure when more is possible."[108] What is more, this arbitrary kind of law, which might be defended as profitable if it were effective, is, in fact, liable to result in miscarriages of justice, in terms of injuries and failure to secure reparation.[109] In the harping on the fact that "the sufferer suffers, and the doer (i.e., criminal) does"[110] I am tempted to see a reference to the Aeschylean conception of justice in the suffering of the criminal,[111] of which this miscarriage of justice is a travesty.

(7) These remarks are supplemented by another passage (apparently from the same work, though preserved in another papyrus) in which Antiphon argues that the ordinary conception of justice, a negative version of the *lex talionis*,—that is, "not to wrong another when one is not oneself wronged,"—is fallacious, since attempts to enforce it in court, by giving evidence, often defeat their very purpose; one may be technically just and essentially unjust.[112] The argument, though so far merely casuistical, nevertheless represents a genuine attempt to reach real rather than apparent justice. It opposes the current notion that justice consists in helping one's friends and hurting one's foes; for if read in the light of the rest of this work and of the work "On Concord," and if compared with other discussions of the same subject that deny the possibility of real justice ever doing injury, we are entitled to see in Antiphon's argument a conception of justice as the equivalent of concord and friendliness among equals.[113]

(8) In still another passage, Antiphon discusses the social implications of nature. "Those descended from noble ancestors we reverence and honor; but those from no noble house we neither reverence nor honor. In this we treat each other barbarously, since by nature we are all alike fully adapted to be either barbarians or Hellenes. We may observe this from the needs which all men naturally have; and these it is possible for all men alike to gain, and in them all none of us is marked off as bar-

[108] D 87 B 44 Frag. A, Col. 4, l. 31—Col. 5, l. 22.

[109] D 87 B 44 Frag. A, Col. 5, l. 25—Col. 7, l. 15.

[110] Col. 6, ll. 10–13: *ἐπιτρέπει τῷ πάσχοντι παθεῖν καὶ τῶ δρῶντι δρᾶσαι.*

[111] *Choeph.*, 313: *δράσαντι παθεῖν*; see above, pp. 98; 129; 131.

[112] D 87 B 44, pp. 353–355 = *Oxyrh. Pap.* 1797.

[113] For the traditional view, cf. Xen. *Mem.* II, 6, 35; III, 9, 8; Plato, *Rep.* 334b; for the refutation, *Crit.* 49a–50a; *Rep.* 335a–d. Cf. Plato (?) *Clit.* 410a: *δικαιοσύνην ἢ ὁμόνοιαν*; 410ab: *εἶπές μοι δικαιοσύνης εἶναι τοὺς μὲν ἐχθροὺς βλάπτειν, τοὺς δὲ φίλους εὖ ποιεῖν. ὕστερον δὲ ἐφάνη βλάπτειν γε οὐδέποτε ὁ δίκαιος οὐδένα· πάντα γὰρ ἐπ' ὠφελίᾳ πάντας δρᾶν.* See further, E. Bignone, "Antifonte Sofista," *Rivista di Filol. e di Istr. Class.*, N.S. 1 (1923), pp. 309–325; W. Aly, "Form-probleme," pp. 137–140.

barian or as Hellene; for we all breathe the air through mouth and nostrils. . . ."[114] Here speaks the leveller, in the line of Hippias; and the doctrine will be continued by the sophists Lycophron and Alcidamas, by the Cynics and the Stoics, by St. Paul, and by Shakspere's Shylock: "Hath not a Jew eyes . . . ?"[115]

The papyrus fragments of Antiphon's work "On Truth" have such implications that they have been interpreted in very different senses. To some, who have remembered the immoral and cynical conclusions to which the appeal to *physis* could be pushed, as by Callicles, in Plato's *Gorgias*,[116] or by the Athenians in the "Melian Dialogue" of Thucydides,[117] Antiphon has seemed to be arguing in favor of rebelling against the law of the state and justifying selfish pleasure-seeking; he is a Machiavelli, if not a Nietzsche.[118] Now, Xenophon's picture of Antiphon is not very attractive; but it is not Xenophon's way to present in a favorable light those who differ with Socrates. Moreover, that Antiphon is impatient of the restrictions of ordinary law, as merely arbitrary, as bungling, as an impediment to the satisfaction of individuals, as an impertinent meddling with the process of nature, cannot be denied; but to find in his work "On Truth" the deliberate justification of violent individualism is unwarranted. Nothing in the evidence points to his having held that the interests of individuals are necessarily hostile to each other; his *physis* is a kindly one, in which social differences are obliterated and men's common qualities are the important consideration; his utilitarianism, or hedonism, is no more dangerous than what Socrates proposes for the consideration of Protagoras.[119] Still more important, the defense of education and *sophrosyne* and the warning against anarchy, in the essay "On Concord," are in the spirit of traditional Greek ethics. Because these sentiments clearly stand in the way of the interpretation of the papyrus fragments as revolutionary documents, the suggestion has been made that these fragments from "On Concord," which have survived by quotation in Stobaeus, should be assigned not to the sophist Antiphon, but to Antiphon the orator.[120] But there is nothing in the manner of citation of

[114] D 87 B 44, frag. B, pp. 352–353, from *Oxyrh. Pap.* 1364.

[115] For Lycophron and Alcidamas, see below, pp. 253 f.; for the Cynics, p. 277 f.; cf. also *Colossians* 3, 11; *Merchant of Venice*, III, 1.

[116] See below, pp. 259–261.

[117] See below, Appendix 38: "Might makes right."

[118] To this effect, in general, Grenfell and Hunt, *Oxyrh. Pap.* XI, pp. 94 f.; Diels, *Monatschrift*; Vinogradoff, *Outlines of Historical Jurisprudence* (London, 1922), Vol. II, pp. 29 ff.; S. Luria, *Hermes* 61, pp. 343–348; Taylor, *P.M.W.*, pp. 271; 119, n. 1; Field, *Plato*, pp. 89 ff.

[119] See below, p. 248.

[120] So Luria, *Hermes* 61, pp. 344 ff., who also agrees with Wilamowitz that the fragments of the *Politicus* of "Antiphon" (= D 87 B 72–76) should be so assigned; I should suppose that Luria would include also fragments 58 and 59, on *sophrosyne*.

these fragments by Stobaeus to support such a division. The more natural explanation of the inconsistency is to admit that the interpretation of the longer fragments as dangerously revolutionary is at fault. Once it is realized that Antiphon's remarks on law and nature have been erroneously fitted into a preconceived notion of what he must have meant, a notion derived from the better known and explicit statements of Callicles and Thrasymachus in Plato, the difficulty disappears. For his work "On Truth" should be interpreted in the light of his earlier work "On Concord," even if it reflects the increasing interest of its period in social problems.

From this point of view, Antiphon stands revealed not as the immoral foe of *nomos* and social control, but as its critic, a realistic but socially minded utilitarian who appeals to *physis* as to a more stable court of last resort than ephemeral and fallacious human agencies. He is a transitional figure between the conservative defenders of *nomos* (men like Protagoras, whose very title, "Truth," he parodies, but whose standard he holds to be mere opinion), and the unscrupulous advocates of *physis* whom we have yet to consider. He does indeed protest against the authority of the state; and freedom from such authority compels a resort to *physis*. Antiphon seems to believe, perhaps too ingenuously, that the change of allegiance leads to a recognition of the equality of man within the law of *physis*. There is danger here, for it may lead next to the individualism and to the wilful violence of a Callicles, and to the perversion of old watchwords which Thucydides says [121] took place under the stress of war and revolution. But there remains one more possibility, as Plato and Aristotle will show: the natural inequality of man as the basis of organic social justice, controlled but not unnatural.[122]

Prodicus seems to share with his contemporary Hippias the distinction of having been concerned both with physical speculations and with ethical and philological matters.[123] His work "On the Nature of Man" (Περὶ φύσεως ἀνθρώπου) was apparently a medical treatise;[124] an ingenious attempt has been made by A. W. Benn to reconstruct his cosmology on Orphic lines from a reference in Aristophanes and three fragments of Euripides.[125] The subject of his discourse near the beginning of

[121] Thuc. III, 82–84.

[122] The "moderate" interpretation of Antiphon here proposed should be supplemented by the reading of E. Barker, *Greek Pol. Theory*, pp. 66–69; F. Altheim, "Staat und Individuum," *Klio* 20 (1926), pp. 257–267; E. Bignone, "Antifonte Sofista," pp. 145–166; 309–332; A. Menzel, *Kallikles*, pp. 59–64; W. Eckstein, *Naturrecht*, pp. 32–40; W. Aly, "Form-probleme," pp. 144–146; W. Jaeger, *Paideia*, pp. 324–328.

[123] Suidas calls Prodicus φιλόσοφος φυσικὸς καὶ σοφιστής (D 84 A 1).

[124] Cf. D 84 B 4.

[125] A. W. Benn, *The Greek Philosophers*, pp. 91–93.

Plato's *Protagoras* is not mentioned; it is the elaborate wrappings of the valetudinarian and the booming of his voice that are featured.[126] Later comes the not ill-natured satire on his habit of obtruding hair-splitting verbal distinctions at every possible point; and this seems to have been his major interest.[127] Apparently Plato does not think of Prodicus, as of Hippias, as having a doctrine or point of view that could elucidate or advance the argument of the dialogue, and uses him chiefly for comic relief. Indeed, it may be that for Prodicus the content of an ethical discussion was of only incidental interest compared with the verbal distinctions involved, and that he was more rhetor than sophist.[128] None the less, Socrates is represented by Plato as having a certain respect for Prodicus, in spite of his pretensions and his fees; he ironically calls himself the pupil of Prodicus,[129] and sends pupils to him.[130] Doubtless Socrates held that the proper use of words is the beginning of clear thinking; and the verbal distinctions of Prodicus may have helped to prepare the way for the Socratic task of definition and moral analysis.

Even the teacher of rhetoric whose first interest is form and style can hardly help having private opinions on problems of the day; and his sample compositions must be on some subject. Our knowledge of the content of the thought of Prodicus, however, is curiously unsatisfactory as to the manner of its transmission; and the fragments are not altogether consistent. The principal items are four in number.

Two of the passages are found only in two spurious "Platonic" dialogues. In the course of the *Eryxias*, a pioneer work on the nature of economic value, based on almost Ruskinian principles, Prodicus is said to have maintained, though without convincing his bearers, that the value of wealth and, indeed, of other things is relative to the character of its possessor; it is good only so far as he is good and makes good use of it. Though the *Eryxias* is not the best sort of evidence, it may at least be adduced as showing that not very long after Plato's day such a doctrine could be plausibly attributed to Prodicus. It is interesting as an attempt to remove "goods" from the realm of absolute *data* and to regard them as relative to man's activities.[131] It is, therefore, akin to such a humanism as we usually associate with Protagoras.

The pseudo-Platonic *Axiochus*, though eclectic in its matter, is one of the earliest extended pieces of "consolation" literature that has been pre-

[126] Plato, *Protag.* 315cd ff. = D 84 A 2.

[127] D 84 A 13; cf. D 84 A 9, 11, 13–20.

[128] Cf. H. Gomperz, *Soph. und Rhet.*, pp. 125 ff.

[129] Plato, *Protag.* 341 a; cf. *Charm.* 163 d; *Cratyl.* 384 b; *Meno* 96 d.

[130] *Theaet.* 151 b = D 84 A 3a.

[131] Prodicus may also have written a "Praise of Poverty"; cf. Diels II, p. 316, note on line 31.

served.[132] The evils of life are recited as Socrates professes to have heard them (for a fee) from the lips of Prodicus, together with the stock answers and consolations (derived from Platonic and Epicurean and other sources). Even the standard point that death concerns neither the living nor the dead is attributed to Prodicus.[133] It appears to be solely on this evidence that Prodicus has been described as "the first pessimist." [134] There is some reason to question, however, whether Prodicus actually held the pessimistic views attributed to him in the *Axiochus*. Not only do the sentiments, both the pessimism and the consolation, clearly come from later sources, but the pessimism is at first sight hard to reconcile with the buoyant tone of the famous "Choice of Heracles" which we shall presently consider. We may admit that the inhabitants of his birthplace, Ceos, had the reputation of being pessimistic;[135] as Scots have sometimes been regarded as "dour," a Cean would be a convenient spokesman for pessimism,[136] which the frail health of Prodicus [137] would make even more plausible. All that we have a right to say is that Prodicus had a better right than most men to be a pessimist. That need not prevent him, to be sure, from trying to overcome evil with good; examples of cheerful invalids are fortunately common, and the most acute realization of the nature of good is not incompatible with, and may even best proceed from, the most acute perception of the nature of evil. The argument, however, which the *Axiochus* puts in the mouth of Prodicus as the last word on the futility of fearing death [138] not only has a later ring but is not at all the sort of argument that Prodicus is described by Xenophon as having used.

The "Choice of Heracles," [139] for which Prodicus is best known, is an

[132] E. Zeller, *Phil. d. Griech.*[6] (1920), I, 2, p. 1315, n. 5; Diels II, p. 318, n. on l. 3; C. Buresch, *Consolationum Historia*, pp. 8–20.

[133] [Plato], *Ax.* 366b–369b; 366 bc = D 84 B 9. It has been suggested that Euripides had Prodicus in mind when he put in the mouth of Theseus a reference to some one "who maintained that mortals have more evils than blessings," and to whom Theseus eloquently replies (*Suppl.* 196–215); but the idea was surely commonplace by now; cf. Antiphor (above, pp. 232 f.); and H. Diels, *Antike Pessimismus*, pp. 20–21.

[134] E.g. by T. Gomperz, *Gr. Denker*, I[4] (Berlin and Leipzig, 1922), p. 355.

[135] That is the implication of Menander, frag. 613 Kock: καλὸν τὸ Κείων νόμιμόν ἐστι, Φανία· | ὁ μὴ δυνάμενος ζῆν καλῶς οὐ ζῇ κακῶς.

[136] Diels, Vorsokratiker[5] II, p. 318, note on line 23, concludes: "Prodikos wird für den Pessimismus vielleicht nur als Keier herangezogen."

[137] See above, p. 241.

[138] *Ax.* 369b; see above, and n. 133.

[139] "The Choice of Heracles" is variously described as being contained in a book of Prodicus entitled "Horai" (Schol. Aristoph. *Clouds* 361 = D 84 B 1), as being one of a number of eulogies composed by Prodicus and other sophists on Heracles and others (Plat. *Symp.* 177b = D 84 B 1), and as having been delivered as a "show speech" to large audiences. These accounts are not necessarily inconsistent with each other. The last, by Xenophon, is the one that gives the full report, extending to several pages. (Xen. *Mem.* II, 1, 21–34 = D 84 B 2). Joel has argued unconvincingly (*Sokrates*, II, 1, pp. 125–206) that the real author of the apologue is Antisthenes.

apologue, the purport of which Xenophon's Socrates professes to recall by memory for the benefit of Aristippus. He does not pretend that it is reported verbatim; Prodicus spoke "somewhat after this fashion, and adorned his thought with rather finer phrases"; and indeed the style is mainly Xenophontic.

There is no need of repeating in detail the story of Heracles as Xenophon, after Prodicus, recounts it, rather tediously, one must admit. The moral is as obvious as it is irreproachable, and no reader can doubt for a moment that young Heracles in the end will prefer the hard path of Virtue to the allurements of Pleasure. The antithesis is not new; Hesiod [140] and Simonides [141] have already expressed it. What is new, and what will persist in Cynic and Stoic literature, is the figure of Heracles as the type of the heroic champion of virtue. (His other aspects, of course, will persist elsewhere.) The story is sometimes criticized, to be sure, as inadequate in its representation of good and evil; for it implies that a choice may be made once and for all, whereas ordinarily a moral struggle must be constant.[142] But it is of the essence of myth and drama to concentrate eternal values as far as possible in the guise of historic events and opposing personages;[143] moreover, the choice of Heracles may be compared with such concentrated phenomena as religious "conversion." Finally, the apologue of Prodicus is valuable as showing the sort of humanism that was to endure in later Greek thought; good is something not given outright by gods or fate but achieved by the human will, the alternative, evil, being equally present and equally real. Here is the antidote to pessimism; and if Prodicus tended to be a pessimist by environment and personal experience, he deserves the more credit for his defeat of pessimism. There remains the further possibility that the apologue is merely a "show speech," delivered without conviction, and based merely on one of the current notions of the day; this possibility one can neither affirm nor deny.

The fourth item to be reckoned with in any attempt to appraise the ethical content of Prodicus is his theory of the origin of religious belief. Our sources are miscellaneous but apparently reliable, and agree in attributing to Prodicus a rationalistic view.[144] The gods are those natural objects and powers which men recognize as useful and endow with a cult, and those discoverers of the arts which are likewise deified. This view was variously described by ancient writers as allegorizing, as

[140] Hesiod, *W.D.*, 289–292; see above, p. 33; and W. Nestle, *Philol. Woch.* 36 (1916), p. 415.

[141] Simonides, 37 Diehl; see above, p. 67.

[142] Cf. Sir A. Grant, ed. Aristotle's *Ethics*, I, pp. 145 ff.

[143] Cf. the myth of Plato's *Protagoras*; see below, pp. 245 f.

[144] D 84 B 5.

Euhemerism, and as atheism.[145] It is open to question whether Prodicus had any sinister motive in advancing his theory. Unlike Critias, whom we must consider later,[146] but like Epicurus and Lucretius and like Comte and his fellow-Positivists, Prodicus seems rather to have been trying to extend the boundaries of a genuine humanism sufficiently to include a religious attitude toward Nature and toward men who have made us at home in the cosmos. That this attempt should have been confused with such an attack as that of Critias is not surprising, for it is an attack on supernaturalism.[147]

4

The sophists thus far considered all ranged themselves on the side of *physis*, as against *nomos*, in seeking the sanctions of conduct. None of them intended to be, or in fact was, subversive of morality; each appealed from the unstable basis of conduct in man to a more stable basis outside of man, in *physis*. We must now consider the sophist who is generally regarded as at once the arch-defender of *nomos* and the chief exponent of relativity. Protagoras is known to us chiefly from the generous though critical treatment of Plato, who presents him in the dialogue that bears his name as the defender of *nomos*, and in the *Theaetetus* as the relativist. The two accounts are complementary, and when Plato wrote the *Protagoras* he undoubtedly felt the implications of the sophist's other teachings which he was later to criticize in the *Theaetetus*. In view of Plato's patent fairness, and in default of any independent tradition of the writings of Protagoras, we are bound to accept Plato as our chief witness, which other evidence will merely amplify. Even the myth of the *Protagoras*, I think, must reflect an essential position of the sophist, however much the details may owe to the literary art of Plato.[148]

Protagoras is interested first of all in the art of the rhetor and literary critic; but he also professes, as Gorgias does not profess, thereby to teach

[145] Cicero, *De Nat. Deorum* I, 118: ". . . *quam tandem religionem reliquit?*" Sextus Empiricus (D 84 B 5) lumps Prodicus with Euhemerus (who saw in gods merely deified heroes) and with Diagoras the Melian (the "atheist" *par excellence*). Cf. J. Adam (*Rel. Teachers*, p. 277), who regards Prodicus as one of the Sophists who "appear to have rationalized the gods out of existence altogether." Adam distinguishes between the allegorizing rationalism of Democritus and other pre-Socratics, and Prodicus, whose "aim is to explain the origin of the belief in gods, on the assumption that the belief is erroneous."

[146] See below, pp. 254 f.

[147] Possibly Prodicus, for all the orthodoxy of his apologue, was suspected of heterodoxy; the *Eryxias* represents him (399a) as having been expelled from the gymnasia for holding views on virtue that would seem to make prayer superfluous; and Suidas, doubtless confusing Prodicus with Socrates, states that Prodicus drank hemlock and died for having corrupted the young. (D 84 A 1, with Diels' note on l. 24.) These are trifling points, based on later traditions; but they show something of the later reputation of Prodicus.

[148] See below, pp. 245 f.

the art of political *arete*, an all-round excellence or culture which is not mere technical proficiency.[149] This involves the intellectual content, as well as the form, of education. A reputable and trusted educator teaching the sons of men of substance and position in democratic Athens, Protagoras naturally adopts the respectable and conservative position; justice, goodness, virtue are a matter of conformity with *nomos*, the social tradition of one's state. It is as if one lived on an island, and were content to abide by its *mores*, with no concern for other islands. So far as Protagoras is an ethical teacher, that is enough for him. But as one interested also in the theory of knowledge, he stresses the relativity of knowledge to the knower. Thus at one stroke he cuts loose his moorings; his island becomes a floating island, adrift on a Heraclitean river. And Socrates, who is after all the true conservative, seeks once more to drop anchor in a secure haven. What that haven may be, we shall inquire later.

The conviction that all men are capable of being educated in *arete*, though not all to an equal extent, nor most men so effectually by some means as by others, is what Plato represents Protagoras as supporting by a myth describing the genesis of man's intellectual and moral faculties. There is no reason why Protagoras may not have used myths, as Prodicus apparently did, nor why the content of the present myth may not express his convictions, with which Plato would also agree; it is only the conclusions to be drawn from the myth with which he will quarrel.[150]

The content of the Myth, a new and ingenious version of the Prometheus myth, suggests that virtue is teachable on the ground that man has a natural endowment given to him by supernatural powers in time past. (The time element is not significant, being merely part of the method of the story-teller; it is the distinctions that matter.) All men were provided by Epimetheus ("Afterthought," who "was not very wise") with the bodily equipment needed for bare survival (their *physis*), and some men were given by Prometheus ("Forethought") the stolen skills (*technai*) which enabled them to compensate for their partial inferiority to the beasts and to progress further in the arts. But a moral or political sense (*arete*) was lacking till finally Hermes (the god of "treasure-trove"), after consultation with Zeus, gave to all men as a free gift to be enjoyed "by the grace of God," as it were, the faculties of conscience and justice (*aidos* and *dike*) so that they may dwell in an orderly society.[151]

The Myth, then, provides a generous recognition of the external *data* of ordinary human existence, and suggests that all men are also capable

[149] Protagoras is here, as in other respects, engaged in a polemic with Hippias; Plato, *Protag.* 317 c d; 318 d e; cf. 311b–312b.

[150] See Appendix 33: *Protagoras* Myth; source.

[151] See Appendix 34: *Protagoras* Myth; meaning.

of virtue (they are, as it were, "social animals"), though how they may advance in virtue is not yet explained. We seem to be back at the level of early Greek poetry where good things are the "gifts of the gods," and where *aidos* and *dike* are the guardians of morality.[152] Protagoras is not opposed to *physis*; in fact, the myth reckons, as does the second book of Plato's *Republic*, with important data as being potentialities for human growth that are beyond human control. Nor would the historic Socrates have any quarrel with Protagoras on this score. But more than *physis* is needed. "Training requires natural gifts [*physis*] and practise [*askesis*]," Protagoras once said;[153] and in the discourse of Protagoras that follows the Myth proper he sketches the system of social control that he advocates, in order to support the claim that virtue not only is, but is generally supposed to be, capable of being taught to all men. We distinguish, he says, between the things that come through *physis* or by chance or automatically, and those things (including virtue) that come through instruction and by taking pains, and by practise; for the latter we hold men morally responsible, and if necessary punish those who are deficient,—which would be illogical if virtue did not belong in this category (323c–324c). Here again Socrates would have no quarrel. But as Protagoras goes on (325c–326c) to dilate on the educative power of early training and of social institutions, in a word of *nomos* in the largest sense, and then proceeds (326c–e) to eulogize *nomos*, the laws of the *polis*, as the pattern or outline of conduct, "discovered"[154] by old legislators to keep citizens to the straight and narrow path, we can feel Socrates silently preparing to dissent. For Protagoras is content with the *status quo*, and is willing to enforce it and to use his best wits to defend it. The *status quo* is always open to attack from the point of view of *physis*; if society is the savior, society is also the corrupter.[155] Moreover Socrates (and Plato) is bent on developing the forces of social control in the service of an ideal as yet only vaguely realized. Protagoras does not ask in what sense the legislators were "discoverers." But the point is fundamental. Is *nomos* "discovered" in the *physis* of man, or in the larger *physis*? At least it involves something not merely spontaneous,[156] but reflective and voluntary. It is accepted by society for its greater good, Protagoras implies; and recalcitrant individuals must be punished.[157] When Archelaus and Antiphon and Hippias and Prodicus argue that "justice" exists merely

[152] See above, p. 18.

[153] D 80 B 3.

[154] *Protag*. 327 d: ἀγαθῶν καὶ παλαιῶν νομοθετῶν εὑρήματα.

[155] Cf. *Rep*. 489 d–495 a.

[156] Cf. *Protag*. 327 d e: ἀνάγκη.

[157] As to the νομοθέτης, Burnet points out, *Essays and Addresses*, p. 27, that θεῖναι is used of the giving, θέσθαι of the adoption of laws.

by *nomos*, they mean that "justice" has very weak credentials, whereas for Protagoras the emergence of "justice" from *nomos* is the vindication of *nomos*. It remains for Socrates (and Plato and Aristotle) to show that a self-imposed or recognized *nomos* is contained in the fully developed *physis* of man.

What, then, of the admitted fact that sons are sometimes inferior to their fathers? Since virtue has been proved to be teachable, and all society teaches it, such a degeneracy must come, argues Protagoras, from a lack of natural aptitude.[158] Here *physis* enters once more, as a stubborn fact. Yet even the most mediocre person, if disciplined by society, would appear to good advantage if compared with those savages among whom some characters in a play exhibited last year innocently enough expected to be happy, — and were, of course, disappointed (327c). Thus the champion of *nomos* and education and civilized society has his fling at primitivism and mere *physis*. But here Protagoras shows a willingness to be content with small mercies, if not a defeatist attitude; he prefers half a loaf to no bread, semi-education to savagery. Like Isocrates, in another generation, he has his roots in actual society and expedients and makeshifts, unlike the visionary Socrates, and unlike the Plato who is for remaking society. For all Protagoras' picture of progress from savagery in the myth, he seems to think that man has reached his limit, and the present pattern is now fixed for all time; education is bound therefore to be a reflection of society's present ideas and standards. It is enough if one can lift a docile person to the level of his community; why expect more (328ab)? Yet Protagoras adds, in justification of his profession, that there are those (among whom he is himself preeminent), who excel others in the ability to advance men in virtue. Since he has hitherto held that all society educates, this must mean merely that he surpasses others in the skill with which he imbues the young with the *nomos* of their *polis*, a rare feat for a foreigner moving from city to city.

For although Protagoras regards *nomos* as the court of last appeal, he is also at pains to emphasize the relativity of all goodness, as of all knowledge. Not only is the good what is useful for something or somebody, as he agrees with Socrates,[159] but, as he hastens to add at length, what is not useful for man may be useful for beast; what is useful for one part of an organism may be injurious to another part, and so forth (334a–c). Such utilitarianism, and its special application to man as a standard, the Socrates of Xenophon would accept,[160] and it is the ancestor of pragmatism and of one variety of "humanism."[161] But Protagoras

[158] N.b. 327 b c: *εὐφυέστατος . . . ἀφυής*.

[159] *Protag.* 333d = D 80 A 22.

[160] Cf. Xen., *Mem.* III, 8, 2–3; see below, p. 273; IV, 6, 8.

[161] See Appendix 35.

instinctively shrinks from accepting the hedonistic calculus which Socrates mischievously proposes for his acceptance (an ethical criterion which the Socrates of the *Gorgias* and later dialogues definitely rejects);[162] he takes the noble and respectable line, and insists on qualitative distinctions rather than on a mere maximum of pleasure, though the argument as a whole is inconclusive. Clearly Plato felt that hedonism was implicit in the utilitarianism and relativism of Protagoras, who had nevertheless not thought out any conceptions of an end to which all minor interests must conduce.[163]

Plato's *Protagoras* does not impute to the sophist the view that knowledge, as well as goodness, is relative; but that latent implication becomes explicit in Plato's *Theaetetus*, where, in support of a sensationalist psychology, Protagoras is said to have upheld the famous doctrine that "man is the measure of all things, of those that are that [or 'how'?] they are, and of those that are not that [or 'how'?] they are not."[164] Plato gives an ironical hint, however, that the sensationalist psychology which is here associated with the theory was not actually put forward by Protagoras but is Plato's own (justifiable) deduction from the theory.[165] The doctrine of *homo mensura* is a logical enough translation into epistemology of the relativity of *nomos*, and it cannot be questioned that Protagoras held it. On the positive side it amounts to nothing more than the statement that every experience implies an experiencer, whose character determines what he experiences. Socrates in the *Cratylus* suggests that Protagoras means to say: "as things appear to me, so they are for me; as they appear to you, so they are for you."[166] The changeable character of both experiencer and experience is easily derived by Socrates from the flux of Heraclitus. We may note that there is no early evidence except Plato's *Theaetetus* to show whether Protagoras meant by "man" the generic Man or the individual man; and Plato's language implies that the individual is meant. Some modern scholars have sought to show that

[162] See below, pp. 260–263; but cf. *Laws* 732 d–734 e (where the hedonistic calculus is defended by the Athenian Stranger on a high ethical level), in the light of 636de, 653ac, 804b, and esp. 644d–645c (where the "iron cords" of conflicting emotions are counteracted by the "golden cord" of reason and law).

[163] *Protag.* 351 b–357 e. Note the repeated references to a τέλος; 353 e 7; 354 b 6; 354 b 7 f.; 354 d 2; 354 d 8; 355 a 5; cf. *Gorg.* 499 e.

[164] Plato, *Theaet.* 151 e–152 a; Sext. Emp. *adv. Math.* VII, 60 = D 80 B 2. The sentence is quoted by Plato as having stood at the beginning of a work by Protagoras entitled "Truth" (Ἀλήθεια); Sextus Empiricus gives the title as the "Throwers" (Καταβάλλοντες), i.e., "Attacking Arguments." For the interpretation of the sentence and its implications, see W. Nestle, *Euripides* (Stuttgart, 1901), pp. 406–410; A. Neumann, "Die Problematik des 'Homo-Mensura' Satzes," *C.P.* 33 (1938), pp. 368–379; both with references to previous discussions.

[165] *Theaet.* 152 c.

[166] *Cratyl.* 385 e = D 80 A 13.

Mankind is intended.[167] Probably Protagoras himself never troubled to raise any distinction between mankind and man.[168] And it is easy then to ask, with Socrates, "Why Man? Why not a dog-faced baboon?"[169] For what guarantee is there that the experience of any percipient is more valid than that of any other percipient?

Each percipient perceives what he perceives, and nothing else. Hence Protagoras held that about anything two contrary propositions (*logoi*) may be made, both of which are equally "true," though one may be "stronger" than the others; and it is the task of the *rhetor* to show how "to make the weaker the stronger case."[170] By a "stronger" case he means such a proposition as would be made by a normal person, and therefore one approved by *nomos*, as distinguished from the sincere opinion of a diseased or queer person. But the result of taking the doctrine of Protagoras at its face value, as Aristotle and others were not slow to point out, is that "being" and "not being," "good" and "evil," and other antithetical terms must have identical force, and all distinctions are wiped out.[171] And the reputation of seeking "to make the worse the better cause" was attached not only to less scrupulous teachers than Protagoras but even to Socrates himself.

Not for these doctrines, however, but for agnosticism Protagoras is reputed, though on poor authority, to have been persecuted for impiety and exiled, and his work to have been burned.[172] Not an atheist, he simply declared that he could not affirm whether gods exist or not, because of the obscurity of the subject and the shortness of human life.[173] Doubtless all that he meant to say was that he did not propose to deal with theology.[174] For so thorough-going a humanist and relativist as Protagoras, this is a natural enough omission; nor is the statement necessarily inconsistent with religious orthodoxy in matters of cult.[175]

Protagoras, the respectable conformist, would have been startled to learn how revolutionary his work was to appear to others. If mere *nomos* was the sole sanction for conduct and was moreover relative to human needs, there remained little to stand in the way of those who wished to

[167] Plato, *Theaet.* 166 d–167 d (= D 80 A 21 a); cf. *Theaet.* 161 c. Arist. *Met.* 1062 b 13 (= in part D 80 A 19) may easily be based on Plato.

[168] See further H. Gomperz, *Soph. und Rhet.*, pp. 217–231; W. Nestle, "Hippocratea," *Hermes* 73 (1938), p. 16.

[169] *Theaet.* 161 c = in part D 80 B 1.

[170] τὸν ἥττω λόγον κρείττω ποιεῖν: *D. L.*, IX, 51 (= D 80 B 6a); cf. Arist. *Rhet.* 1402 a 23 (= D 80 A 21; B 6 b).

[171] D 80 A 19.

[172] D 80 A 23.

[173] D 80 B 4.

[174] G. Grote, *Hist. of Greece*, Chap. LXVII (Vol. VIII), p. 169.

[175] See Appendix 35: Protagoras and Pragmatism.

go to the limit of unscrupulous individualism and to revolt against civic controls. The notion that any argument could be met by another was a dangerous one, as the Athenian courts were to learn. Tragedy[176] and comedy followed suit. And the *Antilogiai* of Protagoras set the fashion for many other documents in which pairs of opposing points of view were set forth.[177] The Just and Unjust Arguments which constitute the *agon* of the *Clouds* of Aristophanes satirize most effectively the unscrupulousness of this sort of eristic in the days of Socrates; but as biting is the satire of Plato's *Euthydemus*, which exposes the fallacious eristic of the next generation, by presenting two brothers who exhibit their ability to take either side of any subject indifferently. No wonder that, as Sextus Empiricus reports, "Some men numbered Protagoras among the philosophers who destroyed all standards of judgement."[178]

An example of the break-down of ordinary standards may be seen in the curious document which happens to have been preserved with the manuscripts of Sextus Empiricus, and which is known as the *Dissoi Logoi* (formerly as the *Dialexeis*).[179] Though Doric in dialect, it seems to show clearly the influence both of Protagoras and of Socrates, and to date from about 400 B.C. It reads like a school exercise; most of it consists of puerile antinomies. For example, the first chapter contrasts two views of good and evil: (a) that they are absolutely different, and (b) that they are the same, but that to different people, or at different times to the same person, they may appear good or evil. The writer, taking up the views in reversed order, first gives many examples showing that "circumstances alter cases"; then in support of the first view he makes the point that unless "good" and "evil" have different meanings, when you do "good" to a person you at the same time do him an "evil." Similar arguments are applied to "noble" and "base," "just" and "unjust," "true" and "false."[180]

More interesting is the political pamphlet which Blass recognized as embedded, in adapted form, in the *Protrepticus of Iamblichus*, and which goes by the title of the *Anonymus Iamblichi*.[181] On grounds of dialect, style, and content, it seems to belong to the end of the fifth century, or to the early fourth century, though it cannot be ascribed to any known

[176] Cf. Soph. *Ant.* 687 (see above, p. 139); *Eur. Antiope* fr. 189: ἐκ παντὸς ἄν τις πράγματος δισσῶν λογῶν | ἀγῶνα θεῖτ' ἄν, εἰ λέγειν εἴη σοφός.

[177] Cf. H. Gomperz, *Soph. und Rhet.*, pp. 130–138; 179–182.

[178] D 80 B 1.

[179] D 90.

[180] See further H. Gomperz, *Soph. und Rhet.*, pp. 138–192; A. E. Taylor, *Varia Socratica*, pp. 91–128, who argues convincingly that the work reflects ideas of the Socratic period, rather than of Plato's maturity.

[181] D 89.

author.[182] It is the work of a convinced conservative, meeting the claims of *physis* to be all-sufficient by a tolerably well reasoned argument in favor of *nomos* as rooted in human nature.

It may be worth while to give a brief outline of the contents of this composition, which professes to be a sort of manual of true success. One who aspires to success in wisdom or courage or eloquence or virtue must be not only well endowed by *physis* (a matter of chance) but desirous of nobility and industrious both early and late. Begin young, and plug away steadily, not intermittently; for well-timed progress averts the jealousy of men, since the gradual conviction of one's deserts emerges, as it does not if success comes suddenly. One's difficulties in matters of benefactions given and received will be best met if one takes the side of *nomos* and justice, the founder and unifier of society.[183] Exhortations to self-control and a generosity that is unsparing even of one's life are followed by warnings against acquisitiveness (i.e., against the ideal of Callicles in Plato's *Gorgias* and of Thrasymachus in the *Republic*), and against supposing the power that it gives to be real virtue, or submission to *nomos* to be cowardice. For if men were naturally incapable of living alone, and came together under compulsion, and so realized all their welfare, and it were impossible for them to dwell in lawlessness (for that would be a worse affliction than the solitary life), then it is through this necessity that *nomos* and justice lord it over men (another glance at Pindar's famous phrase); it is by *physis* that these hardships bind men. In the unlikely event that a superman should appear one would do wrong to suppose that he would find his acquisitive powers sufficient to excuse him from bowing to *nomos*; he could save himself only by siding with *nomos* and justice. For otherwise all men would be ranged against him as his foes, and through their law-abiding character, and through sheer numbers, by skill or by force would get the better of him. So even strength itself is preserved through *nomos* and justice. The advantages of law-abidingness, even if slight, are widely diffused, and so suffice; it saves men from worry, penury, fear, war, and tyranny, all of which come from lawlessness. *Nomos* and justice are the bulwarks against tyranny; and it would take a man of iron to seize power without their being set aside.

Though this is not a profound piece of reasoning, it is valuable because it shows how far the stock ideas and arguments of the age penetrated

[182] See Diels, II, p. 400, note, and references there given. P. Shorey, Φύσις, Μελέτη, Ἐπιστήμη, p. 192, thinks this document reminiscent of Plato and Isocrates, though he finds the commonplace that both nature and art are necessary throughout sixth, fifth, and fourth century literature; see above, pp. 72; 234.

[183] Cf. Eur. *Suppl.*, 312 f.

into rather ordinary minds. Clearly the appeal to *physis* has already taken the inevitable turn that it has never since been able to recall; it is now used to justify the strong man and aggression and acquisitiveness. To it our writer responds that on such terms life must be, in the phrase of Hobbes, "nasty, brutish, and short" even for the aggressor, to say nothing of the rest of his fellow-men. And the source of *nomos* is a sort of compulsion that comes from the nature of man himself,—from his *physis*.[184] This is a major discovery, whoever may first have made it. Finally, our writer, unlike Plato and Aristotle, who both consider the possibility of an enlightened autocracy, regards the autocrat as the portentous product not of superior personality but of anarchy.[185] Another document of similar import is to be found in a pseudo-Demosthenic speech "Against Aristogeiton,"[186] in which the doctrine of the social contract is set forth; but here it is the *physis* of the individual man which must accommodate itself to the ordinances of a more universal *nomos*, god-given and instituted by the wise to correct men's lapses.

## 5

In dealing with Gorgias we are returning to a somewhat earlier period than that in which the works last mentioned were written, although the extraordinarily long life of Gorgias may have overlapped most of them. The relativism of Protagoras can be plausibly connected with the flux of Heraclitus; the renunciation by Gorgias of metaphysics is the result of the *reductio ad absurdum* of Eleatic dialectic. The *physis* of Parmenides and Zeno turns out to be nothing real; from their arid, unknowable, incommunicable "Being" he turns, as does Socrates from *physis* in general, to more practical interests.[187] Though like his master Empedocles he is still interested in *physis* at least to the extent of speculating on the principles of optics,[188] his chief interest is rhetoric, the art of persuasion.[189] In this restriction of interests to the field of practical affairs, in which results may be achieved, his own pupil Isocrates will follow him, in opposition to the greater range of interests that the Platonic Academy will maintain.

Unlike Protagoras, who professes in the course of his rhetorical instruction to impart *arete* to his pupils, Gorgias laughs at those sophists

[184] Diels, *Vorsokratiker*[5], II, p. 402, ll. 24–30: *εἰ γὰρ ἔφυσαν μὲν οἱ ἄνθρωποι, κτλ. . . . διὰ ταύτας τοίνυν τὰς ἀνάγκας τόν τε νόμον καὶ τὸ δίκαιον ἐμβασιλεύειν τοῖς ἀνθρώποις καὶ οὐδαμῇ μεταστῆναι ἂν αὐτά· φύσει γὰρ ἰσχυρὰ ἐνδεδέσθαι ταῦτα.*

[185] Cf. A. Menzel, *Kallikles*, pp. 25–30.

[186] [Demosthenes] XXV, 15–35; 85–91.

[187] Sextus Empiricus reports the reasoning of Gorgias (D 82 B 3); see also Grote, *Hist. of Greece*, Vol. VIII, p. 172; A. W. Benn, *Greek Philosophers*, pp. 80 f.

[188] D 82 B 4; 5.

[189] Plato, *Gorgias*, 452 d e. The phrase "*πειθοῦς δημιουργός ἐστιν ἡ ῥητορική*" here comes from the lips of Socrates, but is doubtless a current phrase; see W. H. Thompson *ad loc.*

who still make such a claim, thinking that "cleverness" is all that one should pretend to teach.[190] Thus he inculcates the principles of style and the famous "figures," and the art of argumentation, preferring the long set speech to the more rapid dialectical method of Socrates. He may have written a treatise on rhetoric (a "*Techne*"); at any rate he provides examples of his art in the form of elaborate show speeches, several of which purporting to be by him have survived. In them, along with much of calculated artifice and superficiality and unreality, one is aware at times also of a certain grandeur of sentiment that does not always seem tawdry; and one feels that Gorgias is interested in the psychological analysis of motives, and in the plausible or sufficient appeal to the feelings. This makes him the ally of the dramatist as well as of the orator. Of special interest for our subject is a passage in the "Encomium of Helen" (if this work be from the hand of Gorgias), in which the speaker analyzes the possible motives of Helen for leaving Greece; in any case, he argues, she was not to blame, whether she was the victim of chance and divine compulsion (Τύχης βουλήμασι καὶ θεῶν βουλεύμασι καὶ Ἀνάγκης ψηφίσμασι) or of force (βία), or of persuasion by words (λόγος) or of love (ἔρως).[191] Neither here nor in the certainly authentic fragments of Gorgias have we anything but stock ideas reviewed in turn and ingeniously manipulated, without any real concern for truth. One need not suspect Gorgias of any moral obliquity; in fact he passed for a virtuous and a pious man.[192] But it is precisely those who are most successful in sharpening weapons to the keenest edges who often are most indifferent to the various or even conflicting uses to which they may be put. Plato's picture of Gorgias very clearly indicates that he was indifferent; he even presents the sophist as priding himself on the power of men armed with rhetoric to persuade men about matters concerning which the speakers are personally ignorant,—as he and his brother had often persuaded recalcitrant patients to take medicines when the physicians could do nothing.[193] This amoralist position, concerned with means but not ends, leads easily to perversions; and it was the fate of Gorgias to have his pupils and followers use his technique for quite different ends, often for ends which he might personally have renounced.

The influence of Gorgias, in a sense a "father of the sophists," was enormous, not only among pupils but in widening circles.[194] Two distinct trends are to be noted among his followers. Lycophron, a pupil,

[190] D 82 A 21.

[191] D 82 B 11, esp. chapters 6–20; see also below, p. 254; and Euripides, *Troad.* 914–1059 (above, p. 193, and n. 84).

[192] D 82 A 8.

[193] Plato, *Gorg.* 456 b = D 82 A 22.

[194] D 82 A 1; 2; 35.

who extended his master's metaphysical scepticism to the limit and denied all possibility of any predication,[195] also leveled all social distinctions, regarding them as mere names;[196] while he found in law (*nomos*) a compact, a surety of justice among men, though it cannot make citizens just and good.[197] Meanwhile the successor of Gorgias, Alcidamas, though taking the side of *nomos*,[198] also attacked slavery more in the spirit of Hippias and Antiphon: "God left all men free: Nature (*physis*) made no man a slave."[199]

It would have been well for the reputation of Gorgias if he had been regarded as the father of these emancipating doctrines alone. But the genius of Plato has connected Gorgias for all time rather with the opposing trend by devoting to it the dialogue named for the great sophist. Here he shows how the profession of Gorgias, however innocent his intentions may have been, inevitably lent itself to the worst excesses of Athenian politics and to the most immoral of philosophical positions. Possibly Gorgias himself begins the debacle in the *Helen*, if that work be his. For one of the defenses of Helen there put forward is that if she did what she did "through the will of Chance and devices of the gods," she is not blameworthy; "for it is a law of nature (πέφυκε) that the stronger is not hindered by the weaker, but that the weaker is lorded and led by the stronger; that the stronger leads and the weaker follows."[200] This is, at any rate, as we shall see, the doctrine that Plato puts in the mouth of Callicles, in the *Gorgias*;[201] it will appear still more explicitly in the position of Thrasymachus, a fellow *rhetor*, in the first book of the *Republic*;[202] the political realization of the doctrine confronts us constantly in Thucydides;[203] and finally it lies behind the theory of religion of Critias, who while in exile in Thessaly came under the influence of Gorgias, and whom we may digress for a moment to consider.

Critias, kinsman of Plato, and friend of Socrates, was among the most dangerous of the Thirty, a fact which, as Xenophon argues,[204] must not be held against Socrates, whose conversation Critias utilized only to sharpen his wits in order to further his own ambitions. As a later writer[205] puts it, he was "a layman among philosophers, a philosopher

[195] D 83, 2.
[196] D 83, 4.
[197] D 83, 3.
[198] Arist. *Rhet.* 1406 a 22 f.; b 11 f.
[199] Schol. to Arist. *Rhet.* 1373 b 18; *Or. Att.* (Didot), Vol. II, p. 316 a.
[200] D 82 B 11, §6; see above, p. 253.
[201] See below, pp. 260 f.
[202] See below, pp. 265–267.
[203] See below, pp. 268–271.
[204] Xen. *Mem.* I, 2, 12–31.
[205] Proclus, commenting on Plato, *Tim.* 21a, and wrongly considering the Critias of that dialogue to be the younger Critias; J. Burnet, *T.-P.*, pp. 338, 351; A. E. Taylor, *Comm.*, pp. 23–25.

among laymen"; we may add perhaps that he was an example of *corruptio optimi pessima*.[206] Of all his many and varied writings, in prose and in verse, we are here concerned with only one, and that a dramatic fragment ascribed on almost as good authority to Euripides as to Critias.[207] It is a fragment of the *Sisyphus*, in which the speaker gives his theory of the origins of law and religion. There was a time when men lived like beasts, without order; there were no rewards for the good, no punishments for the wicked. So men imposed laws (*nomoi*) as chasteners, that justice might be lord (τύραννος) and might enslave *hybris*, and sinners might be punished. This checked open deeds of violence, but not secret ones. So a clever man invented the fear of the gods to quell wicked and secret offenders, saying that there is a *daimon*, immortal, all-seeing, all-hearing, all-knowing, whom none can evade.[208] This is a pleasant deceit, made plausible by the gods being supposed to dwell precisely in the region whence men had most to fear and to hope for, — the sky, region of thunder and lightning and stars, source also of light and rain; hence men's fears and the quenching of lawlessness by law; hence men's belief in gods. Thus Critias, if it is he, does not merely seek to rationalize law and religion, like Antiphon,[209] Prodicus, and the Epicureans,[210] but to degrade it as a pious fraud. In him Drachmann finds "our first direct and unmistakable evidence of ancient atheism." [211]

Plato's *Gorgias* may be regarded as a drama in three acts, in which Gorgias, Polus, and Callicles successively are confronted by Socrates. It cannot be supposed that Plato's chief purpose was to deal with the sophist for whom the dialogue is named; for the exhibition of Gorgias has ended just before the dialogue begins (447ab); and the conversation between Socrates and Gorgias ignores the famous sceptical views of the sophist, and is restricted to the question, "what is the *rhetor*, and what is his profession?" The result of this act is as inconclusive as is the whole of the *Protagoras* or as is the first book of the *Republic*, in which Thrasymachus is apparently confuted. And the sequel passes from the definition of rhetoric to the moral principles that underlie political activity; here Gorgias is all but forgotten.

Gorgias claims to teach the art of rhetoric, and when pressed by Socrates to indicate the specific content of his art, as well as its form, boasts

[206] Cf. *Rep.* 490e–495a, possibly with Alcibiades in mind; see below, p. 306.

[207] D 88 B 25.

[208] Cf. the "Ring of Gyges," Plato, *Rep.* 359b–360d; see below, p. 311.

[209] See above, pp. 235–240.

[210] See above, pp. 243 f.; and below, pp. 334 f. In dealing with Lucretius we must distinguish between his reverence for nature and his contempt for what passed for "religion"; for the latter, compare the present fragment of Critias with Lucretius V, 1161–1240.

[211] A. B. Drachmann, *Atheism*, p. 50.

that it has to do "with words about the greatest and best of known things" (451d), or even more specifically, "with that which is the greatest good and which bestows on men freedom themselves and rule over others in their cities" (452d) by giving them the power of "persuasion" in courts and political bodies (452e–453a) "about the just and the unjust" (454b). It transpires, however, that this "persuasion" may exist without the persuader having any real or expert knowledge of the subject in hand.[212] Gorgias is not so much disturbed as he should be by this fact, and complacently claims that the *rhetor* can speak better about anything than can anybody else,[213] though he blandly assumes that the *rhetor* will not abuse this power; and he holds that the *rhetor* is not responsible if his pupils abuse it (456c–457c).

The lack of a real content in the art of the *rhetor* is becoming apparent, and its dangerous consequences are now pressed by Socrates. If the rhetor is more persuasive (in a mob) than the physician, it is a case of the ignorant seeming to the ignorant to be wiser than the wise (459a–c); yes, a very convenient short-cut, agrees Gorgias, not to have to learn the several arts, but only rhetoric (459e). What, then, of moral considerations, just and unjust, noble and base, good and evil? Socrates proposes four possible answers: (1) There is no need for the *rhetor* himself to have knowledge of them, if he can create the semblance of knowing them; (2) or the pupil must have previously studied these matters *before* he undertakes the study of rhetoric; (3) or, if the pupil has not this preliminary training, it is no affair of the *rhetor*, who will make him seem to the crowd to know what is good; (4) or the *rhetor* cannot teach his art except to those who have already some knowledge of ethics (459c–e). Gorgias, now realizing what is in the air, quickly decides that if his pupils have not previously studied these matters they must learn them, as well as rhetoric, from him; so they will be just, after all (460a). This addendum comes too late; for Socrates now reminds Gorgias of his previous admission[214] that the pupils of the *rhetores* do sometimes abuse their art and so act unjustly. Thus is Gorgias confuted, and the first act of the drama is concluded. Yet it is possible to argue that the self-contradiction of Gorgias is more apparent than real; for the thesis that the man who has "learned justice" will always be just[215] rests on the Socratic identification of virtue with knowledge (developed in other Platonic dialogues, but not here), which is in itself hardly an adequate

[212] 454c–454e. Elsewhere Plato himself admits the practical value of possessing true opinion, the gift of *θεία μοῖρα*, which can give no account of itself. See below, pp. 298–300.

[213] 456c; cf. 458e.

[214] 456c–457c.

[215] 460 b: *ὁ τὰ δίκαια μεμαθηκὼς δίκαιος.*

account of the moral problem.[216] The real answer to Gorgias would have been simply to show that his rhetorical training had no moral content, and therefore was at least potentially immoral. To which Gorgias might honestly have replied that it is not the business of any art, *qua* art, to teach ethics also. And Socrates would then have to take the higher ground of the public interest; and that is what he does anyway. But this involves not so much an investigation of rhetoric itself as an examination of its position in society, and a deeper probing of the sanctions of human conduct. The real, though indirect, answer to Gorgias, therefore, is contained not so much in this first act of the drama as in the sequel, and particularly in the third act, just as the real answer to Thrasymachus is contained not so much in the first book of the *Republic* as in the remaining nine books. Plato recognized this fact when he added to the "*Thrasymachus*" its far more significant sequel.[217] But Plato is fair enough in the *Gorgias* not to make the *rhetor* responsible for more than what an impartial historical appraisal would attribute to him. Vain, shallow, incompetent in dialectic, but not immoral, he paints him; not immoral, but incapable of seeing the potentialities of his art, which was indeed a high explosive, and in the wrong hands a vicious thing. What the wrong hands would do with it we learn from Polus and Callicles.

The young *rhetor* Polus now intervenes, "coltish" as his name (463e). Can Socrates be serious? Yes; and when Polus, himself author of a work on the Art of Rhetoric, asks Socrates to define what sort of art he believes rhetoric to be, he is shocked to hear Socrates declare that it is no art at all, but rather a form of flattery, a sham art or mere knack, like cookery, a phantom of a part of politics; it aims only at pleasure, not at nobility, like other sham arts that minister to the body rather than to the soul (461b–466a). Polus appeals to "facts": are not *rhetores* highly regarded, powerful, able like tyrants to do as they please, even to encompass the death of whomsoever they wish (466a–c)? They have the power, Socrates admits; but that this power is good he denies, unless the end be good. For doing "what one pleases," like any immediate act, is good only as a means to a good end (466e–468e). In fact, to do an injustice is worse than to suffer it, and the tyrant is no more to be envied than a maniac who runs amuck in the Agora (469a–e). Polus cites the case of Archelaus, who criminally and unjustly made himself king of Macedonia, and yet is happy. So the many may believe, replies Socrates; but he is not impressed by popular votes. He himself considers only the just man happy, and the unjust man less unhappy if punished than if unpunished (470c–474b). Polus has enough lingering regard for conventionality to admit that it is more

[216] See Grote, *Plato*, II, 94; and below, pp. 274 f.; 307; 328.
[217] See below, pp. 265 f.

shameful (a greater disgrace) to do than to suffer injustice, but not that it is baser (474cd). He has a momentary bit of satisfaction when Socrates proceeds to define moral concepts in terms of benefits and pleasure; but his satisfaction disappears when Socrates shows that since injustice is not painful his reason for regarding it as shameful must be that it is not beneficial, and therefore evil (474d–475e). Finally, he is compelled to agree that it is better for the guilty to suffer punishment than not, both on the ground that active and passive are correlative, so that if punishment is just, being punished is just, and also on the ground that for injustice (a diseased condition of the soul) punishment is medicinal (476a–479e). It follows that the art of rhetoric is useful not in concealing but only in revealing such a cancer of the soul (one's own, or one's friends') for punishment, or, Socrates maliciously adds, in preventing one's enemy from being cured by being punished (480e–481b).

This paradoxical result certainly does violence to ordinary common sense, as even Socrates (and Plato) must have realized, to say nothing of his critics, — Isocrates, for example.[218] Grote has argued that Plato has no right to condemn Polus, or even Archelaus, on the ground of subjective sentiment, the self-respect which the tyrant is presumed to lose. There is no reason to suppose, he urges, that Archelaus did lose it, or feel pain; what is more, like all "successful" men, he is admired by ordinary people. To make Polus give in on the grounds assigned is to force a concession on the part of *physis* (the natural admiration of crowds for success) to King *Nomos* (the socially useful outward respect for virtue). And it does not follow that Archelaus, who feels no taint of the soul, will profit by being punished; moreover if crime were a real disease of the soul, no punishment would be required to deter the prospective criminal. Punishment *does* profit society, however; and Plato should have emphasized the social, objective aspect of the matter. Hence the frank admission of Callicles in the sequel, that by *nomos* it is indeed more disgraceful to do than to suffer injustice, and his appeal to *physis*. So Grote seeks to save Polus from being crushed by the private code of Socrates (or Plato). It is true, to be sure, that Polus is not condemned by common sense, but rather by an appeal to another standard or level of experience which Grote challenges; the discrepancy appears in the widening gulf between Socrates and Callicles.

The bitterness of Plato's tone throughout the exchange of arguments between Socrates and Callicles may reasonably be attributed to the circumstances under which the dialogue was written. Politically ambitious in his youth, stimulated by Socrates to hope for a realization of the life of the reason in Athens, Plato was completely disillusioned first by the

[218] Cf. Grote, *Plato*, II, 104–112.

excesses of the Thirty, then by the execution of his master, the "just man," at the hands of the restored Athenian democracy (despite its general moderation), a few years after the Peloponnesian War. How he turned once and for all from active politics to the life of the reason, he told as an old man in the (probably genuine) seventh Epistle.[219] The *Apology*, the *Crito*, and the *Euthyphro* were his defense of Socrates, written shortly after the trial.[220] When the sophist Polycrates produced a few years later a pamphlet, of which we have traces in Libanius and elsewhere, defaming Socrates, the anger of Plato was kindled afresh, and he replied by writing the *Gorgias*, which is at the same time a renewed defense of Socrates, Plato's own *Apologia pro Vita Sua*, and a *protrepticus* to a new social philosophy.[221] It is a bitter denunciation of all the forces of evil that had been unleashed during the past two generations of Athenian history: the dreams of material empire fostered by even the greatest statesmen, the spoiling of the aristocracy by the democracy, the unscrupulous efforts of the aristocracy to defend itself from such spoliation by the weapons provided by the *rhetores* and sophists, and behind all these phenomena that utterly selfish will to power of democrats and aristocrats alike which Thucydides also reveals.[222] By exposing this trend as the culmination of that philosophy of *physis* which several of the sophists were upholding, Socrates is represented as making a frontal attack on the real enemy of the good life, that life which Socrates himself lived and died to uphold.

Of Callicles, at whose house the whole conversation takes place, we know nothing except what Plato tells us. It has been suggested by various scholars that he is an imaginary person (an unusual phenomenon in Plato's earlier dialogues), or that he is a disguise for a real person. In any case, he is not himself a sophist; in fact, though he feels for philosophy a condescending tolerance, if it is not taken too seriously or pursued beyond one's youth (484c–486c), he has only contempt for the sophists as a class (519e). He is rather the young politician on the make, the *enfant terrible*, the "democratic man" of the *Republic* (560d), who is not ashamed to avow in all its nakedness the doctrine which Plato does not impute to Gorgias, and which even Polus shrank from pushing to the limit. He is

[219] Plato, *Epistles* 324c–326b; with 326b, cf. *Rep.* 473c, and see below, p. 300.

[220] The *Apology* is probably nearer to historical record than are the dialogues; but for evidences of liberties taken by Plato, see R. Hackforth, *The Composition of Plato's Apology* (Cambridge, 1933).

[221] Cf. J. Humbert, *Polycrates, l'Accusation de Socrate, et le Gorgias* (Paris, 1930), M. Pohlenz, *Aus Platos Werdezeit* (Berlin, 1913), pp. 128–167; but his argument that the *Gorgias* may possibly have preceded the attack of Polycrates is met both by Humbert and by J. Geffcken, *Hermes* 65 (1930), pp. 14–37.

[222] See below, p. 271, and Appendix 38.

no believer in the ideal of political democracy, and respects rather the "gentleman"[223] or the "wise and valiant" man,[224] who as a matter of fact thrives in the democracy which he approximates.[225] He is annoyed with Socrates for forcing Gorgias and Polus to make fatal concessions to the ordinary opinions of mankind (482de) and for using terms in their conventional rather than in their natural sense (482e–483a). And he proceeds in a speech of real eloquence and power to develop the thesis that it is not *physis* but only a slave-morality that finds greater disgrace in doing than in suffering injustice. *Nomos* is the recourse of the many weak, in fear of the stronger; they stamp overreaching acquisitiveness (πλεονεκτεῖν) as shameful, whereas *physis* herself shows that it is just for the better man to have more (πλέον ἔχειν) than the worse, and for the stronger to have more than the weaker; this is in fact in accord with "the law of nature," exemplified by the beasts, by many human clans, and by Xerxes' invasion of Greece.[226] But we tame children into the observance of "equality," whereas a really strong man[227] would throw off these unnatural trammels, as in Pindar's poem, that proclaims *Nomos* as King, Heracles helped himself to Geryon's cattle in high-handed fashion.[228]

Socrates, after ironically congratulating Callicles on his frankness and friendliness, points out that on his own admission the many are more powerful by *physis* than the one; so their *nomoi* prevail, and thus are better by definition; and their opinion that to do injustice is worse than to suffer must therefore be rooted in *physis* as well as in *nomos* (486d–489b). Since Callicles is not at all satisfied with this enthronement of the rabble, Socrates seeks to elicit the more exact meaning of the "stronger" who is to rule; it turns out that Callicles means that the "wiser" should rule and get more (489b–490a). This seems to be the first case in which *physis* is invoked on behalf of the individual's desires. Thus transpires the equivocal character of the appeal to "Nature," which justifies as easily the one strong man as the many weak; and since the appeal to *physis* by

[223] *Gorg.* 484d: καλὸς κἀγαθός.

[224] *Gorg.* 491b: μὴ μόνον φρόνιμοι, ἀλλὰ καὶ ἀνδρεῖοι.

[225] *Gorg.* 513a–c; cf. W. H. Thompson, ed. *Gorgias*, pp. xxiii f.; A. Menzel, *Kallikles*, pp. 20–24.

[226] *Gorg.* 483a–c: τὸν κρείττω τοῦ ἥττονος ἄρχειν καὶ πλέον ἔχειν . . . κατὰ νόμον γε τὸν τῆς φύσεως. Cf. A. E. Taylor, *P.M.W.*, p. 117, n. 1: "The first occurrence, so far as I know, in extant literature, of the ominous phrase 'law of Nature.' Callicles of course intends the words to be paradoxical — 'a convention if you like, but Reality's convention, not a human device.'" Contrast *Tim.* 83e: παρὰ τοὺς τῆς φύσεως νόμους, with Taylor's note. For the "natural man," cf. Eur. *Cyclops*, 316–346, and Shakspere's Caliban.

[227] Contrast *Anonymous Iamblichi* (D 89 1 §6, 2–5), and above, pp. 250–252, noting the reference there also (§6, 1) to Pindar, frag. 152 Bowra, to which Callicles will presently refer, *Gorg.* 483e–484c.

[228] See Appendix 36: *Nomos Basileus*.

democrats and by oligarchs has different results, it is unfair to call the position of Callicles, without qualification, "sophistic."

Of what is the "wiser" to have more? Not more food and drink and clothes, to be sure. No; the "stronger" men of Callicles are those who are "wiser" and more "manly" in statecraft, and so have a right to rule cities and to have more than others (490b–491d). The repeated reference to "rule" suggests a new turn to the thought; do these superior persons rule themselves, asks Socrates, as well as others? The very mention of self-rule, self-control, causes Callicles to launch on a eulogy of self-indulgence on the grand scale as the road to happiness; the many, who cannot realize it, invent temperance and justice as a poor substitute; real virtue (*arete*) and happiness consist in giving free rein to one's desires without let or hindrance; all else is unnatural nonsense (491d–492c). So those who need nothing cannot rightly be called happy?[229] No; nor can stones or the dead. Socrates muses for a moment, almost forgetting Callicles, who, of course, would have no use for such notions, on the mystical idea that this life is really death and death is life, since the soul is here entombed in the body.[230] Or, to develop another mystical view, the myth of the Danaids, who were condemned to draw water in leaky jars, typifies all insatiate desires; whereas the wise man fills his jar and is done (493a–d). No, objects Callicles; pleasure depends on constant flux, the perpetual refilling of vessels that are perpetually emptying.[231] Yet when Socrates presses him hard, even Callicles at last admits that there are differences of quality, as well as of degree, in pleasures; some are better than others; and pleasure is a means to *the* good, but is not itself *the* good.[232]

Since Socrates has now wrung from Callicles the admission that the end of living is the good (499e8), the good life must now be viewed as an art which requires the services of the expert (*technikos*). The argument that follows is long and to some extent repetitious, for Callicles again and again forgets the distinction already made (464b) between arts

[229] 492e; this self-sufficiency was the formula for happiness proposed by Socrates to Antiphon in Xen. *Mem.* I, 6, 10; see above, p. 232.

[230] 492e–493a (σῶμα . . . σῆμα); cf. *Cratyl.* 400bc; *Phaedo* 62 b; and see above, p. 60.

[231] 493d–494b; a doctrine which Plato admits elsewhere for physical pleasure, but not for "pure" pleasures; cf. *Phileb.* 31b–55b; P. Shorey, *Unity*, pp. 20–25; A. E. Taylor, *P.M.W.*, pp. 119–131.

[232] *Gorg.* 494b–500a. The reasoning is less satisfactory here than in the *Philebus*, which has therefore been supposed to have been written in reply to criticisms of this part of the *Gorgias* (cf. W. H. Thompson, ed. *Gorg.* p. 196). Grote, *Plato*, II, 119–131, finds the discussion of the *Gorgias* not only inconsistent with the hedonism proposed by Socrates in the *Protagoras* (see above, p. 248), but less satisfactory in that it denies immediate pleasure to be in itself *a* good; also in that it does not reckon with social ends, but condemns pleasure because it is incommensurable with a superhuman Good which "is discernible only by the Platonic telescope." One does not have to go so far as that to realize that Callicles and Socrates live in different worlds, which is precisely what Plato is trying to show.

that improve and arts that merely flatter, so that Socrates has occasion again and again to restate it (501ab; 513c; 517b–519d). At times Callicles lapses into sullen silence, only to rejoin the discussion when Socrates seems for a moment to make an admission that favors him. And Socrates, who has not attempted to meet the first eloquent speech of Callicles with a similar reply, gradually gathers impetus, and pours forth, in a repeated *leitmotiv*, his conviction that only the good life matters.

He begins with the by now familiar distinction between the two kinds of activity: those that recognize an end in the promotion of goodness, whether of soul or of body, and those that merely flatter. Among the latter are cookery, and music and even poetry (501a; 501e–502d); yes, and rhetoric too (502de; cf. 513c), and its practitioners the statesmen. For if we ask whether they merely gratify the desires of the citizens or whether they educate them and if necessary curb and chasten them (502d–503b; cf. 515d–519d), judged by this rigid test the elder statesmen and even Pericles himself failed, and as a matter of fact were ostracized or at least censured by the citizens whom they had failed to educate.[233] The mention of chastening nettles Callicles; he does not want to be improved (505cd). Socrates patiently recapitulates the discussion (506c–507a) and reaffirms the principle of order and self-control, of not letting the desires get out of hand,[234] and draws once more the conclusion that it is worse to do than to suffer injustice (508bc), even if such a conviction results in leaving one helpless, at the mercy of insults and cruelty (508c–509c; cf. 488bc). For if one attempts to arm one's desire to avoid suffering injustice by ways and means in this world, one must either rule the state or make terms with those who do rule, which will inevitably result in the loss of one's integrity and self-respect (509c–511a). And it is no use to object that the non-conformist may lose his life; of course he may, but mere living is not man's goal. A ship's helmsman keeps his passengers alive; an engineer accomplishes rather more; but neither improves men's lives (511b–512c). Not mere living or length of days is what matters, but the quality of life. Therefore true statesmenship is not the mere imitation of a state's superficial character, but the improvement of its character (513a–514a), a task for which credentials are required such as no statesmen, present or past, can show (514a–517a). And to enforce the point, Socrates restates once more the distinction between flattery and edification; and denounces the

[233] Plato, who in the *Phaedrus* (269a–270a) praises Pericles, is hardly fair to him here. Pericles was precisely the man who *could* on occasion rebuke a mob (*Thuc.* II, 65). As Grote remarks, *Plato*, II, p. 145, Pericles would have agreed with the Gorgias of our dialogue, but not with Callicles.

[234] *Gorg.* 507a–508a: *σωφροσύνη* is here the fundamental virtue; in the *Republic* it is *δικαιοσύνη*. But the point is the same, even if the "order" that is here commended lacks content.

shams of Athenian statesmanship, — past imperialism and militarism and luxury are the cause of present distress; their authors, the statesmen, cannot complain if they are denounced.[235] So, too, the sophists, whom Callicles despises, though Socrates thinks a little better of them: they, or at least some of them, profess to teach virtue (519e–520).

To what service of the state does Callicles at last invite Socrates, to be its physician or its flatterer (521a)? Its flatterer, replies Callicles; for if he refuses — ! Precisely: if he refuses, the old story; Socrates will be at the mercy of the wicked. But it will be a case of a bad man abusing a good man, and since unjustly, shamefully; and since shamefully, basely (521ab). Socrates seems to live in a fool's paradise, in no danger of ever being haled into court by some contemptible person.[236] Not at all; that is just what may happen. Socrates is about the only Athenian who practises the true art of politics; but since he does not curry favors, he will be like a severe physician accused before school-boys by an indulgent cook, with no defense that they will listen to.[237] He stands alone, Socrates *contra mundum*. But what of that? The only thing that a man need fear is, not death, but going to Hades laden with injustice (522c–e).

Is Callicles at last convinced? Not at all; his is a different world from that of Socrates, in spite of the moments in the argument when Socrates has seemed to carry him along with his reasoning. The myth with which Socrates closes the dialogue, the first of Plato's three myths of the future life, may therefore be supposed, though ostensibly still addressed to Callicles (who, be it noted, does not speak again), to express more imaginatively what Socrates holds, or what Plato feels about his master's life and death, stripped of temporal limitations.[238] Like the last part of the *Apology*, spoken (or at least written) not for the unconvinced jurors but for the friends of Socrates, both those present and those of future centuries, so the myth of the *Gorgias* is addressed to sympathetic souls of any age. The myth of the *Republic*, which likewise deals with the destiny of the righteous and the wicked in another world, is prefaced by the remark that such a representation is justifiable since it has been shown on independent grounds that the innocent sufferer is better off than the wicked man who prospers.[239] If Callicles has not been convinced, no ordinary reader of the

[235] 517b–519c; the statesmen are condemned not as democrats (the one exception to the condemnation is the democrat Aristides, 526b), but as flatterers.

[236] 521c; cf. *Meno* 94e.

[237] 521c–522c. The irony of these glances at the trial of Socrates is obvious; even the charge of "corrupting the young" is foreshadowed, 521e; cf. *Apol.* 24b. Grote, *Plato*, II, p. 151, does well to call attention to the boldness of Plato's claims for the rights of conscience, of individual dissent; but he hardly allows sufficiently for the concessions to ordinary moral sentiment by all the speakers.

[238] On Plato's myths generally, see below, p. 314, and Appendix 51.

[239] *Rep.* 612a–c.

*Gorgias* can fail to feel the moral grandeur and the sincerity of Socrates, or to feel with him the ultimate rightness of the Vision of Judgement, a very different sort of trial from the possible travesty of justice to which he and Callicles have just referred, or from the actual trial of Socrates.

We need not suppose that Socrates actually set forth on any occasion the particular myth that Plato puts in his mouth in the *Gorgias*, any more than any of the later myths. The general point of view of the myth, like the paradoxes, of the *Gorgias*, is certainly Socratic; but the literary art is Plato's, while the materials are earlier than Plato. Homer's picture of the land of departed heroes, in the eleventh book of the *Odyssey*, and references to the Islands of the Blessed and to Tartarus; the myth of Prometheus (already used in a different spirit in the *Protagoras*), and above all the Orphic mythology with its strong moral basis, lie behind this myth.[240] Not fate, or favoritism, or chance, but one's deserts determine one's future lot. The special doctrine of reincarnation, however, probably of Pythagorean origin and appearing in several later Platonic myths, docs not appear here. The ideas of judgement, rewards and punishment, of separate realms for the righteous and the wicked (and of purgation, if not here of a separate Purgatory), will recur endlessly in literature after Plato, notably in the sixth book of the *Aeneid*, in Dante, and in Milton.

The chief point of the myth is the change in the system of judgement that was made early in the reign of Zeus in order to prevent miscarriage of justice. Before then, men were judged on the day of death, while still clothed with the body and perhaps surrounded with outward possessions; and the judges were also in the flesh. No wonder that the condition of the soul often escaped detection. So Zeus caused Prometheus to conceal from men the day of their impending deaths;[241] furthermore, he caused their naked souls to be judged by naked judges in the world to come. So rewards and suffering and cures (where curing is needful and possible) are now visited on those who deserve them.[242]

This is the tale that persuades Socrates that he must keep his soul in sound health against the day of judgement, scorning the arguments of Callicles and his world; and since neither the wise Gorgias nor Polus nor Callicles have been able to show him a better way of life, this is the one truth that remains unshaken after all their talk: that one must strive not to seem but to be good. For nothing evil can befall the truly good man.[243] Thus living, whether one turn one's mind to statesmanship or to anything else, and thus dying, one follows the path to which reason points.

[240] Cf. J. Dörfler, "Die Orphik in Platons *Gorgias*," *Wien. Stud.* 33 (1911), pp. 177–212.
[241] Cf. Aesch. *P.V.* 250.
[242] *Gorg.* 523a–526d. See further H. Kuhn, "The True Tragedy" (1942), pp. 56 f.
[243] 526d–527d; cf. *Apol.* 41d.

After the eloquence of the last pages of the *Gorgias* it is something of an anti-climax to return to the argument of Callicles. But Plato thought it worth his while to restate it in the first book of the *Republic*, giving it to the *rhetor* Thrasymachus; in fact, it is from his destructive argument that the stately edifice of the later books springs. Some, indeed, have held that the first book was originally an independent work, a "*Thrasymachus*," a Socratic dialogue of the inconclusive type, like the *Protagoras*, or that it is possibly a first draught for the *Gorgias* which was later expanded.[244] If, however, as seems more probable, it was designed from the beginning as the introduction either of the *Republic* as we know it or of a "first edition" of the *Republic*, it probably followed the *Gorgias*.[245] Even the greater restraint of Socrates in reasoning with Thrasymachus than with Callicles would seem to be a sign that time has elapsed since the events that called forth the special bitterness of the *Gorgias*, and is perhaps sufficient reason for dealing here with Thrasymachus after Callicles. There is little, indeed, in the "*Thrasymachus*" that differs from the Socratic conversations with sophists that we have considered; much in the remaining books of the *Republic* must be Plato's own development; and the Myth of Er with which it concludes rounds off the discussion even more impressively than does the myth of the *Gorgias*. These matters must wait for later consideration;[246] here we shall deal only with the "*Thrasymachus*."

The comparatively little that we know about Thrasymachus tells us almost nothing about his thought; famous as a *rhetor* rather than as a sophist, he was admired for his style.[247] He was capable of composing a forensic speech, in which the claims of moderation and "the ancestral constitution" are advocated;[248] but there is no way of telling whether it is a *bona fide* speech of Thrasymachus, a show speech, or a speech written to order for another person. Since it would not have been like Plato to exaggerate grossly the personal traits of a well-known public figure, it is reasonable to suppose that the violence and bluster of Thrasymachus in the *Republic* are part of the man. Yet it has been doubted whether any *rhetor* who expected to earn his living at Athens in the period that covers

[244] See, *inter alios*, F. Dümmler, *Kl. Schr.* I, pp. 229–270 (Dümmler thought that the myth of Er belonged to the original "*Thrasymachus*"); Wilamowitz, *Platon*, I, 206–208.

[245] So, *inter alios*, on grounds of style or of thought or of references to other dialogues or of internal unity and consistency, W. Lutoslawski, *Origin and Growth of Plato's Logic* (London, 1899), pp. 268–276; 319–322 (*Rep.* I early, but later than *Gorgias*); C. Ritter, *Platon*, I, pp. 273–278; A. E. Taylor, *P.M.W.*, p. 264; cf. p. 20; L. A. Post, "An Attempt to Reconstruct the First Edition of Plato's *Republic*," *C.W.* 21 (Nov. 14, 1927), pp. 41–44; P. Shorey, *W.P.S.*, pp. 3; 213–215; P. Shorey, Loeb ed. *Rep.*, Vol. I, pp. x; xvi; xxv.

[246] See below, pp. 314–316.

[247] D 85 A 1–3; 13; B 1; cf. H. Gomperz, *Soph. und Rhet.*, pp. 49–57.

[248] D 85 B 1.

the first years of the Peloponnesian War [249] would have dared to hold the extreme views attributed to him by Plato; in the *Gorgias* it is not the respected *rhetor* but Callicles who holds them.[250] Among the fragments of Thrasymachus, there is only one which may give a clue, one in which he is reputed to have said in a speech that "the gods have no regard for human affairs; else they would not have disregarded the greatest of goods among men, justice, which, we see, men do not practice," [251] Possibly Plato found in this cynical, though not original,[252] sort of remark sufficient ground for putting in the mouth of Thrasymachus the wild and outrageous ideas which Glaucon and Adimantus were to restate more temperately in the second book, before Socrates was to undertake his serious reply to them. Thrasymachus would serve to bring to a head the conflict of views in the most violent form, and Socrates could provisionally answer him. Their exchange of views may be briefly summarized.

The opening discussion has shown that justice is inadequately defined, by kindly old Cephalus, as equivalent to scrupulous honesty in business, and hardly less inadequately by his son Polemarchus, as the helping of friends and hurting of foes which the gnomic poets have counselled. Thrasymachus has listened impatiently to the reply of Socrates to Polemarchus; and after the conclusion that the just man cannot hurt any one (335d–336a), he bursts into the discussion, and is presently persuaded to give his own definition of justice, as "nothing else than the advantage of the stronger" (338c). Not necessarily the advantage of the physically stronger, as it immediately appears, but the advantage of the particular form of government, or of the particular sovereign of the moment (338de). This does not imply any social contract, but merely a *de facto* government. Justice is thus a matter of mere convention, since other types of government, or other rulers, will have different interests; but because each secures its power at any cost, all are actuated by the same principle, and the definition has a universal validity (339a). Yet it is admitted that rulers may be mistaken as to their real advantage; we must qualify the definition by saying "the advantage of the ruler so far as he is a real ruler and makes no mistakes" (339c–341a). This involves the conception of ruling as an art. Now every art has its special subject-matter or interest to perfect; moreover it seeks to promote the advantage of the weaker, who need it. As physicians, *qua* physicians, seek not their own but their patients' advantage, so rulers rule for the sake of the ruled (341c–342e). But at this

[249] For the dramatic date of the *Republic*, see A. E. Taylor, *P.M.W.*, pp. 263 ff., who convincingly places it about 421 B.C.

[250] See further Grote, *Hist. of Greece*, VIII, p. 194.

[251] D 85 B 8; cf. Ennius, *Telamo*, 353–355 Vahlen, cited below, p. 334; 359.

[252] Cf. Aesch. *Ag.* 369–372; Eur. *El.* 583 f.; Xen. *Mem.*, I, 4, 11.

point Thrasymachus scornfully abandons argument, and makes a cynical speech calling attention to the "facts" of the seamy side of Greek political life. Actual rulers *do* govern in self-interest, fattening their sheep for their own profit; and the real interest of the stronger is what is ordinarily called injustice. Only a precious innocent will fail to realize that "justice" is looking out for the other fellow's good; whereas "injustice," overreaching (πλεονεκτεῖν) on the grand scale, results in happiness and tyranny and the respect of the public; it is "a stronger, more liberal, and more lordly thing than justice" (343a–344c). Thrasymachus is forced, however, to admit the distinction between the specific function of any art and the incidental results, as for example, pay (345c–347e). And now for the real issue, the contention of Thrasymachus that the life of the unjust man is better than that of the just man,—that overreaching is the sole rule of happiness (347e). This was the contention also of Callicles, who, however, deduced it from *physis*, and deemed it therefore right. Thrasymachus makes no such claim; he discards altogether any moral conceptions of right and wrong, and points merely at "facts." He is too wary to be shamed, as Polus was, into damaging admissions.

The question is, then: Does injustice pay? Is it cleverness, in the long run? And Socrates by dialectical skill disproves the contention on three counts. (1) As in medicine, music, and the other arts, an overreaching (πλεονεκτεῖν) or lack of principle, is fatal, so in any art it is folly to ignore limits and to suppose that one cannot have too much of a good thing (349b–350c). Behind this argument lies the Pythagorean analogy between health and music and mathematics, and indeed the more far-reaching Greek instinct for measure, for "the mean," for moderation. (2) Furthermore, injustice is in itself weak; it defeats its own purpose by breeding internal discussion. There must be honor even among thieves (351a–352d). (3) And now that we are examining no longer merely external but internal results, we must observe that as any organ or tool performs its peculiar function only if its specific virtue is unimpaired, so of the soul; its specific virtue is justice, and it functions well and is happy only so far as it is just (352d–354a). This, then, is the provisional reply to Thrasymachus, though Socrates is far from satisfied with his analysis of justice; and the rest of the *Republic* will be devoted to the further analysis.[253] But here it will be more and more Plato, rather than Socrates, whose mind will be felt, so that we had best leave the remaining books of the *Republic*, along with other works of Plato's maturity, for our later discussion.

The consequences of sophistic discussion are to be felt in the drama of

[253] See below, pp. 311–314; cf. also *Laws* 714b–715d: rule of the stronger leads only to *stasis*; rulers must be servants of law.

the period[254] as well as in the political developments which they partly express. For the *polis*, the delicately organized democracy of Pericles, in which rights and duties seemed to be rationally adjusted, was disintegrating under the pressure of the Peloponnesian War, till no positive authority remained to control the individual's natural will to survive and to seize what he could in the war of each against all. Here our best witness is of course Thucydides. In order to appreciate the change of *morale*, one may contrast the "Funeral Oration" of Pericles as reported by Thucydides (II, 35–46), with the historian's own picture of Greek society a few years later.[255] The whole of Thucydides is in fact an epitaph on the *polis* as a moral agent; though the *polis* survived in the fourth century as an administrative unit, intellectual and spiritual ideas found their natural habitat either in more cosmopolitan societies or in the minds of individuals and small groups.

Thucydides studies the whole *physis* of man and his motives as the various medical writers of the Hippocratean Corpus study the physiology and the pathology of the body. For this is the age in which treatises "On Nature" in general are supplanted by medical tracts "On the Nature of Man." The Hippocratean writers, influenced by the atomist Democritus (himself the author of medical treatises),[256] by the Heraclitean conception of the law and the unity of *physis*,[257] and by Pythagorean thought, strive by observation and reason to reduce to scientific method what hitherto has been crude experiment tempered by superstition. They abandon belief in final causes and in supernatural causes and interventions.[258] Hence they conceive of the unity of nature, of nature herself as a norm, and of the uniformity of scientific law which makes it the physician's duty to consider the whole physique of his patient, or indeed his geographic and atmospheric environment as well.[259] Not only has each individual his

[254] For Sophocles, see above, pp. 139 f.; for Euripides, pp. 172–174; for the reaction of Aristophanes, above, p. 250, and below, Appendix 39.

[255] Thuc. III, 81–84; cf. W. Jaeger, "The Problem of Authority and the Crisis of the Greek Spirit" (Harvard Tercentenary Publications, 1936), pp. 3–6.

[256] Cf. D 68 B 26b–26d; W. Jaeger, *Diokles von Karystos*, p. 54, denies Democritean influence on the Hippocratean corpus.

[257] Cf. D 22 B 1; 123; 112.

[258] Cf. Περὶ Ἱερῆς Νόσου, 1; 2; 18: all diseases have natural causes, and none (not even epilepsy, the "divine disease") is more, or less, divine (θεῖον) than others; none occurs ἄνευ φύσιος; and cf. Περὶ Ἀέρων, κτλ., 22. (θεῖον is thus equivalent to κατὰ φύσιν; it is also used chiefly of atmospheric phenomena.) In their discussion of the causes of disease it is to be noted that the Hippocratean writers, like others after them, use indifferently the terms αἰτία and πρόφασις (the latter usually employed of an alleged motive, but here of the exciting cause); e.g. Περὶ Ἀέρων, κτλ., 22; Περὶ Ἀρχαίης Ἰητρικῆς, 2; 20; cf. Xen. *Hell.* VI, 4, 33.

[259] Περὶ Ἀρχαίης Ἰητρικῆς, 20; Plato, *Phaedrus* 270ad: (Hippocrates held that the *physis* of the body can be understood only as a whole); cf. K. Deichgräber, *Berl. Akad. Abhandl.*, 1933, pp. 149–152; Plato, *Charm.* 156 c e; Περὶ Ἀέρων, κτλ., *passim* ("meteorological medicine"); Περὶ Διαίτης, I, 2: παντὸς φύσιν ἀνθρώπου γνῶναι καὶ διαγνῶναι, κτλ.;

own *physis* (ἰδίη φύσις), to which the *techne* of medicine seeks to restore an ailing organism, but there is also a general human *physis* (κοινὴ φύσις) or normal condition of mankind. This uniformity enables the physician who observes symptoms (*tekmeria, semeia*) and who interprets them rationally (by *gnome* and *logos*) under their respective "types" (*eide*)[260] to predict the probability (*eikos*) of his patient's course of health or disease.[261] The writers reckon also with the part played in the formation of individuals and of peoples by the compulsion of *nomos* (environment, customs, institutions, and even psychological motives), which may itself become in time a part of their *physis*.[262] Great shocks may indeed bring about real and far-reaching changes of condition and character,[263] but this is not tantamount to natural evolution or to degeneration, nor is it any abandonment of causality in favor of a capricious *Tyche*; for *Tyche* is merely that part of *physis* that defies man's powers of prediction. The Hippocratean writers, then, separate medicine from philosophy and religion and teleology, with full recognition of cause and effect and scientific law, while keeping a sceptical attitude with regard to the ultimate problems of causality.[264]

Now Thucydides, a man of patent sincerity, seeks "to bring all human action within the realm of natural causes." [265] He distinguishes certain things that he can report with a fair measure of reliability ("what each man said," and "what was done" [266]) from other things which are mere matters of theory. Thus he distinguishes the symptoms and the course of the plague, which he can describe, from hypotheses about its causes, on the "probabilities" of which even physicians could only speculate.[267]

---

the writer of this work goes so far as to refer (I, 5) to the (Heraclitean) operation of natural law in traditional terms that suggest either divine control or fatalism; πάντα γίνεται δι' ἀνάγκην θείην . . . τὴν πεπρωμένην μοίρην ἕκαστον ἐκπληροῖ. W. Jaeger, "Diocles of Carystus: A New Pupil of Aristotle," *Phil. Rev.* 49 (1940), p. 403, points out that Hippocratic medicine was at least not anti-teleological.

[260] Cf. A. E. Taylor, *Varia Socratica*, pp. 212–247; C. M. Gillespie, *C.Q.* 6 (1912), pp. 179–203; G. F. Else, *H.S.C.P.* 47 (1936), pp. 18–20.

[261] Προγνωστικόν, 1 (πρόνοια = "knowing things about a patient before you are told them"; C. Singer, *Greek Biology and Greek Medicine* (Oxford, 1932), p. 85. Thus it includes *prognosis*; it is not used, as by the philosophers, as the antonym of *tyche*.); 25 (σημεῖα); Περὶ 'Αέρων, κτλ., 11.

[262] Περὶ 'Αέρων, κτλ., 16; cf. 14; and Democritus, D 68 B 33.

[263] Περὶ 'Αέρων, κτλ., 23; n.b. ἐκπλήξιες τῆς γνώμης.

[264] See further W. A. Heidel, Περὶ Φύσεως, pp. 91–133; W. Nestle, "Hippocratea," *Hermes*, 73 (1938), pp. 1–38; brief discussion, pp. 32–35, of the chronology and authenticity of some of the more important works in the corpus.

[265] C. N. Cochrane, *Thucydides and the Science of History* (Oxford, 1929), p. 17. This book in general (esp. pp. 3–34) shows the debt of Thucydides to Hippocrates both in vocabulary and in many of his master ideas.

[266] Thuc. I, 22.

[267] Thuc. II, 48: ἀφ' ὅτου εἰκὸς ἦν γενέσθαι αὐτό, καὶ τὰς αἰτίας ἅστινας νομίζει τοσαύτης μεταβολῆς ἱκανὰς εἶναι δύναμιν ἐς τὸ μεταστῆσαι σχεῖν.

That does not mean that he is sceptical about causality as such, or that he has an inadequate conception of scientific law; he simply does not presume to express an opinion on matters concerning which doctors will disagree, and concerning which no classification and no prediction is possible. When he comes to the question of the causes of the Peloponnesian War, he distinguishes between what we should call the proximate causes or "incidents," the accusations (*αἰτίαι*) that started it, and the underlying causes, least talked about at the time, but the real cause of the war (*ἡ ἀληθεστάτη πρόφασις*).[268]

But why write history at all? Because, as Thucydides tells us in as many words, history is likely to repeat itself, "so long as human nature remains the same"; hence knowledge of the past helps one to forecast the future.[269] The essential uniformity and unchanging character of human nature is thus the first postulate of the political philosophy of Thucydides: this it is that makes it possible for him (or for the persons whom he presents) to lay down propositions about it that read like scientific laws.[270] And his second postulate is that all our human life is controlled, not by Fate, or Providence, or the gods, but mostly by human intelligence and shrewdness (*γνώμη*) and political acumen (*ἀρετή*, often compared with the *virtù* of Machiavelli, whose realism is indeed Thucydidean). The one exception to this rule is the incalculable element of *Tyche*, which is not for Thucydides, as for Herodotus, something supernatural,[271] but merely what is external to man and is unpredictable, like Emerson's "Fate."[272] Not that man's intelligence is always reliable; unfortunately, it is a law

[268] Thuc. I, 23. The use of terms here has caused much discussion, but need occasion no misunderstanding if we remember the usage of the medical writers; see above, p. 268, n. 258. Polybius, III, 6–7, prides himself on his stricter use of these same terms; but at any rate Thucydides has made the useful distinction between pretended and genuine motives and has a clear idea also of more remote causes.

[269] Thuc. III, 82, 2: *ἕως ἂν ἡ αὐτὴ φύσις ἀνθρώπων ᾖ*; cf. I, 22: *τῶν μελλόντων ποτὲ αὖθις κατὰ τὸ ἀνθρώπινον τοιούτων καὶ παραπλησίων ἔσεσθαι.* For the *πρόγνωσις* and *πρόνοια* of Pericles, Thuc. II, 65, 3 and 4, and cf. above, p. 269, n. 261.

[270] With Thuc. V, 105 (*ὑπὸ φύσεως ἀναγκαίας . . . νόμον*, cited below, Appendix 38) contrast Herodotus VII, 8 (*νόμος* = custom, tradition); cf. Sir J. R. Seeley, *Introduction to Political Science*, pp. 5 f., on the difference between history and political science, and p. 4: "History without political science has no fruit; political science without history has no root."

[271] Herod., III, 139; IV, 8: *θείῃ τύχῃ*; for this idea of "divine chance," see also below, pp. 272 f.; 299 f.

[272] Thuc., I, 140 (Pericles): *τὴν τύχην ὅσα ἂν παρὰ λόγον ξυμβῇ εἰώθαμεν αἰτιᾶσθαι.* Each such event has its natural cause; but the coincidence (*ξυμβῇ*), as of the plague with a critical moment in Athenian history, remains beyond human prediction. II, 64 (Pericles): *τὰ δαιμόνια* means hardly more than *τύχη*, and the phrase is an obvious borrowing from popular language, rather than the expression of the historian's or the speaker's faith. For Aristotle, see below, pp. 320 f. For Emerson, cf. "Fate," in *The Conduct of Life* (Boston, 1904), p. 31: "Fate then is a name for facts not yet passed under the fire of thought: for causes which are unpenetrated." But the whole of this essay, poetic to the last degree, is a fine acceptance of what is beyond our control as a challenge to realize what is in our power.

of human nature that men do make mistakes: *errare est humanum*.[273] What is more, "all things tend to wax and wane." [274] Hence private virtue is no guarantee of continuous prosperity; otherwise the conventionally pious Nicias, safe and adjusted to normal conditions, would not have met with his terrible end in a disordered state of the world.[275]

Thucydides writes not as moralist, but as observer. The springs of human action, and particularly of public action, he finds to consist in a more or less enlightened self-interest; this is politics serving economics, the acquisitiveness (πλεονεξία) of the sophistic "strong man." He knows all that there is to know about the "economic causes of war," even if he gives no statistics about the balance of trade. For him therefore the essence of Greek politics and the motive force of all history is the will to power,[276] which is little veiled by conventional inhibitions; even these disappear in a crisis, such as the plague, or war, or revolution.[277] For the "rule of the stronger" is a law of nature, and "might makes right." [278]

## 6

The total effect of the activity of the sophists had been to sharpen the intellectual weapons of the Athenians and to dull their consciences. If their attitude was not deliberately subversive of ordinary morality, their less scrupulous followers found it easy to make explicit what had been beneath the surface, — the fact that neither *nomos* nor *physis*, if isolated, had provided any consistent or objective foundation for conduct. The crumbling of inherited beliefs and moral standards under the impact of reason left well-meaning young Greeks sceptical and, as it were, orphaned, and less well-meaning Greeks actually lawless.[279]

During the latter part of the fifth century, then, the same question seems to emerge from every point of view: What is the basis of man's happiness? Or (in another form) what is the nature of the Good? And at every point the scepticism, or anti-nomianism, or cynicism of the sophists is met

[273] III, 45, 3 (Diodotus, excusing the Mitylenaeans): πεφύκασί τε ἅπαντες καὶ ἰδίᾳ καὶ δημοσίᾳ ἁμαρτάνειν, κτλ.

[274] II, 64 (Pericles): πάντα γὰρ πέφυκε καὶ ἐλασσοῦσθαι; cf. below, p. 301, n. 167, for Plato.

[275] See Appendix 37: Thucydides on Nicias.

[276] VI, 85, 1 (an Athenian envoy, justifying the choice of friends or foes, by a ruler or by an empire, according to advantage): οὐδὲν ἄλογον ὅτι ξυμφέρον οὐδ' οἰκεῖον ὅτι μὴ πιστόν· πρὸς ἕκαστα δὲ δεῖ ἢ ἐχθρὸν ἢ φίλον μετὰ καιροῦ γίγνεσθαι.

[277] Thuc. II, 53, 4 (of the moral effect of the plague): θεῶν δὲ φόβος ἢ ἀνθρώπων νόμος οὐδεὶς ἀπεῖργε, κτλ.; III, 82–84 (the transvaluation of moral values that took place after the revolution at Corcyra, due to πλεονεξία).

[278] See Appendix 38: "Might makes right."

[279] For the state of mind, see Plato, *Rep.*, 537d–539a; and J. Adam, *Rel. Teachers*, pp. 270 ff.

by Socrates, and presently by Plato.[280] To the sophists' sceptical and paradoxical transvaluations of all values they oppose new paradoxes: Socrates, the wisest of all men, who knows only that he knows nothing; Socrates, the only true statesman, who shuns all political activity; the good man who prefers to suffer rather than to do injustice; the claim of the good society, grounded in an invisible good that knows no change. If Socrates and Plato do not believe that it is fated that the good shall prevail, they at least recall Greek thinkers to the ancient faith that man must find his good within a beneficent natural order.

That Socrates avoided the investigation of "the Nature of the Universe" and the so-called "cosmos," as a useless inquiry resulting in conflicting opinions, and investigated instead human affairs, and especially the nature of moral ideas, is the explicit testimony of Plato, Aristotle, and Xenophon.[281] That does not mean that Socrates never referred, explicitly or implicitly, to *physis*; on the contrary we find him drawing arguments from the natural affection of even the beasts for their kind;[282] from the fact that men, too, are by *physis* friendly, and need each other;[283] that both natural endowments (*physis*) and practise are needed in the development of courage;[284] that the hands and feet are made for their special services by God (ὁ θεός) or by some divine dispensation (θεία μοῖρα).[285] This alternative account, and the failure here to mention *physis*, does not imply any real change of point of view, just as in the conversation with Hippias, discussed above,[286] Socrates refers to the law or the gods as punishing incest. In Plato's *Meno*, however, Socrates distinguishes *physis* from the gods. The dialogue begins with the question whether virtue can be taught; and it appears that virtue can neither be bestowed by *physis*,[287] nor be taught,[288] but that there is also a kind of virtue, later to be distinguished from "philosophic" virtue, as "popular" virtue, a "right opinion" which is of practical value, and whose source, since it is neither *physis* nor instruction, must be a special divine dispensation.[289] In the myth of the *Protagoras*, such a divine dispensation bestows virtue on *all* men, and makes them morally responsible for practising it, whereas other

[280] Cf. C. Ritter, *Platon*, I, pp. 361 ff.; W. Jaeger, "Problem of Authority," pp. 6–8; G. C. Field, *Plato and His Contemporaries*, pp. 77–106; H. Cherniss, "The Philosophical Economy of the Theory of Ideas."

[281] See Appendix 39: Socratic Problem, II.

[282] Xenophon, *Mem.* II, 34.

[283] II, 6, 21.

[284] III, 9, 1–3; cf. IV, 1, 3; and P. Shorey, **Φύσις, Μελέτη, Ἐπιστήμη**.

[285] II, 3, 18.

[286] IV, 4, 21–23; see above, p. 229.

[287] Plato, *Men.*, 89ab.

[288] *Men.* 89d–96d.

[289] Meno 99e: *ἀρετὴ ἂν εἴη οὔτε φύσει οὔτε διδακτόν, ἀλλὰ θείᾳ μοίρᾳ παραγιγνομένη ἄνευ νοῦ οἷς ἂν παραγίγνεται.* See also R. D. Archer-Hind, ed. *Phaedo*, pp. 149–155.

boons come from *physis*, or chance.[290] The two statements are not incompatible, though that of the *Meno* somewhat fancifully limits the divine dispensation till it becomes equivalent to chance;[291] the *Republic* recurs to the idea, but reckons also with different grades of citizens who are capable of different degrees of virtue.[292]

Thoroughly Socratic is the distinction[293] between "doing well" (εὐπραξία) and "good luck" (εὐτυχία). The first term, ambiguous in ordinary Greek (doing, or faring well), for Socrates has only one meaning; it involves study and practice and activity; but the result of "doing one's work well" is that one is "dear to the gods." ("Heaven helps him who helps himself.") Thus Socrates implies the possibility of a harmonious cooperation between man's activity and his environment, and suggests that his happiness is the result of fulfilling his function. That is the nearest approach to hedonism that Xenophon's Socrates makes; it is rather far from the hedonism proposed by Socrates in the *Protagoras*.[294]

But Socrates goes further; he makes use, adaptation to function, the norm of goodness. To Aristippus, who wishes to trap Socrates into admitting that any good is sometimes bad,[295] Socrates replies that he knows of no good which is not good in relation to some object, nor of any beauty save in what serves some particular purpose.[296] It follows that goods vary with circumstances and persons; what helps one man may hurt another. This view is accepted by the Socrates of the *Gorgias*, who argues[297] that all things are prized according as they conduce to utility or to pleasure or both; the view is stated only to be rejected in the (probably Platonic) *Hippias Major*;[298] and, of course, it is incompatible with the Platonic theory of ideas, eternal and unchanging. Possibly Xenophon's report shows an acquaintance with both the *Gorgias* and the *Hippias Major*, and a desire to affirm as Socratic the utilitarian view of the good and the beautiful (found in the *Gorgias*) and to disclaim Socratic authority for the criticism of the *Hippias Major*.[299]

From the belief that utility is the standard of goodness to the belief that all things contribute to the use of man is an easy step for an optimist; and

[290] *Protag.* 322a–324c; see above, pp. 245 f.

[291] Cf. my "Plato's View of Poetry," pp. 18 ff.; and my "The Spirit of Comedy in Plato," pp. 78 ff.

[292] See below, pp. 299 f.

[293] Xen. *Mem.*, III, 9, 14 f.

[294] See above, p. 248; and for happiness, see also Xen. *Mem.*, I, 6, 9–10 and p. 232 above.

[295] Cf. the *Dissoi Logoi*; see above, p. 250.

[296] Xen. *Mem.*, III, 8, 2–3; IV, 6, 8–9; cf. IV, 7, 2–8 for a utilitarian view of education.

[297] Plato, *Gorg.* 474de; see above, p. 258.

[298] Plato, *Hipp. Ma.*, 289d–290e; 294a.

[299] So argues E. C. Marchant, Loeb ed. of Xenophon, *Memorabilia* and *Oeconomicus*, pp. xvi f.

Socrates crowns his utilitarianism with teleology, taking a rather naïf anthropocentric view of the universe. Xenophon represents him as arguing, in two long conversations, that man's fitness for his external environment, his physical, and above all his intellectual powers, must be the product not of chance but of design, and, what is more, of a loving creator, who cares for man and providentially ordains the whole *cosmos* for man's express advantage.[300] The familiar sign of Socrates, his *daimonion*, which warned him with regard to his actions, is only a special case of this providential care, and is a token of a genuine mysticism in Socrates, which is confirmed by the stories of the trances of Socrates which Plato records.[301]

All this evidence helps us to understand Plato's imaginative reconstruction of Socrates' youthful interests in the *Phaedo*, and the disappointment of young Socrates when he found that the *nous* of Anaxagoras did not dispose all things for the best, but only mechanically.[302] If young Socrates ever did puzzle his head with physical speculation, one gathers both from Xenophon and from the *Phaedo* what a world of difference there was between the *physis* of the Ionian philosophers and that *cosmos* which Socrates light-heartedly described as having been created for man's delight.

It is worth while to dwell for a moment on the teleology of Socrates and its consequences. Socrates simply shuts his eyes to the existence of evil in the *cosmos*, even from man's point of view, assuming that *physis* (or the gods) will realize the good. Moral evil he finds in the ignorance of imperfect human beings, an explanation that leaves both their imperfection to be explained and the place of the will to be discovered. Since he holds that all good is good for something, and man's good is what is to his advantage, Socrates argues that only a fool will fail to do whatever he knows to be a means to that end. In other words, theory and practise are one; virtue is the other face of knowledge.[303] And since knowledge can be taught, virtue can be taught.[304] Now it is true that virtue, as distinguished from innocence, cannot exist without moral insight (*phronesis*); but it does not follow that moral insight will always be translated into moral action. The problem is not so wholly intellectual as Socrates supposes, for tough consciences and weak wills are fairly common; there are moral dullards as well as intellectual dullards. The Socratic teleology

[300] See Appendix 40: Socrates and Teleology.

[301] Plato, *Symp.* 175b. In Plato the warning of the *δαιμόνιόν τι* is always negative (*Apol.* 31cd; cf. [Plato?] *Alc.* I, 103a: *δαιμόνιον ἐναντίωμα*); in Xenophon it is sometimes also a positive power, prompting to action.

[302] *Phaedo*, 96a–97b; see above, pp. 221; 272; below, pp. 285; 292 f.

[303] Xenophon, *Mem.* III, 9, 4; Plato, *Gorg.* 460b: *ὁ τὰ δίκαια μεμαθηκὼς δίκαιος*; Aristotle, *E.N.* 1144b19: *ὅτι μὲν γὰρ φρονήσεις ᾤετο εἶναι πάσας τὰς ἀρετάς, ἡμάρτανεν.*

[304] A position provisionally held by the Socrates of both the *Protagoras* and the *Meno*, though more than one kind of goodness is under consideration; see above, pp. 272 f.

and the concomitant doctrine of action accounts for good, but not for evil.[305]

The naïf teleology of Socrates will be continued by the more metaphysical teleology of Plato and Aristotle, both of whom have a real conception of the meaning of science. They therefore come to realize that the problem of evil is one to which physics, psychology, ethics, metaphysics, and religion all have something to contribute. Plato has recourse to ethical dualism, much in the spirit of the "mystical religions"; he wrestles with metaphysical dualism; but his final philosophy turns the problem of good and evil over to religion. Aristotle "short-circuits" Plato's process, subordinating good and evil alike to the conception of development and of the final cause.[306]

Socrates supplements his faith in the beneficence of the universe by discovering in the flux and chaos of human life certain fixed principles of conduct which are of practical use. Here the precise content of his teaching is less important than his method, which is open to any patient and honest man of intelligence; it is what Aristotle describes as the peculiar contribution of Socrates to philosophy, — namely, the method of inductive reasoning and definition.[307] Xenophon illustrates it meagerly,[308] Plato in the "Socratic dialogues" very richly. Copious material from daily life, and a wise sense of the meanings of words, possibly owing something to Prodicus,[309] are combined in the Socratic dialectic to bring forth exact conceptions of "what each thing is."[310]

Such definitions, however, would have been fruitless if they had not converged in a more general conception of the good, defined as we have already seen in terms of use and fitness for a purpose; this conception of what is good, or of "the good," underlies all the thinking of Socrates and Plato, and finally emerges in Plato's "Idea of the Good." Unlike the accidental and varying customs and laws that serve their temporary and partial purposes, and that are derived merely from the *fiat* of a limited society, what is truly good is, even for Socrates, inherent in the actual nature of things; even *nomos*, at its best, is therefore rooted in *physis*, and the antithesis exploited by the sophists is on its way to being resolved in a

[305] Cf. *Romans*, 7, 19: "For the good that I would I do not; but the evil which I would not, that I do"; Ovid, *Met.* VII, 20 f., *video meliora proboque, deteriora sequor*; and see below, pp. 306 f.; 328.

[306] For Plato, see below, pp. 279–316; for Aristotle, pp. 317–330; on the underlying problems involved, see further A. E. Taylor, *Elements of Metaphysics* (London, 1903), pp. 269–272, including p. 272, note 1; 391–407.

[307] Aristotle, *Met.* 1078 b 23–29.

[308] Xen. *Mem.* IV, 6, 1; 13–15.

[309] See above, pp. 240 f.

[310] Xen., *Mem.*, IV, 6, 1: *τί ἕκαστον εἴη τῶν ὄντων*; cf. IV, 5, 11; Aristotle, *Met.* 1078b24: *τὸ τί ἐστι*; cf. Arist. *de Part. An.* 642a25–31.

"law of nature." But this law, Socrates would say, as against Callicles,[311] is a kindly and rational law including all men and all things, and the way to happiness is not the rebellion but the submission of the individual to its authority. Socrates himself refuses to escape from prison not because of the bidding of the particular law covering his case but because of a loyalty to a whole system of rights and duties which no casuistry may evade.[312]

Thus the supreme contribution of Socrates is not merely a method, or even a doctrine, but an act of faith. His simple religious faith in the ultimate rationality or goodness of that universe of which all partial beings are dependent members requires that he act in accordance with its demands, at whatever cost to himself. Whatever, if realized, is good, the good man is bound to bring to pass; and Socrates refuses to compromise with his conscience. Throughout the "Socratic" dialogues of Plato shines the picture of the just man for whom knowledge instantaneously becomes virtue, whatever may be the case with weaker brothers. He will suffer, rather than do, injustice; he will drink the hemlock, rather than be inconsistent with himself and with the goodness of the universe.[313] His heroism has proved to be an argument more moving and more convincing than any intellectual system. For the fact that to heroism was added happiness, even though that was not his immediate quest, was the practical vindication of his paradoxes and of his faith.

311 See above, pp. 260–263.

312 Plato, *Crito* 50a–54e.

313 "Consistency is, indeed, the one word which, better than any other, expresses the whole character of Socrates, and the whole of philosophy as well." A. W. Benn, *The Greek Philosophers*, p. 126.

# CHAPTER IX

## PLATO

### I

FROM the time of Socrates on, the thinkers of Greece are ranged in two main groups. The one conceives of Nature as the product of necessity, without plan or purpose; here stand the Atomists and their successors the Epicureans, and here, too, the worshippers of the goddess *Tyche*, whose cult becomes of great importance in the Hellenistic and Roman Ages.[1] The other group includes those who believe that the universe is the product not of blind, mechanical necessity but of a law or destiny which is rational and good, whether it be called the will of Zeus or Providence or Fate: here stand Diogenes of Apollonia, Socrates, Plato, and Aristotle, and after them the Stoics and their successors. For the latter group, man's good is either the gift of Fate (or of divine Providence), or is to be won by conformity with the laws of nature which are the expression of Fate (or of the will of the gods).

The discussions of the Sophists and of Socrates had made it clear, as we have observed,[2] that if *Nomos* and *Physis*, Law and Nature, are really opposed, the ground of ethics is swept away. The discovery of Law in Nature and the attempt to base human conduct on the immutable laws of the universe was the great task undertaken not only by Socrates, but by Plato, Aristotle, and the Stoics. We must observe, however, that a partial and one-sided solution was too hastily devised by a younger associate of Socrates, Antisthenes. Like Socrates in his insistence on virtue, like Hippias in his adherence to Nature, he went further than either in his contempt for mere social convention, or indeed for all the arts that have created civilization; and the tales told of him, of Crates, and of Diogenes, his "Cynic" successors, agree in their pictures of simplicity and primitivism carried to the point of eccentricity and boorishness, if not of indecency.[3] So the Cynics became the mendicant friars of the ancient world. Virtue alone matters, and is sufficient for happiness; while happiness, if it is to be won at all, will come only by the surrender of all fears and desires and ambitions and social conformity. Although this seems to be an unnecessarily complete repudiation of a world conceived to be

[1] See also below, p. 368, and Appendix 62; p. 391, and n. 348.
[2] See above, p. 271.
[3] Cf. Lovejoy and Boas, *Primitivism*, pp. 117–152.

wholly bad, and it is hard to see how good or happiness can come therefrom, it was from the Cynics, first of all, that the Stoics were presently to derive their inspiration,[4] only to enrich it and ennoble it; and for the Stoics the Nature to which they were to surrender their wills was to appear as fundamentally rational and good.[5]

Meanwhile the Cyrenaics, led by Aristippus,[6] developed a philosophy of refined hedonism. The chief good of man is pleasure, the pleasure of the moment, divorced from pain or desire or hope. Social life, and even generous acts, are good, but only because they generally conduce to the pleasure of the doer, not because of any concern for society or the needy. This creed is not capable of being connected with any conception of the whole nature of the universe, or of a social order; it is essentially selfish, and is indeed sceptical of the ultimate goodness of the universe. It bids the lucky individual, "*carpe diem*"; but even he has no assurance that another day may not ruin his pleasure. Thus the Cyrenaic is at heart a pessimist; and it is related that a successor of Aristippus, Hegesias, enumerated the discomforts of human life so effectively that many of his hearers committed suicide, and his lectures were finally forbidden by Ptolemy Philadelphus.[7] Yet the Cyrenaics merely stressed as an exclusive ideal what Socrates had discussed as the goal of the utilitarian;[8] what Plato and Aristotle admit as one ingredient of the good;[9] what Aristotle's contemporary, the respectable astronomer Eudoxus, of the Academy, upheld; and what the Epicureans were to justify. But these thinkers made a more determined effort to relate pleasurable conduct to a reasoned theory of the universe and of man's nature as a social being, just as the Stoics sought to justify the Cynic's individualism by a deeper conception of man's moral nature.

## 2

In Plato are fused all the leading forces and problems of the earlier age, and from him issues much of the varied thought of the future. Seldom is it given to a single man to express so completely the searchings of heart of all men, or to sow the seeds from which such endless harvests are to be reaped. In our study of fate, good, and evil, we have already had to reckon with Plato as a witness to the inquiries of the sophistic age and of Socrates, and have had to consider how far he was recording the beliefs of others

[4] See below, pp. 337 f.

[5] See below, pp. 333; 340–342; 343 f.

[6] It has been argued that the specifically hedonistic doctrine of the Cyrenaics is the contribution not of the elder Aristippus, but of his grandson the younger Aristippus; R.P. 264; A. E. Taylor, *Epicurus*, p. 82, n. 1. But cf. also Zeller-Nestle, *Grundriss*, pp. 136–139.

[7] Cic. *T.D.* I, 83–84.

[8] Cf. Plato, *Protag.* 351b–357e; see above, p. 248.

[9] Plato, *Phileb.* 53b; see above, p. 261, n. 231; Aristotle, *E.N.* Book X.

and how far he was expressing his own thought; this problem is indeed always with us, not least because of the dramatic character of almost all of the earlier dialogues.

Born probably in Athens in 427 of an aristocratic family, trained in poetry and rhetoric, and introduced to philosophy possibly first by the Heraclitean Cratylus and then toward the age of twenty by association with Socrates, Plato naturally looked forward to a political career. But the trend of party politics during the later years of the Peloponnesian War and above all the political execution of Socrates in 399 by the restored democracy caused him to abandon all political ambitions and to devote the rest of his life to philosophy.[10] It is not unlikely that during these years Plato made a visit to the Pythagorean communities in southern Italy and Sicily before he established the Academy at Athens, about 388–387, at the age of forty. At any rate, Pythagorean influence is to be seen both in Plato's writings of this period and in much of the programme of the Academy, in which mathematics and ethical and political philosophy were pursued. Half way between the founding of the Academy and his death in 348–347 Plato was persuaded to try to translate theory into practice in Sicily (in 367, and again in 361); but the odds were too great, as he himself realized.

The dialogues of Plato begin[11] with the portrayal of Socrates and his associates: the events attending the trial, his conversations with friends on ethical and other matters, his opposition to certain sophistic doctrines, his championship of the good life[12] as something to be explained neither on the basis of *physis* nor of *nomos* exclusively (*Apology*, *Crito*, *Euthyphro*, *Laches*, *Ion*, *Charmides*, *Lysis*, *Cratylus*, *Euthydemus*, *Protagoras*). Here the Socratic method of inquiry by induction and definition, of irony, of mystical contemplation and ardent pursuit of the good and the beautiful, are in the foreground. They persist in the dialogues that follow, but more and more Plato allows the figure of Socrates to become the spokesman of his own thought. The *Gorgias* shows a new and terrible seriousness, the *Meno* the beginning of a new method, in which the Socratic definition is linked with a theory of knowledge (recollection) of a world of absolute being;[13] this is further developed in the full-fledged Theory of Ideas of

[10] The *Gorgias*, provoked by new attacks on the memory of Socrates, reflects the "conversion" of Plato; see above, pp. 258 f.; cf. *Epistle* VII, 324b8–326b4, and particularly Plato's conviction, reached during the years after the death of Socrates, that good government could exist only when "either true philosophers found their way to political authority or politicians by some divine dispensation (ἔκ τινος μοίρας θείας), take to philosophy"; cf. *Rep.* 473cd, and see below, pp. 298–300, and Appendix 47.

[11] On the chronology of Plato's works, see Ueberweg-Praechter, *Grundriss*, I, 199–218. See also above, pp. 258 f.; 263; 265 f.

[12] See above, pp. 245–247; 271 f.; 275 f.

[13] See above, pp. 223; 258 f.; below, Appendix 30.

the *Symposium*, the *Phaedo*, the *Republic*, and the *Phaedrus*, written when the Academy was well launched. Difficulties of logic and ethics and psychology are analyzed in the later "dialectical" dialogues (*Theaetetus*, *Parmenides*, *Politicus*, and *Philebus*); here Socrates recedes into the background. Finally, in his later years, Plato attempts to fuse religion and science in an imaginative picture of the origin of the *cosmos* (*Timaeus*, and the fragmentary *Critias*), and to set forth in the *Laws*, more realistically than in the *Republic*, the possibilities of political reform in a "second-best" society. In the *Timaeus* Socrates plays no important rôle, while in the *Laws* he is replaced by a "stranger from Athens" who doubtless is Plato in thin disguise.

It must not be supposed that the transition from Socrates to Plato is quite as definitive as this outline would suggest. Plato is present in his work from first to last, selecting, emphasizing, interpreting, developing, retouching, defending, criticizing, restating. Socrates the man, and something of his doctrine, or it would be better to say of his moral attitude, remains from first to last; his *ethos* is translated into the Platonic *logos*, for both Socrates and Plato are fundamentally concerned to discover the basis on which must rest the necessary reply to the challenge of the Sophists. To distinguish the Socratic and the Platonic elements in many of the dialogues would be a difficult if not an impossible undertaking, and is fortunately not wholly necessary for our present purpose. Certain differences which appear may however be set down. As we have already observed,[14] Socrates remains an amateur in scientific matters, and loses interest in "science" when he realizes that it cannot deal with values; Plato's march is toward science, and toward science of the most mathematical sort. Socrates proceeds by inductive reasoning to the formulation of a definition, but his interest is not in dialectic for its own sake: Plato, too, begins with an ethical interest, but turns at times to logic and metaphysics as ends in themselves. Socratic irony has its counterpart in Platonic wit and the brilliant creation of a dramatic *milieu*. The Socratic mysticism, with its trances and its *daimonion*, and the guidance of dreams and oracles, is something personal and psychological, though it is akin to some of the experience of the Orphics or of other mystics; characteristically it is Socrates whom Plato represents as having heard from the lips of the wise woman Diotima about the steps by which, like a mystic, one may rise to the beatific vision of transcendent beauty.[15] It may be doubted whether Plato himself is thus personally given to mystical experience, unless of a somewhat intellectual kind. His Pythagoreanism is acquired, though it leads to a vision of truth or goodness which has something of

[14] See above, pp. 272 f.

[15] *Symp.* 201d–212a.

the immediacy of the mystics'.[16] To this it must be added that Plato has the poet's gift of setting forth in concrete images, or in myths, sometimes in Orphic materials, those realms of experience that defy merely logical expression, of using myths, as it were, like lanterns to illuminate the darkness before the feet of the pioneer.[17]

Before undertaking a more detailed consideration of Plato's contribution to our problem, it will be well to notice in a more general way the character of the task that Plato set himself and the general direction of his thought. Like Socrates, he was troubled by the ignorance of unthinking men, creatures of habit and prejudice; and no less troubled by the diverging paths of the intellectuals who maintained the exclusive claims of *physis* or of *nomos*. *Physis* could be used to justify selfish individualism; *nomos* could be used to support the *status quo*, whether of the many or of the few; either could be used to justify brute force, and was an inadequate rational basis for the good life. As against the sophists, Socrates and Plato undertake to show that there may be discerned a *nomos*, a law of development and control, of harmony and proportion, in the *physis* of man. Furthermore, this law of human nature can exist only within a larger and beneficent order, the *physis* of the *cosmos*. Thus Socrates and Plato are conservatives in opposing the centrifugal and destructive tendencies of sophistic thought, while at the same time they are visionary reformers in seeking to develop human nature in accordance with the laws of an ideal goal, not yet attained and never fully to be achieved by finite man. Good exists; more good is to be created or discovered; yet even this good must be related to the all-embracing frame of the universe.[18]

A part of Plato's programme will therefore be practical, ethical and educational, and in a sense political, even if it will take part in practical politics only exceptionally. There is a good, the good should be pursued, the good should prevail; the better elements in each individual should rule the rest, the better elements in society should control. This is an aristocratic and intellectual ideal, derived in part from the Socratic and Platonic reaction against the working of Athenian democracy, in part from Plato's admiration of Spartan simplicity and discipline, and in part from Plato's increasing sympathy for the Pythagoreans' cult: an ascetic common life, a devotion to the things of the spirit, a harmony or health of the soul to be won by the study of "music" in the full sense of the word, including mathematics and science.[19] In its social aspect the result will be

[16] Cf. *Epistle* VII, 341cd.

[17] See below, p. 314, and Appendix 51.

[18] See Appendix 41: Plato and Rival Thinkers.

[19] On the earlier (religious) contributions of the Pythagoreans, cf. Burnet, *Thales to Plato*, pp. 41–56. The Pythagoreans nearly or quite contemporary with Plato had dropped most of the religious doctrines of their master, and developed the mathematical and scientific doc-

justice, in its intellectual aspect, knowledge of truth, or of the good. In the *Phaedo* we see Plato's interpretation of the life and death of Socrates in (early) Pythagorean terms; the good man whose life has been devoted to the freeing of his soul from dependence on the body, and who therefore faces death in the cheerful faith that his soul shall now find its final freedom. In the *Republic* he traces the growth of the conception of justice, as not merely a natural or a conventional state but a health of the soul which has learned to control its whole being, and (if possible) the society in which it lives, by gradual progress toward the contemplation of a realm of pure and eternal realities.

Contemplation of the good and the beautiful is congenial to the mystic Socrates, as the quest for the meaning of goodness is congenial to his ironical, agnostic nature. With Plato, though he too, and not only in the myths, finds in contemplation and love the ultimate experience of the soul, the quest takes on a more intellectual and a more protracted character, as other objects than values (the good and the beautiful) present themselves. Like the Pythagoreans he investigates also mathematical conceptions; like the Eleatics and Megarians, logical and metaphysical relationships. The result is that over and above the world of the Heraclitean flux, (of which there can be only "opinion") he finds a realm of eternal and unchanging realities, the "Ideas," which alone can be "known." Yet for Plato, too, when he comes to seek a principle of relationship among the Ideas, a master-Idea prior to all the rest, it is the "Idea of the Good," which is higher than knowledge, higher even than existence.[20]

The need of supposing that a stable reality exists, Plato feels alike in dealing with the problems of conduct, of knowledge, and of being, — in the fields of ethics, of epistemology, and of ontology.[21] He hints at such a reality in the *Meno*, in the doctrine of reminiscence; he describes it as an "hypothesis" in the *Phaedo*; he briefly unfolds the doctrine, as if familiar, in the *Republic*; and in later dialogues that deal with the difficulties involved he returns to the point that only if this hypothesis be valid can goodness, knowledge, and being exist.[22]

Yet there are difficulties involved in the famous Theory. If we distinguish, as we ordinarily must, between Mind and Matter, Soul and Body, Thought and Sensation, the Eternal and the Flux, the noumenal and the

---

trines. Burnet, *Thales to Plato*, 87–93; Field, *Plato and His Contemporaries*, pp. 175–187; Erich Frank, *Plato und die Sogennanten Pythagoreer* (Halle, 1923). On the Pythagoreans in general, Burnet in *Enc. Rel. Eth.* X, 520–530, esp. 523–526.

[20] *Rep.* 508e; 509b: ἐπέκεινα τῆς οὐσίας. See also below, pp. 285–287.

[21] For a clear and brief statement of the triple need, and of Plato's approach, see H. Cherniss, "The Philosophical Economy of the Theory of Ideas"; cf. also P. Shorey, Loeb ed. *Rep.*, Vol. II, pp. ix–xxiii, and works by Shorey and by others there cited.

[22] See Appendix 42: Platonic Ideas.

phenomenal, the creator and the created, the One and the Many, and if we suppose the Ideas to correspond only to the first member of each of these pairs, we are in danger of finding ourselves committed to such a dualism as will make most problems insoluble. If the Ideas are indeed "separate from" the phenomenal world, no ingenuity will suffice to effect a reconciliation. That Aristotle held Plato to have made such a separation and therefore regarded the Ideas as superfluous, is common knowledge; what is not so commonly recognized is the extent to which Plato attempted to meet such criticisms.[23]

At this point it may be fair to observe that the term "dualism" merely gives a name to a distinction between two modes of being, such as mind and matter. The aim of most monists[24] is to effect a synthesis or reconciliation of the modes. Now it is one thing to admit that *we* do not understand how mind and matter, the one and the many, Ideas and particulars, are related; it is quite another thing to say that the two are ultimately discrete and are fallaciously wedded by the intellect. Plato takes note of the problem, and deals with it by metaphor ("partakes," "imitates," "is present") or by myth; and his method, that of the mystic, comes perhaps nearer to solving it than does any other, for he neither denies its existence nor pretends to have found a complete solution. Like all "middle of the road" thinkers, however, he remains open to the attack both of the materialists and of the obscurantists who abandon scientific pretensions.

It will help to clear the ground if we admit at once that some sort of dualism is the condition of any ethical system; Good and Evil are absolutely opposed, however much Evil may be minimized or explained away. Nor can the immortality of the soul, in any ordinary sense of the expression, be admitted unless some clear cleavage of soul and body be accepted. Here Plato, both in the *Phaedo* and in the *Republic*, follows the dualism of the Pythagoreans and of most other mystics; and it must be observed that the later Academy, like the Epicureans and like most Stoics, sought to evade such a dualism, and by returning to a monistic and materialistic conception were compelled to abandon belief in immortality.

But in the fields of epistemology and of ontology the case stands otherwise. Knowledge is impossible if predication is not based on the inseparability of subject and attribute; science demands a *cosmos* which is one, and in which every part is linked with every other part. Here the difficulty is of explaining the relation of universal to particular, of law to fact; in terms of Christian theology, it is the difficulty of reconciling the con-

[23] Aristotle, *E.N.* 1095a26: 1096a11–1097a14; also see below, p. 286. For Plato, see below, pp. 283 f.; and L. Robin, *La Théorie Platonicienne des Idées* (Paris, 1908), pp. 30–120 (Aristotle's exposition and criticism, especially in the *Metaphysics*).

[24] E.g. Hegel.

ception of a transcendent God with the conception of God's immanence. The theory of Ideas offers a simple hypothesis with regard to knowledge and with regard to being or goodness; the difficulty comes in the attempt to explain the nature of error and illusion, or again the nature of process, variety, and evil. If there is any break in the totality of being, it would appear *prima facie* to be between the Ideas and phenomena, between what can be known and what cannot be known or can at best be subject only to opinion.[25] There is a danger, in that case, of our being confronted by a stubborn residuum, by portions of the *cosmos* or tracts of human history, which are not amenable to the intelligence;[26] for to "know" anything is for Plato not a casual act but the perception of its necessary relation to the meaning of the whole, in a word, of the nature of causality.[27]

Several of the later dialogues therefore face the possible attacks that could be made on the Theory of Ideas and the defense that the "friends of the Ideas" might reasonably make. The *Theaetetus* disposes of sensation and of opinion as adequate substitutes for knowledge.[28] The *Sophist* upholds the claims of both motion and rest, and shows that the Theory of Ideas will adequately meet them.[29] Plato argues both against dualism and against a superficial monism.[30] The *Parmenides* represents the great Eleatic philosopher as raising objections to such a theory of Ideas as appears in the *Phaedo*, particularly the difficulties involved in stating of what things there are Ideas, how particulars are related to Ideas (whether by "Participation," by "presence in," or by "imitation of" them), and what is the relation of one Idea with another. The "Third Man" argument is here introduced in disparagement of the Ideas, as Aristotle will later use it:[31] the relation between a particular man and the Idea man can be explained only by reference to a third "Man"; this step leads to an infinite regress. Yet Parmenides, after aiming these objections at the hypothesis of ideas, holds that knowledge is nevertheless possible only on such an hypothesis.[32]

In the realm of *physis* Plato gradually shifts the emphasis from science to theology, from astronomy to cosmology, from the Ideas to God; and to

[25] Aristotle seeks to avoid at least any such break; but he permits a break at another point, as we shall see below (p. 322).

[26] The same problem, here stated in terms of Ideas and particulars, appears in the *Timaeus* in the conception of Reason and Necessity (again a stubborn residuum not amenable to intelligence); see below, pp. 302–305. But even the *Timaeus* retains the Ideas (cf. 27d–28b; 29a; 30c; 51a–52a; A. Rivaud, Budé ed. of *Tim.* (Paris, 1925), pp. 34–36; Cherniss, "Economy," pp. 455 f.).

[27] See below, pp. 285–297.

[28] *Theaetetus* 179c–183c; 184b–186e.

[29] *Sophist* 249bc; 254c.

[30] *Sophist* 243de; 244a–245e.

[31] Aristotle, *Soph. El.* 178b36 ff. The argument had previously been used by an Eleatic in disparagement of the sensible world; cf. Burnet, *T.-P.*, 254; 259 f.

[32] *Parmenides* 134e–135c; cf. 128cd. Cf. *Philebus* 16cd.

mathematics he adds mythology. For he is seeking such a conception of causality as will include both mechanical necessity and the recognition of purpose, both fate and good. He will find it necessary to reckon also with evil.

The conception of causality is so familiar to us that we are apt to take it for granted; yet it is by no means simple or obvious. Analyzed by Aristotle, criticized by Hume and Kant, it is assumed in every branch of science. Yet the Greek philosophers who speculated so busily about the *physis* of being did not use the word "cause" (*αἰτία*) in the pre-Socratic period, except with the human association of moral responsibility.[33] It is the medical writers of the Hippocratean *corpus* who first gave currency to the term and to the idea.[34] But that this conception of what we should call "physical causation," is adequate for all purposes Plato denies in that famous passage of the *Phaedo* which is the first inquiry by any Greek into the general nature of causality; and he takes occasion frequently in later writings to oppose the empiricists, who, he believes, have not got at the root of the matter.[35] Their method is at fault in that it leads only by chance to a right opinion,[36] whereas real knowledge is attained only when it has been chained fast by a reasoned knowledge of its cause, of which it is possible to give a demonstration.[37]

It is precisely the apparently mechanical nature of the *Nous* of Anaxagoras which impelled "Socrates" to look further back for something which should explain why it is "good" that phenomena should exist as they do; Socrates is therefore represented as resorting to what he ironically describes as a makeshift,[38] in other words, to the hypothesis of the Ideas. Plato's first far-reaching explanation of causality therefore is the Ideas. But the Ideas themselves need to be examined in the light of a higher hypothesis, if we are to understand why there should be any *physis* at all, or again how the Ideas are related one to another; and that is the function of the Idea of the Good, the source both of knowledge and of being, which gives meaning to all subsidiary modes of being or activity.[39]

[33] G. Göring, *Ursache*, pp. 9; 21; Phillip H. DeLacy, "The Problem of Causation in Plato's Philosophy," *C.P.* 34 (April, 1939), pp. 97 f.; A. W. Pickard-Cambridge, "The Value of Some Ancient Greek Scientific Ideas" (Presidential Address, British Classical Association, 1937), pp. 7–29.

[34] For the medical writers, and for Thucydides, see above, pp. 268–271; for popular use, cf. Herodotus, I, 1, who in his "title page" announces that he proposes to inquire into the **αἰτίη** of the Persian Wars; Plato uses the term **αἰτία** sparingly in the earlier dialogues.

[35] *Phaedo* 96d–e; 100e–101a; cf. *Sophist* 265cd; *Timaeus* 46cd; 68e; 76d; *Laws* 889cd; 894–896.

[36] *Symp.* 202a; cf. *Theaet.* 200e; 206 cd; *Rep.* 431c.

[37] *Meno* 98a: αἰτίας λογισμῷ; *Symp.* 202a: λόγον δοῦναι; cf. *Phaedo* 76b; *Rep.* 534b.

[38] *Phaedo* 99d: δεύτερος πλοῦς. Cf. W. J. Goodrich, *C.R.* 17 (1903), pp. 381–384; 18 (1904), p. 511; N. R. Murphy, *C.Q.* 30 (1936), pp. 40–47.

[39] See Appendix 43: Idea of Good.

We have seen that Plato himself is aware of the difficulty of dealing with the relationship between Ideas and particulars except by metaphor; and the Idea of the Good he expressly declines to elaborate except by the simile of its offspring, the Sun, author of light and visibility and generation.[40] Moreover it is expressly in order to account for becoming and decay, as well as being, that the Ideas are introduced.[41] But the Ideas have had to meet the criticisms of Aristotle and of modern scholars alike on the very ground that whatever else they may explain they do not explain becoming and decay. Aristotle's criticism, put in terms of his own four-fold system of causes,[42] comes down to the charge that the Ideas, which of course are not "material" causes, are not "formal" causes, because form is immanent, while Ideas are transcendent; nor "final" causes, because the "One" (therefore presumably the Idea) is not a cause by virtue of its goodness alone; the Ideas are intended, he admits, to be "efficient causes," but should not be, since the immutable cannot produce the mutable.[43] As a matter of fact, any criticism of the Ideas expressed in terms of Aristotle's four causes is inappropriate, because the assumptions of Plato and of Aristotle as to what constitutes ultimate reality are different. For Plato, phenomena are not ultimately real; whereas for Aristotle the ultimate reality is the concrete object which comprises both form and matter.[44]

A second attempt on the part of modern scholars to interpret the Ideas as the source of all phenomena has consisted in the identification of the Ideas, or at least of the Idea of the Good, with Plato's God.[45] Now it must be supposed that Plato had some conception of a relationship between the Idea of the Good and God; but what it was he has not told us in so many words. The two conceptions play similar parts in his philosophy, as causes and as patterns of goodness. Thus the Good begot its offspring through benevolent design;[46] yet this is an exceptional remark for the *Republic*, such thoughts being reserved in general for the more imaginative *Timaeus*.[47] A decisive difference holds between the two: the Ideas are

[40] See Appendix 44: Figure of Light.

[41] *Phaedo* 95e: ὅλως γὰρ δεῖ περὶ γενέσεως καὶ φθορᾶς τὴν αἰτίαν διαπραγματεύεσθαι (from this phrase Aristotle derives the title of his own *De Generatione et Corruptione*). Cf. 101c.

[42] See below, p. 318.

[43] *Met.* 991a9–b9; 1071b14–23; *De Gen. et Corrupt.* 335b9–20; n.b. 335b18: "If the Forms are causes, why is their generating activity intermittent?"

[44] See further DeLacy, pp. 101–103.

[45] E.g. by J. Adam, *Religious Teachers*, pp. 442–459, who shows the difficulties involved in alternate hypotheses, and the consequences of accepting the identification; Nature becomes the revelation of God, and teleology ceases to be anthropocentric; the problem of evil remains, and at least a partial (moral) dualism. P. Shorey, "The Idea of Good," p. 188, dismisses the question of identification as unprofitable.

[46] *Rep.* 505a; cf. 506e; 508b; 511c; 517b.

[47] Cf. *Tim.* 29c; 32ab; 68e; Shorey, Loeb ed. *Rep.*, Vol. II, p. 102, n.a.

immutable, like the Parmenidean One, while God is living and active like a soul, or acts by means of a soul.[48] Accordingly the middle dialogues, which stress the Ideas, deal with theology only conventionally, even if in a spirit of moral reform; whereas the later dialogues stress theology, and refer to God and soul as the causes of motion, while the Ideas remain, partly for ethical, logical, and epistemological purposes, partly as God's pattern for the creation.[49] In this sense, the Good stands in Plato's thought as something still higher than God; and it is to be noted that Plato, who lectured on the Good even in his old age, never reduced his lecture to writing. Doubtless he never succeeded in effecting a final metaphysical reconciliation of the two conceptions.[50]

For the interpretation of *physis*, however, and of change or motion, subjects which increasingly engage Plato's attention in his later years, he turns from causation by the Ideas to causation by Soul.[51] Plato's earlier depreciation of motion as such has now been abandoned; whatever "completely is" must include movement, life, soul.[52] The physical world, moreover, is a "mixture," involving process into being.[53]

The regular movements of the heavenly bodies have always been for Plato, as for Greeks before and after him, and for many modern men,[54] the occasion of speculation and awe, even of veneration, leading to a conviction about the linked unity of the *cosmos* and a single master, usually

[48] *Phaedo* 80a; *Phaedrus* 246c–d. Yet the Idea of Good is "Father" (*Rep.* 506e) and "King" (509d).

[49] For a possible identification or "confusion" of the Ideas and God in *Timaeus* 29a and 29d, see below, Appendix 45.

[50] See further Burnet, *T.-P.*, pp. 169; 336–337; Taylor, *P.M.W.*, p. 289; Shorey, *Idea of Good*, p. 229; P. E. More, *Religion of Plato*, p. 41. It should be added that Plato nowhere states that "God is a soul," as both Burnet and Taylor imply; so far as the God of his later dialogues is to be identified with anything else, it is perhaps *Nous*, though that is an inference, not a conclusion based on any direct statement; see below, pp. 291–293.

[51] On the subjects discussed in the following pages, see also J. B. Skemp, *The Theory of Motion in Plato's Later Dialogues*, which has appeared since my manuscript was completed.

[52] *Sophist* (248e–249a: n.b. παντελῶς ὄν), a term hitherto used (as in *Rep.* 477a) of the Ideas, which are immutable.

[53] *Philebus* 26d: γένεσις εἰς οὐσίαν; cf. 27b: γεγενημένη οὐσία. So in *Timaeus* 35a, οὐσία is a mixture of the Same and the Other. "In other words, the mature philosophy of Plato found reality, whether intelligible or sensible, in the combination of matter and form, and not in either separately." (Burnet, *T.-P.*, pp. 331 f.) The *Timaeus* elsewhere (27d; cf. 31b) maintains the earlier view of the priority of being to becoming: cf. Taylor, *Commentary*, p. 87, and DeLacy, pp. 109 f.

[54] So George Meredith, in "Lucifer in Starlight":

On a starred night Prince Lucifer uprose . . .
He reached a middle height, and at the stars
Which are the brain of heaven, he looked, and sank.
Around the ancient track marched, rank on rank,
The army of unalterable law.

With "the brain of heaven," cf. Plato's conception of νοῦς: see below, pp. 291–293. For astronomy and theology in antiquity, see F. Cumont, *Astrology and Religion*, pp. 101–138.

not without a feeling that its orderliness provides a pattern for human conduct. Goodness, in the *Gorgias* and the *Philebus*, is due to the presence of order and measure (*τάξις, κόσμος, μετριότης, συμμετρία*) in the soul;[55] the *Republic* testifies to the effect on a philosophic mind of the contemplation of the heavens.[56] Yet merely empirical observation is disparaged by comparison with the rational comprehension of the mathematical relationships that are involved in astronomy.[57] Both observation and speculation had a part in the astronomical studies of the Academy, as of the Pythagoreans, with results of far-reaching importance.[58]

The circular motion or revolution about an axis shown by some heavenly bodies Plato regards as symbolic of the motion of what he calls the "World-Soul."[59] Yet he finds problems in the apparent departure of the planets, or of the sun's course, from the perfect circle; he therefore sets out to "save the appearances," as members of the Academy phrased the ideal of science; in other words, to explain them on the simplest hypothesis by mathematical reasoning.[60] It is certain that he abandoned the geocentric theory of the universe; probably he at last entertained the heliocentric hypothesis.[61]

For the source of the motion of the heavenly bodies Plato turns to the conception of "soul." This new interpretation of causality is for Plato a natural one, for he has already regarded soul as the ruler and orderer of the body,[62] even if the complete explanation of causality will still require the recognition of physical objects as contributory agencies or conditions.[63]

[55] *Gorg.* 504a ff.; *Phileb.* 64de.

[56] *Rep.* 500b–501c. Astronomy and the Ideas are fused: cf. 500c: **τεταγμένα ἄττα καὶ κατὰ ταὐτὰ ἀεὶ ἔχοντα**, of the heavens; and 501b, **τὸ φύσει δίκαιον . . . ἐκεῖν' αὖ τὸ ἐν τοῖς ἀνθρώποις**, of the painting of the Ideas in human characters. (In the passage just cited, n.b. *φύσει*, used of the realm of Ideas; and see below, p. 303, n. 177.) So Kant, in the conclusion of the *Critique of Practical Reason*: "Two things fill the mind with ever new and increasing admiration and awe . . .: *the starry heavens above and the moral law within*."

[57] *Rep.* 528e–530c; cf. *Philebus* 55e for the importance of mathematics for the arts; and the motto (said to have been inscribed over the door of the Academy): **μηδεὶς ἀγεωμέτρητος εἰσίτω.**

[58] It is even possible to regard the "scientist" Democritus as having marked time, by comparison with Plato, whose scientific conceptions have more in common with modern modes of thought. Cf. J. Stenzel, "Platon und Demokritos," *N. Jahrb. f. Kl. Alt.* 45 (1920), pp. 89–100.

[59] *Tim.* 36cd; 47bc; 90cd; cf. *Laws* 897e. See below, p. 291.

[60] Burnet, *T.-P.*, p. 346; cf. pp. 225–227: "Plato conceived the function of Astronomy to be the discovery of the simplest hypothesis which would account for the apparent complexity of celestial phenomena." Cf. Simplicius on Aristotle, *De Caelo*, p. 488, lines 21–24 Heiberg; Simplicius on Aristotle, *Phys.*, p. 292, lines 15–26 Diels.

[61] Theophrastus, quoted by Plutarch, *Quaest. Plat.* 1006c; cf. Burnet, *T.-P.*, pp. 347 f. Unfortunately Aristotle's authority was thrown into the opposite side of the scales, to the great damage of astronomical investigation for some two thousand years.

[62] *Phaedo* 79e–80a; 94b; 105cd; cf. *Gorg.* 504a; 465cd.

[63] See below, p. 305.

A new point of far-reaching importance is a new doctrine of the soul, not set forth in the earlier dialogues: namely that it is the ultimate source of motion, in fact the only self-moved mover, unlike other moving beings which receive their motion from without.[64] Hence soul is logically prior to body; to it must be attributed whatever of intelligence and purposiveness exists anywhere;[65] therefore also not only the motion but the order of the *physis*.[66]

The ground on which Plato discards the adequacy of mere physical causation is that it lacks any purposive element, whereas the structure of the *cosmos* reveals everywhere the fitness of details for some end or purpose. Teleology, the recognition of providence,[67] therefore plays a large part in Plato's mature philosophy. But the teleology is less naïf and anthropocentric and more cosmic than that of the Socrates whom Xenophon reports.[68] An irrational universe is inconceivable.[69]

The *Protagoras* myth has already suggested that all men are divinely and providentially endowed with their *physis* and with the possibilities of *arete*, while some men are also given the *technai*.[70] The *Politicus* myth (268e–274e) somewhat fancifully [71] attempts to account for the existence of evil through an imagined catastrophe, such as Plato's scientific contemporaries conceived as possible.[72] There are reminiscences here of the details of the Hesiodic ages, in which the golden age of Cronos gave place to worse ages,[73] and also of the "reversed evolution" of Empedocles.[74]

[64] *Phaedrus* 245c–246a; *Laws* 894b; cf. anticipations of this doctrine by Anaxagoras, (D59A99 = Arist. *De An.* 404a25); Diogenes of Apollonia (D64A20 = Arist. *De An.* 403a21 ff.); Alcmaeon of Croton (D24A12 = Arist. *De An.* 405a29 ff.); echoes of it in Cicero, *Tusc. Disp.* I, 24.

[65] *Laws* 896cd.

[66] *Laws* 897ab; cf. 903bd.

[67] *Tim.* 30bc; τὴν τοῦ θεοῦ . . . πρόνοιαν; cf. 44c. Favorinus, cited by Diog. Laert. III, 24, says that Plato was the first philosopher to refer to the θεοῦ πρόνοια. This may be true, though the conception is to be found in popular language (e.g. Herodotus III, 108). It was the Stoics, however, who first used πρόνοια, without further qualification, of a divine providence. Cf. Jebb on Sophocles, *O.T.* 978.

[68] See above, pp. 274 f.; also Diogenes of Apollonia (D 64 B 5); Xen. *Mem.* I, 4, 8 and 17; Theiler, *Naturbetrachtung*, pp. 62–82; A. Diès, *Autour de Platon*, pp. 532–545, on Plato's thorough reorganization of his predecessors' tentative arguments from design into a synoptic view of a universe created and maintained by reason; F. W. Bussell, *The School of Plato* (London, 1896), on the relations in Platonic and kindred philosophies between God, Nature, and Man, with emphasis (pp. 47–57; 79–119; 177–182; 220–22; 305–317) on teleological views.

[69] *Sophist* 248b ff.: cf. 265cd: the causation of natural objects and species ἀπό τινος αἰτίας αὐτομάτης καὶ ἄνευ διανοίας is discarded in favor of creation by a θεὸς δημιουργῶν, by θεία ἐπιστήμη, or by θεία τέχνη. Cf. *Philebus* 28e; 30ab.

[70] *Protag.* 320c–323a; see above, pp. 245 f.

[71] *Polit.* 268de.

[72] Cf. also Plato's Atlantis myth; esp. *Tim.* 22cd; 23ab; 25cd; *Critias* 112a.

[73] See above, pp. 31–33; cf. also *Laws* 712e–714a; and *Rep.* 547a.

[74] *Polit.* 271b: εἰς τἀναντία τῆς γενέσεως; D31B61. On the sources of the *Politicus* myth see further P. Frutiger, *Les Mythes de Platon*, pp. 241–244.

The myth stresses the irrationality and blindness of *physis* which is revealed when, as it is imagined, the divine helmsman who has ordered all things (273de) for a time releases his control of the helm of the ship (272e), whether through impotence or through carelessness we are not informed. Fate and inborn impulse[75] and Necessity[76] and Matter[77] therefore temporarily regain the upper hand and man degenerates, till the helmsman once more restores the cosmic regularity. But in the restored order the *cosmos* recovers its equilibrium more fully than does man, who is helpless until the gods intervene and bestow their gifts: Prometheus the gift of fire, Hephaestus and Athena the arts. On the character of even the more primitive man, before the "fall," Plato suspends judgement, being no blind admirer of the "noble savage" or of material well-being, however innocent, without the assurance of philosophy (272bd); and he is less ready than will be the Epicureans to assume that helpless men will find necessity to be the mother of invention.[78] The human ruler, at any rate, and *a fortiori* the tyrant, is inferior to the divine shepherds (271d) who had cared for men under Cronos. The answer of the *Politicus* myth to the problem of evil, then, is a mingling of several conceptions: an incomplete or intermittent control by God; the partial sway of Fate, or Necessity, or Matter; and the innate vice or weakness of man, who is largely free to work out his own salvation.[79]

But it is above all in the *Timaeus* that Plato allows his fancy to play soberly[80] with Pythagorean and Empedoclean materials in the attempt to imagine how the intelligent, benevolent, creator established the structure and processes of the *cosmos*, both in the vast framework of the universe and of the heavenly bodies and in the details of organic life, of human anatomy, physiology, and psychology. This is the work of Plato which during many centuries was considered to be his most characteristic and most important work.[81] For some centuries, before the rediscovery of the

[75] *Polit.* 272e6: εἱμαρμένη τε καὶ σύμφυτος ἐπιθυμία.

[76] *Polit.* 274a2: ἀνάγκη; cf. 262d 2–3.

[77] *Polit.* 273b4: τὸ σωματοειδές; and see below, pp. 301 f.

[78] With *Polit.* 274c: διὰ τὸ μηδεμίαν αὐτοὺς χρείαν πρότερον ἀναγκάζειν, contrast Lucretius V, 868–877; 1029; 1105–1107; 1452–1457; cf. Virgil, *Georg.* I, 145 f.

[79] For the interpretation of the *Politicus* myth see further: L. Campbell, ed. *Politicus*, pp. xxviii–xli; B. Jowett, IV, 431–435; J. Adam, ed. *Rep.*, Vol. II, pp. 293–298; J. A. Stewart, *The Myths of Plato*, pp. 173–211; A. E. Taylor, *P.M.W.*, pp. 395–397.

[80] The result is only a "likely story," a myth with a high degree of probability, *Tim.* 29cd; certainty is not of the world of becoming, but only of the immutable; "as being is to becoming, so is truth to belief" (29c).

[81] Note how largely it bulks in the epitomes of Platonism of Albinus (see below, p. 372) and of Diogenes Laertius III, 69–109, esp. 68–91; 101–105; and how it appealed to the eclectic Stoic-Platonic thinkers of the Hellenistic and Roman periods, like Cicero, who translated it. Helpful works for the study of the *Timaeus* are: L. Robin, *Études sur la Signification et la Place de la Physique dans la Philosophie de Platon* (Paris, 1919); A. E. Taylor, *A Com-*

complete works of Plato in the Renaissance, the *Timaeus* was the work of Plato that was best known (through Latin translations) to western Europe.

As in Greek mythology the Olympian gods are not supposed to have created the universe or the materials of which it consists, but rather to have succeeded to the management of a ready-made universe, so the divine artisan or Demiurge whom Plato represents in the *Timaeus* as having brought into being the *cosmos* is not conceived as having created its materials; these, as we shall see, are in part given, and will at times even offer resistance to his purpose.[82] His is the intelligence and the benevolence and providence which brings order out of chaos; he it is who takes three elements, Sameness, Otherness, and a mixture of these two, and from them creates soul, and invests it with a bodily frame, both in the *cosmos* (the "World-Soul") and in the lesser individual souls of his agents and of men.[83]

The very multiplicity of beings to whom Plato at one time or another attributes the term "god" or "divine" raises an important and difficult question: where in Plato's theology is the "God" by reason of whom Plato deserves to be called theist?[84] The Demiurge, the created universe,[85] the stars and planets,[86] the gods of popular mythology,[87] and the good souls,[88] are all called "gods," or at least "divine." Yet if God must be conceived of both as what is independent of and prior to everything else, and also as what is the cause of the good and the rational, it appears that God is not a soul. For soul has *genesis*, and is indeed created by *Nous*[89] or by the Demiurge,[90] who therefore is prior to soul.[91] Moreover, as we shall

---

*mentary on Plato's Timaeus* (London, 1928); F. M. Cornford, *Plato's Cosmology* (London and New York, 1937).

[82] *Tim.* 47e ff.; see below, pp. 302–305. On the Demiurge in general, see also Cornford, *Plato's Cosmology*, pp. 34–39, who warns against reading (with Taylor and others) "into Plato's words modern ideas that are in fact foreign to his thought," — e.g. monotheism, omnipotence, creation *ex nihilo*. On the whole those are salutary warnings; but Cornford perhaps does less than justice to the *goodness* of the Demiurge. Granted that he is a mythological, not a religious figure (an object of worship), he is the earliest philosophical expression of a creative agency who is at once powerful (though not omnipotent), rational, and good; it is no falsification of Plato's thought to see in the Demiurge a God who is the personification of *Nous*.

[83] *Tim.* 35ab. Judiciously read, Plutarch's *De Animae Procreatione in Timaeo* provides an interesting commentary on this passage; but see below, pp. 309–311.

[84] A. Diès, *Autour de Platon* (Paris, 1927), pp. 522–574, "Le Dieu de Platon," esp. pp. 555 ff.; R. Hackforth, "Plato's Theism," *C.Q.* 30 (1936), pp. 4–9.

[85] *Tim.* 34b, 92c.

[86] *Tim.* 40d.

[87] *Tim.* 40d–41a.

[88] *Laws* 897c–899b.

[89] *Philebus* 30b.

[90] *Tim.* 34c; cf. 30b.

[91] See below, p. 292, and n. 99.

see, soul is in itself neutral, capable either of good or of evil,[92] and achieves goodness through association with *Nous*.[93] There is no "one best soul" which creates all things; for the language of the *Laws*[94] implies the possible existence of many good souls, and argues that it is the "best kind of soul" that controls the regular movements of the heavenly bodies; nevertheless the monotheism of the *Timaeus* is patent. Nor is it pertinent to object that Plato is committed to the doctrine that *Nous* cannot arise apart from soul; for his statements to that effect refer only to the *cosmos*, not to its creator.[95]

In the *Philebus* (23c–30e) it is Reason (νοῦς) which is the "cause of the mingling" (αἰτία τῆς συμμίξεως, 27b9; it is also τὸ δημιουργοῦν, 27b1, or τὸ ποιοῦν, 26e7); the more mythical, personal terminology of the *Timaeus* gives the same rôle to a divine artisan, or Demiurge (ὁ ἄριστος τῶν αἰτιῶν, 29a6). In each case it is the necessary cause,[96] which brings order and soul into the world.[97] The rôle of *nous* in making cosmos of chaos naturally recalls that famous attempt of Anaxagoras to explain the creation by a similar formula, which Plato and Aristotle both found unsatisfactory; the older philosopher might now feel that he was having his vengeance for their criticism.[98] But Plato can point to the intermediary rôle which soul plays in his scheme, something more explicit than any motive power which Anaxagoras ascribed to *nous*, and something which translates reason into action; and Plato explicitly distinguishes soul (*psyche*) from the reason (*nous*) or God which creates it.[99] One is forced to the conclusion that Plato's ultimate God is viewed as the impersonal *Nous*, or in mythical terms as the personal Demiurge, both of which impart their goodness to the world through the creation of Soul.[100] What is God *in himself*? Plato will not answer directly, any more than he will describe the Idea of the Good directly,[101] but only by an image, by re-

[92] *Laws* 896d6; and see below, p. 306.

[93] *Laws* 897b.

[94] *Laws* 897c7: τὴν ἀρίστην ψυχήν; cf. 898c4; see below, pp. 310 f.

[95] *Philebus* 30c; *Tim.* 30b; cf. Hackforth, p. 7. R. G. Bury remains unconvinced on this point: see *Rev. des Études Grecques* 50 (1937), p. 317.

[96] *Philebus* 26e2–4; *Tim.* 28a 4–5.

[97] *Phileb.* 26d; 27b; 30b; 64c; *Tim.* 53b; 34c.

[98] *Philebus* 28e3: νοῦν πάντα διακοσμεῖν; cf. Laws 966e: νοῦς τὸ πᾶν διακεκοσμηκώς; Anaxagoras, as quoted in *Phaedo* 97c; νοῦς ἐστιν ὁ διακοσμῶν τε καὶ πάντων αἴτιος. The mention of Zeus, *Philebus* 30d1, recalls also the reference to Zeus by Diogenes of Apollonia (Diels 64A8).

[99] *Phileb.* 30b; *Tim.* 30b; cf. *Sophist* 249a: soul is the bearer of *nous*. Platonism, for all its apparent dualism, is a constant struggle to close the gap between contrasted aspects of reality: "Ideas," Eros, Soul, *Daimon*, Moderation, the "mixed life," grades of cognition, are some of the devices for bridging it. Cf. J. Souilhé, *La Notion Platonicienne d'Intermédiaire.*

[100] Cornford, p. 197, reaches the conclusion that "the Demiurge is to be identified with the Reason in the World-Soul." Such, too, is the point of Hackforth's article.

[101] See above, p. 286.

ferring to the regular revolution of a globe.[102] So in the *Timaeus* (28c) he declares: "As for the maker and father of this universe, to find him out is hard, and to speak of him, when one has found him, before all mankind is impossible"; and he proceeds to discuss the problem of models and likenesses. It is as if he were to reply to the question "Where are God and his goodness to be found?" with the simple answer, "In his works." Thus once more his God, *Nous*, or Reason, is both transcendent and immanent, both perfect and outgoing, unlike Aristotle's God, whose activity is confined to self-contemplation.[103] Soul, however, is not transcendent, since it operates only through *genesis* and *kinesis*. *Nous* and *Psyche* together comprise Plato's conception of God's manifestation in the *cosmos*: The Word was made Spirit and dwelt among us.

The material causes proposed by the Ionian physicists and even the *Nous* of Anaxagoras had failed to explain "*how* it is best" that so-and-so should be.[104] The *Timaeus* seeks to find this teleological explanation, by conceiving of the Demiurge as combining with intelligence and power a desire for the good, and as creating this visible universe of becoming on the pattern of the eternal and self-same.[105] The fundamental question, then, is posed: "*Why* becoming and the universe were framed by him who framed them." [106] The answer follows: "He was good, and none that is good is ever subject to any grudgingness with regard to anything; being without grudgingness, he desired all things to become as far as possible like himself. This one might most rightly accept from wise men as the sovereign source of becoming and of the *cosmos*. For God desired that all things should be good, and that nothing, so far as might be possible, should be bad." [107]

This benevolent, outgoing character of the divine Demiurge is a magnificent conception of considerable originality. Xenophanes and Parmenides have sought by negative restrictions to save their One God from any imperfection, but at the expense of reducing him to pure being, immutable and without offspring. The expurgation of the popular mythology, by Xenophanes, by Euripides, and by Plato himself, has removed from the gods a good deal that was unsavory, but has not suggested, by way of compensation, any positive content.[108] In the *Euthyphro* Socrates is represented as laying down the principle that "every blessing that we

[102] *Laws* 897d–898b.

[103] *Met.* 1074b15–35; see below, p. 322.

[104] *Phaedo* 97c–98b.

[105] *Tim.* 28c–29b.

[106] 29d: *δι' ἥντινα αἰτίαν, κτλ.*

[107] See Appendix 45: Demiurge, in *Timaeus.*

[108] Xenophanes, D 21 B 10–16; Euripides, *I.T.* 385–391; *Belleroph.* fr. 292, 7 Nauck; see above, pp. 184; 200.

enjoy is the gift of Heaven."[109] In his "Outlines of Theology" in the *Republic*[110] Plato sketches a moral expurgation of myths, forbidding the representation of the gods as evil, as lying or deceiving, or as the source of anything evil. It follows that the famous remarks of Homer attributing both good and evil to Zeus are false;[111] likewise any story about human woes inflicted by God except as remedial punishment for sin.[112] Plato is indeed the first Greek to deny explicitly the vindictiveness or jealousy of the gods.[113] The Olympian gods claim sacrifice, and do not really love men save as they receive worship from men; they are also supposed to feel *phthonos*, grudgingness or jealousy of human prosperity.[114] Even the gods of the Hesiodic Myth of the Ages and similar myths serve chiefly as symbols of good or evil tendencies, and seldom suggest a divine Providence. The Platonic Ideas may be thought to give form and meaning and value to individual beings, but not through any love of them; save for the Idea of the Good the world as we know it would never have come into being. The God of Aristotle no more loves this world than do the Epicurean gods; for the "love of the lover for the beloved" of which Aristotle conceives is all in one direction, from the creation toward the creator.[115] But the *Timaeus* seeks to fill this gap, and to conceive of God as forthgoing, allowing his perfection to flow into innumerable and endless forms of expression. The Neo-platonists will find in the emanations of the One a kindred doctrine.[116] There is more than a little justification for seeing, along with much difference, a likeness between the doctrine of the *Timaeus* and the Christian doctrine of the incarnation. "For God so loved the world that He gave His only begotten Son"; "The Word was made flesh and dwelt with us."[117] It is interesting, moreover, to observe that

[109] Plato, *Euthyphro* 14e; a remark which moves Archbishop Arethas, in the early tenth century, to refer in the margin of his beautiful manuscript of Plato to the verse: "Every good gift and every perfect gift is from above."

[110] *Rep.* 379a: τύποι περὶ θεολογίας. Adam, note *ad loc.*, regards Plato as here advancing even beyond Socrates, as well as the poets.

[111] *Il.* 24, 527–532, adapted or misquoted by Plato; see above, p. 27.

[112] *Rep.* 379d–380c.

[113] But cf. also Aeschylus, *Ag.* 750–762 (see above, p. 107); Bacchylides, XIV, 51–63 (see above, pp. 81; 83). With *Tim.* 29e, quoted above (p. 293), cf. *Phaedrus* 247a: φθόνος γὰρ ἔξω θείου χόρου ἵσταται; *Theaet.* 151cd: οὐδεὶς θεὸς δύσνους ἀνθρώποις; Aristotle, *Met.* 983a2–5. The reference (*Rep.* 451a) to the placation of Adrasteia (= Nemesis), who might bring bad luck, is hardly more than a comic aside.

[114] See above, pp. 19; 48; 74 f.; 84–88.

[115] See below, p. 318. This is the Aristotelian counterpart of the intellectual love of the Ideas portrayed in the *Symposium* and the *Phaedrus*.

[116] See below, p. 377; and for Milton, pp. 394 f.

[117] The *Timaeus*, too, relates the expression of the Word (or Reason) in an "only begotten" offspring (92c9: μονογενής). In the Hebrew account of the creation (*Genesis* 1), we are not told that Jehovah's love caused the act of creation; but after each stage He "saw that it was good." A. O. Lovejoy, *The Great Chain of Being*, pp. 49 f., sees in the fecundity

Plato's instinct has brought him to realize that if a purpose is to be found anywhere at all in the *cosmos* it must be at the very beginning. A mechanistic astronomy or biology will seek in vain to import any explanation of the origin or purpose of the universe, or of life; they cannot assimilate such alien conceptions. As a matter of fact, sensible scientists do not try to do so, realizing that this is the province of metaphysics, of theology, of myth. Plato frankly admits that his account is myth, and at the end of the *Timaeus* makes it clear that the "soul" which the Demiurge put into the world is not different from what Plato has elsewhere called the "soul of Zeus," the divine power recognized by all the pre-Socratic philosophers.[118]

The benevolence of the creator, as well as his power, is suggested by various figurative expressions. He is the "father" of the world,[119] and its "begetter";[120] he is its "master,"[121] its "king,"[122] or "ruler."[123] To the world he is as soul is to body;[124] and his activity results in the creation of the "world-soul."[125] But this doctrine leads to pantheism and an overemphasis on the immanence of the creator which Plato seems anxious to avoid; his transcendence is accordingly stressed in the figure of the "maker" (ποιητής)[126] or "artisan" (Demiurge)[127] of the universe. Here Plato stands revealed as a theist, even at the risk of representing his creator in anthropomorphic terms.

The Natural Theology of the *Timaeus* is supplemented by an important discussion in Plato's last great work, the *Laws*. In the tenth book Plato urges that a chief obstacle to morality and political security is religious heresy, whether in the form of outright atheism, the assertion that gods do not exist (889a–890a); or of the supposition that gods exist but are indifferent to men's conduct (899d–905d), as the Epicureans will later maintain; or again of the belief that the gods can be bribed (905e–907d). These three forms of heresy are mentioned in the *Republic* (365d) only to be set aside, at least for the time, so that the possibilities of a purely humanistic ethics without theological sanctions may be explored.

For the first position Plato seems in the *Laws* to blame the Ionian

---

of God here set forth by Plato a reversal of Plato's earlier championship of God's self-sufficiency.

[118] *Tim.* 92c; *Philebus* 30d; cf. *Laws* 899b (of astronomy): θεῶν . . . πλήρη πάντα, echoing Thales (Diels 11 A 22); see above, pp. 220 f. Cf. *Genesis* 1, 1: "In the beginning God created Heaven and Earth"; *John* 1, 1: "In the beginning was the Word."

[119] *Polit.* 273b; *Tim.* 28c: 41a.

[120] *Tim.* 41a.

[121] *Epist.* VI, 323d.

[122] *Phileb.* 30d; *Cratyl.* 396a.

[123] *Cratyl.* 396a; *Epist.* VI, 323d.

[124] *Phaedrus* 246cd, in a provisional tone; *Phileb.* 30ab, more confidently.

[125] *Tim.* 30ab, etc.

[126] *Tim.* 28c.

[127] *Soph.* 265b; *Polit.* 273b; *Tim.* 28a: 41a, etc.; *Laws* 892b.

physicists (889b) and certain poets (886bd; 890a) who ascribed to *physis* or to *tyche*,[128] and "not to mind (*nous*) or any god or art (*techne*)," the origin of the *cosmos*; while to *techne* (art, or design), a later, human artificial invention, or to *nomos*, and not to *physis*, they ascribe such "toys" as the fine arts, statecraft, justice, and the gods.[129] The answer to such atheism is to insist on the priority of the soul, author of the motion of the body, and on the fact that the universe manifests the working of such a soul; in a word, to insist that it reveals design rather than mere chance, and that indeed soul is really more "natural" than body.[130]

The second position may possibly be illustrated by a fragment from the *Melanippe* of Euripides;[131] can it be supposed that the gods bother to keep a record of every man's deeds? The answer is that for God to neglect man's conduct would be inconsistent with his nature. This answer is of course valid only on the assumption that God's existence has been granted, and furthermore that his nature has been subjected to such a scrutiny or moral expurgation as Xenophanes and Euripides and Plato himself have already made.[132]

The notion that the gods could be bribed is met with contempt; it implies that God would neglect his own interests in permitting the corruption of men, his own property. This argument, too, rests on the hypothesis of a reformed theology.

In his teleological arguments Plato has been anticipated at least by Diogenes and Socrates; he implies that such arguments are now commonplace. The same speaker (not Socrates) who is made to refer to them also observes that all men believe in gods.[133] The arguments from design and from the *consensus gentium* are not original with Plato. His refutation of atheism, however, and his proof of the existence of God, both in the *Timaeus* and in the *Laws*, rests less on these arguments than on the conception of soul as the prime mover. This doctrine in turn leads to the conception of the heavenly bodies as endowed with life, — in other words,

[128] But the atomists, at least, do not ascribe all to *τύχη*; e.g., Leucippus, (D 67 B 2): *οὐδὲν χρῆμα μάτην γίνεται, ἀλλὰ πάντα ἐκ λόγου τε καὶ ὑπ' ἀνάγκης*; Democritus (D 68 B 119): *ἄνθρωποι τύχης εἴδωλον ἐπλάσαντο πρόφασιν ἰδίης ἀβουλίης.*

[129] *Laws* 888e–890a; cf. Pindar, frag. 152 Bowra (and see above, p. 260); Critias, *Sisiphus*, frag. 1 Nauck (= D 88 B 25), and see above, p. 254 f.; also Euripides, *Bellerophontes*, frag. 286 Nauck, and see above, p. 217; F. Solmsen, "The Background of Plato's Theology," *T.A.P.A.* 67 (1936), pp. 210–212. See also J. Tate, "Greek for 'Atheism,'" *C.R.* 50, 1 (Feb. 1936), pp. 3–5, showing that one of the accusations against Socrates was that he disbelieved in the existence of gods, not merely that he did not worship them. On Greek atheism generally, a rather rare phenomenon, see A. B. Drachmann, *Atheism in Pagan Antiquity* (London, 1922).

[130] *Laws* 891e–892c; cf. *Tim.* 33d1: *ἐκ τέχνης.*

[131] Frag. 506, Nauck; Solmsen, "Background, etc.," p. 211.

[132] See above, pp. 293 f.

[133] *Laws*, 886a.

to the doctrine of astral gods, deserving of worship in the state which the *Laws* contemplates.[134]

The astral gods are to have a future in the Hellenistic and later ages; but it is not they whom Plato trusts to explain the ways of God to man and the divine providence.[135] Here he resorts once more to the purified gods of popular mythology, enriched by the conception of the Demiurge and his beneficent design for the universe and for every individual human soul.[136] This discrepancy, or failure to reconcile two apparently independent sources of being, will be of importance when we turn, as we now must, to Plato's treatment of the problem of evil. This problem involves for him at least three questions: the source of the good or evil in the *cosmos*; the nature of human (moral) good or evil; and the relation between man's goodness and his fortunes (the problem of divine justice).

Two facts, neither questioned by Plato, force upon him the problem of evil: the goodness of God, and the existence of evil in the world as we know it.[137] And it may be well at once to admit that the problem remains for him a paradox, not unlike the relation of his Ideas to the world of phenomena. The latter relation he discusses, as we have seen, but leaves ultimately to the language of metaphor, merely insisting on the validity of the Ideas, if being, meaning, and value exist.[138] The problem of evil he approaches also in metaphysical terms, suggesting that good and evil are correlative;[139] or that evil is somehow mere non-existence (*μὴ ὄν*), or better, is "otherness";[140] or again, that evil is absence of limit and order,[141] or, finally, that the created is inferior to the creator.[142] But in the end he leaves the problem to mythology, whether by imagining the way in which the *cosmos* was created and is governed or by depicting the fortunes of the human soul in its relation to the *cosmos*.

Two further concessions on Plato's part must be recognized. Like other Greeks, but unlike Jews and Christians, he does not suppose God, though

[134] See Appendix 46: *Epinomis*.

[135] E.g., *Laws* 900c–903b1.

[136] Solmsen, "Background, etc.," pp. 216–218, has distinguished the three avenues by which Plato approached the problems of theology: (1) the further elaboration of existing speculations on the nature of the gods, and (2) on teleology, and (3) the new doctrine of the soul as the source of motion. The same author has more recently discussed these and related matters in his *Plato's Theology* (Ithaca, 1942), esp. pp. 131–174.

[137] For a sketch of the problem, see C. M. Chilcott, "The Platonic Theory of Evil," *C.Q.* 17 (1923), pp. 27–31, a paper which escaped my notice till after I had written these pages. For the more general question, cf. P. E. More, *Religion of Plato*, pp. 232–261, (n.b. diagram, p. 234, of the treatment of the problem of evil by the schools).

[138] See above, p. 283.

[139] *Theaet.* 176a, quoted below, p. 302; cf. P. Shorey, *W.P.S.*, p. 578.

[140] *Parm.* 160c–162a; *Soph.* 237a–245e; 255a–259d.

[141] *Gorg.* 492d–494d.

[142] See below, Appendix 49.

perfectly good, to be omnipotent. God indeed does what he can to impart his goodness to the world, by the continuous ordering of given materials (neither by an original *fiat*, a creation *ex nihilo*, nor again by special interventions on behalf of individuals);[143] but that is all, and evil still remains, neither minimized nor explained away as the condition of a greater good. Thus this is not the best of all possible or conceivable worlds (as in the philosophies of St. Augustine and St. Thomas Aquinas and Leibnitz), but it is the best world possible under the conditions given. Only to that extent is Plato an optimist; to that extent therefore it may be felt that Plato fails to answer man's demand for an explanation of the ultimate "Why" of the whole universe. And if Plato fails us here, he declines also to explain why every detail of history has taken place, or to predict in detail what will occur. That, he might say, is the province of history, not of philosophy; and a "philosophy of history," an *a priori* account of all events, is in the nature of things impossible, in spite of the grandeur and the ingenuity of the *Timaeus* myth. For such a conception would ignore both that "Necessity" which even God can only incompletely "persuade" and that freedom of the human will in which Plato believes.[144]

In his "Outlines of Theology,"[145] the pattern which must guide those who are to educate the young citizens of his Republic, Plato affirms both of the facts which will occasion the paradox of evil: the goodness of God, and the fact of evil. God is good, and not the cause of anything evil; "but for mankind he is the cause of few things, but of many things not the cause. For good things are far fewer with us than evil, and for the good we must assume no other cause than God, but the cause of evil we must look for in other things and not in God."[146] This is the first distinct statement in Greek literature of the problem of evil, which hitherto has been only implicit.[147] The affirmation of divine goodness and freedom from responsibility from evil will be often echoed.[148]

What is more, Plato, like Pindar[149] and like Socrates,[150] frequently

[143] Unless θεία μοῖρα (τύχη) be so regarded; see below, pp. 299 f.; Appendix 49.

[144] For further salutary cautions, from different points of view, cf. D. Morrison, "The Treatment of History by Philosophers," *Proceedings of Aristotelian Society*, N.S. 14 (London, 1914), pp. 291–321; A. W. Pickard-Cambridge (cited above, p. 285, n. 33); both stress the danger of abstracting portions of a whole and treating them as complete explanations of the whole, and in particular of ignoring the personality or will of the individual. See below, pp. 306 f.

[145] See above, p. 294.

[146] *Rep.* 379c; cf. Proclus *ad loc.*, Vol. II, pp. 27–41 Kroll.

[147] See Index, *s.v.* Evil, problem of.

[148] Cf. *Rep.* 617e; see below, p. 315; *Tim.* 41ab; 42d; *Laws* 900e; 904a.

[149] For Pindar, see above, pp. 72 f.; for Aristotle's reference to this popular conception, see below, p. 324.

[150] Xen. *Mem.* II, 3, 18: θείᾳ μοίρᾳ; see above, p. 272; cf. also the Socratic θεῖον τι καὶ δαιμόνιον (Plato, *Apol.* 31cd); see above, p. 274.

ascribes, seriously or playfully, to "a divine dispensation" or "a divine chance" (*θεία φύσις*, or *θεία μοῖρα*, or *θεία τύχη*) whatever unexpected agency or coincidence [151] may from time to time seem to save men's weakness or folly or vice from bringing about the sad consequences that might be expected,[152] tempering, as it were, the wind to the shorn lamb. Many Greeks in fact piously ascribe good luck to *Agathe Tyche*, whose name they ejaculate when an issue hangs in the balance,[153] and to whom, sometimes in association with *Agathos Daimon*, they in time give a cult. Plato's use of terms varies according to his emphasis. Sometimes he stresses the fact that certain precious things *are*, after all, given to man; here he tends to speak of *physis*: sometimes the fact that for many a narrow escape man can thank nothing less than the "grace of God" (either *moira* or *tyche*): or, again, he will point to the fact that such miracles are nothing that man could count on or foresee; here it is *tyche*. According to circumstances, then, one may be either grateful for a "divine dispensation" or regretful for its precariousness; certainly it is better than nothing, when it appears, but it seems to bear no relation to man's calculations, and little relation to his deserts. Just as "right opinion," which may happen to be right, but which cannot justify itself rationally, is *ipso facto* inferior to knowledge, and as "popular virtue," utilitarian or habitual or drilled into one by one's betters, is inferior to that "philosophic virtue" which is derived from real knowledge of the good, so "divine dispensations" fall something short of perfection, however much they may be regarded as marks of divine goodness and providence.[154] One feels here the survival in Plato of the Socratic optimism and teleology, which holds that somehow all must be for the best, together with a deepening sense of the narrow margin by which the good prevails.

Chance uncontrolled by reason, mere *tyche*, is for Plato at best of dubious value, and may be a cause of evil. Yet he is aware of its potency in the *cosmos*, as the ally of *ananke*;[155] and he realizes that it may even conspire, though blindly, to make possible what is actually good. In the *Republic*, Plato makes the question of the possibility of the ideal state becoming a reality turn on the possibility of the philosophical and the political power being united in the same person,—an off chance, yet a barely possible

[151] Cf. *Tim.* 25e: δαιμονίως ἔκ τινος τύχης οὐκ ἀπὸ σκοποῦ. The result of the coincidence is (ironically) described as miraculous, just what a god might have bestowed; actually, Plato is manipulating the conversation ἀπὸ σκοποῦ so that the convergence of two themes may *appear* accidental.

[152] Cf. J. R. Lowell, *The Present Crisis*: "behind the dim unknown, | Standeth God within the shadow, keeping watch above his own."

[153] E.g., *Tim.* 26e.

[154] See Appendix 47: Θεία Μοῖρα.

[155] Cf. *Rep.* 499b5: ἀνάγκη τις ἐκ τύχης.

one.[156] This hypothesis involves the fortunate appearance of the right kind of human nature, a matter of *physis*,[157] and no less the fortunate environment in which, like a plant, it is to be fostered; this is a matter of nurture, or *trophe*.[158] The happy combination is very precarious, and Plato harps on the vocabulary of *tyche* as he calls attention to the dangers that beset the tender plant;[159] in fact only such a special stroke of fortune will avail to save it as might be called "divine."[160] Yet it is rash to assume that such a consummation is absolutely impossible, however difficult it may be to bring it to full fruition: "all noble things are difficult," as the Greek proverb has it.[161]

Plato's own attempt, reluctantly undertaken, to realize in Syracuse such a consummation failed, as we perceive, through a combination of circumstances, among them the weak *physis* of the young tyrant Dionysius and the murder of his uncle, the philosophically minded Dion. If at least some of the Platonic *Epistles* are genuine, we have a striking expression of the way in which Plato viewed these tragic events. He alludes to the conviction which he has expressed before his first visit to Sicily, that "the human race will not find respite from evils until through some divine dispensation (*moira*) either philosophers gain political power or statesmen become real philosophers."[162] As one reads the epistles that deal with these events, one is struck by the constant references to *tyche*, whether good or evil, and by the author's evident hesitancy at times in deciding whether to apportion the responsibility to human agencies, to mere luck, or to a divine dispensation.[163]

If the goodness of God be thus unquestioned by Plato, and the fact of evil be removed from God's responsibility, how does Plato conceive of the

[156] *Rep.* 473cd; n.b. 473c: *ἑνὸς . . . μεταβαλόντος, . . . οὐ μέντοι σμικροῦ γε οὐδὲ ῥᾳδίου, δυνατοῦ δέ*; cf. 491ab: *ὀλιγάκις ἐν ἀνθρώποις φύεσθαι καὶ ὀλίγας*; 496a: *πανσμίκρον*; 503b: *ὀλίγοι . . . ὀλιγάκις*; 503d1: *σπάνιον*.

[157] N.b. the emphasis on the *physis* of the philosopher, *Rep.* 490d; cf. 367e6; and *passim*; cf. *Tim.* 17c–18a.

[158] *Rep.* 491d–492a; cf. *Tim.* 18ab; 20a1; 20a7 (*physis* and *trophe*). The terms are of course medical, and invite comparison with the Hippocratean writings and with Thucydides (see above, pp. 268 f.).

[159] *Rep.* 491d2: *τὸ μὴ τυχόν*; 491e2: *τυχούσας*; 492a2: *τύχῃ*; 492a5: *ἐὰν μή τις . . . βοηθήσας θεῶν τύχῃ*; 495b5: *τύχωσι*; 495d4; 495e2; 497a: *μὴ τυχὼν πολιτείας προσηκούσης*.

[160] *Rep.* 492e: *θεῖον ἦθος* contrasted with *ἀνθρώπειον ἦθος* (cf. 497bc); 499c1: *ἔκ τινος θείας ἐπιπνοίας*; *Rep.* 592a8: *ἐὰν μὴ θεία τις συμβῇ τύχη*; cf. *Meno* 94b, 99cd, on statesmen described ironically as *θεῖοι*; cf. *Gorg.* 454c–454e, and above, p. 256; but *Laws* 951b, more seriously; in any case, one cannot bank on their appearance. Cf. also *Laws* 710cd; 875cd.

[161] *Rep.* 473c: *δυνατοῦ*; cf. 499cd; 502ac; 497d10: *τὰ καλὰ . . . χαλεπά*; cf. 502c6–7, *et passim*.

[162] *Epist.* VII 326ab; cf. *Rep.* 473c (but n.b. in the epistle the addition of *ἔκ τινος μοίρας θείας*). The reference may be to the famous passage in the *Republic*, if the fifth book was written as early as 388 B.C.; more probably to some oral discussion.

[163] See Appendix 48: Θεία Τύχη.

origin of evil, whether cosmic or moral, and the question of divine justice to the individual? It is idle to seek in Plato for a single solution of these problems. There are in fact two solutions, and to speak of either as "Platonic" and of the other as "un-Platonic" means a failure to recognize essential Platonism.[164]

The simplest solution of the problem is an absolute dualism of soul and body, mind and matter; good comes from soul or mind, evil from body or matter. Such a solution is often suggested by Plato. In the *Phaedo*, the *Symposium*, and the *Phaedrus*, an Orphic emphasis on the importance of the soul and its sad plight when lodged in the prison-house of the body is the basis of the asceticism, of the argument for the immortality of the soul, and of the conception of philosophy as a delivery of the soul from the body.[165] Only the rational part of the soul is really divine,[166] and may be corrupted by the accidents of man's bodily state.[167] This simple conception Plato elaborates in the *Politicus* myth, as we have seen,[168] by connecting an imagined "fall of man" with a temporary neglect on the part of the divine helmsman and the resurgence of the pre-existing and disorderly materials of the world thereby permitted; thus "Fate and inborn impulse" once more get the upper hand.[169]

These are "bodily" sources of evil; but we shall not be false to Plato's

[164] So the second century Platonist Maximus of Tyre asks, *Philosophoumena*, XLI, ivb, "What is the cause of evil (ἀτασθαλίης αἰτία)?" and rightly replies that it is twofold, to be traced both to matter and to soul: διττὴ δὲ αὕτη, ἡ μὲν ὕλης πάθος, ἡ δὲ ψυχῆς ἐξουσία. Taylor's statement that the ascription of evil to matter is "quite un-Platonic" (*Commentary on Timaeus*, p. 117; cf. his *P.M.W.*, p. 492) is criticized by H. B. Hoffleit, "An Un-Platonic Theory of Evil in Plato," *A. J. P.*, 58 (1937), pp. 45–58. On the error committed by Plutarch, who interpreted Plato as imputing evil to an evil World-Soul, see below, pp. 309–311.

[165] *Phaedo*, esp. 63e–68b; 81c–83e; *Symp.* 207c–212a; *Phaedrus*, 245c–249d. The positive counterpart to asceticism is "becoming like God," *Theaet.* 176a, cited below, p. 302. See also Adam, *R. T.*, pp. 375–387; G. Entz, *Pessimismus und Weltflucht bei Platon* (Tübingen, 1911).

[166] *Phaed.* 79a; 80ab; cf. *Rep.* 518c; 540a; 611e; *Tim.* 41b–42a; *Laws* 899d.

[167] *Cratyl.* 403e–404a; cf. *Tim.* 86b; see below, p. 306; *Protag.* 326b; *Rep.* 546a: γενομένῳ παντὶ φθορά ἐστιν, κτλ.; cf. Thuc. II, 64 (Pericles on the tendency of all things to "wax and wane": πάντα γὰρ πέφυκε καὶ ἐλασσοῦσθαι); *Rep.* 611cd (in this life we behold the soul marred by association with the body). In the Orphic myth of Dionysus the evil in man is traced to man's half-Titanic origin; see above, pp. 59 f.

[168] See above, p. 290.

[169] *Pol.* 272e: τότε δὲ δὴ κόσμον πάλιν ἀνέστρεφεν εἱμαρμένη τε καὶ σύμφυτος ἐπιθυμία. For the primordial "bodily" source of evil cf. 269d: σώματος . . . φύσις; 273b: τὸ σωματοειδές. These stubborn and disorderly forces are conceived in the *Politicus* myth as regaining their power only in that part of the cycle in which God has retired from the helm; whereas in the *Timaeus* myth, as we shall see, the corresponding force (ἀνάγκη) is a permanent recalcitrant accessory of the divine power. The element of time in both dialogues is part of the myth, as Proclus saw; *chaos* is not something prior to *cosmos*, or alternating with it, but is what is present at all times, except so far as Reason prevails (and it never prevails altogether); leave Reason out, and *chaos* is what is left. Cf. Cornford, Plato's *Cosmology*, pp. 206–210.

meaning if we regard them as falling under a larger conception, which we may call that of "matter." The usual later Greek philosophic expression for matter, *hyle*, so common in Aristotle, is hardly to be found in Plato in this sense.[170] But Plato constantly, though in different terms, conjures up a sense of that inert, negative, imperfect kind of being which is opposed to mind or soul, to purpose or good, and which as such is a source of evil, or is indeed evil itself. Without it, soul cannot achieve its ends, for soul must have something to work upon; but matter alone, unformed and uncontrolled, is of no value, and seems to be imperfectly obedient, or even to offer resistance to the good offices of soul. In either case it is evil.[171]

In the spirit of Pythagorean mathematics, Plato finds the relation of pleasure and the good to turn on the relation between limit and the unlimited, terms which the Pythagoreans equated with good and evil respectively.[172] Here is a preliminary study, as it were, of that opposition between the One and the Duality of the Great and Small, or the Indeterminate Dyad, which Aristotle says that Plato taught in the Academy, and which Aristotle asserts that Plato held to be the causes, respectively, of good and of evil.[173]

The stubbornly resistant character of this negative substratum is more explicitly named "necessity." "It is not possible that evils should cease to be, for it is necessary (*ἀνάγκη*) that something should always exist contrary to the good. Nor can they have their seat among the gods, but of necessity (*ἐξ ἀνάγκης*) they haunt mortal nature and this region of ours. Wherefore we should seek to escape hence to that other world as speedily as we may; and the way of escape is by becoming like to God so far as we can; and the becoming like is becoming just and holy by taking thought." [174]

On necessity (*ἀνάγκη*) as the antithesis to the good Plato rings changes in a variety of senses. It may be simple physical compulsion.[175] Our appetites may be divided into two categories: those "necessary" appetites which we either cannot suppress or the satisfaction of which is beneficial, both of which our nature requires us (*ἡμῶν τῇ φύσει ἀνάγκη*) to seek to satisfy; and those "unnecessary" appetites which can be suppressed, or

[170] In *Tim.* 69a6, ὕλη includes both "divine" and "necessary" causes. "*Timaeus Locrus*" (a later imitation), characteristically *does* use ὕλα of "matter." Cf. A. Rivaud, *Le Problème du Devenir*, pp. 2; 275–276; 285–315.

[171] Cf. Rivaud, pp. 316–353.

[172] *Phileb.* 13b–18d; for the Pythagoreans, see Appendix 28.

[173] *Met.* 988a8–16. For analogies with Empedocles, cf. *Met.* 984b32 (= D31A39).

[174] *Theaet.* 176a; the opposite movement of human degeneration, caused by sinfulness, is impressively described by stages in books VIII and IX of the *Republic*.

[175] *Gorgias* 447a: cf. schol. *ad loc.*, from Olympiodorus; *Rep.* 347c1: *ἀνάγκην . . . καὶ ζημίαν*. Cf. 500d; *Laws* 818b (a criticism of the popular saying that the gods themselves cannot fight against *Ananke*).

which are harmful.[176] The "necessary," then, is not always evil; it may be merely the *condicio sine qua non* of the attainment of good; it is the confession of a limitation in our natures, or in the nature of all being.[177] Plato is fond of qualifying a general assertion by a glancing allusion to such a limitation. Thus, for example, we should be concerned with bodily matters only so far as is absolutely necessary.[178] Hence it is commonplace in Plato to refer to an inevitable occurrence, or to a logical conclusion which forces itself upon one, as "necessity."[179] The definition of the nature of the true philosopher is set forth "as it must of necessity be."[180] Here the necessary comes close to the rational; but even so, there is a note of reluctance at yielding to such compulsion; one does not give in to *ananke* more than one must; a young man who is influenced by his environment more than is necessary perforce yields to false standards.[181] Plato is never weary of drawing the antithesis between this dead-weight of necessity and the spontaneous, deliberately sought good; the necessary is what one puts up with, *faute de mieux*.[182]

Plato's resort to matter (conceived as body or as necessity), so far as we have yet considered it, has been offered by him chiefly as his explanation of moral evil, though it has also had a larger bearing, particularly in the *Philebus* and the *Politicus*. It is in the *Timaeus* that Plato makes his most determined effort to represent the origin of cosmic good and evil. Here the dualism is complete. God, the Demiurge, Providence, *Nous*, soul, represent the living, intelligent, purposeful source and agencies of good; and the resistance to the divine act of creation comes from the blind, inert, recalcitrance of "necessity" or matter. The dualism reflects perhaps the Pythagorean coloring of much of the argument; but the choice of terms may owe something also to Anaxagoras, who also has tried to describe the *cosmos* as the ordering of primordial *chaos*. Wishing to find a teleological explanation of *physis*, and noting that such powers as *Ananke* and *Heimarmene* have hitherto been generally conceived as hostile to man, he has resorted to *Nous* as the reason of things being well disposed.[183] So

[176] *Rep.* 558de.

[177] Rep. 597c: *ὁ μὲν δὴ θεός, εἴτε οὐκ ἐβούλετο εἴτε τις ἀνάγκη ἐπῆν μὴ πλέον ἢ μίαν ἐν τῇ φύσει ἀπεργάσασθαι αὐτὸν κλίνην, οὕτως ἐποίησεν μίαν μόνον αὐτὴν ἐκείνην ὃ ἔστιν κλίνη.* The uniqueness of each Idea (supported in the sequel by the *τρίτος ἄνθρωπος* argument) is thus referred to God's will, or alternatively to the *ananke* to which even God is subject. In this passage, 597b–598a, n.b. the repeated use of *φύσις* as the equivalent of the realm of Ideas; cf. also 501b, and see above, p. 288, n. 56.

[178] *Phaedo* 64e: *καθ' ὅσον μὴ πολλὴ ἀνάγκη.* Cf. *Rep.* 383c: *καθ' ὅσον ἀνθρώπῳ ἐπὶ πλεῖστον οἷόν τε.*

[179] *Rep.* 495e2; *Tim.* 28c3: *ἀνάγκη*; *Rep.* 492d2, 496a4, *et passim*: *πολλὴ ἀνάγκη.*

[180] *Rep.* 490d5–6: *ἐξ ἀνάγκης*; see my note, *C. P.* 22 (1927), pp. 220 f.

[181] *Rep.* 494d: *πέρα τῶν ἀναγκαίων, ἡ Διομηδεία λεγομένη ἀνάγκη, κτλ.*

[182] *Rep.* 347cd; 493c; 358c; 540b; *Laws* 628cd; cf. 858a.

[183] Cf. *H.S.C.P.* 47 (1936), pp. 118–123; and Göring, p. 8.

Plato, too, opposes God's will and goodness to the works of nature, *Nous* to *Ananke*.

After dealing at length with the creation in terms of the divine purpose,[184] Plato pauses to remark: "Now what we have said thus far, save for a few things, has displayed the creations of Reason (*Nous*); but our discourse must also set by their side the effects of Necessity (*Ananke*). For the generation of this world of ours came about from a combination of Necessity with Reason, but Reason overruled Necessity by persuading her to conduct most of the effects to the best issue; thus, then, was this universe compacted in the beginning by the victory of reasonable persuasion over necessity. Wherefore if one would tell the tale of the making truly, one must bring the errant cause (πλανωμένη αἰτία) also into the story, so far as its nature permits."[185] And Plato makes a fresh attack on his account of the creation, manipulating Empedoclean "elements" and Pythagorean geometry to show how the *cosmos* was conditioned by matter, space, and form, — in a word, by Necessity.

The *Ananke* of the *Timaeus* is not the goddess *Ananke* who "holds lots" and governs all things in the poem of Parmenides,[186] nor the goddess *Ananke* who in the Myth of Er presides over the destinies of the cosmos and of individual souls;[187] for that goddess, as befits her Pythagorean and Orphic background, symbolizes divine intelligence and providence, as well as power.[188] Nor is the *Ananke* of the *Timaeus* any longer, as often elsewhere in Plato, a logical necessity, a scientific law;[189] nor is it, like the Necessity of the Stoics, equivalent to Reason, Providence, *Fatum*.[190] Whatever in the *Timaeus* can be reduced to law or uniform sequence, and whatever is providential, is due to *Nous*. That is why *Ananke* is called an "errant" cause, — errant in that we cannot see in it any purpose;[191] it is what Aristotle would call accidental or contingent.[192] It is one of the reasons, as we have seen, why a complete science, a complete philosophy of history, is impossible,[193] and why myth is often appropriate. So the Creator, seeking to make the creation as nearly as possible like its eternal model, has created time, the "moving image of eternity."[194] Moreover

[184] *Tim.* 27d–47e.

[185] *Tim.* 47e–48a; cf. the important recapitulation, 68e–69a.

[186] D28A37.

[187] *Rep.* 614c–621d; see below, pp. 314–316.

[188] Cf. Proclus on *Rep.*, Vol. II, pp. 204–208 Kroll.

[189] See above, p. 303.

[190] Cf. Horace, *Odes* I, 35.

[191] Cf. *Tim.* 69b; ὅσον μὴ τύχῃ.

[192] κατὰ συμβεβηκός. See below, p. 321.

[193] Another reason is that *a priori* history inevitably omits the rôle of personality or will. See above, p. 298.

[194] *Tim.* 37d.

by a strange "bastard" kind of reasoning we deduce from the consideration of changing phenomena a conception of the unchanged, indeterminate "receptacle" or "foster mother" in which phenomena take place,—in other words, of what we call "space."[195] This is another of the stubborn data of experience which Plato conceives as "necessary."

The creation, then, is an amendment, by the introduction of a benevolent purpose, to the primordial rule of Nature. The purpose cannot be carried out in a void, or without materials; it would be idle to suppose otherwise. The bird and the aviator can soar only because the air resists their wings; the painter's visions must be embodied in pigments, and in spatial relations; even the musician's conceptions have no validity except in a temporal sequence. *Nous*, in other words, must "persuade" *Ananke*.[196] But she can persuade *Ananke* only imperfectly;[197] that is, there is a residuum of "brute fact" in the world that cannot be rationalized. *Ananke*, being itself without purpose, is the negative substratum of phenomena;[198] in itself indeterminate, it is essential for all determination. Even the work of Reason, which is the true cause of becoming, requires the coöperation of secondary or contributory causes (συναίτια), which must not be confused with the true cause; they are, as we might say, the mechanical conditions of locomotion, vision, and so forth, and unless guided by Reason can only accidentally achieve such effects.[199] Finally, apart from Plato's delimitation of the power of the Creator, a concession to the intractability of his materials, we must also recognize another element, inconsistent with Plato's scheme, which he perhaps does not himself recognize, or which he perhaps would not trouble to explain, since his whole account is a myth. Although Plato represents the Demiurge as creating soul expressly in order to account for the introduction of motion into what would otherwise be without motion, he also represents a state of affairs as existing (logically, we must suppose, rather than in time) prior to the operations of the Demiurge, in which the visible world was moving at random and without order,[200] and which therefore had to be reduced to order.

For one who is busy with the conception of a good and divine Creator building the *cosmos* it is natural to ascribe whatever of imperfection and evil there may be to the material substratum. But it is not the only conceivable explanation of evil. Indeed, when one is busy with a different order of problems, particularly with moral problems, it is as natural to find good and evil in the soul of the individual. This, in fact, is Plato's

[195] *Tim.* 48e–52c.
[196] *Tim.* 48a.
[197] See Appendix 49: Finite God of *Timaeus*.
[198] Cf. στέρησις in Aristotle, *Phys.* 192a3 ff.; 209b11 ff.
[199] See Appendix 50: Secondary Causes in *Timaeus*.
[200] *Tim.* 30a. Aristotle calls attention to the inconsistency, *De Caelo* 300b 18.

tendency in the "Socratic" dialogues.[201] Moreover the tripartite psychology of the *Republic* and of the *Phaedrus* myth (with its charioteer driving two ill-matched steeds) is based on the possibility of a moral conflict, which points to a higher and a lower self, a dualism of the soul; the good man is he in whom the higher rules, and the result is "self-mastery,"[202] a state of moral health or harmony which is justice. In spite of the unity and individuality of the soul, then, Plato recognizes the fact that the soul may be the cause either of good or of evil;[203] even for evil ends, some internal consistency or self-control, some sort of *arete*, is demanded.[204] In fact the worst men are simply the perversions of the best natures.[205] Though the soul may be marred by its association with the body and by its environment,[206] only its own evil, which is injustice, can really injure it; yet even this cannot actually destroy it, since it is immortal.[207]

The autonomy of the soul implies the freedom of the will. This conception, in fact, is implicit in the earlier dialogues, in which the several virtues are analyzed, as well as in the psychology of the *Republic*, which explains man's self-mastery. It will be even more clearly defined in the Myth of Er[208] and in the account, in the *Timaeus*, of the creation of men's souls, which are to prosper or suffer according to their actions.[209] Later in the *Timaeus* (86b–87c), to be sure, Plato suggests that to a certain extent disease in the soul (vice or folly) may be the product of evil heredity, bodily habit, and social environment. Nevertheless even here Plato goes further than do most "behaviorists" in recognizing a clear distinction between good and evil, and in suggesting the possibility of overcoming evil by the proper care of the soul, our God-given guardian spirit (*daimon*) that lifts us toward heaven which is our home, like plants whose roots are not in earth but in heaven.[210] Freedom of the will is even more explicitly

[201] E.g., *Lysis* 220e; cf. also *Phileb.* 35d.

[202] *Rep.* 430e: *κρείττω αὑτοῦ*; cf. *Gorg.* 491d; *Laws* 726a. The part of Plato's criticism of contemporary poetry that is based on psychological grounds (*Rep.* 602c–605c) accuses poetry of making the momentary emotion supreme at the expense of the reason.

[203] *Rep.* 435c–441c; cf. *Laws* 904a: *ἐμψύχους οὔσας τὰς πράξεις ἁπάσας καὶ πολλὴν μὲν ἀρετὴν ἐν αὐταῖς οὖσαν, πολλὴν δὲ κακίαν.*

[204] *Rep.* 352c: *οἵ γε παμπόνηροι . . . πράττειν ἀδύνατοι*; cf. *Laws* 626cd; and Aristotle, *Pol.* 1255a16, on the contradictory nature, the weakness, of evil.

[205] *Rep.* 490e–495b: "*corruptio optimi pessima.*"

[206] *Rep.* 611cd; see above, p. 301.

[207] *Rep.* 608d–611a.

[208] See below, pp. 314–316.

[209] *Timaeus* 42bc; see below, pp. 308 f.

[210] *Tim.* 87c–90d. Taylor, *Commentary*, pp. 610–620, holds that this passage is inconsistent with the teaching of Socrates, with Platonism, and with the brand of Pythagoreanism which Plato elsewhere ascribes to Timaeus; he suggests that it may be merely Plato's record of a current medical theory. Cornford, *Plato's Cosmology*, pp. 343–349, finds in the passage not sheer determinism but a recognition, *inter alia*, of physical factors in moral health or disease.

upheld in an impressive passage in the *Laws* bespeaking honor for the soul, which ranks second only to God; honor is shown neither when one is prone to self-indulgence nor "when a man thinks that he himself is not responsible for his various sins and the many and great evils of his life, but holds others responsible and always excepts himself as guiltless."[211]

Why, then, should a man who is captain of his soul ever be guilty of evil? The Socratic identification of virtue with knowledge requires vice to be some sort of ignorance. Plato, too, holds that "no man willingly sins."[212] If then he sins, it is because of a mistaken conception of what is good, either through simple ignorance of essential facts (ἄγνοια), or through a deeper ignorance in the soul (ἀμάθια), a moral blindness, the very opposite of the Socratic agnosticism, which is the recognition of one's own limitations. Worst of all is that self-delusion, born of self-love, which makes man the victim of flattery and cuts him off from true education, the turning of the soul to the light. "The greatest evil of all is one which in the souls of most men is innate, and which every man excuses in himself, and so has no way of escaping."[213] How men's eyes may be opened, and how they may be brought to knowledge of the truth, both intellectual and moral, Plato suggests in the Parable of the Cave.[214]

In the *Republic* Plato is thinking of the individual soul. In the *Timaeus* his Demiurge invests the World-Soul with a bodily frame; but he also creates the souls of individuals, both those of the inferior *daimones* and the gods of mythology (39e–40d) and those of human beings. The created gods his goodness will not suffer to die (41a), and he presently uses them as his agents in the creation of men: he creates men's souls out of the same materials of which he composed the soul of the universe, though in a second or third blending (41d), and shows them the laws of their destiny,[215] and gives them all the same "first birth" (41e3–4); and when they are "of necessity"[216] implanted in bodies, they are "necessarily"[217] subject to the same natural sensibility to violent impressions and emotions (42a5–6). All men are created equal, as it were. Then, however, they experience different careers according as they master these emotions or are

[211] *Laws* 727bc; cf. 861a–864c; 903d–904c (cited below, p. 313); and 728cd: "the soul is the possession of a man above all adapted by nature to flee evil and to pursue and capture the supreme good."

[212] *Laws* 731c: πᾶς ὁ ἄδικος οὐχ ἑκὼν ἄδικος; cf. 860d: οἱ κακοὶ πάντες εἰς πάντα εἰσὶν ἄκοντες κακοί; see also above, pp. 256 f.; 274; and below, p. 328.

[213] *Laws* 731d–732a; cf. *Rep.* 382ab, on the "lie in the soul." On this whole subject see the penetrating discussion of P. E. More, *Religion of Plato*, pp. 242–261.

[214] *Rep.* 514a–518b.

[215] *Tim.* 41e2–3: νόμους τοὺς εἱμαρμένους; cf. *Laws* 904c: κατὰ τὴν τῆς εἱμαρμένης τάξιν καὶ νόμον; see below, p. 313.

[216] *Tim.* 42a3–4: ἐξ ἀνάγκης; n.b. the recurrent references to Necessity in this sentence and in the parallel passage, 69cd, quoted in part below, p. 308, n. 223.

[217] *Tim.* 42a5: ἀναγκαῖον.

mastered by them; and they experience metempsychosis, with a chance of winning an ultimate happiness (42bc). Here is freedom of the will, and a prospect of individuality. The Demiurge has created the immortal element in men's souls, and has promulgated the ordinances governing their careers "so that he may be guiltless of their several wickednesses thereafter."[218] The "weaving of mortality upon immortality" (41d1–2),—the creation of mortal bodies and of the mortal parts of the souls,[219]—is now delegated to the new gods, the "children" of the Demiurge, "to fashion and rule over all that must yet befall a human soul, with whatsoever is incidental to these tasks, and to govern and guide the mortal creature to the best of their powers, save in so far as it should be a cause of evil to itself" (42de). Then the Demiurge rests (like Jehovah after the Creation, and like the God of the *Politicus* myth, who retires to his watchtower),[220] while his "children" do his bidding.[221]

The conception of a partly delegated creation is certainly introduced to save the divine Demiurge from responsibility for presiding over all the contingencies involved in the world of "Necessity," and in particular for the creation of human bodies, which are destructible. These matters are stressed more later (69d ff.); but we must not overlook the fact that the Demiurge himself contemplates the "necessary" housing of the soul in the body;[222] and it is this incorporation which subjects the soul to great tides of emotion, to "dread and inevitable passions" and a precarious life, unless it be rightly nurtured and educated.[223] The details may be delegated, but the initial responsibility belongs to the Demiurge, whose act alone makes possible both moral good and moral evil. As in the Myth of Er, God is blameless of man's evil deeds, for man has freedom of the will; even the children of the Demiurge cannot save men from such evils as

[218] *Tim.* 42d: ἵνα τῆς ἔπειτα εἴη κακίας ἑκάστων ἀναίτιος; cf. *Rep.* 617e: θεὸς ἀναίτιος; and see below, p. 315, and n. 272.

[219] *Tim.* 69c; see below, n. 223. These "mortal parts of the soul" correspond to θυμός and ἐπιθυμία in the psychology of the *Republic*, or to the two steeds in the *Phaedrus* myth (see above, p. 306). W. F. R. Hardie, *A Study in Plato* (Oxford, 1936), pp. 141–146, argues that θυμός in the psychology of the *Republic* is introduced only because of an ambiguity in the highest part of the soul, which is both morally active and (as if disembodied) speculative. But the moral agent, it may be said in reply, needs a nervous system, as a government needs a police force. See further, A. E. Taylor, *P.M.W.*, pp. 281 f.: Plato is telling "about rival springs of action, and the decline, as represented in the *Republic*, has no reference to anything but action and '*active* principles,' or 'determining motives.' "

[220] *Polit.* 272e.

[221] *Tim.* 42e; cf. 69ad, recapitulating the present passage as an introduction to the detailed story of the activity of the "children," which now takes into account the secondary causes.

[222] *Tim.* 42a; see above, p. 307, and n. 216.

[223] *Tim.* 42ae; 43a–44c; cf. 69c: ἄλλο τε εἶδος . . . ψυχῆς προσῳκοδόμουν τὸ θνητόν, δεῖνα καὶ ἀναγκαῖα ἐν ἑαυτῷ παθήματα ἔχον . . . αἰσθήσει δὲ ἀλόγῳ καὶ ἐπιχειρητῇ παντὸς ἔρωτι συγκερασάμενοι ταῦτα, ἀναγκαίως τὸ θνῆτον γένος συνέθεσαν.

they bring upon themselves;[224] the source of moral evil, as of good, is the soul.

What, then, once more, of cosmic good and evil, if the soul be the only source of motion? The explanation of motion by the Good and the Ideas suggested in the *Phaedo,* which is not myth, was only quasi-teleological; it observed that natural events seem to point to a purposive mind. In the mythical parts of the *Timaeus* and the *Laws*, the teleology becomes explicit; the regularity of the heavens is not regarded as proceeding "as if" planned by a mind, but as uncontrovertible evidence of a divine Creator.[225] The agency of the divine Creator (Mind) in producing motion is soul; since he is good, the World-Soul is good.[226] In the *Laws*, thinking of the part played by soul in the *cosmos*, and remembering its priority to body, Plato remarks: "Then the properties and affections of soul will be antecedent to those of body. . . . Therefore we must further admit that soul is the cause of goodness in things and of evil, of beauty and ugliness, justice and injustice, if we reckon it the cause of all. Then if soul is the indwelling cause in all things that are in any way moved, we must say that it orders the heavens also. Shall we say one soul or more than one? I shall answer not less than two, the one beneficent, the other of opposite potency. . . . And in whatsoever soul is engaged, if she takes to herself Reason (*Nous*) as her godlike helpmate, she guides everything rightly and happily; but if she takes Unreason (*Anoia*) as her associate, all her works are of the opposite character."[227]

Plutarch, concerned like Plato to save God from responsibility for having created cosmic evil, and interpreting the *Laws* in the light of the *Timaeus*, derives the doctrine of an eternal evil World-Soul, a sort of Devil, a Manichaean "bad god." "It is impossible," he writes, "that a single being, good or bad, should be the cause of all that exists, since God cannot be the author of any evil. . . . We must admit two contrary principles, two rival powers, of which one marches always to the right and on a uniform plan, the other always to the left, and follows an opposing direction. . . . If nothing happens without a cause, and a good being can produce nothing

[224] *Tim.* 42e: ὅτι μὴ κακῶν αὐτὸ ἑαυτῷ γίγνοιτο αἴτιον.

[225] W. F. R. Hardie, *A Study in Plato*, p. 147: "It is just this insistence on the literal efficacy of a benevolently purposive mind which seems to distinguish the teaching of the *Timaeus* and the *Laws* from that of the *Phaedo* or the *Republic*." Cf. Taylor, *Commentary*, p. 299, on *Tim.* 47e4–5.

[226] Taylor, *Commentary*, p. 77, on *Tim.* 29d7–30c1: "It is the activity of soul, acting for the sake of what it believes to be good, by which the actual course of nature is made an approximate, though never a complete realization of good, an 'imitation' of the perfect order of the Forms."

[227] *Laws* 896ce; 897b; W. Jaeger, *Aristotle*, p. 132, and *Journal of Religion*, 18 (1938), pp. 128–131, discusses "the interest of the Academy in Zoroaster" and "Chaldaean dualism." Cf. also [Plato] *Epinomis* 988e, and *Des Places* (cited below, Appendix 46), p. 327.

evil, there must be in nature a special principle of evil as there is of good."[228] Plutarch goes on to deny that the same being [Homer's Zeus] dispenses good and evil to men from two jars; there are rather two rival powers; hence the mingling of good and evil in human life, as in the physical world.

This is not the place to pursue further Plutarch's own philosophy.[229] But it is important to note that it was such misinterpretations of Plato that enabled his successors to find in him sanctions for demonology, and to blame evil *daimones* for cosmic catastrophes, false oracles, human misfortunes, and even human immorality.[230] Plato occasionally uses, of course, the popular conception of *daimones*, as divine intermediaries, as men's guardian spirits, or even as rational souls.[231] They are dramatically described in the Laws:[232] "the world is full of many goods and also of evils, and of more evils than goods; and there is a deathless battle going on among us, which requires marvellous watchfulness, and the gods and *daimones* are our allies." But Plato does not use the *daimones* to excuse moral evil; rather man's own will is the responsible moral agent.[233]

Plutarch's doctrine of cosmic evil also is certainly a misinterpretation of Plato; for the *Timaeus*, which does speak of a good (created) World-Soul, has not a word to say of any evil World-Soul, and ascribes cosmic evil to the "errant cause," Necessity, and only moral evil to soul. Even the *Laws*, the supposed warrant of the doctrine, does not specify one good soul and one evil soul, but merely "not less than two" altogether (896e5); and presently the same phrase is used again (898c7–8), this time of the good soul, which is therefore to be set down as itself "one or more,"—the number does not seem to matter. Nor can one even deduce a *single* good soul from the description of the ruler of the heavenly bodies as

[228] Plutarch, *De Iside et Osiride* 369a–d. In other work, *De Animae Procreatione in Timaeo* (1014d–1015b), Plutarch identifies the power of evil also with Plato's *ἀπειρία* (cf. *Philebus*), *ἀνάγκη* (cf. *Timaeus*), and *σύμφυτος ἐπιθυμία* (cf. *Politicus*); Taylor, *Commentary*, pp. 115–117; Hoffleit, pp. 51 f. Unlike earlier Platonists, Plutarch argues that matter, as such, is "formless," and therefore cannot be, like Soul, the cause of evil or of good; in favor of such an interpretation, cf. *Tim.* 50d–51a, on the "formless" or neutral receptacle, which is space (see above, p. 305).

[229] But see below, pp. 368–370.

[230] Cf. Plutarch, *De Defectu Oraculorum, passim.*

[231] E.g., *Phaedrus* 240ab; 247e–250b; see also P. E. More, *Religion of Plato*, pp. 128–136; J. A. Hild, *Démons*, pp. 268–285; L. Robin, *La Théorie Platonicienne de l'Amour*, pp. 130–148; J. Souilhé, *Intermédiaire*, pp. 197–202.

[232] *Laws* 906a; cited also by Clement of Alexandria, *Strom.* V, 93, in confirmation of Pauline theology.

[233] Cf. *Rep.* 617e: *οὐχ ὑμᾶς δαίμων λήξεται, ἀλλ' ὑμεῖς δαίμονα αἱρήσεσθε*; see below, p. 315. Such a literary use of popular notions as *Epist.* VII 336b (*ἤ πού τις δαίμων ἤ τις ἀλιτήριος*) does not prove that Plato seriously believed in evil *daimones* as the source of human sin. On the whole subject of the debasement of the conception of *daimones* in the age following Plato, cf. Hild, pp. 286–337; and see above, p. 297; below, pp. 368 f.

ἡ ἀρίστη ψυχή (897c7; 898c4), for that phrase means merely that it is the "best kind of soul," as distinguished from the evil kind.[234] Furthermore, Plato does not say that either kind of soul, good or evil, is a god.[235] Finally, Plato has in the *Politicus* myth explicitly rejected the explanation of cosmic good and evil as due, respectively, to two gods.[236]

Plato, then, identifies the source of moral evil at first chiefly with body or matter,[237] and then more and more with soul.[238] Cosmic evil he ascribes to "Necessity"[239] everywhere except in one passage of the *Laws*, where he ascribes it to one or more unreasoning souls.[240] Whenever he deals with cosmic evil, he uses myth. Plutarch's error consists in taking with too great literalness what Plato has written as myth, and in forcing the language of the *Laws* to explain the *Timaeus* myth. He also overlooks the fact that Plato's God is not omnipotent, and is mind, rather than soul. The unresolved residuum, or evil, in the world, as Plato sees it, may confidently be assigned to matter or "Necessity," once and once only (apart from passing allusions to evil *daimones*) conceived as endowed with life (soul).

There remains the problem of the relation between man's goodness and his fortunes, the problem of the divine justice. Since God is good, it is reasonable to suppose that he provides for his creatures. Early in the *Republic*, however, Glaucon and Adimantus, restating more powerfully the position of Thrasymachus[241] which they personally disclaim, point out that justice is often less profitable in this life than injustice. For injustice is "natural," argues Glaucon, and is best for the strong who can practice it with impunity; justice is a mere "social contract," the device of the weak who fear that the danger of suffering from the unbridled licence of others will outweigh their chances of gaining from such licence on their own part.[242] Left to themselves, and unobserved, all men alike would naturally be unjust; such is the lesson taught by the fable of the magical ring of Gyges, which made one invisible.[243] Hence it is not justice itself but the appearance of justice that is profitable. And Glaucon

[234] Cf. *Laws* 897b7: πότερον . . . ψυχῆς γένος. The interpretation given above is that of E. B. England, ed. *Laws*, and of Hackforth, p. 6. See above, p. 292.

[235] *Pace* Burnet, *T.-P.*, pp. 335–338; and Taylor, *P.M.W.*, p. 492; *Commentary*, p. 77; see above, p. 287, n. 50. But Burnet and Taylor of course reject Plutarch's misinterpretation. W. D. Ross, ed. Aristotle, *Metaphysics*, vol. II, pp. 266–268, entertains a similar misinterpretation; see below, p. 320, n. 28.

[236] *Polit.* 270a: μητ' αὖ δύο τινὲ θεὼ φρονοῦντε ἑαυτοῖς ἐναντία.

[237] See above, pp. 301–303.

[238] See above, pp. 305–309.

[239] See above, pp. 303–305.

[240] See above, pp. 309–311.

[241] See above, pp. 265–267.

[242] *Rep.* 358e–359b; cf. Antiphon (see above, pp. 236 f.). N.b. in Glaucon's argument the contrast of *physis* and *nomos* here and in 364a4. These terms were used by Antiphon and by Callicles (*Gorg.* 483a–486c; see above, p. 260), but not by Thrasymachus.

[243] *Rep.* 359b–360d; cf. the *Sisyphus* of Critias (see above, p. 255).

sketches the careers of two men: the perfectly just man with a reputation for injustice will suffer persecution and torment, while the perfectly unjust man with a plausible exterior will prosper.[244] How can it be held that justice is in itself preferable to injustice? Even the gods can be bribed to condone injustice. And to Glaucon's argument his brother Adimantus adds that the poets and others say that "the gods themselves assign to many good men misfortunes and an evil life, but to their opposites a contrary lot."[245] The two brothers beg Socrates to vindicate their instinctive feeling that all these arguments are false.[246]

The major argument of the *Republic* therefore turns on the attempt of Socrates to see the internal working of justice in the soul, or in the state, as its own sufficient reward regardless of material consequences.[247] As he traces in imagination the growth of early society, and draws up "Outlines of Theology" for a state that is in process of purification, he lays down the principle that the gods are good and are authors only of good;[248] but he is unwilling to leap at once to the conclusion (though it represents his conviction) that poets "shall not be allowed to say that many unjust men are happy, and just men are miserable"; for that is precisely the question under discussion, and therefore must not be prejudged.[249] In this life man is subject to the vicissitudes of *physis*, and the misunderstanding of his fellow men, from which not even God can save him. Yet he may still be true to the divine part of his own nature and keep his soul pure. Only after this conception of justice has been vindicated does Plato feel free, toward the end of the Republic, to reckon in results of a different order, God's dealings with man both in this life and in the life to come. "All things that come from the gods work together for the best for him that is dear to the gods, apart from the inevitable evil caused by sin in a former life."[250] And now, with a sweep forward, Plato takes in the life to come. "This then must be our conviction about the just man, that whether he fall into poverty or disease or any other supposed evil, for him all these things will finally prove good, both in life and in death. For by the gods assuredly that man will never be neglected who is willing and eager to be

[244] *Rep.* 360e–362a; cf. *Gorg.* 508c–509c, and above, p. 262.

[245] *Rep.* 364b.

[246] *Rep.* 357a–358e; 366b–367e.

[247] The Socrates of the *Republic* actually proves that justice leads to what amounts to blessedness, and not necessarily to happiness in the ordinary sense; cf. my "The Spirit of Comedy in Plato," *H.S.C.P.* 31 (1920), p. 103, and n. 6.

[248] *Rep.* 379a–391e.

[249] *Rep.* 392ac; cf. *Laws* 660e, for the converse; and *Laws* 899d–900c: the apparent "success" of the wicked, celebrated in song and in tales, is an argument for the "Epicurean" tenet that the gods are heedless of men's conduct. The notion of "poetic justice" is involved; see above, pp. 93–96.

[250] *Rep.* 613a. The last phrase is a glancing allusion to metempsychosis and freedom of the will; cf. *Tim.* 42e: "save in so far as it should be a cause of evil to itself"; see above, p. 308.

righteous, and by the practise of virtue to be likened unto God, so far as that is possible for man."[251] And now it is time for myth, as Plato unfolds the richness of Orphic and Pythagorean religious faith and traces the fortunes of the soul in a future life. The soul is now free from the body, and God's sovereignty is absolute.

To such a conviction it is still possible to object that in this life, at least, the sufferings of the righteous and the victories of the wicked are only too obvious. Plato will agree;[252] but he will also urge, first, that the God who so magnificently controls the *cosmos* is not likely, through ignorance or indolence, to neglect smaller tasks;[253] second (in what is described as a "myth"), that God's interest is in the care of the whole *cosmos*, of which individual men are but puny parts; what happens to him is "best for the whole and for [him], so far as the common creation permits."[254] This may seem to have a certain abstract justice about it; but so far it lacks any consideration of individual personality; it is far from the conception of the Father who knows of the fall of every sparrow, and *a fortiori* of every human soul. But a third argument, also part of the "myth," continues to follow the fortunes of this individual soul, "appointed now to one body, now to another," and endowed with growth and moral freedom, as he is moved (like a chessman) to that abode which he comes to deserve, throughout eternity. The development of our particular characters, however, God has left to the will of each of us; "for every one of us becomes what he is for the most part by the bent of his desires and the nature of his soul."[255] "For the most part," be it noted, and "so far as the common creation permits"; for an element of "Necessity" or Fate remains here and in the brief sketch of the "order and law of destiny" that follows;[256] but the great emphasis is laid on the moral justice of the divine economy as it continues in successive lives throughout eternity. It does not mercifully forgive sin, as the Christian God may; and it offers no vicarious atonement for sin. It admits freedom of the will, and thus tolerates moral evil; but it also offers mercy in the large, by providing through successive lives for more than mere *tlemosyne*, in fact for education and purification and "growth in grace" and a possibility of ultimate blessedness. Thus each body is no longer an Orphic prison-house or tomb but a school and a battle-ground, like that in heaven itself, where victories may be won.[257]

An abstract freedom of the will and an abstract necessity, each claiming

[251] *Rep.* 613ab.
[252] *Laws* 899d–900b, in his Reply to the Atheists; see above, pp. 295–297.
[253] *Laws* 901b–903a.
[254] *Laws* 903ad.
[255] *Laws* 903de; 904bc.
[256] *Laws* 904c–905d: n.b. 904c8–9: κατὰ τὴν τῆς εἱμαρμένης τάξιν καὶ νόμον.
[257] *Laws* 906a, quoted above, p. 310.

to be absolute, admit of no metaphysical reconciliation.[258] Plato says as much when he finally leaves to myth and eschatology the problem of divine justice. Such has been his method in the myths of the *Gorgias*[259] and the *Phaedo*;[260] such, too, in the myths of the *Politicus*[261] and the *Timaeus*,[262] and in the suggestion of a myth in the *Laws*.[263] But his supreme effort to justify the ways of God to men is the Myth of Er, which closes the *Republic*.

The Myths of Plato, it may suffice to remark here, complete the work of reason by suggesting imaginatively what may reasonably be supposed to be true with regard to those ultimate reaches of speculation which immediate human experience cannot embrace: God, the origin and destiny of the soul, and divine justice. These ultimates correspond roughly to the three postulates of Kant's ethical theory: God, immortality, and freedom. They cannot be proved; and to affirm the details of a myth is not the part of wisdom, but rather to argue that something like them would be the completion of the broken arc of our moral experience. They may be further tested pragmatically by living on the assumption that they are true (a good risk, a good "bet"); so proved, the mystic turns out to be the realist, after all.[264]

The Myth of Er is a vision of last things, reported by a slain warrior marvelously restored to life. The details of the myth are in the main traditional, but their use by Plato is original. It embraces Hell and Purgatory and Heaven in its scope, as it follows the fortunes of souls, born and reborn, passing before a judgement seat, and receiving their just deserts. The landscape is vague; and nowhere in Plato is the language more full of tense feeling and overtones that recall Plato's own discussions, that echo earlier literature, and that indeed appeal to the whole moral experience of the human race.[265] Most of the details must here be overlooked; but "the chief point"[266] is the solemn yet hopeful conviction that man's happiness or misery throughout eternity depends on his justice or injustice in this life, or in the series of lives that awaits him. Thus popular mythology, which portrayed some men as blessed at once or as incurable and so damned forever, is combined with the Orphic and philosophic conception of an escape from the "cycle of generation."[267]

[258] See also below, pp. 350 f.

[259] *Gorgias* 523a–526d; see above, pp. 263 f.

[260] *Phaedo* 107d ff. (but see also below, Appendix 52); cf. *Phaedrus* 248a–249d.

[261] See above, pp. 289 f.; 301.

[262] *Tim.* 39e–42d; see above, pp. 307–309.

[263] *Laws* 903a–905d; see above, p. 313.

[264] See Appendix 51: Platonic Myths.

[265] Of later works reminiscent of the Myth it must suffice here to mention Cicero's *Somnium Scipionis;* the sixth book of Virgil's *Aeneid;* and vaguer echoes in Dante and Milton.

[266] *Rep.* 615a: τὸ κεφάλαιον.

[267] See above, pp. 60 f., and other pages there cited.

With this picture of human destinies is connected a picture of the cosmic order. On the knees of Necessity (*Ananke*) rests the Spindle which governs the movement, in concentric spheres or "whorls," of the heavenly bodies. Something like this conception was perhaps held by Parmenides, and possibly by some earlier Pythagorean; and Parmenides may also have seen in this same figure the power that moves (in the falsely conceived world of appearance) both the *cosmos* and human destinies.[268] So, at least, Plato now conceives the case, not (as in the *Timaeus* [269]) opposing Necessity to Reason, but seeing Necessity herself in the guise of Providence. Her daughters are the *Moirai*, who assist in turning her spindle, and whose very names are significant: Lachesis (who presides over lots), Clotho (the spinner), and Atropos ("the inflexible"). As they spin, they sing, with the Sirens, the music of the spheres; Lachesis the past, Clotho the present, Atropos the future.[270]

The allotment of human destinies is described in terms that emphasize both the element of encompassing Necessity or determinism and, within it, that of human freedom of choice. From the lap of Lachesis a "prophet" takes both lots and patterns of lives, and in quaintly archaic style utters a proclamation. "Souls that live for a day, now is the beginning of another cycle of mortal generation that will end in death. No *daimon* will cast lots for you, but you shall choose your own *daimon*.[271] Let him to whom falls the first lot first select a life to which he shall cleave of necessity (*ἐξ ἀνάγκης*). But virtue has no master over her, and each shall have more or less of her as he honors or dishonors her. The responsibility is his who chooses; God is without responsibility." [272] The order of choice is determined by the lots which are now flung before the souls.[273] The "patterns of lives" from which the souls now choose are far more numerous than those who choose,[274] and are of every variety; that is, there is a real choice, even for the last comer. But there is no determination from with-

[268] Cf. my "Fate, Good, and Evil in Pre-Socratic Philosophy," pp. 108–110.

[269] See above, pp. 303–305.

[270] *Rep.* 617bd; cf. Catullus, 64, 303–322; Virgil, *Buc.* IV, 46–47.

[271] See Appendix 52: *Daimon* and Choice.

[272] *Rep.* 617e: *αἰτία ἑλομένου· θεὸς ἀναίτιος*; cf. *Tim.* 42d; and see above, p. 308. This is the supreme comment in Greek literature on the complaint of Zeus that men are apt to blame the gods for their own delinquencies (*Od.* 1, 32; see above, pp. 22 f.), and the supreme affirmation of human freedom of the will and moral responsibility. The conception of metempsychosis combining fatalism and freedom of the will recurs in later thought; e.g. in the Hermetic writings; Stobaeus, *Anth.* (ed. Wachsmuth and Hense), p. 322: *ψυχὴ ἐν ἀρχῇ ἑλομένη βίον τὸν καθ' εἱμαρμένην*; and V. Cioffari, *Fortune and Fate*, pp. 33–39. For resemblances and differences between the doctrine of Plato and that of Philo Judaeus (which is typical of much later thought), cf. H. A. Wolfson, "Philo on Free Will," *Harv. Theol. Rev.* 35 (1942), pp. 131–169.

[273] See Appendix 53: Use of Lots.

[274] *Rep.* 618a; cf. 619b, the second proclamation of the "prophet"; 619de.

out of the quality of soul, for the choice of a life inevitably (ἀναγκαίως) determines the character of the soul, mingled though it is with external conditions of living.[275] This it is that enhances the solemnity of every choice, and the supreme importance of such education as will ensure moral discrimination, a proper sense of the conditions under which the soul will prosper (that is, become more just), and a refusal to be dazzled by externals.[276]

In the shrewd account of the choices made by the various souls, some famous and some obscure, some choosing wisely and some foolishly, there is not a little humor, and no little pathos. The great point to observe is the extent to which the several souls have been educated by past experience, and the folly of those who rely on habit, even on good habit, rather than on "philosophy," for guidance.[277] Now that the choices have been completed, it remains for each soul to pass before the three *Moirai*. To each Lachesis assigns the *daimon* that he has chosen as his guardian and the fulfiller of his choice; the *daimon* leads the soul to Clotho, who turns the spindle to ratify the destiny that he has got "by lot and choice" (ἣν λαχὼν εἵλετο μοῖραν); and then to Atropos, to make the web of destiny irreversible. Finally it passes beneath the throne of Necessity. Choices, once made, therefore cannot be unmade or undone. So Fate enters in at the beginning and at the end of the process, while freedom of the will is master of the central portion. Reason and Necessity, often in conflict in this life (as the *Timaeus* insists) are thus seen at last reconciled in this mythical pageant of last things.

That is the saving myth, then, belief in which will keep the soul unspotted. The kernel of the myth is simply this: that the soul is immortal and capable of enduring every evil and every good. Believe this, "and thus both here and in our journey of a thousand years . . . we shall fare well."[278]

[275] *Rep.* 618b; cf. *Laws* 904bc, quoted above, p. 313.

[276] *Rep.* 618b: ἔνθα . . . ὁ πᾶς κίνδυνος ἀνθρώπῳ. With this concentration of a whole moral life in a moment of choice may be compared the "Choice of Heracles" of Prodicus; see above, pp. 242 f.

[277] *Rep.* 619bd; cf. *Phaedo* 82b; and, for those who blame τύχη and the gods, rather than themselves, for bad choices, *Rep.* 619c; *Phaedo* 90d; *Od.* 1, 32; and see above, p. 315.

[278] *Rep.* 621cd. The conviction that the soul can endure (ἀνέχεσθαι) every evil is an interpretation of the old philosophy of τλημοσύνη. It is also a foreshadowing of the Stoic ideal of endurance and forebearance (ἀνέχου καὶ ἀπέχου); see below, Appendix 58. The final words of the *Republic*, with their calm and confident hopefulness, remind one of the spirit in which Socrates himself found in the prospect of death not sorrow but hope (cf. *Phaedo* 114d, quoted below, Appendix 51; cf. p. 276). They have often been compared with Dante's use of the word "*stelle*" at the close of each of the three divisions of the *Divine Comedy*.

# CHAPTER X

## ARISTOTLE

THE thought of Aristotle is in part a development of Plato's thought, in part a reaction against it. His earlier works, and the earlier strata of those works which he later revised, are in general representative of his Platonic period;[1] while his later writing tended more and more to emphasize his independent modes of thought, though it still preserved much that was Platonic. With the greater part of Aristotle's philosophy we need not here concern ourselves. But we must consider his approach to cosmology and theology; the theory of causality that is set forth in the *Physics* will need interpretation in the light of the *Metaphysics*; and within the realm thus sketched we shall find that the field of the *Ethics* is a province; minor points will send us to various other works.

At first, then, "young Aristotle walked in the footsteps of old Plato."[2] We have seen that Plato in his later years was less interested in the everlastingness of the Ideas than in the eternal order of the heavens; the stars have souls, and are thus endowed with sense-perception and self-movement; they are in fact "visible gods."[3] Such was the view of Aristotle not only at first but even in the transitional dialogue "On Philosophy," in which he also criticized the theory of Ideas; the heavens are divine, rational, self-moving.[4] When he wrote the treatise "On the Heavens," he adopted the view of Eudoxus, perhaps already hinted at in the *Laws*, of concentric celestial spheres whose motion causes the stars that are set in them to move.[5] Aristotle no longer found, as he formerly did, a stumbling

[1] Cf. W. Jaeger, *Aristotle*; esp. pp. 24–38; 293–308; note the wholesome warning, pp. 294 f., against supposing that an exact chronology can be established on the basis of cross-references in the works; the evidence points to reworking.

[2] W. Theiler, *Naturbetrachtung*, p. 83.

[3] Plato, *Tim.* 40d; cf. 34b; *Laws* 931a; 894c–899a; [Plato] *Epinomis* 982c; 983a; see also above, pp. 287 f.; 296 f.; Appendix 46.

[4] Cic. *N. D.* I, 33; II, 42, 44 (= Arist. frags. 26, 23, 24 Rose); cf. II, 95 (= frag. 12 Rose). Cf. W. Jaeger, *Aristotle*, pp. 138–141; 148–151; W. K. C. Guthrie, "Aristotle's Theology," *C.Q.* 27 (1933), pp. 162–171; 28 (1934), pp. 90–98; Guthrie, Loeb ed. of Aristotle, *De Caelo*, pp. xv–xxxvi. In view of the traces of "reworking," it seems to be impossible to say whether Aristotle had reached (as Jaeger holds, and Guthrie disbelieves) the doctrine of the "prime mover" when he began the composition of the "On Philosophy" or even of the "On the Heavens" (*De Caelo*); there are certainly inconsistencies to be explained on either hypothesis.

[5] *De Caelo* 291a11, 17; 293a7; cf. Plato, *Laws* 899a.

block in circular motion, which was now conceived to be as "natural" as is rectilinear motion; whether any transcendent source of motion, an "unmoved mover," was yet assumed, may be doubted. Later, however, Aristotle introduced such a principle, in order to explain the change from potentiality to actuality, and in order to avoid an infinite regress in the explanation of causality. This is the "first mover," or "unmoved mover," [6] the cause of the diurnal circular movement of the starry heavens, of the variously timed rotations of the planets, of the rhythm of the seasons. It is conceived at different times as actuality, as form or mind, as a personality, and as God. But it acts on the several parts of the universe not by planning or willing or exerting force, but solely by being the object of their desire, their "beloved," as it were.[7] Thus it is at once the supreme final cause and an efficient cause; the heavens are so far related to it, operating partly through their own (living) *physis* and partly through the attraction of the "unmoved mover." How inadequate this conception must be for religion and for ethics, we shall presently observe.[8] But we may trace in Aristotle another conception, derived in part from previous thought and penetrating his own earlier writings, which comes to play an even more significant part in his thought: I mean his analysis of the nature of causality, and in particular his teleological conception of nature.

The *Physics*, dealing like the works of the pre-Socratics with Nature, takes change for granted, and analyzes phenomena in terms of substance, or substratum (ὕλη, ὑποκείμενον), and grades of form (εἶδος) or of privation (στέρησις), that is to say of the modes of being that we predicate of things, whether they are actual or only potential. What causes them to be what they are, rather than something else? Aristotle recognizes four kinds of causality: (1) material, (2) efficient, (3) formal, and (4) final. Thus, for example, a statue (1) is of bronze, (2) is made by a sculptor, (3) in certain proportion, (4) in order to be set in a temple.[9] These causes may be combined in various ways as the necessary conditions of individual existence; one or another may interest us most in a given case. In the first book of the *Metaphysics*, Aristotle suggests, though somewhat unfairly, that all his predecessors have done little more than speculate concerning the material cause.[10] It is true that they are little interested, before Diogenes of Apollonia and Socrates, in asserting a teleological interpretation of nature; whereas Aristotle is very much concerned to

[6] *Phys.* 241b34–243a12; 256a4–260a19. It may be added that Aristotle still later revised the doctrine, now conceiving of a number of "unmoved movers," for the several heavenly bodies; *Met.* Λ, 8, with the commentary of W. D. Ross; W. Jaeger, *Aristotle* 342–367.

[7] *Met.* 1072a26: τὸ ὀρεκτόν; 1072b3: ὡς ἐρώμενον.

[8] See below, p. 322.

[9] Cf. *Phys.* 194b16–195b21, = (almost) *Met.* 1013a24–1014a20.

[10] See above, p. 221, and below, Appendix 28; and H. Cherniss, *Aristotle's Criticisms.*

establish it. Nothing occurs without a sufficient cause; and although there are many phenomena, such as the unimportant differentiae of individual animals, that can be adequately explained on mechanical grounds, without invoking a final cause or purpose, there are others, both within the field of human activity (such as the arts) and in nature generally (such as the functioning of an organism), in which the adaptation of means to end is the all-important fact.[11] Against Empedocles, the evolutionist who has explained natural selection merely as survival of those natural species that are (accidentally) fitted to survive, Aristotle argues that the permanence of coëxisting species and the breeding of animals true to type is proof of a design in nature, whose course normally prevails.[12]

Plato in his later years came to think of *physis* as a totality with a trend, even an ethical trend.[13] In the *Laws*, although he opposes to the *physis*, the *tyche*, and the *ananke* of the materialists the more spiritual terms *psyche*, *nous*, *theos*, and *techne*,[14] he also argues that it must not be supposed that the Gods, Good, and Right subsist merely by reason of *techne* or *nomos*, and not by reason of *physis*.[15] Thus Plato here, at least, tacitly uses, like any sophist, the term *physis* of a moral order. But whereas Plato regularly employs *psyche* as the prime source of motion,[16] Aristotle assigns the same rôle more and more to *physis*, which for him, far more than for Plato, becomes personal, teleological, and quasi-divine.[17] For this *physis* is not the mere "stuff" or "process" of the pre-Socratics; it is a creative, willing, purposive *demiurge*, like that of the *Timaeus*;[18] it is a cunning craftsman, moulding matter to form;[19] it is indeed the pattern

[11] *Phys.* 199b34–200b8. For the adaptation of various organs to purposes, the advantages of man's erect position, of teeth, hands, feet, etc., cf. *De Part. An.* 658b14; 660a17; 661b7; 662b18; 686a33; 687a5; and S. O. Dickerman, *De Argumentis Quibusdam*, cited below, Appendices 33 and 40.

[12] *Phys.* 198b17–199b32.

[13] See above, p. 281, and Appendix 41.

[14] Plato, *Laws* 899a ff.

[15] *Laws*, 889e; see above, p. 296.

[16] *Phaedrus* 245d; *Laws* 896b; cf. [Plato] *Epinomis* 988d.

[17] Aristotle, *Phys.* 200b11: ἡ φύσις μέν ἐστιν ἀρχὴ καὶ μεταβολῆς; cf. 192b13–21. On this whole subject, cf. W. Theiler, *Naturbetrachtung*, pp. 83–101; C. Werner, *La Philosophie Grecque* (Paris, 1938), pp. 148–156; A. S. Pease, *Caeli Enarrant*, pp. 171–175; also, for Aristotle's *physis* as the reconciliation of the old antithesis of *nomos* and *physis*, J. L. Myres, *Political Ideas of the Greeks* (New York, 1927), pp. 298–308.

[18] Aristotle, *Protrepticus*, frag. 50–61 Rose: τιμιώτατον δέ γε τῶν ἐνταῦθα ξῴων ἄνθρωπός ἐστιν, ὥστε δῆλον ὅτι φύσει τε καὶ κατὰ φύσιν γέγονε . . . ἡ φύσις ἡμᾶς ἐγέννησε καὶ ὁ θεός (scil. for the theoretic life); *De Caelo* 290a30: οὐδὲν ὡς ἔτυχε ποιεῖ ἡ φύσις; 291a25: ὥσπερ τὸ μέλλον ἔσεσθαι προνοούσης τῆς φύσεως (contrast *Tim.* 30c: πρόνοια τοῦ θεοῦ); 288a: ἡ φύσις . . . ἐκ τῶν ἐνδεχομένων ποιεῖ τὸ βέλτιστον (contrast *Tim.* 30a; and see above, p. 293); *Pol.* 1254b27: βούλεται . . . ἡ φύσις, κτλ. (contrast *Laws* 897a1, βούλεσθαι, κτλ., of the world-soul).

[19] *De Part. An.* 654b29; ὥσπερ οἱ πλάττοντες . . . ἡ φύσις δεδημιούργηκεν (contrast *Tim.* 42d; 74c; 92b).

for art,[20] and is even personified.[21] Nature does nothing in vain, nothing superfluous, nothing without a purpose;[22] and "Nature acts as if she foresaw the future."[23] "Even in the lower creatures there is a natural good above their own level, which strives after the good that is proper to them."[24] This is not an abandonment of causality; it is an argument that the future, no less than the past, may determine the present.

What of the origins of good and evil? The regularity of the movements of the heavenly bodies Aristotle interprets as evidence not of mechanical causation but of an absolutely reasonable purpose; they are eternal, and admit of no imperfection. Ordinary terrestrial phenomena, on the other hand, show less perfection. Some of nature's failures Aristotle is content to explain by referring them not to any fault in the design but rather to defects in the material, inasmuch as matter,[25] though not essentially evil, may be good for one purpose and unsatisfactory for another purpose; hence the imperfections of the individual members of a species.[26] The terms "good" and "evil" may be applied to every category within the realm of nature, Aristotle holds, and not to special, separable categories of being, as he argues Plato to have held.[27] Potentialities (*dynameis*) are for either good or evil, and the corresponding actualities (*energiai*) are likewise either good or evil; but there is no evil apart from individual evil things, least of all any eternal evil principle in the universe.[28] The result is that evil, for Aristotle, exists only as a by-product in the world-process, in particular things, through some failure on their part to reach their appropriate perfection, which is goodness. The cause of this failure is either matter[29] or necessity, neither of which is evil in itself.

What, then, of necessity itself; is it absolute, or does it admit of modes

[20] *Phys.* 194a21 (*et passim*): ἡ τέχνη μιμεῖται τὴν φύσιν.

[21] *De Part. An.* 687a10: ἡ φύσις ἀεὶ διανέμει, καθάπερ ἄνθρωπος φρόνιμος, ἕκαστον τῷ δυναμένῳ χρῆσθαι.

[22] *De Caelo* 291b13; *De Gen. An.* 744a36; b16; *De An.* 432b20.

[23] *De Caelo* 291a25; see above, n. 18. Cf. *De Part. An.* 686a22.

[24] *E.N.* 1173a4.

[25] Matter, ὕλη, like τύχη, τὸ αὐτόματον, ἀνάγκη, and στέρησις, for Aristotle implies the unlimited, formless, irrational, and is so far evil. Absolute primal matter (πρώτη ὕλη) in fact, has no predicates, being a sheer abstraction; but it is none the less for Aristotle the source of becoming and change (cf. A. Rivaud, *Devenir*, pp. 416–433); it corresponds to the ἀνάγκη of Plato's *Timaeus* which νοῦς seeks to "persuade" (see above, pp. 302–305).

[26] *Phys.* 192a15; *Met.* 1027a13; cf. *E.N.* 1099b19: τοῖς πεπηρωμένοις πρὸς ἀρετήν (happiness is available for all whose moral powers have not been "maimed"). See below, p. 325.

[27] *Met.* 1091a29–1092a21; cf. *E. N.* 1096a19.

[28] So Aristotle argues in the difficult passage, *Met.* 1051a4–21; see W. D. Ross (ed. *Met.*, Vol. II, pp. 266–268), who suggests that Aristotle is answering "the Platonic belief in an Idea of evil (*Rep.* 476a; cf. 402c; *Theaet.* 176e)," and "The Platonic belief that the first principles of the universe, the one and the indeterminate dyad, are a good and bad respectively (*Met.* 988a14; 1075a35; 1091b31). Aristotle may have the bad world-soul of the *Laws* (896e, 898c) especially in mind." (On the latter point, see above, pp. 309–311.) Cf. also *Met.* 1075b1–7, where Aristotle blames Empedocles for having made strife (which Aristotle takes to be equivalent to evil) imperishable. And see *H.S.C.P.* 47 (1936), pp. 110–115.

[29] See above, n. 25.

or degrees? What room is left for chance? Would it be fair to call Aristotle a determinist? [30] Necessity he defines as having several meanings: (1) a condition without which one cannot live, or as that without which the good cannot be or come to be (οὗ ἄνευ οὐκ, i.e., a condition *sine qua non*); (2) the compulsory, operating negatively; and (3) that which cannot be otherwise.[31] Nevertheless he recognizes, as men commonly do, the rôle of chance (τύχη), the contingent or accidental (τὸ κατὰ συμβεβηκός), that which happens neither always nor for the most part, but which nevertheless *does* occur. Of this he maintains that we can have no scientific knowledge.[32] Aristotle did not realize how far mathematicians and actuaries can reduce to formulas the field of chance and probability. These apparent exceptions to the usual course of nature may be merely the insignificant concomitants of events (such as the accidental fact that an architect may happen to be pale, a fact which has nothing to do with his function as an architect); but they may at times contribute to events of importance. Though they have their own causes, they are for us indeterminate if we do not know their causes, and are so far mere chance. Moreover, an event which is sufficiently explained by a simple cause may also contribute to a result, good or bad, which we might have planned or tried to avoid, but which we did not so anticipate. For example, a man going to market to buy something may unexpectedly meet there some one who owes him money, and may thus collect the debt. This would be termed luck, or chance. But it could not have been foreseen or planned, nor could one count on its happening again.[33] Of wider application than the term chance, or luck, is the spontaneous (τὸ αὐτόματον), which includes, Aristotle says, not merely the fortunes of animate beings capable of purposive action but also the activities of lower animals or of lifeless things, as when a stolen horse happens to return to its master. Here again there is no denial of causality, but merely of the possibility of foreseeing the convergence of two chains of causation.[34] We have not yet raised, it should be noted, the question of the freedom of the human will, the existence of which, to be sure, Aristotle never doubts.[35]

[30] It seems unnecessary even to ask whether Aristotle was a fatalist; but it may be worth recording that the word μοῖρα is not to be found in his works except in what amounts to quotation.

[31] *Met.* 1015a20–1015b15 for (1), cf. also *Phys.* 199b34; τὸ ἐξ ὑποθέσεως; and F. M. Cornford, *Plato's Cosmology*, pp. 165–170; 173–175 (on "hypothetical" as contrasted with "absolute" necessity).

[32] *Met.* 1026a33–1027b16; 1064b15–1065a26; cf. Thuc. I, 140; above, p. 270, and n. 272.

[33] The possibility of seeing in τύχη the work of divine power in us Aristotle recognized in the *Eudemian Ethics* 1248a16–b4 (cf. Plato on θεία τύχη, above, pp. 299 f.; also below, pp. 324 f.), but the author of the *Magna Moralia* finds (1206b30–1207b19) that the luck of unworthy persons requires that τύχη be set under φύσις.

[34] See Appendix 54: Contingency in Aristotle.

[35] See below, p. 327.

The perfection of the heavens, the evidences of design in the *physis*, and (in the dialogue "On Philosophy")[36] the argument that the existence of a better proves the existence of a best, which must be the divine, the necessity for conceiving of a prime mover: such are the arguments by which Aristotle has built up a theology. In Book Λ of the *Metaphysics*, moreover, he attempts a brief but systematic treatment of theology, culminating in the account of the prime mover, which is now described as God.[37] When we seek in this work and elsewhere in Aristotle, however, for the content and attributes of this divine being, the result is disappointing. Aristotle's God is saved from all contact with evil or imperfection by being allowed no activity except thought, and no object of thought except himself; for thought about any less perfect object would detract from his perfection.[38] The price of this perfection is that Aristotle's system admits of no divine creator of the universe, of no divine love or providence or governance. Not only is there in Aristotle no beginning or end to the substratum, or to the cosmic process, but there is no conception of the unfolding of any divine plan, any "far-off divine event, to which the whole creation moves," or any "philosophy of history" in Aristotle, as there is, in a limited sense, in Plato.[39] There is no theory of any moral relationship between God and man, or any suggestion of divine rewards and punishments.[40] It may be added that Aristotle, unlike Plato, has little to say of personal immortality; man's "active" reason, though not his receptive mind, is held to persist;[41] but this does not lead to any picture of a future life. Aristotle's God thus turns out to be as completely transcendent, as little immanent in the world, as Aristotle accused Plato's ideas of being.[42] Aristotle's God is in fact as speculative, as content with theory, as was Aristotle himself; for, unlike the restless Plato, the reformer and revolutionary, whose chief interest was the production of a better society of better citizens, Aristotle was content to describe and to analyze, whether his material was the structure of animals or the anatomy of human nature.[43] The God of Aristotle is a monarch who reigns, but does not rule. Such theism is so far from satisfactory to most later theists, whether pagan or Christian, that they either criticized it or sought to accommodate it to Christian theology.[44]

[36] Περὶ Φιλοσοφίας, frag. 16 Rose.

[37] *Met.* 1072b25–30.

[38] *Met.* 1074b15–35; see above, p. 293.

[39] Cf. Cic. *T.D.* I, 70; *Acad. Pr.* II, 118, 119; for Plato, see above, pp. 295 f.; 305.

[40] The suggestion in *E.N.* 1178b24–29 that the gods care for men, and requite the rational, being themselves rational, is a mere concession to popular religion.

[41] *De Anima* 413a6; b24–27; 430a22.

[42] Cf. W. A. Heidel, *The Necessary and the Contingent*, pp. 21–24.

[43] Note the emphasis in the last book of the *Nicomachean Ethics* (a late book) on contemplation rather than action as the ideal of happiness; see below, p. 328.

[44] See further W. D. Ross, ed. *Metaphysics*, Vol. I, pp. cxlix–cliv; also, on the importance

There are straws, to be sure, that point in another direction, toward a less absolutely transcendent God. Aristotle gives a (qualified) praise to Anaxagoras, for having appeared to see in *Nous*, Reason, the cause of the *cosmos* and of all order.[45] He asks whether goodness is a separate, transcendent element in the universe or is immanent in its order, and decides that it is both, just as in an army goodness resides both in its general and in its discipline, but chiefly in the general, since he causes the discipline, not the discipline the general.[46] There is nothing grudging in the divine nature.[47] Once Aristotle remarks that "God and Nature do nothing in vain."[48] But usually it is Nature alone that is described as so acting.[49] Aristotle's teleology remains therefore as an unconscious but definite trend of nature. It is a purpose that is no one's purpose, bringing about a result that is of value for no specified kind of being, except in the production and maintenance of the *status quo*; it implies a plan, but no planner. It is worthy of note that whereas the Peripatetic medical writer Diocles of Carystus maintains Aristotle's teleological doctrines,[50] Aristotle's chief successor Theophrastus practically abandons the notion of an unmoved first mover in favor of movement inherent in things; and though he echoes Aristotle's phrase about "nature doing nothing in vain,"[51] he also gets rid of much of Aristotle's teleology by recognizing the rôle of necessity and coincidence in many celestial and terrestrial phenomena. The antithesis of good and evil he resolves into the recognition of various kinds of being by no means all of which subserve any one purpose; yet evil does not prevail on the whole.[52] His pupil Strato, "ὁ φυσικός," who combines Aristotelian with Democritean principles, abandons teleological explanations of the world and indeed the conception of God as distinct from the world.[53]

Even if Aristotle's theology be dropped out of view, however, there remains an impressive body of evidence for a natural order that is systematic, in whose embrace all parts are interdependent, and of whose general trend goodness may be predicated (despite minor lapses and failures)

---

(and the difficulty) of giving the final cause its due in theology and in science, A. W. Pickard-Cambridge, "The Value of Some Ancient Greek Scientific Ideas," esp. pp. 13–16; 27–29.

[45] *Met.* 984b15; see above, p. 221.

[46] *Met.* 1075a11–25.

[47] *Met.* 983a2.

[48] *De Caelo* 271a33; *De Gen. et Corr.* 336b32.

[49] Cf. above, p. 319 f., and nn. 17–24.

[50] W. Jaeger, *Diokles von Karystos*, pp. 51–54; W. Jaeger, "Diocles of Carystus: A New Pupil of Aristotle," *Phil. Rev.* 49 (1940), pp. 402–406.

[51] Theophrastus, *De Causis Plantorum*, I, 1, 1.

[52] Theophrastus, *Metaphysics* 10a9–21; 7a22–b5; 10b26–12a2; 8a21–b9; cf. the edition of this work by W. D. Ross and F. H. Fobes, pp. xi–xviii; xxiv–xxvi.

[53] Cic. *Acad. Pr.* II, 121; *N.D.* I, 35; cf. R. D. Hicks, *Stoic and Epicurean*, p. 23.

because of its self-sufficiency and eternality and intelligibility. And within this order one may find room for the recognition of human values, in the well-being of individuals or of groups, either as a gift of nature or as something which men may achieve for themselves. Thus Aristotle's ethical theory can stand on a humanistic basis, without support from his theology.

That man's chief good is happiness (*eudaimonia*) is for Aristotle beyond question, because happiness is sought by all men as good in itself, not as a means to some ulterior end.[54] As to its content, questions may well be asked, for men's tastes and experience vary; yet in the end it will be found that the highest form of happiness of which man is capable is the use of the reason.[55] But a prior question is the source of happiness: "The question is raised whether happiness is something that can be learned or acquired by habit or by discipline of any other kind, or whether it comes by divine dispensation (κατά τινα θείαν μοῖραν) or even by chance (διὰ τύχην)."[56] In other words, is happiness a gift or an achievement? The latter alternative is set down innocently enough, in deference to popular opinion, for the very word *eudaimonia* still carried something of the original suggestion that its possessor was under the favor of a friendly divinity (*daimon*).[57] Later in the *Ethics*,[58] kinds of causality are named in what purports to be an exhaustive list: *physis*, *ananke*, *tyche*, *nous*, and all that is human (δι' ἀνθρώπου). The last kind includes all that is in our power (ἐφ' ἡμῖν); and by the elimination of the other forces, which man's deliberation cannot affect, man and his mind is left as the source of moral action, and therefore of happiness, even though the field of such action admits of less exact knowledge than does that of the theoretical sciences, and is subject to variability and contingency.[59] These lists, then, express not so much Aristotle's own analysis of the kinds of causality, — his are "the four Causes," — as his use of traditional and popular notions; yet his analysis uses and criticizes the implications of these popular notions.

[54] *E.N.* 1097a34–1097b6.

[55] *E.N.* 1177a12–1179a32; see below, p. 328.

[56] *E.N.*, 1099b9–11; cf. Archilochus frags. 8 and 14; see above, p. 34.

[57] J. Burnet, ed. *Nicomachean Ethics*, p. 46: "Aristotle admits the *prima facie* plausibility of the naive religious view that εὐδαιμονία is good fortune sent by dispensation of divine providence. Θεία μοῖρα is the religious equivalent of τύχη, and is commonly so used by Plato." (See above, pp. 299 f., and Appendices 47 and 48.) The alternatives are set forth more fully in the corresponding passage of Aristotle's (earlier) *Eudemian Ethics* (1214a14–26): the list, held to be exhaustive, includes φύσις, μάθησις (through ἐπιστήμη), ἄσκησις (ἔθος), ἐπιπνοίᾳ δαιμονίου τινός (ἐνθουσιάζειν), τύχη; cf. also the early *Protrepticus*, as quoted by Iamblichus, p. 49 Pistelli.

[58] *E.N.* 1112a32.

[59] It is interesting to observe that it is in this field (together with astronomy and natural history) that Aristotle uses the term "reasonable" (εὔλογος), as the sophistic age and Thucydides used εἰκός. Cf. J. M. LeBlond, *Eulogos et l'Argument de Convenance chez Aristote*, Paris, 1938, and my review, *A.J.P.* 61 (1940), pp. 503 f.

Ethics (and politics) must operate in the field of the contingent; necessity is often opposed to the rational and the good, yet provides the materials or the tools which they must use. Spontaneity (τὸ αὐτόματον) and chance (τύχη), or what simple people call a divine dispensation (θεία μοῖρα) will occasionally produce the same results that purpose would have produced.[60] Nature, though close to necessity and matter, has her unconscious purposes,[61] which art may complete,[62] and which the ethical and political thinker must heed; but the chief rôle in the production of the good remains for conscious reason, or for man so far as he deliberates and acts rationally. Thus we may list in rising order the powers to be reckoned with, from the less to the more rational: necessity, spontaneity, fortune, nature, man. None of these powers can operate without a greater or a less interference from one or more of the rest.[63]

Let us return to Aristotle's question [64] about the source of happiness. The idea that happiness is a gift of the gods he urbanely dismisses, with the remark that "if there is anything in the world that is a gift to men, it is reasonable to suppose that happiness is a divine gift, especially as it is the best of human things." [65] He proposes to discuss the point later, but never does.[66] Moreover, he continues, happiness will be capable of wide diffusion among all who are not morally "maimed," and will not be limited to a few favored people.[67] And just as we find increasing evidence of purpose as we rise higher in the scale of causes, so it is reasonable to suppose that the best and noblest of things, happiness, will be the product not of chance but of man's intelligence.[68]

Since Aristotle holds that the good of man is not a condition but an activity of soul in accordance with virtue, it follows that happiness rests chiefly with the human agent, and is only secondarily the product of external goods which are the antecedent conditions or the tools of activity.[69] But to the extent to which these external factors must be reckoned with it is necessary to deny the possibility of real or complete happiness to certain

[60] See above, p. 321.

[61] *Phys.* 193a28–33.

[62] *Phys.* 199a15–17; see above, pp. 319 f.

[63] See further W. L. Newman, ed. Aristotle, *Politics* (Oxford, 1887–1902), Vol. I, pp. 15–24; Cic. *N.D.* II, 43: *neque naturam neque fortunam* (the heavenly bodies move not through nature or chance, but by divine and rational wills of their own); cf. J. B. Mayor's long note *ad loc.*, comparing Aristotle and Plato on the priority of reason to other kinds of causality. For the persistence of lists of powers in the Peripatetic and related schools, see the (pseudo-Aristotelian) *De Mundo* 401b8, and below, p. 373, and n. 246.

[64] See above, p. 324.

[65] *E.N.* 1099b11–13.

[66] Unless in *E.N.* 1177a12–1179a32; see below, p. 328.

[67] See above, p. 320.

[68] *E.N.* 1099b19–24.

[69] *E.N.* 1099a31–b8; 1100b4–11; cf. *Pol.* 1323a36–b29.

classes of beings: animals, children, the prosperous who, like Priam, fall late in life into calamities. Yet as soon as we begin, like Solon in the story,[70] to count no man "happy" till he has died without a reversal of fortune, still more, as we attempt to reckon prospectively with the fortunes of a man's descendants, we become involved in absurd suspensions of judgment which do violence to the common man's realistic recognition of happiness whenever and wherever it is found. Furthermore, "if we follow the changes of fortune, we shall often call the same person happy at one time, and miserable at another, representing the happy man as 'a sort of chameleon without any stability of position.' It cannot be right to follow the changes of fortune. It is not upon these that good or evil depends; they are necessary accessories of human life, as we said; but it is man's activities in accordance with virtue that constitute his happiness and the opposite activities that constitute his misery." [71] In other words, as Aristotle goes on to show, character is more stable than fortune, and happiness may outlive mere external good fortune, — an important point to bear in mind in the consideration of tragedy. For though small incidents, good or evil, do not turn the scale of life, and great events enhance or mar one's happiness, still even in disaster "nobility shines out, when a person bears the weight of accumulated misfortunes with calmness, not from insensibility but from innate dignity and magnanimity." [72] From the calamity of a Priam, to be sure, it is not reasonable to expect a recovery of happiness; from most great misfortunes, however, a recovery may be won, though "only in a long and complete period of time and after attaining in it to great and noble results." [73] One thinks of Oedipus at Colonus.

What is the source and what is the specific character of that virtue or goodness in accordance with which man must act, if he is to achieve happiness? It is habitual conduct, the result of repeated actions. As such it is not mere nature, for repeated acts do not alter natural trends: nor again can it be absolutely contrary to nature. "It is neither by nature then nor in defiance of nature that virtues are implanted in us; nature gives us the capacity of receiving them, and that capacity is perfected by habit." [74] And what kind of acts are to become habitual, thus producing virtue and ultimately happiness? What, in other words, is the formal cause of virtue? Aristotle's answer develops the universal Greek hatred of *hybris* and instinct for moderation [75] into his doctrine of the mean; virtue, he argues,

[70] Herodotus I, 32; see above, pp. 84–86; 161 f.; below, Appendix 11.

[71] *E.N.* 1100b4–11.

[72] *E.N.* 1100b30–32.

[73] *E.N.* 1101a6–13.

[74] *E.N.* 1103a24–26.

[75] μηδὲν ἄγαν: cf. E. G. Wilkins, *The Delphic Maxims in Literature* (Chicago, 1929), pp. 19–48.

lies somewhere between the excess and the deficiency of a given emotion or action: it is "a state of deliberate moral purpose consisting in a mean that is relative to ourselves, the means being determined by reason, or as a prudent man would determine it." [76] Thus neither the ascetic's condemnation of all natural impulses nor the behaviorist's acceptance of all impulses is adequate; the prudent man, whose standards are those of reason and experience, mediates between them, as a pilot sails between Scylla and Charybdis. Now this rather quantitative notion of virtue is open to criticism, as Aristotle himself realizes. Some vices have no real opposites; some virtues cannot be given a place in any merely quantitative scale. In many moral choices the conception of a mean is of no practical value whatsoever. Nevertheless, Aristotle is at least right in seeing the need of reducing warring impulses to some sort of proportion or symmetry; this is the ethical counterpart of the harmony or healthy functioning which the Pythagoreans found in mathematics and music and medicine. The mean, then, is a good relative to the extremes that flank it; and as a moral good, it is an extreme, and the object of whole-hearted pursuit.[77]

If the doctrine of the mean defines the formal cause of virtue, it is next in order to define the efficient cause that brings it into being; and this Aristotle does in the opening chapters of the third book of the *Nicomachean Ethics* [78] in his analysis of the will. What gave special point to this analysis in his day was the question of moral and legal responsibility which was constantly discussed in the courts of justice. How far should a man receive credit (or blame) for an act? Did he act under compulsion, or ignorance? Does he now feel remorse? Did he choose a lesser evil in order to avoid a greater evil? Starting with such questions, Aristotle shows that what he calls *proairesis* (moral purpose, or will in the fullest sense), involves both an element of desire for an ultimate end and an element of deliberation in the choice of means; and these means are such matters as lie within our power.[79] Thus virtue and vice are equally voluntary; for the ability to act implies the ability to refrain from acting, and *vice versa.* Finally, it will not avail to plead with the behaviorist in excuse of evil action that no other action was at the time possible for a person of such-and-such a character, and that he acted according to his lights; his character is the result of habits which in turn were produced by previous choices: "for one's character depends upon the way in which one exercises one's powers." [80]

[76] *E.N.* 1106b36–1107a2.

[77] *E.N.* 1107a6–8; see further W. J. Oates, "The Doctrine of the Mean," *Phil. Rev.*, July, 1936, pp. 382–398.

[78] *E.N.* 1109b30–1115a3.

[79] *E.N.* 1113a10: *καὶ ἡ προαίρεσις ἂν εἴη βουλευτικὴ ὄρεξις τῶν ἐφ' ἡμῖν.*

[80] *E.N.* 1114a7.

Such, in brief, is Aristotle's defense of the "freedom of the will." Its scope is severely limited by the nature of the problem (chiefly the question of legal responsibility) that he seems to have in mind; it is common sense, and is far from metaphysical. It does not attempt to give, and perhaps no psychological system has ever succeeded in giving, a satisfactory explanation of the process by which a choice or volition is translated into action, beyond a recognition of the fact. But at least Aristotle admits, what Socrates had denied, and what Plato but only partially realized,[81] the possibility of involuntary error, of error that is not committed through mere ignorance; this he does by describing "weakness of will" or "incontinence" (ἀκρασία).[82] It is a fact that we sometimes know the better and do the worse; the difficulty is often that the desire for immediate pleasure overcomes the will to attain to the ultimate good. Pleasure, indeed, is a good, or an ingredient of the good, but is not identical with the good.[83] Aristotle, then, like Plato, tends to feel very strongly the opposition of reason and the senses, and to derive his ethical sanctions ultimately from the goodness and rationality of nature or of God. "Freedom with [Aristotle] means primarily the freedom of reason, not that of the 'will'. . . . Since reason is the highest realization of human capacities, men's actions will be truly free, in his sense, only when they are wholly governed by rational purposes."[84] Thus Aristotle paradoxically contrasts the greater apparent freedom of the slaves in a household to do as they please with the devotion to duty of the "free" master; so mankind is more "free," but less divine, than the heavenly bodies which are bound by necessity.[85] And indeed it is true that increasing years and wisdom and responsibilities mean in a sense a loss of freedom, though they bring also a new kind of freedom to approach a more austere moral and intellectual ideal.[86] For Aristotle the highest ideal is not merely active, or even aesthetic or moral, but reflective; it means the free functioning of the highest part of man, his reason, not in creation but in contemplation.[87] Such a life indeed approximates as closely as is humanly possible the life which Aristotle ascribes to God.

Not all men, to be sure, are equally capable of reaching and enjoying such an ideal of happiness. Yet ordinary men should be enabled to develop their full potentialities, and, if need be, should be checked in any

[81] See above, pp. 274; cf. 256 f.; 306 f.

[82] *E.N.* 1145b22–1152a36; cf. 1144b28–30.

[83] *E.N.* 1152b1–1154b31; 1172b19–1176b29.

[84] W. A. Heidel, *The Necessary and the Contingent*, pp. 35 f.

[85] *Met.* 1075a18–25. Cf. Sir A. Grant, *Ethics*, Vol. I, p. 286, quoted by Ross *ad loc.* Aristotle assumes freedom for man "not so much from a sense of the deep importance of morality, but rather from a sense of the slightness of man and of his actions in comparison with nature, and with what he would call the 'diviner parts' of the universe."

[86] Cf. St. Augustine and Dante; see below, pp. 386–388.

[87] *E.N.* 1177a12–1179a32.

undesirable propensities. This is the office of the state, whose nature Aristotle examines in the *Politics*, a work no less ethical than the *Ethics* (for both treatises are concerned with the moral nature of man). What strikes the modern reader of the *Politics*, however, quite as much as its ethical purpose is the extent to which Aristotle is content to deal with human nature as it is, or with Greek institutions of the fourth or even of the fifth century. (There is hardly a suggestion that Alexander's empire was to supersede the small *polis*.) No crusader following a visionary ideal, like Plato in the *Republic*, Aristotle seeks merely to realize the possibilities of the *polis* as an ethical agent. He analyzes types of government, as in other works which he wrote or supervised (such as the *Constitution of Athens*) he describes existing constitutions. But his description of an ideal state turns out to be no Utopia, but a series of remarks on ways and means, in the spirit of Plato's *Laws*, and a dissertation on liberal education. He remarks that the best practicable constitution is the one that suits the circumstances of a given people; any absolute best is hardly worth discussing.[88] On the whole, he seems not deeply interested in any thoroughgoing reform of society.

Aristotle does not abandon his teleology in the *Politics*. Society, the family and the state alike. are rooted in nature, for "man is by nature a political animal";[89] "the state comes into being for the sake of life [the satisfaction of man's elementary needs]; it continues to exist for the sake of the good life."[90] Thus man by taking thought merely completes what nature began, by a more complete realization of what nature intended. And nature's intentions are respected, Aristotle believes, in the recognition of the division of labor, even in the recognition of the fact that some men seem to be living tools intended by nature to be slaves.[91]

What is most striking, to the modern reader, but what an ancient Greek would find quite natural, is the emphasis on the exclusive claims of the state, which is to be in fact all but "totalitarian." Athenians and Spartans not only were used to dying for the fatherland but looked to the state for the direction of much of their lives; there was no separation of church and state, as we might put it. The "Funeral Oration" of Pericles[92] sums up, even if it idealizes, fifth century feeling in the matter; and Plato's *Republic* hardly finds it necessary to argue the point, though it does show, in its quasi-historical account of the development of a primitive society into a Utopia, that it is only in the full-fledged state that man reaches his fullest stature. Aristotle agrees.

If the justification of the claims of the state is the fact that the state

[88] *Pol.* 1288b25.
[89] *Pol.* 1253a2.
[90] *Pol.* 1252b29.
[91] *Pol.* 1254a15: φύσει δοῦλος.
[92] Thuc. II, 35–46.

realizes the end toward which nature tends, it becomes of supreme importance to define this end. Neither Plato nor Aristotle, as a matter of fact, considers the state as an end in itself; the state exists for the sake of man, not man for the state, if any such absolute pair of alternatives be presented. But even so, what is the end of man-in-the-state? Multiplication of lives, improvement of the human stock, economic production, military security, self-sufficiency, the pursuit of knowledge? All these, and others, are ends which Plato and Aristotle recognize, and the question is one of reconciling them and of subordinating all the rest of them to whichever may prove to be the chief end. Aristotle, despite his more realistic view of human nature and its possibilities, shares with Plato a tendency to subordinate all else to the life of reason. And since this is admittedly a life into which only the few can fully enter, it follows that the rest of mankind must become hewers of wood and drawers of water in the service of such a society as shall best foster the emergence and the free functioning of superior minds. This is not political tyranny, for careers are to be open to talents, the economic interests of the middle class are to be deliberately fostered in the interest of political stability, and more or less democratic concessions abound. It is rather the benevolent despotism of an intellectual *corps d'élite* who are natural, not merely *de facto*, rulers. It is as if the whole of a mediaeval town, well defended against neighbors outside the pale, and provided with material necessities, were banded together actually, though without its full knowledge, for the perpetuation of the monastery, or institute for scientific research, which in turn ruled it, and which through impersonal laws wisely promoted the virtue and thus the happiness of all its citizens, so far as they were severally capable of virtue and happiness. Such societies have existed, and perhaps as happily as most others. What Aristotle fails to realize is the dangers of a static and isolated community which resists the infiltration of new experience from without, and which imperfectly appreciates how far all virtue and all happiness must come through the efforts of individuals, often of humble natural gifts. Aristotle, in a word, like Plato, risks losing the world through pride of intellect.[93]

So much should be said by way of criticism. Yet it would be ungrateful to take leave of Aristotle[94] without acknowledging the tremendous impetus that he gave to men's efforts to discover how man could by rational means establish good in the world within the scope defined for him by nature. After Plato, there is no greater single power, unless it be that of the Stoics, in the history of this heroic struggle.

[93] See further, W. L. Newman, ed. Aristotle, *Politics*, Vol. I, pp. 61–83; A. W. Benn, *Greek Philosophers*, pp. 253 f.; 264.

[94] For Aristotle's discussion of tragedy, see above, pp. 92–99; 101; cf. 326.

# CHAPTER XI

## FATE AND PROVIDENCE

### I

AFTER the magnificent achievement of Plato and Aristotle, Greek philosophy seems to decline. Yet it is not merely that less great minds inevitably must follow; it is in part the case that Plato's and Aristotle's thought so far outsoared the comprehension, and indeed the needs, of ordinary men that it was only hundreds of years later that they could be fully appreciated. So the Academy and the Lyceum busied themselves less with metaphysical flights than with specialized investigations or with preserving the works of their masters. The Academy continued, and for centuries concerned itself mostly with ethics, mathematics, and logic; but it soon learned from contemporary sceptics [1] to adopt a critical attitude and to suspend judgement, rather than to dogmatize. So Carneades (214–129 B.C.) opposed the contemporary Stoic dogma that recognized the existence of Fate or Providence and that reckoned with the possibility of divination; "probability" (what his predecessor Arcesilaus (315–241) had called "the reasonable" in thought) was for him the only guide to action; "opinion" was to be entertained about such phenomena as affected conduct, but not about the ultimate causes of things, such as gods or fate.[2] Eventually mathematics and ethics were appropriated by more effective teachers than those of the Academy. The Lyceum continued, and made fruitful researches in botany and medicine [3] and music. But it was left almost wholly to new philosophic schools, the Epicureans and the Stoics, to deal with the fundamental problems of ethics and religion; and even these philosophers were far from seeking, like Plato and Aristotle, to build up methods of scientific investigation, to plan political systems, or to speculate about spiritual things. Revolting against intellectualism, they endeavored to give practical advice and comfort to ordinary people. Popularizers, rather than

[1] E.g. Pyrrho of Elis (d. 275 B.C.), who denied that it is possible to predicate of a given thing one quality any more than its opposite; and the sillographer Timon (c. 320–230 B.C.), who admitted that honey *seems* sweet, but not that it is sweet. But such men do not even attempt hypotheses to account for phenomena.

[2] For Carneades, see also below, pp. 347 f.; 351; 356; 358; 360–365.

[3] W. Jaeger, "Die Pneuma im Lykeion," *Hermes* 48 (1913), pp. 29–74; W. Jaeger, *Diokles von Karystos*, showing the Peripatetic and (pp. 51–54; cf. 154–180) the teleological character of the medical theory of Diocles.

researchers, prophets instead of sceptics, materialists and not believers in any separate spiritual order, they seem to recall us to the age and the occupation of the Sophists (mostly non-Athenian, as the Stoics are mostly non-Greek), before Plato and Aristotle made of philosophy a technical subject for the expert. But with this difference: the *polis* is no longer the self-sufficient, successful, all-providing institution that it was in the earlier period. Large kingdoms are eclipsing the small *polis*; the law and custom of the state is open to question; the individual is coming to rely on himself; social, national, and racial distinctions are tending to mean less for any who can think of themselves as citizens of the world. The broad humanity of Menander has replaced the parochial concerns of Aristophanes. So, too, these newer philosophers seek to find the good for man, even for men who have failed in every worldly sense,—for the outcast, the poor, the weak.

The philosophic literature of the Hellenistic period is also for us singularly like in form to that of the pre-Socratic and Socratic periods. Instead of the majestic unity and completeness of the works of Plato and Aristotle, we return once more to fragments, isolated quotations preserved by doxographers or excerptors. Even the longer works that have survived in more nearly complete form tend to be polemic essays (*diatribai*), sermons,[4] or letters, though longer and more systematic treatises are also written. Among the literary forms most often practised during the Hellenistic period and in the Roman period is the "Consolation"[5] addressed to the bereaved, the discouraged, the oppressed. As we approach the Roman period, the several schools often influence one another, especially the Academy and the Porch (the Stoics), a circumstance which, combined with Cicero's own eclectic leanings, renders his philosophical writings a treasure-house for those who wish to know the state of mind of a thoughtful, though not profound or original, Roman who has made Greek philosophy his own.

All the philosophical schools after Aristotle tended to divide their inquiries into three questions. These may be phrased quite simply: "How does one know the world? What is the nature of the world? How can one live happily in such a world?" The three departments of philosophy dealing with these problems were termed respectively, Logic, Physics, and Ethics.[6] The Epicureans, to be sure, developed an empirical method of Logic in opposition to the rationalistic method of the Stoics, but resorted to an even more naively sensationalist psychology than that of the

[4] Cf. the Cynic χρεῖαι, "useful things."

[5] See above, p. 241 f.; below, pp. 336, n. 25; 355; 368; 388–391.

[6] The division was first made by Xenocrates of the Academy; cf. Sextus Emp. *adv. Math.* VII, 16 (= R. P. 316).

Stoics.[7] We are concerned, therefore, chiefly with Physics and Ethics,—with Nature and Man. And it will simplify matters if we realize how much the Epicureans and the Stoics have in commmon. Both schools, abandoning the idealism of the Academy and the Lyceum, conceive of matter as the sole reality, and indeed revive earlier conceptions of matter: the Epicureans, the atomism of Leucippus and Democritus; the Stoics, the notions of fire and breath of Heraclitus and other pre-Socratic thinkers. Both schools, moreover, seek to find man's good in happiness, in peace of mind, in "freedom from perturbation."[8] The difference, as we shall see, is in the means invoked: the Epicurean seeks to free man's will from nature's law, while the Stoic seeks to submit to it.

2

Epicurus (341–270 B.C.) states clearly the motive that impelled him to study nature: it is to free the mind from passion and fear, especially from the fear of death and the superstitions that often attend it,—in a word, to achieve *ataraxia*.[9] And this is precisely the avowed motive also of his devoted Roman follower, Lucretius. Epicurus himself is not uncommonly regarded as a scientist of the first order, whose discoveries anticipated those of modern physics. It is true that he claimed to be self-taught, and that there is much in his speculation that modern experiment has confirmed. But with one important exception there is not much in Epicurean science that is not already in the system of Democritus, with its atoms streaming downwards in a void, in accordance with what Lucretius will call "the decrees of fate" (*foedera fati*).[10] The exception is the highly original notion of an occasional "swerve" in the direction of the streaming atoms.[11] This is intended first of all to explain how the atoms can meet and form the world and all therein is. But this freedom of the will on the part of the atoms is also the device of Epicurus by which he seeks to escape from a purely mechanistic, fatalistic system; the *foedera fati* of Lucretius are indeed broken by the *foedera naturai*, the laws and internal constitutions of groups of atoms, or organisms.[12] "It were better," writes Epicurus, "to follow the myths about the gods than to become a slave to the 'destiny' (*heimarmene*) of the natural philosophers [the atomists?]: for the former

[7] Cf. Seneca, *Epist.* 89, 11 (= R.P. 458), denying the Epicureans a Logic apart from Physics; but see P. H. and E. A. DeLacy, *Philodemus: On Methods of Inference: A Study in Ancient Empiricism*, Monograph X of Am. Philol. Assoc. (Philadelphia, 1941).

[8] For Epicurus on ἀταραξία, D. L. X, 136; for the Stoics on "freedom from perturbation," SVF III, 443–455; Cicero, *T.D.* IV, 9–23 (= R.P. 521).

[9] See Appendix 55: Epicurus; bibliography.

[10] Lucretius II, 251–260.

[11] D. L. X, 43; C. Bailey, *Epicurus*, p. 24; the idea is more fully expressed by Lucretius, II, 216–293; cf. Cic. *De Fin.* I, 18; *De Fato* 22; *N. D.* I, 69.

[12] Cf. A. W. Benn, *Greek Philosophers*, pp. 406 f.; 414–418.

suggests a hope of placating the gods by worship, whereas the latter involves a necessity that knows no placation."[13] Ethics, in other words, is impotent without freedom of the will. It is true, of course, that the "swerve" is unaccountable, contingent, practically causeless, and amounts almost to chance,[14] at least in the physical world, though it will serve a purpose in human psychology and therefore in ethics.

Except for the "swerve" of the atoms, an endless chain of causation[15] is supposed to account for everything. Clearly there is in Epicurean physics hardly an explanation, surely there is no guarantee, of good for the *cosmos*; there is not even any purpose or trend on the part of nature, unless it be a tendency to degenerate. This pessimistic strain appears also in Lucretius,[16] though Lucretius also thinks of Nature as a vivifying, creative force, *Natura daedala rerum*. Certainly there is no implication that Nature is interested in creating good for man, his happiness or well-being; and there is no providence, no special divine intervention at any point, no future reward or punishment for the (material) soul after its temporary identity is dissolved by death.

The existence of the gods, to be sure, and their immortality and blessedness, Epicurus takes for granted, for all men have a "common idea" of them engraved in their minds.[17] He is no atheist, say what his later critics may. But at any rate his gods, like the still more remote God of Aristotle, have no interest in the operation of the *cosmos*, which indeed shows many flaws, especially from the point of view of man's well-being.[18] It was a commonplace for others beside Epicureans to remark that the gods do not care for human affairs,—otherwise the good would not suffer and the wicked prosper.[19] But the anthropomorphism, the inactivity, and the lack of benevolence of the Epicurean gods were especially open to criticism;[20] these gods seemed as superfluous as fifth wheels, unless perhaps in one respect. For though they have little enough to do with man, they do un-

[13] C. Bailey, *Epicurus*, pp. 90 f.; Bailey, *Greek Atomists and Epicurus*, p. 318.

[14] See Appendix 56: Epicurus, "Swerve," and *τύχη*.

[15] Yet Epicurus insists that a given event, such as the position of the sun and moon, could be explained by more than a single chain of causes; D. L. X, 93; 113; R. P. 464a.

[16] Lucretius IV, 823–842 (absence of design in Nature); II, 1105–1174; V, 826–833 (Nature's weariness and degeneration); see further W. M. Green, "The Dying World of Lucretius," *A.J.P.* 63 (1942), pp. 51–60.

[17] D. L. X, 123; C. Bailey, *Epicurus*, p. 84.

[18] Cf. Cic. *N. D.* I, 18; Lucretius V, 195–234; II, 167–181.

[19] This remark is especially common in Latin literature; e.g., Ennius, *Telamo*, 353–355 Vahlen: *Ego deum genus esse semper dixi et dicam caelitum,* | *sed eos non curare quid agat humanum genus:* | *nam si curent, bene bonis sit, male malis, quod nunc abest* (see also above, p. 266; and below, p. 359)); Virgil, *Aen.* II, 536: *Si qua est caelo quae talia curet; Buc.* VIII, 35: *nec curare deum credis mortalia quemquam.*

[20] Cic. *N.D.* I, 71–124; cf. C. Bailey, *Greek Atomists and Epicurus*, pp. 438–481. But C. Jensen, *Ein Neuer Brief Epikurs* (Berlin, 1933), finds evidence that the gods of Epicurus

consciously, like Aristotle's god, serve as ideals of *ataraxia*, of purity and passionless contentment, for man to emulate. In this sense it might be held that the gods help mankind; not that they need man's worship, but that man needs the gods to help him "to be able to contemplate all things with a mind at rest."[21] Nevertheless, what good, what human happiness can exist in this bleak Epicurean universe must be chiefly man's own creation. Here, then, is the field of human resourcefulness and enterprise, which Lucretius pictures in his stirring account of the rise of civilization;[22] here, too, is the field of ethics.

Democritus, besides setting forth the atomic system, also taught quite independently an ethical system of eudaemonism, a cheerfulness won through moderation, taking for granted the freedom of the will, and building good on the foundation of human intelligence and purpose. What Democritus had to do as an independent matter, Epicurus is able to undertake as a related inquiry, since his "swerve" has freed man in part from the grip of mechanical necessity; man's mind is composed of atoms whose spontaneous swervings, *as a group*, are conceived as an act of the will.[23]

If neither the *polis* of his fathers nor the *cosmos* that scientific speculation disclosed could any longer guarantee a lordly and a happy life to Epicurus, he had additional excuses for discouragement in his personal history, if he chose to take advantage of them: poverty, exile, and poor health. But he rose to the challenge, and proclaimed that pleasure (*hedone*) or happiness (*eudaimonia*) are within man's grasp if he will but use his reason and his will. Man need no longer be haunted by superstitious myths. He may indeed not expect immortality; but the fear of death is cast forth, and the first office of "consolation" is performed. "Become accustomed to the belief that death is nothing to us . . . since so long as we exist, death is not with us; but when death comes, then we do not exist." Yet foolish is "the man who says it is good not to be born, but 'once born make haste to pass the gates of Death.' "[24] For "the right understanding of [desires] enables us to refer all choice and avoidance to the health of the body and ⟨the soul's⟩ freedom from disturbance, since this is the aim of the life of blessedness. . . . [The wise man] laughs at ⟨des-

---

were indifferent to bad men, benevolent to good men.

[21] Lucretius V, 1203, the poet's ideal of "pure religion and undefiled." See further G. D. Hadzits, "The Significance of Worship and Prayer among the Epicureans," — *T.A.P.A.* 39 (1908), pp. 73–88, noting citations from Philodemus. Cf. also Euripides, fr. 910 Nauck, and see above, p. 216.

[22] Lucretius, V, 925–1457.

[23] Cf. C. Bailey, *Greek Atomists and Epicurus*, pp. 319–327; 435–437; A. W. Benn, as cited above, p. 688, n. 12. With the importance of the group, cf. "*Gestalt*" psychology.

[24] A retort to the old notion of μὴ φῦναι; see above, p. 42.

tiny⟩, whom some have introduced as the mistress of all things. ⟨He thinks that with us lies the chief power in the determining of events, some of which happen by necessity⟩, and some by chance (*tyche*), and some are within our control; for while necessity (*ananke*) cannot be called to account, he sees that chance is inconstant, but that which is in our control (τὸ παρ' ἡμᾶς) is subject to no master. . . . As to chance, he does not regard it as a god as most men do (for in a god's acts there is no disorder), nor as an uncertain cause [of all things]: for he does not believe that good and evil are given by chance to men for the framing of a blessed life, but that opportunities for great good and great evil are afforded by it."[25]

Pain is evil, but can be endured (and Epicurus bore it nobly), and is in any case outweighed in the hedonistic calculus by greater or more enduring pleasure. Pleasure is good, greater pleasure is a greater good; but the best pleasure is not the mere momentary gratification of the senses, which is generally preceded by previous pain,[26] and is moreover itself subject to natural limits (one cannot go on eating, for example, indefinitely), but rather the "static" pleasure of a calm mind, which includes the pleasures of memory and of anticipation and of scientific speculation. To this extent Epicurus, who has begun by recognizing only a quantitative standard in his hedonism, tacitly admits a qualitative standard; thus he differs with Aristippus,[27] though not with the partly Epicurean Horace. Abate one's ambitions; learn to live in obscurity (λάθε βιώσας),[28] giving full expression to friendliness and gentleness of spirit; live and let live.[29] As regards the "social virtues," such as justice, Epicurus holds to the theory of the "social contract," considering justice to be merely an inconvenient concession, which is nevertheless conducive to the greatest amount of pleasure of which the individual is capable. Epicurean life at its best will mean positive joy, not merely the virtue and emotional suppression of the Cynics and Stoics; not, again, merely the simple satisfaction of the senses; but something of the rarer intellectual and aesthetic joy that Epicurus supposes his gods to enjoy in some celestial retreat. Such is the message of his letters and of his "Principal Doctrines"; such is the gospel that he taught in the Garden, his school in Athens. No wonder that his message came

[25] D.L. X, 124–126; 128; 133–134, from the Letter to *Menoecus*; C. Bailey, *Epicurus*, pp. 84–91. For other passages in the literature of consolation that are indebted to the earlier part of the passage here quoted (esp. Lucretius III, 830–1094), and for other commonplaces, possibly Epicurean (e.g. leaving life, as a courteous guest a banquet), cf. Buresch, *Consolationum Historia*, pp. 60–64.

[26] See above, pp. 248; 261.

[27] See above, p. 278.

[28] Epicurus, frag. 551 Usener; 86 Bailey.

[29] Cf. N. W. DeWitt, "Epicurean *Suavitas*," *Trans. Royal Soc. of Canada*, 32 (1938), pp. 41–48.

as a new religion, or that Lucretius revered him as a very god, and gave lyric expression to his debt to Epicurus.[30]

The Epicurean philosophy, as an ethical system, is nobler than its critics [31] have usually admitted; it is not necessarily either sensual or selfish. Yet there is in it, probably unrealized, a certain negative attitude, a surrender, a retreat from life, an avoidance of the grudging, possibly vindictive power of Nature, a refusal to be entangled in politics, an unwillingness to recognize the sharp moral antitheses of the Stoics. Epicurean happiness, or at least freedom from pain, is something that seeps through when one has determined not to ask much of life. There is something exquisite in scarcity, that bids one seize the day, and gather rose buds. Yet the spring poems of Horace surprise the reader by the tinge of melancholy with which they are apt to be suffused; for the Epicurean, indeed, the annual cycle of nature knows no counterpart of human renewal.[32] Thus the Epicurean, even in the act of seeking to be freed from the domination of Nature's law, finds himself hemmed in by it.[33]

## 3

While Epicurus and his school was seeking a release from Nature, a rival school was teaching in the Painted Porch (Stoa) at Athens a philosophy of obedience to Nature. Zeno (c. 336–264) of Citium in Cyprus, like practically all of his Stoic successors, was non-Athenian; indeed, many Stoics had, like Zeno, a Semitic or at least Oriental background. This appears in their prophetic fervor, and in their conception of an eternal antithesis between good and evil. Thus Zeno himself, with his authoritative moral apothegms, seems remote from the spirit of inquiry, of irony, of Socrates; he stands nearer to Heraclitus, both in his style and in the conceptions of fire, and of universal reason which he borrowed from him. But his first impulse to philosophy, we are told by Diogenes Laertius,[34] came at the age of thirty, when he was in Athens. In a bookseller's shop he picked up and read Xenophon's *Memorabilia*, and "was so pleased that he inquired where men like Socrates were to be found. Crates [the Cynic] passed in the nick of time; so the bookseller pointed to him and said,

[30] See further W. H. Sellar, *Roman Poets of the Republic*, pp. 308–384; W. H. Mallock, *Lucretius on Life and Death* (New York, 1900) (selected passages of Lucretius, translated into the metre of Omar Khayyam); G. Santayana, in *Three Philosophical Poets*, (Cambridge, 1910); A. E. Taylor, *Epicurus*, pp. 80–96; G. F. Else, "Lucretius and the Aesthetic Attitude," *H.S.C.P.* 41 (1930), pp. 149–182.

[31] E.g., the pseudo-Platonic *Axiochus*, and Plutarch, *Against Colotes*.

[32] Catullus 5, 4–6; Horace, *Odes* III, 21; IV, 7, 13–16; see above, p. 50; cf. F. Villon, *Ballade des Dames des Temps Jadis*; William (Johnson) Cory, *Mimnermus in Church:* "But oh, the very reason why I clasp them is because they die."

[33] See further my *The Achievement of Rome* (Cambridge, Mass., 1933), pp. 379–383; 488.

[34] D.L. VII, 2–3.

'Follow yonder man.' The crude naturalism and personal independence of the Cynic, with its insistence on the absolute claims and the sufficiency of virtue, served for a time to develop his native ethical bias. Presently he built a foundation of physics for his ethics, by appropriating Ionian conceptions of fire and air. To this he added a naively materialistic logic and psychology. Even Aristotelian terms and conceptions appear in his work or that of his successors. Thus his system is a synthesis of earlier ingredients, inspired by a practical purpose. Expanded, interpreted, and defended by his immediate successors, Cleanthes (c. 304–233 B.C.) and Chrysippus (c. 208–281 B.C., the "second founder of Stoicism"), Stoicism underwent even further modifications in its "middle" period at the hands of Panaetius and Posidonius (second and early first centuries), drawing nearer to Platonism; further adaptations were made by the later Stoics, such as Seneca. Thus Stoicism differs from Epicureanism, which never was modified in any important way. Nevertheless it is possible to see in the work of Chrysippus the standard form of Stoicism. Not only is it far more abundant than the meagre fragments of Zeno and Cleanthes, but later philosophers, whether Stoics or opponents of Stoicism or Stoicizing eclectics like Cicero, tend to refer particularly to Chrysippus for the points to be established or attacked. Moreover, it is Chrysippus who especially realizes that the Stoic system contains a problem of fate, good, and evil. This is the system which we must first examine in its general outlines; we must then see what problems it left, and what solutions were offered.[35]

To the Stoic, as to the Epicurean, an interest in "Physics," Nature, is secondary to an interest in Ethics; but it is the subject that he must deal with first, for one's conception of what one must do, or even of what one may do, is determined by one's idea of the structure of the universe of which we are parts. The Stoic, speculator rather than experimenter, and chiefly a borrower or synthesizer, is about as much and about as little a scientist in the modern sense as is the Epicurean.

The Stoic is a monist, and a thorough-going materialist. He opposes not matter and spirit, for spirit is a subtle kind of matter, but rather the passive and the active, — terms which however are relatively rather than absolutely opposed, somewhat as in Aristotle's conception of matter and form. The active principle in the world is variously described by terms, largely inherited from early thinkers, which tend to be identified with one another: it is Fire, Breath, Nature, Reason, Law, God, Providence, Fate.[36] At one time Stoicism seems to be pantheism; at other moments, as in the *Hymn* of Cleanthes, it is a theistic religion.

[35] See Appendix 57: Stoics; bibliography.

[36] Cf. D.L. VII, 135.

O God most glorious, called by many a name
Nature's great king, through endless years the same;
Omnipotence, who by thy just decree
Controllest all, hail, Zeus, for unto thee
Behoves thy creatures in all lands to call.
We are thy children, we alone, of all
On earth's broad ways that wander to and fro,
Bearing thine image wheresoe'r we go.
Wherefore with songs of praise thy power I will forth shew.
Lo! yonder heaven, that round the earth is wheeled,
Follows thy guidance, still to thee doth yield
Glad homage; thine unconquerable hand
Such flaming minister, the levin-brand,
Wieldeth, a sword two-edged, whose deathless might
Pulsates through all that Nature brings to light;
Vehicle of the universal Word, that flows
Through all, and in the light celestial glows
Of stars both great and small. O king of kings
Through ceaseless ages, God, whose purpose brings
To birth, whate'er on land or in the sea
Is wrought, or in high heaven's immensity,
Save what the sinner works infatuate.[37]

So the *Hymn* begins; with the rest of it we shall be concerned later.[38]

How the Stoics reconciled the various manifestations of the active principle, Diogenes Laertius explains. "God is one and the same with Reason (Νοῦς), Fate (Εἱμαρμένη), and Zeus; he is also called by many other names. In the beginning he was by himself; he transformed the whole of substance through air into water, and just as in animal generation the seed has a moist vehicle, so in cosmic moisture God, who is the seminal reason (σπερματικὸς λόγος) of the universe, remains behind in the moisture as such an agent, adapting matter to himself with a view to the next stage of creation. Thereupon he created first of all the four elements: fire, water, air, earth."[39] The orderly process by which the *cosmos* comes into being is rational and divine; it exhibits the creative, or artistic power of fire;[40] it will some day end in a universal conflagration (ἐκπύρωσις), which only the immortal Zeus will survive, to begin a new cycle of cre-

[37] SVF I, 537, lines 1–13; trans. (with sundry textual variants) by J. Adam, *Vitality of Platonism*, p. 105; Adam's discussion follows, pp. 108–189.

[38] See below, p. 345.

[39] D.L. VII, 135–136, tr. R. D. Hicks.

[40] D.L. VII, 156: *φύσιν εἶναι . . . πῦρ τεχνικὸν ὅδῳ βαδίζον εἰς γένεσιν, ὅπερ ἐστὶ πνεῦμα πυροειδὲς καὶ τεχνοειδές*; cf. Cic. *N.D.* II, 57 (both are in SVF I, 171); the "way up and the way down" of Heraclitus (D22B60) underlies the conception.

ation.[41] Since the reason and providence of Zeus pervades all things, the *cosmos* may be described as a living creature endowed with reason (*ζῷον ἔμψυχον καὶ λογικόν*),[42] and having aether, or heaven, or the sun, as its ruling principle (*τὸ ἡγεμονικόν*). Evidence of the providential care (*πρόνοια*) of God and grounds for optimism is found in the perfection of the *cosmos*, its regularity and relative permanence, its adaptation of means to ends,[43] an adaptation particularly fitted to man's needs [44] and to his aesthetic sense.[45] Since the events in the cosmic process are connected in an endless chain of causation, they may also be described as all occurring through Fate.[46] This ultimate connection of every least detail in the universe, past, present, and future, here and in remotest space, with every other detail, — for example of the aspects of the stars with human actions, — is a bond of "sympathy" between all the parts of the universe, and serves, together with the providence of Zeus, as the basis of the Stoic belief in the possibility of foretelling future events by divination.[47] Chance (*tyche*) is excluded from serious consideration, as merely a cause inaccessible to man's reckoning.[48] Finally, man is a part of this cosmic system, and especially his soul, which is part of the soul of the universe, a spark of fire, or a "breath innate in us." [49]

Such, in the briefest possible compass, is the Stoic physics. What, next, of ethics and of man? The connection is supplied by the fact, just noted, that man is rational, that his reason is a part of the divine reason. What must be, must be; but man, by his insight, may will to do what must be done, and so may act in harmony with nature; or, again, he may resist. The result, considered externally, will be the same in either case, for man

[41] SVF II, 585–595. Some later Stoics, such as Panaetius, rejected the conception of the ἐκπύρωσις.

[42] D.L. VII, 139; cf. Plato, *Tim.* 30b: *τὸν κόσμον ζῷον ἔμψυχον ἔννουν.*

[43] Cic. *N.D.* II *passim*, esp. 78–80.

[44] Cic. *N.D.* II, 133; 154; 37; 160 (= SVF II, 1131; 1153; 1154).

[45] Cic. *N.D.* I, 47; *De Fin.* III 18 (= SVF I, 1165; 1166).

[46] *καθ' εἱμαρμένην δέ φασι τὰ πάντα γίγνεσθαι Χρύσιππος ἐν τοῖς περὶ εἱμαρμένης καὶ Ποσειδώνιος ἐν δευτέρῳ περὶ εἱμαρμένης καὶ Ζήνων, Βόηθος δ' ἐν τῷ πρώτῳ περὶ εἱμαρμένης. ἔστι δ' εἱμαρμένη αἰτία τῶν ὄντων εἰρομένη ἢ λόγος καθ' ὃν ὁ κόσμος διεξάγεται* (D.L. VII, 149 = SVF II, 915; cf. also Cic. *De Div.* I, 125 = SVF II, 921). The etymology here suggested (*εἱμαρμένη — εἰρομένη*), though incorrect, (see below, Appendix 4; and A. S. Pease on Cic. *De Div.* I, 125: *fatum autem*) is common enough in ancient literature. See further the definitions of *εἱμαρμένη* attributed to Chrysippus, SVF II, 913.

[47] D.L. VII, 149; Cic. *De Div.* I, 127 (= SVF II, 944); *De Div.* I, 82–84 (= SVF II, 1192); *De Div.* II, 34, and A. S. Pease *ad loc.*, on *consensu*; and see below, pp. 352; 357; 362. For something like *συμπάθεια*, cf. also Theophrastus, *De Causis Plantorum* II, 19, 4: *φαίνεται γοῦν συμπάσχειν οὐ μόνον τὰ ἐπὶ γῆς ἀλλὰ καὶ τὰ ὑπὸ γῆς ὕδατα, κτλ.*

[48] *ἄδηλος αἰτία ἀνθρωπίνῳ λογισμῷ*; SVF II, 965–967; 979.

[49] *τὸ συμφυὲς ἡμῖν πνεῦμα*, D.L. VII 156 (= SVF II, 776); cf. R. K. Hack, *La Sintesi Stoica*: II, *Pneuma*, in *Ricerche Religiose*, 2 (1926), pp. 297–325; and for the development of such ideas in later Stoicism, C. P. Parker, *Sacer Intra Nos Spiritus*, *H.S.C.P.* 17 (1906), pp. 149–160; and see below, p. 343, and n. 61.

cannot overrule Nature, or Fate; but by willing coöperation, by making its law his law, he can find happiness, or by resignation he can at least find peace. Thus Cleanthes once more sums up the conflicting elements in religious terms:

> Lead me, O Zeus, lead Thou me, Destiny,
> By whatsoever path ye have ordained.
> I will not flinch; but if, to evil prone,
> My will rebelled, I needs must follow still.[50]

To live "according to nature": that is the phrase, often repeated by the Stoics, which sums up their ethical ideal, or rather the means by which they expect to achieve first virtue, and thereby whatever happiness is humanly possible.[51] This is man's whole business; it leads to self-preservation; it involves action, not mere contemplation; it is attended by pleasure, though that is a by-product, not in itself the goal. Although the Stoics hold virtue to be the only good,[52] they also conceive of good as that which conduces to happiness (*εὐδαιμονία*) on the smooth current of life (*εὔροια βίου*).[53] All things else,—health, wealth, pleasure, even life itself,—may be used either well or ill, and therefore are "matters of indifference" (*ἀδιάφορα*), though later Stoics will distinguish them as "to be preferred" or "not to be preferred." [54] Here enters the question of value judgements, which the Stoic must needs transfer from external nature to the province of his own will.[55] Because even life is "indifferent," Stoics sometimes hold that there are circumstances in which suicide is justified. Virtue, on the other hand, is "a harmonious disposition, choiceworthy for its own sake and not from hope or fear or any external

[50] SVF I, 527; trans. R. D. Hicks, *Stoic and Epicurean*, p. 76; Seneca's version adds another line: *ducunt volentem fata, nolentem trahunt* (also in SVF I, 527).

[51] *Πρῶτος ὁ Ζήνων . . . τέλος εἶπε τὸ ὁμολογουμένως τῇ φύσει ζῆν, ὅπερ ἐστὶ κατ' ἀρετὴν ζῆν· ἄγει γὰρ πρὸς ταύτην ἡμᾶς ἡ φύσις*, D.L. VII 87 (= SVF I, 179, where see other passages from other authors); also SVF I 552 (Cleanthes); SVF III, 12 (Chrysippus): *ἴσον ἐστὶ τὸ κατ' ἀρετὴν ζῆν τῷ ζῆν κατ' ἐμπειρίαν τῶν φύσει συμβαινόντων.* We need not here dispute Diogenes' "*πρῶτος*," assigned to Zeno, though the conception of "life according to nature" has been foreshadowed by Heraclitus, certain Sophists, the Cynics, and Speusippus. It is on the cult of "Nature" that such a Stoic as Seneca based his primitivism, a respect for simple, uncorrupted, natural man, qualified only by his realization that primitive man is not a Stoic philosopher; *Epist.* 90; cf. Lovejoy and Boas, *Primitivism*, pp. 260–286; 364 f.

[52] See below, n. 57.

[53] Cf. Sextus, *adv. Math.* XI, 30 (= SVF III, 73); Sextus XI, 33 in SVF III, 75: *ἀγαθόν ἐστιν ἀφ' οὗ συμβαίνει τι τῶν ἐν τῷ βίῳ ὠφελεῖσθαι*; and, for further traces of utilitarianism, SVF III, 86; 95; 107; 108.

[54] D.L. VII, 102 (= SVF III, 117); cf. Plutarch in SVF III, 123.

[55] On this whole subject, see E. Grumach, "Physis und Agathon in der Alten Stoa," *Problemata*, 6 (1932), esp. pp. 16–43.

motive,"[56] and is the only absolute good;[57] moreover, it is in itself sufficient to ensure happiness.[58] Thus the Stoic "accepts the Universe,"[59] and attempts the possible, — that is, he seeks to discipline his life into conformity with what his reason tells him is nature's intention; he cannot change nature, except in minor details, but he can change himself. Especially does the Stoic, unlike the Peripatetic, distrust the emotions, as being merely erroneous opinions, and endeavor to attain to a passionless condition.[60] The will, or the motive, is more important than the deed, and is far more important than external circumstances. The Stoic does not expect happiness to offer herself to him without his effort; but he can find happiness within himself, even if the *polis* fails, even if he is poor, or old, or in pain. Such is the resoluteness, we may even say the resiliency, of the Stoic.

From diverse sources the early Stoics made this synthesis, which had the appearance of logical consistency, and which met for countless men the practical tests of life. Once it is granted that everything comes from Fate or Providence, two faces of a single reality, all the rest seems to follow necessarily. Nevertheless Stoicism almost immediately found that it contained inconsistencies, and that its attempts to deal with practical issues required reinterpretations and compromises. Quite naturally it was criticized by Epicureans, who denied Providence and whose conception of the good was pitched nearer to the heart of the average man; by Peripatetics, who strove to break down absolute antitheses into delicate gradations; by Academics, who met dogmatism with scepticism. But the Stoics themselves almost immediately took in hand the business of reinterpretation: Chrysippus differed with Zeno, Panaetius was in some ways heretical; and Posidonius in his day differed with his master Panaetius; Cicero borrowed from many sources. The result was an eclectic Stoicism. Some of these criticisms and modifications we must now consider.

A primary source of perplexity is the ambiguity of the conception of "Nature." Is Nature a fact (things as they are) or an ideal (what will be, what should be)? Acquiescence is the result of the first interpretation, eager activity of the second. And again, may the command "Follow Nature" mean not only our surrender to the universal Nature but also the development of our specific natures, of those functions with which Nature

[56] D.L. VII, 89; 127 (= SVF III, 37; 40; cf. 43, Cicero).

[57] D.L. VII, 101 (= SVF III, 30; cf. 37, Cicero).

[58] D.L. VII, 127 (= SVF III, 49); cf. Cic. *T.D.* V, 48–50 (= SVF III, 59).

[59] As Margaret Fuller said she did; to which Carlyle, hearing of her remark, retorted, "Egad, she'd better!"

[60] D.L. VII, 110–117; n.b. 117: *φασὶ δὲ καὶ ἀπαθῆ εἶναι τὸν σοφόν*; cf. Cic. *T.D.* IV, 43; Seneca, *Epist.* 116, 1 (= SVF III, 443): [*adfectus*] . . . *nostri illos expellunt, Peripatetici temperant.*

has endowed us as individuals? On the extent to which such a secondary meaning is admitted will depend the limits of self-surrender and self-realization. The trend of Stoicism was on the whole in the direction of a recognition of the value of the individual and of his specific *arete*, as a part of the whole. Of his duty, his conscience is the only judge.[61] But since he is rational, he will appreciate more and more, as he grows older and wiser, the claims of the whole: "An animal's first impulse . . . is to self-preservation, because nature from the outset endears it to itself, as Chrysippus affirms in the first book of his work 'On Ends,' saying that 'the nearest and dearest thing to every animal is its own constitution and its consciousness thereof.' . . . But when reason in accordance with a more perfect leadership has been bestowed on the beings we call rational, for them life according to reason becomes the natural life. . . . By the nature with which our life ought to be in accord, Chrysippus understands both universal nature and more particularly the nature of man, whereas Cleanthes takes the nature of the universe alone as that which should be followed, without adding the nature of the individual."[62] A corollary of this doctrine is the attitude of the Stoics toward political activity, which turns on the question of "nearness and dearness" (οἰκείωσις).[63] Shall the Stoic, like the Epicurean, shun the activities of the state and cultivate his own garden, shall he take part in politics, or shall he feel himself a member of a larger society, a citizen of the *cosmos*? Usually he takes the last course, whether as the rational rebel against a tyrannical Roman emperor, or as a rational emperor who writes: "The poet cries, 'O beloved city of Cecrops!' Wilt thou not say, 'O beloved city of Zeus'?"[64] It is as a believer in the participation of each rational soul in the universal Reason or Nature (not merely the national custom) that the Stoic, both in the Hellenistic age and in the Roman empire bases human law on nature, thus effecting a reconciliation between the rivals which the sophistic age had divorced.[65]

[61] The Stoic believes that he can recognize goodness by a sort of intuition (πρόληψις). Cf. also Seneca, *Epist.* 41, 1: *Prope est a te Deus, tecum est, intus est . . . sacer intra nos spiritus sedet bonorum malorumque nostrorum observator et custos.* See above, p. 340, n. 61; and cf. A. W. Benn, *Greek Philosophers*, pp. 349 f. Plutarch relates (*Cicero*, 5) that when Cicero consulted the Delphic oracle to learn "how he should become most famous," the reply came that "he should make his own nature (φύσις), not the opinion of the many, his guide in life."

[62] D.L. VII, 85–89; cf. above, p. 341, n. 51; Cic. *De Fin.* III, 16–21; 27; IV, 14; 32–39; 46–48; V, 17; 24–27; 33–44; 59–60; 65; *T.D.* V, 82; also R. D. Hicks, *Stoic and Epicurean*, pp. 77–80; A. W. Benn, *Greek Philosophers*, pp. 339–341.

[63] This question had interested also the Peripatetics; cf. F. Dirlmeier, "Die Oikeiosis-Lehre Theophrasts," *Philologus*, Supplementband 30, 1 (1937).

[64] M. Aurelius, *To Himself*, IV, 23.

[65] Cf. Justinian's *Digest* I, 3, 2; J. L. Myres, *Political Ideas of the Greeks* (New York, 1927), pp. 308–318; and see above, p. 227.

In his prophetic fervor, Zeno has championed the absolute claim of virtue on man, and the absolute opposition of good and evil, of saints and sinners. If virtue is the result of rational activity, a rigid logic must proclaim that most men, being largely irrational, are incapable of virtue, — a conclusion which common sense was bound to reject in favor of a conception admitting degrees of moral progress. Such was to be the compromise of Panaetius. That virtue alone is sufficient for happiness is another hard saying which offends common sense: do not the "good things of life" contribute at least something? So at length "Panaetius and Posidonius deny that virtue is self-sufficing: on the contrary, health is necessary, and some means of living and strength."[66] Similar concessions to the Academy and to the Peripatetics are made by the less extreme Stoics in the matter of "advantages," or "preferred things."[67] The result is a working philosophy of conduct not very different from that of the Peripatetics, except in the tremendous emphasis still placed on the will.

These, however, are minor accommodations to the necessities of living. There remain difficulties in the original Stoic creed that demand nothing less than a frontal attack. Is it true, after all, that the evidence justifies the simple optimism of Zeno, or the theodicy set forth at length by the Stoic Balbus in the second book of Cicero's *De Natura Deorum*, which holds that the universe is governed not only by Fate but by Providence, that it is the best of all possible worlds (if not of all conceivable), nay even that it is designed for the good of man? Granted the orderliness of the physical *cosmos*, there remain the ugly facts of the world of animals and men: natural catastrophes, pain, starvation, disease, cruelty, crime, mutual destruction, — in a word, the problem of evil. Can this be the purpose of a kindly Providence? And if physical evils can be explained away, or even given a moral justification, what of moral evils, that are seated in the wills of supposedly rational creatures? If sin is folly, and no absolutely wise man has yet been produced by the *cosmos*, is not the whole scheme of the creation a failure?[68] Is it then the part of discretion to relieve Fate and Providence from at least some of its moral responsibility by recognizing the freedom of the will of man, a freedom to create either good or evil? In this case Fate is deprived to that extent of any moral purpose, and seems to have no other purpose than the production of the next universal conflagration. Here, then, is a second major problem.

Cleanthes, perceiving the fact of evil, sought to relieve Providence, though not Fate, from responsibility for it, arguing (unlike Chrysippus) that though all that comes through Providence is also fated, not all that is

[66] D.L. VII, 128; see further, Cic. *T.D.* V, *passim*.

[67] See above, p. 341; D.L. VII, 106–107; but cf. Cic. *T.D.* V, 47 in criticism.

[68] So Plutarch, *De Communibus Notitiis*, 1076b.

fated is providential.[69] He goes further, and places the moral responsibility for evil squarely on the shoulders of man, holding that God nevertheless knows how to make evil contribute to good. Thus in his *Hymn*, of which we have already quoted the opening lines,[70] he continues, attributing all to God's purpose:

> Save what the sinner works infatuate,
> Nay, but thou knowest to make crooked straight.
> Chaos to thee is order; in thine eyes
> The unloved is lovely, who did'st harmonize
> Things evil with things good, that there should be
> One Word through all things everlastingly.[71]

And Cleanthes proceeds to castigate human folly, and to pray that God may deliver men from such darkness and lead them to wisdom.

Chrysippus (and others following in his footsteps) also has to admit the fact of evil, and to see it as caused, like everything else, by common "Nature";[72] but he invents elaborate and ingenious arguments to minimize evil or to reduce it to an incidental place in the scheme of things. Some of his arguments are of a purely logical type. So, for example, he maintains that such terms as good, justice, courage, and truth would be meaningless apart from their correlative terms.[73] Or again, just as coarse wit may be in itself offensive but may contribute to the charm of a comedy, so evil may have its place and be not without its uses in the whole of reality.[74] Moreover some evils are the necessary consequence of a plan that is on the whole good,—as the head is delicately contrived, but liable to injury.[75] Or good may come from evil, as war may relieve overpopulation; or earthquakes and other disasters may get rid of wicked persons.[76] And there may be still other apparent evils, as there are many animals, whose uses still elude us.[77]

[69] Chalcidius, *in Timaeum*, chap. 142 = SVF II, 933.

[70] See above, p. 339.

[71] *Hymn* of Cleanthes, SVF I, 537, lines 13–17, tr. J. Adam.

[72] Plut. *De Stoic. Repugn.* 1050a (= SVF II, 937).

[73] A. Gellius VII, 1, 1–6 (= SVF II, 1169); cf. Plato, *Theaet.* 176a (see above, pp. 297; 302); Seneca, *Epist.* 124, 19: *nulli vitium est, nisi cui virtus potest esse.*

[74] Plut. *De Comm. Not.* 1065d; *De Stoic. Repugn.* 1050 f. (both in SVF II, 1181); cf. *De Stoic. Repugn.* 1054 f. (= SVF II, 550): τέλεον μὲν ὁ κόσμος σῶμά ἐστιν, οὐ τέλεα δὲ τὰ τοῦ κόσμου μέρη, τῷ πρὸς τὸ ὅλον πως ἔχειν καὶ μὴ καθ' αὐτὰ εἶναι; *De Stoic. Repugn.* 1051a (= SVF II, 1182): κακίαν δέ φησι καθόλου ἆραι οὔτε δυνατόν ἐστιν οὔτ' ἔχει καλῶς ἀρθῆναι.

[75] A. Gellius VII, 1, 7–13 (= SVF II, 1170): *per sequellas quasdam necessarias* (κατὰ παρακολούθησιν); cf. also Philo *De Fortitudine* Vol. II Mang. p. 413 (= SVF II, 1171): the doctor should be praised for saving a life, not blamed for the amputation that was necessary to save it.

[76] Plut. *De Stoic. Repugn.* 1049a–d (= SVF, II, 1177); cf. SVF II, 1174 (Origen).

[77] Lactantius, *De Ira* 13 (= SVF II, 172).

Another group of arguments turns on the possible moral or educative uses of adversity. It is no more fair to blame God's providence when men abuse it than to blame a father because his children squander their patrimony.[78] Again, God disciplines men by hardships,[79] and warns them by natural calamities;[80] he may let the guilty man escape, and take vengeance on his descendants.[81]

Chrysippus clearly has his back to the wall, or he would not have resorted to some of these arguments; a number of them are reported to us by later critics of Stoicism who scornfully point out their fallaciousness. Chrysippus is determined not to admit that God can be responsible for anything shameful,[82] or that anything can be truly good except a good will; but in the end his Fate has been drained of most of the moral quality that entitles it to be called also Providence. He even admits that God cannot know everything;[83] and, as to his power, that "there is a good deal of necessity mixed in" with the governance of the *cosmos*.[84] In other words, Fate is not wholly providential, after all, and some good and some evil, at least, must be traced to other sources, perhaps to human wills. Later Stoics, indeed, like Cicero (partly a Stoic),[85] and Seneca, Epictetus and Marcus Aurelius,[86] tend to accept divine providence as a fact hardly open to argument, and to remove the problem of good and evil from the field of physics to ethics, to the province of human emotions and actions. Let us see how far the fatalism of Chrysippus, or of Stoicism generally, admits of human freedom of the will.[87]

In the first place, the whole physical theory of the Stoic committed him deeply to determinism. A work attributed to Plutarch reports the four

[78] Cic. *N.D.* III, 70 (= SVF II, 1186); see below, p. 359; Cotta implies that this is a common Stoic argument. Cf. also the *Hymn* of Cleanthes.

[79] Seneca, *De Providentia* I, 2, 6; I, 4, 7; Epictetus *Disc.* I, 24, 1 (comparing God to an athletic trainer); these almost amount to "whom the Lord loveth He chasteneth."

[80] Plutarch *De Stoic. Repugn.* 1040c (= SVF II, 1175).

[81] Cic. *N.D.* III, 90 (= SVF II, 1180); see above, pp. 36; 41 f.

[82] Plut. *De Stoic. Repugn.* 1049e (= SVF II, 1125).

[83] Philodemus, Περὶ θεῶν διαγωγῆς col. 7, 28 = SVF II, 1183.

[84] Plut. *De Stoic. Repugn.* 1051c = SVF II, 1178; cf. Cic. *N.D.* II, 167: *magna di curant, parva neglegunt.* But the Stoic speaker is perhaps thinking of physical evils; see J. Mayor *ad loc.*, and below, p. 358.

[85] For Cicero, see below, pp. 354–365.

[86] See Appendix 58: Seneca, Epictetus, M. Aurelius.

[87] The Stoic expression for freedom, borrowed from the Peripatetics, refers to "what is in our power" (τὸ ἐφ' ἡμῖν; see above, p. 327; below, Appendix 58); Epicurus uses τὸ παρ' ἡμᾶς (see above, p. 336); later writers use also the expression τὸ αὐτεξούσιον. See also O. Rieth, "Grundbegriffe," p. 156 (and cf. p. 133), who holds that the Stoics were concerned to establish moral responsibility, rather than "freedom of the will." But it comes to the same thing. For the whole subject in its relation to both ancient and modern thought, see G. L. Fonsegrive, *Le Libre Arbitre*: chap. v traces the increasing libertarianism of the Stoics; chap. vi ("Les Traités *de Fato*") deals with the works *On Fate* of Cicero, Plutarch [?], Alexander of Aphrodisias, and others; later chapters, with the debate in Christian theology.

chief arguments by which Chrysippus supported it: that nothing happens without a cause; that the universe is an orderly, self-contained organism; that the existence of divination proves that everything occurs according to fate (*moira*); and that every proposition is either true or false (the "law of contradictories").[88] To these may be added the argument that God's foreknowledge, which is infallible, includes all details, among them our characters and education, our actions, and the results of them; therefore all is predestined, and we are at best the agents of fate.[89] All these arguments might be summarized in the proposition that the future is wholly contained in the present, or indeed in the past.

The extreme position of Chrysippus, however, is open to objections; and Chrysippus himself appears to have betrayed some uneasiness about it. If the practise of divination is to be of any use, by allowing us to be on our guard against a fated disaster, not everything is then fated, "since it is in our power either to be on our guard or not to be on our guard" (*ἐφ' ἡμῖν ὄντος τοῦ φυλάξασθαί τε καὶ μὴ φυλάξασθαι*); otherwise "we shall be on our guard only if it is fated that we shall be so, and we shall not be on our guard, if it is not so fated, even if all the soothsayers give us warning of what is to be." And Chrysippus gives what is to become the commonplace illustration for the argument: Oedipus, whose parents, though forewarned, and attempting to forestall the predicted calamity by slaying him, were unable to do so. The warning, therefore, as Chrysippus concludes, was useless to them, because all was caused by fate.[90] The argument will be attacked by the Academic Carneades, on the ground that Apollo could not on Stoic principles foretell the death of Laius without knowing the chain of natural causes leading to it,[91] and more devastatingly by the Peripatetic Alexander of Aphrodisias.[92]

In his contention that every proposition is either true or false, and that what happens is the product of antecedent causes, Chrysippus is attempting to establish, as Cicero will point out, just that fatalism which Epicurus (with his "swerve") sought to escape.[93] But it is open to Carneades to point out that though a proposition must be true or false, events need not be the results of eternal causes inherent in nature or the universe, but may in part, at least, be the product of more immediate and fortuitous causes,[94]

[88] [Plut.] *De Fato*, Chap. 11 (= SVF II, 912); see also below, pp. 370–372.

[89] Chalcidius *in Timaeum*, chaps. 160–161 (= SVF II, 943); cf. Cic. *De Div.* I, 127 (= SVF II, 944), cited above, p. 340; and see below, p. 362.

[90] So Diogenianus reports Chrysippus, in Eusebius, *Praep. Evang.* IV, 3 (= SVF II, 939); cf. also Cic. *De Div.* II, 21: *si fato omnia fiunt, nihil nos admonere potest ut cautiores simus;* and A. S. Pease, *ad loc.*; and see below, pp. 348; 350; 364 f.; 372; 385, for the oracle given to Laius.

[91] Cic. *De Fato* 33 (= SVF II, 955); see below, p. 365.

[92] Alexander of Aphrodisias, Περὶ Εἱμαρμένης, 30–31; see below, p. 375.

[93] Cic. *De Fato* 20–21 (= SVF II, 952); see below, p. 364.

[94] Cic. *De Fato* 28 (= SVF II, 953).

a distinction which Chrysippus, too, is forced to make, as we shall presently observe.[95] Carneades, moreover, presses a number of other logical objections, the strongest of which is that the test of experience, by which alone the truth or falsity of a proposition can be established, is lacking in the case of propositions directed to the future; one may assert of the future that an event is possible, but not that it is necessary. The Stoics who argue otherwise "are not establishing the necessity of fate, but are merely interpreting terms." And, above all, "they are binding the human soul, deprived of freedom of the will, to the necessity of Fate." [96]

As a matter of fact, Chrysippus himself was unwilling to remain an out and out fatalist, and sought, as did Epicurus, to reconcile fate with freedom of the will, having it both ways, or even inclining a little to the side of freedom, but becoming involved in verbal tangles that caused him involuntarily to confirm the fatalist position.[97] His method is of two kinds. He observes the paralyzing effect of that form of fatalism, known as the "lazy fallacy," or the "argument of sloth" (ἀργὸς λόγος, *ignava ratio*), which runs: "If it is fated that you shall recover from an illness, you will recover whether you call a physician or not; if it is fated that you shall not recover, you will not recover, whether you call a physician or not; one of these alternatives is your fate, therefore it is of no avail to call a physician." [98] Because such an argument frustrates all activity, Chrysippus distinguishes two types of prediction: the simple type, as "Socrates will die on a certain day"; and a complex or conditional type, in which events are jointly dependent on fate (*συνειμαρμένα*, *confatalia*), as "A son will be born to Laius," the truth of which is not regardless of the relations of Laius and Iocasta. And if the rôle of deliberation, of the will, and of action, is recognized in this case, the inference is that it may apply also in the case of the patient and the physician.[99] Aristotle had already based his ethical conception of the voluntary on the naïf consciousness of freedom of the ordinary man and on what he assumes to be in our power (ἐφ' ἡμῖν);[100] and a Peripatetic work expressly deals with the "lazy fallacy." [101] This argument, by the way, Carneades had avoided, preferring an even

[95] See below, p. 349.

[96] Cic. *De Fato*, 11–16; 20 (= SVF II, 954). Here as elsewhere the Academic Carneades is using Peripatetic arguments to attack Stoic doctrines; cf. W. A. Heidel, *Necessary and Contingent*, pp. 37–42.

[97] Cic. *De Fato* 39; and cf. SVF II, 974; see also below, p. 349.

[98] Cic. *De Fato* 28–29 (not in SVF).

[99] Cic. *De Fato* 28–30 (of which 30 = SVF II, 952); cf. Origen, *Contra Celsum* II, 20 (= SVF II, 957); Serv. *ad Aen.* IV 696 (= SVF II, 958), distinguishing *condicionalia fata* from *denuntiativa.* Laius (or Oedipus) becomes the commonplace illustration for this argument; see also above, p. 347; and below, pp. 364; 372; 375.

[100] See above, p. 327.

[101] The (Peripatetic) *De Interpretatione* 18b31; cf. W. A. Heidel, *Necessary and Contingent*, pp. 42–45.

more direct attack on Stoic fatalism based on freedom as an immediate *datum* of experience. "If all occurs through fate, then nothing is in our power; but something is in our power, therefore not everything occurs through fate."[102]

Akin to the conception of jointly dependent events (*confatalia*) is the other chief argument of Chrysippus in support of at least a partial freedom, one which "avoids necessity but retains fate."[103] This turns on the distinction between two kinds of causes: principal and perfect (*προηγουμένη αἰτία, causa perfecta et principalis*), and proximate or auxiliary (*προκαταρκτική, proxima*). The Stoics had other terms as well to characterize types of causality.[104] Thus it is the nature (or, as Aristotle would have said, the formal cause) of a cylinder that permits it to roll down hill; that is the principal cause of its rolling. But it will not roll unless some one sets it in motion; that is the proximate or auxiliary cause (or, as Aristotle would have said, the efficient cause). What is true in this physical illustration holds also in the moral sphere: as the agent may or may not start the cylinder rolling, so the moral agent may give or withhold his assent (*συγκατάθεσις, assensio*) to the images (*φαντασία, visa*) provided by his experience; assent being "in our power," moral responsibility for action follows, and with it praise or blame.[105] For "the peculiar properties of our minds are subject to fate only according their individuality and quality."[106] The continuation of this argument, as reported by Gellius,[107] is intended as an answer to a determinist, "behaviorist" psychology, and is followed[108] by the illustration of the cylinder and the free agent, and by similar arguments from Pythagorean sources, and even by the famous speech of Zeus in the *Odyssey* blaming men, not gods, for folly and evil.[109] Nevertheless, it is so phrased as to leave practically no room for freedom; no wonder that Gellius concludes[110] by quoting Cicero (from a lost portion of his *De Fato*) to the effect that Chrysippus became flushed and strained and inextricably involved in the difficulties of the problem in his effort to explain how "every thing is ruled by fate, but that we nevertheless have some control over our conduct."

[102] Cic. *De Fato* 31; cf. also 32 and 33; and see above, p. 348; and below, pp. 364 f.

[103] Cic. *De Fato* 41.

[104] *σμῆνος αἰτίων καταλέγουσιν, τὰ μὲν προκαταρκτικά, τὰ δὲ συναίτια, τὰ δὲ ἑκτικά, τὰ δὲ συνεκτικά, κτλ.*, Alexander Aphr. Ch. 22 (= SVF II, 945); cf. Clem. Alex. *Strom.* VIII, 9 (= SVF II, 351), which adds *τὰ συνεργά*. On this whole subject, see O. Rieth, "Grundbegriffe," esp. pp. 134–155.

[105] Cic. *De Fato* 39–44 (= SVF II, 974); cf. A. Gellius VII, 2, 1–14 (= SVF II, 1000).

[106] A. Gellius VII, 2, 7, cited in previous note.

[107] A. Gellius VII, 2, 8–10.

[108] A. Gellius VII, 2, 11–14.

[109] *Od.* I, 32; see above, p. 22.

[110] A. Gellius VII, 2, 15.

The result, then, is a partnership of fate and freedom, or what a critic of Chrysippus, the Cynic Oenomaus, calls "half-slavery"; indeed Chrysippus himself is said to have used the figure of a dog, tethered to a moving vehicle, who may choose to run with it but who will be dragged by it, willy-nilly, if he does not so choose.[111] But this is not real freedom; for a real freedom to choose one of a pair of mutually exclusive terms implies an equal freedom to choose its opposite.[112] It is not surprising that the critics of Chrysippus, such as Plutarch, Origen, and Nemesius, should have protested that he only seemed to save freedom, and that fatalism remains.[113]

As in the case of Aristotle, and perhaps of all rigorous ancient thinkers who did not resort to a facile dualism, the difficulty arises from an initial assumption, the absolute power of an all-inclusive Fate. If Fate determines all, then *ex hypothesi* there is no room for freedom.[114] And especially is this the case where, as with the Stoics, the primary conception of Fate is abstracted from ordinary experience. For a Stoic, or a "behaviorist," to debate the problem of freedom is as futile and unreal as for a physicist to trifle with the question "What happens when one irresistible force meets another irresistible force?" The very question is a self-contradiction. So an abstract Fate, or Necessity, or Law, assumed by definition to be omnipotent, leaves no room for any freedom. Behavior, assumed to be the product of calculable past and present forces, can be of only one kind; there can be no question of moral responsibility. The abstract future is contained in as abstract a present; and both were long since contained in the abyss of the past. It is not asserted that any given person can predict the future, even with respect to a well-defined event; for human knowledge is limited. But it is asserted that there are at present in existence all the factors which, if fully known, would enable one to predict infallibly what must be.

From such a position the means of escape are of two kinds. First, one may deny the validity of the abstractions, and proceed to reckon with a

[111] For the partnership, Aetius *Plac.* I, 27, 3 = SVF II, 976, comparing the Stoics on this point with Plato, who is described as recognizing both *εἱμαρμένη* and *ἡ παρ' ἡμᾶς αἰτία*; so the Stoics *τὴν μὲν ἀνάγκην ἀνίκητόν φασιν αἰτίαν καὶ βιαστικήν, τὴν δὲ εἱμαρμένην συμπλοκὴν αἰτιῶν τεταγμένην, ἐν ᾗ συμπλοκῇ καὶ τὸ παρ' ἡμᾶς, ὥστε τὰ μὲν εἱμάρθαι.* Cf. Epiphanius *Adv. Haeres.* III, 2, 9 (H. Diels, *Doxogr. Gr.*, p. 592, 24–26) dealing with Zeno: *τὰς δὲ αἰτίας τῶν πραγμάτων πῇ μὲν ἐφ' ἡμῖν, πῇ δὲ οὐκ ἐφ' ἡμῖν, κτλ.* For "half-slavery," *ἡμιδουλεία*, cf. Eusebius *Praep. Evang.* VI, 7 = SVF II, 978 (see also below, p. 385); n.b. also the suggestion that Laius could have escaped his death by not begetting a son, but once his son was born there was no escape, and this Apollo knew. For the dog, cf. Hippolytus *Philos.* 21 (Diels *Dox. Gr.* p. 571, 11) = SVF II, 975.

[112] So Alex. Aphr. *Quaestiones* II, 4 and 5 (= SVF II, 1007); and for Aristotle, see above, p. 327.

[113] SVF II, 988–994; 996, 997.

[114] See also above, pp. 313 f. On this whole subject, cf. A. O. Lovejoy, *The Great Chain of Being*, on a similar conception, long entertained but here analyzed as a failure.

world that is alive, creative, evolutionary, in which growth, emergent organisms, and personalities or souls play a part.[115] This is compatible with, but does not require, a dualistic scheme of matter and spirit, or body and soul. And in the second place, one may argue that there is no more reason in strict logic or in experience to begin with the concept of necessity than with the concept of freedom; one is entitled therefore in view of what Kant called the antinomies of the pure reason, which involve an intellectual stalemate, to proceed on the hypothesis that what the practical reason demands for moral responsibility, namely freedom, is valid. And that, of course, is the actual procedure not merely of some metaphysicians, including the Academics and the Stoics in their less fatalistic moods,[116] but of modern "pragmatists," and indeed of the ordinary man.

We have been pausing to observe the efforts of Chrysippus, as the "standard" Stoic, to reconcile fatalism and freedom. We must now notice how later critics, incidentally or of set purpose, dealt with the problem, and with good and evil. For of course it entered into many general discussions of religion and ethics and metaphysics, and a considerable literature of special treatises "On Fate" grew up.[117]

The issue has now been clearly drawn between the fatalists, represented on the one hand chiefly by Chrysippus in his most characteristic expressions, and on the other hand by the defenders of freedom and by the humanistic theory of good and evil, represented by such Academic critics as Carneades, Clitomachus, and Antimachus, or by such a figure as Posidonius. In the absence of surviving works of these men, we are dependent on quotations from them, or criticisms of them, in later writers such as Cicero, Seneca, Plutarch, and Alexander of Aphrodisias, who indeed all find much of their ammunition in these earlier writers.

It has been the custom to regard Posidonius (135–51 B.C.) as a Platonizing, dualistic, mystical, Stoic, on whom could be fathered most of the innovations in Stoicism for which no other plausible source could be found; for example, the first book of Cicero's *Tusculan Disputations*, his *Somnium Scipionis*, and the second book of the *De Natura Deorum*, and

[115] Such, in general, is the direction taken by thinkers as different as Plato, Aristotle, Cicero, and St. Augustine, among the ancients; among modern trends, mention may be made of H. Bergson's "creative evolution," of Lloyd Morgan's "emergent evolution," the "vitalism" of H. Driesch, and B. Croce's conception of "history."

[116] The Stoics could consistently argue that this solution of the problem recognizes the life "according to Nature" and recognizes also man's rational nature. Cf. O. Rieth, "Grundbegriffe," pp. 156–168. For an astronomer's defense both of a mechanistic theory of nature and of man's freedom, together with the "conservation of character," cf. H. N. Russell, *Fate and Freedom* (New Haven, 1927).

[117] A partial list of the treatises *On Fate* (*pro* and *contra*) may be found in W. Gundel's article *Heimarmene*, *P.W.* VII, 2624–2626; 2643–2645. Cf. also G. L. Fonsegrive, *Libre Arbitre*, Livre I, Chap. VI, "Les Traités *de Fato*"; and see below, pp. 367 f.; 384 ff.

even the eschatology of the sixth book of Virgil's *Aeneid*.[118] His importance as a scholar in many fields, and as a consolidation of strictly Stoic ideas with ideas from other sources, is not diminished but is rather enhanced if the little that we really know to be Posidonian is subjected to close examination; he turns out to be of greater originality than was suspected.[119] The Stoic conception of "sympathy," to be sure, which has been supposed to be especially Posidonian,[120] now appears to be merely the normal Stoic doctrine. But Posidonius himself makes several innovations, the more important of which, for our special interest, may be summarized.

As to "Physics," Posidonius holds that unqualified matter is only a logical presupposition, while "God is intellectual spirit extending throughout all substance,"[121] not as creator, apparently, but acting within the world. But the God of Posidonius is not, as for other Stoics, identical with Nature or with Fate, but "Fate is in the third place from Zeus. The first is Zeus; the second, Nature; the third, Fate."[122] By "Nature," Posidonius means the systems of heaven and earth and the creatures therein contained,[123] which he considers to be animate;[124] soul, warm breath, holds together and moves organic beings. (There is no evidence in the fragments that Posidonius believed in personal immortality, or dealt with eschatology.) Inorganic bodies, on the other hand, consisting of eternal material qualities and forms, are the source of all movement, and may be called Fate.[125] Thus Posidonius recognizes three types of causality: "The cause of something is that through which it exists [matter], or the prime active power [soul], or the principle of activity [God, or Reason]."[126] Furthermore, he is a believer in divination.[127]

[118] See, for example, A. Schmekel, *Philosophie der Mittleren Stoa*, esp. pp. 85–154; 238–290; R. Hirzel, *Untersuchungen*, esp. Vol. I, pp. 191–243; Vol. II, pp. 516–535; 772–789 (but see also Vol. III, pp. 342–438, part of which opposes P. Corssen's attempt to find Posidonius extensively in Cicero); E. Bevan, *Stoics and Sceptics*, pp. 85–118; K. Reinhardt, *Poseidonius* (München, 1921); K. Reinhardt, *Kosmos und Sympathie*; J. Haussleiter, in *Jahresbericht* 255 (1937), pp. 22–27.

[119] J. F. Dobson, "The Posidonius Myth," C.Q. 12 (1918), pp. 179–195; L. Edelstein, "The Philosophical System of Posidonius," *A.J.P.* 57 (1936), pp. 286–325. (The author accepts as Posidonian only such matter as is connected by ancient notices with the name of Posidonius; to his article I am especially indebted in the following paragraphs; all passages therein cited are quoted in it.)

[120] W. Jaeger, *Nemesios von Emesa* (Berlin, 1914), pp. 97–133 ("Syndesmos"), finds the doctrine especially in Posidonius, whom he regards as "the first Neoplatonist," and traces the doctrine to Plato, *Tim.* 31bc. But Plato is at least no fatalist or materialist. See also above, p. 340, and n. 47.

[121] Commenta Lucani, p. 305 Usener.

[122] H. Diels, *Dox. Gr.* p. 324a4; Edelstein, *op. cit.*, pp. 292–305.

[123] D.L. VII, 138.

[124] Galen, *De Placitis*, p. 457, 2 Müller.

[125] D.L. VII, 149: *καθ' εἱμαρμένην δέ φασι τὰ πάντα γίνεσθαι . . . καὶ Ποσειδώνιος ἐν δευτέρῳ Περὶ εἱμαρμένης.*

[126] *Dox. Gr.* p. 457, l. 14 (Arius Didymus); cf. Edelstein, p. 302.

[127] See below, p. 361.

So far, God, Nature, and Fate have found a place in the philosophy of Posidonius; Good and Evil enter only when he turns to "Ethics," which he handles in a manner more akin to that of Aristotle than to that of the older Stoics. "From the right understanding of the emotions there may be derived the right understanding of things good and evil, of the virtues and of the aim of life."[128] And by "emotions" Posidonius does not, like the Stoics, mean judgements, but what the man in the street means: feelings, sufferings, bodily or psychic. These are partly the result of outward conditions, but may be disciplined and educated; here Posidonius sides with Plato and attacks Chrysippus. Among the "good things," not "matters of indifference," he includes health and wealth,[129] though he admits that wealth may be ill used and thus become a source of evil.[130] His teacher Panaetius does not believe that virtue is self-sufficient for happiness; therefore with the greater justification Posidonius discusses the rational control of life in accordance with conceptions of duties (*καθήκοντα*, or, in Cicero's term, *officia*), and especially, since Panaetius has not fulfilled his promise of dealing with the subject, he discusses conflicts between expediency and right.[131] And, again more like Aristotle than like the Stoics, he admits the possibility of moral progress. Finally, as to the aim of life, Posidonius though asserting, like Zeno, that it is living in agreement with Nature (that is, living in accordance with virtue), expressly rules out pleasure as an immediate goal, and also the ideal of "experiencing the happenings in the whole of nature."[132] Since discrimination is required, he puts his finger on the fallacy of such an ideal: to the emotions, the irrational and godless part of the soul, our brutish and evil *daimon* (something like "original sin"), it sacrifices the better *daimon* that is born in us and that has the same nature as the *daimon* that governs the whole *cosmos*.[133] There is a suggestion here of the dualistic psychology of Plato's *Phaedrus*. And Posidonius, once more nearer to Aristotle than to the Stoics, sets as his goal "the contemplation of the truth and order of all things, and the fashioning of oneself as far as possible in accordance therewith, being led aside as little as possible by the irrational part of the soul."[134] Yet Posidonius is not content with resignation to Fate, but counsels men not to rely on Fortune but to do battle with their own weapons,[135] thus assuming freedom of the will.

[128] Galen, *De Placitis*, pp. 448, 9–11; cf. 397, 5–8.
[129] D.L. VII, 103; cf. *Dox. Gr.*, p. 593, 9 (Epiphanius).
[130] Seneca, *Epist.* 87, 35; cf. 87, 31.
[131] Cic. *De Offic.* III, 7–8.
[132] Galen, *De Placitis*, p. 450, 5.
[133] Galen, *De Placitis*, p. 448, 15.
[134] Clem. Al. *Strom.* II, 129, reading, with Sylburg and Dindorf, *αὑτόν* ("oneself"); Dobson, *C.Q.* 12 (1918), p. 192, retains the Ms. reading *αὐτήν*, and translates: "helping to establish it" (sc. the orderliness of the Universe).
[135] Seneca, *Epist.* 113, 28.

The new Posidonius who stands thus revealed is not the mystic, the religious seer, the transmitter of Platonism and of oriental thought, the inspirer of eschatologies and the forerunner of Neo-platonism. A dualist in his own right he may possibly be, a humanistic ethical thinker (here certainly a dualist), a notable scientist, with a synoptic view of human experience. But we shall not find him greatly influencing later thought. Stoicism will continue to be chiefly the Stoicism of Chrysippus; those who do not find it wholly to their taste, like Cicero, will temper it with Academic criticism or with genuine Platonism, or will turn to quite different ways of thought.

4

In Cicero we meet the best example of the accomplished amateur of philosophy, the man of affairs whose early training under masters of several different schools (Epicurean, Stoic and Academic) has aroused a deep interest, especially in the problems of religion and conduct, and who in the last two years of his life, excluded by circumstances from action, resorts to philosophy both as a personal consolation and as a means of enriching the life of his fellow-countrymen. Hostile to Epicureanism, and both by his temperament and by his experience as a lawyer inclined to weigh opposing arguments and to choose the more likely conclusion, Cicero favors the sceptical trend of the New Academy,[136] rather than the dogmatism of the Stoics. In the time of national stress, however, and after domestic sorrows, above all after the loss of his daughter Tullia, he tends to turn more to the truly Platonic conviction of personal immortality, as well as to the dogmatic Stoic defense of divine providence. His rôle as a writer on philosophy is that of the gifted and well-read eclectic, who is seeking not so much to force conflicting doctrines into a consistent scheme as to give each its day in court. The dialogue form (closer to that of Plato's last works and of Aristotle's early works than to that of the earlier Platonic dialogues)[137] lends itself to this purpose. Though he modestly says of these works, in an oft-quoted remark, "They are copies, and so made with the less effort; I merely supply the words, of which I have an abundance,"[138] he is also correct in asserting that he treats his Greek originals with some independence of judgement.[139] In any case it was an amazing achievement for him to produce the notable series of works,

[136] See above, p. 331.

[137] R. Hirzel, *Der Dialog* (Leipzig, 1895), I, pp. 457–459; 550–559.

[138] *Ad Att.* XII, 52, 3.

[139] Cic. *De Off.* I, 6; M. van den Bruwaene, *La Théologie de Ciceron* (Louvain, 1937), finds in Cicero much more than a compiler of Greek excerpts. His suggestion (due in part to Hirzel) that Cicero's late works in part utilized his own earlier studies helps to explain his achievement in the last crowded years.

imperfect in arrangement and repetitious at times though they are, that were crowded into two brief years.[140]

Most interesting for our subject, apart from the ethical treatises on the various conceptions of the "end" of life, or the chief good and the chief evil (*De Finibus Bonorum et Malorum*) and on the practical problems of conduct in determining the claims of right and of expediency (*De Officiis*), are the (lost) *Consolatio*, written immediately after the death of Tullia, the *Tusculan Disputations*, and the group of theological works *On the Nature of the Gods*, *On Divination*, and *On Fate*.

We know that the death of Tullia profoundly affected Cicero. He wrote to Atticus that he wished to build for her not a tomb but something more like a shrine (*fanum*) suggestive of her *apotheosis*.[141] That, of course, is not good Stoic doctrine. And what we know of the *Consolatio*, as well as the whole of the *Tusculan Disputations* (which might have been entitled "*De Vita Beata*," or "the ways of attaining to a happy life," show that Cicero opens his mind to the Platonic doctrine of immortality as at least a live hypothesis. A dozen years earlier, in his *Republic*, he has written the impressive *Somnium Scipionis* as a tribute to this attitude. Yet he borrows also from the consolatory work of the Academic Crantor, *On Suffering*, sides with the Stoics as to the possibility of rising superior to pain and passion, and uses arguments from all the schools in support of the proposition that virtue is sufficient for happiness. If we had to label his attitude, it would be to call him a follower of the sceptical and critical New Academy, not expecting to reach dogmatic certainty, yet inclined to find the greater measure of probability in the Stoic emphasis on virtue, and in the Platonic doctrine of the soul and its destiny.[142]

A similar attitude is to be seen in the group of theological works. The *De Natura Deorum* is written with a serious feeling that atheism or the denial of divine providence is dangerous: "in all probability the disappearance of piety toward the gods will entail the disappearance of loyalty and social union among men as well, and of justice itself, the queen of all the virtues."[143] Cicero undoubtedly had little personal faith in the rites of divination in which he himself, as an augur, was supposed to engage, and which indeed he criticized in the second book of his work *On Divination*.[144] And the pontiff Cotta is paradoxically made the mouthpiece, in

[140] For Cicero's achievement in providing a Latin vocabulary for the expression of Greek philosophic terms, cf. M. O. Lişcu, *Étude sur la Langue de la Philosophie Morale chez Ciceron* (Paris, 1930); also Rieth (cited above, n. 104).

[141] Cic. *Ad Att.* XII, 36.

[142] For Cicero's sources in the *Tusculan Disputations*, cf. R. Hirzel, *Untersuchungen*, Vol. III, pp. 342–492.

[143] *N.D.* I, 4; cf. II, 168, put in the mouth of the Stoic Balbus. Cf. also Plato, *Laws* X; and see above, pp. 295 f.

[144] See below, pp. 362 f.

the *De Natura Deorum*, of the sceptical views of the New Academy, though in his official capacity he believes in upholding the state religion, which he accepts on authority.[145] Probably there is at work here not only the attitude of the official, who appreciates the social value of religion as a disciplinary and cohesive force, even if it be merely "the opiate of the people," but also, at least on Cicero's part, a genuine and deep-seated temperamental inclination, in a world in which there is much to be said on both sides of the ultimate problems of existence and of the ways of God to men, to admit that certainty cannot be found by the pure reason, and therefore that one must for practical purposes live by faith, testing one's faith by its moral results.[146] It is to be observed that Cicero himself, who takes hardly any part in the discussion, remarks at the very end that in his opinion the discourse of the Stoic Balbus "approximated more nearly to a semblance of the truth" than did the more sceptical discourse of the Academic Cotta. That was perhaps as far as the Academic Cicero could go in accepting Stoic dogmatism.[147]

In the first book of the *De Natura Deorum*, the Epicurean point of view is presented by Velleius and criticized by Cotta. The Epicurean conception of gods is easily demolished as inadequate and indeed superfluous. Not quite so easily to be met, and in fact never quite met in the present work is the Epicurean attack on the theology and cosmogony of Platonists and Stoics, on Plato's divine artisan of the world and the Stoic's Providence. Velleius mercilessly launches question after question. How could a creator build the world? If created, how could it be indissoluble? Or, on the other hand, why should Providence create a mortal world. "Why did these deities suddenly awake into activity as world-builders after countless ages of slumber?" And why all the details of the firmament, — for self-gratification, or for the delectation of a handful of wise men or of many fools? And if the world itself is to be deified, why should it be spherical and rotating? And why should the earth, part of the world, be so obviously imperfect? [148]

[145] *N.D.* III 5–7; cf. 44 (on Carneades); 93, 94.

[146] See above, pp. 350 f. "I believe in God," said a recent theologian, "until you demonstrate His existence." "And then?" asked his friend. "And then I disbelieve the proof."

[147] For the interpretation of this final remark see A. S. Pease, "The Conclusion of Cicero's *De Natura Deorum*," *T.A.P.A.* 44 (1913), pp. 25–37 (the work is descriptive, not polemic; Cicero is dealing with method, rather than dogma; his sympathies are divided); N. G. McCrea, "Cicero and the Academy," *P.A.P.A.* 66 (1935), pp. xxviii f. (Cic. holds to the Academy and probability, but also through temperament rather than reason, to a spiritual view of the universe as the basis of a virtuous and active society); and in general, J. B. Mayor, ed. *N.D.* vol. III, pp. ix–xxv. We shall meet a similar attitude in the problem of fatalism and freedom of the will; see below, p. 365. The reading of Cicero's work may well be followed by the reading of the *Octavius* by the Christian Minucius Felix (on which cf. E. K. Rand, *Founders of the Middle Ages*, pp. 41–49).

[148] *N.D.* II, 18–24.

process the active principle, and supposes it to be intelligent and operating in time; whereas on the Stoic's own hypothesis the active principle should consistently be regarded only as logically distinguishable but not as actually separate from the attributes of matter.[176] Thus we may say that matter behaves according to physical "laws," but only by the license of personification may we say that laws, like living creatures, *cause* events. The Stoic universe is supposed to be alive and rational; it is the Academy's business to show that the matter of the Stoics, being passive, corruptible, and finite, cannot be identified with a divine and eternal and intelligent being, much as the Epicureans proved that an immortal soul cannot be derived from mortal matter.[177] If this be granted, all the rest follows, and the arguments against belief in the special interest of Providence in human affairs must be granted also, unless Providence is conceived to be of a quite different order of being. Provisionally we are left, then, with the conception of Nature as a System of neutral creative forces, operating in general ways which are as a matter of fact on the whole to the advantage of man, who must however work out for himself within this field of neutral forces whatever may conduce to his own specific interest or good. Cotta professes to suspend judgement, but has no positive creed to put forward except that of the state, as we have seen,[178] while Cicero himself is inclined to accept, also on faith, the Stoic Providence as the more likely hypothesis.[179]

The *De Natura Deorum* was followed almost immediately by the *De Divinatione*, which is linked with the former work very closely by its subject-matter. But whereas Cicero has perhaps betrayed in the earlier work a temperamental leaning toward Stoicism, in spite of the Academic criticism, in the *De Divinatione* he writes with real fervor in criticism of the Stoic belief in divination, — and that, too, in spite of his own office as an augur. Doubtless his realization of the cynical misuses and political perversions of the practises of divination in his own day makes him eager to divorce it from the other religious institutions whose utility he appreciated.[180]

The arguments in favor of divination are set forth in the first book chiefly by Quintus Cicero (who though partly a Stoic was actually more a Peripatetic), and are drawn chiefly from Posidonius, though they refer

[176] That is, there is no difference between *Natura naturans* and *Natura naturata*. Cf. Lactantius, *Inst. Div.* VII, 3: *interdum sic confundunt* [*Stoici*], *ut sit Deus ipsa mens mundi, et mundus corpus Dei*; and see T. W. Levin, *Six Lectures Introductory to the Philosophical Writings of Cicero* (Cambridge, 1871), p. 85, n. 3.

[177] *N.D.* III, 29–31; cf. Lucretius III.

[178] See above, pp. 355 f.

[179] See above, p. 356.

[180] Cf. A. S. Pease, ed. *De Div.*, Intro., pp. 10–13.

also to the older Stoics.[181] They are illustrated by countless anecdotes and by quotations from Roman and from Greek poets. They proceed from the common (Epicurean, as well as Stoic) belief in weather signs derived from the behavior of animals ("natural divination"), to the belief in tokens expressly sent by the gods, such as portents and dreams, and "artificial divination" elicited by the arts of haruspices and augurs. The possibility of divination is quite explicitly deduced from the standard Stoic theory of Fate, and from such a notion of the causal nexus of everything ("sympathy") as regards the future as contained in the present.[182]

In the second book, Marcus Cicero replies, using arguments drawn chiefly from Carneades (probably through Clitomachus), but partly from the Stoic Panaetius, who was a heretic with regard to divination. He begins by eliminating one by one the fields within which divination may be supposed to operate, — fields in which the senses or the arts give reliable information; only one field seems to be left, that which chance controls.[183] But this is precisely the field in which determinism, and therefore divination, is ruled out.[184] Or if chance is ruled out, and we return to Stoic fatalism, of what avail is divination in avoiding calamity, since all is now supposed to be predestined? [185] Indeed a knowledge of the sad and inevitable future might be a disadvantage.[186] After this preliminary skirmish Cicero deals systematically with the various kinds of divination practised in Rome, not denying the existence of "sympathy," but denying any special interpretation of it that would connect rites of divination with knowledge of particular events.[187] An admirably rational attack is made on the Stoics who rest their case for theism on divination: rather than prove the existence of gods from the existence of divination, one should argue that the futility of divination proves the non-existence of gods, — a conclusion which, of course, Cicero does not seriously accept (II, 41). Quite admirable, too, is Cicero's naturalistic explanation of various phenomena commonly ascribed to the success of divination: the cult of Fortuna and "lots" at Praeneste (85–87), astrology (87–99), and dreams (119–142; 146–147). Belief in oracles receives a sharp reproof (110–118). And Cicero sums up his purpose and achievement in this work by distinguishing between *superstitio*, which he hopes he has overthrown, and

[181] Pease, pp. 18–24.

[182] *De Div.* I, 125–128; n.b. 127: *Qui enim teneat causas rerum futurarum idem necesse est omnia teneat quae futura sint.*

[183] *De Div.* II, 9–14.

[184] II, 15–18.

[185] II, 19–21; cf. *N.D.* III, 14; see also above, p. 347.

[186] II, 22–26. On the commonplace that not even Jupiter can overrule Fate (25), see the passages collected by Pease, *ad loc.*

[187] II, 34; cf. 37, a thoroughly "naturalistic" statement; also 142.

*religio*, which he seeks to uphold, but maintaining once more his Academic suspension of judgement (148–150). It is clear, however, that he feels that no further defense of divination could be made in rebuttal.

From the writing of the *De Divinatione* Cicero had planned to proceed to a similar treatise on fate, which was also to argue both sides of the question in two books, the first setting forth the Stoic doctrine, the second the Academic criticism of it.[188] Perhaps it was the pressure of events that caused him to condense this undertaking probably into a single book, the *De Fato*.[189] Accordingly in the present work Cicero does not, as in the *De Natura Deorum* and the *De Divinatione*, set forth at length the position of one school through the mouth of one speaker, and then make another speaker criticize it at length from the point of view of an opposing school; he himself carries on the discussion continuously, more (as in the *Tusculan Disputations*) moving from topic to topic, and bringing into juxtaposition at each point the views of the opposing schools. Of the work a small portion at the beginning[190] has been lost; also the last part of the work; and there are some *lacunae*. It is fairly clear that for the Stoic argument Cicero made use of the work by Posidonius, *On Fate*, reflecting the work of like name by Chrysippus, and that for the Academic criticism he utilized a work of Antiochus (probably the one of the same name) which presented the doctrine of Carneades.[191] His own point of view is not explicitly stated, unless in the sections on fortune,[192] or unless it was indicated in the lost exordium; but it is not difficult to perceive his general sympathy with the thought of Antiochus, which seeks to save the freedom of the will from Stoic fatalism, just as in the previous work Cicero had sympathized with the Academic attack on that divination which was supposed by the Stoics to be a deduction from the same fatalism. But he is anxious also to see in Chrysippus whatever admissions favor freedom, and to suggest that both schools really believe in freedom, differing in terms, rather than in substance.[193]

Although we have already considered a number of passages from

[188] *De Div.* II, 3; II, 19; I, 125. Cf. A. Loercher, *De Compositione et Fonte Libri Ciceronis Qui est De Fato* (Halle, 1907), pp. 342–345; A. Yon, ed. *De Fato* (Paris, 1933), pp. vi–x.

[189] Cf. *De Fato* 1: *casus quidam.*

[190] Possibly to be supplied from Aulus Gellius VII, 2 (see above, pp. 347; 349), from Servius on *Aen.* III, 376, and from other authors; cf. Loercher, pp. 371–375; Yon, pp. xxxiv–xl.

[191] But Cicero supplemented Posidonius, who seems to have upheld, like other Stoics, "sympathy," but not astrology, by interpolations from Chrysippus; while with the matter taken from Chrysippus he interpolated direct borrowings from Carneades and Diodorus of Megara (*De Fato* 13; 17–18, for Diodorus); he also added some rhetorical flourishes of his own. For the sources, see A. Schmekel, *Phil. der Mittl. Stoa*, pp. 155–184; A. Loercher, *op. cit.*, pp. 339–340; 347; 354–361; 369; 375; A. Yon, *op. cit.*, pp. xl–xlvi, holds that Cicero used only Antiochus.

[192] See below, and n. 196.

[193] *De Fato*, 44: *verbis eos, non re dissidere.*

Cicero's *De Fato*, because they preserve respectively the arguments of Chrysippus or of Carneades,[194] we may here survey the work as a whole. Where the text proper begins (after the introduction, and a *lacuna*), Cicero is criticizing Posidonius for attributing to fate and "sympathy" what may be due to mere chance.[195] Chrysippus also is at fault in attributing too much in men's conduct to climate; nature (climate, for example) may determine our temperaments to some extent, but not every detailed choice or act, as to where and when we shall walk.[196] The attempt of Chrysippus to base divination on determinism fails to distinguish between the possible and the necessary;[197] which Diodorus the Megarian, in his discussion of "possibles," arguing that only that is possible which either is or will be, and furthermore that what will be must be of necessity, goes beyond the evidence.[198] Epicurus, in seeking to avoid such determinism by means of the "swerve," unnecessarily admits events without any cause;[199] whereas Chrysippus, by insisting that every proposition is either true or false (the "law of contradictories") and that every event is dependent on a chain of causation, reaches an even more dangerous conclusion.[200]

Carneades is called in as conciliator, one who is able to recognize both freedom and causality, since the human will is itself a cause. And this does not invalidate the law of contradictories; true propositions directed to the future need not imply that all future events are inherent in the whole nature of things and of the world; there is room for contingency.[201] The "lazy fallacy"[202] is no serious obstacle; for even Chrysippus admits that there are events which are conditional on other events (*confatalia*), and which are thus not absolutely determined in themselves; for example, the birth of Oedipus.[203] Carneades, on the other hand, avoids such reasoning, and gives the lie direct to determinism; starting with human freedom as an indisputable *datum* of experience, he argues that it is therefore determinism that is ruled out.[204] Mere futurity is not the same as

[194] See above, pp. 347–349; for Chrysippus, *De Fato*, 20–21; 28–30; for Carneades, 7–8; 28; 31–33; 41–44.

[195] *De Fato*, 5–6.

[196] 7–9 (= SVF II, 950–951): *nam nihil esset in nostra potestate, si ita se res haberet.* The emphasis of Chrysippus on climate recalls the theories of the Greek medical writers of the fifth century B.C.; see above, pp. 268 f. Cf. also Cicero's criticism of astrology, *De Div.* II, 87–99, and above, pp. 362 f.

[197] *De Fato*, 11–12.

[198] 18–19. On Diodorus and his logic, and the "dominative argument" (κυριεύων), see Yon, *op. cit.*, pp. xxi–xxii; T. W. Levin, *Lectures*, pp. 89 f.

[199] *De Fato*, 18–19.

[200] 20–23; see above, p. 347.

[201] 23–28; see above, pp. 347 f.

[202] See above, p. 348.

[203] 28–30; see above, pp. 347 f.; and below, pp. 372; 375.

[204] 31; see above, p. 349.

necessity; so not even Apollo could foretell future events whose causes are not wholly contained in nature, and therefore could not foretell the career of Oedipus.[205] But a further analysis of the concept of causality is possible. One should distinguish mere antecedence (which is *not* causality) from the necessary efficient cause (34–35), and this in turn from the *sine qua non* which is not in itself sufficient to cause an event (36). Only after the event, indeed, is it sometimes possible to assign the cause, even though it was true before the event that it was to occur (37–38). Now Chrysippus attempted to mediate between determinism and freedom of the will, and in fact inclined toward freedom; but his terminology committed him to determinism.[206] The defenders of freedom assert that one's tendencies and desires (*adpetitus, adsensiones*) are free, since otherwise all moral responsibility would be impossible (40). In order to avoid determinism, while retaining causality, Chrysippus devised his distinction of principal (or perfect) causes and auxiliary (or proximate) causes; among the latter he includes those that are "in our power," and illustrates the point by the simile of the cylinder and the agent who starts it rolling.[207] Thus the quarrel between Chrysippus and his opponents is merely as to whether the term "fate" is to be used of our tendencies and desires; it is agreed that the sense impressions which precede them are external and necessary (44–45). In any case, Cicero concludes, such reasoning is preferable to the Epicurean "swerve," which is without causes; and yet the atomic system, even with the swerve, he regards as in the highest degree fatalistic.

In the *De Fato*, as in the two preceding theological treatises, Cicero's usually sceptical attitude is allowed to serve as the chief means of attack on the dogmatism of the fatalists. The reason is patent. In merely intellectual or speculative matters, the sceptical position is safe, and nothing is lost if certainty is frankly dismissed as unattainable. But in the question of fatalism and freedom of the will, the foundations of ethics and of patriotism are at stake; Cicero's choice, in view of his rôle as humanist and patriot, could not be doubtful: freedom must be upheld. Many modern men have made similar choices; one cannot fail to compare Kant's appeal from the pure reason to the practical reason.[208]

We have considered Cicero's treatise *On Fate* in some detail as an example of the way in which the conflict between the Stoic fatalists and their more humanistic critics was conducted. The debate continued, with shifting strategy. In the field of poetry, the great name is Virgil.

[205] 32–33; see above, p. 349. [206] 39; see above, p. 349.

[207] 41–43; see above, p. 349.

[208] See above, p. 351; also M. Y. Henry, "Cicero's Treatment of the Free Will Problem," *T.A.P.A.* 58 (1927), pp. 32–42, with many modern illustrations.

Virgil's treatment of fate issues from an even richer fund of ideas than does Homer's. He moves from one philosophy to another, or fuses them at will; Epicureanism (in the *Bucolics* and *Georgics*) is followed by Stoicism and a Platonic mysticism (in the *Aeneid*) which is congenial to Virgil's personal mysticism. The Trojan legend is seen by him as providentially destined by gods not wholly unlike those of Homer to culminate in the greatness of Augustan Rome and her mission in the history of the world.[209] Even divine opposition to this consummation finds a reconciliation foreshadowing the ineluctable facts of Roman history, facts which must have been in some sense fated. Obstacles of another sort, in the persons of Dido and Turnus, each the victim of a tragic fault, occasion a swerve in the epic scheme that suggests Greek tragedy.[210] Their suffering and death, and the sufferings of Aeneas himself, at first hardly understood by him, yet borne with Stoical fortitude, and later (after the vision vouchsafed in the lower world) accepted as the price of progress, are part of the divine plan for a Rome whose task is beneficent. Yet as to the precise cause for many an event, whether it is natural causality, or chance, or fate, or a divine purpose, Virgil very often suspends judgement, or gives alternative explanations.[211]

Virgil employs all the means of divination and prophecy that are at the disposal of the epic poet,[212] — dreams, omens, oracles, sooth-sayers, the Sibyl, the didactic and prophetic speech of Anchises in the Elysian Fields, the scenes depicted on the shield of Aeneas, and messages from the gods, — to establish a conviction of what must take place. But it is above all the will (*numen*, the "nod") of a god or "what has been said" (*fatum*) by a seer or (later) by a god, that Virgil employs to give a sense of fatality.[213] *Fatum* indeed absorbs the ideas that were wrapped up in most of the Greek conceptions of fate: the Homeric conception of Moira ("the allotted portion"), the will of Zeus, *Ananke*, *Heimarmene*, *Tyche*, and *Pronoia*.[214] Yet what is "fated," that is, "said" by Jupiter, or by another god, though effective, is possibly not omnipotent; for gods may be in conflict, and even the "things said" by Jupiter himself on different occasions

[209] See Appendix 60: Polybius; Livy; Diodorus Siculus.

[210] See above, p. 117, and n. 73.

[211] See Appendix 61: Virgil; Tacitus; Lucan.

[212] Cf. C. H. Moore, "Prophecy in the Ancient Epic," *H.S.C.P.* 32 (1921), pp. 99–175; for Virgil, pp. 133–142.

[213] Less often, Virgil also uses the *Parcae* (= the *Moirai*, as spinners and birth-goddesses and prophets), and *Fortuna* (something between Luck, Fate, and the gift of birth; see C. Bailey, *Religion in Virgil* (Oxford, 1935), pp. 234–240; and see below, n. 217).

[214] With *Il.* 1, 5: Διὸς δ' ἐτελείετο βουλή, cf. *Aen.* I, 2, *fato profugus*, and Servius *ad loc.* The word *fatum* is, of course, older than Virgil; cf. Ennius (in Cic. *De Div.* I, 66) line 58 Vahlen: *Apollo fatis fandis dementem invitam ciet.* But it is Virgil who most exploits the word: e.g., *Aen.* I, 254–262: [*Jupiter*] *fatur . . . manent immota tuorum fata tibi: . . . fabor enim . . . et volvens fatorum arcana movebo.*

may seem to be inconsistent or at least in need of being brought into some final harmony with an even more inclusive and ultimate power. Personal fortunes may have to bow to a more universal destiny. Thus fates may be "weighed" against contrary fates.[215]

It is an illuminating experience to read the *Aeneid* with an eye to the way in which all these matters present themselves to Aeneas himself as his fortunes develop. At Troy, he is the Homeric hero, who would rather die fighting than yield, but who has become convinced by his successive visions of Hector and of the gods, and finally of Creusa's shade, that Troy is doomed by the will of the gods, and that his task lies elsewhere. Just where, he gradually learns, after disappointments and neglected or misunderstood warnings, during his voyages. The storm and shipwreck are serious reverses; Carthage seems a happy refuge, but the gods overrule his free will; he at last leaves, not gladly, but resolutely, for he has learned the futility and the wrongness of resisting what he now recognizes as no longer merely "things said" to him but as fate. But that this fate is not only cruel, but is in the end to be also providential, as the Fatum Romanum, is the lesson that he learns from the lips of Anchises. Henceforth he is the willing servant of fate: *fors et virtus miscentur in unum.*[216] The Italic *socii* must be crushed, as indeed their descendants were all but crushed in the Social War, and absorbed, by Rome only twenty years before Virgil's birth. So Aeneas, something more and something less than a Stoic saint, is Virgil's symbol of man's fated pilgrimage through a world of heroism and devotion and, it must be added, of precious human affections.[217] Yet for Virgil there remains at the heart of things the mystery, unsolved by man, on the one hand, of suffering not wholly deserved, of single wills thwarted for reasons which we can imperfectly understand; and on the other hand the possibility and the duty of retrieving from evil and from failure something noble and good.

## 5

In the centuries after Virgil the great debate continued. Treatises on Fate and Providence multiplied.[218] Seneca, whose prose occasionally

[215] *Aen.* I, 239: *fatis contraria fata rependens.* On this and other aspects of the problem, cf. L. E. Matthaei, "The Fates, the Gods, and the Freedom of Man's Will in the *Aeneid*," *C.Q.* 11 (1917), pp. 11–26.

[216] *Aen.* XII, 714; cf. Seneca, *De Providentia* III, 4; IV, 12: *paulatim* [*fortuna*] *nos sibi pares faciet* (cf. p. 346 above; also pp. 27 f.).

[217] See further my "Self-Revelation in Virgil," *C.W.* 24 (1932), pp. 169–173; 177–181, with other literature there cited; C. Bailey, *Religion in Virgil*, Chapter IX, "Fate and the Gods," with an Appendix on "*Fortuna*"; T. Frank, *Vergil* (New York, 1922), pp. 182–192; E. K. Rand, *The Magical Art of Virgil* (Cambridge, Mass., 1931), pp. 363–372; A. S. Pease, ed. *Aen.* IV (Cambridge, Mass., 1935), pp. 38 f., 54 f., 554 (Index, s.v. "fate").

[218] Besides the works dealt with in the text, mention may be made of Philo Judaeus (b. *circ.* 20–10 B.C.), Περὶ Προνοίας, now extant only in an Armenian version (but long

touches on fate (or fortune), reverts to the theme often in the choruses of his tragedies, and especially to the mutability of human affairs.[219] The sometimes eclectic Platonism of the second century of our era, best represented by Plutarch and Albinus, and the Peripatetic Alexander of Aphrodisias, turned to our problem, which engaged the interest of the Neoplatonists and in due season, of course, of such Christians as St. Augustine.

Meanwhile the Graeco-Roman world had been further penetrated by the "mystery religions," which moved west and which promised their initiates personal salvation and an escape from the harshness of Fate. This was the age, too, when the cults of *Nemesis* and *Tyche* were renewed (*Tyche* often in association with the fortune of a ruler or of a city);[220] when *daimones* became demons; when magic and astrology flourished;[221] when oracles were still in honor, even if they temporarily ceased (before Plutarch's time);[222] when the cult of the Sun was associated with rulers, even with the cult of the Roman emperor.[223] But our concern must be less with the popular trends of religious expression than with the more philosophical expressions of the period. We may begin with the "Middle Platonists."

Not a profound or original thinker, Plutarch (*c.* 46–120) is a noble student of life and letters. To such an *anima candida*, much in the way of superstition and of intellectual perverseness may be forgiven. If he upbraids Stoics and Epicureans alike, it is because he feels that the doctrines that he attacks impede the best way of life, and this is something that really matters. If he writes for Apollonius a merely conventional anthology of consolation,[224] his letter to his wife on the death of their daughter is a moving document. And his *Moral Essays*, like his *Lives*, are the product both of reading and of ripe reflection.[225]

Like the other "Middle Platonists" of the second century, Plutarch professes to return to the Platonism of Plato himself, resisting both the scepticism of the New Academy and the dogmatism of Stoics and Epicureans. A good deal of his philosophical work is therefore devoted to the discussion of problems on what he conceives to be Platonic lines. Thus scattered passages in Plato are made to serve a single philosophy of

---

fragments are excerpted by Eusebius, in the *Praeparatio*; cf. Loeb ed. of Philo, Vol. IX, pp. 454–507), and of Seneca, *De Providentia;* and see also above, pp. 346; 351, and n. 115, and below, pp. 384 f.

[219] Seneca, e.g., *Thyestes*, 596–622; *Oedipus*, 980–994; and see above, p. 112, n. 46.

[220] See Appendix 62: Τύχη: Fortuna.

[221] See Appendix 63: Astrology.

[222] See Appendix 64: Oracles.

[223] See Appendix 65: Ideas in Roman Period: bibliography.

[224] It has been suspected that the *Consolatio ad Apollonium* is not by Plutarch himself.

[225] Of Plutarch's religious and ethical thought, a popular account may be found in J. Oakesmith, *The Religion of Plutarch* (London, 1902).

history. Plutarch rightly holds that Plato combined the God of the theologians and poets with the matter of the physicists; but he mistakenly argues that Plato derived evil not from matter but from a pre-existent, disorderly soul which an absolutely good God is able partially, but not wholly, to convert into the world-soul which in turn is the author in time of the *cosmos*.[226] God is transcendent, and not in direct contact with earthly things; and Plutarch attacks the Stoics whose materialistic pantheism makes God responsible for evil, and yet a punisher of evil. It is assumed that man's will is free. Plutarch believes in divination and in demons, beings intermediate between gods and men, some good and others evil; these he finds not only in Hesiod but in Homer, and he uses them to explain various phenomena, such as divination and the cessation of oracles.

Throughout the *Moral Essays* of Plutarch the reader catches glimpses of this dualistic theology and its implications. To Epicurean taunts as to why the mills of God grind so slowly, he replies in the essay *On the Instances of Delay in Divine Punishment* that the gods are not vindictive, like men, but leave room for repentance and reform. To the human conception of retribution, which he finds expressed in the Aeschylean phrase, "suffering for the doer,"[227] Plutarch opposes the conception of rewards and punishments hereafter, a conception which postulates, of course, a belief in the immortality of the soul. The myth that follows has something of the flavor of the Platonic Myth of Er, with its proclamation in the name of "Adrasteia, daughter of Zeus and Necessity,"[228] but it more definitely suggests the possibility of moral reformation.

Thus Plutarch answers the Epicureans. It may be they whom he answers also in his *Essay on Chance* (*Tyche*). He begins with the quotation of a line by the tragic poet Chaeremon: "Chance, not wisdom, rules the life of men."[229] This Plutarch scornfully refutes. Was it by chance that all the heroism, all the villainy of human history has occurred? No, the moral, dominating qualities of man depend on sagacity, self-control, and reason, man's special gift, that distinguishes him from the beasts. Even the arts rarely succeed by chance, *a fortiori* the whole conduct of life, which includes all the arts.

If Plutarch recoils against the Epicureans, he has almost as little use for the Stoics, not because of their dogmatism, for he is equally dogmatic, but because of their materialism and fatalism, which even their conception of

[226] Plato, *Phaedrus* 245c; *Politicus* 273b; *Timaeus* 52d ff.; *Laws* 896d; Plutarch, *De Animae Procreatione in Timaeo Platonis*, 1014b–1016d; see above, pp. 309–311, and R. M. Jones, *The Platonism of Plutarch* (Chicago, 1916), pp. 81–86.

[227] Aesch. *Choeph.* 313; see above, p. 98; 107; 114, n. 57; 131.

[228] Plutarch, *De Sera Num. Vind.* 564e.

[229] Nauck, *T.G.F.*, p. 782.

providence cannot redeem. Moreover he finds the Stoics inconsistent. (He it is who damagingly quotes some of the sayings of Chrysippus which we have already considered above.)[230] Chrysippus makes God both creator and brutal destroyer of human life, upholder of moral law and instigator of wars; his God is "author of nothing base," and at the same time author of every least event, which must include evil and vice. Moreover his God punishes not merely the vicious (whom, however, he has tolerated as a necessary part of the whole scheme of things) but also good men, through a sort of neglect, or even through impotence; "there is a large admixture of necessity (*ananke*) in things."[231] Thus either the goodness or the power of the Stoic God is defective.[232] Furthermore, Plutarch satirizes eloquently, yet not quite fairly, the notion that good cannot exist without evil, virtue without vice: destroy evil, and will no good remain? And what useful rôle does vice play in the world?[233]

On grounds of content and of style it is clear that the essay *On Fate* which is preserved among Plutarch's *Moral Essays*[234] is not the work of Plutarch himself; in it Platonism, Peripatetic doctrine, Stoicism, and what will become Neoplatonism all find a place. Yet it will serve as a fair sample of the somewhat eclectic kind of treatment that was current in this period with regard to Fate and related problems,[235] and may be read for its general interest. It purports to be a letter to one Piso, setting forth the writer's views about Fate. He begins by distinguishing (somewhat in the Neoplatonic fashion) Fate as energy and as substance, and proceeds (chapters 1 and 3) to explain the former aspect as set forth by Plato.[236] Fate, though all-inclusive, he continues, is in itself not infinite, but determinate and finite. Disputing the doctrine of "sympathy," he argues that in nature's cycles like causes produce like results (3). But Fate, like Law, legislates only in general terms, not absolutely determining particular events (though some [the Peripatetics?] may object that particulars are prior to universals): this involves the admission that Fate is to some extent conditional, though still universal, a point upheld by reference to Plato's description of Adrasteia's decree.[237]

[230] See above, pp. 345 f.

[231] Plut. *De Stoic. Repugn.* 1051bc (= SVF II, 1178).

[232] *De Stoic. Repugn.* 1049a–1051d.

[233] Plut. *De Comm. Not.* 1065b–1066e; 1076a–1077a; cf. Plato, *Theaet.* 176a, and see above, pp. 297; 302. Here the Stoic would seek to distinguish moral vice from physical evil.

[234] See also above, pp. 346 f.

[235] See Appendix 66: Source of [Plutarch] *On Fate*.

[236] The conception of Adrasteia, *Phaedrus* 248c; the laws which God established in the nature of the universe for immortal souls, *Timaeus* 41e; the speech of the maiden Lachesis, daughter of Necessity, *Rep.* 617d.

[237] Chap. 4; cf. Plato, *Phaedrus* 248c: the soul will be saved if it sees the truth. Pseudo-Plutarch uses here the false etymology of εἱμαρμένη; see above, p. 340, n. 46.

The writer now considers the relations between Fate, Providence, and Fortune, "that which is in our power," and contingency (5). Fate is an inclusive term, so that it may be said that everything is included "in Fate"; but not all things occur "according to Fate," as law covers all human actions, but not all actions are lawful. So there is room within Fate for other kinds of causality and potentiality; many antecedent conditions may consist with Fate; for example, the "possibles," some of which will be realized, some will not, thus differing from the necessary; while the contingent is partly in our power (6).

Fortune (*tyche*) is also a kind of causality, but "a cause by accident." When an accident occurs in a case in which free will is exercised for an end, we call it Fortune, — as when one finds treasure when digging a hole to plant a tree. Some say that *Tyche* is merely a cause unknown or unforeseen by the human reason; better is the Platonist definition of *Tyche* just given. The writer cites the case of the sailing of the ship for Delos the day before the sentence was passed on Socrates, an accident or concurrence of events which prolonged his life for some days, and which was therefore *Tyche* for him.[238] Still a larger category is chance (*τὸ αὐτόματον*), what occurs of its own accord; this includes Fortune, but of itself has nothing to do with the purposes of animate beings, as Fortune has.[239]

Fate, then, includes various kinds of eventuality, none of which are absolutely determined (according to *Heimarmene*); but Fate is itself included in Providence.[240] Here the writer recognizes three kinds of Providence, basing his classification on a theology and demonology which may be called Platonic, but in a special Plutarchan sense. "The supreme and first Providence is the understanding or will of the first God, doing good to everything, by which in the beginning (*πρώτως*) all divine things have universally been most excellently ordained; the second is that of the second gods, who go through the heavens, by which mortal things are brought into being in an orderly fashion, and all that pertains to the continuation and preservation of every kind; the third might probably be called the providence and forethought of the *daimones* who are set on earth as guardians and overseers of human actions." "Hence," the writer urges, "in contradiction of the sentiments of some [Stoic] philosophers, all things are done according to Fate and Providence, but not according to Nature" (9). The subordination of Fate to Providence is derived from Plato's *Timaeus*;[241] God comes first, then his Providence; next the "sec-

[238] Chap. 7; cf. Plato, *Phaedo* 58a, which is quoted; and see above, pp. 299 f.

[239] The author's treatment of *τύχη* and *τὸ αὐτόματον*, despite the reference to Plato, is Peripatetic; see above, p. 321; also below, pp. 373 f.

[240] *πρόνοια*; chap. 8.

[241] Plato, *Tim.* 29d; 41d; 42d; *Laws* 875c; see above, pp. 290–297.

ond" Providence, in the creation by the "young gods," which excuses God from causing any evil: here enters Fate, for God, being free from all evil, has no need of laws or Fate. The third Providence, that of the *daimones*, is also "a Kind of Fate," being engendered after Fate, and comprehended by it, as are free will and fortune. And yet in a more inclusive sense all that is done is comprehended under Fate; and even the first Providence, "as having engendered Fate, does in some sense comprehend it" (10).

These conclusions may seem to mark a return not exactly to Plato, but to the benevolent fatalism of Chrysippus, or to the three-fold classification of Posidonius: Zeus, Nature, Fate.[242] But the author concludes by registering his explicit disagreement with those whose "sentiment not only includes all things in Fate but affirms them all to be done by and according to Fate"; and he mentions, only to dismiss as sophistry, the usual arguments: among them, the "lazy fallacy"; the argument that "nothing is without a cause" (which is used to support divination); "sympathy" (used to support an attitude of resignation); and the argument that every proposition is either true or false (the "law of contradictories"[243]). He regards his own essay as an introduction to a future discussion of particulars.

In general, the "Platonist" Albinus (who flourished about the middle of the second century of our era) agrees with Plutarch and pseudo-Plutarch. He is no fatalist, and suggests that Plato upholds freedom in order to avoid an infinite regress in the chain of causation, and also in order to save a basis for ethics. Astrology he rejects. Necessary consequences follow free choices, as in the case of Apollo's prophecy to Laius;[244] possibility is indeterminate, and is consistent with freedom. Much of this, of course, is not strictly derived from Plato; but Albinus, like Plutarch, emphasizes the Platonic affirmation that God is not to blame for men's evil deeds and men's suffering. Yet he does not, like several Platonists of his age, attribute to Plato the doctrine that matter is identical with evil;[245] nor does he, like Plutarch, ascribe to Plato (on the strength of *Laws* 896e) the doctrine of an evil world-soul.

The later Peripatetic writers also discuss the relation of fate to the whole scheme of things, not uninfluenced by Stoic thought. The pseudo-Aristotelian work *De Mundo*, which is largely Stoic, draws up a list of the "many-named" powers to be reckoned with, and goes so far as to equate Zeus with *Ananke*, *Heimarmene*, *Pepromene* (with an incorrect

[242] H. Diels, *Dox. Gr.* p. 324a4; see above, p. 352.

[243] See above, pp. 347 f. and 364.

[244] See above, pp. 348; 364; below, 375.

[245] Albinus, *Didaskalikos*, chap. xxvi; R. E. Witt, *Albinus*, pp. 5 f.; 120; cf. below, Appendix 66. For the confused theory of Albinus with regard to the "world-soul" see R. M. Jones, *The Platonism of Plutarch*, pp. 88 f.

etymology), *Moira*, *Nemesis*, *Adrasteia*, and *Aisa* (also wrongly explained).[246] More in the Peripatetic tradition is Bishop Nemesius of Emesa (fl. *circ.* 390 A.D.), whose treatment of the voluntary and the involuntary and of freedom of the will, is quite Aristotelian.[247]

The chief late Peripatetic writer of interest for our problem, however, is the greatest of the commentators on Aristotle, Alexander of Aphrodisias (beginning of the third century of our era), whose treatise *On Fate* is devoted to a defense on Aristotelian principles of the freedom of the will against the fatalism of the Stoics.[248] Alexander distinguishes between *heimarmene* and what is in our power (τὸ ἐφ' ἡμῖν). The existence of the former is admitted by common consent; but failure to agree as to its nature leads to inconsistency and confusion in the matter of awarding blame or credit to men.[249] All of Aristotle's four kinds of causality are recognized, and illustrated, as by Aristotle, by reference to a statue.[250] On the basis of a threefold distinction of efficient causes between (1) acts "existing in nature," which have the principle and cause of their creation in themselves, and (2) acts "according to reason," willed from without, as by a craftsman, and (3) acts "produced for the sake of some end," but not for the sake of the end actually realized (in other words, accidental occurrences),[251] Alexander inquires as to the place of fate. Though it implies a purpose, it cannot be among the acts "according to reason"; for here, as in the arts, freedom to act argues equal freedom not to act. Fate is therefore to be found among acts "existing in nature," and is indeed equivalent to nature in all but name.

This does not mean, however, that nature is controlled throughout by necessity (even if all growth is ultimately caused by the movement of the heavenly bodies); for nature is at time impeded, and so admits what is "contrary to nature." Though each individual's life is for the most part, for better or for worse, the product of his personal nature (οἰκεία φύσις) or character, and Heraclitus was right in proclaiming that "a man's character is his destiny,"[252] it is not possible to predict with absolute certainty

[246] [Aristotle], *De Mundo* 401b8 ff.; see above, p. 325, n. 63. This work was written about 100 A.D.; J. P. Maguire, *Yale Classical Studies* 6 (1939), pp. 111–167 finds the sources of the greater part of it, and (p. 162) in particular of this passage, to be Stoic, and in fact Chrysippean.

[247] Nemesius, Περὶ Φύσεως Ἀνθρώπου, chapters 30–40; for Aristotle, see above, p. 327.

[248] See Appendix 67: Alexander of Aphrodisias; bibliography.

[249] Alexander, *De Fato* 2; in his *De Anima*, p. 182, lines 19–29, Alexander points out that even those who profess to believe in the inevitability of Fate resort also to Fortune, prayers to gods, and oracles, in order to avoid Fate.

[250] See above, p. 318.

[251] *De Fato* 4: αὐτομάτως τε καὶ ἀπὸ τύχης; cf. *De Fato* 7 and 8 and see below, p. 374; cf. Alexander, *De Anima*; pp. 176–179 Bruns (περὶ τύχης); p. 177, l. 19: κατὰ συμβεβηκὸς αἴτιον ἡ τύχη; see above pp. 321; 324 f.

[252] *De Fato* 6; for Heraclitus, D22B119, and below, Appendix 52.

what a man will do in the future on the basis, for example, of physiognomy or of soothsaying; for one's personal nature or properties may be changed by effort, as Socrates asserted that he had "become better than his nature through the practise of philosophy."[253] Such, then, is the Peripatetic view of fate in broad outline, a view that recognizes fate in the form of natural propensities, but that also asserts freedom of the will.

The rest of Alexander's work *On Fate* is an amplification of this thesis, with refutation of Stoic fatalism. Not only is fatalism a moral evasion, when men attribute evils to fate rather than to their own acts, but is also disproved by the consensus of opinion which holds that at least some things are the result of chance (*tyche*), as in the discovery of treasure by one who is digging for something else.[254] Moreover the Stoics, in reducing all things to the realm of necessity, do not recognize the true nature of possibility; we should not blame on our own ignorance of causes alone the failure of some things to occur; statements of fact are not true because the fact is presumed to have occurred through necessity, but only because the fact *did* occur.[255] Furthermore, if everything proceeded from preexisting causes, nature (who does nothing in vain) would have provided man with his deliberative faculties in vain, since deliberation and choice are exercised only about "what is in our power" (τὸ ἐφ' ἡμῖν).[256] The Stoics try to save both fate and free will; but the latter they reduce to animal instinct (resembling the "natural" notion of a falling stone), whereas free will really implies assent after rational deliberation, on the part of one who has *within himself* the source (ἀρχή) or cause (αἰτία) of action.[257] The denial of this principle precludes moral responsibility (and is therefore the evasive resort of the vicious); but it also precludes the reward of virtue by Providence (which would on this showing itself be predestined, apart from man's merits), and precludes the possibility of divination.[258] In a word, only on the hypothesis of human free will are virtue and vice, reward and punishment possible.[259]

Against the Stoic conception of nature as an endless chain, each link both in turn an effect and a new cause, Alexander argues that in fact

[253] *De Fato* 6; cf. *Macbeth*, I, 4, 11 f.; "There's no art | To find the mind's construction in the face."

[254] *De Fato* 7 and 8, with further examples borrowed from Aristotle (see above, p. 321); cf. 4, and above, p. 373; and Alexander, *De Anima*, as cited above, n. 251.

[255] *De Fato*, 9 and 10.

[256] 11 and 12; cf. Aristotle, above, pp. 319 f.; 324 f.; also Alexander, *De Anima*, p. 170, l. 2, p. 171, l. 27, on "non-being" as the source of free will in us (and of chance outside of us); this is hardly Aristotelian.

[257] *De Fato* 13–15: n.b. 15: ὁ γὰρ ἄνθρωπος ἀρχὴ καὶ αἰτία τῶν δι' αὑτοῦ γινομένων πράξεων.

[258] 16–18.

[259] 19–20; cf. 33–39, and see below, n. 265.

natural tendencies often do not find their fruition.[260] Again, though everything has a cause, not everything may therefore be inferred to be the cause of something else; a house requires a foundation, but a foundation will not necessarily be capped by a house; and, as we have seen, there are also "accidental" causes.[261] Mere priority is not causality. But a first cause is required, else causality becomes an infinite regress and nothing is really caused.[262]

It is "in our power" to resist our impulses; some qualities indeed are innate (παρὰ τῆς θείας φύσεως δῶρον), but even so we (unlike stones) are free to make either much or little of them by training and practise, and so to acquire habits that are stable.[263] Yet a sagacious man may once in a while act out of character for the express purpose of spiting a soothsayer who incautiously ventures to say that he will "of necessity" do thus and so.[264] This unexpected sally brings Alexander to the remaining subject of real interest: the question of the possibility of foretelling the future.[265]

Fatalism cannot be argued on the ground that the gods have absolute foreknowledge of future events; they cannot know that that will be which is in its nature impossible; and of events whose very nature is that they may or may not be, the utmost that may be said of them is that they are *possible*. Divination may exist only in this limited sense, enabling men by divine counsel to protect themselves against something. For if all things take place by necessity, why do men consult the gods, whose oracles resemble counsels? Above all, why adduce the oracle given to Laius, warning him against having a child? "If thou shalt beget a son, he shall slay thee, and thy whole house shall go through blood." The Stoics say that the god rendered the oracle in this form not knowing that it would be disobeyed (whereas he really knew this better than anyone else), but that if he had not given such an oracle none of the events in the story of the reversal of fortune (*peripeteia*) which befell Laius and Oedipus would have taken place. And Alexander proceeds to impute to the Stoics the desire of preserving the drama of destiny (τὸ τῆς εἱμαρμένης δρᾶμα) even at the cost of attributing the series of unholy events to the god Apollo himself, who knew the future, and who yet by the oracle deceived Laius into supposing that disaster could be avoided by exposing his child; this is a more impious doctrine than the Epicurean doctrine of the improvidence of the gods.[266] It is indeed to be noted that the responses of Greek

[260] 23. [261] 24; cf. 8. [263] 27.

[262] 25; cf. Aristotle, and see above, pp. 318; 322. [264] 29.

[265] 30–32. The remaining sections, 33–39, accomplish little more than a recapitulation of the earlier argument, with emphasis on the effect of fatalism in removing the possibility of virtue.

[266] 30–31; for the Epicurean opposition to "destiny," cf. D.L. X, 134, and see above,

oracles are very commonly conditional.[267] Thus Alexander, like Aristotle in his ethical approach to the subject, rejects fatalism, not following Aristotle's arguments in favor of the first mover and necessity.[268] It may be added that Alexander's conception of tragedy, recognizing free will, does not easily admit a blameless hero, for his suffering must be self-imposed; on the other hand, the tragic fault (*hamartia*) consists in a fatal and inexcusable lack of perception for which the hero is responsible, as in the cases of Laius and Oedipus.[269] Complete consistency is not to be found in Aristotle's handling of the problem, perhaps partly because the problem itself was not so pressing before the Stoics asserted fatalism, and became involved in difficulties in defending it: Alexander, using only part of Aristotle's materials, achieves a greater degree of consistency. He at least provides the materials for a theory of freedom, with due recognition of the importance of external necessity and of chance (something not uncaused, but not aiming at the goal that interests us); and he duly stresses the conscious effort of the moral agent as a principal source of action.

It was the aim of Plotinus (c. 205–270) and of the Neo-Platonists who followed his lead to escape from the confused and evil world about them to a pure and stable reality. This Plotinus terms the One (or the Good), the source of all being, and the goal of his own and of every eager spirit, with which he seeks to merge himself. In his quest he has unquestionably been aided by the Parmenidean One, and by the Platonic theory of Ideas or of the Good, and by the Platonic conception of cosmology (in the *Timaeus*) as well as by the Platonic lover's flight (in the *Symposium* and the *Phaedrus*) from earthly beauty to the contemplation of celestial beauty and truth.[270] In his repudiation of Stoic and Epicurean materialism and of scepticism, he has a right to regard himself as the successor of the Plato who repudiated the materialistic atheism of his own day. So much may be said without detracting from the debt of Plotinus to other sources.[271]

---

p. 333; for the prophecy, Euripides, *Phoen.* 19 f.; Cicero, *De Fato* 30, uses this illustration, in distinguishing, with Chrysippus, conditional from absolute events (see above, pp. 348; 364).

[267] E. Ehnmark, *The Idea of God in Homer*, pp. 75 f., quoted below, Appendix 6. Thus oracles admit of fulfilment or of evasion on the part of enlightened persons who have freedom of will. For the interpretation of the present passage in Alexander, see further R. A. Pack (*op. cit.* in Appendix 67), pp. 428–436.

[268] Cf. R. A. Pack, pp. 430; 433 f.

[269] Pack, pp. 434–436.

[270] Note the negative character of the descriptions of the One of Xenophanes, Parmenides, and Plotinus (*Enneads*, VI, 9, 3–11), and of Plato's ideal world (*Symp.* 211ab).

[271] For the debt of Plotinus to Platonism, cf. E. R. Dodds, "The *Parmenides* of Plato and the Origin of the Neoplatonic One," *C.Q.* 22 (1928), pp. 129–142; for Posidonius as "the first Neoplatonist, cf. W. Jaeger, *Nemesios von Emesa*, pp. 68–137, whose discussion, how-

An absolute so perfect as the One of Plotinus, which is above Being, Mind, and Soul, cannot strictly be known to the intellect alone; and there is a sense in which it is true to say that the approach of Plotinus to the One is that of the religious mystic. But that is not the whole truth; for it is by sheer intellectual ingenuity that he seeks to explain by a hierarchy of graduated conceptions how the world of our experience, with its imperfections, has come out of the absolute perfection of the One. His treatment of the problem is indebted in part to Plato's account of the creation (in the *Timaeus*), in part to Aristotle's conception of the potential, which is now conceived to overflow, though without diminution of itself, into the actual.

Like Plato, Plotinus faces the problem of both moral evil and cosmic evil. As virtue is the result of an activity of the soul which rises above the body, so moral evil is the result of laziness or arrogance on the part of the soul which is involved in body. Cosmic evil, however, is a more difficult problem, since the very suspicion of its existence seems to detract from the perfection of the One whence all proceeds. The realization of the One through the activity of Soul requires a gradual process by which the individuality of phenomena is achieved in space and time;[272] nor can the process become actual without the existence of matter (*hyle*). Matter itself, to be sure, is mere privation or abstraction (*steresis*), the ultimate limit in the process that can be conceived;[273] for body is for Plotinus, as for Aristotle, a union of form and matter. Matter is therefore not in itself equivalent to positive evil as such;[274] what is evil in matter is rather its remoteness from the source of good, and its inertness. To this extent, matter is mere absence of good. But Plotinus, also like many another, sometimes seeks to explain away what looks like positive evil in the details of the *cosmos* by supposing that it must subserve some greater good of the whole *cosmos*; or, again, that evil, even moral evil, is justified because it may be the arena in which virtue is fostered. Such, in the briefest possible compass, and ignoring much of the metaphysical detail, is the Plotinian conception of what must be, of good, and of evil: rather than amplify this sketch [275] it may be more profitable here to quote or para-

ever, should be supplemented by that of Dodds; for the transitional Middle Platonism, cf. R. F. Witt, *Albinus* (and see above, p. 372); for the influence of Aristotle and (through Numenius) of Jewish thought, P. E. More, *Hellenistic Philosophies*, pp. 205–225; for the background of Plotinus more generally, W. R. Inge, *The Philosophy of Plotinus*, Lectures IV and V, "The Forerunners of Plotinus"; this work is indispensable for the study of Plotinus.

[272] Cf. W. R. Inge, Vol. I, pp. 155–187.

[273] *Enneads* III, 6, 7; W. R. Inge, Vol. I, pp. 128–131; (and cf. Aristotle's πρώτη ὕλη; see above, p. 320, and n. 25).

[274] Plotinus even conceives of matter at the upper, as at the lower, end of the scale; soul is the matter of spirit; cf. W. R. Inge, Vol. I, pp. 139–143.

[275] For a more detailed discussion of matter and of evil in Plotinus, see B. A. G. Fuller,

phrase certain passages of the *Enneads* of Plotinus that deal rather systematically with our problem.[276]

Since "the Good is that on which all else depends," if evil exists at all, it must be some mode of non-being (*Enneads* I, 8, 2; I, 8, 3). How then do we explain [Plato's] teaching that evils can never cease to be, but "exist of necessity," that "while evil has no place in the divine order, it haunts the mortal nature and this region of ours"? [277] "Given that the Good is not the only existent thing, it is inevitable that by the outgoing from it there should be produced a Last, something after which nothing more can be produced: this will be Evil. This Last is Matter, the thing which has no residue of good in it: here is the necessity of Evil" (I, 8, 7). Matter is Evil, not in the sense of having quality, but precisely in not having it (I, 8, 10). The soul has a mingled nature: it possesses the Good as its Essence, the Evil as an Accidental (I, 8, 10); hence the possibility of both Virtue and Vice (I, 8, 10–12).

The first three books of the third *Ennead* deal with Fate and Providence. Causality is upheld within the realm of Nature; the Epicurean "swerve" therefore is rejected (III, 1, 1). But superficially identical conditions have different results; whereas attempts to go deeper to an atomic *Ananke* assumed to include even mental processes, or to planetary and astral influences, or again to the linked unity of all phenomena, result alike in fatalism (III, 1, 2). But random atomic movements can explain neither this orderly Universe, nor mental and spiritual acts and states and personality (III, 1, 3). Another kind of fatalism, that derives everything from one prime Cause, ignores the descending chain of causes, and among them the rôle of the mind and the will; on this showing, we are no "We," and nothing is our act.[278] To the claims of astrology and "sympathy" we may reply that they ignore human personality, acts and wills, sacrificing them to the stars; granted that place and climate and heredity exert general influences, nevertheless there are individual differences and individual efforts; moreover how can horoscopes be retroactive, determining

---

*The Problem of Evil in Plotinus*, pp. 63–298; E. Schröder, *Plotins Abhandlung* ΠΟΘΕΝ ΤΑ ΚΑΚΑ (*Enn.* I, 8), with sketch of the problem before Plotinus, and of his influence; W. R. Inge, *The Philosophy of Plotinus*, Vol. I, pp. 131–137; R. Jolivet, *Plotin et le Problème du Mal*, pp. 87–156; R. Jolivet, *Problème du Mal chez Saint Augustin* (Paris, 1929), pp. 89–106; for the Thomist position, cf. E. Gilson, *The Philosophy of St. Thomas Aquinas* (Eng. trans., Cambridge, 1929), pp. 151–162.

[276] In the following quotations and paraphrases, I have used the Greek text of the *Enneads* (ed. R. Volkmann, Leipzig, 1883), consulting also the translation by S. Mackenna (and B. S. Page) (London, 1917–1930), which I have in some cases adapted or corrected. (In dealing with so difficult an author as Plotinus, one must be grateful for every kind of assistance; Mackenna's translation, though able and stimulating, is marred by errors.)

[277] *Enneads* I, 8, 6; cf. Plato, *Theaet.* 176a; and see above, p. 302.

[278] III, 1, 4; cf. III, 1, 7.

living thing on earth" (III, 2, 9). If men's sins were involuntary in the sense that they were wholly the result of external Necessity, the consequent suffering would be unjust; the fact is that men are themselves moral agents, sources of action, moved by their own natures, and therefore free.[283] As in a drama, or in a painting, the perfection of the whole requires grades of being, the less perfect as well as the more perfect (III, 2, 11–12). In the vicissitudes of time, the justice of inevitable Retribution (*Adrasteia*) is to be seen, a principle that operates also in the least details of the organic world; leaf and bloom and fruit, and, still more, man, testify to the care of Providence (III, 2, 13–14). Even man's inhumanity to man, war, the devouring of kind by kind, if viewed objectively, is but that changing in the *dramatis personae* without which the drama cannot go on, a drama of struggle and final harmony (III, 2, 15–16). All the world's a vaster stage, and each man plays the part that suits his character, and reaps his fitting reward; his lapses are no reflection on the skill of the playwright. "The whole is not fair if each individual is a stone, but if each one throws in his voice towards one harmony, singing out his life, thin, harsh, imperfect though it be" (III, 2, 17).

But if Reason be exonerated from responsibility for such evil as souls perpetrate, is not Reason likewise deprived of credit for the good? No; Unity is ramified in diversity, with differences or even contraries of function; a general plans a campaign, but leaves details to his subordinates, who act according to their respective natures, natures more and more fallible as they stand lower in the scale of being. The wonder is not that there is so much failure, but that there is so much nobility in inferior creatures.[284] Yet man stands apart from the other creatures, and is justly called to account for his deeds, because his nature is in part free to act, free, that is to say, within the all-comprehending Providence. If he acts in an evil manner, it is because he fails to assert his freedom, yielding to the substratum of Matter which is the other part of his nature, perhaps through a weakness and degradation occasioned by a transmigration of his soul such as Plato described (III, 2, 4). Providence, then, permeates the *cosmos* in various degrees, as creatures varying in receptivity react to her. "But all sums up to a unity, a comprehensive Providence; from the inferior grade downwards is Fate, the upper is Providence alone." All that is well done is done according to Providence, though not therefore by Providence, since free agents may cause it; even the evil done by free agents, like the wounds and the broken bones of an organism, may be healed by Providence.[285] Divination of the evil along with the good is

[283] III, 2, 10: *ἀρχαὶ δὲ καὶ ἄνθρωποι. Κινοῦνται γοῦν πρὸς τὰ καλὰ οἰκείᾳ φύσει καὶ ἀρχὴ αὕτη αὐτεξούσιος.*

[284] III, 2, 18; III, 3, 1–3; cf. III, 3, 7.

[285] III, 2, 5; cf. *Natura medicatrix.*

conceivable only as the disorderly submits to the orderly and so falls within the train of observable sequences.[286]

To appraise the value of the system of Plotinus as a whole is a difficult task. But one may readily perceive that his treatment of fate, good, and evil attempts the impossible. The attempt to explain evil by the conception of matter promises, like Plato's later discussions of non-being as "otherness," to provide an explanation of the principle of individuality in the phenomenal world; but it ends by identifying matter with the merely indeterminate, and fails to explain how this is derived from the One which is supposed to be the source of all things. For the doctrine of emanation, even if it could account for quantitatively endless expansion and differentiation in the creative process, cannot explain how perfection creates imperfection, because the latter conception involves a qualitative contradiction, good becoming evil. Plotinus, therefore, resorts at times to the explanation of moral evil in terms of the behavior of individual souls. As the world soul becomes incarnate in the universe, else the creation could not proceed, so the individual soul's errand requires it to unite with body. But if it becomes self-willed, interested in its immediate environment and forgetting its original errand, then it becomes a fallen soul.[287] A moral distinction, we must observe, is already here, one between "higher" and "lower." And if we ask whether the soul's choice to remain at the lower level is free or is determined, the answer of Plotinus will be that it is both; it is caused by the law of emanation, and it is caused also by the soul's own nature. But that is only another way of saying that the Soul's choice is neither determined nor free. In either case, moreover, no rational motive has been given for the choice of the lower. Plotinus in seeking both to eat his cake and to have it has achieved only one sure result: namely, the conclusion that somehow perfection has caused imperfection.[288] There remains the attempt to justify by commonplaces the presence of evil in a good world; in this attempt Plotinus succeeds no better and no worse than Chrysippus and his Stoic successors.[289]

The grandeur of the system of Plotinus and its far-reaching influence have justified us in spending some space in examining his attempt, however unsatisfactory the result, to achieve a monistic metaphysical solution of our problem. Far less space will suffice to give due recognition to the followers of Plotinus, of whom the most interesting for our purpose is Sallustius, friend of the emperor Julian, possibly consul in 363 A.D., high-

[286] III, 2, 6. So Plotinus rejects the evil *daimones* that Plutarch entertained: Inge, Vol. II, pp. 192–199; J. A. Hild, *Démons*, pp. 323–331.

[287] *Enneads* V, 1, 1; cf. IV, 8, 4–5.

[288] See further B. A. G. Fuller, *The Problem of Evil in Plotinus*, pp. 299–333.

[289] See above, pp. 377; 379–382; cf. pp. 344–351.

minded defender of paganism against the Christianity that was now all but triumphant, and author of the treatise *On the Gods and the World*.[290]

Two chapters in the treatise deal especially with our problem: the ninth, on Providence, Fate, and Chance, and the twelfth, on the origin of evil.[291] In the former, Sallustius finds evidence of the existence of Providence in the order of the *cosmos* and in the details of human bodies, as well as in divination; nor does this "incorporeal Providence of the gods for bodies and souls" cost them any effort (thus the Epicurean objection to the idea of Providence may be met). Fate, on the other hand, is a "providence exercised from bodies upon bodies"; hence the term *Heimarmene*, because the *Heirmos* (chain) appears more clearly in bodies;[292] hence also the art of astrology, which is based on the belief that human affairs generally, and especially our bodily nature, health and disease, good and evil fortune, is governed by the gods and by the celestial bodies. "But to suppose that acts of injustice come from *heimarmene* is to make us good and the gods bad, unless what is meant thereby is that everything happens for the good of the universe as a whole and of all things in a natural condition, but that evil education or weakness of nature changes the blessings of Heimarmene to evil, as the sun, good as it is for all, is found to be harmful to those suffering from inflammation of the eyes or from fever." Traditional arguments against astral fatalism follow: If fate rules all, why do whole nations, whose horoscopes must vary, have strange customs? And why are astrologers inconsistent in dealing with the influence of the same planets? At most, horoscopes have a limited validity; and they cannot affect the past. Finally, as *Pronoia* and *Heimarmene* exist for tribes and cities as well as for individuals, so also *Tyche*, which is that power of the gods that orders for the good diverse and unexpected happenings; she should therefore enjoy a corporate worship, since every city has diverse elements.[293] But the power of *Tyche* does not extend above the moon.[294] And if the bad prosper and the good suffer, we must not be surprised; for prosperity will not take the badness from the bad, while the good will be content with virtue alone.

[290] Sallustius: text in Mullach, *Fragmenta Philosophorum Graecorum*, Vol. III, pp. 30–50; brief discussion and English translation in G. Murray, *Five Stages*, pp. 211–238; 241–267; edition, with translation and invaluable Prolegomena, by A. D. Nock (Cambridge, 1926), showing the debt of the eclectic Neoplatonist author to the Neoplatonist Iamblichus, to current handbooks of Platonism, and to commonplace books in general.

[291] Sallustius in his fifth chapter also gives a preliminary list of topics: the First Cause, Providence, Fate, Chance, Virtue, Vice, Good and Evil constitutions arising therefrom, the question whence evils came into the universe.

[292] But on this etymology see above, pp. 340, n. 46; 370, n. 237; below, Appendix 4.

[293] For this friendly aspect of *Tyche*, Nock well compares, pp. lxxiv f. the anonymous choral lyric, Diehl, Vol. II, p. 158, no. 4 (cited also above, p. 124, n. 104); also the cult of *Agathe Tyche*.

[294] See Appendix 63.

This thesis, which was not confined to Stoic circles though it was most often argued in them, Sallustius supports also by Platonic arguments. In his twelfth chapter he goes on to inquire, "How is it, if the gods are good and make everything, that there are evils in the *cosmos*?" To this old question, debated especially by Stoics and Neoplatonists, Sallustius replies that evil can have no objective existence (*physis*), but "come into being through the absence of good, just as darkness has no absolute existence, and comes into being through the absence of light." This analogy, which has the flavor of Plotinus, Sallustius develops, denying inherent or natural evil in gods, in minds, in souls, in bodies, in the union of soul and body, or in *daimones* (unlike Plutarch, and unlike his own friend Julian). If then "natural evil" does not exist, evil must be something that appears in connection with certain human activities, when men err in what they conceive to be good: even such error may be averted by divinely instituted arts and sciences and rites, or by laws and punishments, and sins may be purged away after death by gods and *daimones*.[295]

Such, in brief, is the creed of Sallustius, further set forth in supplementary chapters that follow. It is a popular or introductory work, neither very original nor very profound; but it is not on that account of less value as testimony to the modes of thought of paganism in its last stand against Christianity. And its burden, perhaps deliberately calculated to disarm the hostility of other sects (including the Gnostics and the "atheist" Christians), is the greatness and goodness of the gods, and the possibility of human blessedness to be gained through virtue.

## 6

To extend our inquiry to the treatises on Fate and Providence and Evil written in the succeeding centuries would require more space that is here available; for the material is abundant. For Neoplatonism, we might examine Archbishop William of Moerbeke's Latin versions of three lost treatises of Proclus (410–485): *De Providentia et Fato, et eo quod in Nobis; De Decem Dubitationibus circa Providentiam; De Malorum Subsistentia*,[296] and observe how ingeniously he develops the Plotinian system so as to bring all things under the control of Providence, and how he explains evil (whose objective reality he denies) as a "parhypostasis" or "deviation from subsistence." Or we might consider in the work of another Neoplatonist, Hierocles of Alexandria (fl. 430), *On Providence and Fate and What is in Our Power*, as it is summarized by Photius; the

[295] Sallustius, chapter 12; the ethical argument is contained also in 10, 14–16, 19–21.

[296] V. Cousin, *Procli Philosophi Platonici Opera* (Paris, 1820), Vol. I; Eng. Translation by T. Taylor, London, 1833; cf. E. Schröder, *Plotins Abhandlung* ΠΟΘΕΝ ΤΑ ΚΑΚΑ, pp. 196–202; V. Cioffari, *Fortune and Fate*, pp. 59–65.

attempt to reconcile Platonic with Peripatetic doctrine, Fate with a Providence in which the existence of law and of punishment is itself proof of the existence of free-will.[297] We could then consider the sixth book of the *Praeparatio Evangelica* of Eusebius (265–340), which defends freedom of the will against several types of fatalism, supporting the argument of the Christian author by long quotations from various works both pagan and Christian, such as "The Detection of Impostors" of the Cynic Oenomaus (dealing largely with oracles, including that about the death of Laius),[298] the "Answers to Chrysippus" of Diogenianus, the essay *On Fate* of Alexander of Aphrodisias, and the arguments against astrology of the Syrian Bardesanes (b. *circ.* 155 A.D.) and of Origen (185–254).[299] Or we might examine the treatise of Diodorus, Bishop of Tarsus, *Against Fate*, who criticized Bardesanes for not going far enough in the assertion of freedom of the will;[300] and the commentary of Chalcidius (*c.* 300 A.D.) on Plato's *Timaeus*, defending the divine law, Providence, which resides in the *anima mundi*, from being identified with the Stoic Fate; the latter he also distinguishes from Fortune in Aristotelian fashion;[301] and the six vigorous orations of St. John Chrysostom (345–407) *On Fate and Providence*.[302] Surely a full study of our problems should lead us to that pagan

[297] Hierocles, Περὶ προνοίας καὶ εἱμαρμένης καὶ τῆς τοῦ ἐφ' ἡμῖν πρὸς τὴν θείαν ἡγεμονίαν συντάξεως, in Photius, *Bibliotheca*, 214 and 251; also in Migne, *Patrologia Graeca*, Vols. 103 and 104; cf. the Latinized "Compendium" in Grotius (see below, p. 393), pp. 17–35; and Hierocles on the *Aureum Pythagoreum Carmen*, in Mullach, *F.P.G.*, Vol. I, 408–484, esp. chap. XI, pp. 438–446; Grotius, pp. 3–17. Hierocles shows the influence of Origen (for whom see below, n. 299).

[298] See also above, p. 350, and n. 111.

[299] Eusebius, *The Preparation for the Gospel*, ed. E. H. Gifford, (4 vols., including Greek text, English translation and notes, Oxford, 1903). For Bardesanes, see Eusebius, *P.E.* VI, 10; in Latin, Grotius, *De Fato*, pp. 336–348; also the Greek text, with the translation of Grotius, in I. C. Orelli, *De Fato*, pp. 202–219. The argument turns on the difference between the beasts, whose conduct is determined by their natures, and man, who though in part determined by his nature (*physis*), is also partly free; in different regions, he orders his laws and customs (*nomoi*) differently, not because of astral influence (for there are differences within a given region) but because of a God-given freedom to exercise the will. It is the argument of Dr. Isaac Watts (*Divine Songs*, XVI): "Let dogs delight to bark and bite," etc. There is considerable anthropological detail (partly fanciful) to illustrate the varieties of human behavior. For Origen, cf. also H. Koch, *Pronoia und Paideusis: Studien über Origenes und sein Verhältnis zum Platonismus* (Berlin and Leipzig, 1932), pp. 280–291.

[300] Diodorus of Tarsus, Κατὰ Εἱμαρμένης, summarized by Photius, *Bibliotheca*, 223; Photius bestows on Diodorus and his reasoning only a partial approval.

[301] Chalcidius *In Platonis Timaeum*, chap. 147, Wrobel: *Sic fatum quidem ex providentia est, nec tamen ex fato providentia.* Freedom of will is, of course, upheld; conditional necessity, the necessary consequence of an action which lies within the power of an agent, is illustrated by the prophecy given to Laius (chap. 153) and by the fruit forbidden to Adam and Eve (chap. 154). For other points, see Chalcidius, chaps. 145–188; E. Steinheimer, *Untersuchungen über die Quellen des Chalcidius* (Aschaffenburg, 1912); V. Cioffari, *Fortune and Fate*, pp. 71–78; and see below, Appendix 66.

[302] Migne, *Patrologia Graeca*, Vol. 50, pp. 749–774.

who became one of the greatest of the Christian fathers, St. Augustine (354–430), whom we must pause to consider, however briefly.

After a Platonic period, in which he believed on rational grounds in the reality of an absolute though impersonal goodness beyond the evils of this transitory and illusive world, Augustine passed through a period in which the dualism of the contemporary Manichaean sect convinced him that good and evil are equally real and eternal. In his final, Christian period he held that God is absolute, and that his goodness appears in its true light to the good, though to others it seems evil. After the sack of Rome by Alaric (410 A.D.), when the power of the temporal state and even of the Church seemed to many of the faithful to be discredited, Augustine argued in his *De Civitate Dei* that "the most glorious city of God" is seated partly in this declining world and partly in the stable estate of eternity.[303] In this life the righteous and the wicked alike enjoy a common lot (with room for patience and for repentance, respectively); it is only in the world to come that fit rewards and punishments are to be expected.[304]

Neither Fate (apart from Providence) nor Chance, neither the claims of astrology nor God's fore-knowledge of future events, will Augustine allow to be grounds for a fatalistic philosophy;[305] for God's providence includes man's freedom of will to choose.[306] Even in his Christian period Augustine retains an affection and respect for Plato, whose natural theology is the nearest of pagan philosophies to Christian doctrines;[307] but this admiration does not extend to the Platonists and to others who uphold the existence of (sometimes evil) *daimones*, intermediaries between God and man, instead of good angels and the mediator, Christ.[308]

The source of evil Augustine finds to be in the wills of the angels and of the men, created by God with freedom to sin or not to sin, who "fell" through their own choice;[309] this is not a "natural" or "original" evil, but a perversion of good, for evil is not an absolute.[310] The devil's nature is good; only his will is evil.[311] But God can use evil for good ends, as antithesis may adorn a poem.[312] The body hinders the soul, but cannot

[303] St. Augustine, *De Civ. Dei*, I, 1.

[304] I, 8; cf. V, 21.

[305] V, 1–7, for astrology; V, 8–10, for the problem of fore-knowledge, here connected with the Stoic (and Ciceronian) tradition.

[306] V, 10 and 11, the latter a lyric chapter.

[307] VIII, 1–13.

[308] VII, 14–X, 23.

[309] XI, 11; XII, 1–7; cf. *Confessions* VII, 4–7.

[310] *De Civ. Dei*, XI, 9, end: *Mali enim nulla natura est; sed amissio boni mali nomen accepit* (cf. XI, 22; contrast *Confessions*, IV, 24; V, 20, of his Manichaean heresies); for Augustine's debt in this matter to Plotinus, *Confessions* VII, 18 and 23.

[311] *De Civ. Dei*, XI, 17.

[312] XI, 18.

compel it to sin.[313] And in the life hereafter, which Augustine describes with the eloquence of yearning, free will takes on an even more glorious aspect as the moral agent is united with God: "For the first free will, given to man when he was first created righteous, had the power not to sin, but had the power also to sin: but this last free will shall be the more powerful than the first, in that it shall not be able to sin; but this, too, is by the gift of God, not by the possibility of his own nature."[314] As against the Pelagian sect, the humanists among contemporary theologians, who recognize only what Augustine calls the "first free will," an indifferent power of sinning or not sinning, Augustine holds in his late treatise *On Grace and Free Will* that through the Fall even such power is removed, and man is free only to sin (more or less), save as God gives him grace to choose good. Thus freedom of will turns out to be the result of a combination of divine grace and human acceptance of grace, limited by God's fore-knowledge (but not determination) of the extent to which individuals (conceived as the "elect") will actually avail themselves of their freedom. Implicit in the doctrine is "predestination," and the damnation of all but the elect (something which Plato[315] and Cicero[316] and later the Arminians and Milton[317] seek to avoid, but which Calvinism[318] and Jansenism accept); surely the doctrine risks the loss of man's moral responsibility, in spite of the assertion of man's freedom of the will.[319]

Dante, heir to much else both in the pagan and in the Christian tradition, is an Augustinian both in the conception of the stages of the soul's ascent[320] and in his vindication of the soul's freedom, here supported also

[313] XIV, 3; cf. XIV, 5, preferring the Platonic to the Manichaean doctrine, against which Augustine in the *De Libro Arbitrio* has already insisted that the origin of evil lies in man's free will.

[314] XXII, 30 (contrast Aristotle, above p. 327); and cf. Dante, below, p. 388.

[315] Cf. A. E. Taylor, *Platonism*, pp. 94–96.

[316] See above, p. 365, and M. Y. Henry cited in n. 208.

[317] For a comparison of Milton's views with St. Augustine's, cf. D. Saurat, *Milton: Man and Thinker* (New York, 1925), pp. 273–279. Saurat, however, exaggerates the rôle of matter (which is for Milton divine) in St. Augustine as a cause of evil; both stress primarily the will. It is in the question of predestination that Milton differs most with St. Augustine; see below, pp. 394–396.

[318] For an account of the consequences, for good and for evil, of the Augustinian and Calvinistic doctrine in modern times, cf. P. G. E. Miller, *The New England Mind* (New York, 1939), esp. Chap. I, "The Augustinian Strain of Piety"; and for the revolt of one who soared with the wings of an Augustine and of a Dante, but who was no Puritan at heart, G. Santayana, Sonnet XXIII: "Is this the heaven, poets, that ye paint? | Oh, then, how like damnation to be blest! | This is not love: it is that worser thing — | Hunger for love, while love is yet to learn."

[319] On the whole subject, see further Fonsegrive, *Libre Arbitre*, pp. 97–112; R. Jolivet, *Le Problème du Mal chez Saint Augustin*, with full references to passages, and a note on the debt of Augustine to Plotinus.

[320] St. Augustine, *De Quantitate Animae*; cf. E. K. Rand, *Founders of the Middle Ages*, chap. VIII, "St. Augustine and Dante."

by the philosophy of St. Thomas Aquinas.[321] Though Dante's scheme reckons with stellar influences, the will is nevertheless free;[322] indeed the greatest gift of God is this freedom of the will.[323]

The *Civitas Dei* was inspired by St. Augustine's confidence, amid the general evils of his age, in the universal goodness of the divine order. It was a more personal experience that inspired another Christian, a century later, to find consolation in philosophy. Boethius (c. 480–524) had already attempted in earlier works to show the real unity of Plato and Aristotle, and in theological treatises to profit by Aristotelian modes of thought in dealing with the problems of the Christian faith. In the last year of his life, after a distinguished career, he was unjustly imprisoned and finally executed. His days in prison were spent, as they were by certain other fellow spirits, — by Socrates and Bunyan, and Grotius, and in another sense by the blind Milton, — in brooding on the vicissitudes of this life, and in justifying the ways of God to men. In each case the sense of personal wrongs led to a conviction that if injustice is too often the way of this world, there must be an ultimate justice elsewhere, in heaven and in the eternal purposes of God; the result, in other words, is a theodicy.

The *Consolation of Philosophy* of Boethius has its high place in literature, and falls within, or fuses, several distinct literary types: the consolation, the Platonic or Ciceronian dialogue, the allegorical discourse of a personified virtue (here the physician, Lady Philosophy), the *protrepticus*, or hortatory introduction to a field of learning, and the Menippean *satura*, with alternating prose and verse. Of singular charm and effectiveness are some of the lyrics and elegies that relieve the argument. To some it has seemed strange that this work is devoid of any specifically Biblical or even Christian matter; the fact is that Boethius is working out his problem on such terms as may appeal to all men of good will, whether pagan or Christian, and is using chiefly the Platonic approach;[324] yet

[321] Dante, *Par.* IV, 76: *chè voluntà se non vuol, non si ammorza* (with Grandgent's notes on lines 58–76); cf. *Summa Theologica*, Prima Secundae, q.6, a. 4.

[322] *Purg.* XVI, 52–84; cf. XXVII, 140.

[323] *Par.* V, 19–24. Cf. E. G. Gardner, *Dante and the Mystics* (London, 1913), p. 180: "The whole *Divina Commedia* is, in a sense, the story of the liberty of man's will, in time and in eternity." And for a concise statement of Dante's ideas about providence, good, and evil, of his emphasis on God's love and on the varying degrees of freedom of will, and of Dante's relation to his predecessors, cf. C. H. Grandgent, ed. *Divina Commedia* (Boston, 1933), pp. xix–xxiii; for his relation to Aristotle and to St. Thomas Aquinas, especially in the matter of chance, destiny and providence, cf. V. Cioffari, *The Conception of Fortune and Fate in the Works of Dante* (Cambridge, Mass., 1940).

[324] A. E. Taylor, *Platonism*, p. 19: "Here the Platonic cosmology and natural theology is expanded with singular charm and grace as a basis for the justification of God's mysterious ways with man." For Boethius generally, cf. E. K. Rand, *Founders of the Middle Ages*, chap. v, "Boethius, The First of the Scholastics"; E. K. Rand, "On the Composition of

there is little in the *Consolation* which is inconsistent with the argument of the *City of God*, or with Christian theology in general.

To the lamentations of Boethius over his own misfortune and over the fact that in the world at large, over which God is supposed to rule, the wicked flourish and the righteous suffer,[325] Lady Philosophy offers her "remedies," first the milder sort (consolation of the feelings), and then the more forcible sort (metaphysical argument).[326] There have been other martyrs, in whose train Boethius might well follow, defying the assaults of the mad, leaderless wicked.[327] This defiance of the wicked is an imaginative expression of the metaphysical denial of the reality of evil.[328] Nor is there anything exceptional in the way that Fortune has treated Boethius; she is always fickle, for better or for worse.[329] He may, indeed, like Dante, decline the suggestion that there is consolation in the memory of happier things;[330] yet his remaining blessings, a noble and devoted family, serve as anchors of comfort in the storm.[331] The goods of Fortune not only are bestowed capriciously but even when bestowed are not absolutely good, but depend for their value on the character of the recipient; this is a part of the "stronger remedy." "Wherefore, O mortal men, why seek you abroad for your felicity, which is placed within yourselves?"[332] "If blessedness be the chief good of a nature that is endowed with reason," it cannot depend on unstable fortune (unless in the revelation of the uses of adversity); on the other hand, it is impossible to impose imperiously upon a free mind.[333] Blessedness (*beatitudo*) is a conception most often associated in the minds of Romans with material things, as was felicity (*olbos*) by the Greeks; here we find it on its way to the full Christian ideal, which we may remember is linked in the "Beatitudes" of Christ with suffering, and in the tradition of the Church often with martyrdom. The further analysis of the goods of this world, both the apparent goods and the real goods, leads to the Platonic conclu-

---

Boethius' *Consolatio Philosophiae*," *H.S.C.P.* 15 (1904), pp. 1–28, with analysis of the argument; H. F. Stewart and E. K. Rand, *The Theological Tracts*, and *The Consolation of Philosophy* (London and New York, 1918), the Loeb edition, from which citations are made in the following notes; V. Cioffari, *Fortune and Fate* (1935), pp. 82–91; E. T. Silk, "Boethius's Consolatio Philosophiae as a Sequel to Augustine's Dialogues and Soliloquia," *Harvard Theological Review* 32 (1939), pp. 19–39.

[325] Boethius, *Cons.* I, pr. 4, 105: *si quidem deus . . . est, unde mala?* (quoted from some Epicurean); cf. I, prosa 4, 120–123; I, metrum 5, 25–48.

[326] I, pr. 5, 38–44; cf. I, pr. 6, 46–62.

[327] I, pr. 3, 15–49.

[328] Cf. III, pr. 12, and see below, p. 390.

[329] II, pr. 1 and 2.

[330] II, pr. 3, 14–51; II, pr. 4, 1–6; Dante, *Inf.* v, 119–121.

[331] II, pr. 4, 1–34.

[332] II, pr. 4, 38–73.

[333] II, pr. 4, 79–85; II, pr. 8, 7–26; II, pr. 6, 24–26; cf. III, pr. 2, 5–79; III, pr. 8, 31–35.

sion that no goods can of themselves lead men to blessedness;[334] indeed they are but imperfect images of the true and perfect good, the fountain of all goodness, at which man should aim directly.[335] It is a good which is not really to be distinguished from God,[336] source of everything except evil; "wherefore evil is nothing, since he cannot do it who can do anything."[337]

So the "stronger," metaphysical remedy is applied. The fourth and fifth books of the *Consolation* deal more fully with the fundamental problem of evil, and with related problems. "This is the chief cause of my sorrow, that though the governor of all things is good there can either be any evil at all or that it pass unpunished."[338] Lady Philosophy's reply, based largely on Plato's *Gorgias*, is that the good are always rewarded, and the evil punished; for evil men are impotent, indeed purely and simply are not.[339] The argument, like its Platonic original, is full of paradox. To the good, goodness is its own reward, and to the evil wickedness is its own punishment;[340] hence it is better not to succeed than to succeed in doing evil; and better, if wicked, to be punished than to escape.[341] Yet the argument would be convincing were it not for the confusion of rewards and punishments which chance seems to introduce into the divinely ordained system.[342] The point requires a new departure in the discussion,[343] and a new division of the hydra-headed problem: the simplicity of providence, the chain of fate, chance, divine knowledge and predestination, and freedom of the will.[344]

Providence and fate, as Boethius explains them, are but obverse and reverse of one truth; the "simplicity of divine providence" is the source of all things, viewed "in the purity of God's understanding," while fate is the manifold, active course of these same things, viewed from below, or in time.[345] Hence every fortune is good; even adversity can be turned to good account; "it is in your hands to frame for yourselves what fortune you please."[346] Like Plotinus, Boethius sees goodness radiating or un-

[334] III, pr. 8, 31–35.
[335] III, pr. 9, 91–94; III, pr. 10, 7–9.
[336] III, pr. 10–12.
[337] III, pr. 12, 80–82; cf. III, pr. 12, 96 f.: *nec ullam mali esse naturam*; cf. IV, pr. 2, 104–106; 118–120; cf. Plotinus and St. Augustine, above, pp. 378; 792, and n. 310.
[338] IV, pr. 1, 9–12.
[339] IV, pr. 1, 24–31; IV, pr. 2–4.
[340] IV, pr. 3, 36–38.
[341] IV, pr. 4, 9–14; 42–44; cf. Plato, *Gorgias*, 469a–479e; 508bc; and see above, pp. 257 f.; 262.
[342] IV, pr. 5.
[343] IV, pr. 6, 21: *velut ab alio orsa principio.*
[344] IV, pr. 6, 7–14.
[345] IV, pr. 6, 22–101.
[346] IV, pr. 6, 2–3; 38–45; 53–54.

folding from a central, divine power, and fatality or evil only in remoteness from this prime source; but he interposes less in the way of elaborate intermediate grades of being and activity than do the Neoplatonists.[347] Chance, or fortune, is not the negation of law, but "an unexpected event of concurring causes in those things which are done to some end or purpose"; the definition, and even the illustration given (a farmer's digging up buried treasure) is Peripatetic.[348] As fate is subordinate to providence, so fortune is subordinate to fate.

Boethius goes on to affirm the freedom of the will: "for there can be no reasonable nature, unless it be endowed with free will."[349] In fact, the more men engage in contemplation of God, and the less they are fettered by the body, the greater is their freedom.[350] The fore-knowledge of human actions on the part of God may seem to imply that these actions are predestined; and some attempts to avoid this conclusion are fallacious or futile.[351] All things are foreseen by the divine mind; but that does not mean that all (including voluntary actions) happen of necessity.[352] But the really important point for Boethius is the timelessness of God's knowledge, which is not so much prescience of a future as knowledge of a never fading present.[353] "Doubtless all those things come to pass which God foreknows shall come, but some of them proceed from free will, which though they come to pass by being, yet they lose not their own nature, because before they come to pass, they might also not have happened."[354] And Boethius ends his work with an impressive tribute to that eternal witness of all things who is God, in whose sight we must live uprightly.[355]

The discussions of fate and providence, of chance, of causality, and of free will after Boethius belong almost wholly to Christian theology, and cannot be here pursued. The learned John of Salisbury, to be sure, a mediaeval humanist with something of the scepticism of Montaigne or of Erasmus, doubts whether it is possible for philosophy to solve the ultimate

[347] For the figure of concentric revolving "orbs" (IV, pr. 6, 65–76), and the indebtedness of Boethius both to Proclus and to Plotinus, cf. H. R. Patch, "Fate in Boethius and the Neoplatonists," *Speculum* 4 (1929), pp. 62–72 (with a minor correction by V. Cioffari, *Fortune and Fate* [1935], pp. 64 f.): "The more the soul is freed from things corporeal and thus, according to both Proclus and Plotinus, from Fate, the more it may attain to that centre of stability and simplicity which, according to Plotinus, is Providence, or God" (Patch, pp. 71 f.).

[348] V, pr. 1, 6–7; 18–22; 35–58; Aristotle, *Phys.* 195b31–198a13; and see above pp. 321; 374; for further details, cf. V. Cioffari, *Fortune and Fate* [1935], pp. 82–91; and for the enormous cult of Fortuna and her wheel in later times, cf. H. R. Patch, *The Goddess Fortuna in Mediaeval Literature* (Cambridge, 1927).

[349] *Cons.* V, pr. 2, 5–6.

[350] V, pr. 2, 16–21.

[351] V, pr. 2, 27–29; pr. 3.

[352] V, pr. 4, 11–27; 53–54.

[353] V, pr. 6, 66–72; cf. 77–80; 115–116.

[354] V, pr. 6, 120–124.

[355] V, pr. 6, 163–176.

problems of fate, good, and evil. Yet it is interesting to observe how Platonic, Aristotelian, and Stoic ideas and terminology continue to be manipulated, for example, by Albertus Magnus and by S. Thomas Aquinas, with chief emphasis on Aristotle.[356] Of particular interest to us is the later revival of Platonism, especially by Georgius Gemistus Pletho (*c.* 1355–1450) and by his pupil the Cardinal and Patriarch Bessarion, who sought anew to reconcile Platonism and Aristotelianism; and the attempt of Theodorus Gaza (*c.* 1400–1478) to defend Aristotelianism. For more than twenty years, tracts and letters passed back and forth between these and other scholars. A good deal of the argument was concerned with the question whether Plato or Aristotle afforded the better basis for belief in the freedom of the will and moral responsibility, and for the teleological conception of the universe, doctrines that were, of course, orthodox. Pletho and Bessarion gave Plato the greater credit in this matter, and held that Aristotle attributed to Nature causality (and spontaneity) but not purpose (unless an immanent purpose); Pletho moreover stressed the necessary bond of cause and effect, rejected spontaneity, and carried his belief in the unchangeability of God's law to the point of regarding prayer as futile and impious. Gaza replied in a treatise *On the Voluntary and the Involuntary* which has only recently been printed for the first time. He argues that there is essential agreement between Plato and Aristotle both as to free will and necessity and as to chance and necessity. The argument turns on the Platonic thesis that "no one is voluntarily evil" and on the Aristotelian distinctions between involuntary, non-voluntary, and voluntary action, considered in relation to the extent of the agent's knowledge or ignorance of immediate and of ultimate good, and also on the various meanings of the terms "necessity" and "chance" or "contingency." The argument is intricate, nor are all the details valid; but Gaza is satisfied that he has saved both fate (or necessity) and the voluntary (with contingency); and, what is more, that he has vindicated the Christian conception of prayer.[357]

Such was the controversy among Greeks under Italian skies about the middle of the fifteenth century. In the succeeding two centuries greater

[356] For Albertus Magnus and for St. Thomas Aquinas, cf. V. Cioffari, *Fortune and Fate* (1935), pp. 92–118; G. L. Fonsegrive, *Le Libre Arbitre*, pp. 113–129; H. O. Taylor, *The Mediaeval Mind* (London, 1911), Vol. II, pp. 420–432; 475–483.

[357] Most of the documents in this controversy are in Migne, *Patrologia Graeco-Latina*, volumes 160 and 161; for the history of the controversy, cf. J. W. Taylor's Chicago dissertation, "Georgius Gemistus Pletho's Criticism of Plato and Aristotle" (Menasha, Wisconsin, 1921), pp. 6–19; 55–65. For Pletho's essay *On Fate*, and for the exchange of letters between Pletho and Bessarion on the subject, see Migne, vol. 160, pp. 961–964; vol. 161, pp. 716 f.; 720 f. (also in Orelli, *De Fato*, pp. 224–247, with Latin translation). The text of Theodorus Gaza's treatise was first published, with introduction, translation, and notes, by J. W. Taylor (*University of Toronto Studies*, Philological Series, No. 7, 1925).

minds struggled with the same problems in northern Europe. We may conclude our study by taking brief note of two of these figures.

When Boethius was imprisoned, his beloved library was not among his consolations, and he wrote from the fulness of his well-stored mind. A different fortune befell the Dutch jurist and theologian Hugo Grotius (1583–1645). When, in 1619, in the course of the religious struggles of his day, he was imprisoned at Louvain, as a sympathizer with the Arminians (or Remonstrants), who denied predestination, he was allowed a plentiful and ever-changing supply of books; indeed, it was in a chest supposedly filled with books that he finally made his escape, thanks to the help of his devoted and capable wife. During his months in prison he naturally brooded much on the problem of fate and free will, and occupied his time in reading ancient works that deal with it; such of them as were in Greek he translated into Latin. After his escape, he published his collection of passages, under the title: *Philosophorum Sententiae De Fato, et de eo quod in nostra est potestate, collectae partim, et de Graeco versae.* The work must have appealed to Greekless readers, and passed through several editions. Here in succession are marshalled the arguments of more than a score of authors, classified as "Pythagoreans," "Platonists," "Peripatetics," "Stoics," "Epicureans," "Jews," and finally "Christians." It is as if a great company of the ancients, pagans and Christians alike, had visited Grotius in his cell, and had counselled him to believe that man's spirit need not be cast down by the idea of Fate; for all that matters most is either in the gift of a kindly providence or is within man's own power to achieve.[358]

Milton concerns us not only as an English poet but as a thinker in the Greek tradition. Puritan though he was, he was more than Puritan; the way in which he wore his "singing robe" and the texture of his thought are alike classical, are indeed the finest and most personal English expression of the Hellenism of the high renaissance. Both personal and public events prompted in him a growing sense of the power of evil, but no loss of his belief in the ultimate goodness of God;[359] here was a problem that demanded his deepest probing. The native appeal of virtue is the theme of much of his early poetry; the necessity of liberty is the burden of the

[358] The edition of Grotius, *De Fato*, in the Harvard College Library was published by Elzevir, Amsterdam, 1648, with a preface by the widow; it is a volume of 384 pages, followed by another work by another author, and once belonged to C. E. Norton. The *De Fato* may also be found in the collected theological works of Grotius. Some of his translations have also been used by later scholars in similar works; e.g. by I. C. Orelli, in his edition of the essays *De Fato* of Alexander and four others (Zurich, 1824).

[359] Milton's arguments for the existence of God are the orderliness of the world and the existence of conscience in man; *De Doctrina Christiana* IV, 14; cf. Kant (above, p. 288, n. 56); and Wordsworth: "Whose dwelling is the light of setting suns . . . and in the mind of man."

prose works of his maturity; as an old man, blind and disheartened by the palpable failure of all that he has championed, he turns, like St. Augustine and Boethius and Grotius, to the task of somehow vindicating the divine justice. The less orthodox his Christianity becomes, and the more independent his thought, the more he seems to return to Greek conceptions of fate, good, and evil. We are concerned chiefly with his later poems, which must be supplemented by his posthumous treatise *De Doctrina Christiana*.[360]

Early in *Paradise Lost* Milton sets forth his purpose:

> That to the height of this great argument
> I may assert eternal Providence
> And justify the ways of God to men.[361]

The action of the poem turns on the "first disobedience" of man, and the fall of Adam. But the fall cannot be understood unless it is seen in the frame of a larger conception, which is nothing less than the whole scheme of divine providence, including the creation, the conditions under which the fall is possible, and, in the sequel, the terms on which regeneration may proceed.

Milton is so far orthodox as to see in the fall both original and personal sin.[362] Man is capable of both good and evil, and is responsible for his acts; once created, he is left by the Creator to his own devices with a minimum of special intervention. If he perversely chooses evil, it is because he allows his reason to be thwarted by his passions. But we cannot fail to ask why God permitted the fall to take place. Milton's answer involves his whole conception, first of the relation of the imperfect creation to the perfect creator, and, second, of the nature of evil itself. When Raphael is relating the story of the creation, Adam asks:

> what cause
> Moved the Creator in his holy rest
> Through all eternity so late to build
> In chaos.[363]

In his reply, Raphael repeats the speech of "the Omnipotent Eternal Father" about the creation, a part of which is of extreme importance for our inquiry.

[360] Cited here by the pages of Bishop Sumner's translation, contained in Volumes IV and V of Bohn's edition of Milton's *Prose Works* (London, 1875).

[361] *P. L.* I, 24–26.

[362] *De Doctr. Christ.* IV, 253–263.

[363] *P.L.* VII, 90–93. Earlier the poet has asked (*P.L.* I, 28–33) "what cause moved" our parents to fall. With the question about the cause (*aitia*) of the creation, cf. Plato, *Tim.* 29d; see above, pp. 293–295; for Plato's question about the cause of human evil, see above, pp. 307–309.

I uncircumscribed myself retire,
And put not forth my goodness, which is free
To act, or not; necessity and chance
Approach not me, and what I will is fate.[364]

God, in other words, is free, and self-sufficing, like Aristotle's God; there is no compulsion for Him to propagate the Creation (the Son, Who is the Word); if He acts, it is because He wills to act.[365] He does will to act, gloriously and with immediate effect, in the creation. Yet something of his goodness is not "put forth"; and to the extent to which he "retires himself" and leaves the created world free to go its own way, to that extent evil and the fall are made possible.[366]

Why, then, should free beings do evil? Everything comes from God; even evil may exist potentially in Him:

Evil into the mind of God or man
May come and go, so unapproved, and leave
No spot or blame behind.[367]

But whereas God's very nature expels evil in his "retiring," man entertains evil when he allows his reason to be beguiled by his senses. Not that matter is in itself evil, or that the body and its normal desires are to be utterly repressed; matter is actually divine, a part of God, and soul and body are one.[368] Here speaks the humanist who cannot deem evil the manifold beauties of this visible world and the endearments of the senses. Not passion itself, but enslavement by passion (the loss of *sophrosyne*, as it were), is evil, and was the cause of the fall.[369] It follows that regeneration comes about when "one greater Man," the divine reason incarnate in Christ, by taming passion is able to "restore us."[370] This, too, is part of God's plan for man, and His final justification; grace is added to freedom of the will.

Man shall not quite be lost, but saved who will;
Yet not of will in him, but grace in me
Freely vouchsafed.[371]

[364] *P.L.* VII, 170–173; cf. I, 116 f.: "By fate, the strength of gods . . . can not fail" (Satan is speaking).

[365] Cf. *P.L.* VIII, 403–432, for the contrast between God's self-sufficiency and man's need of "collateral love and dearest amity"; 415 f.: "Thou in thyself art perfect, and in thee | Is no deficience found. Not so is Man," etc.; *De Doctr. Christ.* IV, 83; cf. Plato, with Lovejoy's criticism, cited above, p. 294, n. 117; Aristotle, above, pp. 322 f.

[366] See Appendix 68: Milton and "Retraction."

[367] *P. L.* V, 117–119; the speaker is Adam.

[368] *P.L.* IV, 724–775; V, 404–426; 469–490; 496–501; VIII, 422–432; 618–629; *De Doctr. Christ.* IV, 175–180; 188 f.

[369] *P.L.* IX, 1009–1045; XII, 83–90; cf. VIII, 635–637; IX, 21–31; St. Augustine, *De Civ. Dei* XIV, 11–28.

[370] *P.L.* I, 4 f.; *P.R.* I, 150–167; *De Doctr. Christ.* IV, 284–286; 327–330.

[371] *P.L.* III, 173–175.

It involves a second act of creation; Christ is formed within the Son whom God has already created. The story of the Temptation, in *Paradise Regained*, represents Milton's almost Hellenic idea of regeneration as a sort of recovery for man of the *sophrosyne* that was lost by the fall.[372] But the result of the regeneration, unlike anything Greek, is positive gain: man "is raised to a far more excellent state of grace and glory than that from which he has fallen"; [373] thus evil is turned to good.[374]

God's fore-knowledge of what shall be does not in Milton's view lead to Calvinistic pre-destination or pre-election. In other words, men's freedom of will is really free, even though God knows what uses they will make of it, and thus can employ men's wills as materials in His total plan. Again and again Milton's characters reiterate the full moral responsibility of angels and men, who stand or fall by their own act, and cannot "justly accuse their Maker, or their making, or their fate." [375] But God in the fulness of His Knowledge can contemplate with a certain irony or compassion the futile rebellion of the fallen angels or the ignorance and weakness of man.[376] The problem of fate, good, and evil, then, is not one that admits of any final intellectual solution; it remains partly, to be sure, within the realm of human activity and human suffering, but it lies partly on the knees of the inscrutable gods. That is what Homer and Greek tragedy have said, once and for all. Man is free, but only within limits; therefore life demands of him the patient endurance of evil, the hand of compassion for fellow-sufferers, and the smile of irony at fortune's ways. Above all, it demands the performance of God's will, which works through us, and which is the source, if not of worldly success (for chance has a part in that), at least of human good and human happiness. This may not be "poetic justice," as the older critics understood the term; [377] but it is the divine justice.

It was the fallen angels who

[372] We are not here concerned with Milton's Arianism, which consists in the conception of the Son (and Christ) as not co-eternal with the Father. But we must note the complete subordination of the Crucifixion to the Temptation; this, of course, lends itself to Milton's intellectual treatment of his theme. There is no suggestion of vicarious atonement.

[373] *De Doctr. Christ.* IV, 284; cf. *Areopagitica*: "Good and evil we know in the field of this world grow up together almost inseparably. . . . He that can apprehend and consider vice . . . and yet prefer that which is truly better, he is the true wayfaring Christian."

[374] *P.L.* I, 162–166; VII, 186–188; 615 f.; XII, 469–477; cf. St. Augustine on the "last free will," see above, p. 387.

[375] *P.L.* III, 98–128; IV, 66–67; V, 233–237; 538–541; X, 43–47; cf. *De Doctr. Christ.* IV, 30–77, an interesting passage which revives many of the Greek arguments against fatalism from Homer down.

[376] *P.L.* V, 718–734; VIII, 75–84; 398–406; XII, 48–62; *Samson*, 682–686; 705–709; cf. Saurat, *Milton*, pp. 229–232.

[377] See above, pp. 93–96.

reasoned high
Of Providence, foreknowledge, will, and fate,
Fixed fate, free will, foreknowledge absolute;
And formed no end, in wandering mazes lost.
Of good and evil much they argued then,
Of happiness and final misery,
Passion and apathy, and glory and shame,
Vain wisdom all, and false philosophy;
Yet with a pleasing sorcery could charm
Pain for a while or anguish, and excite
Fallacious hope, or arm th' obdured breast
With stubborn patience as with triple steel.[378]

Yet it is Satan, no mere spirit of evil, but virtue gone wrong, who has mastered a working philosophy of considerable value:

The mind is its own place, and in itself
Can make a heaven of hell, a hell of heaven.[379]

This is not to be dismissed as wishful thinking; it is the Homeric *tlemosyne*, the *arete* of tragedy and of all humanism, the Stoic inner fortitude that is not humbled by fate. It is, in fact, very near to Milton's own stubborn, heretical defiance, except that Satan's defiance is of God Omnipotent. But Milton is himself even more akin to blind Samson; both have been schooled by suffering.

Milton's last great work, the *Samson Agonistes*, abandons any attempt to phrase a philosophical justification of God's ways; it rather exhibits, for the purgation of pity and fear,[380] the spectacle of Samson first humiliated and then triumphant in death. It is triumph that the Chorus would fain claim for him, a little before the catastrophe,[381] yet patience, as they know, that "is more oft the exercise of saints, the trial of their fortitude"; either is in Samson's lot, though his blindness marks him as likely to be crowned at last by patience.[382] His revenge, as it proves, is "dearly bought, yet glorious";[383] and both Manoah and the Chorus derive from

[378] *P.L.* II, 557–569; cf. *Samson*, 652–709 (the Chorus, before the catastrophe, reasoning with God).

[379] *P.L.* I, 254 f.; St. Augustine, *Enarr. in Ps.* VI, 10: *nam locis corpora continentur, animo autem locus est affectio sua.*

[380] Milton's prefatory remarks, "of that sort of dramatic poetry which is called tragedy," call attention to Aristotle's phrase, with the added words, "that is, to temper and reduce them to just measure with a kind of delight, stirred up by reading or seeing those passions well imitated." See above, p. 97.

[381] *Samson Agonistes*, 1268 ff.: "Oh, how comely it is, and how reviving | To the spirits of just men long oppressed, | When God into the hands of their deliverer | Puts invincible might," etc.

[382] *Samson*, 1287–1296.

[383] *Samson*, 1660.

his death not sorrow alone but pride, a sense of calm, and a conviction of divine justice reasserting itself.[384] The calm Milton would attribute, as we have seen, to the process of purgation. Yet that is not all. "Nothing is here for tears"; yet what consoles Manoah is not merely Samson's heroism, but,

> which is best and happiest yet, all this
> With God not parted from him, as was feared,
> But favouring and assisting to the end.[385]

And it is left for the Chorus, entirely in the Greek tragic manner,[386] to proclaim its simple religious faith:

> All is best, though we oft doubt,
> What th' unsearchable dispose
> Of highest wisdom brings about,
> And ever best found in the close.
> Oft he seems to hide his face,
> But unexpectedly returns . . .
> His servants he, with new acquist
> Of true experience from this great event,
> With peace and consolation hath dismissed,
> And calm of mind, all passion spent.[387]

[384] The Chorus has wavered, like Samson himself, with regard to divine justice. Contrast Samson, 703 f.: "Just or unjust, alike seem miserable. | For oft alike both come to evil end;" with 293 f.: "Just are the ways of God | And justifiable to men."

[385] *Samson*, 1718–1721.

[386] On this and much else that is of interest for our subject, cf. W. R. Parker, *Milton's Debt to Greek Tragedy in Samson Agonistes* (Baltimore, 1937); see also above, pp. 99 f.

[387] *Samson*, 1745–1750; 1755–1758.

# APPENDICES

## APPENDICES

Each Appendix bears especially on the page to which a reference is given (in parenthesis) immediately after its number.

1 (10): *Themis. Themis,* as her name probably indicates, is concerned with "dooms," "judgments," the fixed laws and sanctions of civil society. (Cf. *Il.* 11, 807; contrast *Od.* 9, 106; 112–114.) Yet the etymology is not certain (cf. R. Hirzel, *Themis,* etc., pp. 53–56; and Hirzel regards *Themis* as older than *Dike*). There are traces of an early association of *Themis* with natural forces, and with oracular counsel. In the "Hymn" of the Kouretes, the young men are bidden to "leap" for full jars and flocks and fields and hives and cities and ships and young citizens "and for goodly *Themis*" (J. E. Harrison, *Themis,* pp. 8; 515–519; 533–535); "Hesiod" marries *Themis* to Zeus (*Theog.* 901); and Aeschylus, *P. V.* 211 f., treats *Themis* (who actually superseded the oracle of Earth at Delphi) as but another name or "form" of Gaea. See further K. Lehrs, *Populäre Aufsätze,* pp. 95–108; J. E. Harrison, *Themis,* pp. 483–485; L. R. Farnell, *Higher Aspects of Greek Religion,* pp. 69–78; 91; R. Hirzel, *Themis,* etc. pp. 1–53.

2 (11): *Afterlife in Homer.* The interest in what may lie beyond this life, which doubtless was prominent in the pre-Homeric world, as it was destined to become very important in the seventh and later centuries which returned to pre-Homeric sources, has been eclipsed for Homer by the interests of this world; there is hardly any cult of the dead, and there are no ghosts, possibly because cremation has supplanted inhumation. The great eleventh book of the Odyssey is exceptional, probably an interpolation, and based on pre-Homeric and post-Homeric beliefs; but even here the picture of the life after death is gloomy, and hardly recognizes moral rewards and punishments. Elysium (a pre-Hellenic name) is reserved by Homer for Menelaus, favorite of Zeus (*Od.* 4, 563); only later does it, or something like it, become the reward of virtue, or of religious initiation. The idea that the innocent descendants of the guilty are punished after them is rooted in the early tribal stage of society; it does not appear in Homer, but will emerge later, and will be rejected (see above, pp. 29, and n. 97; 36; 41; 61); but see also p. 87 (Herodotus).

3 (12): *Daimon.* M. P. Nilsson (*History of Greek Religion,* pp. 112; 165) and E. Ehnmark (*The Idea of God in Homer,* pp. 59–73) well distinguish between the undefined power attributed to *daimones* and the individual, personal *theos,* who is anthropomorphic, and receives a cult. *Theos* is used normally with the definite article, of a particular god, though in more or less philosophic Greek the word sometimes drops the article, and means something like a monotheistic god; *daimon* often dispenses with the article, and is almost equivalent to Fate, indifferent, good, or evil. Yet thrice in a single book of the *Iliad* (7, 291; 377; 396) "ὁ δαίμων" means neither abstract fate nor any particular god, but "some god."

4 (14): *Etymologies of Moira, etc.* Cf. H. Ebeling, *Lexicon Homericum,* s. v. μοῖρα (by C. Mutzbauer), noting first the definition of the *Etymologicum*

*Magnum*, and the abundant Homeric examples; see also s.vv. *μόρος* and *εἱμαρμένη*. The stems of these words, as is universally recognized, are derived from the verb *μείρομαι*, "receive one's portion." F. M. Cornford, and Mauss and Durkheim (cited by G. Murray, *The Rise of the Greek Epic* (Oxford, 1911), Appendix D, p. 337) trace *μοῖρα* to the special divisions or portions of primitive tribes, and the shares of land, etc. that they held. (Νόμος, "law," is similarly akin to *νομή*, "pasture.") For *Aisa*, often equivalent to *Moira*, see Ebeling, s.v. *αἶσα* (by B. Giseke), connecting the stem with *ἴση*, "equal," i.e., "a just share." See further s.v. *πότμος* (Giseke), cognate of *πίπτω* "befall" (cf. Latin *casus*); i.e., a "chance," or "doom," never of good luck; and s.v. *πεπρωμένον* (Giseke), from stem *πορ-*, "give," "bestow"; hence "what is accomplished, predestined." Cf. also C. F. von Nägelsbach, *Homerische Theologie*[3], pp. 116–141; W. E. Gladstone, *Juventus Mundi* (London, 1869), pp. 358–360; St. George Stock, "Fate (Greek and Roman)," in Hastings, *Enc. of Rel. and Eth.* V, pp. 786–790; S. Eitrem, *P. W.* s.v. *Moira*; E. Leitzke, *Moira und Gottheit im alten griechischen Epos: Sprachlichen Untersuchungen* (Göttingen, 1930); S. Eitrem, "Schicksalsmächte," *Symbolae Osloenses*, 13 (1934), pp. 47–64; E. Ehnmark, *The Idea of God in Homer*, pp. 86–103.

5 (19): *"Odyssey" ethical.* Aristotle, *Poetics* 1459b14–16; cf. L. A. Post, "The Moral Pattern in Homer," *T.A.P.A.* 70 (1939), pp. 158–190; S. E. Bassett, "'Η δ' Ὀδύσσεια . . . ἠθικόν," in *Classical Studies presented to E. Capps* (Princeton, 1936), pp. 3–13; L. A. Post, *T.A.P.A.* 69 (1938), pp. 1–18; S. E. Bassett, *The Poetry of Homer* (Berkeley, 1938), pp. 187–207; and, for even greater emphasis on the tragedy of Achilles, S. E. Bassett, "The Ἁμαρτία of Achilles," *T.A.P.A.* 65 (1934), pp. 47–69; and P. C. Wilson, "The *πάθει μάθος* of Achilles," *T.A.P.A.* 69 (1938), pp. 557–574; and see above, pp. 26 f.; for the differences, as well as the resemblances between the two poems, W. Jaeger, *Paideia*, pp. 42–54.

6 (24): *Conditional Prophecy.* Of the "twain fates" of Achilles, E. Ehnmark writes, *The Idea of God in Homer*, pp. 75 f.: "This conditional prediction is typical. It is extremely common for an oracle to answer: if you act in such and such a way, the result will be such and such. . . . The oracle foretells the future subject to certain conditions; it can predict the consequences of a certain course of action. Such prophecies presuppose the existence of an order, or regularity in what happens, which yet leaves some scope for the free decisions of the individual. Life is not foreordained except in so far as its events are the effects of definite causes. This order is something altogether abstract, being neither power, nor will, nor person. It is a scheme of events, not a power that controls them." On the oracle given to Laius, sometimes stated in conditional form, but a stock instance for later philosophical speculation on predestination, see above, p. 159, n. 84; fuller references in *Index*, s.v. Oracle given to Laius. See further R. Hirzel, *Themis*, etc., pp. 7–9.

7 (31): *Golden Age.* M. Croiset, *Hist. de la Litt. grecque*[3] (Paris, 1910), I, p. 506. Cf. J. R. Lowell, *Literary Essays*, II (Boston, 1892), p. 98: "From the days of the first grandfather, everybody has remembered a golden age behind him. No doubt Adam depreciated the apple which the little Cain on his knee was crunching, by comparison with those he himself had tasted in Eden." By this reasoning, the first grandfather, or perhaps Adam himself, was the first *laudator temporis acti*. There are surprisingly few traces of such an attitude in

Homer; it begins in earnest in Hesiod. On the Ages generally and especially on the Golden Age and on the later tradition of the idea, among mystics, philosophers, and poets, Greek and Roman, see further: H. T. Buckle, *Hist. of Civilization in England*, I (New York, 1858), p. 96 (on the idea of the Golden Age as a phase of an irrational and erroneous "indulgence of a poetic sentiment in favour of the remote and unknown"); E. B. Tylor, *Primitive Culture*, I (New York, ed. of 1920), pp. 26–39, on "progression-theories" and "degeneration-theories" of civilization (both spring from theology rather than from history, which recognizes a "development-theory"); G. Norlin, "Ethnology and the Golden Age," *C. P.* 12 (1917), pp. 351–364, on the tendency of the Greeks to see the past (and contemporary barbarians) as happy or as unhappy by contrast with the disillusionment or with the success of their own epochs; J. A. K. Thomson, *Greeks and Barbarians* (London, 1921), pp. 13–31, for racial contrasts; W. R. Hardie, "The Age of Gold," in *Lectures on Classical Subjects* (London, 1903), pp. 102–131; E. Graf, "Ad aureae Aetatis Fabulam Symbola," *Leipziger Studien zur cl. Philol.* 8 (1885), pp. 1–84; K. F. Smith, "Ages of the World (Greek and Roman)," in Hastings, *Enc. of Rel. and Eth.* I, pp. 192–200; also his *Elegies of Albius Tibullus* (New York, 1913), notes on Tib. 1, 3, 35–48, and on 1, 3, 45–46; K. Seeliger, "Weltalter," in Roscher, *Ausf. Lex. s.v.* (For several of these references I am indebted to the kindness of Professor A. S. Pease.) Of the ideas found in later elaborations of the Golden Age, several, though not all, are implicit in Hesiod: the rule of Cronos (Saturn), not of Zeus (Jupiter); blessings that come of their own accord, without toil; piety; communism; vegetarianism; the simple life, according to nature, without the arts and sciences, and without navigation, trade, or war. That man's fall came through his restless invention of these dangerous devices, is a later notion. With the contrary idea of the progress of man (cf. Aesch. *P. V.* 440–455; Lucret. V, 925–1457), and with the idea that the Golden Age may return (cf. Plato, *Polit.* 269c; Virg. *Buc.* 4) we are not here concerned; Hesiod's interest is in explaining how evil entered the world.

8 (41): *Theognis on Zeus.* A. Croiset, *Hist. de la Litt. grecque*[3], II (Paris, 1914), p. 156. Cf. *Jeremiah*, 12, 1: "Righteous art thou, O Lord, when I plead with thee: yet let me talk with thee of thy judgments. Wherefore doth the way of the wicked prosper? Wherefore are all happy that deal very treacherously?" This is the first time in Hebrew literature (early sixth cent.) that the problem of the prosperity of the unrighteous is raised, probably after Jeremiah has narrowly escaped from a plot against his life. The answer of Yahweh is simply that Jeremiah has worse sufferings still to face. Inconsistent are the two strains in *Job*, the prose (early, orthodox) and the poetry (later, heterodox), being hardly reconciled; but the outcome is (1) resignation (19, 25; 40, 3–5; 42, 1–6), as in Theognis, and (2) recourse from the contemplation of God's dealings with man to God's majestic ways in Nature (36, 24 — 41, 34), a magnificent if unethical retreat from *Dike* to *Physis.* J. M. Edmonds, *Elegy and Iambus* (Loeb ed.), I, p. 13, n. 2, regards Theognis 373–392 as late, remarking that both it and 731–752 (quoted above, p. 41) "take Zeus to task (contrast 687) in the manner of late-fifth-century Athens." But we have already met the germ of the protest in Homer (see above, p. 24). The metrical arguments which Edmonds chiefly stresses (based on the frequency of the masculine caesura in the 3rd foot of the hexameter) seems to me inconclusive for the two passages in question (1 such caesura in 1.66 and in 1.83 lines, respectively; even in

Tyrtaeus, however, I find such variations as 1 in 5.3 lines (T. 6; 7), 1 in 1.7 (T. 8), and 1 in 1.2 (T. 9)).

9 (52): *Orphism*. Pausanias, VIII, 37, 5; Aristotle Pseudepig. Fr. 10 [7] Rose. On the Orphic religion in general, see M. P. Nilsson, *History of Greek Religion*; M. P. Nilsson, "Early Orphism and Kindred Religious Movements," in *Harvard Theological Review* 28 (1935), pp. 202–204; W. K. C. Guthrie, *Orpheus and Greek Religion*; E. Rohde, *Psyche: The Cult of Souls and Belief in Immortality among the Greeks*, pp. 335–347; O. Kern, *Orphicorum Fragmenta*; J. Adam, *The Religious Teachers of Greece*, Lecture V, "Orphic Religious Ideas," pp. 92–114. A. D. Nock, "Orphism or Popular Philosophy?" *Harv. Theol. Rev.* 33 (1940), pp. 301–315, shows how nebulous and lacking in specific Orphic character are many of the ideas often associated with Orphism. I. M. Linforth, *The Arts of Orpheus* (Berkeley, 1941), reviewing all the evidence with great care, comes to a sceptical conclusion: although there were rites and a literature of various ages associated with the name of Orpheus, there was never a distinctive Orphic religion. It is doubtless true that most accounts of Orphism (including my own) fail to distinguish as carefully as Linforth has done the varying value of the evidence; and also that they tend to read into Orphism greater religious and philosophic value than it had for the average Greek.

10 (58): *Orphic Cosmogony*. D1 B12, second half; much fuller account in Kern, *Orphicorum Fragmenta*, 140–248; see also above, pp. 52 f. There were clearly both more and also less orthodox versions, the less orthodox becoming more coarse and grotesque, though they also included abstractions such as Necessity ('Ανάγκη or 'Αδράστεια); cf. D1 B13. The Orphic goddess Necessity, goddess or judge of the dead, or queen of the world, mother of *Heimarmene*, sometimes displaced by *Themis* or by *Dike*, will become important in different ways in later philosophy, though not in cult. For Parmenides, see Appendix 28; for Plato, see above, pp. 302–305; 315 f.; cf. W. Gundel, *Ananke und Heimarmene*, pp. 25 f.; R. Hirzel, *Themis, Dike, und Verwandtes*, pp. 353, 389. The Orphic "Hymns" are mostly still later than the "Rhapsodies."

11 (100): "*Count no man happy*." Sophocles, *O.T.* 1524–1530, on which see Jebb's note on 1529, and below, pp. 161 f.; 325 f.; and Sir R. W. Livingstone, "The Exodus of the *O.T.*," in *Greek Poetry and Life* (Oxford, 1936), pp. 158–163, esp. p. 163: "The words of the chorus, conventional and familiar, recall us from these remote and tragic happenings to the world of everyday. . . . That undoubtedly is the artistic effect of these words (1524 f.) which seem and are platitudinous and inadequate to the tragedy." Cf. *Trach.* 1–3; *Tyndareus*, frag. 546 Pearson; Euripides, *Phoen.* 1758–1763 (the first two lines an echo of the passage in *O.T.*); also, for the sentiment, *And.* 100–102; *Troad.* 509 f.; *Her.* 1291 f.; *I. A.* 161 (these, however, not in the exodus). It may be added that F. Ritter, *Philologus* 17 (1861), pp. 422–436, rejected, but without sufficient reason, all the *clausulae* of all seven surviving tragedies of Sophocles. For the ending of Milton's *Samson*, see below, p. 398; and cf. W. R. Parker, *Milton's Debt to Greek Tragedy in Samson Agonistes* (Baltimore, 1937), pp. 70 f.

12 (117): *Interpretations of "P.V."* For brief accounts of the various interpretations of the *Prometheus Bound* and of the figure of Prometheus by poets

and scholars in different ages, cf. N. Wecklein, ed. *Prometheus* (English trans. by F. D. Allen, Boston, 1891), pp. 14–18; J. E. Harry, ed. *Prometheus* (New York, 1905), pp. 71–74; H. W. Smyth, *Aeschylean Tragedy*, pp. 92–97. For the suggestion that the present play represents a reworking of an earlier play, and may be dated as late as B.C. 410, see C. B. Gulick, *H.S.C.P.* 10 (1899), pp. 103–114. In more recent years it has even been suggested that the play is not at all the work of Aeschylus; cf. Schmid-Stahlin, *Geschichte der Gr. Litteratur* (München, 1934), I, 2, p. 193, and n. 5.

13 (133): *Second stasimon of "Eumenides." Eum.* 490–516. This is a test case: if Orestes escapes, fallen is the house of *dike*; license will follow; in vain will the murdered cry for vengeance. (This is the argument for punishment as a deterrent.) 517–525: The need of fear (τὸ δεινόν) as inquisitor; it is well to be chastened by suffering (520 f.; cf. *Ag.* 177, and see above, p. 108; one thinks, too, of the Socratic paradox that it is better, if guilty, to be punished than not; see above, pp. 257; 272). *Eum.* 526–537: A digression in praise of *sophrosyne*, τὸ μέσον (529), as opposed to anarchy (526 f.); *hybris* is child of impiety, *olbos* of ὑγίεια φρένων (533–537). 538–549: Digression continued to include *Aidos* (expanded to include guests as well as parents); show *aidos* for the altar of *dike*, else shall *poine* follow. 550–552: he who is voluntarily just shall prosper (ἑκὼν δ' ἀνάγκας ἄτερ δίκαιος ὤν, κτλ.; cf. Solon 1, 7–16, and see above, p. 36; contrast Simonides 4 Diehl, who excuses involuntary failure due to ἀνάγκη; see above, p. 68; cf. also Psalm 1.) 553–565: The way of the transgressor, scorned by *daimon*, caught by a storm, and wrecked on the reef of *dike*. (Again cf. Solon and Psalm 1.)

14 (135): *Blood-vengeance.* There is no warrant for seeing, as some scholars do, evidence in the *Eumenides* for a transition from a matrilinear to a patriarchal society; the Erinyes really avenge offences against either a father or a mother (*Eum.* 513 f.; cf. *Choeph.* 924 f.; *Il.* 9, 453–457; 571; and see H. J. Rose, *Folk-Lore*, 37 (1926), pp. 229 f.; and, for the *Suppliants*, see above, p. 110); it merely happens in the present myth to be the mother who has been slain. For the history of the successive stages in Greek blood-vengeance or punishment, cf. H. J. Treston, *Poine: A Study in Ancient Greek Blood-Vengeance* (London, 1923), which distinguishes, pp. 422–424, (1) the tribal custom of earliest Greece, *Wergeld*, with exile or death as alternatives, under group control; private vengeance, but not *vendetta*; (2) "Homeric" custom; homicide normally punished by death (avoided in practise, though not in theory, by flight); no regular trial, but etiquette distinguishing murder and vengeance, thus preventing wholesale vendetta; (3) "Hesiodic" vendetta, with no control; ancestral "curses"; blood-thirst of the dead; mutilation of murdered corpses; deprivation of burial; (4) "Apolline" code: murderer "god-hated," shunned, slain or banished; courts for murder, if for nothing else; right of suppliant till guilt is proved; no *wergeld*, but minor appeasement of relatives, after exile, for minor degrees of guilt; (5) code of *polis* (Draco, etc.); compromise of old and new. (So in *Eumenides*, religion of cleansing and political synoecism overcome the resistance of the clans.)

15 (137): *References for "Eumenides."* On the far-ranging ideas dealt with in this paragraph, see further G. Murray, *Aeschylus*, pp. 177–183; 196–201 (on pity in Aeschylus); 203 f.; W. Headlam (and A. C. Pearson), ed. *Agamemnon*,

Intro., pp. 27–31; G. Thomson, ed. *Oresteia*, Vol. I, Intro., pp. 1–5 (on Greek conceptions of progress); 49–69 (on the conflict and the reconciliation in the *Eumenides*); B. A. G. Fuller, "The Conflict of Moral Obligation in the Trilogy of Aeschylus," *Harvard Theological Review* 8 (1915), pp. 459–479; H. W. Smyth, *Aeschylean Tragedy*, pp. 230–234; for Plato, *Tim.* 48a (on "persuasion"; cf. F. M. Cornford, *Plato's Cosmogony*, pp. 162–177, 361–364, comparing the *Eumenides*; see above, pp. 304 f., and below, Appendix 49); *Politicus* 294a (on personal rule); for Aristotle on *epieikeia*, *E.N.* 1137a31–1138a3.

16 (144): *Fate and Character in Sophocles.* Among critics who have emphasized fate and irony, mention may be made of C. J. Ehlinger, *De Fati apud Sophoclem Notione, Indole, Vi* (Berlin, 1852); J. Wieberg, *De Fato Graecorum* (Jena, 1869); J. H. Schlegel, *Die Tragische Ironie bei Sophokles* (Tauberbischofsheim, 1874); F. Wisbacher, *Die Tragische Ironie bei Sophokles* (München, 1895); H. F. Müller, *Die Tragödien des Sophokles* (Heidelberg, 1909); for C. Thirlwell and L. Campbell, see above, pp. 102–104; for M. B. O'Connor, p. 138, n. 3. For the emphasis on character, C. R. Post, "The Dramatic Art of Sophocles," *H.S.C.P.* 23 (1912), pp. 71–127 (especially pp. 81–90, emphasizing the surmounting of successive obstacles by the protagonist); K. Reinhardt, *Sophokles* (Frankfurt, 1933), p. 12 and passim, on the pathetic isolation of the characters; similarly, W. Schadewaldt, "Monolog und selbstgespräch," *Neue Philol. Unters.* 2 (1926), pp. 55–93, and "Sophokles; Aias und Antigone," *Neue Wege zur Antike* 8 (1929), pp. 61–109 (which however goes too far in denying Sophocles effective characterization, and sees in these dramas chiefly the intellectual conflict of ideas). F. Allègre, *Sophocle, Étude sur les Ressorts Dramatiques de son Théâtre et la Composition de ses Tragédies* (Lyons and Paris, 1905), maintains that in Sophocles there is an imperfect reconciliation between character and fate, but that the imperfection is the less apparent in that fate and characters play their parts chiefly in different portions of the dramas, so that the characters have at least the illusion of freedom. M. Croiset, in a review of Allègre, *Journal des Savants*, 1906, pp. 289–302; 353–359, holds that Sophocles and his contemporaries were not aware of any such contradiction between forces which only modern theorists have made absolute; dramatic action, like all action, goes on in the narrow space between two unknowns, the past and the future (external forces and human impulses), and Sophoclean tragedy exhibits the two shadows as they fall over the action. In my discussion I attempt to reckon with both points of view.

17 (174): *"Rhesus."* The discussion above of the seventeen plays of Euripides leaves out of consideration the *Cyclops* (a satyr play) and the *Rhesus*. Though few recent scholars besides Murray have accepted the *Rhesus* as a genuine (probably early) work of Euripides, it has considerable interest, whoever its author may have been. It deals with the material of the tenth book of the *Iliad* (the *Doloneia*), but with chief emphasis on the fate of the Thracian king, Rhesus, the ally of Hector, who is murdered by the wiles of Odysseus helped by Athena. For our special subject it must suffice to note here: (1) the piety of Hector, who attributes fortune to the gift of the gods (*Rhesus* 56; 64; 103), and (2) the similar piety of the Chorus (199; 317 f.; contrast 332; 882–889; the concluding prayer, 995 f., has in its setting an ironical effect); (3) the rationalizing attitude of Aeneas (105–108); (4) the daring of Dolon, throwing dice with the gods (183); (5) the confidence of Rhesus (390; 488; only a slight

concession to caution, 468); (6) the caution of Odysseus, who will not force the issue against *Tyche* (583 f.; cf. 594, Diomedes); (7) the intervention of Athena, who in this play represents or interprets the power of fate (n.b. 595–598; 634–636; 640), helping Odysseus and deceiving Paris; (8) her action, though not her identity, is recognized by the charioteer (729; 852–855); (9) the mother of Rhesus, the Muse of the Mountains, who had foreknowledge of his doom (935; cf. also 974 f., of the doom of Achilles), holds Athena accountable (*αἰτία*) for it (938–940). The *Rhesus* thus shows a vigorous action controlled chiefly by divine forces, and characters triumphing or stricken as they yield to them or challenge them. No moral is pointed, unless it be the importance of cautious collaboration with the gods, whose justice, however is not evident.

18 (175): *A. W. Verrall.* It is noteworthy that *Alcestis*, *Iph. Taur.*, and *Ion*, together with *Phoen.* (from the next group), form Verrall's materials for his *Euripides the Rationalist*, while in his *Four Plays of Euripides* he draws on the *Helen*, and the *Orestes* (of the next group), together with *Andromache* and *Heracles*. His thesis (*E. the R.*, pp. 231 f.), if I may paraphrase it, is that the poet's orthodox (and miraculous) conclusions were composed with tongue in cheek, while his real intent was left to the wits of the reader, who has only to study the incidents and language in order to draw quite different (and sceptical) conclusions. One may admit that in most of the plays discussed by Verrall the sense of the dramatically effective is of paramount importance, without accepting Verrall's thesis. Is the *Philoctetes* of Sophocles, which presents several analogies with these plays and has been suspected of showing Euripidean influence, written in a cynical spirit?

19 (186): *Euripides, "Heracles."* J. Burnet, "The Religious and Moral Ideas of Euripides," in *Essays and Addresses*, pp. 61 f., generalizes even further the idea set forth in my discussion: "The strong man is only of value so long as he uses his strength in the service of mankind. When he is released from that service, his strength becomes a danger to himself and to those who are nearest and dearest to him." Cf. also J. Burnet, *Thales to Plato*, p. 121, on the *Heracles* as a study of the problem of might and right comparable to the Melian Dialogue of Thucydides (see Appendix 38); and R. S. Conway, "An Unnoticed Aspect of Vergil's Personality," in *Harvard Lectures on the Vergilian Age* (Cambridge, Mass., 1928), pp. 68–71, showing that Virgil regards Augustus as a divine epiphany only when acting as a benefactor of mankind. I have not thought it necessary to deal with A. W. Verrall's theory of the *Heracles* (expressed in his *Four Plays*, pp. 134–193, and briefly summarized by G. Norwood, *Greek Tragedy*, pp. 229–234), which rejects all the supernatural (including, of course, Hera's part) in the play, and sees in the hero "a mighty misbegotten intellect," deluded and deluding not only in the mad scene but more or less at all times, and Iris and *Lyssa* a dream of the Chorus. The less radical interpretation suggested above will, I think, "save the appearances."

20 (196): *Vocabulary of "Alcestis."* The vocabulary of the play is varied, and only a full commentary would suffice to elucidate it; but in addition to the cases cited above, for "fate" (p. 195, n. 90), note ὀφείλω, of the "debt" of nature, 419; 682; 712; 782 (cf. 686: ἔφυς); οὐκ ἔστι, 53; 1076 (cf. 135; 146);

*οὐδ' οἷόν τ' ἐμοί*, 487; *ἀνάγκη*, of moral necessity, 378; 416; 617; *χρή* (*χρῆν, χρεών, δεῖ*), of moral necessity or propriety, 107; 501; 523; 619; 633; 655; 686; 709; 737; 840; 939; 1008; 1071; 1105; 1110; *οὔπω θέμις*, of a taboo, 1144; *τύχη*, of one's personal "plight," 213, 240, 395 (and elsewhere *συμφορά, κακόν, δαίμων, πῆμα, πένθος, ἄλγος, νόσος*, etc.); but *τύχη*, of a stroke of "luck," 1070 (cf. 1071: *θεοῦ δόσιν*); 1130; and for "endurance" and active courage and will power, *τλῆναι* (*τολμᾶν, φέρειν, καρτερεῖν*), 1; 275; 277; 397; 411; 462; 552; 572; 644; 742; 752; 837; 887; 891; 892; 907; 955; 1068; 1071; 1078 (cf. Soph. *Ajax* 528; *Phil.* 82; 110; 481; *O.C.* 184).

21 (196): *"Alcestis" and Verrall.* See *Euripides the Rationalist*, pp. 1–128. It is true that Heracles is annoyed on learning that Admetus, with old-fashioned courtesy, has kept his guest in ignorance of his own bereavement (821–833; 1008–1018); but he nevertheless sets at once about the rescue. The Chorus, at first critical of such hospitality (551 f.; 560 f.), acquiesce with Admetus' explanations, and sing his praises (569–605), concluding that piety must find its reward (604 f.). Heracles in the last scene seems to me to commend, rather than to reprove, Admetus (1147: "just man that thou art, hereafter show thy piety toward strangers"), while the last speech of Admetus does not seem to me to suggest so much a promise of reform as relief at escape from bereavement (1157 f.); *aliter* Verrall, pp. 40 f.

21 *bis* (200): Τύχη *in "I. T."* For *τύχη*, 89 (contrasted with *τέχνη*); 475–478, Iph. on the inscrutability of *τύχη*, here identified with *τὰ τῶν θεῶν*; 490 (O. of his personal "fortune"; cf. 647); 500 (O.): *Δυστυχὴς καλοίμεθ' ἄν* (cf. Soph. *O.T.* 1080–1085; see above, p. 158); 721 f. (Pylades, on the inevitable *μεταβολή* of good fortune succeeding misfortune); 850 (O. contrasting his "happy" birth with his *συμφοραί*); 865 f. (Iph.): *ἄλλα δ' ἐξ ἄλλων κυρεῖ δαίμονος τύχῃ τινός*; 873 f. (Iph.): *τίς τελευτά; | τίς τύχα μοι συγχωρήσει*; 895 (Iph.): *τίς ἂν οὖν τάδ' ἂν ἢ θεὸς ἢ βροτὸς ἢ | τί τῶν ἀδοκήτων* (cf. the repeated recessionals); 909–911 (O.): *τῇ τύχῃ δ' οἶμαι μέλειν τοῦδε ξὺν ἡμῖν*: ("Heaven helps him who helps himself"); 1410 (Messenger): *τύχας* ("events"); cf. also 620: *ἀνάγκην*.

22 (201): *Divine Interference in "Helen." Helen* 44–46 (Hermes brought Helen to Egypt at the behest of Zeus; cf. 670 f.; 695; 708); for the rôles of Hera, Kypris, and Helen's fatal beauty, 260; 363; 584–586; 653; 674–681; 704; 708; 1024–1027; 1093–1106; more generally, 663; 704: *πρὸς θεῶν δ' ἦμεν ἠπατημένοι*; 744–760 (distinction between the actual will of the gods and the revelation of soothsayers; with 756, cf. Iocasta in Soph. *O. T.*; see above, p. 159); 1642–1679, the Dioscuri, connecting the will of the gods (1648, 1669), with fate (1646: *πεπρωμένοισιν*; 1651: *ἐχρῆν*; 1677: *μόρσιμον*); and, speaking of themselves, 1660 f.: *ἀλλ' ἥσσον' ἦμεν τοῦ πεπρωμένου θ' ἅμα | καὶ τῶν θεῶν, οἷς ταῦτ' ἔδοξεν ὧδ' ἔχειν*; 1686 (Theoclymenus): *εἰ θεοῖς δοκεῖ*.

23 (202): Τύχη *in "Helen."* For *Tyche* as an active force in the plot of the *Helen*, cf. 285 f. (with contrast of *πράγμασιν*, fortune, and *ἔργοισιν*, Helen's own deeds); 293; 321; 412: *ἀνελπίστῳ τύχῃ* (of the escape of Menelaus and the phantom "Helen" from the shipwreck); 477–479 (where contrast *καιρὸν . . . οὐδέν' ἦλθες* with 1081, *ἐς καιρόν*); 645; 698 f.; 738; 742; 857 (of Theonoe's sudden entrance); 891 (of Menelaus' arrival); 925 (of the reunion of Helen and Menelaus); 1217 (of the sailors falling in with M.); 1291; 1296; 1300; 1374;

1409; 1424 (Helen): τῆς τύχης με δεῖ μόνον; 1636 (Theocl.): ἀλλ' ἔδωκεν ἡ τύχη μοι, with the retort of the servant, τὸ δὲ χρεὼν ἀφείλετο. For gnomic utterances, cf. 267 f.: τύχην πρὸς θεῶν; 403: πρὸς θεῶν τυχεῖν; 641–645; θεὸς . . . τύχας (cf. 855 f.: θεοὶ . . . εὐτυχές); 711–719 (Messenger, on the inscrutability of human vicissitudes; n.b. θεὸς . . . τύχης, and contrast of σπεύδων with αὐτόματα); 1137–1143 (Chorus, on the same theme; n.b. θεὸς ἢ μὴ θεὸς ἢ τὸ μέσον . . . ἀνελπίσταις τύχαις); 1441–1451 (Prayer of Menelaus; n.b. Ζεῦ . . . θεὸς . . . τῆς τύχης . . . εὐτυχῇ); 1688–1692, the repeated recessional, on the unexpected (cf. 657: ἀδόκητον; 813: δεῖ δὲ μηχανῆς τινος).

24 (215): *Palace Miracle in "Bacchae."* For the "Palace Miracle" (and related matters), see G. Norwood, *The Riddle of the Bacchae* (with useful bibliography of works on Euripides and on the *Bacchae* down to the year 1908); A. W. Verrall, *The Bacchants of Euripides* (Cambridge, 1910), pp. 1–163; C. Norwood, *Greek Tragedy*, pp. 281–285; G. Murray, *Euripides and his Age*, pp. 183–197; C. E. Whitmore, *The Supernatural in Tragedy*, pp. 82–89; G. M. A. Grube, "Dionysus in the *Bacchae*," *T.A.P.A.* 66 (1935), pp. 37–54, esp. 44–47, dealing sceptically with the "Palace Miracle," as only an "earth-tremor" with no serious consequences except to the imagination of the Chorus, but accepting the divinity of the "stranger" and his delusion of Pentheus by an apparent conflagration (623–626) and by a phantom (629 f.); the latter are perhaps "miracles." Verrall, *The Bacchants*, pp. 107–125, argues that Dionysus achieves his control over Pentheus simply by use of a (poisoned?) drink; n.b. 913, reading σπένδοντα with Ms. P; and 1157: πίστον ("potion").

25 (218): *Fate in Euripides.* The evidence for the generalization made in the text need not be repeated, but may be summarized, with references to previous discussions. *Medea*, no recourse to fatalism (pp. 178 f.); *Hippolytus*, hardly any fatalism, unless in 1256 and in the speech of Artemis (p. 182); in the *Heracles* and in the *Heraclidae*, the fatalism of the Chorus turns to confidence in Zeus, and fate saved Heracles so long as he was fulfilling his destiny (pp. 185 f.); *Hecuba*, only conventional phrases, with reservations (p. 189); *Alcestis*, the tricking of the Moirai, and other divine interventions, with constant allusions to fate and necessity (pp. 195–197); *I. T.*, fate only in the speech of Athena, 1486: τὸ χρεών (p. 201); similarly (if not seriously), in *Electra*, 1248, 1301 (p. 204), and in *Orestes* (pp. 205 f.); fatalism seen in the guise of divine interferences in *Helen* (p. 201), of *tyche*, in *Electra* (pp. 203 f.), of heredity, in *Orestes* (p. 206), and of oracles and divine acts, in the *Phoenician Women*, a "drama of doom" (W. Jaeger, *Paideia*, p. 352; above, pp. 206–208); in *Bacchae*, no fate, but divine power and miracles, and (at the end) the association of Zeus and *ananke*, 1349, 1351 (pp. 211; 215).

26 (218): Τύχη *in Euripides.* Again a summary, with references, will suffice. *Medea*, no recourse to *tyche; Heracles*, 309, 509, 1314, conventional references, and 1347–1357, H. yields bitterly to his *tyche*, not however to the later personified goddess *Tyche* (pp. 184 f.); similarly *Hecuba*, though 786 and 488–491 mark a closer approach to personification and to *tyche* as a philosophic idea (p. 189); as do *Suppliant Women* 549–557 (p. 190), and *Trojan Women* 67 f., 692, 697, 1203–1206, all significant lines, though only in passing, for the *Trojan Women* is not a drama of chance (pp. 193 f.); *Alcestis*, the chance arrival of Heracles, to whom is given the speech on rising superior to *tyche* (p. 196);

*Ion*, a drama of chances and of allusions to chance, e.g. 512–515 (pp. 197–199); likewise *I.T.* (p. 200, and Appendix 21 *bis*), and *Helen*, where *θεῖα τύχη*, providence, is superficially suggested (pp. 201 f.); but *tyche* is a more grim affair, nearer to fate, in *Electra* (p. 203), in the *Phoenician Women* 1653 (p. 208) and in *I.A.*, where it is closely associated with the divine power (p. 210); *Bacchae*, no recourse to *tyche* (p. 211). For further discussions of *tyche* in *Euripides*, cf. H. Meuss, *Tyche bei den attischen Tragikern* (Hirschberg, 1899), pp. 10–14; G. Busch, *Untersuchungen zum Wesen der* Τύχη *in den Tragödien des Euripides* (Heidelberg, 1937), and my review thereof, *A.J.P.* 59 (1938), pp. 364–367; E. G. Berry, ΘΕΙΑ ΜΟΙΡΑ, pp. 26–33, esp. pp. 29–33, tracing in Euripides the reflection of the contemporary transition from the conception of *tyche* as allied with the older divinities to the conception of *tyche* as pure chance, or even to the personification of Chance as *Tyche*, with her cult. The idea that *Tyche* is a goddess mightier than the gods is rejected by Odysseus, in *Cyclops*, 606 f. It is instructive, for the thought of the next century, to compare Menander, frags. 482, 483, 594, 598 Kock. See also above, p. 94, n. 20.

27 (220): *Physis*. On *Physis* in general, see also above, pp. 223–228; for a list of works bearing on *Physis* and related matters, Appendix 31. For the present point, see Burnet, *E.G.P.* pp. 10 f.: "the stuff of which anything is made" (in the second edition, p. 14, Burnet's phrase was "the permanent and primary substance"); also his Appendix, pp. 363 f., "On the Meaning of Φύσις"; Burnet, "Law and Nature"; Burnet, *T.-P.*, p. 27. His view is supported on the whole by A. O. Lovejoy, "Meaning of Φύσις" (n.b. p. 376, defining *φύσις* in pre-Socratic usage as "the intrinsic and permanent qualitative constitution of things, what things really are"); also by Lovejoy's review of Heidel (*Phil. Rev.* 19 [1910], pp. 665–667). That Burnet's view, though true in part, does not adequately recognize the use in early Greek philosophy of *φύσις* to describe not merely material substance but also origin, process of growth, law of change, cause, normal character, the totality of things, is the contention, explicit or implicit, of F. J. E. Woodbridge, in *Phil. Rev.* 10 (1901), pp. 359–374; F. M. Cornford, *Rel.-Phil.*, emphasizing the animate, divine character of *physis*; W. A. Heidel, Περὶ φύσεως (n.b. pp. 97, synopsis; 129, summary); J. W. Beardslee, *Use of* Φύσις (n.b. pp. 65–67; Beardslee himself emphasizes the use of *φύσις* as "character," "quality," of a person or thing); Lovejoy and Boas, *Primitivism*, pp. 103–116, "Genesis of the Conception of Nature as Norm" (and cf. pp. 447–456, Appendix, "Some Meanings of 'Nature'"; this work goes further than Lovejoy's earlier works in admitting a considerable variety of meanings). For *φύσις* as normal constitution (opposed to the product of *τέχνη*, *ἄσκησις*, or *διδαχή*, or to physical deformity), see Democritus frag. 242 Diels; the Hippocratean Περὶ Ἀέρων 14 (II, 58 Littré) and A. Chiapelli, *Sofistica Greca*, pp. 6–11; Heidel, Περὶ φύσεως, pp. 102–104; 114–126; Beardslee, pp. 31–42; W. Jaeger, *Paideia*, pp. 303 f., on the new conception of human nature, extended from man's physique (studied by the Ionian medical writers) to his social and moral nature (by the sophists and Thucydides).

Of prime importance for the view that *Physis* at least sometimes meant origin, genesis, is Empedocles, frag. 8 Diels: *φύσις οὐδενὸς ἔστιν ἁπάντων | θνητῶν, οὐδέ τις οὐλομένου θανάτοιο τελευτή, | ἀλλὰ μόνον μῖξις τε διάλλαξίς τε μιγέντων | ἔστι, φύσις δ' ἐπὶ τοῖς ὀνομάζεται ἀνθρώποισιν.* Cf. also Plato, *Phaedo* 95e9; the discussion involves an inquiry into causality (*δεῖ περὶ γενέσεως καὶ φθορᾶς τὴν αἰτίαν πεπραγματεύσασθαι*) and reminds Socrates of his youthful interest in the investigations of his predecessors and contemporaries into the question of *physis*, that is, of causes (περὶ φύσεως ἱστορίαν . . . εἰδέναι τὰς αἰτίας ἑκάστου, διὰ τί γίγνεται ἕκαστον καὶ διὰ τί ἀπόλλυται καὶ διὰ τί ἔστι); see above, p. 285. This passage, it may be remarked in passing, supplied Aristotle with the title of his work Περὶ Γενέσεως Καὶ Φθορᾶς (*De Generatione et Corruptione*). Not sufficiently stressed, I think, is the fact that Aristotle in his *ex parte* account of the pre-Socratics and their explanations of αἰτίαι frequently substitutes for φύσις the term ἀρχή, which for him means both "beginning" and "cause"; and Aristotle is not disposed to grant his predecessors any more than he can help in the way of an explanation of causality.

The passages which Burnet cites, *E.G.P.*, pp. 10; 363 f., from Plato (*Laws* 891c7; 892c; 891c70), from Aristotle (*Phys.* 193a9; etc.; *Protrep.* fr. 52 Rose), and from Euripides (frag. inc. 910 Nauck) prove indeed that φύσις often means "stuff, make-up," but not that this is the exclusive meaning. Aristotle's doubts (*Met.* 1014b16, cited by Burnet, p. 364) about the short upsilon in the noun φύσις, as compared with the long upsilon in the verb φύω(φυίω) are not conclusive, even for Aristotle; cf. *Pol.* 1252b32: οἷον ἕκαστόν ἐστι τῆς γενέσεως τελεσθείσης, ταύτην φαμὲν τὴν φύσιν εἶναι ἑκάστου; and *passim*; see also above, pp. 318 f.

28 (221): *Pre-Socratic Philosophy.* It has been argued in the text that Plato and Aristotle fail to recognize the living, divine causality which is implicit in each of the pre-Socratic systems. Such are the living, cosmogenetic god of Thales, an efficient cause, and Anaximander's conception of process and natural law, with moral implications in the survival of the fit, which Aristotle slights. Anaximenes provides both a material and a formal cause, though without ethical implications. The One God of Xenophanes is both Fate and Good; Evil is only in the world of appearance. The Pythagoreans and the mystics find Good in Limit or Proportion, with important applications not only in medicine and music but in ethics. Their religion defines the limits within which Good may be realized; they discard external Fate as an all-sufficient cause; and they believe that the immortal soul passes through a succession of lives. Heraclitus includes both Good and Evil, as correlatives, within a natural system which presents an analogy with primitive moral law; human good and evil, however, are related to a specifically human attitude and activity, as with the Atomists and the Stoics. The (monistic) Way of Truth of Parmenides defines a formal, but not an efficient, cause; Being is controlled by Justice, which is identified with Fate; his (dualistic) Way of Opinion deals with a mingling of opposites under the control of a divine power (δαίμων) who is Fate (or Justice, or Necessity). Empedocles reckons with forces, Love and Strife, controlled by the "law of the mingling," which though apparently equivocal are ultimately productive of Good and of Evil respectively; his religion is closely bound to his philosophy. The *Nous* of Anaxagoras is formal and efficient, but not final, as Plato and Aristotle point out; they criticize him the more severely because he superficially seems to promise more than his predecessors, yet has no better grounds for the optimism which he shares with Plato and Aristotle. Diogenes of Apollonia, however, is a full-fledged teleologist, a fact which Aristotle chooses to ignore. The Atomists are determinists within the limits of their physical philosophy (but see above, pp. 296, n. 128; 333 f. and Appendix 56); but Good and Evil are the province of a quite distinct and humanistic inquiry, in the course of the quest for "cheerfulness" (see above, pp. 334 f.).

29 (222): *Sophists.* In Plato, *Rep.* 492a–493c, Socrates maintains that the general public is the arch-sophist, whose opinions the politicians and the so-called "sophists" merely express; doubtless we have here a vicious circle. Among general discussions of the Sophists, some polemic or defensive may be mentioned: G. Grote, *Hist. of Greece,* Ch. 67; Sir A. Grant, ed. *Nicomachean Ethics of Aristotle,* Vol. I, Essay II, esp. pp. 104–153; H. Jackson, *Enc. Britannica,* s.v. Sophists; A. Chiapelli, *Sofistica Greca*; A. W. Benn, *The Greek Philosophers,* Ch. II; H. Diels, *Frag. d. Vorsokratiker,* Vol. II, pp. 252–416 (for texts); H. Gomperz, *Sophistik und Rhetorik*; W. Jaeger, *Paideia,* pp. 283–328.

30 (223): *Socratic Problem, I.* As to the "Socratic problem," my position is conservative; I believe that the Socrates whom we meet in the Platonic dialogues is more and more developed by Plato as a dramatic figure for the exposition of his own views (till he is dropped altogether), and that we must find "the historic Socrates" partly in Plato, but also in Xenophon and Aristotle and in the varying trends of the minor Socratics. For the purposes of this discussion I draw chiefly on the earlier Platonic Dialogues, including the *Protagoras,* the *Gorgias* (with some reservations), and the first book of the *Republic,* supplemented by Xenophon and Aristotle, leaving the later dialogues, as Platonic, for consideration in the following chapter. The *Gorgias* or the *Meno* may well be the transitional dialogue (from Socrates to Plato); for the *Meno,* see K. Buchmann, *Philologus,* Supplementband 29, 3 (1936), and my review of it, *C.P.* 35 (1940), pp. 210–212.

For convenient recent discussions of the "Socratic problem," cf. Ueberweg-Praechter, *Grundriss*[12] (1926), pp. 133–140; H. Maier, *Sokrates* (Tübingen, 1913); G. C. Field, *Plato and His Contemporaries,* pp. 50–55; 61–63; 202–238; W. D. Ross, "The Problem of Socrates" (Proceedings of the English Classical Association, 30 (1933), pp. 7–24); A. K. Rogers, *The Socratic Problem* (New Haven, 1933); R. Hackforth, *The Composition of Plato's Apology* (Cambridge, 1933); A. D. Winspear and T. Silverberg, *Who Was Socrates?* (New York, 1939), and my review of this work, *C.W.* 33 (1939), pp. 18 f. The dissenting views of J. Burnet (e.g. ed. *Phaedo,* 1911; also *T.-P.,* 1914, and "The Socratic Doctrine of the Soul," 1916), and of A. E. Taylor (e.g. in *Varia Socratica,* Oxford, 1911; and in *Socrates*), who attribute much to Socrates (including the Theory of Ideas) that is ordinarily regarded as Platonic, and who regard Socrates in turn as substantially a Pythagorean, are criticized by Field, Ross, and Rogers, and perhaps most effectively by A. M. Adam, "Socrates, 'Quantum Mutatus ab Illo,' " *C.Q.* 12 (1918), pp. 121–139. Burnet and Taylor, in spite of their great learning, err, as it seems to me, in treating Plato too much as a reporter, instead of as a free dramatic artist. It goes without saying that Xenophon was incapable of appreciating or of recording many aspects of Socrates; in the case of Plato, the question is not so much one of capacity as of intention. "We can never know exactly how far Xenophon has told us too little, and Plato too much." (Sir A. Grant, ed. Aristotle's *Ethics,* I, p. 155.) An extraordinary result of Plato's dramatic success may be found in the fact (noted by Grant, p. 158) that Aristotle in the *Politics* 1265a11 refers to the *Laws* of Plato as one of the "discourses of Socrates," even though Socrates does not appear in the dialogue. On the "Socratic problem" see further above pp. 231; 259; 264; 267; and below, Appendix 39: Socratic Problem, II; on Xenophon's contribution, E. C. Marchant, intro. to Loeb ed. of *Memorabilia.*

31 (224): *Physis and Nomos; bibliography.* The literature on *Physis* and *Nomos* is very extensive. The following works, arranged here in a roughly chronological order, may be found helpful. (For full titles of those abbreviated, see bibliography; and see also Appendix 27.)

A. Chiapelli, *Sofistica Greca* (1889–90).
J. Burnet, *E. G. Phil.*[4] (1930); pp. 10 f.[4] (= p. 14[2]); pp. 363 f. (Appendix), "On the Meaning of φύσις." (The first edition was 1892.)
J. Burnet, "Law and Nature in Greek Ethics," *Internat. Journ. of Ethics*, April, 1897; also in *Essays and Addresses*, pp. 23–28 (1929).
C. Huit, *La Philosophie de la Nature* (1901).
F. J. E. Woodbridge, "The Dominant Conception of the Earliest Greek Philosophy," *Phil. Rev.* 10 (1901), pp. 359–374.
J. Adam, *Rel. Teachers* (1901), Chap. XIII.
R. Hirzel, Ἄγραφος Νόμος (1901).
K. Joel, *Naturphilosophie* (1903).
R. Hirzel, *Themis, Dike*, etc. (1907).
A. O. Lovejoy, "Meaning of φύσις," etc. *Phil. Rev.* 18 (1909), pp. 369–383.
W. A. Heidel, "Περὶ Φύσεως," etc. (1910).
A. O. Lovejoy, Review of Heidel, *Phil. Rev.* 19 (1910), pp. 665–667.
J. E. Harrison, *Themis* (1912), pp. 531–535.
F. M. Cornford, *Rel.-Phil.* (1912), pp. 125–142.
A. W. Benn, *Greek Philosophers*[2] (1914), Chap. II "Nature and Law."
J. W. Beardslee, *Use of* Φύσις (1918).
E. Barker, *Greek Pol. Theory: Plato and Predecessors* (1918), pp. 50–77.
A. Menzel, *Kallikles* (1922).
Sir P. Vinogradoff, *Outline of Historical Jurisprudence*, Vol. II (1922), ch. II, "The Concept of Law."
W. Eckstein, *Naturrecht* (1926).
J. L. Myres, *Pol. Ideas of the Greeks* (1927), pp. 241–318.
H. Stier, *Nomos Basileus* (1928).
R. Scoon, *Greek Philosophy before Plato* (1928).
A. O. Lovejoy, and G. Boas, *Primitivism* (1935).
W. Jaeger, *Paideia* (Eng. trans., 1939), pp. 283–328.

32 (231): *Xenophon and Socrates.* Xenophon's account of the conversation between Socrates and Hippias (above, p. 229) may, to be sure, be indebted to the very passage of Plato under consideration; or both Xenophon's and Plato's accounts may come from a common source; this source might indeed be a lost writing of Hippias to which we possess no other reference. K. Joel, *Der Echte und der Xenophontische Sokrates*, II, pp. 1106 ff., like Dümmler, is inclined to find here, as almost everywhere, traces of Antisthenes and the Cynic tradition. I cannot follow them so far; but it is true that the conversation between Socrates and Hippias becomes fully significant only when read in the light of *Protag.* 337c; for the defense of *nomos* is necessary only when it is attacked in the name of *physis*. W. Nestle, *Philologus* 67 (1908), pp. 568 f., argues that Hippias is the source of the remarks of Herodotus (III, 38; VII, 152; see above, p. 226), as well as of the *Dialexeis* (*Dissoi Logoi*) 2, 18 (above, p. 250); the connection, I think, can be neither proved nor disproved; what is clear is that these ideas were current in the mid-fifth century.

33 (245): *"Protagoras" Myth; source.* Plato, *Protag.* 320c–322d (= D 80 C 1). Attempts have been made to identify the *Protagoras* myth with a work by the Sophist (listed by D. L., IX, 55) entitled Περὶ τῆς ἐν ἄρχῃ καταστάσεως. Diels held that the title itself may have been evolved from the present imitation of Protagoras by Plato; cf. D 80 A 1, and Diels II, p. 267, with note on l. 9. W. Nestle, *Philologus* 67 (1908), pp. 533 ff., accounts for parallels between *Protag.* 321b and Herodotus II, 108 by supposing a common source in Protagoras himself. E. Norden, *Agnostos Theos*, pp. 368–374; 397–400, points to Ionic traits of style in the myth (which he thinks may be derived by Plato from Protagoras) and finds traces of the title, as of the thought, in the famous Critias fragment (D 88 B 25; see above, p. 255); of the word κατάστασις in the Hippocratean corpus and in Democritus. S. O. Dickerman, *De Argumentis Quibusdam*, pp. 73–92, discussing the source of various arguments about the structure and fitness of animal and human bodies that are to be found in *Xenophon* (see above, p. 274), Plato, and Aristotle (above, p. 319, and n. 11), concludes that they all go back to sophistic debates of which the *Protagoras* myth (and Euripides, *Suppl.* 201–213) preserve some record, debates which emphasized now the perfection, now the weakness, of the human body; the position of Protagoras, as Dickerman points out, required him to emphasize the weakness of man, as compared with the beasts, except so far as man improves his lot by training his mind. The myth itself Dickerman attributes to Protagoras, rather than to Plato. So also P. Frutiger, *Les Mythes de Platon*, pp. 181–185, who, however, does not think very highly of it. P. Friedländer, *Platon* I, pp. 203 f., and H. Gomperz, *Soph. und Rhet.*, pp. 129 ff., find both substance and style Platonic. Among others who favor Platonic authorship of the myth are G. Grote, *Plato*, II, pp. 46 ff., in extravagant admiration; J. A. Stewart, *The Myths of Plato*, pp. 220–222, who contends also that the myth is "a true Myth, not an Allegory"; P. Shorey, *W.P.S.*, p. 124: "otherwise Plato would owe to Protagoras the greater part of his own social and political philosophy." Contrast also the religiosity of *Protag.* 322a, with the scepticism of D 80 B 4, unless the former is marked as ironical by the use of θεία μοῖρα (cf. Appendix 34). Perhaps the upshot of the discussion may be thus stated: the substance of the myth owes much to sophistic discussions in which Protagoras may have taken part, and preserves something of his style and point of view; but it is shaped by Plato's literary art, and is used by Plato in the sequel as a stepping stone to a point of view that Protagoras could not have held.

34 (245): *"Protagoras" Myth; meaning. Protag.* 322cd: note the teleological emphasis here, as well as earlier (e.g., 321a: even the myopic Epimetheus providing against the extermination of species); Zeus acts with sufficient cause, and for a purpose (322c: ἵνα εἶεν, κτλ.); see further Stewart, *Myths of Plato*, pp. 220–227. Throughout the myth, note also, beside the stylistic archaisms discussed by Norden (see above, Appendix 33) the recurrence of terminology reminiscent of earlier conceptions of fatality and of the "gifts of the gods"; 320d1–2: χρόνος . . . εἱμαρμένος γενέσεως (cf. 321c6: ἡ εἱμαρμένη ἡμέρα); at least nine examples of the verb νέμω, "apportion," with which compare also 320c4: νόμην, "distribution"; and 327d4: νόμον, the "law" of Zeus that they shall die who cannot partake of *aidos* and *dike*; other terms significant of contriving (321a2), bestowing (321b2; d3; e3), equipping (320e1) man's "nature" (320e2: φύσιν). Finally, not to be overlooked is the sly use of the expression θεία μοῖρα, "divine lot" (322a3), ordinarily used by Plato of a free gift of god

to man (see also above, pp. 272; 298–300; and below, Appendix 47), but here of the gifts stolen by Prometheus.

35 (249): *Protagoras and Pragmatism.* In recent years Protagoras has been claimed as the forerunner of philosophical "empiricism," "pragmatism," and "humanism" (e.g. as represented by such men as C. S. Peirce, W. James, J. Dewey, H. Bergson, G. Santayana, F. C. S. Schiller), as the thinker whose sound appreciation of the fact that truth cannot be found except in terms of human needs and experience was obscured by the misunderstanding of the "intellectualist" Plato. The relationship can best be examined in the brilliant writings of Schiller, notably in "From Plato to Protagoras," in his *Studies in Humanism* (London, 1907), pp. 22–70 (cf. also pp. 298–348); and in his *Plato or Protagoras?* (Oxford, 1908). It is argued that the humanism of Protagoras is not sceptical, and is in fact a better instrument for dealing both with science and with ethics than is Plato's teleological, transcendental conceptualism, which is held to be an abstraction from personality and from the growth of truth; moreover that in the *Theaetetus* Plato never answers (because he fails to understand) the arguments of Protagoras which he fairly enough reproduces; finally, that Plato fails to explain error because he makes truth wholly objective. It may be pointed out, however, that even the Platonic Ideas, and above all the Idea of Good (see above, pp. 285–287, and below, Appendix 43), are in part examples of *concepts in use* (cf. J. A. Stewart, Plato's *Doctrine of Ideas*, pp. 1–127; see below, Appendix 42), and that to that extent Plato himself is a pragmatist; furthermore, what is a Platonic myth (even though conceived as an object of contemplation), if not pragmatic? Even so, Plato distrusts mere sensation, and makes man not the measure but the measurer of all things; his ideal of science is mathematical, and he therefore, unlike Protagoras, contributes to the advance of objective science. His final retort to Protagoras reads: "The measure of all things is God." (*Laws* 716c.) For a suggestive reply to Schiller, see C. P. Parker, "Plato and Pragmatism," in *Harvard Essays on Classical Subjects* (ed. H. W. Smyth, Boston, 1912), pp. 175–206.

36 (260): *Nomos Basileus. Gorg.* 483e–484c. The fragment of Pindar (151 Boeckh = 169 Bergk, Christ, Schroeder = 152 Bowra) here quoted is perverted to suit the purpose of Callicles. Pindar undoubtedly wrote δικαιῶν τὸ βιαιότατον, "justifying the extreme of violence," whereas Plato makes Callicles quote him as saying βιαιῶν τὸ δικαιότατον, "doing violence to the most established claim." (This reading of the Platonic manuscript should stand in the Platonic text, which should not be emended to agree with the indirect Pindar tradition.) Here Pindar, a deeply religious man, seeks to reconcile the material principle of might with the idea of a divine order (cf. Pindar, frag. 70 Bowra, which also refers to the myth of Heracles and Geryon, expressing sympathy for Geryon, while disclaiming whatever is not sanctioned by Zeus). Callicles, however, puts a partial construction on Pindar's meaning, in that it recognizes only the principle of might; hence the verbal change. Probably Pindar's words had already been quoted and misquoted by many other authors as the dignity and authority of *nomos* declined; for *Nomos* as king, or rather as tyrant, cf. Herodotus III, 38 (see above, pp. 226; 230; 232). Plato himself refers three times in the *Laws* (690bc; 714e; 890a) to the Pindaric passage; of these references, the second clearly is intended to represent what Pindar actually said; while the third, roughly agreeing with the words of Callicles, is given in ex-

planation of the claim of might to be accepted as right, or of "life according to *physis*" which leads to impiety; this is also satirized in the first of the three references. The third reference attributes these views to "wise men, both laymen and poets," in such a way as to suggest that this particular perversion of Pindar's words may have been current before Plato put it in the mouth of Callicles. In any case it should be noted that it is not Socrates but Callicles (or Plato) who misquotes Pindar; so the present passage of the *Gorgias* cannot be the ground of one of the accusations of Polycrates against Socrates, that he perverted and misquoted the poets. See further above, p. 251; Wilamowitz, *Platon*, II, 95–105; A. Menzel, *Kallikles*, pp. 30–35; 41–44; 93–96; H. E. Stier, "*Nomos Basileus*," pp. 225–258; J. Humbert, *Polycrates*; A. E. Taylor, *P.M.W.* 103, n. 1; 117, n. 2.

37 (271): *Thucydides on Nicias.* Thucydides, VII, 77; 86; cf. II, 51, on the conscientious persons whose very dutifulness during the plague was their undoing. These remarks are not ironical, or sardonic, but realistic; the tragic poets and even Plato would agree (see above, pp. 95–98; 99 f.; 101; 311–313). W. Bagehot, *Physics and Politics*, though more cautious than Plato and other teleologists, recognizes as contributing to "verifiable progress" certain physical, moral, intellectual, and social qualities: "The better religions . . . have given what I may call a *confidence in the universe*." This is the sort of statement that Thucydides, and all scientists *qua* scientists, would regard as belonging to the realm of speculative philosophy, rather than to science.

38 (271): *"Might makes right."* I, 76, 2 (the Athenians to the Lacedaemonians, before the war): *αἰεὶ καθεστῶτος τὸν ἥσσω ὑπὸ τοῦ δυνατωτέρου κατείργεσθαι*; II, 63, 2 (Pericles, justifying the war): *τυραννίδα ἔχετε*; IV, 61, 5 (Hermocrates the Syracusan, blaming not the self-seeking Athenians but those who submit to them): *πέφυκε γὰρ τὸ ἀνθρώπειον διὰ παντὸς ἄρχειν μὲν τοῦ εἴκοντος, φυλάσσεσθαι δὲ τὸ ἐπιόν*; V, 89; 105 (the Athenians to the neutral Melians, who do not wish to enter the war, in the so-called "Melian Dialogue"): *δυνατὰ δὲ οἱ προύχοντες πράσσουσι καὶ οἱ ἀσθενεῖς ξυγχωροῦσιν . . . ἡγούμεθα γὰρ τό τε θεῖον δόξῃ, τὸ ἀνθρώπειόν τε σαφῶς διὰ παντὸς ὑπὸ φύσεως ἀναγκαίας, οὗ ἂν κρατῇ ἄρχειν*; III, 39 (Cleon, cynically exploiting the doctrine, and blaming the rebel Mytileneans for presuming to put might before right): *ἰσχὺν ἀξιώσαντες τοῦ δικαίου προθεῖναι.*

F. M. Cornford, in an interesting book, *Thucydides Mythistoricus* (London, 1907), pp. 58–68, denies that Thucydides has any clear conception of a universal reign of causality in Nature; he argues, pp. 97–108, that by *Tyche* (which he finds operative in several crucial cases) Thucydides does not mean merely the operation of unknown natural causes but the irruption of undetermined agencies; and he suggests, pp. 110–250, that consciously or unconsciously the historian casts his story in the pattern of tragic drama, with emphasis on *hybris* and *nemesis*, so that the result represents the victory of art (or myth) over science. The large part in the story that is played by the unexpected may be admitted, but not the denial to Thucydides of a belief in causality and in natural law, as I have indicated above. The dramatic pattern, too, though recognizable here and there, — for example, in the sequence of "Melian Dialogue" (*hybris*) and Sicilian Expedition (*nemesis*), — has been exaggerated by Cornford. (See also above, p. 191.) On these and other matters, see P. Shorey, "On the Implicit Ethics and Psychology of Thucydides," *T.A.P.A.* 24 (1893), pp. 66–88;

J. B. Bury, *Ancient Greek Historians*, pp. 92–95; 123–149; E. Barker, *Greek Political Theory*, pp. 73 ff.; W. R. M. Lamb, *Clio Enthroned*, pp. 34–68; 125–134; W. Nestle, "Thukydides und die Sophistik," *N. Jahrb.* 33 (1914), pp. 649–685; G. F. Abbott, *Thucydides*, pp. 6–92; C. N. Cochrane, *Thucydides and the Science of History*, pp. 35–137.

39 (272): *Socratic Problem, II.* Plato, *Apol.* 19b–d; Xenophon, *Mem.*, I, 1, 11–16; cf. IV, 7, 2–8; Aristotle, *Met.* 987b1; *De Part. An.* 642a29. (See also above, Appendix 30, Socratic Problem, I; and pp. 279 f.) Against this testimony I cannot accept *Phaedo* 96a–97b as sober Socratic autobiography, nor the *Clouds* of Aristophanes as any witness at all for the historic Socrates. As to the evidence of the *Phaedo*, it may be admitted that young Socrates would naturally take a layman's interest in the Ionian science of the day, without claiming any expert knowledge of it; but he immediately lost interest in it when he perceived that it had no answer to the questions of meaning, of causality, of goodness, in which he was interested (see above, p. 274). So he could truthfully say at the end of his life (*Apol.* 19b–d) that he had never concerned himself with scientific speculations. The *Clouds* is comedy, and deliberately confuses the well-known moralist and reasoner Socrates with the speculations of the earlier physicists and of certain contemporary sophists, even these being travestied. The *Birds* of Aristophanes refers (1555; cf. 1282) to Socrates as a sort of necromancer, conjuring up a "spirit" (*psyche*); a legitimate enough comic treatment of the mystic Socrates, who may have had Orphic leanings, and who certainly had much to say about the care of the *psyche* as the supreme duty of man (cf. *Apol.* 29d–30a); but neither this nor the doctrine of the *Phaedo* warrants Burnet and Taylor in representing Socrates as a full-fledged Pythagorean (J. Burnet, ed. *Phaed.*, pp. xliii–lvi; "The Socratic Doctrine of the Soul," *Proc. of the British Academy*, 1916; A. E. Taylor, *P.M.W.*, pp. 174–183); the Pythagoreanism is better to be explained as Plato's own contribution, derived from his travels in Italy and Sicily. My account of Socrates draws more from Xenophon than some scholars would approve (e.g., A. K. Rogers, *The Socratic Problem*, pp. 165–180). I am not blind to the possibility that some of Xenophon may be his well-intended invention, and that much else may be derived from Plato. It seems to me worth while, however, to let Xenophon's admittedly inadequate picture speak for itself, and then to note how it is modified by the testimony of Plato and Aristotle.

40 (274): *Socrates and Teleology.* Xenophon, *Mem.*, I, 4, 4–18; IV, 3, 3–14. The passages have been held by some scholars to be un-Xenophontic, though without sufficient reason; by others to be un-Socratic. The doctrine attributed to Socrates by Xenophon has much in common with that of Diogenes of Apollonia, the first real teleologist; cf. D64B2, with W. Theiler, *Naturbetrachtung*, pp. 4–6; *H.S.C.P.* 47 (1936), pp. 123 f.; A. S. Pease, *Caeli Enarrant*, pp. 163–170; F. Solmsen, *Plato's Theology*, pp. 49–52. Theiler believes (pp. 14–54) that Xenophon, writing his memoirs long after the death of Socrates, combined materials derived from Diogenes and other sources, in the light of his own pious theology. If he is right, similar passages in Plato (not merely *Phaedo* 97c, but *Phileb.* 28dff.; *Rep.* 507c; 530a; and *Tim.* 27d–29d) would imply that Plato, too, was indebted to Diogenes rather than to Socrates. See also S. O. Dickerman, *De Argumentis Quibusdam*, cited above, Appendix 33, on similar arguments in Plato's *Protagoras* and in Aristotle.

In the discussions reported by Xenophon, note the contrast between τύχη and γνώμη, I, 4, 4; the tribute to the "natural" desire for motherhood and child-rearing, I, 4, 7; the argument from the existence of the unseen soul to the existence of unseen gods who requite men's service, I, 4, 9; I, 4, 17; the emphasis on the gods' providential care for men, I, 4, 11: φροντίζειν; I, 4, 14 and I, 4, 18: ἐπιμελεῖσθαι; IV, 3, 5: φιλάνθρωπα; IV, 3, 6: προνοήτικον; IV, 3, 8: ἀνθρώπων ἕνεκα; IV, 3, 9: ἀνθρώπους θεραπεύειν; IV, 3, 12: ἀνθρώπων ἐπιμέλεια; cf. I, 1, 9; I, 3, 4.

41 (281): *Plato and Rival Thinkers.* G. C. Field, *Plato and His Contemporaries*, pp. 91–92; 98 f.; 102–105; cf. 116–121, discusses alternative attempts to escape the evils of the world, by Cynics, Stoics, and Christians. Burnet, *Thales to Plato*, p. 122, well sums up the quarrel of Plato with the Sophists, whose opposition between Law and Nature "tended to do away with the distinction between right and wrong." (See also above, pp. 221–228; 246 f.; 271 f.) Burnet holds that Plato's final judgment on the Sophists is to be found in the *Laws* (889e; see above, pp. 295 f.), and that he is there still giving "an impartial historical judgment" on the Sophists of the closing decades of the fifth century. That is doubtless true; but it is also true that Plato in his old age is battling with contemporary "naturalists" who still use a materialist metaphysics. *Laws* 890a 7–9; cf. Aristotle, *E.N.* 1094b16; Field, pp. 91–92; 116 f.; 131; J. Tate, "On Plato, *Laws* X 889cd," *C.Q.* 30, 2 (April, 1936); but see also F. Solmsen, "The Background of Plato's Theology," *T.A.P.A.* 67 (1936), pp. 209 f. M. Pohlenz, in *Hermes* 53 (1918), pp. 416 f., holds that *Laws* 889a ff. is directed against Democritus; but see above, p. 296, n. 128. It may be noted that Plato himself is working his way toward a conception of *physis* that shall embrace all reality, whether material or immaterial: cf. *Rep.* 597b6, c2, d2, d7, e4, 598a1, in which the term *physis* is equated with truth (597e7; cf. 501b2); and see above, pp. 287 f., and n. 56; 303, and n. 177. In the *Timaeus* and the *Laws*, reason is at work in *physis*. See further A. W. Benn, *Greek Philosophers*, pp. 233–242, "Note on the Idea of Nature in Plato"; W. Eckstein, *Naturrecht*, pp. 55–71.

42 (282): *Platonic Ideas.* J. A. Stewart well distinguishes, in *Plato's Doctrine of Ideas*, two uses of the Ideas: (1) The Ideas as objects of aesthetic, mystical, religious contemplation. (See also Stewart's *The Myths of Plato*, on the "objects of transcendental feeling," — something, I think, perhaps more Socratic in its psychological background than Platonic, though Plato is the craftsman who gives expression to it in the Myths; see further above, p. 314. (2) The Ideas as "concepts in use," methodological assumptions, principles of the scientific understanding. This is the more Platonic attitude. It ought to be unnecessary to add that the Ideas in this sense are not mere mental concepts, something which the thinker attributes to reality; the thinker, if he holds to the Ideas at all, does so because the Ideas really exist, and are the sole condition on which reality exists. Plato rejects, in the *Parmenides* (132bd) the suggestion that an idea is merely a "thought," existing in a soul.

43 (285): *Idea of Good. Rep.* 505d; 508e–509b; cf. 517bc; *Phileb.* 20d; *Laws* 716c. P. Shorey, in "The Idea of Good in Plato's Republic," Univ. of Chicago *Studies in Classical Philology*, Vol. I (1895), argues that the Idea of Good is "a regulative ethical concept" (p. 208), not "a transcendental ontological mystery"

(p. 230), and not a personal divinity like the Demiurge of the *Timaeus* (p. 239). For its content we must look to the ethical discussions in the minor dialogues as well as to the *Republic*; it presents itself as the ἀρχὴ ἀνυπόθετος, the last frontier in any series of questions that ask "Why?"; therefore as the "end of controversy" which saves us from an infinite regress (pp. 230 f.). "It means . . . a rational, consistent conception of the greatest possible attainable human happiness, of the ultimate laws of God, nature, or man that sanction conduct, and of the consistent application of these laws in legislation, government, and education" (p. 239). See further P. Shorey, Loeb ed. *Rep.*, vol. II, pp. xxiii–xlii, and works by Shorey and by others there cited.

44 (286): *Figure of Light. Rep.* 506e; 508ac; 509bc. Greek literature abounds in figures drawn from the idea of the sun, light, and vision, as symbols of the good, the intelligible, the true, in contrast with darkness and blindness, the symbols of evil and mere semblance; a few examples must suffice. On the Proem of Parmenides, cf. C. M. Bowra, *C. P.* 32 (1937), pp. 99–100; on Pindar (e.g. *Pyth.* 8, 95–98; *Nem.* 7, 23), L. W. Lyde, *Contexts in Pindar* (Manchester, 1935); for Sophocles, *O.T.* 369–375; 412–419; 454 f.; 1186–1196 (see above, p. 156; cf. 103, and H. Kuhn there cited); for Plato, *Rep.* 514a–521c, 529cd, 533d (the Parable of the Cave and its sequel), on which see A. S. Ferguson, *C.Q.* 15 (1921), pp. 131–152, and 16 (1922), pp. 15–28, with N. R. Murphy, *C.Q.* 26 (1932), pp. 93–102; the imagery of the *Symposium* and the *Phaedrus*, and *Phaedo* 77e (with the recurrent refrain of Lucretius II 55–61, III 87–93, VI 35–41, and the figure of light and darkness, *passim*). The figure always implies that darkness is to daylight as daylight is to the light of reason. The symbolism of light of course pervades also Mithraism, the sayings of Jesus, and the poetry of Dante, Milton, Newman, and the sonnet of Blanco White (see above, p. 358).

45 (293): *Demiurge in Timaeus. Tim.* 29e–30a; cf. 30bc. It should be noted that the same rôle is assigned to the "pattern of the eternal" (*Tim.* 29a) and to the creator "himself" (29e). Diès, pointing out that Plato constantly emphasizes the rôle of intellect as organizer of the *cosmos* (*Cratylus* 400a; *Phaedo* 97c; *Phaedrus* 246e; *Sophist* 265c; 266c; *Phileb.* 28de; 30cd; *Laws* 967b), raises the question whether Demiurge and Model are identical, and decides that though both symbolize the supreme divinity they must be distinguished as subject and object. (*Autour de Platon*, pp. 550–555.) Taylor, *Plato*, p. 142, speaks of the distinction between the personal and the impersonal as being less sharp among classical Greek thinkers than among modern men, and writes that "'The good' figures so manifestly in the *Timaeus* as the model contemplated by the divine artist in constructing his work that we cannot without confusion of thought identify it at the same time with the artificer." We are confronted again by the problem, in another form, of the identification of the Idea of the Good with God (see above, pp. 286 f.). The solution (if we may call it a solution) proposed in the *Timaeus* is myth. Cf. Cornford, *Plato's Cosmology*, pp. 23–32; 40–41.

46 (297): *"Epinomis."* It may be noted that the *Epinomis*, which appears, at least, to be a sequel or appendix to the *Laws*, develops the doctrine of astral gods, emphasizing the importance of astronomical and therefore of mathematical studies, and ironically or seriously advocating a religious cult of the

astral gods. Whatever may have been Plato's intention, the suggestion was seriously entertained by some of his successors; so that he deserves not a little of the credit, or blame, for Greek astrology and demonism. On the *Epinomis*, cf. Taylor, *P. M. W.*, pp. 14–15; 497–501; Taylor, "Plato and the Authorship of the Epinomis," *Proc. Brit. Academy*, 1930, upholding Platonic authorship; *contra*, W. Jaeger, *Aristotle*, pp. 150–154; F. Müller, *Stilistische Untersuchungen der Epinomis des Philippus von Opus* (Lüneburg, 1927); B. Einarson, "Aristotle's *Protrepticus* and the Structure of the *Epinomis*," *T.A.P.A.* 67 (1936), pp. 261–285. See also E. des Places, "La Portée Religieuse de l'Epinomis," *Rev. des Études Grecques* 50 (1937), pp. 321–328.

47 (299): *Θεία Μοῖρα*. For the *Protagoras* myth, which emphasizes φύσις, see above, pp. 245 f. In *Meno* 99e–100b, what comes θείᾳ μοίρᾳ is opposed both to φύσις, what is innate and instinctive, and to what is deliberately acquired either as διδακτόν or as ἀσκητόν; cf. *Meno* 89a and 89d, and above, pp. 272 f.; also E. S. Thompson, ed. *Meno*, pp. 161 f.; 227–230; here of politics, and perhaps ironically; certainly so in *Ion* 534c (θείᾳ μοίρᾳ), of poetry (see my "Plato's View of Poetry," pp. 15–18; and my "The Spirit of Comedy in Plato," p. 74); similarly in *Rep.* 366c7, θείᾳ φύσει is contrasted with ἐπιστήμη, as a basis for justice; and cf. 368 af: θεῖον γένος. But θεία μοῖρα is associated, or identified, with φύσις in *Laws* 642c and 875c, of politics; cf. *Apol.* 22c, of poetry; *Phaedrus* 230a; 244c. *Rep.* 492e–493a is a line case: ἦθος . . . θεῖον, first contrasted with ἦθος . . . ἀνθρώπειον, and then identified with θεοῦ μοῖρα; what the natural man cannot do, God's grace can save. Thus *Phaedo* 58c: μηδ' εἰς Ἅιδου ἰόντα ἄνευ θείας μοίρας ἰέναι, ἀλλὰ καὶ ἐκεῖσε ἀφικόμενον εὖ πράξειν (i.e., the life of Socrates is divinely, and, it is now implied, is rightly crowned by a happy death). On "popular" and "philosophic" virtue, cf. R. D. Archer-Hind, ed. *Phaedo*, Appendix I (pp. 149–155). For θεία τύχη, see above, pp. 299 f., and Appendix 48; and on all these matters see further E. G. Berry, ΘΕΙΑ ΜΟΙΡΑ, pp. 49–85.

48 (300): *Θεία Τύχη*. For mere chance, *Epist.* VII 324c; 324d; 325b; 329a; 337d; 350de; for "divine chance," 326a: ἄνευ παρασκευῆς θαυμαστῆς τινος μετὰ τύχης; 326b: ἔκ τινος μοίρας θείας; 327c: συλλαμβανόντων θεῶν; 327e: θείᾳ τινὶ τύχῃ; 336e: θεία τις τύχη; 337d: ἀγαθῇ . . . μοίρᾳ καὶ θείᾳ τινὶ τύχῃ; for a combination, or for rival explanations, *Epist.* III 316a: εἴτ' ἄνθρωπος εἴτε θεὸς εἴτε τύχη τις; VII 326e: ἴσως μεν κατὰ τύχην, ἔοικεν μὴν τότε μηχανωμένῳ τινὶ τῶν κρειττόνων; 336b: ἤ που τις δαίμων ἤ τις ἀλιτήριος (see above, p. 310, n. 233); VIII 353b: εἴτε δὴ θείαν τις ἡγεῖσθοι βούλεται τύχην καὶ θεὸν εἴτε τὴν τῶν ἀρχόντων ἀρετὴν εἴτε καὶ τὸ συναμφότερον μετὰ τῶν τότε πολιτῶν τῆς σωτηρίας αἰτίαν συμβῆναι γενομένην, ἔστω ταύτῃ ὅπῃ τις ὑπολαμβάνει. With these rival explanations, cf. Virgil's habit of mind (see above, p. 366, and below, Appendix 61); also Livy I, 4, 4: *forte quadam divinitus*; Tennyson, *Lancelot and Elaine*: "chanced divinely."

49 (305): *Finite God of "Timaeus."* The divine creator expressed his goodness in the creation only "so far as was possible." *Tim.* 29e3; 31c3; 32d: ὅτι μάλιστα; 30d: μάλιστα; 30a3; 38c1: κατὰ δύναμιν (cf. *Laws* 903d: κατὰ δύναμιν τὴν τῆς κοινῆς γενέσεως; see below, p. 313): *Tim.* 37d2: εἰς δύναμιν; 32b4–5: καθ' ὅσον ἦν δύνατον; 69b: ὅπῃ δύνατον ἦν. On δύναμις see J. Souihlé, *Étude sur le terme* ΔΥΝΑΜΙΣ *dans les Dialogues de Platon* (Paris, 1919). Cf. further

*Tim.* 35a: δύσμεικτον . . . βίᾳ; 37d: τοῦτο . . . οὐκ ἦν δύνατον; 48a7: ᾗ φέρειν πέφυκεν; 69d7: ὅτι μὴ πᾶσα ἦν ἀνάγκη (this of the delegated creation). In view of these reiterated expressions qualifying the operation of the divine Creator, it is hard to accept Taylor's denial, *Commentary*, p. 79, n. 1, that the God of the *Timaeus* is "finite" on the ground that all that is implied is that image is inferior to original. If God wished to express "as nearly as possible" the eternal pattern (28a; 29a), or to make everything become "as like as might be to himself" (29e), and evil remains, God must be to that extent finite. Cf. Cornford, *Plato's Cosmology*, pp. 162–177, "Reason and Necessity," esp. pp. 164–165; 172–177; and for Cornford's comparison with the conclusion of the *Eumenides* of Aeschylus, pp. 361–364, and above, pp. 135–137.

50 (305): *Secondary Cause in "Timaeus." Tim.* 46ce: ταῦτ' οὖν πάντα ἔστιν τῶν συναιτίων οἷς θεὸς ὑπηρετοῦσιν χρῆται τὴν τοῦ ἀρίστου κατὰ τὸ δύνατον ἰδέαν ἀποτελῶν . . . λεκτέα μὲν ἀμφότερα τὰ τῶν αἰτίων γένη, χωρὶς δὲ ὅσοι μονωθεῖσαι φρονήσεως τὸ τυχὸν ἄτακτον ἑκάστοτε ἐξεργάζονται. 69e: δύ' αἰτίας εἴδη, . . . τὸ μὲν ἀναγκαῖον, τὸ δὲ θεῖον. Cf. 46e6; 76d6–8. For συναίτια as agents of a principal, cf. *Gorg.* 519ab; *Laws* 936d; *Phaedo* 99b: ἄλλο μὲν . . . τὸ αἴτιον τῷ ὄντι, ἄλλο δὲ ἐκεῖνο ἄνευ οὗ τὸ αἴτιον οὐκ ἄν ποτ' αἴτιον. Aristotle goes further than Plato in admitting this ἄνευ οὗ οὐ (the *condicio sine qua non*) as a real cause; see above, p. 321.

51 (314): *Platonic Myths. Gorg.* 524ab; 526d; 527c; *Phaedo* 114d: τὸ μὲν οὖν ταῦτα διισχυρίσασθαι οὕτως ἔχειν ὡς ἐγὼ διελήλυθα, οὐ πρέπει νοῦν ἔχοντι ἀνδρί· ὅτι μέντοι ἢ ταῦτ' ἐστὶν ἢ τοιαῦτ' ἄττα περὶ τὰς ψυχὰς ἡμῶν καὶ τὰς οἰκήσεις, ἐπείπερ ἀθάνατον γε ἡ ψυχὴ φαίνεται οὖσα, τοῦτο καὶ πρεπειν μοι δοκεῖ καὶ ἄξιον κινδυνεῦσαι οἰομένῳ οὕτως ἔχειν — καλὸς γὰρ ὁ κίνδυνος — καὶ χρὴ τοιαῦτα ὥσπερ ἐπᾴδειν ἑαυτῷ; *Rep.* 621cd: "The tale will serve us if we believe it, and . . . we shall fare well"; *Epistle* VII 335ac; and *Juvenal*, II, 153: *sed tu vera puta.* See further J. A. Stewart, *Plato's Doctrine of Ideas*, esp. pp. 1–13; 129–197; J. A. Stewart, *The Myths of Plato*; both these works stress the "transcendental feeling" aroused by the myths, and at times by the Ideas, and find a pragmatic sanction for them in their moral effect on believers in them (see above, Appendix 42; P. Frutiger, *Les Mythes de Platon*); P. Stöcklein, "Ueber die philosophische Bedeutung von Platons Mythen," *Philologus*, Supplementband 30, 3 (1937), and my review of the latter work, *C.P.* 33 (1938), pp. 221–225, with brief reference to other literature on the myths. Taylor, *Platonism*, pp. 105 f., well speaks of a moral law of "gravitation" by which "like is attracted to like," without any special intervention of God. In *Laws* X we have the substance of eschatological myths without their imaginative details; "these pictorial details probably form no part of Plato's serious belief." Similarly, Stöcklein regards *Mythos* as "Vorstufe des Logos."

52 (315): *Daimon and Choice. Rep.* 617de is perhaps a deliberate correction by Plato of *Phaedo* 107d, where each man's *daimon* is assigned to him by lot in this life, and escorts him in the next life. The spirit of the present passage is nearer to that of Heraclitus: ἦθος ἀνθρώπῳ δαίμων (D22B19; cf. above, pp. 307–309); also to that of *Rep.* 329d: not γῆρας but ὁ τρόπος τῶν ἀνθρώπων is the αἰτία of misery. (That, near the beginning of the *Republic*, is the opinion of the aged Cephalus, who must expect soon to face death, but who does not fear such terrors in another life as the myths of the poets depict, because he has

been just. Here, at the end of the *Republic*, we are told again, in a myth, that the just man need not fear death; but "justice" is now understood to be an inward quality of soul.) For the emphasis in the Myth of Er and elsewhere, on "choice," cf. further H. Kuhn, "The True Tragedy," *H.S.C.P.* (1942), pp. 71–78.

53 (315): *Use of Lots.* For the manipulation of lots (a form of *tyche*) in Plato's proposals for the marriage of the best citizens, cf. *Rep.* 460a; *Tim.* 18e. The Greeks probably thought of the lot as resting not on mere luck but on the will of the gods (as in the choice by lot of certain priests); but the choice by lot of certain Athenian officials in the classical period was favored merely because the method seemed to be democratic. Cf. J. W. Headlam (Headlam-Morley), *Election by Lot at Athens*[2], revised by D. C. Macgregor, Cambridge, 1933; S. Dow, "*Prytaneis*," *Hesperia*, Suppl. I (Athens, 1937), esp. pp. 198–207; S. Dow, "Aristotle, the Kleroteria, and the Courts," *H.S.C.P.* 50 (1939), pp. 1–34. The purpose was at first to leave choices to the will of the gods; later it was simply to avoid favoritism and corruption.

54 (321): *Contingency in Aristotle. Phys.* 195b31–198a13; cf. W. D. Ross, *Aristotle*, pp. 75–78; Ross, ed. *Physics* (Oxford, 1938), pp. 38–41; W. A. Heidel, *The Necessary and the Contingent in the Aristotelian System*, a paper which brings out the extent to which Aristotle's difficulties in this, as in other problems, arose from his having abstracted (and hypostasized) too much, from the concrete whole of experience, such conceptions as matter and form, means and ends, causality, and indeed necessity itself. The result is that "Aristotle recognizes only a conditional or hypothetical necessity in nature in so far as it proceeds purely in accordance with purpose." (Heidel, p. 30.) Matter thus becomes merely the negation of purposiveness, unrealized potentiality. Yet Aristotle also holds that the necessary is eternal, as hypostasized meaning. The field of chance, or contingency, is precisely where we are unable to define the extent to which potentiality has achieved realization; here, then, is room for freedom of human action, and therefore for moral choice — unless, as the Stoic fatalists will point out, the future is already wholly contained in the present (see above, p. 362). Both the contingent and the necessary have meaning only within a limited scope defined by a particular end, and should not be generalized into absolutes (Heidel, p. 46). On this treatment of chance (τύχη and τὸ αὐτόματον) by Aristotle, see further V. Cioffari, *Fortune and Fate*, pp. 16–32.

55 (333): *Epicurus; bibliography.* Diogenes Laertius preserves the three letters and the "Principal Doctrines" of Epicurus in his tenth book. Quotations from Epicurus by later writers, the poem of Lucretius, fragments of Philodemus recovered at Herculaneum, and the moving appeal of Diogenes of Oenoanda (second century of our era) inscribed on a wall (*Diogenis Oenoandensis Fragmenta*, ed. I. William, Leipzig, 1907; R. D. Hicks, *Stoic and Epicurean*, pp. 309–311; J. L. Stocks, in Powell and Barber, *New Chapters in the History of Greek Literature* (Oxford, 1921), pp. 31–36) show that the essentials of his philosophy were faithfully preserved by his followers without serious modification. For collections of Epicurean writings see H. Usener, *Epicurea*; H. Bignone, *Epicuro* (Bari, 1920); C. Bailey, *Epicurus*; on Epicurus and Epicureanism generally, see also A. E. Taylor, *Epicurus*; C. Bailey, *The Greek Atomists and Epicurus*, pp. 128–142; R. D. Hicks, *Stoic and Epicurean*, pp.

153–311; A. W. Benn, *The Greek Philosophers*, pp. 365–418. B. Farrington suggests that the letters of Epicurus are a reply to the religious legislation of Plato, *Laws* X; C. Bailey thinks the polemic to be incidental; *Proc. of (Eng.) Classical Assoc.* 36 (1939), pp. 52–54; see further B. Farrington, *Science and Politics in the Ancient World* (New York, 1940), pp. 101–110; 130–147.

56 (334): *Epicurus, "Swerve," and τύχη.* Apparently Epicurus himself does not use the word *tyche* of the "swerve"; but Plutarch sees *tyche* in the result of its working; *De Sollert. Anim.* 964c, in H. Usener, *Epicurea*, p. 351. Epicurus reckons freely with *tyche* in his ethical writings. For the connection between these ideas and those of the Atomists, see further my "Fate, Good, and Evil in Pre-Socratic Philosophy," *H.S.C.P.* 47 (1936), p. 125. I should now add, however, that the cosmos of the Atomists admits Chance (τὸ αὐτόματον) in the heavens, and to a less extent it admits Purpose on earth. Thus Aristotle attributes to the Atomists an account of animals and plants not ἀπὸ τύχης, but using φύσιν ἢ νοῦν ἤ τι τοιοῦτον ἕτερον (*Phys.* 196a24 = D68A69); he also implies that they inconsistently assign astronomical movements, including the cosmic whirl (δίνη) to τὸ αὐτόματον. See C. Bailey, *The Greek Atomists and Epicureans*, pp. 138–146; 316–327; 433–436; also V. Cioffari, *Fortune and Fate* (1935), pp. 1–15, criticizing Bailey's interpretation; Cic. *De Nat. Deorum* I, 66: [from the atoms] *effectum esse caelum atque terram nulla cogente natura sed concursu quodam fortuito; T.D.* I, 22; 42; Dante, *Inf.* 4, 136: *Democrito che il mondo a caso pone.* Aristotle himself understands by τὸ αὐτόματον merely an indeterminate or unknown cause (see above, pp. 320 f.; 324 f.; and for similar Stoic doctrine, p. 340). Moreover, it is in the sublunary realm, not in the heavens, that Aristotle and the Peripatetics find τύχη and imperfection (see pp. 320; 325; below, Appendix 63).

57 (338): *Stoics; bibliography.* For the study of Stoicism, useful works are: A. C. Pearson, *The Fragments of Zeno and Cleanthes* (London, 1891); H. von Arnim, *Stoicorum Veterum Fragmenta* (3 vols., Leipzig, 1903–05; vol. 4 (M. Adler), 1924; cited as SVF); A. Schmekel, *Die Philosophie der Mittleren Stoa* (Berlin, 1892); R. D. Hicks, *Stoic and Epicurean*; E. Bevan, *Stoics and Sceptics*; E. V. Arnold, *Roman Stoicism.* The earlier Stoic literature has reached us chiefly by way of doxographies. The seventh book of Diogenes Laertius (on the Stoics), for example, seems to be compiled from a general account of Stoicism (possibly by Chrysippus himself), interlarded with specific accounts of the several philosophers. (Cf. SVF, I, p. xxxv; R. D. Hicks, Loeb ed. of D.L., Vol. I, pp. xxii–xxxii; R. Hope, *The Book of Diogenes Laertius; Its Spirit and Its Method*, New York, 1930; H. Diels, *Doxog. Gr.*, 161–168.) So, too, Cicero in his philosophical works often leans hard on doxographical works, perhaps sometimes prepared for the purpose; but he also is able to deal specifically with individual Stoics. Cf. R. Hirzel, *Untersuchungen*, as cited above, p. 352, n. 118; H. Usener, *Epicurea*, pp. LXV–LXVIII; H. von Arnim, SVF, pp. xix–xxx.

58 (346): *Seneca, Epictetus, M. Aurelius.* For Seneca, see *De Providentia* (*Quare aliqua incommoda bonis viris accidant, cum providentia sit*), *passim*, and esp. VI, 1–5: God protects the good man from moral evils, but allows him hardships, thus giving him every good, including the good fortune not to need good fortune. But Seneca tries also to be a scientific determinist (*Nat. Quaest.*

II, 36), and even admits planetary influence on human affairs (*Ad Marciam De Consolatione*, 18, 3); see also above, pp. 367 f.

For Epictetus, see Arrian's *Discourses of Epictetus*, IV, 12, 7–8: "No man is master of another's moral purpose; and in its sphere alone are to be found one's good and evil. It follows, therefore, that no one has power either to procure me good or to involve me in evil, but I myself alone have authority over myself in these matters." Cf. *Disc.* I, 1, "On things in our power (ἐφ' ἡμῖν) and things not in our power," and the *Encheiridion* of Epictetus, *passim*, as to the distinction between the things under our control (ἐφ' ἡμῖν) and those not under our control. The practical conclusion to be drawn with regard to the latter is the often quoted maxim of Epictetus: "Endure and Renounce" (ἀνέχου καὶ ἀπέχου, Epict. frag. 10 = 179 Schweighäuser, from A. Gell. XVII, 19), a Stoic version of the earlier philosophy of τλημοσύνη, with something of the religious resignation of Meister Eckhart. (See also above, p. 316 and n. 278.)

For a collection of passages in M. Aurelius bearing on Providence, see R. D. Hicks, *Stoic and Epicurean*, pp. 46–53. Marcus, like Epictetus, is worth reading not so much for any new thought as for the powerful expression of the Stoic commonplaces, enhanced by the fact that the slave and the emperor express a common creed. Marcus states the alternatives thus: "The universe must be governed either by a fore-ordained destiny, — an order that none may overstep, — by a merciful Providence, or by a chaos of chance devoid of a ruler. If the theory of an insuperable fate be true, why struggle against it? If Providence watches over all, and may be inclined to mercy, render thyself worthy of celestial aid. But if leaderless chaos be all, rest content that in the midst of this storm-swept sea Reason still dwells and rules within thee." (*To Himself*, XII, 14.)

59 (358): *Argument from Design*. Cic. *N.D.* II, 87–90; 93. This argument, of course, recalls earlier teleological arguments (see above, pp. 221; 273–276; 289; 309), and becomes a commonplace in literature. Such reasoning is in fact the starting point of the famous work of William Paley, *Natural Theology, or Evidence of the Existence and Attributes of the Deity, Collected from the Appearances of Nature*, London, 1802 (3rd ed., 1803, from which I cite below). Thus a watch, even if imperfect or if imperfectly understood, implies not only a design (adaptation of means to end) but a designer. Subsequent arguments Paley bases, as does Balbus, largely on human and comparative anatomy, above all on the human eye. The Deity is not only intelligent, but kind. Of the origin of evil, Paley attempts no single or simple explanation, but shows an almost Stoic ingenuity in suggesting (pp. 497–572) possible causes for what appear to us to be physical evils, in a varied world of conflicting interests, with possible moral compensatons. Human life is conceived as a period of moral probation (pp. 561–568), and must be judged in the light of a future life, "natural theology" being crowned by revealed religion (pp. 574–579). For a more general discussion, cf. A. S. Pease, *Caeli Enarrant*.

60 (366): *Polybius; Livy; Diodorus Siculus*. The sense of Rome's mission under divine guidance developed as the actual success of Roman arms pointed to her "manifest destiny." The conception meets us possibly first in Polybius, who begins by seeing the consolidating power of *Tyche* at work (I, 4, 1; I, 4, 5; cf. W. W. Fowler, *C.R.* 17 (1903), pp. 445–449, "Polybius' Conception of Τύχη," which is more than chance, sometimes almost equivalent to Stoic

Nature or Fate; but Polybius also records the popular ideas of τύχη, as chance or *nemesis* or special divine intervention; see below, Appendix 62). But Polybius tends more and more (perhaps under Stoic influence) to emphasize human wills and institutions and national character as determining forces, with some notion of cycles in history (I, 63, 9; XXXVI, 17, 1–4; VI, 5, 5, cycles; VI, *passim*, constitutions; and cf. J. B. Bury, *The Ancient Greek Historians*, New York, 1909, pp. 193–207). Rome's destiny is a master idea in the work of Virgil's contemporary, the historian Livy, who finds the secret of Rome's national greatness in her ancient manliness, honor, and piety, qualities which, we must add, he failed to perceive in the "decadence" of his own age. Livy is not quite consistent in referring the course of events now to fate, now to gods, now to human wills; cf. Livy V, 49, 1 (gods and men); V, 19, 8 (luck following *ratio* and *consilium*); V, 36, 6 (Fate pressing hard on Rome); V, 37, 1 (Fortune blinding the Romans); all these passages are cited by J. W. Duff, *Literary History of Rome* (London, 1927), p. 652. Diodorus Siculus (*c.* 90–30) attempted a universal history, seeing all peoples as members of one human family under that divine providence which orders alike the stars and the natures of men; but his achievement is disappointing.

61 (366): *Virgil; Tacitus; Lucan.* I have discussed Virgil's suspended judgement, with illustrations of the "fate or gods or men" type of explanation, from the major works and also from the possibly Virgilian poems of the *Appendix*, in "Young Virgil and 'The Doubtful Doom of Human Kind,'" *A.J.P.* 43 (1922), pp. 344–351; e.g. *Aen.* XII, 320 f.: *incertum . . . casusne deusne*; cf. R. S. Conway, *Harvard Lectures on the Virgilian Age* (Cambridge, Mass., 1928), pp. 64–66; 99–112. Tacitus, inclined like Virgil to suspend his judgement as to causes and motives, devotes a notable chapter (*Annals* VI, 22; see the notes of H. Furneaux *ad loc.*, also his introduction, Vol. I, pp. 29–30) to the question whether human affairs are subject to fate and immutable necessity or to chance; whether the Epicureans are right who deny divine interest in men, or the Stoics who derive all things not from roving stars but from the chain of natural causes, leaving room, however, for human choice (with results following inevitably), and for the wise or foolish use of what fortune sends; or, finally, whether the claims of astrology, as most men believe, deserve some respect, in spite of the frauds of its weaker practitioners. (Cf. also *Annals* III, 18, on *ludibria rerum mortalium.*) Lucan, imitator of Virgil in many things, and a convinced Stoic, normally holds to the supremacy of Fate. But he finds divination hard to reconcile with Fate; once, after asking whether Law or Chance is supreme, he prays for hope (II, 1–15; cf. IX, 566–586; the Stoic Cato refuses to question Ammon's oracle about his own fate). Caesar leaves all to Fortune (V, 510; 593; 668), — and loses. It should be added that Lucan, like others, is sometimes precise in distinguishing *Fatum* and *Fortuna*, sometimes uses them interchangeably (cf. Polybius, and Appendix 60).

62 (368): Τύχη; *Fortuna.* For *Tyche*, cf. Demosthenes, *Second Olynthiac*, 22 (the power of τύχη; yet Heaven helps him who helps himself); Demetrius of Phalerum, from whose *Treatise on Fortune* Polybius quotes, XXIX, 21, on the vicissitudes of fifty years of Greek history, and the moral to be drawn from them: the power, the amoral nature, and the fickleness of Fortune; Polybius (see Appendix 60); Plutarch, *On the Fortune of Alexander* (two essays) and *On the Fortune of Rome*, stressing the rôle of Fortune and (only less) of Virtue;

Pacuvius, 366–375 Ribbeck; Pliny, *Nat. Hist.* II, 22: "Throughout the whole world, at every place and hour by every voice *Fortuna* alone is invoked and her name spoken. . . . She is worshipped with insults, courted as fickle and often as blind, wandering, inconsistent, elusive, changeful, and friend of the unworthy. . . . We are so much at the mercy of chance (*sors*) that Chance is our god." On Fortune in Italy, see also Cic. *De Div.* II, 85–86 with the notes of A. S. Pease (the Praenestine "lots"); Horace, *Odes* I, 34 (for the un-Epicurean ideas here suggested, cf. W. Jaeger, *Hermes* 48 (1913), pp. 442–449); I, 35 (*Fortunae Antiates*).

63 (368): *Astrology.* Plato's respect for astronomy almost verged on astrology; it culminated in the Myth of Er (which however preserved human freedom, though it was astrology that later writers sometimes drew from it; cf. Proclus on *Rep.* 620de, Vol. II, pp. 341–345 Kroll), and (if the *Epinomis* be Platonic) in the cult of astral gods. Here Plato was probably indebted to Oriental influences. (See above, pp. 287 f.; 295 f.; 314 f.; and cf. F. Cumont, *Astrology and Religion*, pp. 45–57.) Babylonian astronomy had become astrology by the time that the Greeks under Alexander conquered Mesopotamia. Plato's pupil Eudoxus rejected astrology in favor of pure astronomy (Cic. *De Div.* II, 87). Aristotle, followed by Ptolemaeus, distinguished between the celestial and the sublunar regions and their respective kinds of Fate, divine or physical (cf. W. Gundel, *Ananke und Heimarmene*, pp. 78–80). There was earlier warrant for the notion that the sublunar realm is disorderly (for Pythagorean tradition, D44A16; D58B37; for a somewhat doubtful derivation from Heraclitus of the doctrine that evil rules the sublunar region, Hippolytus, *Refut. Omn. Haeres.* I, 4); and the idea that τύχη exists only in the sublunar realm is common after Aristotle (see above, p. 383, for Sallustius). So Aristotle finds absolute necessity only in the outer heavens; and Cicero writes (*Somnium Scipionis* 9): *infra autem iam nihil est nisi mortale et caducum praeter animos munere deorum hominum generi datos, supra lunam sunt aeterna omnia.* Cf. also W. Farnham, *The Mediaeval Heritage of Elizabethan Tragedy* (Berkeley, 1936), pp. 26–29. The Stoics, most of whom had oriental roots but had absorbed Greek thought, found in the "sympathy" of the cosmos the warrant for divination. (See above, pp. 340; 347; 352; 357; cf. K. Reinhardt, *Kosmos und Sympathie*, pp. 92–138; how much of this doctrine is due to Posidonius remains doubtful.) Astrology and the casting of horoscopes was now justified by a great philosophical sect. Horace in Epicurean mood may deplore the resort to the "Babylonian numbers" of the Chaldaeans (*Odes* I, 11); but even legislation is impotent to check it (Tacitus *Hist.* I, 22; cf. also *Annals* VI, 22, and above, Appendix 61). Cicero as a Stoic may admit "sympathy" but as an Academic exclude astrology (see above, pp. 361–363); nevertheless it is Cicero who in the *Somnium Scipionis* as a Platonist and a forerunner of Dante links with men's fortunes the starry spheres which are also to be the abode of the blessed, and such eschatological beliefs become widespread in the Roman Empire. Meanwhile not merely the populace but even emperors now resort to astrology; and the deterministic foundation of the pseudo-science is reaffirmed in the poem of Manilius (first century of our era) in fatalistic terms (e.g. IV, 14–16; *Fata regunt orbem, certa stant omnia lege | longaque per certos signantur tempora casus. | Nascentes morimur, finisque ab origine pendet*). On the whole subject see A. Bouché-Leclercq, *Histoire de la Divination* (Paris, 1880), I, pp. 205–257; IV, 325–334; F. Cumont, *Astrology and Religion*, pp. 28–35; 45–56; 66–

72; 81–100; 153–161; 167–202; F. Boll, *Sternglaube und Sterndeutung*[3] (Leipzig, 1926); and, for the surprising prevalence of belief in the pretensions of astrology even in our day, B. J. Bok and M. W. Mayall, "Scientists Look at Astrology," *Scientific Monthly* 52 (1941), pp. 233–244.

64 (368): *Oracles.* On Greek oracles generally, see A. Bouché-Leclercq, *Histoire de la Divination*, Vol. II, pp. 227–409; Vol. III, pp. 1–414; F. W. H. Myers, "Greek Oracles," in *Hellenica* (ed. E. Abbott, London, 1880), and in Myers, *Essays, Classical* (London, 1883), the later pages, on the Neoplatonic attitude towards oracles, being of special interest; W. R. Halliday, *Greek Divination* (London, 1913); for Plutarch's explanation of the temporary cessation of oracles in his time, cf. Plutarch, *De Defectu Oraculorum*, and see above, pp. 310; 369.

65 (368): *Ideas in Roman Period; bibliography.* For a survey of this period, see A. D. Nock, *C.A.H.*, Vol. XII, "The Development of Paganism in the Roman Empire"; for certain phases of it, G. Murray, *Five Stages in Greek Religion*, Chap. 4, "The Failure of Nerve" (which Murray sees beginning in the Hellenistic Age); also F. Cumont, *Textes et Monuments Figurés Relatifs aux Mystères de Mithra* (Bruxelles, 1899), Vol. I, pp. 293–312, for the doctrine of Mithraism; R. Reitzenstein, *Poimandres*, and W. Scott, *Hermetica*, for the fusion in Egypt of Greek philosophy with religious and magical ideas in the second and third centuries; C. H. Dodd, "Hellenism and Christianity" (in *Harvard Tercentenary Publications: Independence, Convergence, and Borrowing in Institutions, Thought, and Art*, Cambridge, 1937), pp. 109–131; A. W. Benn, *Greek Philosophers*, Chap. XIII, "The Religious Revival"; W. R. Inge, *The Philosophy of Plotinus*, Lectures II and III, "The Third Century"; F. Allegre, *Tyché*, pp. 165–240; J. A. Hild, *Démons*, pp. 286–331; E. Tournier, *Némésis*, pp. 225–258. W. Gundel, *Ananke und Heimarmene*, pp. 93–100 (Εἱμαρμένη in inscriptions sometimes now a death-goddess, though hardly personified; Ἀνάγκη, more personal, in magical, mystical, Hermetic literature).

66 (370): *Source of [Plutarch] "On Fate."* G. L. Fonsegrive, *Le Libre Arbitre*, pp. 74 f., accepts the work as genuine. But a now lost work appears to have been a common source of the essay *On Fate* attributed to Plutarch, of chapter XXVI of the Διδασκαλικὸς τῶν Πλάτωνος δογμάτων of Albinus (C. F. Hermann, ed. Plato, Vol. VI, p. 179), who was also a "Middle Platonist," of the essay *On Fate* written by Alexander of Aphrodisias, of parts of the Commentary on the *Timaeus* of Plato by Chalcidius, and of other works; this common source seems to have been close to the thought of Antiochus, who was probably, as we have seen, one of Cicero's sources with regard to Fate; it is in turn a stage on the road toward the Neo-Platonism of Nemesius and of Plotinus himself. R. E. Witt, *Albinus and the History of Middle Platonism*, pp. 86 f. (and my review of this work, *C.P.* 34 (1939), pp. 176–178); A. Gercke "Eine Platonische Quelle des Neuplatonismus," *R.M.* 41 (1886), pp. 266–291; Ueberweg-Praechter. *Grundriss*, pp. 555 f.; A. D. Nock, *Sallustius*, pp. xxxvii f.

67 (373): *Alexander of Aphrodisias; bibliography.* Alexander of Aphrodisias, Περὶ Εἱμαρμένης (here cited as "*De Fato*"); text, ed. I. Bruns (in *Supplementum Aristotelicum*, vol. II, Part II, Berlin, 1892); J. F. Nourrisson, *Essai sur Alexandre d'Aphrodisias*, with French translation (Paris, 1870); A. Fitzgerald, text with (careless) English translation (London, 1931); R. A. Pack, "A Passage in Alexander of Aphrodisias Relating to the Theory of Tragedy,"

*A.J.P.* 58 (1937), pp. 418–436; cf. also above, pp. 92; 94. Alexander's more systematic treatise Περὶ Ψυχῆς (with "Mantissa") is also important for this subject: ed. Bruns (in *Suppl. Aristot.* Vol. II, Part I, esp. pp. 169–186). Aristotle himself had relatively little to say about fatalism, writing before the Stoic dogma was formulated; it is the more interesting to learn from Alexander how a Peripatetic would meet the dogma.

68 (395): *Milton and "Retraction."* One is reminded of the divine "helmsman" in Plato's *Politicus* myth (see above, p. 289) who temporarily "retires" from the control of the world; or again of the delegation of parts of the creation, in Plato's *Timaeus*, to the created gods (see above, p. 301); also of the attempts of Plotinus to secure both the perfection of the *One* and the individuality of phenomena, and of St. Augustine's doctrine that freedom of the will is the source of evil (see above, pp. 386 f.). Milton's answer to the problem has been called "retraction" by D. Saurat, *Milton: Man and Thinker* (New York, 1925), p. 124: "According to his eternal plans, God withdraws his will from certain parts of Himself, and delivers them up, so to speak, to obscure latent impulsions that remain in them. Through this 'retraction,' matter is created; through this retraction, individual beings are created. The parts of God thus freed from his will become persons." This doctrine, which is not orthodox Christian theology, Saurat traces (pp. 281–309) to Milton's acquaintance with the thirteenth-century non-orthodox Jewish *Zohar*. On Milton's theological and philosophical thought in general, see Saurat, pp. 80–243: E. M. W. Tillyard, *Milton* (London, 1930), pp. 213–274.

# SELECT BIBLIOGRAPHY

The following bibliography lists only those works which have proved most valuable or which bear most directly on the subject of this book, and includes the titles of less than a quarter of the works cited in the text; sufficient description of the other works cited will, however, be found in the notes. In a few cases the abbreviated titles of works frequently cited are given below. Works which appeared after May 1942 are not listed.


Abbott, E., "The Theology and Ethics of Sophocles," in *Hellenica* (London, 1880), pp. 33–66.

Adam, J., *The Religious Teachers of Greece* (Edinburgh, 1909).

—— *The Vitality of Platonism* (Cambridge, 1911).

Allègre, F., *Sophocles: Étude sur les Ressorts Dramatiques de son Théâtre et la Composition de ses Tragedies* (Lyons and Paris, 1905).

—— *Étude sur la Déesse Grecque Tyché* (Paris, 1889).

von Arnim, H., *Stoicorum Veterum Fragmenta* (3 vols., Leipzig, 1903–05; vol. 4, M. Adler, 1924). [SVF]

Arnold, E. V., *Roman Stoicism* (Cambridge, 1911).

Bailey, C., *Epicurus, the Extant Remains* (Oxford, 1926).

—— *The Greek Atomists and Epicurus* (Oxford, 1928).

Beardslee, J. W., Jr., *The Use of Φύσις in Fifth Century Literature* (Chicago, 1918).

Benn, A. W., *The Greek Philosophers* (New York, n.d.).

Berry, E. G., *The History and Development of the Concept of* ΘΕΙΑ ΜΟΙΡΑ *and* ΘΕΙΑ ΤΥΧΗ *down to and including Plato* (Chicago, 1940).

Bevan, E., *Stoics and Sceptics* (Oxford, 1913).

Buresch, C., "Consolationum Historia" in *Leipziger Studien*, 9, (1886–87).

Burnet, J., *Early Greek Philosophy*[4], (London, 1930). [*E.G.P.*]

—— *Greek Philosophy, I: Thales to Plato* (New York, 1914). [*T.-P.*]

—— "Law and Nature in Greek Ethics," in *Essays and Addresses* (New York, 1930).

Busch, G., *Untersuchungen zum Wesen der* Τύχη *in den Tragödien des Euripides* (Heidelberg, 1937).

Bussell, F. W., *The School of Plato* (London, 1896).

Butcher, S. H., *Some Aspects of the Greek Genius*[3], (London, 1904).

Canter, H. V., "Ill Will of the Gods in Greek and Latin Poetry," *C. P.* 32 (1937), pp. 131–143.

Cherniss, H., *Aristotle's Criticism of Pre-Socratic Philosophy* (Baltimore, 1935).

—— "The Philosophical Economy of the Theory of Ideas," *A. J. P.* 57 (1936), pp. 445–456.

Chiapelli, A., "Sofistica Greca," *Arch. f. Gesch. der Phil.* 3 (1889–1890), pp. 1–21; 240–274.

Chilcott, C. M., "The Platonic Theory of Evil," *C.Q.* 17 (1923), pp. 27–31.

Cioffari, V., *Fortune and Fate from Democritus to St. Thomas Aquinas* (New York, 1935).

Cornford, F. M., *Plato's Cosmology* (London and New York, 1937).

—— *From Religion to Philosophy* (London, 1912), [*Rel.-Phil.*]

Cumont, F., *Astrology and Religion among the Greeks and Romans* (New York, 1912).

Decharme, P., *Euripides and the Spirit of his Dramas* (Eng. trans., New York, 1906).

DeLacy, P. H., "The Problem of Causation in Plato's Philosophy," *C. P.* 34 (1939), pp. 97–115.

Dickerman, S. O., *De Argumentis Quibusdam apud Xenophontem, Platonem, Aristotelem Obviis e Structura Hominis et Animalium Petitis* (Halle, 1909).

Diels, H., "Der Antike Pessimismus," *Schule und Leben*, Heft I (Berlin, 1921).

—— *Doxographi Graeci* (Berlin & Leipzig, 1929).

—— *Die Fragmente der Vorsokratiker*[5] (W. Kranz) (Berlin, 1934–1937). [*Vorsokratiker*; or *D.*]

Diès, A., *Autour de Platon* (Paris, 1927).

Dixon, W. M., *Tragedy* (London, 1925).

Dodds, E. R., "Euripides the Irrationalist," *C. R.* 43 (1929), pp. 97–104.

Drachmann, A. B., *Atheism in Pagan Antiquity* (Eng. trans., London, 1922).

Dutoit, E., *Le Thème de l'Adynaton dans la Poésie Antique* (Paris, 1936).

Eckstein, W., *Das Antike Naturrecht in Sozialphilosophischer Beleuchtung* (Wien und Leipzig, 1926).

Edelstein, L., "The Philosophical System of Posidonius," *A. J. P.* 57 (1936), pp. 286–325.

Ehnmark, E., *The Idea of God in Homer* (Uppsala, 1935).

von Erffa, C. E. frhr., "ΑΙΔΩΣ und verwandte Begriffe in ihrer Entwicklung von Homer bis Demokrit," *Philologus*, Supplementband 30, 2 (1937).

Farnell, L. R., *Higher Aspects of Greek Religion* (London, 1912).

Fonsegrive, G. L., *Essai sur le Libre Arbitre* (Paris, 1887).

Frutiger, P., *Les Mythes de Platon* (Paris, 1930).

Frye, P. H., *Romance and Tragedy* (Boston, 1922).

Fuller, B. A. G., *The Problem of Evil in Plotinus* (Cambridge, 1912).

Girard, J., *Le Sentiment Religieux en Grece d'Homère à Eschyle*,[3] (Paris, 1887).

Gomperz, H., *Sophistik und Rhetorik* (Leipzig and Berlin, 1912).

Göring, C., *Über den Begriff der Ursache in der Griechischen Philosophie* (Leipzig, 1874).

Greene, W. C., "Plato's View of Poetry," *H. S. C. P.* 29 (1918), pp. 1–75.

—— "The Spirit of Comedy in Plato," *H. S. C. P.* 31 (1920), pp. 63–123.

—— "Fate, Good, and Evil in Pre-Socratic Philosophy," *H. S. C. P.* 47 (1936), pp. 85–129.

Grote, G., *Plato*, 3 vols. (London, 1865).

Gundel, W., *Beiträge zur Entwickelungsgeschichte der Begriffe Ananke und Heimarmene* (Giessen, 1914).

Guthrie, W. K. C., *Orpheus and Greek Religion* (London, 1935).

Hack, R. K., *God in Greek Philosophy to the Time of Socrates* (Princeton, 1931).

Hackforth, R., "Plato's Theism," *C. Q.* 30 (1936), pp. 4–9.

Harrison, J. E., *Prolegomena to the Study of Greek Religion* (Cambridge, 1903).

—— *Themis* (Cambridge, 1912).

Heidel, W. A., *The Necessary and the Contingent in the Aristotelian System* (Chicago, 1896).

—— "Περὶ φύσεως. A study of the conception of Nature among the Pre-Socratics," *Proc. Am. Acad. Arts and Sciences*, 45 (1910), pp. 77–133.

Hicks, R. D., *Stoic and Epicurean* (Oxford, 1928).

Hild, J. A., *Étude sur les Démons* (Paris, 1881).

Hirzel, R., "Ἄγραφος Νόμος" (*Abh. d. Sächs. Gesellsch. d. Wissenschaft*, 20 [1901]), pp. 1–98.

—— *Themis, Dike and Verwandtes* (Leipzig, 1907).

—— *Untersuchungen zu Cicero's Philosophischen Schriften*, 3 vols. (Leipzig, 1877–1883).

Huit, C., *La Philosophie de la Nature chez les Anciens* (Paris, 1901).

Inge, W. R., *The Philosophy of Plotinus*, 2 vols. (London, 1923).

Jaeger, W., *Aristotle: Fundamentals of the History of his Development* (Eng. trans., Oxford, 1934).

—— *Diokles von Karystos* (Berlin, 1938).

—— *Paideia* (Eng. trans., Oxford, 1939).

—— in *Sitzber. preuss. Akad. Wiss.* (Berlin, 1926).

Joel, K., *Der Ursprung der Naturphilosophie aus dem Geiste der Mystik* (Basel, 1903).

Jolivet, R., "Plotin et le Problème du Mal," in *Essai sur les Rapports entre la Pensée Grecque et la Pensée Chrétienne* (Paris, 1931).

Kern, O., *Orphicorum Fragmenta* (Berlin, 1922).

—— *Religion der Griechen*, Vol. I (Berlin, 1926).

Kitto, H. D. F., *Greek Tragedy, A Literary Study* (London, 1939).

Kuhn, H., "The True Tragedy. On the Relationship between Greek Tragedy and Plato," *H. S. C. P.* 52 (1941), pp. 1–40; 53 (1942), pp. 37–88.

Leach, A., "Fatalism of the Greeks," *A. J. P.* 36 (1915), (abridged, as "Fate and Free Will in Greek Literature," in *The Greek Genius and its Influence*, ed. L. Cooper, New Haven, 1917).

Lehrs, K., *Populäre Aufsätze aus dem Altherthum*[2] (Leipzig, 1875).

Linforth, I. M., *The Arts of Orpheus* (Berkeley, 1941).

—— *Solon the Athenian* (Berkeley, 1919).

Lovejoy, A. O., *The Great Chain of Being* (Cambridge, Mass., 1936).

—— "Meaning of φύσις," *Phil. Rev.* 18 (1909), pp. 369–383.

Lovejoy, A. O., and Boas, G., *Primitivism and Related Ideas in Antiquity* (Baltimore, 1935).

Macurdy, G. H., *The Quality of Mercy* (New Haven, 1940).

Matthaei, L. E., *Studies in Greek Tragedy* (Cambridge, 1918).

Menzel, A., *Kallikles* (Wien and Leipzig, 1922).

Meuss, H., *Tyche bei den attischen Tragikern* (Hirschberg, 1899).

Mondolfo, R., *Problemi del Pensiero Antico* (Bologna, 1935).

More, P. E., *The Religion of Plato* (Princeton, 1921).

Murray, G., *Aeschylus, the Creator of Tragedy* (Oxford, 1940).

—— *Euripides and His Age* (New York, 1913).

—— *Five Stages in Greek Religion* (Oxford, 1925).

Nägelsbach, C. F. von, *Homerische Theologie*[3] (Nurnberg, 1884).

—— *Nachhomerische Theologie* (Nurnberg, 1857).

Nestle, W., "Der Pessimismus und seine Überwindung bei den Griechen," *N. Jbb. f. kl. Alt.* 47 (1921).

Nilsson, M. P., *History of Greek Religion* (Oxford, 1925).

Nock, A. D., ed. *Sallustius* (Cambridge, 1926).

Norwood, G., *Greek Tragedy* (London, 1920).

Pack, R. A., "Fate, Chance, and Tragic Error," *A. J. P.* 60 (1939).

—— "A Passage in Alexander of Aphrodisias Relating to the Theory of Tragedy," *A. J. P.* 58 (1937).

Pease, A. S., ed. Cicero, *De Divinatione* (Univ. of Illinois, 1920).

—— "Caeli Enarrant," *Harv. Theol. Rev.* 34 (1941), pp. 163–200.

Rand, E. K., "On the Composition of Boethius' *Consolatio Philosophiae*," *H. S. C. P.* 15 (1904).

Reinhardt, K., *Kosmos und Sympathie* (Munich, 1926).

Rieth, O., "Grundbegriffe der Stoischen Ethik," *Problemata* 9 (1933).

Ritter, H., and Preller, L., *Historia Philosophiae Graecae*[8] (Gotha, 1898). [R. P.]

Rivaud, A., *Le Problème de Devenir dans la Philosophie Grecque depuis les origines* (Paris, 1906).

Robin, L., *Études sur la Signification et la Place de la Physique dans la Philosophie de Platon* (Paris, 1919).

Rohde, E., *Psyche* (Eng. trans., New York, 1925).

Royce, J., *The World and the Individual:* Vol. II, *Nature, Man, and the Moral Order* (New York, 1901).

Russell, H. N., *Fate and Freedom* (New Haven, 1927).

Schröder, E., *Plotins Abhandlung* ΠΟΘΕΝ ΤΑ ΚΑΚΑ, *Enn.* I, 8 (Rostock dissertation, 1916).

Shorey, P., "The Idea of Good in Plato's Republic," *Univ. of Chicago Studies in Classical Philology*, I (1895).

—— *The Unity of Plato's Thought* (Chicago, 1904).

—— *What Plato Said* (Chicago, 1933). [W.P.S.]

—— Φύσις, Μελέτη, Ἐπιστήμη, *T.A.P.A.* 40 (1909), pp. 185–201.

Skemp, J. B., *The Theory of Motion in Plato's Later Dialogues* (Cambridge, 1942).

Smyth, H. W., *Aeschylean Tragedy* (Berkeley, 1924).

Solmsen, F., "The Background of Plato's Theology," *T.A.P.A.* 67 (1936).

—— *Plato's Theology* (Ithaca, 1942).

Souilhé, J., *La Notion Platonicienne d'Intermédiaire* (Paris, 1919).

Stewart, J. A., *The Myths of Plato* (London, 1905).

—— *Plato's Doctrine of Ideas* (Oxford, 1909).

Stickney, J. T., *Les Sentences dans la Poésie grecque* (Paris, 1903).

Stier, H., "Nomos Basileus," *Philologus*, N. F. 37 (1928), pp. 225–258.

Stöcklein, P., "Über die philosophische Bedeutung von Platons Mythen," *Philologus, Supplementband* 30, 3 (1937).

Taylor, A. E., *A Commentary on Plato's Timaeus* (London, 1928).

—— *Epicurus* (London, 1911).

—— *The Faith of a Moralist:* Vol. I, *The Theological Implications of Morality* (London, 1930).

—— *Plato* (London, 1911).

—— *Plato: The Man and His Work* (New York, 1927). [P.M.W.]

—— *Platonism and Its Influence* (Boston, 1924).

Theiler, W., *Zur Geschichte der Teleologischen Naturbetrachtung bis auf Aristoteles* (Zurich, 1924).

Thirlwall, C., "On the Irony of Sophocles," *Philological Museum* 2 (1833), pp. 483–537; *Philologus* 6 (1841), pp. 81–104; 254–277.

Thomson, J. A. K., *Irony* (Cambridge, Mass., 1927).

Tournier, E., *Némésis et la Jalousie des Dieux* (Paris, 1863).

Treston, H. J., *Poine: A Study in Ancient Greek Blood-Vengeance* (London, 1923).

Ueberweg, F., and Praechter, K., *Grundriss der Geschichte der Philosophie*,[12] Vol. I (Berlin, 1926).

Usener, H., *Epicurea* (Leipzig, 1887).

Verrall, A. W., *The Bacchants of Euripides* (Cambridge, 1910).

—— *Four Plays of Euripides* (Cambridge, 1905).

—— *Euripides the Rationalist* (Cambridge, 1913).

Wehrli, F., ΛΑΘΕ ΒΙΩΣΑΣ (Leipzig and Berlin, 1931).

Whitmore, C. E., *The Supernatural in Tragedy* (Cambridge, Mass., 1915).

Wieberg, J., *De Fato Graecorum Quid maxime probabile sit Quaeritur* (Iena, 1869).

Witt, R. E., *Albinus and the History of Middle Platonism* (Cambridge, 1937).

Zeller, E., *History of Greek Philosophy* (Eng. trans., London, 1881).

# INDEX OF NAMES AND SUBJECTS

Further references to Greek words which appear in this Index in transliterated English form, and to certain other Greek words, may often be found in the Index of Greek Words and Phrases. Such words as Fate, Good, Evil, and God (gods) occur so frequently that they are listed here only in special connections. References under *Moira* are only to that word, not to other expressions of the idea of Fate, references to which will be found elsewhere. Under the names of major authors, principal discussions are indicated by italic numerals.

# INDEX OF GREEK WORDS AND PHRASES

## *Etymologies of Certain Greek Words*



## *Greek Words and Phrases*

(Many of the following words, and certain other Greek words, will be found in their transliterated English forms in the Index of Names and Subjects)